InfoTrac® College Edition offers:

- More than 10 million articles from nearly 5,000 academic journals and other sources
- Daily newspapers and monthly magazines
- Online help with research papers
- Easy-to-use search features

Log On & Get Started

ISBN: 0-534-27494-3

Here is your FREE passcode to InfoTrac College Edition®

Only available with NEW copies of Thomson Learning textbooks

PG5JB986MX / 0097775A

Management and Supervision in Law Enforcement

Fourth Edition

Wayne W. Bennett, LL.B.
Former Chief of Police
Edina, Minnesota and
Boulder City, Nevada

Kären M. Hess, Ph.D.
President, Institute for Professional Development
Instructor, Normandale Community College
Bloomington, Minnesota

THOMSON
WADSWORTH

Australia • Canada • Mexico • Singapore
Spain • United Kingdom • United States

THOMSON
WADSWORTH

Senior Executive Editor, Criminal Justice: Sabra Horne
Assistant Editor: Dawn Mesa
Editorial Assistant: Paul Massicotte
Technology Project Manager: Susan DeVanna
Marketing Manager: Dory Schaeffer
Marketing Assistant: Neena Chandra
Advertising Project Manager: Stacey Purviance
Project Manager, Editorial Production: Jennie Redwitz
Print/Media Buyer: Doreen Suruki
Permissions Editor: Sarah Harkrader
Production Service: Peggy Francomb, Shepherd, Inc.
Photo Researcher: Suzie Wright
Copy Editor: Cindy Blum
Illustrator: Donna Lennox
Cover Designer: Bill Stanton
Cover Image: Top: © Najlah Feanny/Corbis Saba; center: © Reuters NewMedia Inc./Corbis; bottom: Michael Heller/911 Pictures
Compositor: Shepherd, Inc.
Text and Cover Printer: Phoenix Color Corp
Indexing: Christine M. H. Orthmann

Printed in the United States of America
1 2 3 4 5 6 7 07 06 05 04 03

Library of Congress Control Number: 2003106242

ISBN 0-534-61605-4

Wadsworth/Thomson Learning
10 Davis Drive
Belmont, CA 94002-3098
USA

Asia
Thomson Learning
5 Shenton Way #01-01
UIC Building
Singapore 068808

Australia/New Zealand
Thomson Learning
102 Dodds Street
Southbank, Victoria 3006
Australia

Canada
Nelson
1120 Birchmount Road
Toronto, Ontario M1K 5G4
Canada

Europe/Middle East/Africa
Thomson Learning
High Holborn House
50/51 Bedford Row
London WC1R 4LR
United Kingdom

Brief Contents

Contents

SECTION II **Basic Management/Personal Skills**

Preface

Welcome to the fourth edition of *Management and Supervision in Law Enforcement.* Based on feedback from students and instructors, we have made several changes in this edition, but we have retained our focus on writing a reader-friendly text that provides a comprehensive, up-to-date overview of management and supervision in law enforcement, blending theory and practice. The content applies to agencies of all sizes at all levels: local, county, state and federal.

Key Themes

Although significant changes have been made, three themes continue from previous editions. First, managers and supervisors need to move from an authoritative style to a participative leadership style—empowering all personnel to become contributing team members. Second, community policing and problem solving are key to preserving the peace and fighting crime. Citizens can become allies in both. Law enforcement cannot go it alone any longer. How community policing and problem solving affects management is illustrated throughout the text. Third, change must be viewed as an opportunity rather than something to resist. Not only must managers help their people grow and develop, they, themselves, must continuously grow and develop, looking for new and better ways to accomplish their mission. As futurist Alvin Toffler asserts: "The illiterate of the 21st century will not be those who cannot read and write, but those who cannot learn, unlearn and relearn." This text is a beginning toward opening your mind to new ways of thinking and doing.

Organization of the Text

Section One, Management and Supervision: An Overview, takes a broad look at management, beginning with the law enforcement organization itself and the challenges this organization presents (Chapter 1). Next the role of the manager and the various levels of management and leadership in law enforcement are discussed, including the challenge of participatory management (Chapter 2).

Section Two, Basic Management/Personal Skills, focuses on basic skills that affect everything done by law enforcement managers at all levels. A critical basic skill that can make or break a law enforcement manager is skill in communication. Effective communication is at the core of effective management (Chapter 3). The manager's role, by definition, includes decision making and problem solving (Chapter 4). How decisions are made and by whom are vital management questions. Among the most important decisions are those involving how time will be spent—the time of individual managers, officers and the agency as a whole (Chapter 5). Other important decisions involve how resources other than time can be most effectively managed, that is, the ongoing task of budgeting, which has a direct effect on what individual managers, their officers and ultimately the agency can accomplish (Chapter 6). The second section concludes with a discussion of the selection process and dealing with unions (Chapter 7).

Section Three, Managers and the Skills of Others, focuses on how managers can develop the numerous talents of their subordinates through participatory leadership. It first explains the importance of training (Chapter 8) and then suggests ways managers can go beyond training to fully develop the potential of all personnel (Chapter 9). Managers must not only build on the strengths of their people and accommodate their weaknesses, but also motivate their officers to be as effective as possible. Research has shown that tangible rewards such as pay raises and fringe benefits are not necessarily the most motivating influences. In fact, they are often thought of as givens, making managing much more challenging. Managers who can develop and motivate their team members will make a tremendous contribution to the department and to accomplishing its goals and objectives, thereby also accomplishing its mission. In addition, many concepts basic to motivation are directly related to keeping morale high. Attending to employees' motivation and morale is critical to being an effective manager (Chapter 10).

Section Four, Managing Problems, discusses problems to be anticipated in any law enforcement organization. They are an inevitable part of the challenge of accomplishing work through others. Managers must recognize problem behaviors and use an appropriate combination of constructive criticism, discipline and incentives to correct the problems (Chapter 11). In addition, supervisors and managers will be faced with numerous complaints and grievances from their subordinates, their superiors and the public they serve. They or their officers may, in fact, be the objects of civil lawsuits. Effectively handling such matters requires great knowledge as well as skill in communication (Chapter 12). Conflicts, disagreements, differences of opinions and outright confrontations may also occur and must be dealt with diplomatically by law enforcement managers (Chapter 13). Finally, all the preceding, plus the challenges inherent in law enforcement work itself, can result in extreme stress for supervisors, managers and subordinates. Reducing such stress is a critical role of administrators (Chapter 14).

Section Five, Getting the Job Done—Through Others, focuses on getting the job done through effective leadership. (People would rather be led than "managed.") Personnel must be effectively deployed and their productivity enhanced (Chapter 15). Evaluation should be continuous and should include both formal and informal evaluation. The results should be used to help employees continue to grow and develop and to make the department more effective as well (Chapter 16). The section concludes with a discussion of the need for managers to be forward looking, considering what the future of law enforcement and the entire criminal justice system may hold (Chapter 17).

New to this Edition

The text has been completely updated, with over 500 references from 2000 or more recent and only 28 "classic" references retained. The impact of the 9/11 attack on America in many areas of management and supervision is included. Among the numerous additions to this edition are the following:

- Chapter 1 The Law Enforcement Organization—the emerging law enforcement agency; the contributions of Max Weber, Frederick Taylor, Elton Mayo (the Hawthorne Effect) and Peter Drucker; Enterprise Resource Planning.
- Chapter 2 The Role of the Manager and Leadership in Law Enforcement—mechanistic vs. organic models of management/leadership; developing a strategic plan; essential traits for effective leadership.
- Chapter 3 Communication: A Critical Management Skill—making important messages stand out in the Information Age; difficulties in dealing with the media and suggested policies and procedures for dealing with the media; guidelines to build relationships with the media; the cultural barrier; wearable computers; communication problems on September 11th, 2001; communication and homeland security.
- Chapter 4 Problem Solving and Decision Making—the Abilene Paradox; the difference between handling a call and solving a problem; problem-oriented policing by the 2001 winner of the Herman Goldstein *Excellence in Problem-Oriented Policing Award,* the California Highway Patrol's Corridor Safety Program.
- Chapter 5 Time Management: Minute by Minute—scheduling time; time maps; defragmenting the computer.
- Chapter 6 Budgeting and Managing Costs Creatively—the lead federal funding agency for law enforcement; the Regional Intelligence Sharing System (RISS); contracting; grant-writing skills; obtaining federal grants.
- Chapter 7 Hiring Personnel and Dealing with Unions—recruiting for diversity; recruiting Generation Xers; new applicant screening tests; assuring that physical fitness tests are nondiscriminatory under the Civil Rights Act of 1991; innovations in selection, including the human resource roundtable and candidate ride-alongs; union votes of no-confidence.
- Chapter 8 Training and Beyond—asynchronous vs. synchronous learning; pedagogy vs. androgogy; August Vollmer's contribution to criminal justice education; avoiding failure-to-train lawsuits; differing training needs of the four generations typically found in most law enforcement agencies; characteristics of effective trainers; using case studies in training; the best practices training model.
- Chapter 9 Promoting Growth and Development—where officers' first loyalty must be; expanded discussion on the code of silence; supervisory challenges arising from racial profiling legislation efforts, including ghosting and balancing.
- Chapter 10 Motivation and Morale—turnover problems in law enforcement; strategic career planning.
- Chapter 11 Discipline and Problem Behaviors—discussion of insubordination; expanded discussion of use of force and the Amadou

Diallo shooting; early warning systems (EWS) to identify problem performers.

- Chapter 12 Complaints and Grievances—role of the civilian ombudsman; expanded discussion of internal affairs investigations; officers' rights under *Garrity.*
- Chapter 13 Conflict—It's Inevitable—common mistakes committed by new supervisors; using ombuds.
- Chapter 14 Stress—burst stress; 10 reasons cops' stress is different; overtime and fatigue; depression; the organizational consultant program.
- Chapter 15 Deploying Law Enforcement Resources and Improving Productivity—using scheduling software; steady tours; core principles of Total Quality Management.
- Chapter 16 Performance Appraisals and Evaluation—recognizing value in policing; shortcomings of most current performance appraisals; rater bias; fitness-for-duty evaluations (FFDE), both physical and psychological; evaluating training; the four levels of the Kirkpatrick Model of training evaluation.
- Chapter 17 Challenges in Managing for the Future—an exemplary mission statement for the future; advances in technology; major challenges in the twenty-first century; urban terrorism; homeland security; four broad categories of obstacles facing state and local law enforcement agencies in the terrorism intelligence effort; strategic objectives of homeland security; privitization.

Learning Aids

Management and Supervision in Law Enforcement, fourth edition, is a planned learning experience. It uses *triple strength learning,* presenting all key concepts at least three times within a chapter. The more actively you participate, the better your learning will be. You will learn and remember more if you first familiarize yourself with the total scope of the subject. Read and think about the table of contents; it provides an outline of the many facets of law enforcement management and supervision. Then follow these steps as you study each chapter.

1. Read the objectives at the beginning of the chapter. These are stated as "Do you Know?" questions. Assess your current knowledge of each question. Examine any preconceptions you may hold.
2. Read the list of key terms and think about their possible meanings.
3. Read the chapter, underlining, highlighting or taking notes if that is your preferred study style. Pay special attention to all information that is highlighted. Also pay special attention to all words in **bold** print—these are the key terms for the chapter.
4. When you have finished reading the chapter, reread the "Do You Know?" questions to make sure you can give an educated response to

each. If you find yourself stumped by one, find the appropriate section in the chapter and review it. Also define each key term. Again, if you find yourself stumped, either find the term in the chapter or look it up in the glossary.

5. Read the discussion questions and be prepared to contribute to a class discussion of the ideas presented in the chapter.
6. Periodically review the "Do You Know?" questions, key terms and chapter summaries.

By following these steps, you will learn more, understand better and remember longer.

A Note: The material selected to highlight using the triple-strength learning instructional design includes only the chapter's key concepts. While this information is certainly important because it provides a structural foundation for understanding the topics discussed, you may not simply glance over the "Do You Know?" questions, highlighted boxes and summaries and expect to master the chapter. You are also responsible for reading and understanding the material that surrounds these basics—the "meat" around the bones so to speak.

Exploring Further

The text also provides an opportunity for you to apply what you have learned or to go into greater depth in specific areas through discussions, InfoTrac® College Edition assignments and Internet assignments. Complete each of these areas as directed by the text or by your instructor. Be prepared to share your findings with the class. Good learning!

Ancillaries

To further enhance your study of management and supervision, these supplements are available:

- **Instructor's Manual** Completely updated from the previous edition, the Instructor's Manual includes the following resources for each chapter of the text: a chapter outline, a summary, learning objectives, key terms, possible answers to the discussion questions, InfoTrac College Edition assignment(s) that differ from those in the text, an assignment and application exercise and a test bank. The test bank includes multiple choice, true/false, fill-in/short answer, matching and essay questions.
- **ExamView® Computerized Testing** Create, deliver and customize tests and study guides (both print and online) in minutes with this easy-to-use assessment and tutorial system. ExamView offers both a Quick Test Wizard and an Online Test Wizard that guide you step-by-step through the process of creating tests, while its WYSIWYG capability allows you to see the test you are creating on the screen exactly as it will print or display online. You can build tests of up to 250 questions using up to 12 question types. Using ExamView's complete word processing capabilities, you can enter an unlimited number of new questions or edit existing questions.

Acknowledgements

We would like to thank Christine M. H. Orthmann for her careful editing, indexing and preparation of the Instructor's Manual and ancillaries. We would also like to thank Tim Hess for his review of and contributions to the manuscript. In addition, a heartfelt thanks to the reviewers of the past editions of the text and their valuable suggestions: Timothy Apolito, University of Dayton; Tom Barker, Jacksonville State University; A. J. Bartok, Regional Law Enforcement Academy, Colorado; Lloyd Bratz, Cuyahoga Community College; Gib H. Bruns, Arizona State University; David Carter, Michigan State University; Dana Dewitt, Cadron State College; Larry Gould, Northern Arizona University; Joseph J. Hanrahan, Westfield State College; Robert G. Huckabee, Indiana State University; Alan Lawson, Ferris State University, Michigan; Muriel Lembright, Wichita State University; William McCamey, Western Illinois University; Robert L. Marsh, Boise State University; Robert G. May, Waubonsee Community College; John Maxwell, Community College of Philadelphia; Dennis M. Payne, Michigan State University; Carroll S. Price, Penn Valley Community College; Lawrence G. Stephens, Columbus State Community College; W. Fred Wegener, Indiana University of Pennsylvania; Stanley W. Wisnoski, Jr., Broward Community College; and Solomon Zhao, University of Nebraska, Omaha.

We would like to thank the following reviewers for their insightful suggestions for this fourth edition: Bill Bourns, California State University—Stanislaus; Michael Buckley, Texas A&M University; Dana DeWitt, Chadron State College; Bill Formby, University of Alabama—Tuscaloosa; Lori Guevara, University of Texas—Arlington; Stan Malm, University of Maryland; William McCarney, Western Illinois University. We are deeply indebted to these reviews. Any errors, however, are the sole responsibility of the authors.

Finally, a special thanks to our executive editor, Sabra Horne, our assistant editor, Dawn Mesa, and our production editor, Jennie Redwitz, at Wadsworth and to our production editor Peggy Francomb at Shepherd, Inc.

About the Authors

The content of this text is based on the practical experience of Wayne W. Bennett, who has spent 45 years in law enforcement and has taught various aspects of management and supervision over the past 30 years, as well as the research and experience of Kären M. Hess, Ph.D., who has been developing instructional programs for over 30 years. The text itself has been reviewed by several experts in management and supervision in law enforcement. Any errors, however, are the sole responsibility of the authors.

Wayne W. Bennett is a graduate of the FBI National Police Academy, holds an LL.B. degree in law and has served as the Director of Public Safety for the Edina (Minnesota) Police Department as well as Chief of Police of the Boulder City (Nevada) Police Department. He is co-author of *Criminal Investigation,* 7th edition.

Kären M. Hess holds a Ph.D. in English from the University of Minnesota and a Ph.D. in criminal justice from Pacific Western University. Other West/Wadsworth texts Dr. Hess has co-authored are *Corrections in the 21st Century: A Practical Approach, Criminal Investigation* (Seventh Edition), *Criminal Procedure, Introduction to Law Enforcement and Criminal Justice* (Seventh Edition), *Introduction to Private Security* (Fourth Edition), *Juvenile Justice* (Third Edition), *The Police in the Community: Strategies for the 21st Century* (Third Edition), *Police Operations* (Third Edition), and *Seeking Employment in Criminal Justice and Related Fields* (Fourth Edition).

Dr. Hess is a member of the Academy of Criminal Justice Sciences (ACJS), the American Society for Law Enforcement Trainers (ASLET), the International Association of Chiefs of Police (IACP), the National Institute of Justice (NIJ), the Police Executive Research Forum (PERF) and the Textbook and Academic Author's Association (TAA).

CHAPTER 1

The Law Enforcement Organization

Good organizations are living bodies that grow new muscles to meet challenges.
—Robert Townsend, corporate consultant

Do You Know?

- How law enforcement agencies were traditionally organized?
- What three eras of policing have been identified?
- What should drive an organization?
- How goals differ from objectives and work plans?
- What line and staff personnel are?
- What advantages and disadvantages are associated with specialization?
- What the chain of command is?
- What unity of command refers to?
- What the span of control is?
- What authority should be coupled with?
- What type of organization law enforcement managers should recognize?
- What management tools help coordination?
- What the emerging law enforcement agency looks like?
- What needs to be reexamined in light of the challenges facing law enforcement and our country?
- What three approaches to address the causes of crime, fear of crime and other community issues are promoted by community policing?
- What community-oriented policing and problem solving (COPPS) may offer?

Can You Define?

accountability
administrative services
authority
bifurcated society
chain of command
channels of communication
community era
community policing
coordination
decentralization
delegation
empowered
field services
flat organization
formal organization
generalists
goals
guiding philosophy
Hawthorne Effect
hierarchy
informal organization
key result areas
line personnel
mission
mission statement
objectives
organization
organizational chart
paradigm
paradigm shift
political era
proactive
problem-solving policing
professional model
pyramid of authority
reactive
reform era
responsibility
scuttlebutt
span of control
specialists
spoils system
staff personnel
stakeholders
unity of command
values
Wolf Pack syndrome
work plans

INTRODUCTION

An **organization** is an artificial structure created to coordinate either people or groups and resources to achieve a mission or goal. Organizations exist for many different reasons. One important reason is that a group can accomplish things an individual could never do alone. For example, no single individual could have put a person on the moon, but an organization—NASA—was successful.

The need for organizing has been recognized for centuries. Since recorded time people have banded together into societies. Within these societies they have sought ways to protect themselves from nature and from those who would harm them or their possessions. They made rules, set up ways to enforce these rules and provided swift punishment to those who did not obey. Modern-day law enforcement agencies are an outgrowth of this need for "law and order."

To understand the present, it is often helpful to look at the past—where traditions and the status quo originated. Therefore, the chapter begins with a brief history of the development of law enforcement agencies and the organizational structure that became typical. It examines the traditional military, pyramid-style structure and the generalists and specialists usually found within this organization. The chapter next looks at the mission of law enforcement agencies and the functions they serve. The effect of this mission on an organization's goals, objectives and work plans is then described. This is followed by a discussion of the formal and informal organization within a department and the importance of coordination. The chapter concludes with an exploration of the change occurring in many departments from a focus on crime fighting to a focus on community policing and problem-oriented policing.

The Evolution of Law Enforcement Organizations

Most agencies have an organization with a rich tradition going back to the 1800s in England. In England the Industrial Revolution changed the country from a rural to an urban society, with the accompanying problems of unemployment, poverty and crime. One result was the founding of the Metropolitan Police in London in 1829. The fundamental principles on which this police force rested were set forth by Sir Robert Peel, often called the "Father of Modern Policing." They included the following:

- Police must be stable, efficient and organized militarily.
- Police must be under governmental control.
- The deployment of police strength by both time and area is essential.
- Public security demands that every police officer be given a number.
- Police headquarters should be centrally located and easily accessible.
- The duty of the police is to prevent crime and disorder.
- The power of the police to fulfill these duties is dependent on public approval and on their ability to secure and maintain public respect.
- The police should strive to maintain a relationship with the public that gives reality to the tradition that *the police are the public and the public are the police.*

- The test of police effectiveness is the absence of crime and disorder, not the visible evidence of police activity in dealing with these problems.

The first five principles were embraced almost immediately in the United States, as its cities developed police departments modeled after the London Metropolitan Police. The last four principles, however, were not fully accepted until the advent of community policing, discussed later in the chapter.

New York City established the first modern American city police force in 1844, modeled after London's Metropolitan Police Department. In 1874 the Texas Rangers were commissioned as police officers and became the first agency similar to our present-day state police. Federal agencies were also established, with the FBI created in 1908. In addition to these, many jurisdictions established county law enforcement agencies. These early organizations were modeled after the military, with ranks, levels of command and uniforms. Just as the military has a commander in chief, law enforcement agencies also have chiefs (or sheriffs). Likewise, just as the commander in chief is ultimately responsible to the citizens of the United States, law enforcement chiefs are ultimately responsible to the citizens of the political entity their department serves.

The traditional law enforcement organizational design is that of a pyramid-shaped hierarchy based on a military model.

Law enforcement agencies provide their services to the political entity from which they derive their authority and responsibility. Providing services is their sole reason for existence. It is highly likely that newly created municipalities would expect *someone* to respond to their needs for the many services provided by police. Americans have come to expect and demand reasonably safe communities, so they demand law enforcement organizations. As such organizations develop, they resemble those already in existence in other communities because tradition and experience are enduring.

Further, most present-day law enforcement managers inherited their organizations when they assumed their positions. Many have perpetuated the traditional organization, diagrammed in Figure 1.1, because it has worked.

The Traditional Law Enforcement Organization

Pre-World War II law enforcement agencies followed the industry pattern by placing maximum emphasis on the job and minimum attention on the human interrelationships of people filling the positions. Rigid rules and regulations were used excessively, along with frequent use and abuse of the threat of firing. Individual needs were almost totally ignored. Early law enforcement management was characterized by the general attitude of, "If you don't like the job, plenty of others want it."

Law enforcement organizations were simple. The typical **pyramid of authority** predominated with its **hierarchy** of authoritative management. Command officers and supervisors had complete authority over subordinates, and there was little tolerance for departmental appeal except through the courts.

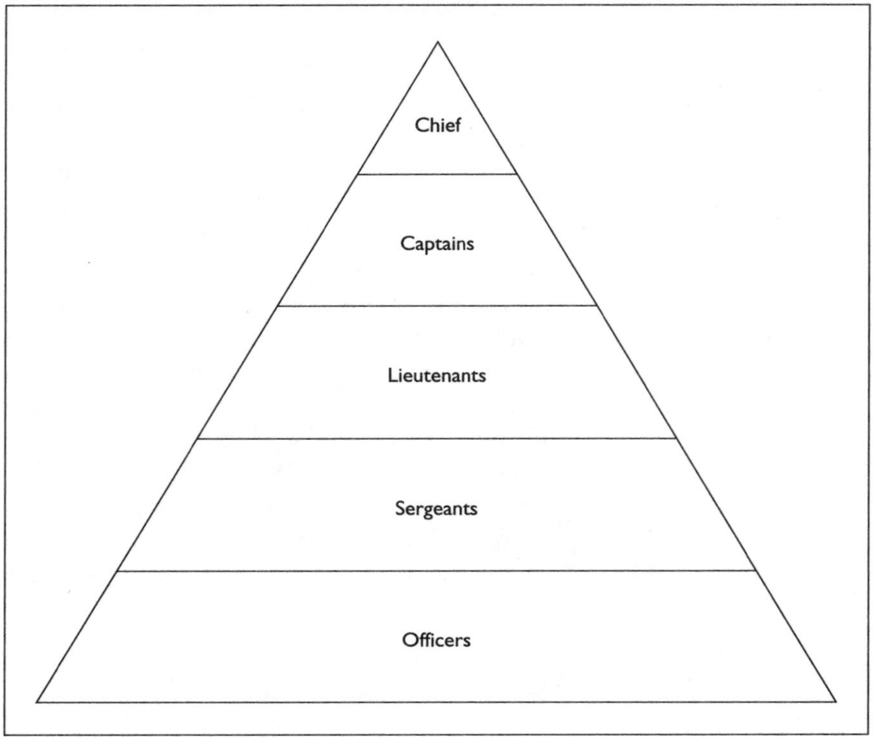

Figure 1.1
The Pyramid of Authority—Organizational Hierarchy

Communication flowed downward. Little or no specialization existed, and training was nonexistent or minimal. Selection was based largely on physical qualifications, and most applicants had military experience.

The majority of personnel were assigned to foot patrol. Police radio communications systems and other technology were virtually nonexistent. University- or college-level training, programs and even courses were unheard of. Ten-hour days and six-day weeks were common, accompanied by extremely low salaries. Flexibility was nonexistent, and fringe benefits were few. As a line in the operetta *The Mikado* puts it: "A policeman's lot was not a happy one."

The Three Eras of Policing

Policing has evolved in the way it views itself, its responsibilities and the most effective means of meeting those responsibilities.

Three distinct eras of policing have been identified: the political era, the reform era and the community era.

The Political Era (1840–1930)

In the **political era,** policing was characterized by police authority coming from politicians and the law, a broad social service function, decentralized organization, an intimate relationship with the community and extensive use of foot patrol. Because of the close tie between police authority and politics during this era, corruption was common. One factor underlying this corruption was the prevalent **spoils system,** whose motto, "To the victor go the spoils," resulted in political interference with policing. The prevailing party believed its members should be immune from arrest and receive other special privileges. Furthermore, the spoils system encouraged politicians to reward their friends by giving them key positions in police departments. A major step toward reducing corruption within police departments occurred in 1883, when Congress passed the Pendleton Act, which created the civil service system in which job applicants were tested and awarded jobs based on their test scores. Promotions were to be based on merit, not politics. The Act also made it unlawful to fire or demote a government employee for political reasons.

During the political era police served a broad social service function, with some even running soup lines. Police were also close to their community, with foot patrol bringing beat officers into contact with the people.

In 1929 President Herbert Hoover appointed the National Commission on Law Observance and Enforcement to examine the American criminal justice system. The commission, named after chairman George Wickersham, devoted two reports to the police. Report 11, *Lawlessness in Law Enforcement,* described the problem of police brutality, concluding that "the third degree—the inflicting of pain, physical or mental, to extract confessions or statements—is extensively practiced." Report 14, *The Police,* focused on police administration and called for expert leadership, centralized administrative control and higher personnel standards. In other words, Report 14 called for police professionalism, which led to the second era.

The Reform Era (1930–1980)

The reform era developed in reaction to the political. During the **reform era** policing was characterized by police authority coming from the law and professionalism, crime control as the primary function, a centralized and efficient organization, a professional remoteness from the community and an emphasis on preventive motorized patrol and rapid response to crime. J. Edgar Hoover (1895–1972) was director of the FBI from 1924 to 1972 and placed the agency's emphasis on catching criminals.

As early as the 1920s, August Vollmer, often called the father or dean of modern police administration, was calling for reforms in policing. He developed the first degree-granting program in law enforcement at San Jose State College and advocated that police function as social service workers and act to prevent crime. A Vollmer protégé, O. W. Wilson, became the main architect of the reform era and the style of policing known as the **professional model.** Like Vollmer, Wilson advocated police efficiency through scientific techniques. His classic text, *Police Administration,* was considered the bible of police administration during the 1950s. It outlined specific ways to use one-officer patrol cars, to deploy personnel and to discipline officers. In 1947 Wilson founded the first professional school of criminology.

Reformers who sought to disassociate policing from politics advocated professional law enforcement officers charged with enforcing the law fairly and impartially. The social service function so prevalent during the political era became less important, even nonexistent in some departments, as police turned greater attention to fighting a war on crime. Two key strategies in this war were preventive automobile patrol and rapid response to calls. This style of policing is what most Americans are familiar with and have come to expect.

Reform that had begun during the 1930s and thrived during the 1950s and 1960s began to erode during the 1970s. One event in 1972 had a great impact on eroding the reform strategy. The classic Kansas City Preventive Patrol Experiment called into question the effectiveness of preventive patrol and rapid response—the two central strategies of the reform era. Wrobleski and Hess (2003, p.28) remark:

> The professional model faced many challenges including the inability of "traditional" police approaches to decrease crime; the rapidly escalating drug problem; the pressing problems associated with the deinstitutionalization of thousands of mentally ill people, many of whom became homeless; dealing with thousands of immigrants, some legal, some illegal, many speaking no English; and the breakdown of the family unit.

To meet these challenges, many departments turned to community-oriented policing—COP.

The Community Era (1980–Present)

Following changes occurring in corporate America, many police departments became customer-oriented, viewing citizens as consumers of police services. Policing during the **community era** is characterized by police authority coming from community support, law and professionalism; provision of a broad range of services, including crime control; decentralized organization with greater authority given to patrol officers; an intimate relationship with the community; and the use of foot patrol and a problem-solving approach.

Community policing is discussed in greater depth later in this chapter and throughout the text, as it affects all aspects of the police organization and function. Table 1.1 summarizes the distinguishing characteristics of the three eras of policing.

Other Influences on the Evolution of Police Management

Management principles evolving in the business world have directly influenced how police executives have managed their forces. Such changes have taken police management and leadership philosophies from a strict control approach to an approach that delegates increased responsibility to the line officer.

Max Weber (1864–1920), a German sociologist and economist, helped establish the foundations of modern sociology. He considered bureaucracy to be the most important feature of modern society. Weber believed that business was conducted from a desk or office by preparing and dispatching written documents through an elaborate hierarchical division of labor directed by explicit rules impersonally applied. Bureaucracy was (and is) important in the organization of police departments.

Table 1.1
The Three Eras of Policing

	Political Era 1840 to 1930	Reform Era 1930 to 1980	Community Era 1980 to Present
Authorization	Politicians and law	Law and professionalism	Community support (political), law and professionalism
Function	Broad social services	Crime control	Broad provision of services
Organizational Design	Decentralized	Centralized, classical	Decentralized, task forces
Relationship to Community	Intimate	Professional, remote	Intimate
Tactics and Technology	Foot patrol	Preventive patrol and rapid response to calls	Foot patrol, problem solving, public relations
Outcome	Citizen, political satisfaction	Crime control	Quality of life and citizen satisfaction

Source: Linda S. Miller and Kären M. Hess. *The Police in the Community: Strategies for the 21st Century*, 3rd ed. Belmont, CA: West/Wadsworth Publishing, 2002, p.14. (Summarized from George L. Kelling and Mark H. Moore, "From Political to Reform to Community: The Evolving Strategy of Police." In *Community Policing: Rhetoric or Reality.* Edited by Jack R. Green and Stephen D. Mastrofski, New York: Praeger Publishers, 1991, pp.6, 14–15, 22–23.)

Also influential and living in the same time period was Frederick W. Taylor (1865–1915), an American industrial engineer, sometimes referred to as the father of scientific management. His book *The Principles of Scientific Management* (1911) called for a small span of control, a clear chain of command, a tall organizational hierarchy and centralized decision making modeled after the military. This method of management style became standard in police organizations during the reform era.

Another influence on management was Elton Mayo's experiment from 1927–1932 at the Hawthorne Plant of the Western Electric Company in Cicero, Illinois. According to Clark (2002): "The major finding of the study was that almost regardless of the experimental manipulation employed, the production of the workers seemed to improve. One reasonable conclusion is that the workers were pleased to receive attention from the researchers who expressed an interest in them." This became known as the **Hawthorne Effect.** Production increased not as a consequence of actual changes in working conditions introduced by the plant's management but because management demonstrated interest in such improvements. Says Clark: "For decades the Hawthorne studies provided the rationale for human relations within the organization." The Hawthorne Effect also needs to be taken into account when research is being conducted.

During the 1940s American economist and management specialist and consultant Peter Drucker (1909) became influential, asserting that productivity was the result of self-starting, self-directed workers who accepted responsibility. He advocated a shift from traditional production lines to flexible production methods. Among his most quoted statements are the following:

- Efficiency is doing better what is already being done.
- There is nothing so useless as doing efficiently that which should not be done at all.

- Today knowledge has power. It controls access to opportunity and advancement.
- Management is doing things right; leadership is doing the right things.
- The individual is the central, rarest, most precious capital resource of our society.

Drucker's ideas were influential in the shift in management styles discussed in the next chapter. Although police departments have changed substantially since their early beginnings in this country, from their very beginnings police departments have had a mission, stated or unstated.

The Law Enforcement Mission

The primary purpose of most law enforcement agencies has become less clear over the past decades. Traditionally, as the name implies, the mission was to enforce the law, that is, to fight crime. In the 21st century, however, many departments have changed their focus to providing services while other departments seek a combination of the two. It is important for departments to clearly articulate their **mission** or purpose in writing.

The **mission statement,** the organization's overriding purpose, should be the driving force of any organization, including law enforcement, focusing its energy.

Mission statements articulate the rationale for an organization's existence. A mission statement can be the most powerful underlying influence in law enforcement, affecting organizational and individual attitudes, conduct and performance. Mission statements are best developed by an appointed committee, representative but not too large for individual participation. Developing the statement is only the first step. It must then be distributed, explained, understood and accepted by all department members. A mission statement is not automatically implemented or effective. It must be practiced in everyday actions and decision making by management and field personnel.

The mission statement of a law enforcement agency should be believable, worthy of support, widely known, shared and exciting to key stakeholders. **Stakeholders** are those *affected by* the organization and those in a position *to affect it.* In a law enforcement organization, stakeholders include everyone in the jurisdiction. Two key questions to answer are (1) what do the stakeholders *want?* and (2) what do the stakeholders *need?* What people want and what they need are *not* necessarily the same. Stakeholders should, however, have input into what is provided for them.

An example of an effective mission statement is that of the Charlotte (North Carolina) Police Department:

> The Charlotte Police Department is committed to fairness, compassion, and excellence while providing police services in accordance with the law and sensitive to the priorities and needs of the people.

A mission statement such as this can both guide and drive an organization. Mission statements are usually part of an organization's overall guiding philosophy.

An Organization's Guiding Philosophy and Values

A **guiding philosophy** consists of an organization's mission statement *and* its basic **values,** the beliefs, principles or standards considered worthwhile or desirable. Consider, for example, the values set forth by the International Association of Chiefs of Police (IACP):[1]

> The members of IACP are committed to the values that are reflected in the association's constitution, member Code of Ethics and Strategic Plan. These include:
>
> A commitment to fair and impartial enforcement of laws and ordinances and respect for fundamental human rights.
>
> A commitment to advancing the principles of respect for individual dignity and respect for constitutional rights of all persons with whom their departments come into contact.
>
> A commitment to the highest ideals of honor and integrity to maintain the respect and confidence of their governmental officials, subordinates, the public and their fellow police executives.
>
> A dedication to innovative and participative management, at all times seeking to improve their departments, increase productivity and remain responsive to the needs of their jurisdiction.
>
> A commitment to friendly and courteous service by striving to improve communications with all members of the public, at all times seeking improvement in the quality and image of public service.
>
> A dedication to improve their personal knowledge and abilities and those of their colleagues through independent study, courses, meetings and seminars.
>
> A reverence for the value of human life and commitment to conduct themselves so as to maintain public confidence in their profession, the department and their performance of the public trust.

You may be thinking that mission statements and value statements are fine but are simply words. How do such words get translated into action?

Our Declaration of Independence was a statement of the guiding philosophy of our country, but it did not establish how the United States should be structured or governed. This was accomplished through our Constitution and Bill of Rights. A statement of philosophy is meaningless without a plan or blueprint for accomplishing it. Goals, objectives and work plans provide this blueprint.

Goals, Objectives and Work Plans

Goals, objectives and work plans are interdependent. All three are needed to carry out an organization's mission.

Goals are broad, general, desired outcomes. **Objectives** are specific, measurable ways to accomplish the goals. **Work plans** are the precise activities that contribute to accomplishing objectives.

[1]Reprinted from *The Police Chief,* Vol. LXI, No. 11, November 1993, p.14. Copyright held by The International Association of Chiefs of Police, Inc., 515 N. Washington St., Alexandria, Virginia 22314. Further reproduction without express written permission from IACP is strictly prohibited.

Goals

Goals are visionary, projected achievements. They provide guidelines for planning efforts. They are what in business would be called the **key result areas.** Goals provide the foundation for objectives and ultimately for work plans. Among the commonly agreed-upon goals of most law enforcement agencies are to enforce laws, prevent crime, preserve the peace, protect civil rights and civil liberties, provide services and solve problems.

Few people would argue about the value of these goals. The disagreements arise over which are most important and how resources should be apportioned. For example, providing how much service and of what kind, compared with how much enforcing of laws? It is also often difficult to determine which objectives might accomplish the goals.

Objectives

Objectives are needed before work plans can be developed. They are much more specific than goals and usually have a time line. Objectives are critical to planning, assigning tasks and evaluating performance. For example, one objective might be to reduce traffic accidents by 20 percent by the end of the year.

Good objectives are clear and understandable, especially to those who will be responsible for carrying them out. They are also practical; that is, they are realistic and achievable. Personnel must have the knowledge, skill and resources to accomplish their objectives. Effective objectives deal with important matters. They should motivate and energize each person to perform not only at a high level individually but also as a team member.

Law enforcement managers are obligated to support the objectives of both the organization and the employees. Regardless of position all employees must act responsibly toward the organization and each other. Good objectives provide the basis for a department's work plans.

Work Plans

Work plans, sometimes called *tactical and strategic plans,* are the detailed steps needed to accomplish objectives. They are tied to a time line and are an effective way to evaluate an organization's performance. To accomplish the objective of reducing traffic accidents, a department might establish the following work plans (in January):

- Analyze where accidents are happening to determine their cause by July1.
- Based on this analysis, take steps to correct identified problems by December 1.
- Conduct 10 educational meetings regarding traffic safety for the public by June 1.
- Design and display 5 educational billboards regarding drinking and driving by April 1.

After a law enforcement agency has determined its goals and objectives and developed work plans, these plans must be put into action—by people organized to do so.

The Formal Organization

The **formal organization** is put together by design and rational plan. The essential elements of a formal organization are:

- A clear statement of mission, goals, objectives and values (as discussed on the previous page).
- A division of labor among specialists.
- A rational organization or design.
- A hierarchy of authority and responsibility.

Typical Divisions in Law Enforcement Agencies

Law enforcement agencies typically are divided into field and administrative services, with personnel designated as line and staff personnel.

Field services using **line personnel** *directly* help accomplish the goals of the department. **Administrative services** using **staff personnel** *support* the line organization.

Field services' main division is the uniformed patrol. Larger agencies may have other divisions as well, such as investigations, narcotics, vice and juvenile. Line personnel fulfill the goals and objectives of the organization. This is what most people think of as law enforcement—the uniformed police officer on the street.

Field service divisions are typically further broken into shifts to provide service within a framework of geographical space and extended time. Continuity of service must be provided between areas and shifts. Larger departments may divide the political entity they serve into distinct *precincts* or *district stations,* the geographical areas served by a given portion of the officers, essentially forming a number of smaller organizations subject to overall administration and operational command. Time is typically divided into three eight-hour shifts so that service can be provided continuously. Officers frequently rotate through these shifts. Personnel assigned to specific divisions and shifts vary depending on the community's size and service needs.

Administrative services, which are usually centralized, include recruitment and training, records and communications, planning and research, and technical services. Staff personnel assist line personnel, including supervisors. The laboratory staff, for example, assists line personnel, acting as liaisons, specialists or advisory personnel. They are technical experts who provide specialized information. Legal staff (city, county or district attorneys) act as legal advisors to all members of the agency.

Conflicts can and do arise between line and staff, particularly when staff attempts to act in a capacity beyond advisory or informational. Both line and staff are necessary components of the law enforcement organization. They must, however, be coordinated and controlled to achieve department goals.

Division of Labor—Generalists and Specialists

Law enforcement agencies, despite their organizational hierarchy, are basically decentralized units, with most decisions made at the level of the patrol, detective, juvenile and narcotics officers and that of the first-line supervisor. Even the authority to arrest is made at the lowest level of the organization. Most arrests are made by patrol officers, detectives and juvenile officers.

Law enforcement agencies cannot function without division of work and, often, specialization. Neither can they function without maximum coordination of these **generalists** and **specialists.** As the organization grows in size, specialization develops to meet the needs of the community. The extent of specialization is a management decision.

Specialization occurs when the organizational structure is divided into units with specific tasks to perform. The patrol unit is assigned the majority of personnel and provides the greatest variety of tasks and services. Even though specialized units are formed, the patrol division often still performs some tasks of these units.

For example, patrol officers may investigate a crime scene up to the point at which they must leave their shift or area to continue the investigation. Or they may investigate only to the point of protecting the scene and keeping witnesses present, or making an immediate arrest of a suspect. At this point they may complete their report on tasks performed relating to the specific crime and either turn it over to another shift of patrol officers or to the investigative unit. Regardless of the division of tasks performed by generalist or specialist units, close communication about cases must occur or problems develop.

Specialization creates a potential for substantially increased levels of expertise, creativity and innovation. The more completely an employee can perform a task or set of tasks, the more job satisfaction the employee will experience. When specialization is not practical, people must understand why the division of labor is necessary. It must also be clear where patrol's responsibility ends and that of the investigative unit begins.

The greater the specialization, necessary as it is, the greater the difficulties of coordination, communication, control and employee relationships. Conflicts and jealousies may arise: "Let the expert do it if he or she is going to get the credit."

Officers in a small agency must perform all tasks. They cannot afford the luxury of specialization. However, with more standardized training requirements and accreditation, all officers have similar backgrounds for performing tasks, regardless of the size of the agency. The major difference is the frequency of opportunity.

Specialization can enhance a department's effectiveness and efficiency, but overspecialization can impede the organizational purpose.

Overspecialization fragments opportunity to achieve the organizational purpose of providing courteous, competent, expeditious law enforcement services. The more specialized an agency becomes, the more attention must be paid to interrelationships and coordination.

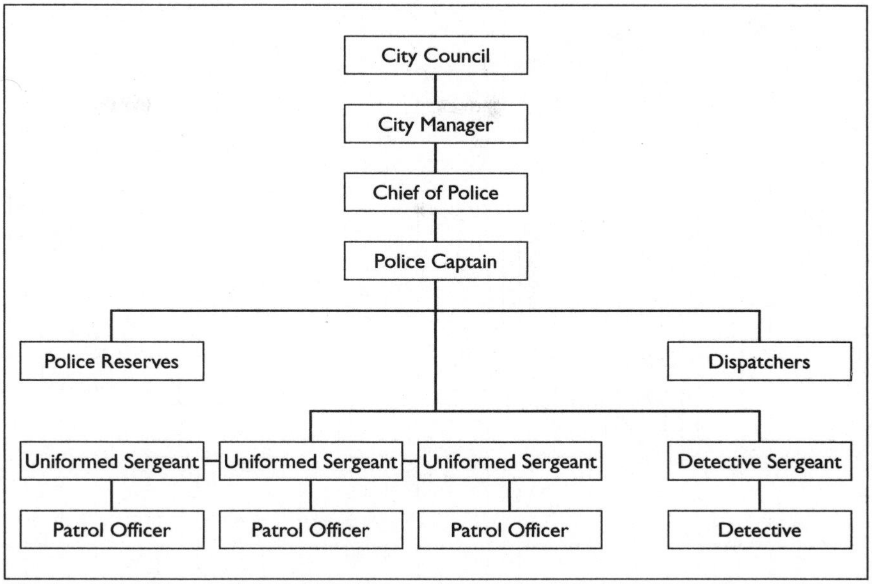

Source: Courtesy of the Boulder City Police Department.

Figure 1.2
A Typical Small Police Department Organizational Chart

Rational Organization and Hierarchy of Authority

The structure of most police departments, as noted, has traditionally been a semi-military, pyramid-shaped hierarchy with authority flowing from the narrow apex down to the broad base. This hierarchical pyramid is often graphically represented in an organizational chart.

The Organizational Chart

An **organizational chart** visually depicts how personnel are organized within an agency and might also illustrate how the agency fits into the community's political structure. Figure 1.2 shows the organization of the police department of Boulder City, Nevada, a community with a population over 15,000 and a police department of 29. This is typical of how police departments are organized in smaller cities. The figure also shows how the police department fits into the city's organizational structure.

This formal organization is generally supported in writing by rules and regulations, department operational manuals and job descriptions. All provide control and a foundation from which actions can be taken.

The larger the agency and the jurisdiction it serves, the more complex the organization and the chart depicting it. Figure 1.3, a chart of the Minneapolis Police Department, shows how a large police department is organized.

Chain of Command

The **chain of command** is the order of authority. It begins at the top of the pyramid with the chief or sheriff and flows downward through the commissioned ranks in the agency—from deputy chief to captain to lieutenant to sergeant and finally to the patrol officer.

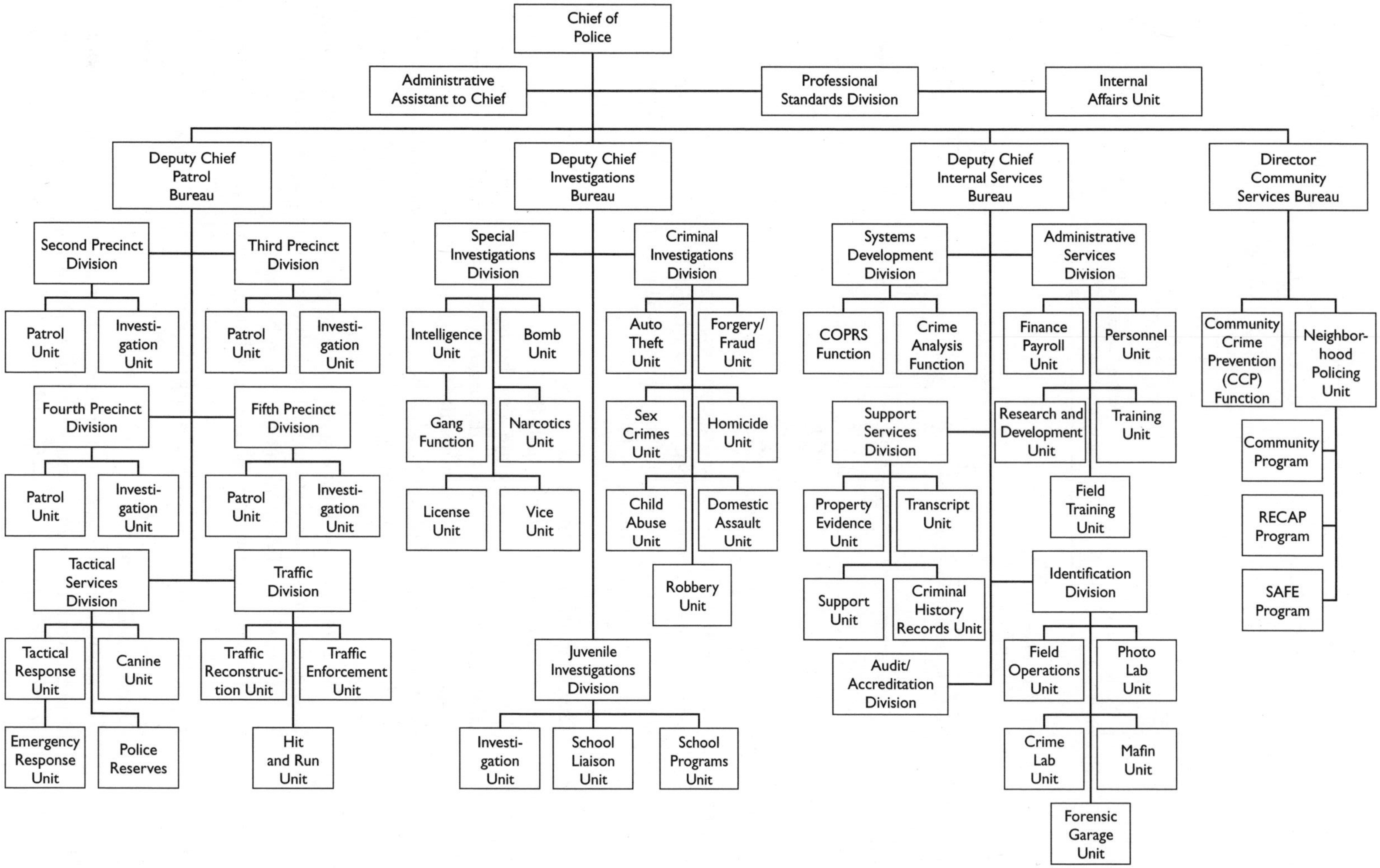

Source: Courtesy of the Minneapolis Police Department.

Figure 1.3
A Typical Large Police Department Organizational Chart

The chain of command establishes definite lines of authority and **channels of communication.**

Each level must forward communications to the next higher or lower level. Channels of communication are the official paths through which orders flow from management to workers. Most companies set up these channels carefully and for good reasons. They are the "highways" for orders and communications to follow and, as such, keep everyone aware of events. They coordinate the organization into a whole unit instead of a series of parts. When an individual leaves these channels and takes a shortcut, he or she is apt to run into problems. For example, a patrol officer who takes a complaint directly to the chief rather than to the sergeant would probably fall out of favor in the department.

Sometimes in law enforcement work, however, emergencies exist that cannot wait to send information through the expected channels. This is one of the challenges of police work.

Unity of Command

Another important part of the organizational design is unity of command.

Unity of command means that every individual in the organization has only one immediate superior or supervisor.

Unity of command is extremely important and needs to be ensured in most instances. Each individual, unit and situation should be under the control of one—and only one—person.

Span of Control

Another factor in most law enforcement organizations is the number of people one individual manages or supervises.

The **span of control** refers to the number of people or units supervised by one manager.

Participants in management classes frequently ask, "What is a reasonable number of people for one person to supervise or manage?" No absolute answer exists. Historically three or four people were considered the maximum that could be effectively managed in a law enforcement agency. However, because of technological advances such as communications with personnel in the field, higher levels of education and training and the extent of the empowerment and flattening of the organization, this number may rise. The span of control also depends on the department's size, the supervisors' and subordinates' abilities, crime rates, community expectations and the political environment. Often the greater the span of control, the less effective the management or supervision.

Do not confuse span of control with how many people one person has authority over. The chief, for example, has authority over everyone in the department, but the chief's span of control extends to only those who report directly to him or her.

The span of control must be realistic. If too few people report to a manager, that manager is not earning his or her salary. If too many people report to a manager, that manager cannot do a good job with all of them. Within a law enforcement agency, the more levels in the pyramid, the smaller the span of control. A number of factors must be considered:

- Distance in space and time between manager and subordinate.
- Difficulty of the tasks performed.
- Types of assistance available to the manager.
- Extent of direction subordinates need.
- Extent of subordinates' skill and experience.

Each factor must be considered as personnel are assigned. Other important considerations are who has authority, who has responsibility and what can be delegated.

Authority, Responsibility and Delegation

Authority, responsibility and delegation are key factors in any organization. Without them organizations could not exist.

Authority is the power to enforce laws, exact obedience and command. **Responsibility** is the state of being answerable, liable or accountable. Thus, managers have the authority to give commands, and subordinates have the responsibility of carrying out the commands. This is very much in keeping with the militaristic model.

The third concept, **delegation,** is also crucial in any organization. Organizations exist because they can accomplish what no one person can accomplish. That single person, the chief, must be able to assign (delegate) tasks to others, who may, in turn, further delegate.

When authority is delegated, it should be coupled with responsibility.

This concept is *key* for all managers, at whatever their level within the police organization, for this is how **accountability** can be ensured. Accountability makes people responsible for tasks assigned to them. Accountability is needed because all the tasks specified in the agency's work plans must be accomplished by someone if the organization is to fulfill its mission. As important as the formal organization of a police department is, as in any group, an informal structure also exists.

The Informal Organization

The formal organization groups people by task and responsibility and clearly delineates the chain of command and channels of communication. The **informal organization** exists side-by-side with this formal organization and may in fact be a truer representation of the way the department actually functions (Figure 1.4).

Within any organization some people may emerge as leaders, regardless of whether they are in a leadership position. In addition, within any organization people will form their own groups—people who enjoy being together and perhaps working together. In Figure 1.4, can you identify the various individuals and groups depicted in the informal organizational chart?

Managers should recognize the informal organization that exists within any law enforcement agency.

Recall the Hawthorne Effect discussed earlier in the chapter. The Hawthorne researchers also found that the workplace had a social system and that this informal organization affected productivity (Clark). The informal organization operates without official sanctions, but it influences agency performance. It may help or harm the goals of the formal organization, and it may support the organization or cause dissention.

Inasmuch as informal organizations are going to exist regardless of whether the supervisor likes them, it might be wise to view them as a positive force and use them to facilitate the work of the department. This can be done by thinking of the informal leader not as a ringleader but as a person "in on things," one whose talents can benefit the whole group.

One aspect of the informal organization is **scuttlebutt,** that is, gossip or rumors. Scuttlebutt can undermine morale and reduce productivity. Also of importance is the **Wolf Pack syndrome,** thought by some to be a vestige of primitive male hunting groups. Within these groups no weaknesses were tolerated because the deficiency of one individual could mean dire consequences for all. Any weak member was attacked by the others. Such aggressive behavior helped ensure that the group would be strong when it faced danger. For example, if one police officer sees another's unoccupied squad car with its window open, the officer may put all the police gear in the car on the unsecured squad's hood and then hide to watch the errant officer return to the very visible evidence of his mistake.

Successful managers are able to coordinate the efforts of both the formal and the informal organization.

Coordination

Coordination ensures that each individual unit performs harmoniously with the total effort to achieve the department's mission.

Management tools for coordination include:

- A clear chain of command and unity of command.
- Clear channels of communication and strict adherence to them.
- Clear, specific job descriptions.
- Clear, specific goals, objectives and work plans.
- Standard operating procedures for routine tasks.
- An agency regulation guidebook.
- Meetings and roll calls.
- Informational bulletins, newsletters and memos.

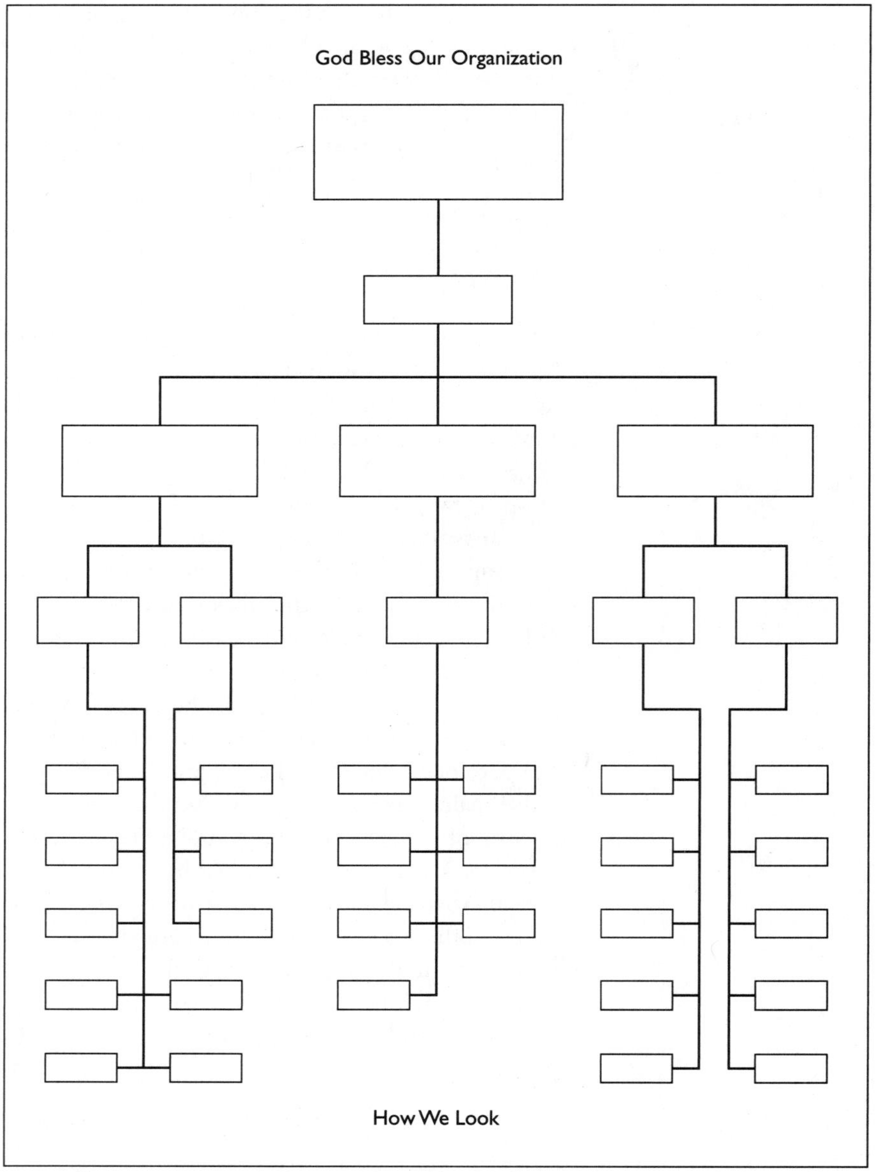

Figure 1.4
Formal and Informal Organizational Charts

Source: Kären M. Hess, ed. From *The Positive Manager* by Wilson Learning Corporation. Copyright © 1985 by Wiley Publishing, Inc. All rights reserved. Reproduced here by permission of the publisher. (***continued***)

Coordinating efforts should be a part of an agency's work plan. Coordination is especially important in departments that are changing their focus from crime fighting to community policing and problem solving.

The Emerging Law Enforcement Organization

Business and industry are undergoing sweeping changes in organization and management styles to remain competitive. Law enforcement agencies are also facing the need for change to meet the competition of private policing. Harr and

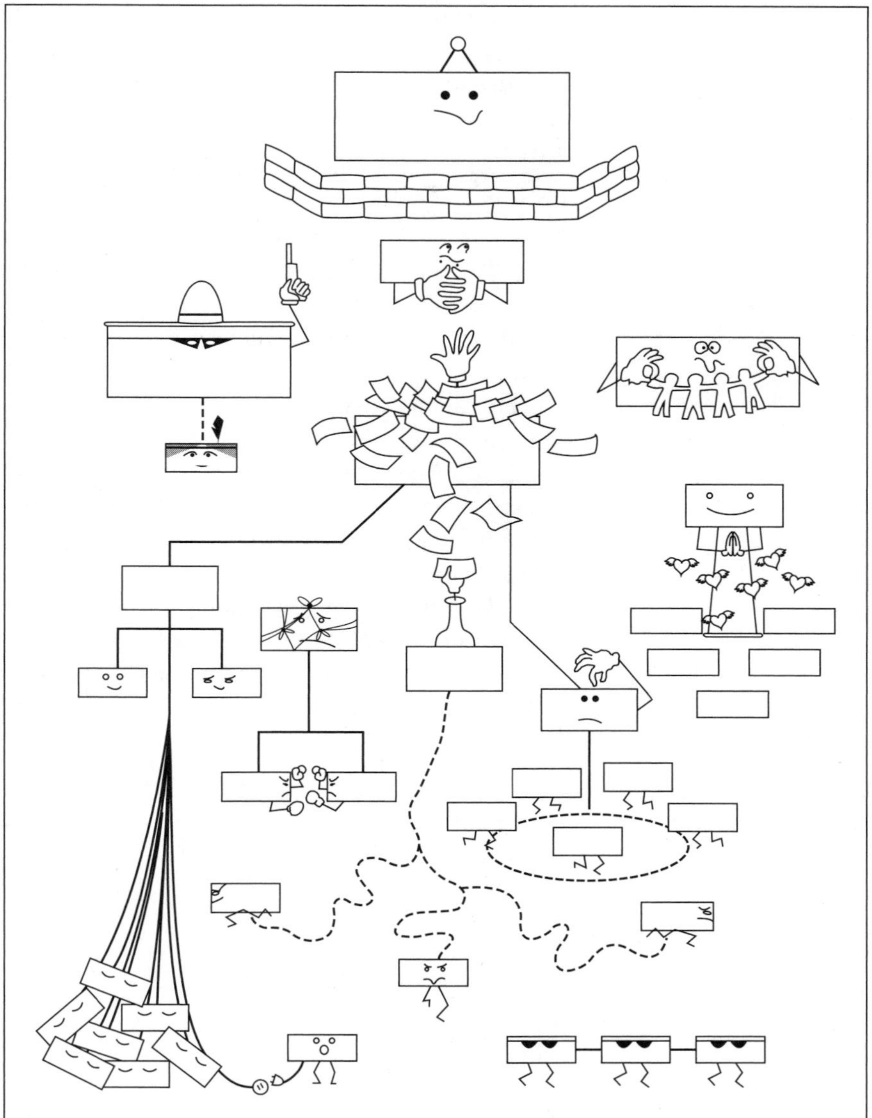

Figure 1.4
Continued

Hess (2002, p.65) note: "Private security is now clearly the nation's primary protective resource, outspending public law enforcement by more than 73 percent and employing nearly three times the people."

Police departments and other law enforcement agencies not only must compete with private police but also must compete for the bright, young college graduates entering the work force. No longer will law enforcement agencies be recruiting a majority of candidates with a military background. Instead they will be recruiting college graduates who will not accept authority blindly. Other changes are also evident in police departments across the country.

The emerging law enforcement agency has a flattened organization, is decentralized and empowers its employees.

Like businesses, for the sake of efficiency, many police departments are turning to a **flat organization,** one with fewer lieutenants and captains, fewer staff departments, fewer staff assistants, more sergeants and more patrol officers. Typical pyramid organization charts will have the top pushed down and the sides expanded at the base. Some police departments are beginning to experiment with alternative organization designs. One example of such experimentation places the patrol officers at the top with everyone under them playing a supporting role (Figure 1.5).

Top-heavy organizational structures are no longer tolerated in business. Progressive firms are flattening their structure, restructuring top-heavy organizations, and pushing authority and decision making as low as possible. Accompanying this change in organizational structure is decentralization.

Decentralization according to Turner (2000, p.50) generally refers to a department's organizational structure and operations: "It is an operating principle that encourages flattening of the organization and places decision making authority and autonomy at the level where information is plentiful. In police organiza-

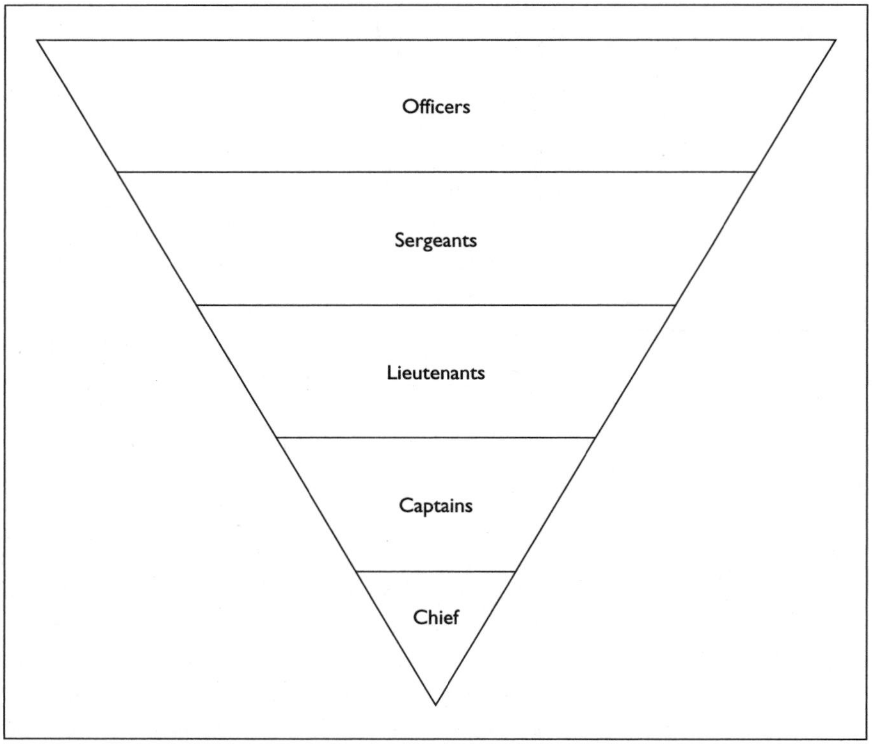

Figure 1.5
The Inverted Pyramid of Authority—Organizational Hierarchy

tions, this is usually at the level of the patrol officer, where officers interacting with the public need the freedom to exercise discretion within predetermined parameters." Flattened, decentralized organizations empower line personnel.

Successful businesses concentrate on soliciting ideas from everyone in their organizations about every facet of their operations. This approach should be applied to policing, especially in larger departments. If officer retention is to be maintained and loyalty and morale preserved and heightened, officers must be **empowered.** Empowered officers are given legal authority to act on their own discretion. As noted by French and Stewart (2001, p.14): "Today's law enforcement organizations engage new organizational practices that focus on empowerment, teamwork and participative management." This is a dramatic change from the old classic overseer management using POSDCoRB (Planning, Organizing, Staffing, Directing, Coordinating, Reporting and Budgeting) to the newer interpersonal close-to-the-boss organizational style and structure. This change is discussed in detail in Chapter 2.

In summary, Maloney and Moty (2002, p.9) state: "Research consistently found that organizations of the future will look flat, lean, flexible and decentralized, with responsibility and accountability pushed to the lowest levels."

Why the Need to Change?

Some readers may be thinking, "If it ain't broke, don't fix it. What's wrong with the way the law enforcement agencies are organized? They have worked fine for the past 200 years."

However, law enforcement must now deal with disruptive social, demographic and technological changes. America is becoming increasingly diverse, with more minorities and more elderly people. Immigrants, legal and illegal, are streaming into our country. People with disabilities are entering into mainstream America after the passage of the Americans with Disabilities Act, and thousands of mentally ill people have been released from institutions, often becoming homeless. In addition, America is becoming a **bifurcated society** with more wealth, more poverty and a shrinking middle class. The gap between the "haves" and the "have nots" is widening. Other social and cultural changes include the weakening influence of family, church and school.

Technology is also forcing policing to change. Technology has revolutionized law enforcement, affecting everything from crime scene investigations to law enforcement gear, weapons and police vehicles.

Finally, the inability of law enforcement to win the "war on drugs" has shown that the police cannot fight crime and disorder by themselves. They need the help of the citizens within their jurisdiction. This need has become even greater after the tragic events of September 11, 2001. The fear of terrorism affects all Americans. Combatting this heightened threat to our national security requires a combined effort.

The challenges facing not only law enforcement but also our entire country necessitate reexamining our public organizations, including law enforcement.

These changes may require a **paradigm shift,** *a dramatic change in how some basic structure is viewed.* A **paradigm** is a model, theory or frame of reference. For example, in the early beginnings of our country, we were an agricultural society. The Industrial Revolution dramatically changed how we viewed our society. We have since shifted to an information-based society. Likewise, law enforcement appears to be undergoing a paradigm shift from an emphasis on crime fighting to an emphasis on order maintenance and peace keeping.

It is important that law enforcement managers at all levels re-examine past assumptions, consider future projections and think very carefully about the future of policing, law enforcement and the entire criminal justice system, including the move toward community involvement in every aspect of policing, courts and corrections.

Community-Oriented Policing and Problem Solving (COPPS)

Gerber (2001, p.40) notes: "The face of law enforcement is changing from report-writing investigators who respond to emergencies and catch criminals to multi-faceted neighborhood workers tasked with affecting quality-of-life issues in the communities they serve. . . . Today's police officer must be part cop, part social worker, part paramedic, part teacher, part computer technician, part pastor, part parent and part politician." He suggests that "community policing initiatives pick up steam as the face of law enforcement changes."

Miller and Hess (2002, p.483) define **community policing** as: "A philosophy or orientation that emphasizes working with citizens to solve crime-related problems and prevent crime." They (p.xix) note:

> Community policing offers one avenue for making neighborhoods safer. Community policing is not a program or a series of programs. It is a philosophy, a belief that working together, the police and the community can accomplish what neither can accomplish alone. The *synergy* that results from community policing can be powerful. It is like the power of a finely tuned athletic team, with each member contributing to the total effort. Occasionally heroes may emerge, but victory depends on a team effort.

The Upper Midwest Community Policing Institute says:

"Community policing is an organization-wide philosophy and management approach that promotes (1) community, government and police partnerships; (2) proactive problem solving; and (3) community engagement to address the causes of crime, fear of crime and other community issues."

Table 1.2 compares traditional policing with community policing.

Hochstetler (2002, p.34) points out: "Community policing is not new; it is based on Sir Robert Peel's belief that 'the police are the public, and the public is the police.' " You may want to return to page 4 and look again at Peel's last four principles. Hochstetler (p.36) contends: "The community must be engaged in its own protection, and it should sense that officers are willing to help to make the quality of life better in non-traditional ways. Community policing gives officers the tools to effect those changes in not only behavior but in attitude, and both police and citizens can benefit from that."

Table 1.2
Comparison of Traditional Policing and Community Policing

Question	Traditional Policing	Community Policing
Who are the police?	A government agency principally responsible for law enforcement.	Police are the public and the public are the police: the police officers are those who are paid to give full-time attention to the duties of every citizen.
What is the relationship of the police force to public service departments?	Priorities often conflict.	The police are one department among many responsible for improving the quality of life.
What is the role of the police?	Focusing on solving crimes.	A broader problem-solving approach.
How is police efficiency measured?	By detection and arrest rates.	By the absence of crime and disorder.
What are the highest priorities?	Crimes that are high value (e.g., bank robberies) and those involving violence.	Whatever problems disturb the community most.
What, specifically, do police deal with?	Incidents.	Citizens' problems and concerns.
What determines the effectiveness of police?	Response times.	Public cooperation.
What view do police take of service calls?	Deal with them only if there is no real police work to do.	Vital function and great opportunity.
What is police professionalism?	Swift, effective response to serious crime.	Keeping close to the community.
What kind of intelligence is most important?	Crime intelligence (study of particular crimes or series of crimes).	Criminal intelligence (information about the activities of individuals or groups).
What is the essential nature of police accountability?	Highly centralized; governed by rules, regulations and policy directives; accountable to the law.	Emphasis on local accountability to community needs.
What is the role of headquarters?	To provide the necessary rules and policy directives.	To preach organizational values.
What is the role of the press liaison department?	To keep the "heat" off operational officers so they can get on with the job.	To coordinate an essential channel of communication with the community.
How do the police regard prosecutions?	As an important goal.	As one tool among many.

Source: Malcolm K. Sparrow. *Implementing Community Policing.* U.S. Department of Justice, National Institute of Justice, November 1988, pp. 8–9.

Partnerships are an integral part of community policing. Abshire and Paynter (2000, p.50) describe how the San Diego Police Department has partnered with the community to make the most of limited resources and bring citizens the high level of service they've come to expect. However, as their police chief cautions: "To do it well, community policing should be viewed as a constant work in progress. We've been able to do a lot more based on the community support and the spirit of community policing. But success doesn't happen overnight. It's been 12 years and we're still identifying some areas where we can really improve and expand community policing throughout our department" (p.54). Chief Bejarano also stresses: "It [community policing] is not a project. It's not a program. It's a culture" (Abshire and Paynter, p.56).

Tony Freeman/PhotoEdit

Partnerships and communication are important elements of community policing. Here, residents receive updates during a Neighborhood Watch information meeting.

Ramsey (2000, p.25) stresses the importance of sharing information and teamwork: "Police share critical information more directly and thoroughly with each other, with the community, and with other agencies on the public safety team. Responding to problems with a broad range of resources, this public safety team gets better results and all team members can take credit for the win. This is community policing. It is ensuring that everyone with a stake in safe neighborhoods has the opportunity to participate."

Smith and Lingerfelt (2000, p.68) note: "Law enforcement executives, among other public safety officials, are striving to implement community policing programs and integrated justice operations that mobilize both government and community resources in constructive partnerships. The intent of these partnerships is to reduce crime, disorder and the fear of crime." They suggest that departments wishing to implement community policing make use of Enterprise Resource Planning (ERP): "ERP is a planning methodology to be used for applying organizational resources (i.e., people, process, and technology) to the mission and operational goals of that enterprise. It is executed at three levels: strategic, process and technical. The strategic plan describes the mission, operational goals and strategies of the organization. The process layer describes how the work will be done so that the mission and goals can be accomplished [similar to the traditional work plans]. The technical layer describes the individual IT projects that will support execution of the process."

One impetus for the development of community policing across the country has been the COPS program (Office of Community Oriented Policing Services), an important part of the Violent Crime Control and Law Enforcement Act of 1994. COPS was created to promote community policing and to add 100,000 community policing officers to our country's streets. The COPS Web site, http://www.usdoj.gov/cops, houses information on COPS initiatives plus details about training and technical assistance, as well as resources to implement community policing. A national evaluation of the COPS program (Zhao and Thurman, 2001, p.2) reports: "COPS hiring grant programs appear to have a significant crime reducing effect on the vast majority of the population of the United States. In addition, COPS' innovative grant programs appear to produce a strong reduction in crime for all COPS grantees included in the study."

Problem solving is also an integral part of community policing efforts, as Miller and Hess (p.86) note: "A problem-solving approach involves identifying problems and making decisions about how best to deal with them. . . . A basic characteristic of community policing is that it is proactive rather than reactive. Being **proactive** involves recognizing problems and seeking the underlying cause(s) of the problems." **Problem-solving policing** is in contrast to the traditional **reactive** approach of simply responding to calls for service.

Solar (2001, p.39) emphasizes: "Community oriented policing promises higher levels of effectiveness by giving officers greater autonomy and encouraging them to become problem solvers and partnership builders." The importance of and approaches to problem solving are the focus of Chapter 4.

Community-oriented policing and problem solving (COPPS) appear to offer an answer to more effective law enforcement for the future.

What has worked in policing in the past may not work today or tomorrow. The chapters that follow reflect this reality and how COPPS is affecting all aspects of law enforcement. This is important because according to *Community Policing in Local Police Departments, 1997 and 1999*: "Community policing appears to be taking hold as a widespread innovation in the nation's approach to law enforcement." In fact, according to Oliver (2000, p.367), community policing is more than an innovation: "Community policing has become the paradigm of contemporary policing, evolving significantly over the past 20 years . . . . [It is] the primary formulation for police practices and the provision of police services in the United States." He describes the evolution of community policing as encompassing three distinct periods:

> The first generation of community policing spans the period 1979 through 1986 and is labeled the *innovative* generation. . . . [beginning with] the seminal work of Goldstein (1979) . . . coupled with the "broken windows" theory by Wilson and Kelling (1982) (pp.374–375).
>
> The second generation of community policing spans the period from 1987 through 1994; it is properly considered the *diffusion* generation. The term *diffusion* used here to describe this generation is derived from the public policy diffusion literature (p.375).
>
> The third and current generation of community policing spans the period from 1995 to the present, and it is properly considered the *institutionalization* generation. This specific term is used to denote the fact that community policing has seen widespread implementation across the United States and has become the most common form of organizing police services (p.378).

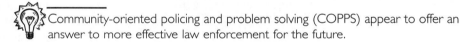

Summary

Managers need to understand the organizational structure within which most law enforcement agencies function. The traditional organizational design is that of a pyramid-shaped hierarchy based on a military model. Three distinct eras of policing have been identified: the political era, the reform era and the community era.

The mission statement should be the driving force of any organization, including law enforcement agencies. This mission statement can direct the development of meaningful goals and objectives and realistic work plans. Goals are broad, general, desired outcomes. Objectives are specific, measurable ways to accomplish the goals. Work plans are the precise activities that contribute to accomplishing objectives. Along with a mission statement, goals, objectives and work plans, a formal organization of personnel is mandatory to accomplish the tasks.

One aspect of an agency's organizational structure is division into field services with line personnel and administrative services with staff personnel. *Line* personnel *directly* help accomplish the goals of the department. *Staff* personnel *support* the line organization.

An organization typically relies on a chain of command, unity of command, a span of control and set channels of communication. The chain of command establishes definite lines of authority and channels of communication. Unity of command means that every individual in the organization has only one immediate superior or supervisor. The span of control refers to the number of people or units supervised by one manager.

These organizational features are necessary to ensure the efficient delegation of tasks. The delegation of authority should go hand-in-hand with responsibility.

As agencies become larger, they often become specialized. Specialization can enhance an agency's effectiveness and efficiency, but overspecialization can impede the organizational purpose. Specialization also requires a higher degree of coordination, although coordination is critical for any department, large or small, specialized or not. In addition to the formal organization depicted in an organizational chart, any law enforcement agency also has an informal organization that managers should recognize. The informal organization can help or hinder accomplishment of the agency's mission.

Management tools for coordination include a clear chain of command and unity of command; clear channels of communication and strict adherence to them; clear, specific job descriptions; clear, specific goals, objectives and work plans; standard operating procedures for routine tasks; an agency regulation guidebook; meetings and roll calls; informational bulletins, and newsletters and memos.

The emerging law enforcement agency has a flattened organization, is decentralized and empowers its employees. It also has adopted community policing: "Community policing is an organization-wide philosophy and management approach that promotes (1) community, government and police partnerships; (2) proactive problem solving; and (3) community engagement to address the causes of crime, fear of crime and other community issues."

The challenges facing not only law enforcement but also our entire country necessitate reexamining our public organizations, including law enforcement.

Community-oriented policing and problem solving (COPPS) appear to offer an answer to more effective law enforcement for the future.

Discussion Questions

1. Who is a law enforcement manager?
2. Is there a difference between the terms pyramidal structure and hierarchy?
3. What is the difference between unity of command and chain of command?
4. What are staff positions in a typical police department?
5. What is the purpose of law enforcement management?
6. What does delegation mean? Can you delegate authority? Responsibility?
7. What does an organizational chart indicate?
8. How could you reorganize to force decision making downward? Is this desirable?
9. What is an informal organization?
10. What changes do you foresee in law enforcement agencies in the 21st century?

InfoTrac College Edition Assignment

Use InfoTrac College Edition to help answer the Discussion Questions as appropriate.

Select one of the following assignments to complete and be prepared to share your findings with the class.

- Find two journal articles on *strategic planning* and summarize them. Include the full reference citation along with your summary.
- Find and outline the article "Organizational Development in a Law Enforcement Environment" by Barbara French and Jerry Stewart.
- Find and outline the article "A Systems Approach to Organizational Transformation" by Brian Ursino.

References

Abshire, Richard and Paynter, Ronnie. "Putting the 'Community' in Community Policing." *Law Enforcement Technology,* October 2000, pp.50–58.

Community Policing in Local Police Departments, 1997 and 1999. Annapolis Junction, MD: Justice Statistics Clearinghouse. www.ojp.usdoj.gov/bjs

Clark, Donald. "The Hawthorne Effect." http://www.nwlink.com/~donclark/hrd/history/history.html (Updated April 2, 2000)

French, Barbara and Stewart, Jerry. "Organizational Development in a Law Enforcement Environment." *FBI Law Enforcement Bulletin,* September 2001, pp.14–19.

Gerber, Greg. "Local-motive." *Law Enforcement Technology,* October 2001, pp.40–49.

Harr, J. Scott and Hess, Kären M. *Seeking Employment in Criminal Justice and Related Fields,* 4th ed. Belmont, CA: Wadsworth Publishing Company, 2002.

Hochstetler, Steven. "Increasing Community and Officer Involvement." *Law and Order,* April 2002, pp.34–36.

Maloney, Mike and Moty, Leonard. "The Impact of Community Growth on the Staffing and Structure of a Midsized Police Department." *FBI Law Enforcement Bulletin,* January 2002, pp.6–12.

Miller, Linda S. and Hess, Kären M. *The Police in the Community: Strategies for the 21st Century,* 3rd ed. Belmont, CA: West/Wadsworth Publishing Company, 2002.

Oliver, Willard M. "The Third Generation of Community Policing: Moving through Innovation, Diffusion and Institutionalization." *Police Quarterly,* December 2000, pp.367–388.

Ramsey, Charles H. "Organizational Change: Preparing a Police Department for Community Policing in the 21st Century." *The Police Chief,* March 2000, pp.16–25.

Smith, Karenne T. and Lingerfelt, James A. "How Law Enforcement Executives Can Use Enterprise Resource Planning to Improve Their Agency's Effectiveness." *The Police Chief,* September 2000, pp.68–72.

Solar, Patrick. "The Organizational Context of Effective Policing." *The Police Chief,* February 2001, pp.39–47.

Turner, Yvonne C. "Decentralizing the Specialized Unit Function in Small Police Agencies." *The Police Chief,* February 2000, pp.50–51.

Wrobleski, Henry M. and Hess, Kären M. *An Introduction to Law Enforcement and Criminal Justice,* 7th ed. Belmont, CA: Wadsworth Publishing Company, 2003.

Zhao, Jihong "Solomon" and Thurman, Qunit. *A National Evaluation of the Effect of COPS Grants on Crime from 1994 to 1999.* Unpublished paper, December 2001.

Book-Specific Web Site

Go to the *Management and Supervision in Law Enforcement* Web site at http://info.wadsworth.com/0534616054 for student and instructor resources, including Internet Assignments and Case Studies.

CHAPTER 2

The Role of Management and Leadership in Law Enforcement

The watchwords of the new leadership paradigm are coach, inspire, gain commitment, empower, affirm, flexibility, responsibility, self-management, shared power, autonomous teams and entrepreneurial units.

—Donald C. Witham, Chief, FBI Strategic Planning Unit

Do You Know?

- How authority and power are alike? How they differ?
- What basic management skills are important?
- What four tools successful managers use?
- What management by objectives (MBO) involves?
- What Theory X/Theory Y, the Four-System Approach, the Mature Employee Theory and the Managerial/Leadership Grid say about management style?
- What management style is best suited for law enforcement work?
- What typical levels of management exist in law enforcement?
- What essential functions chief executives perform?
- How strategic and tactical planning differ?
- With whom law enforcement chief executives typically interact?
- What three management challenges are common?
- What basic difference exists between managers and leaders?
- What theories of leadership have been researched?
- What types of leadership styles have been identified and what their main characteristics are?
- What constitutes effective leadership training?
- What the attributes of a high-performing team are?

Can You Define?

administrative skills
aligned on purpose
authority
Authority–Compliance Management
autocratic leadership
chief executive officer (CEO)
conceptual skills
consideration structure
consultative leadership
Country Club Management
creative talents
cybertribe
delegation
democratic leadership
executive manager
facilitators
first-line managers
focused on task
Four-System Approach
free-rein leadership
future focused
high communication
holistic management
Impoverished Management
initiating structure
interactors
interfacers
laissez-faire leadership
leader
leadership
manage
management
management by objectives (MBO)
Managerial/Leadership Grid
managers

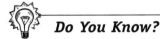

Mature Employee Theory
mechanistic model
middle management
Middle-of-the-Road Management
organic model
participative leadership
people skills
power
rapid response
roll call
seagull management
shared responsibility
situational leadership
SMART goals and objectives
strategic planning
supervision
supervisors
synergism
tactical planning
Task Management
team
Team Management
technical skills
Theory X/Theory Y
Total Quality Management (TQM)
trait theorists
traits
transformational leadership
Wallenda Effect

INTRODUCTION

The organizational chart discussed in the preceding chapter is inanimate, similar to a house without people. The form and foundation exist and are necessary, but it is in no sense vital or exciting.

Vitality and excitement come when the boxes in the chart are filled with people, men and women patrol officers, investigators, sergeants, lieutenants, captains and chiefs interacting, working together to accomplish their mission—"to serve and protect." The organization accomplishes its mission through management directing and guiding employees and resources, both internal and external to the organization.

Managers in law enforcement face unique problems because of the extended period of service (24 hours a day, 365 days a year). The chief executive officer (CEO) of the law enforcement agency obviously cannot be physically present for this extended period and must therefore rely on the organizational structure to permit other members to perform administrative and operational functions. In addition, challenges facing today's law enforcement administrators are huge, including strained budgets and cutbacks, greater citizen demands and expectations for service and an increasingly diverse society.

This chapter examines the complex role of the law enforcement manager, the challenges presented by management and the relationship between authority and power. This is followed by an overview of the basic skills and tools required of an effective manager. Contributions to management from the business world, including management by objectives and total quality management, are the next area of discussion, followed by an analysis of the various management styles. The chapter then examines the levels of management typically found within law enforcement agencies, responsibilities at each level, management challenges most commonly encountered and a look into law enforcement management as a career. Next is a discussion of the differences between managing and leading and a review of key characteristics of leaders. This is followed by a review of research on and theories related to leadership, the various leadership styles and the apparent need for change within law enforcement agencies. Next is a discussion of leadership training and development, the new skills required and guidelines for effective leadership. The chapter concludes with a discussion of holistic management and a team approach to law enforcement.

Managers and Management

Manage means to control and direct, to administer, to take charge of. Those who undertake these activities are called **managers. Management** is the process of using resources to achieve organizational goals.

Managers and supervisors control and direct people and operations to achieve organizational objectives. Managers and supervisors are also jointly involved in planning, organizing, staffing and budgeting. In fact, many gray areas exist in the duties of managers and supervisors. This is increasingly true in organizations that have been "flattened" by eliminating some middle-management positions and empowering employees at the lowest level.

Law enforcement management is a process of deciding goals and objectives, adopting a work plan to accomplish them, obtaining and wisely using resources and making decisions that result in a high level of performance and productivity. As Alsabrook et al. (2001b, p.111) note: "Realizing that agencies are continuously asked to do more with less, improvements in organizational effectiveness and efficiency become vital for any agency."

Managers must also support the development of *individual* responsibility, permitting all employees to achieve maximum potential while simultaneously supporting organizational needs. The sum total of individual member energy is transferred to the organizational energy needed for success.

Authority and Power

Authority, responsibility and accountability were discussed in the preceding chapter. Consider now the relationship between the authority and the power of police managers.

Authority is the legal right to get things done through others by influencing behavior. **Power,** on the other hand, is the ability to get things done with or without a legal right. Authority is generally granted by law or an order. Power is the influence of a person or group without benefit of law or order.

> Authority and power both imply the ability to coerce compliance, that is, to *make* subordinates carry out orders. Both are important to managers at all levels. However, authority relies on a law or order, whereas power relies on persuasion.

In a democracy authority and power are not always regarded as desirable. Even though managers may use both and employees recognize management's right to use both, a limitation exists in the employees' mindset as to how much is acceptable. They expect some freedom of choice.

Managers should never manipulate employees and should avoid **seagull management.** According to management guru Ken Blanchard: "[Seagull managers] hear something's wrong, so they fly in, make a lot of noise, crap on everybody and fly away" (Smith, 2000, p.18).

Delegation

Transferring authority, called **delegation,** is a necessary and often difficult aspect of management because it requires placing trust in others to do the job as well as, or better than, you would do yourself.

Theodore Roosevelt once said: "The best executive is the one who has enough sense to pick good people to do what he wants done, and self-restraint enough to keep from meddling with them while they do it." Yet many managers fail to delegate effectively because they believe "If you want something done right, you have to do it yourself."

Delegation is *not* passing the buck, shirking personal responsibility or dumping on someone. It is the way managers and supervisors free up time to get their work done. Fulton (2001, p.126) suggests: "If you are bogged down in routine actions and 'administrivia' that other people in your unit could easily handle, you are not as productive as you could be." He also suggests: "Learning to properly delegate tasks and responsibilities requires 'letting go' to some degree. But it is also an opportunity to truly work with your people. You get to watch them slowly grow, develop and mature. And someday they will be ready and capable of taking over your job."

Fulton (2002, p.110) contends: "The delegation of work to your people should be a win-win-situation. The employees win because you are delegating meaningful work to them to help them learn and grow. Your department wins because delegation helps future leaders develop within the organization. And you win because delegation of some of your work to others frees you up to concentrate on other areas of your command." Fulton suggests delegation is appropriate for recurring problems with routine solutions such as scheduling.

Basic Management Skills and Tools

To be effective, managers at all levels must be skilled at planning, organizing, coordinating, reporting and budgeting. Equally critical, however, are people skills such as communicating, motivating and leading, as will be discussed throughout the book.

Basic management skills include technical skills, administrative skills, conceptual skills and people skills.

Technical skills include all the procedures necessary to be a "good cop": interviewing and interrogating, searching, arresting, gathering evidence and so on. Police officers often become sergeants because of their technical skills.

Administrative skills include organizing, delegating and directing the work of others. They also include writing proposals, formulating work plans and developing budgets.

Conceptual skills include the ability to problem solve, plan and see the big picture and how all the pieces within it fit. Managers must be able to think in terms of the future, synthesize great amounts of data, make decisions on complex matters and have broad, even national, perspectives. They must see the organization as a whole, yet existing within society. They must also have a sensitivity to the spirit—not just the letter—of the law.

People skills include being able to communicate clearly, to motivate, to discipline appropriately and to inspire. People skills also include working effectively

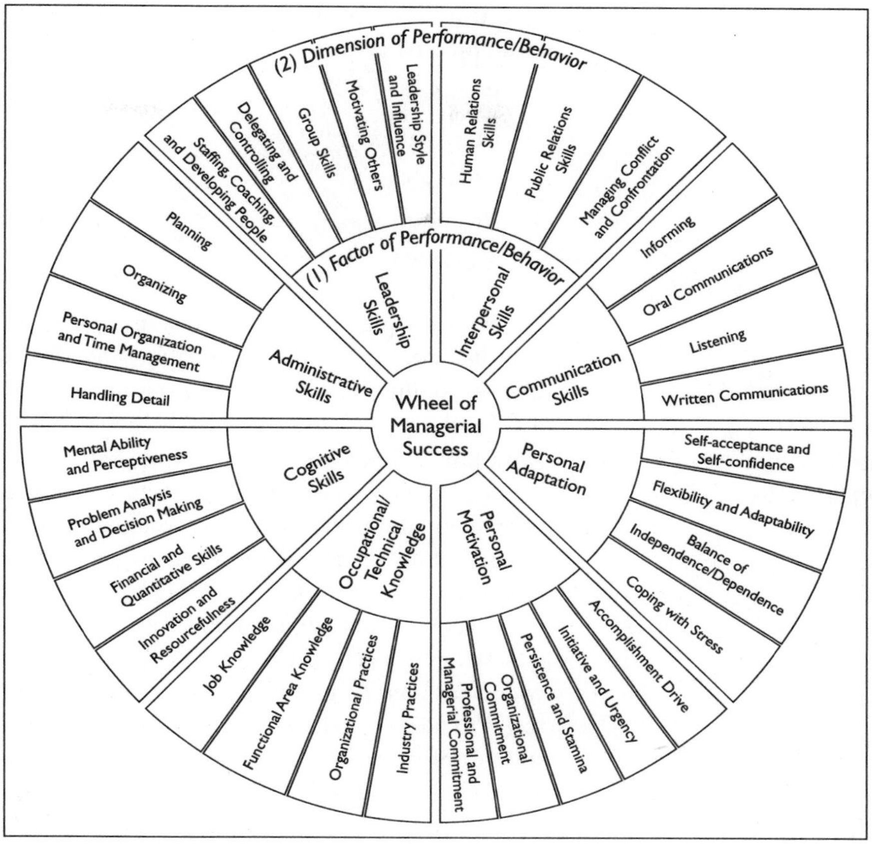

Figure 2.1
The Wheel of Managerial Success

Source: Joy Fisher Hazucha and Robert J. Schneider, Personnel Decisions, Inc. *The Wheel of Managerial Success.* Copyright © 1982 by Personnel Decisions, Inc. Reprinted by permission.

with managers up the chain of command, as well as with the general public. The higher the management position, the more important people skills become.

A Balance

Successful managers balance these skills and more, as illustrated in the Wheel of Managerial Success (Figure 2.1).

Basic Tools

According to management guru Blanchard (1988, p.14): "Successful managers use four tools to accomplish their goals."

Successful managers have:
- Clear goals.
- A commitment to excellence.
- Feedback.
- Support.

"Good performance," says Blanchard, "starts with clear goals." The importance of goals cannot be overemphasized. Just as important, however, are the objectives developed to meet the goals. According to Blanchard, **SMART goals and objectives** are:

Specific.
Measurable.
Attainable.
Relevant.
Trackable.

For example, to say that you want to lose 50 pounds in two months is specific and measurable, but it probably is not attainable. To say that you want to lose two pounds a week, however, meets the criteria for a SMART objective.

The Role of Self-Confidence

Most police supervisors and managers have been promoted into their positions because they possessed or had learned the necessary skills and tools. But with the excitement and pride of promotion often comes an instinctive tinge of self-doubt. Taking on a new level of management is a major challenge and involves risk. Even though initially daunting, change can serve as a catalyst for growth.

Change frequently requires that a person use already acquired skills in a new context, which can be threatening. Asking a person to walk across a six-inch-wide board on the ground poses no threat. Put it 40 feet in the air, and the person is unlikely to take even the first step. To maintain self-confidence, seek the support of your peers, set goals for yourself in mastering the skills you need and get feedback.

Lessons Learned from Business

Just as the development of the law enforcement organization has been influenced by business, law enforcement management has followed the lead of business in some important ways, including management by objectives (MBO) and Total Quality Management (TQM).

Management by Objectives

Management theorist Peter Drucker is credited with first using the term **management by objectives (MBO)** in the early 1950s. It has been popular for over 50 years.

Management by objectives involves managers and subordinates setting goals and objectives together and then tracking performance to ensure that the objectives are met.

The key to the MBO system is to get workers to participate in deciding and setting goals, both individually and in work groups. The performance achieved is then compared to these agreed-upon goals.

Total Quality Management

The pioneer in **Total Quality Management (TQM)** was W. Edwards Deming, a management guru who assisted Japanese businesses in recovering and prospering.

Although Deming's famous "14 Points" were originally aimed at business, several are applicable to the public sector as well—including law enforcement:

- Create constancy of purpose for improvement of product and service.
- Adopt the new philosophy.
- Improve constantly.
- Institute modern methods of training on the job.
- Institute modern methods of supervision.
- Drive fear from the workplace.
- Break down barriers between staff areas.
- Eliminate numerical goals for the work force.
- Remove barriers that rob people of pride of workmanship.
- Institute a vigorous program of education and training (Deming, 1982, p.17).

Stevens (2000, p.204) contends that managers should adopt TQM because: "Community policing strategies and TQM have similar ideals that seem to promote each other, [and] community policing type strategies are at the core of future police services."

Management Styles

Just as different managers use different types of authority and power, they also have varied personalities and management styles. Managers at any level may be sociable and friendly, firm and hard driving or analytical and detail oriented. Several theories regarding management style have been developed, including those of McGregor, Likert, Argyris, and Blake and Mouton. Within each theory "pure" or ideal types are described, but in reality management style should be viewed as a continuum, with "pure" types at the opposing ends.

Theory X/Theory Y—McGregor

This theory from the 1960s is concerned with why workers work and how management views them and their work. Douglas McGregor claimed that how workers were regarded was largely due to two approaches to management, which he labeled Theory X and Theory Y.

In **Theory X,** the organization managed with the following assumptions:

- Workers need control by coercion, threats and punishment.
- The average worker frequently has an aversion to work.
- Management makes all decisions and directs employees to carry them out.
- Workers are dull and lazy.
- Workers desire secure jobs above all else.

Under Theory X, management's responsibility is to provide constant employee supervision. Employees do not want responsibility. They are primarily interested in wages, fringe benefits and avoiding punishment.

Theory Y, in contrast, operates under these assumptions:

Table 2.1
McGregor's Assumptions of Theory X and Theory Y

Theory X	Theory Y
1. The average person inherently dislikes work and will avoid it when possible.	1. The expenditure of physical and mental effort in work is as natural as the expenditure of physical and mental exertion in play or rest.
2. Most people must be coerced, controlled, directed or threatened with punishment to get them to put forth adequate energy in achieving organizational goals.	2. An employee will exercise self-direction and self-control in the service of objectives to which he or she is committed.
3. The average person prefers to be directed, wishes to avoid responsibility, and has relatively little ambition; he or she wants security above all.	3. Commitment to objectives is a function of the rewards associated with their achievement.
4. The average person is inherently self-centered and indifferent to organizational needs.	4. The average person learns, under proper conditions, not only to accept but also to seek responsibility.
5. The average person is by nature resistant to change.	5. The capacity to exercise high degrees of imagination, ingenuity and creativity in solving organizational problems is widely, not narrowly, distributed in the population.
6. The average person is gullible, not very bright, the ready dupe of the charlatan and the demagogue.	6. The intellectual potentialities of the average person are only partially utilized under the conditions of modern industrial life.
	7. The essential task of management is to arrange organizational conditions and methods of operation so people can achieve their own goals best by directing their own efforts toward organizational goals.

Source: Douglas McGregor. *The Human Side of Enterprise*. © 1960 McGraw-Hill Book Companies. Reprinted by permission.

- Employees can be trusted to do a good job.
- Employees are willing workers.
- Employees can be given reasonable goals to accomplish.
- Employees should share in decision making.

McGregor favored the humanistic approach reflected in Theory Y. He believed management should encourage self-motivation and fewer outside controls. Decisions could be delegated. Employees would be responsive to management's goals if management set the proper environment for work. Theory X might have worked in the past, but with better-educated workers, it could create hostility.

McGregor's Theory X/Theory Y says that managers act toward subordinates in relation to the views they have of them. Theory X views employees as lazy and motivated by pay. Theory Y views employees as committed and motivated by growth and development.

Table 2.1 summarizes McGregor's assumptions of Theory X/Theory Y.

The Four-System Approach—Likert

Rensis Likert divided managerial approaches into four different systems. System 1, similar to McGregor's Theory X, is the *traditional,* dictatorial approach

Table 2.2
Likert's System 1 and System 4 Compared

System I (Traditional)	System 4 (Participative)
Leadership is not based on confidence and trust. Subordinates don't feel free to discuss ideas with managers, and managers don't use subordinates' opinions in decision making.	**Leadership** is based on confidence and trust in subordinates. Subordinates discuss their ideas with managers, and their ideas and opinions are used in decision making.
Motivation is based on fear, threat, punishment and some rewards. Responsibility for achieving goals decreases down the hierarchy.	**Motivation** is through economic rewards and involvement in setting goals. People at all levels feel a responsibility for reaching goals.
Communication flows downward from the top of the hierarchy and is viewed with suspicion. There is little feedback.	**Communication** flows freely throughout the organization. There is much feedback.
Interaction between managers and employees is minimal and is viewed with fear and distrust. There is little teamwork.	**Interaction** between managers and employees is extensive, friendly and based on a high degree of confidence and trust. There is a great deal of teamwork.
Decision making takes place primarily at the top of the hierarchy with little subordinate involvement. Acceptance of the decision is usually not considered.	**Decision making** is dispersed but linked through teamwork. Subordinates are fully involved in decisions relating to their work.
Goals are set at the top of the organization. Goals are resisted. Performance goals are relatively low.	**Goals** are set through participation at the level where they will be achieved. Goals are accepted. Performance goals are high.
Controls are concentrated in top management and are used in a punitive way.	**Controls** are widespread and are used for self-guidance and for coordinated problem solving.

Source: Rensis Likert. *The Human Organization: Its Management and Values.*

to managing people. In this system, which generally exploited employees, coercion and a few economic rewards would suffice.

System 2 is similar to System 1, except that economic rewards replace coercion. Some information on organizational development is permitted but not in opposition to management's control.

System 3, which is more liberal, uses employee initiative and gives employees more responsibility. System 4 is participative management, which is the complete opposite of System 1. Participative management is closely allied with the democratic approach except that employees do not vote. Final decisions are made by management but only after employees have added their input.

System 4 also includes team management, which is widely used today. The participative approach encourages support of employees because decisions are made partially on their suggestions. It is easier to support your own suggestion or someone else's if you have a part in it. System 4 draws on the thoughts and backgrounds of all members associated with a particular problem area.

Likert's **Four-System Approach** to management goes from System 1, which is a traditional, authoritarian style, to System 4, which is a participative management style.

The characteristics of Likert's System 1 and System 4, the two extremes, are compared in Table 2.2.

The Mature Employee Theory—Argyris

Another approach to management is the **Mature Employee Theory,** devised by Chris Argyris. This theory emphasizes employees' growth and development as a means of increasing their contributions to the job. Argyris analyzed the relationship between the demands of the organization and those of the individual members, believing that both have an effect on the end result. He determined that the work force has energy to be released if management recognizes it.

Argyris' Mature Employee Theory views employees and their organization as *interdependent.*

Organizations and individuals exist for a purpose. If organizations keep employees dependent, subordinate and restrained, employees cannot help the organization meet its objectives. Both are interdependent: Organizations provide jobs and people perform them.

As individuals develop, they mature from passive to active and from dependent to interdependent. Individuals and organizations need to develop together in much the same way. They need to grow and mature together to be of mutual benefit. Organizations tend to restrict individuals, which results in frustration, failure, short-term perspectives and conflict. A comparison of immature and mature behaviors is contained in Table 2.3.

The Managerial/ Leadership Grid Theory—Blake and Mouton

In the 1960s Dr. Robert R. Blake and Dr. Jane S. Mouton designed the **Managerial Grid** behavioral model, which has also gained wide acceptance. The Managerial Grid, republished as the **Leadership Grid** figure in 1991, identifies different managerial styles and seeks to bring management's needs and the individual's needs closer together for mutual benefit. Manager behavior patterns are placed on a square grid (Figure 2.2).

Blake-Mouton's Managerial/Leadership Grid describes five management styles: Authority–Compliance Management, Country Club Management, Impoverished Management, Middle-of-the-Road Management and Team Management.

Table 2.3
Argyris's Seven Development Dimensions

Childlike Behaviors	Mature, Adult Behaviors
Passiveness	Activeness
Dependent upon others	Relatively independent
Few reactive behaviors	Many reactive behaviors
Shallow, brief, erratic interests	Intense, long-term, coherent commitments
Engages in brief, unconnected jobs	Seeks long-term challenges that link the past and the future
Satisfied with low status	Seeks advancement
Low self-awareness, impulsive	Self-aware and self-controlled

Source: Paul R. Timm. *Supervision,* 2nd ed. St. Paul, MN: West Publishing Company, 1992, p. 119.

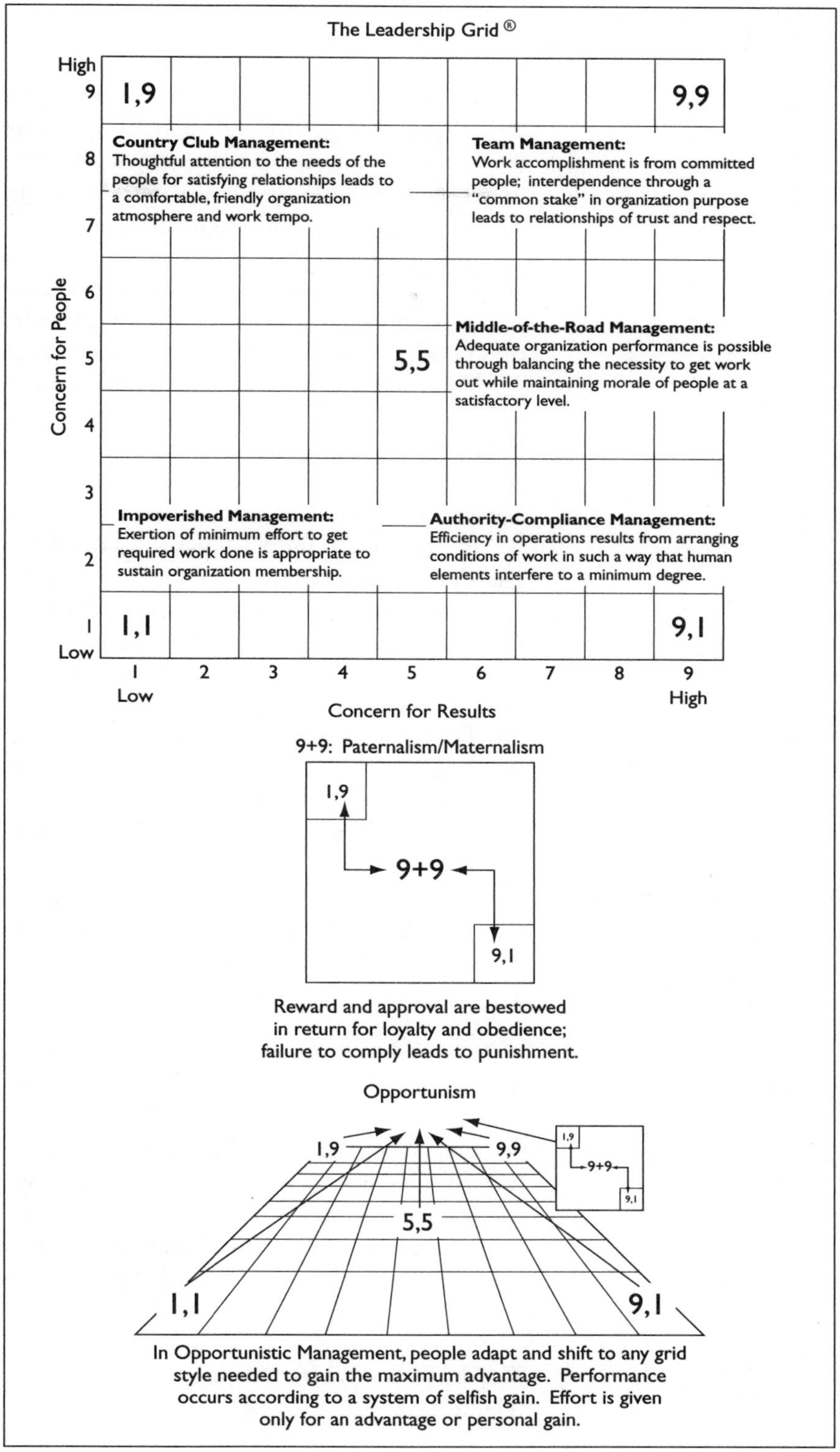

Figure 2.2
The Leadership Grid® Figure, the Paternalism/ Maternalism Figure and the Opportunism Figure
The grid can also be used to demonstrate opportunism and paternalism/ maternalism as shown in the figure.

Source: The Leadership Grid® figure, Paternalism/Maternalism and Opportunism from *Leadership Dilemmas—Grid Solutions,* by Robert R. Blake and Anne Adams McCanse.

(Formerly the Managerial Grid figure by Robert R. Blake and Jane S. Mouton) Houston: Gulf Publishing Company (Grid Figure: p.29, Paternalism Figure: p.30, Opportunism Figure: p.31).

In the lower right is the **Authority–Compliance Management** style, the early autocratic, authoritarian approach. The manager is a no-nonsense taskmaster. Concern is for manager authority, status and operation of the organization. Employees have little say and less influence, and production is the only concern. This is also known as **Task Management.**

The upper left corner is the opposite, the **Country Club Management** style. Managers are overly concerned with keeping employees happy at the expense of reasonable productivity. The work atmosphere is friendly and comfortable. Concern for employees is utmost; concern for productivity is limited.

The lower left corner illustrates the **Impoverished Management** style, which permits workers to do just enough to get by. Managers and employees put in their time and look ahead to retirement. Little real concern exists for employees or management. Little is expected and little is given. Minimal effort is made. The prevailing attitude: ignore problems and they will go away.

In the center is the **Middle-of-the-Road Management** style, with the manager showing some concern for both employees and management but in a low-key manner that is not really productive. The manager is a fence straddler, appeasing both sides, avoiding conflict and satisfying no one.

The upper right corner is the **Team Management** approach, suggested as the ideal. The manager works with employees as a team, providing information, caring about their feelings and concerns, assisting, advising and coaching. Managers encourage employees to be creative and share suggestions for improvement. Employees are committed to their jobs and organization through a mutual relationship of trust and respect. Goals are achieved as a team.

Which Management Style to Select?

The management style selected depends on the individuals involved, the tasks to be accomplished and any emergency the organization is facing, such as a hostage incident, a multiple-alarm fire or an officer down.

No one management style is more apt than another to achieve the agency's mission. The selected style must match individual personalities and situations.

It was once thought that fist-pounding, authoritarian managers were the greatest achievers. People now believe that many styles of management or combinations of several can be effective.

Next consider some specific functions performed at the three basic levels of management, beginning with the first-line, supervisory level.

Levels of Managers

The organizational chart depicts the number of management levels of the agency. (Figure 2.3).

Management typically has three levels:

- The top level or CEO (chief, sheriff).
- The middle level (captains, lieutenants).
- The first-line level (sergeants).

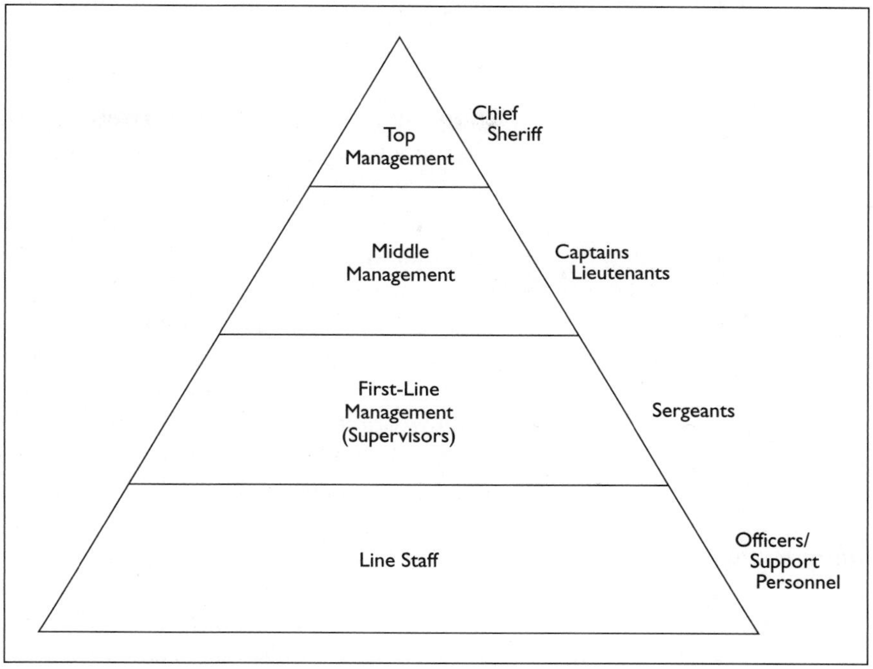

Figure 2.3
The Levels of Management

First-Line Managers

Brewer and Hazlette (2002, p.16) suggest: "Adjusting to the new role of supervisor is arguably the most difficult step in an officer's career." As Harrison (2001, p.151) points out: "Although some may minimize the impact of the sergeant's role, it is the most important level of management; they are the ones who implement philosophy and turn intent into reality. Their work will either motivate or discourage those around them. . . . They alone view, monitor and interact with those who are performing the core functions of policing . . . . The success of the chief or sheriff rests in their hands."

The critical importance of first-line supervisors is well stated in the adage: "Generals win battles but sergeants win wars." Most **first-line managers** or **supervisors** are sergeants, who are responsible to the next highest rank in the organization unless their positions are specialized. Management consultant Drucker says: "Supervisors are, so to speak, the ligaments, the tendons and sinews of an organization. They provide the articulation. Without them, no joint can move."

Supervisors' fundamental responsibility is to ensure that what needs to be accomplished during any given shift *is* accomplished effectively and legally. They are concerned with **supervision** of the day-to-day concerns of law enforcement officers, that is, overseeing the activities of all nonranking employees in the agency. Among their functions are:

- Managing line personnel in the field.
- Supervising patrol activities.
- Conducting inspections.
- Maintaining discipline.
- Enforcing rules and regulations.

- Conducting roll call.
- Managing field operations.

Roll call is the meeting of officers before each shift when officers check in and receive a briefing before going on duty. Field operations include all activities patrol officers undertake.

Supervisors frequently are not trained in the new skills they need. Initial training should concentrate on the "people activities" performed by supervisors, with particular emphasis on motivating others. As Harrison (p.152) suggests: "New sergeants should keep in mind their new job is managing people. The most powerful single word in the manager's vocabulary is: please. The most powerful two-word phrase is: thank you. The most powerful three-word phrases are: I don't know, or can I help?" Harrison recounts what General George Patton wrote in his battle journal: "Don't tell people what to do. Tell them what you want done and let them surprise you with their ingenuity."

Middle Management

Middle management usually includes captains and lieutenants. Captains have authority over all officers of the agency below the chief or sheriff and are responsible only to the chief or sheriff.

Lieutenants are second in rank to captains. They are in charge of sergeants and all officers within their assigned responsibility, and they report to captains. Captains and lieutenants may perform the following functions:

- Inspecting assigned operations
- Reviewing and making recommendations on reports
- Helping develop plans
- Preparing work schedules
- Overseeing records and equipment

The Top Level—The Executive Manager

The **executive manager,** or the **chief executive officer (CEO),** is the top official in any law enforcement agency. The title may be chief of police, director, superintendent or sheriff, but the authority and responsibility of the position are similar. The executive manager is either elected or appointed by the city council, the county commission or the city manager, subject to approval of the city council.

Executive managers have full authority and responsibility as provided by the charter provisions of their local jurisdictions. People appointed to this position are to enforce the applicable laws of the United States, as well as state and local jurisdiction and all rules and regulations established by local government or the civil service commission.

Executive managers are responsible for planning, organizing and managing the agency's resources, including its employees. They are responsible for preserving the peace and enforcing laws and ordinances. The duties and responsibilities of executive managers often include:

- Developing a mission statement.
- Formulating goals and objectives.

- Preparing an annual budget.
- Preparing and periodically reviewing agency rules and regulations, and general and specific agency orders.
- Developing strategic long-term and tactical short-term plans for organizational operations.
- Attending designated meetings of the city council or other organizations.
- Preparing required reports for the governing authority or person.
- Coordinating with other law enforcement agencies.
- Participating in emergency preparedness plans and operations.
- Developing public relations liaisons with the press.
- Administering ongoing, operational financial processes.
- Developing training programs to meet local needs.
- Acting as a liaison with community agencies.

Texts on management often convey the image of an executive working at an uncluttered desk in a spacious office. The executive is rationally planning, organizing, coordinating and controlling the organization. After careful analysis the executive makes critical decisions and has competent, motivated subordinates readily available to offer insightful input. The executive has a full schedule but no unexpected interruptions. Time lines are met without problem.

Several studies, however, indicate that this is *not* a realistic portrayal. In fact, most executives work at an unrelenting pace, are frequently interrupted and are often more oriented to reacting to crises than to planning and executing.

The executive manager's roles in law enforcement may differ from other levels of managers. Executive managers are responsible for the big picture, for not only accomplishing the department's mission through goals and objectives but also for interacting with the community, its leaders, organizations and individual citizens.

Essential Functions of Law Enforcement Executives

Acting in a *managerial* capacity, law enforcement executives serve as:
- Planners.
- Facilitators.
- Interfacers.
- Interactors.

Planners

Law enforcement managers must possess basic skills for planning, that is, the ability to set goals and objectives and to develop work plans to meet them. Whether managers personally formulate these goals and objectives or seek assistance from their staff, plans are essential. Law enforcement organizations cannot function efficiently without tactical and strategic planning.

Tactical planning is short-term planning. **Strategic planning** is long-term planning.

Tactical planning includes the year's work plans. Strategic planning, on the other hand, is futuristic planning.

Some people may use the term *tactical* in an operational or military sense to refer to unusual situations in which combat might be expected. In law enforcement this might include serving warrants, conducting drug raids, dealing with hostage situations and the like. In this context tactical planning would mean planning designed to carry out a tactical operation.

Tactical planning is most often necessary to provide the flexibility needed for change; determine personnel needs; determine objectives and provide organizational control; handle large incidents such as drug raids and special events such as sports competitions, popular concerts, large conventions and parades.

A meeting of line and staff personnel can determine the events for which tactical planning is necessary. Special problems can then be resolved and personnel needs assessed and assigned. A review of similar past events may require assistance from other police agencies in the area, or state or federal aid. Tactical planning should be flexible because of changing conditions such as the number of people involved. Tactical plans are sometimes cast in the form of an action plan such as that shown in Figure 2.4.

Strategic plans, in contrast, focus on the future and on setting priorities. Arnold (2000, pp.61–62) identifies eight steps in developing a strategic plan: "(1) develop a mission statement, (2) set goals, (3) identify project team, (4) conduct environmental and organizational analysis, (5) identify stakeholders, (6) consider alternatives, (7) select a strategy, and (8) implement the plan."

However, as Brissett (2001, p.44) suggests: "Strategic planning is kind of like exercising. You know you should do it, and everyone seems to think it's important, but it's so time consuming." Nonetheless, strategic planning is important because as Drucker says: "Long-range planning does not deal with future decisions, but with the future of present decisions."

A department might decide to place more emphasis on the use of technological advances, including communications and technology training. It might decide to continue the same emphasis on the level of recruitment and in-service training for sworn personnel and to place less emphasis on the use of sworn personnel for nonsworn duties. In addition it might identify new activities such as developing accurate job descriptions and career paths for all employees and eliminating other activities such as free services that most agencies charge for (e.g., fingerprinting, alarms and computer entry).

Kurz (2000, p.28) describes the strategic planning process of the Durham (New Hampshire) Police Department: "The Durham strategic plan project consisted of three phases: a survey of citizen satisfaction with police services; a survey of police officer satisfaction with the department; and a one-day planning session attended by police officers and community leaders." Based on the findings of the surveys and the results of the planning session, the department drafted its strategic plan. Says Kurz (p.34):

> The Durham Police Department 2000 Strategic Plan is designed to be an evolving document, constantly reviewed, updated, and brought into line with the desires of the community. It is the culmination of a series of exercises all designed to ensure

OBJECTIVE: ____

____

____

STRATEGY: ____

____

____

WHAT IS KNOWN ABOUT THE SITUATION (+'s and –'s): ____________________

____

____

What will be done (Tasks)	Who will do it (People)	When will it be done	Resources needed	Evidence of accomplishment

Figure 2.4
Action Plan Sample Worksheet

that the vision, mission, and objectives of the agency are successfully achieved. . . . An outgrowth of this process is the enhanced ability to effectively manage resources, provide accountability through measured results and adjust to change. Successful planning requires the fortitude to change courses when opportunities and community demands arise. Ultimately, it is the planning process itself that keeps the agency focused on what it wishes to accomplish and the best route to get there.

Officers report that they are getting more respect and better cooperation from residents since the department launched the strategic plan initiative three years ago.

Both tactical and strategic planning are essential in the country's war on drugs and terrorism.

Facilitators

Facilitators assist others in performing their duties. Law enforcement managers at any level do not personally bring the agency goals, objectives and work plans to fruition. This is accomplished through a joint agency effort, as well as with the assistance of others external to the agency.

Rules, regulations, personal rapport, communications, standards, guidelines, logic, basic principles and direction all assist others in performing their duties. After managers have directed subordinates on what to do and how, they should let people carry out their duties independently. Trust, honesty and integrity are important in the manager-subordinate work relationship.

Operating within this environment is constant change. All levels of management must recognize change and be flexible enough to adapt to its demands.

Interfacers

Law enforcement executive managers must be **interfacers** who communicate with all segments of the agency, from chief deputy to patrol officer. They must have knowledge of communications and specialized staff activities and relationships, and must understand the division of labor and the allocations of personnel.

They must set agency goals and work plans with input from all agency members. They are the interfacers between all actions of agency personnel and all other people and agencies in contact with these personnel. Like good drivers they can look toward the horizon without losing sight of immediate concerns.

Interactors

Law enforcement managers also must be **interactors** who work effectively with a number of groups. They act as the department's official representative to the press, other local government departments, the business community, schools and numerous community committees and organizations.

Figure 2.5 illustrates the interactions of a typical law enforcement executive and, to some extent, all law enforcement managers.

This diagram shows that only one-fifth of the executive manager's role is with the law enforcement organization. Executive managers have political, community, interorganizational and media roles as well.

Each organization with whom the executive interacts sees the importance and conduct of the position from different viewpoints. Law enforcement managers must determine these varied expectations and develop goals and work plans to meet them effectively.

Law enforcement executives typically interact with politicians, community groups, the media and executives of other law enforcement organizations, as well as individuals and groups within the agency itself.

Attendance at intergovernmental staff meetings is mandatory. Law enforcement agencies need services and information exchange from engineering, finance, planning, building inspections and other departments, just as other departments need the services of the police department.

Although media communications have some undesirable aspects, if reporters and law enforcement personnel establish honest, forthright rapport, they can

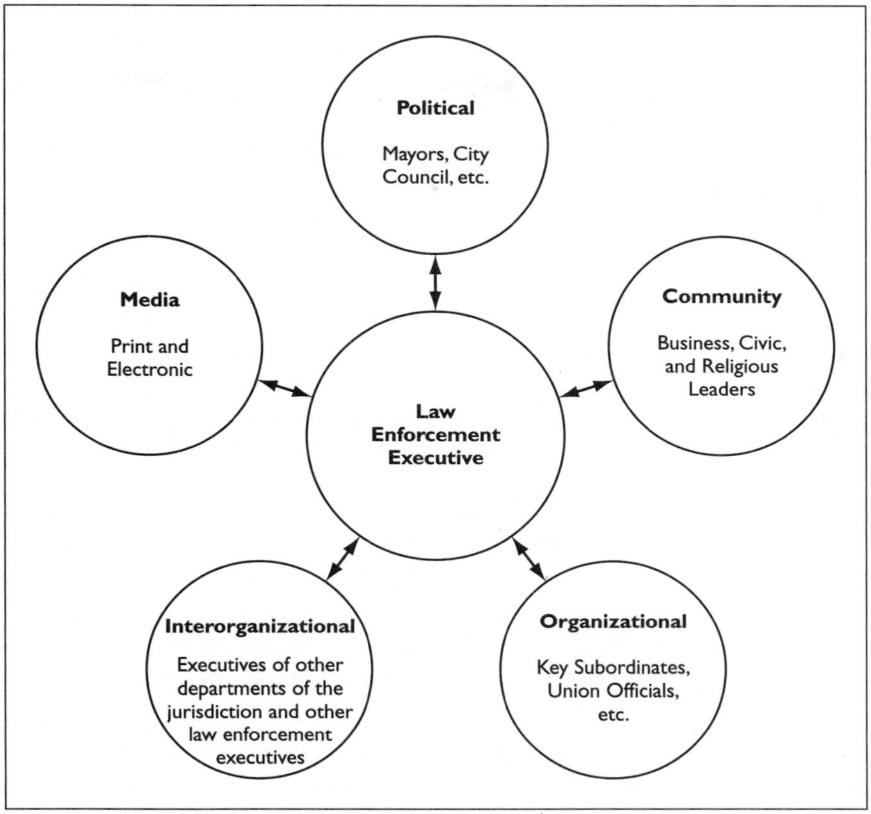

Figure 2.5
Typical Role Set of a Law Enforcement Executive

Source: Donald Witham and Paul Watson, *The Role of the Law Enforcement Executive.* FBI Management Science Unit, 1983. Reprinted by permission.

establish generally good working relationships. Law enforcement needs the media as much as the media need it. (Dealing effectively with the media is discussed in depth in Chapter 3.) Personal contact with representatives of all groups develops an atmosphere of trust, integrity and respect for each other's duties and responsibilities.

On Becoming an Executive Manager

Robert Frost once said: "By working faithfully eight hours a day, you may eventually get to be boss and work twelve hours a day!" When a person first becomes a chief of police, whether selected from within the department or as an outsider, many rumors concerning the appointment will precede the new chief's first day on the job. New chiefs should call a department meeting as soon as possible. At this meeting they should openly state that they understand the officers' concerns and past loyalties but expect to earn their respect. They should also describe the working relationships they seek. Such an open meeting will help allay fears, squelch rumors, decrease suspicions and establish an early rapport with the staff and line personnel.

A chief's management style should be adjusted to the department's needs. Some important changes should be made as soon as possible, but lesser changes should be instituted slowly. Change is stressful for an organization as well as individuals. People will have different opinions about the need for change. A participative approach that invites input from all employees usually works best, as discussed later in the chapter. Decisions should be based on what is good for the community and the department, not on what pleases specific individuals or interest groups.

Whether the department is small or large, the chief of police holds a powerful position in the governmental structure and in the community. The position is also challenging, exciting and filled with barriers and pitfalls. Chiefs should allow time for contemplation, innovation and creative thinking. They must be both managers and leaders. Their responsibilities are heavy, but their rewards are great.

If chiefs adopt a coequal management approach with the department's formal and informal leaders, they may find that their organizational philosophy will be accepted more readily, thus enabling the organizational changes to occur with less resistance.

A major goal of chief executive officers should be to establish an environment in which success is expected and excellence is desired. Ideally, the chief of police is also a leader within the community, particularly in interactions with the city council and the city manager.

Politics

Having to operate in a political environment may be stressful for chiefs. According to Stover (2002, p.6): "From the very beginnings of our noble profession, politics has been a part of policing. But today, politics plays a bigger role in law enforcement than ever before, and today, you also have to add into the mix the need to be politically correct." He suggests that politics sometimes influence who gets policed, who gets hired, retained, promoted and how policing is done.

With a clear mission, goals and objectives, politics should *not* influence the day-to-day operations of the department. However, chiefs must recognize that politics can influence how much funding the department receives. As Slahor (2000, p.235) contends: "Knowing the best ways to create good working relationships with politicians is critical to getting the best for your department. . . . When telling about something, you must be truthful. That candidness wins over the respect of politicians. The biggest way to lose their confidence is to lie to them. . . . Cultivating good relationships also means being in touch with your representative even when you are not drumming up support for a cause or issue."

The political nature of police administrative positions also requires chiefs to keep abreast of changes in legislation. Police administrators must become proactive in the legislative process to effectively serve their departments and communities.

What City Managers Expect from the Chief of Police

Many police chiefs operate under the city manager form of government and report directly to the city manager, not to the city council. In fact, the city manager acts as a buffer between the chief and the council. The chief expects loyalty from his or her personnel, and the city manager expects loyalty from the chief of police. If city managers change during a chief's tenure, the chief should request a meeting to establish a new working relationship. The chief should not expect that the new manager's policies and procedures will be the same as those of the previous city manager. Trust, loyalty and integrity are essential elements for good rapport. The governing philosophy of the city manager and the chief of police must be within acceptable working parameters. However, the city manager is in charge, and flexibility may be required of the chief of police if philosophical differences arise. The chief should determine what the city manager's expectations are:

- What kinds and frequency of reports? Written or oral?
- Who should the chief notify immediately of serious events or incidents?
- What circumstances should the chief deal with directly?
- Should the chief attend city council meetings?
- Should disciplinary actions be reported?

The city manager and the police chief should get together both formally and informally. The chief might invite the city manager to inservice training sessions, roll calls, ride-alongs, stakeouts and the like. The chief should also learn exactly what the city manager expects from the police department and its chief. A chief's success—indeed, the chief's very job—may depend on an effective relationship with the city manager. To be continually at odds with the city manager is a form of career suicide.

Common Management Challenges

Three important management challenges for law enforcement are:
- Administering the budget.
- Maintaining effective community relations.
- Establishing and administering personnel systems and procedures, including recruitment, selection, training and discipline of key employees.

Each decade has its unique changes and challenges. Police chiefs must be constantly alert to the following areas of major concern:

- Employees—Chiefs must evaluate their employees but also be aware that employees are evaluating them.
- Conflict—This must be resolved as soon as possible.
- Politics—Although it is impossible to remain aloof from politics, chiefs should remain objective.
- Communication—Chiefs should keep their department members, their superiors, the media and the community informed.
- Priorities—Few chiefs have sufficient time for everything. They must establish priorities wisely and learn to delegate.

- Street wisdom—Chiefs should get out in the community, ride with officers occasionally, talk with staff and get to know the informal as well as the formal organization.
- Personal conduct—Chiefs are constantly under scrutiny and must perform professionally at all times.

Indicators of Organizational Problems

The following indicators of organizational problems and possible underlying causes are each addressed in depth at appropriate places later in the text.

The manager at higher levels has to make too many decisions. Even though managers are decision makers, decisions should be made at the lowest level practicable. First-line managers should encourage subordinates in the field to exercise independent decision making.

Failure to achieve organizational goals and objectives may be caused by unrealistic goals and objectives or by inadequate manager review or follow-up. *Ineffective, inefficient use of resources* is usually due to a poor organizational design. It may have too little or too much specialization, too many or too few managers, poor division of workload, poor communications flow or a combination of these factors. *Failure to be aware of technology that would improve operations* is usually due to insufficient attention devoted to research and development. *Failure to provide adequate services* is usually due to administrative and operational failures.

Duplication of services or tasks frequently happens because of lack of planning and coordination at the command level. *Lack of coordination between management and subordinates or between work shifts or specialized divisions* is usually due to failure to exercise command responsibility.

Excessive conflict not due to personality clashes indicates low morale and lack of proper communication throughout the organization. *Low morale* is indicated by increases in subordinate complaints, grievances, absenteeism, unvalidated sick leave or work performance and productivity decreases. Department meetings should be held to determine the needs of individuals and the organization. Emphasis should be on performance, with proper recognition when it is achieved. *Lack of opportunity for creativity and innovation* is usually due to lack of proper support and recognition for new ideas. Brainstorming sessions are needed.

Law Enforcement Management as a Career

Deciding to become a law enforcement officer is an exciting career choice, but becoming a manager in law enforcement is even more challenging. It is an opportunity to develop personally and a responsibility to develop others. You can become a successful law enforcement manager in many ways.

Prepare and develop yourself for promotion. Study, attend training programs, take correspondence courses, read trade journals, attend academic courses, use the public library and the law enforcement agency's library and listen to contemporaries. Be ready when opportunity arises.

Be available. Once prepared, you become a valuable resource to the law enforcement organization. Assert yourself at appropriate times. Support your organization's goals and objectives. Participate in work programs. Volunteer to do more than others. Become so valuable to the organization's future that it cannot do without you. Become an information source who is willing to selflessly share information.

Support your manager. An old adage advises: "If you want your manager's job, praise and support him or her because soon that person will move up the ladder. Be derogatory to your manager and he or she will be there forever." Complaining, continually finding fault, being negative or nonsupportive are fast tracks to organizational oblivion. You may accomplish a short-term goal, but in the long run you will destroy your career. Be supportive; if you criticize, make it constructive criticism. Be positive. Praise the good things happening.

Select an advisor or mentor. These are people within or outside the police organization who can assist and counsel you. Advisors can point you in the right direction. They can be a sounding board.

Be positive at and toward work. Either like what you do or change to another job. Rarely can you excel at something you hate. Work longer, more diligently and more competently than anyone else in the organization. Before you know it, you will be an expert.

Nurture interpersonal relationships. Management is getting things done through others. This is impossible to do without treating others as important. Working with others is one of the keys to success. Working alone is a long, hard road. Develop your interpersonal relationships. Combine their strengths with your weaknesses and their weaknesses with your strengths.

According to Booth (2002, p.71): "In any competition, success depends upon the knowledge, skills, and abilities contestants have developed and practiced over time." He suggests: "The very best candidates emerge from a point where three factors converge. The first factor is how well the candidate knows himself or herself. . . . The second emergent element is an understanding of the

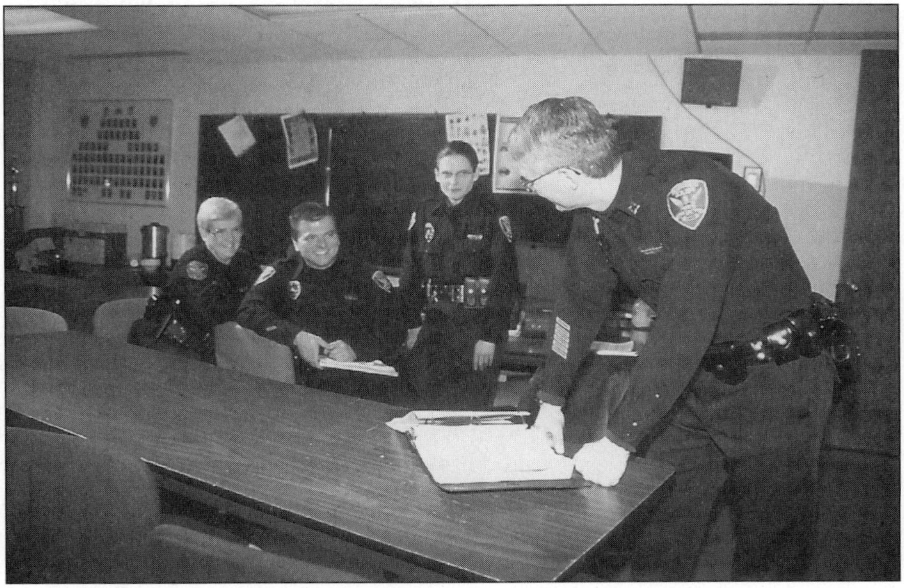

A team approach is becoming more popular in departments across the country. Here officers brainstorm solutions to crime problems identified in their precinct.

© Jim Shaffer

expectations of the organization. . . . The third element is an understanding of the problems being addressed." Fulton (2000a, p.118) stresses: "Your best chance for getting promoted is to be a professional at every rank you hold, prepare for the next rank, and always do the best you can."

Management and Leadership

Leadership has been defined as "working with and through individuals and groups to accomplish organizational goals" (Hersey and Blanchard). Centuries ago, Lao Tsu observed: *The good leader is he who the people revere. The great leader is he whose people say, "We did it ourselves."* Fulton (2000b, p.166) recalls the definition of leadership given by President and World War II Commanding General Dwight Eisenhower: "Leadership: The art of getting someone else to do something you want done, because he wants to do it."

Alsabrook et al. (2001a, p.112) contend: "The job of management is leadership, not supervision. . . . Police managers lead by example." In addition, as Field (2002, p.41) stresses: "Leaders must constantly retool and become perpetual students or risk becoming obsolete." Arnold (2001, p.1) describes the "visionary leader": "True 'visionary leaders' are those who know the direction they want their agencies to go, have the skills to adequately communicate this to their organizations, and, most difficult to fulfill, have the ability to marshal the resources to 'move' the organization in the desired direction."

According to DePree: "Leadership is much more of an art, a belief, a condition of the heart, than a set of things to do. The visible signs of artful leadership are expressed ultimately in its practice" (Tirozzi, 2001, p.434). As Benjamin Franklin wrote over 200 years ago: "Well done is better than well said." Franklin's *Poor Richard's Almanac* set forth many principles of practical leadership:

- He that speaks much is much mistaken. Great talkers should be cropped, for they have no need of ears. [Be a good listener.]
- Promises may get thee friends, but non-performance will turn them into enemies. [Keep your promises. Do what you say you'll do.]
- If your head is wax, don't walk in the sun. [Choose your leadership situations carefully and thoughtfully.]

Managing vs. Leading

Over 20 years ago Drucker conducted a study of the Los Angeles Police Department requested by the chief. Among Drucker's findings was: "You police are so concerned with doing things right that you fail to do the right things." In other words the administration was so concerned with managing that they failed to lead. He also said: "Police are so concerned with doing things right [that] you promote for the absence of wrongdoing rather than for the presence of initiative, innovation and leadership." Recall Drucker's quote: "Managers do things right; leaders do the right thing." Millwee (2000, p.1) describes several other differences between managers and leaders: "Managers inherit goals; leaders set them.

Table 2.4
Management vs. Leadership

Management	Leadership
Does the thing right	Does the right thing
Tangible	Intangible
Referee	Cheerleader
Directs	Coaches
What you do	How you do it
Pronounces	Facilitates
Responsible	Responsive
Has a view of the mission	Has vision of mission
Views world from inside	Views world from outside
Chateau leadership	Front-line leadership
What you say	How you say it
No gut stake in enterprise	Gut stake in enterprise
Preserving life	Passion for life
Driven by constraints	Driven by goals
Looks for things done wrong	Looks for things done right
Runs a cost center	Runs an effort center
Quantitative	Qualitative
Initiates programs	Initiates an ongoing process
Develops programs	Develops people
Concerned with programs	Concerned with people
Concerned with efficiency	Concerned with efficacy
Sometimes plays the hero	Plays the hero no more

Source: Bill Westfall."Leadership: Caring for the Organizational Spirit." *Knight Line USA,* May–June 1993, p.9. Reprinted with permission of *Executive Excellence,* Provo, Utah. September 1992, p.11.

Managers are conformers; leaders are reformers. Managers control; leaders empower. Managers assist; leaders persist. Managers protect; leaders delegate. Managers supervise; leaders coach. Managers are efficient; leaders are effective. Managers are position-oriented; leaders are people-oriented." Table 2.4 presents some striking differences between management and leadership.

A basic difference between managers and leaders is that managers focus on tasks, whereas leaders focus on people.

A manager operates in the status quo, but a leader takes risks. Police administrators must be both skilled managers and effective leaders. Leaders solve problems, maximize potential with competent associates, take safe risks, take responsibility, move forward, lead by example and have vision.

Managers may or may not be leaders, and leaders do not have to be managers. As Kokkelenberg (2001, p.9) states: "Bosses have subordinates, but true leaders have followers regardless of their rank or title. Historically, when individuals thought of leadership, they thought of rank. For rookies, it was the field training officer and for everyone else it was the level(s) above their rank." A true leader has the potential to influence from any position in the organization, formal or informal.

Characteristics of Leaders

A **leader** in the purest sense influences others by example. This characteristic of leadership was recognized in the sixth century B.C. by Chinese philosopher Lao-Tzu when he wrote:

> The superior leader gets things done
> With very little motion.
> He imparts instruction not through many words
> But through a few deeds.
> He keeps informed about everything
> But interferes hardly at all.
> He is a catalyst,
> And although things wouldn't get done as well
> If he weren't there,
> When they succeed he takes no credit.
> And because he takes no credit
> Credit never leaves him.

Leadership creates a special bond that has to be earned. To build and maintain credibility, it is necessary to clarify values, identify the wishes of the community and employees, build a consensus, communicate shared values, stand up for beliefs and lead by example. Taylor (2002, p.29) stresses: "Employees want a leader who knows them, understands them, treats them fairly, and is someone whom they can trust." Fulton (2000c, p.106) adds other traits successful leaders must possess: honesty, confidence, humility, optimism, personal energy, courage, loyalty, adaptability and tenaciousness.

A good leader knows being the boss does not mean bossing. Rather it means giving employees the resources, training and coaching they need and providing them with information so they can see their organization's mission. Stevens (p.197) reports on a study conducted among 97 police commanders and supervisors in 18 police agencies across the country that found that "police leadership isn't prepared as well as expected." Respondents were surveyed on 13 traits considered essential for effectiveness leadership. They were asked to indicate how often they displaced these traits, with 1 being *never* and 5 being *always.* Respondents rated themselves highest on "taking action" and lowest on "creative ability" (the percentage indicates the mean or average response):

Taking action	4.38
Toughness	3.91
Integrity	3.82
Sharing command	3.55
Police decision	3.43
Delegation of responsibility	3.35

Trust subordinates	3.09
Public trust	3.09
Commitment	2.93
Organizational change	2.73
Visionary	2.72
Communication	2.69
Creative ability	1.78

Interestingly, toughness was the second most prevalent trait, yet this may not be entirely positive, especially if leaders are acting as coaches and mentors. As Heller (2002, p.76) suggests: "Two directions I suggest for all educators are the wisdom of the ancient East and brain-based research. The former suggests the incredible power that can result from kindness and compassion. The latter reveals in a painfully empirical manner the physical and psychological harm that can result from a lack of these qualities."

Research on and Theories Related to Leadership

Leadership has been studied over the past several decades from many different perspectives.

Theories about leadership include the study of traits, the classic studies conducted at Michigan State and Ohio State Universities, the Managerial/Leadership Grid and situational leadership.

Trait Theorists

The first group of researchers, the **trait theorists,** examined the individual. They looked at leaders in industry and government to determine what special characteristics or **traits** these people possessed. They found that most leaders are *goal oriented,* stimulating employees to achieve goals by following rather than being forced or commanded to achieve. Leaders are *motivated* and expect the same of those they work for and with. They are *planners and prioritizers* who consider alternatives and variations and lay out realistic courses of action according to the circumstances.

Leaders are *intelligent,* having sufficient knowledge to make decisions. They are *observant,* absorbing information that may not be immediately usable and retaining it for future use. They are also *inquisitive,* delving, probing, pondering and searching. They question everything and do not accept things as they are simply because "that's the way we've always done it."

Leaders are *able to seek out problems.* They foresee problems and prevent them. They are proactive rather than reactive. They are also *creative and innovative thinkers,* spending a certain portion of their time "contemplating their navels," that is, sitting back, thinking and dreaming, yet being practical and realistic. Like Walt Disney, they believe: "If you can dream it, you can do it."

Leaders look at everything they do and ask: "How can I do this differently? Better?" When they discover the answer, they do it.

Leaders are *persevering,* determined, yielding only when proved wrong. Leaders are *risk takers.* They do not want to make mistakes but accept that doers will make mistakes, learn from them and move forward. Remember the saying, "The person who makes no mistakes usually makes nothing." Consider the example of Tom Watson, founder of IBM. When Watson learned that a promising young junior executive had entered into a risky business venture that lost over $10 million dollars, Watson called the man into his office. When the junior executive asked whether Watson wanted him to resign, Watson replied, "You can't be serious. We've just spent $10 million dollars educating you."

Although by definition leaders need others to be followers, most leaders are not governed or unduly influenced by others. They are *independent* and confident in their choices. Leaders are also *effective communicators,* having above-average verbal and written skills. They are *people oriented* because they recognize that they accomplish things *through* others. Ability is important, but the ability to discover ability in others and then help them develop it is the true test of leadership. To accomplish goals with the help of others, leaders need a *high level of personal strength, energy and good health.*

Leaders *know their own limitations.* They neither underestimate nor overestimate their potential. Leaders *live by personal principles and values.* They must have a guiding philosophy similar to that of their organization. Truly effective leaders are *visionary,* working creatively and innovatively, with a clear idea of where they are going and how they are going to get there.

Leaders are *honest* people who are role models in integrity. Although they know their own limitations, they are also *self-confident and optimistic.* A graphic example of the consequences of lack of self-confidence is the death of tightrope aerialist Karl Wallenda. In 1968 Wallenda said: "Being on the tightrope is living; everything else is waiting." He loved his work and had total confidence in himself. Ten years later he fell to his death. His wife, also an aerialist, said that he had recently been worried about falling. This was in total contrast to his earlier years, when all his energy was focused on succeeding.

The **Wallenda Effect** is readily seen in sports when a team that is ahead starts playing simply to keep its lead rather than to increase it. Such a team, playing not to lose rather than to win, often loses its momentum and can be defeated.

Although many leadership traits have been identified, none dominate. Leadership trait theory was highly popular because it simplified the process of selecting leaders. Guaranteed leadership through possession of specific traits, however, was never fully realized because of the number of traits identified and the fact that no single person possessed them all. No criteria determined which traits were more desirable than others. Even possession of all the traits did not guarantee leadership success.

After many studies and experiments, trait theorists could not empirically document leadership characteristics. Researchers in the 1940s and 1950s turned their attention to the situations in which leaders actually functioned.

The Michigan State and Ohio State Universities Studies

Research conducted at Michigan State University and Ohio State University also provides insights into effective leadership. These studies determined that leaders must provide an environment that motivates employees to accomplish organizational goals.

The Michigan State study looked at how leaders motivated individuals or groups to achieve organizational goals. It determined that leaders must have a sense of the task to be accomplished and the most favorable work environment. Three principles of leadership behavior emerged from the Michigan State study:

- Leaders must give task direction to their followers.
- Closeness of supervision directly affects employee production. High-producing units had less direct supervision; highly supervised units had lower production. Conclusion: Employees need some freedom to make choices. Given this, they produce at a higher rate.
- Leaders must be employee oriented. It is the leader's responsibility to facilitate employees' accomplishment of goals.

The Ohio State study on leadership behavior used similar methods. This research focused on two dimensions: initiating structure and consideration structure.

Initiating structure looked at the leader's behavior in assigning *tasks.* It focused on leaders who assigned employees to specific tasks and asked them to follow standard rules and regulations. **Consideration structure** looked at establishing the *relationship* between the group and the leader. It focused on leaders who found time to listen to employees, were willing to make changes and were friendly and approachable.

The Ohio study used these two variables—focus on task and focus on relationships—to develop a management quadrant describing leadership behavior.

The Managerial Grid from a Leadership Perspective

Blake and Mouton developed their Managerial Grid from the studies done at Ohio State University and the Group Dynamics Leadership studies. As Figure 2.2 (p.39) showed, the grid illustrates five types of management or leadership styles based on concern for production (task) versus concern for people (relationship).

Hersey and Blanchard (1977, p.96) summarized the attitudinal preferences of each management style in several areas, including their basic production/people beliefs, guiding slogans, decision making, conflict with superiors and peers, conflict with subordinates, creativity and promotion of creative effort (Table 2.5).

Situational Leadership

Hersey and Blanchard took existing leadership theory a step further. They viewed leadership as an interplay between the amount of direction (task behavior) a leader gives, combined with the amount of relationship behavior a leader provides (the Managerial/Leadership Grid) *and* the readiness level that followers exhibit on a specific task the leader is attempting to accomplish through the individual or group.

Table 2.5
Attitudinal Preferences of Various Management Styles

	Authority-Compliance Management	Country Club Management	Middle-of-the-Road Management	Impoverished Management	Team Management
Basic Production–People Beliefs	Sees good relationships as incidental to high production. Supervisors achieve production goals by planning, directing and controlling all work.	Sees production as incidental to good relations. Supervisors establish a pleasant work atmosphere and harmonious relationships between people.	Sees high production and sound relations in conflict. Supervisors stay neutral and carry out established procedures.	Seeks a balance between high production and good human relations. Supervisors find a middle ground so a reasonable degree of production can be achieved without destroying morale.	Sees production resulting from integrating task and human requirements. Good relationships and high production are both attainable. Supervisors get effective production through participation and involvement of people and their ideas.
Guiding Slogans	Produce or perish.	Try to win friends and influence people.	Don't rock the boat.	Be firm but fair.	People support what they help create.
Decision Making	Inner-directed, depending on own skills, knowledge, attitudes and beliefs in approaching problems and making decisions.	Other-directed, eager to find solutions that reflect the ideas and opinions of others so solutions are accepted.	Avoids problems or defers them to others.	Samples opinions, manipulates participation, compromises and then sells the final solution.	Seeks emergent solutions as the result of debate, deliberation and experimentation by those with relevant facts and knowledge.
Conflict with Superiors and Peers	Takes a win-lose approach, fighting to win its own points as often as possible.	Avoids conflict by conforming to the thinking of the boss or peers.	Keeps its mouth shut and does not express dissent.	Expresses opinions and then tries to find reasonable compromises.	Confronts conflict directly, communicating feelings and facts as a basis to work through conflict.
Conflict with Subordinates	Suppresses conflict through authority.	Smooths over and tries to release tension by appeals to the "goodness of people."	Does not get involved with conflict. It usually avoids issues that might give rise to conflict by simply not discussing them with subordinates.	Deals with surface tensions and symptoms only, letting conflict situations "cool off" for a while, working for a blending of different positions so a somewhat acceptable solution is reached.	Confronts conflict directly and works through it at the time it arises. Conflict is accepted so the clash of ideas and people can generate creative solutions to problems. Those involved are brought together to work through differences.
Creativity	Considers ideas the responsibility of the few, not expected of the majority.	Expects no one to be creative, but a creative person is congratulated.	Sometimes has good ideas "pop up," but ideas are usually unrelated to company goals or morale.	Values creativity and seeks it from everyone, usually under nonthreatening conditions that will not disturb staff or the authority structure.	Expects those interested in and able to tackle a problem to do so. A high degree of interplay of ideas exists. Experimentation is the rule rather than the exception. Innovations further shared goals and solve important problems.
Promotion of Creative Effort	Promotes innovation by rewards and promotions. When a conflict of ideas arises, it is "survival of the fittest."	Encourages innovations by accepting all ideas uncritically. Ideas that will generate conflicts are side-stepped.	Discourages creativity. Ideas are not discussed on the job, so conflicts are unlikely.	Encourages innovation under controlled conditions. Brainstorming and "idea of the month" campaigns are used.	Uses feedback of results of experiments as a basis for further development and thinking. Open expression of differences and mature conflict are accepted. Everyone encourages innovations by defining and communicating problems.

Source: Adapted from Hersey and Blanchard (1977).

Situational leadership specifies that initially workers need support and direction. As they become more task-ready, they need less direction and more support, up to the point where even support can be reduced. The basic premise of situational leadership theory is that as the followers' readiness level in relation to task increases, leaders should begin to lessen their direction or task behavior and simultaneously increase their relationship behavior. This would be the leaders' strategy until individuals or groups reach a moderate level of task-readiness.

As followers or groups move into an above-average level of readiness, leaders would decrease both their task behavior and their relationship behavior. At this point followers would be ready not only from the task point of view but also from the amount of relationship behavior they need.

Once a follower or group reaches this level of readiness, close supervision is reduced and delegation is increased, indicating the leader's trust and confidence.

Transformational Leadership

The most recent form of leadership to be recognized is **transformational leadership,** which treats employees as the organization's most valuable asset. It is employee-centered and focused on empowerment.

An important aspect of transformational leadership is its employee-orientation. Transformational leadership seeks to empower people to make the fullest possible contribution to the organization. What is often lacking, however, is a model for effective *followership.* A leader cannot simply tell people they are empowered and expect them to instantly know how to perform. Employees need training, resources and authority if they are to be empowered.

The focus on leadership rather than management complements the move toward community-oriented, problem-solving policing because it stresses resolving problems and not simply reacting to incidents. It encourages experimenting with new ways and allows honest mistakes to encourage creativity.

Ford et al. (1999, p.14) have developed a road map for making the change to community policing through transformational leadership. They suggest:

> A leader needs three things to build this road map: an understanding of the stages one must go through to make transformational change happen in an organization; an understanding of the underlying elements for change in the move to community policing; and an understanding of key challenges a leader must face in any transformational change effort.

Their road map is shown in Table 2.6.

Leadership Styles

Management literature has identified many leadership styles, several of which can be found in police organizations.

Leadership styles include autocratic, democratic or participative and laissez-faire.

Autocratic leadership is most frequently mentioned in connection with the past. Many early leaders inherited their positions. They were members of the aristocracy, and through the centuries positions of leadership were passed down to family members.

Table 2.6
Community Policing:
A Road Map for Change

TIME LINE

Exploration	Commitment	Planning	Implementation	Monitoring and Revision	Institutionalization
	Concept	**Action Items/ Bench Marking Recommendations**	**New Knowledge and Implementation**	**Movement and Impact Data**	**Examples of Practices**
Organizational Structure	Roles and Responsibilities	Blend specialist Community Policing Organization's into overall patrol units. Define those task areas requiring specialization department-wide and train accordingly. Develop teams utilizing a combination of specialists whenever possible. Review other best practices.	■ Redo job descriptions ■ Redefine relationships across functions and work groups ■ Reduce reporting lines	■ Identify key "generalist" roles and evaluate the number of personnel who participate in this role ■ Track the efficiency of services/systems likely to be affected by a more generalist role and evaluate whether improvements are made as a result of new rules ■ Evaluate the amount of extra work that is avoided through generalist approach (fewer call backs, fewer referrals, etc.)	*Baltimore, MD*—Over the past decade, the agency has evolved from specialized community policing units with a rather narrow focus to a department-wide community policing mandate. Every facet of the agency is geared toward meeting the goals of community policing. Relationships throughout the department have been restructured to allow information, guidance, and authority to flow through the organization without supervisory barriers or traditional "chain-of-command" restraints.
	Divisional Alignment	Geographic subdivisions developed, with internal and external input for assignment of personnel. Reporting lines tailored to activity and geographic area of accountability, rather than function. Review other best practices.	■ Assign areas of geographic responsibility for all personnel ■ Study feasibility of organization for better accountability ■ Decentralize organization into geographic areas as appropriate ■ Assign cross functional teams to areas	■ Evaluate departmental effectiveness in key roles/geographical areas and note improvements as well as areas of weakness ■ Identify key problems unique to each area and track improvements over time (e. g. , less crime, fewer complaints, quality of life issues)	*Grand Rapids, MI*—One centralized agency is in the process of moving into five district areas. Officers are responsible for a geographical area within their district. *Lansing, MI*—Decentralized the department in top problem solving areas and made officers accountable for a specific area. Two new precincts were created to decentralize services. *St. Petersburg, FL*—The city was divide into geographic regions and all employees are accountable for activities in the area to which they are assigned.
	Organizational Accountability to Community	Expand measures beyond crime statistics and response times to include citizen perceptions of safety and security (quality of life). Review other best practices.	■ Create atmosphere soliciting public input ■ Survey community ■ Add citizens to internal planning processes	■ Send customer satisfaction survey following interaction with department to obtain feedback ■ Survey citizen perceptions of safety and quality of life in neighborhood ■ Develop systems for community input, suggestions, and feed-back (e. g., toll-free line, Web page, surveys, suggestion box)	*Sagamore Hills, OH*—An agency serving a rural community initiated their change to community policing by surveying residents. Based on survey, strategies for decreasing residents' fear of crime were developed.

Source: Ford et al. "Transformational Leadership and Community Policing: A Road Map for Change." *The Police Chief,* Vol. LXVI, No. 12, December 1999, p.19. Reprinted by permission. Copyright held by The International Association of Chiefs of Police, Inc. 515 N. Washington St., Alexandria, VA 22314. Further reproduction without express written permission from IACP is strictly prohibited.

In early industrial production efforts, the boss was often a domineering figure. He (bosses were invariably men) was specifically chosen because he displayed traits associated with autocratic leadership. His authority was uncontested, and employees did what they were told or else. This style of management emerged in response to the demands of the Industrial Revolution, when masses of illiterate workers used expensive machinery and needed to follow explicit orders.

Managers who used autocratic leadership made decisions without participant input. They were completely authoritative and showed little or no concern for subordinates. Rules were rules, without exception. According to Johnson (2001, p.29): "This **mechanistic model** of management, or 'Taylorism,' divides tasks into highly specialized jobs where job holders can become experts in their field and demonstrate the 'one best way' to perform their respective cog in the wheel." Says Johnson (2002, p.65): "This model emphasizes the values of neutrality, conformity, impersonality and crime control in the context of law enforcement agencies." Certain circumstances may call for autocratic leadership.

Consultative, Democratic or Participative Leadership

Consultative, democratic or **participative leadership** has been evolving since the 1930s and 1940s. Democratic leadership does not mean that every decision is made only after discussion and a vote. It means rather that management welcomes employees' ideas and input. Employees are encouraged to be innovative. Management development of a strong sense of individual achievement and responsibility is a necessary ingredient of participative or consultative leadership.

Democratic or participative managers are interested in their subordinates and their problems and welfare. Management still makes the final decisions but takes into account the input from employees. Johnson (2002, p.65) says this type of leadership is a good fit with the **organic model** of management: "This model of policing represents a flexible, participatory, science-based structure that will accommodate change. It is designed for effectiveness in serving the needs of citizens rather than the autocratic rationality of operation. It is democratic in that it requires and facilitates the involvement of citizens and employees in the process." Johnson concludes: "While the mechanistic model seeks to maximize efficiency and productivity, the organic model seeks to maximize workers satisfaction, flexibility and personal development."

Laissez-Faire Leadership

Laissez-faire leadership implies nonintervention and is almost a contradiction in terms. Let everything run itself without direction from the leader, who exerts little or no control. This style arises from the concept that employees are adults, should know as well as the manager what is right and wrong and will automatically do what is right for themselves and the organization.

Laissez-faire leaders want employees to be happy and believe that if employees are happy, they will be more productive. Employees *should* feel comfortable and good about their work, but this should be because they participate. Even when they participate, employees must still do the job and meet the organization's goals and objectives. Leaderless management, sometimes called **free-rein leadership,** may result in low morale, inefficiency, lack of discipline and low productivity. Figure 2.6 shows the continuum of leadership styles.

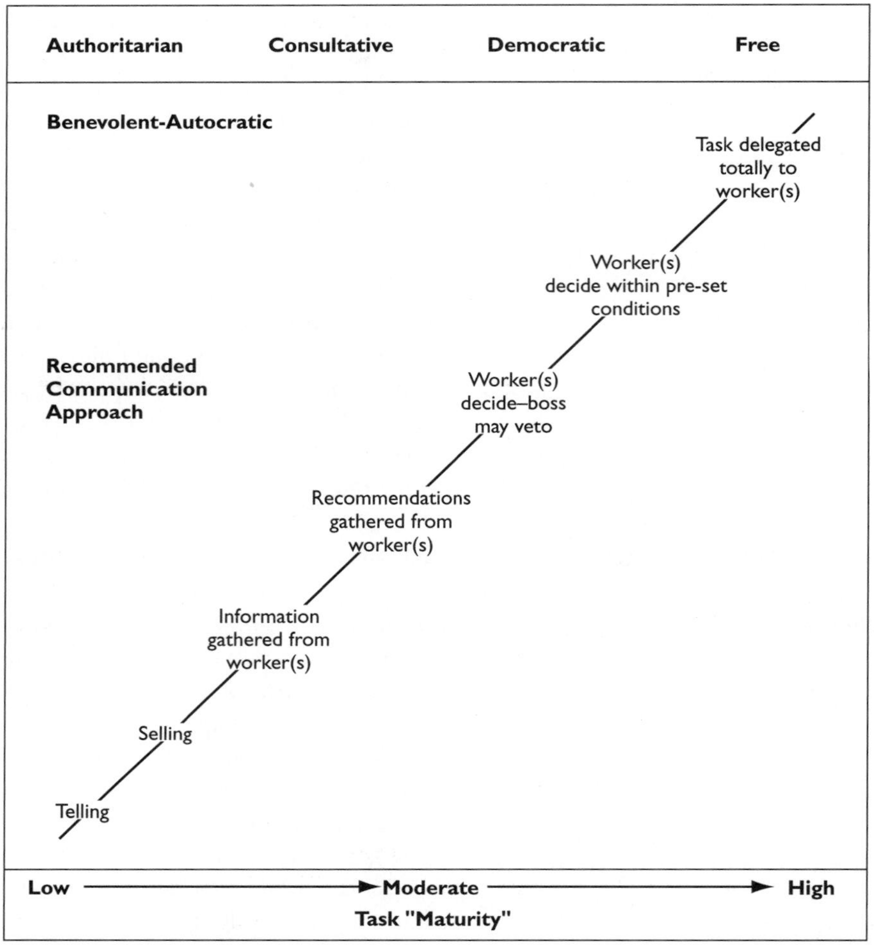

Figure 2.6
Continuum of Leadership Styles

Source: Paul R. Timm. *Supervision,* 2nd ed. St. Paul, MN: West Publishing Company, 1992, p.269. Reprinted by permission. All rights reserved.

Implications

Research on leaders and leadership is abundant. Each theory offers something to the law enforcement manager. However, no one type of leader or leadership style will suffice in all situations.

Leaders must often be autocratic in one situation and democratic or participatory in another. They must know when to make an immediate decision and when to make a decision only after input, discussion and consideration.

Emergency situations rarely permit the opportunity for democratic or participatory decision making. Employees in nonemergency situations rarely respond well to autocratic leadership for routine task performance over the long term.

Leaders know what to do, how to do it, when to do it and with what type of employee, according to the demands of the individual situation. Internationally, leaders have been recognized because of the leadership abilities they displayed for a particular time, place and need. Put into another situation and time, they might not have become leaders.

Table 2.7
Authoritarian and Participatory Leadership Styles Compared

Authoritarian (Mechanistic) Style	Participatory (Organic) Style
Response to incidents	Problem solving
Individual effort and competitiveness	Teamwork
Professional expertise	Community orientation; ask customers what they want
Go by the "book"; decisions by emotion	Use data-based decision making
Tell subordinates	Ask and listen to employees
Boss as patriarch and order giver	Boss as coach and teacher
Maintain status quo	Create, innovate, experiment
Control and watch employees	Trust employees
Reliance on scientific investigation and technology rather than people	Reliance on skilled employees—a better resource than machines
When things go wrong, blame employees	Errors mean failed systems/processes—improve them
Organization is closed to outsiders	Organization is open

Leadership—A Call for Change

Managers must pay attention to the new ideas and trends emerging from America's businesses: a commitment to people, the development of a people-oriented workplace and the belief that leadership can and does make a difference. Leadership in law enforcement historically depended on a strong, authoritarian chief. However, this style of leadership neglects everything known about people and their behavior. Coercion discourages creativity and risk taking and often causes people to rebel.

President Eisenhower used to demonstrate this aspect of leadership with a simple piece of string. He would put the string on a table and say: "Pull it and it'll follow wherever you wish. Push it and it'll go nowhere at all." It is the same with people: "I don't mind being pushed as long as I can steer."

Managers must shift from telling and controlling the people they work with to developing and enhancing them. They must ask for their input before making critical decisions that affect them. They must also listen to their customers—the citizens—in new and more open ways. Managers must stop reacting to incidents and begin solving problems. They must permit risk taking and tolerate honest mistakes to encourage creativity and achieve innovation. To better understand this change in leadership style, compare the key concepts from each, summarized in Table 2.7.

Changing from autocratic management to any other style is a slow, evolutionary process. Developing a new corporate culture for an organization can take years. Part of the challenge is the bureaucracy within most law enforcement agencies, as discussed previously.

Leadership Training and Development

An appointment to fill a position on an organizational chart does not automatically make one a leader. By the same token, relatively few leaders are able to simply step into the role without needing to develop and refine their leadership skills and abilities.

Leaders who have adopted a specific leadership style can change that style through training. They can turn their weaknesses into strengths through studying, working with mentors or observing other leaders in action. Leaders are not born; they are developed. Task-oriented leaders can become people-oriented leaders.

Leadership training before appointment is highly desirable. If not possible, it should happen soon after appointment. Each leader must be an individual, not a mirror image of the predecessor. According to Green (2001, p.385): "Throughout police leadership development the following things are essential: knowing the traits of a leader, presenting a positive role model, having training available, giving others the opportunity to develop and providing feedback."

Leadership can be developed through comprehensive training programs, including participative management and team-building theory, motivational theory, communications and decision making.

Porter and Neal (2000, p.179) discuss leadership development at the executive level and identify eight factors of importance along with the competencies needed for each:

- Thinking (seasoned judgment, visionary thinking, financial acumen, global perspective, research orientation)
- Strategic management (shaping strategy, driving execution)
- Leadership (attracting and developing talent, empowering others, influencing and negotiating, leadership versatility, political versatility)
- Interpersonal (building agency relationships, inspiring trust, moral courage)
- Communication (fostering open dialogue, high-impact delivery, community teaching, community involvement)
- Motivation (drive for stakeholders' success, entrepreneurial risk taking)
- Self-management (mature confidence, adaptability, career and self direction)
- Breadth and depth (cross-functional capability, industry knowledge)

Table 2.8 summarizes the skill layers for law enforcement managers/leaders.

A study by Krimmel and Lindenmuth (2001, p.481) found that the most effective police chiefs (as judged by their city managers) tended to be educated, groomed for leadership through participation in the FBI National Academy's program, were promoted from within and worked in a union environment.

Guidelines for Effective Management/Leadership

- Know your work and those you manage.
- Know how to get and maintain cooperation.
- Learn as much as possible about decision making.
- Learn as much as possible about how to be a leader.
- Learn how to give praise and constructive criticism.

Table 2.8
Skill Layers for Managers/Leaders

A	B	C
When used alone, these skills are suited to a rigidly traditional workplace.	Combined with the skills in column A, the skills below are needed in today's progressive workplace.	Combined with columns A and B, these skills are needed to build and maintain a team environment.
Direct people.	Involve people.	Develop self-motivated people.
Get people to understand ideas.	Get people to generate ideas.	Get groups of diverse people to generate and implement their own best ideas.
Manage one-to-one.	Encourage teamwork.	Build teams that manage more of their own day-to-day work.
Maximize the department's performance.	Build relationships with other departments.	Champion cross-functional efforts to improve quality, service and productivity.
Implement changes from above.	Initiate changes within the department.	Anticipate, initiate and respond to changes dictated by forces outside the organization.

Source: John H. Zenger et al. "Leadership in a Team Environment." *Security Management*, September 1992, p. 29. Reprinted with permission from Achieve Global.

- Learn to think positively; create rather than destroy.
- Learn to handle bad situations as well as good ones.
- Know when to discipline and when to be authoritarian or democratic/participatory.
- Help your employees improve themselves. Doing so will in turn improve you. Give them responsibility, tell them your expectations and provide instructions.
- Be honest with yourself and your officers. Expect honesty from them. Maintain integrity in yourself and demand it in others.
- Use your employees' abilities. They can provide new approaches to problems. Establish two-way communication to capture the vast amount of information contained within the group. Use participation to achieve more acceptance of decisions.
- Do not over supervise. Employees do not like managers constantly breathing down their necks.
- Remember that you are part of management, and never downgrade management or managers. If a problem exists, help solve it rather than creating a worse one.
- Keep your perception of your leadership abilities in line with subordinates' perceptions. Ask them what you can do better for them.
- If you call a meeting, make it worthwhile. Excessive meetings that provide a façade of participation are worse than no meetings. Every meeting should produce a result.

- Treat employees' mistakes as a teaching responsibility, not a punitive opportunity.
- Develop officers who differ with you, rather than clones. Develop officers who can compensate for your weaknesses. The tendency is to do the opposite.
- Be consistent. Be direct. Be honest. Be fair.
- Listen. Lead by example.
- Develop people skills.
- Be a risk taker.

Holistic Management

Police officers feel a high sense of peer identification—no call has higher priority than a fellow officer in danger. Police officers also receive an ego boost by the fact that they are readily identified by their uniforms and have certain powers above and beyond those of the average citizen.

The police manager is responsible for ensuring that the officer does not lose this feeling of ego satisfaction (e.g., after a citizen has flashed an obscene gesture to the officer) and continues to develop this sense of belonging to a unique profession geared toward helping one's fellow human beings. The **holistic management** approach views law enforcement officers and support personnel as total individuals who make up a *team.*

The Team Approach

A **team** consists of two or more people who must coordinate their activities regularly to accomplish a common task. The team approach builds on the concept of **synergism,** that the group can channel individual energies to accomplish together what no individual could possibly accomplish alone—that the whole is greater than the sum of its parts (for example, when 2 + 2 = 5).

Synergism is all around. Athletics provides countless examples of how a team, working together, can defeat a "superstar." Examples of synergism also come from the music world. Consider the power and energy produced by a top-notch marching band or symphony orchestra. Every musician must know his or her part. Individual players may have solos, but ultimately what is important is how it all sounds together.

The Wilson Learning Corporation has identified eight attributes of high-performing teams (Buchholz and Roth, 1987, p.14).

Attributes of high-performing teams are:

- **Participative leadership**—creating interdependency by empowering, freeing up and serving others.
- **Shared responsibility**—establishing an environment in which all team members feel as responsible as the manager for the performance of the work unit.
- **Aligned on purpose**—having a sense of common purpose about why the team exists and the function it serves.

- **High communication**—creating a climate of trust and open, honest communication.
- **Future focused**—seeing change as an opportunity for growth.
- **Focused on task**—keeping meetings focused on results.
- **Creative talents**—applying individual talents and creativity.
- **Rapid response**—identifying and acting on opportunities.

Although Buchholz and Roth were speaking of teams in the business world, the same eight attributes are likely to be present in a high-performing law enforcement agency. In addition, administrators and their subordinates can learn some lessons about teamwork from nature, for example, from geese ("The Lessons from Geese," 1994):

> *Fact:* As each goose flaps its wings, it creates uplift for the birds that follow. By flying in a "V" formation, the whole flock adds 71% greater flying range than if each bird flew alone. *Lesson:* People who share common directions and sense of community get where they are going quicker and easier because they are traveling on the thrust of one another.
>
> *Fact:* When a goose falls out of formation, it suddenly feels the drag and resistance of flying alone. It quickly moves back into formation to take advantage of the lifting power of the bird immediately in front of it. *Lesson:* If we have as much sense as a goose, we stay in formation with those headed where we want to go. We are willing to accept their help and give help to others.
>
> *Fact:* When the lead goose tires, it rotates back into formation and another goose flies to the point position. *Lesson:* It pays to take turns doing the hard tasks and sharing the leadership. As with geese, people are dependent on each others' skills, capabilities and unique arrangement of gifts, talents and resources.
>
> *Fact:* The geese flying in formation honk to encourage those up front to continue their speed. *Lesson:* We need to make sure our honking is encouraging. In groups where there is encouragement, the production is much greater. The power of encouragement (to stand by one's heart or core values or encourage the others) is the greatest quality of honking we seek.
>
> *Fact:* When a goose gets sick, wounded, or shot down, two geese drop out of formation and follow it down to help and protect it. They stay with it until it dies or is able to fly again. Then they launch out with another formation or catch up with the flock. *Lesson:* If we have as much sense as geese, we will stand by each other in difficulties as well as when we are strong.

True leaders are not intimidated by outstanding team members. They do not fear for their jobs. They develop followers who will surpass them. Athletes, for example, will become coaches and train other athletes who will break their records.

One way to initiate action is to encourage employees at the lowest level to work together to solve their problems, with or without manager involvement. These are not highly organized, trained teams but rather groups of employees with a common problem who band together. They are organized informally from anywhere in the organization to focus on a specific problem or project. They are usually self-formed, self-managed and highly productive. When they have met the need, the group dissolves.

McDonald (2000, p.19) presents an innovative approach to teams: "Originally, work was organized around individuals. But as production became more complex, the idea of structured teams emerged. Now with the advent of the

Internet, people can work from anywhere at any time. Physical teams no longer fit. Enter the concept of a **cybertribe,** a group of bright people all sharing the same enthusiasm for their company's goal, but bringing a wide range of complimentary skills to bear on the effort." Although speaking about business, the same ability to share ideas with other departments facing similar problems is an exciting notion.

Summary

Managers have authority and power, which both imply the ability to coerce compliance, that is, to *make* subordinates carry out orders. Both are important to managers at all levels. However, authority relies on force or on some law or order, whereas power relies on persuasion and lacks the support of law and rule.

Basic management skills include technical skills, administrative skills, conceptual skills and people skills. Successful managers have clear goals and a commitment to excellence, feedback and support. Management by objectives (MBO) involves managers and subordinates setting goals and objectives together and then tracking performance to ensure that the objectives are met.

Several management theories have evolved over time. McGregor's Theory X/ Theory Y says that managers act toward subordinates in relation to the views they have of them. Theory X views employees as lazy and motivated by pay. Theory Y views employees as committed and motivated by growth and development. Likert's Four-System Approach to management goes from System 1, which is a traditional, authoritarian style, to System 4, which is a participative management style. Argyris's Mature Employee Theory views employees and their organization as interdependent. Blake-Mouton's Managerial/Leadership Grid describes five management styles: Authority–Compliance, Country Club, Impoverished, Middle-of-the-Road and Team Management. No one style is more apt to achieve the department's mission than another. The selected style must be matched to individual personalities.

Management typically has three levels: the top level (chief, sheriff), the middle level (captains, lieutenants) and the first-line level (sergeants).

Law enforcement executives are planners, facilitators, interfacers and interactors. They are responsible for both tactical and strategic planning. *Tactical planning* is short-term planning. *Strategic planning* is long-term planning. In addition to these roles and responsibilities, law enforcement executives typically interact with politicians, community groups, the media and executives of other law enforcement organizations, and individuals and groups within the law enforcement agency itself.

Three important management challenges for law enforcement are administering the budget, maintaining effective community relations, and establishing and administering personnel systems and procedures, including recruitment, selection, training and discipline of key employees.

The basic difference between managers and leaders is that managers focus on tasks, whereas leaders focus on people. A leader in the purest sense influences others by example. Theories about leadership include the study of traits, the classic studies conducted at Michigan State and Ohio State Universities, the Managerial Grid, situational leadership and transformational leadership.

Trait theorists identified characteristics leaders possessed. The Michigan and Ohio studies determined that leaders must provide an environment that motivates employees to accomplish organizational goals. Situational leadership specifies that initially workers need support and direction. As they mature they need less direction and more support, up to the point where even support can be reduced. Transformational leadership treats employees as the organization's most valuable asset. It is employee-centered and focused on empowerment. Research has also identified several leadership styles, including autocratic, consultative, democratic or participative and laissez-faire.

Leadership can be developed through comprehensive training programs, including participative management and team building theory, communications and decision making.

Attributes of high-performing teams are participative leadership, shared responsibility, aligned on purpose, high communication, future focused, focused on task, creative talents and rapid response. Leaders must balance the need for synergism and the need for survival of the organization.

Discussion Questions

1. Who should be responsible for law enforcement planning? How should it be accomplished?
2. Why is coordination important? What are some examples?
3. What are the main problem areas of the different levels of law enforcement managers?
4. How do you develop yourself to be a law enforcement manager?
5. What is your definition of leadership?
6. What traits do you attribute to successful law enforcement leaders? If you had to select one most important characteristic of a law enforcement leader, which would you select?
7. Which style of leadership do you prefer? Which style do you perceive you use most of the time?
8. What are the merits of the holistic approach to leadership?
9. What direction should law enforcement leaders take for the future?
10. What leadership traits do you possess? What leadership traits do you need to develop?

InfoTrac College Edition Assignment

Use InfoTrac College Edition to help answer the Discussion Questions as appropriate.

- Find one journal article on *decentralization in the business world* and one journal article on *decentralization in law enforcement.* Compare the advantages each article sets forth for this change in management. Be sure to include the full reference citation along with your information.

References

Alsabrook, Carl L.; Aryani, Giant Abutalebi; and Garrett, Terry D. "Five Principles of Leadership." *Law and Order,* May 2001a, pp.112–115.

Alsabrook, Carl L.; Aryani, Giant Abutalebi; and Garrett, Terry D. "The Five Principles of Organizational Excellence in Police Management." *Law and Order,* June 2001b, pp.109–114.

Arnold, Jon. "Strategic Planning for Career Development." *The Police Chief,* April 2000, pp.61–63, 196.
Arnold, Jon. "Leadership and Policing." *Subject to Debate,* October/November 2001, pp.1,9.
Blanchard, Ken. "Getting Back to Basics." *Today's Office,* January 1988, pp.14,19.
Booth, Walter S. "Three Common Factors of Successful Promotion Candidates." *The Police Chief,* July 2002, pp.71–75.
Brewer, Rodney and Hazlette, Tim. "Police Leadership in Kentucky: A Thoroughbred Approach." *The Police Chief,* April 2002, pp.16–20.
Brissett, Liz. "Make the Best Strategic Plan." *Ventures,* July 2001, p.44.
Buchholz, Steve and Roth, Thomas. *Creating the High-Performance Team.* New York: John Wiley and Sons, 1987.
Deming, W. Edwards. *Quality, Productivity, and Competitive Position.* Cambridge, MA: Institute of Technology, Center for Advanced Engineering Study, 1982.
Field, Mark W. "Surviving and Thriving in a Radically Changing World: Learning Never Stops for the Successful Leader." *The Police Chief,* March 2002, pp.41–44.
Ford, J. Kevin; Boles, Jerome G.; Plamondon, Kevin E.; and White, Jane P. "Transformational Leadership and Community Policing: A Road Map for Change." *The Police Chief,* December 1999, pp.14–22.
Fulton, Roger. "10 Steps to a Promotion." *Law Enforcement Technology,* May 2000a, p.118.
Fulton, Roger. "What Is Leadership?" *Law Enforcement Technology,* July 2000b, p.166.
Fulton, Roger."What Is a Leader?" *Law Enforcement Technology,* November 2000c, p.106.
Fulton, Roger. "The 7 Benefits of Proper Delegation." *Law Enforcement Technology,* August 2001, p.126.
Fulton, Roger. "Delegation Fears." *Law Enforcement Technology,* August 2002, p.110.
Green, Don. "Developing Police Leaders." *Law and Order,* February 2001, pp.383–385.
Harrison, Bob. "Policy and Procedure: What New Sergeants Need to Know." *Law and Order,* October 2001, pp.151–153.
Heller, Daniel A. "The Power of Gentleness." *Educational Leadership,* May 2002, pp.76–83.
Hersey, Paul and Blanchard, Kenneth H. *Management of Organizational Behavior,* 3rd ed. Englewood Cliffs, NJ: Prentice–Hall, 1977.
Johnson, Daniel V. "Strategic Planning and Leadership." *Minnesota Police Chief,* September 2001, pp.29–44.
Johnson, Dan. "A Call for Strategic Planning and Leadership." *The Police Chief,* June 2002, pp.65–68.
Kokkelenberg, Lawrence D. "Real Leadership Is More than Just a Walk in the Park." *Law Enforcement News,* February 14, 2001, p.9.
Krimmel, John T. and Lindenmuth, Paul. "Police Chief Performance and Leadership Styles." *Police Quarterly,* December 2001, pp.469–483.
Kurz, David L. "Strategic Planning and Police–Community Partnership in a Small Town." *The Police Chief,* December 2000, pp.28–36.
"The Lessons from Geese." Sioux Falls, SD, Central Plains Clinic, Ltd., Employee Newsletter *Vital Sign,* January 14, 1994.
McDonald, Tom. "Smark, Quick, and Powerful." *Successful Meetings,* May 2000, p.19.
Millwee, Steven C. "Defining a Leader." *ASIS Dynamics,* September/October 2000, pp.1, 23–24.
Porter, Constance and Neal, Susan. "Leadership Development at the Executive Level." *The Police Chief,* October 2000, pp.179–187.
Slahor, Stephenie. "Cultivating Good Political Relations." *Law and Order,* October 2000, pp.235–236.
Smith, Scott. S. "Pulse: Talking with Ken Blanchard." *Entrepreneur,* January 2000, p.18.
Stevens, Dennis J. "Improving Community Policing: Using Managerial Style and Total Quality Management." *Law and Order,* 2000, pp.197–204.
Stover, Brian. "Police and Politics." *Police,* April 2002, p.6.
Taylor, Craig R. "Focus on Talent." *TD,* December 2002, pp.26–31.
Tirozzi, Gerald N. "The Artistry of Leadership." *Phi Delta Kappan,* January 2001, pp.434–459.

WWW Book-Specific Web Site

Go to the *Management and Supervision in Law Enforcement* Web site at http://info.wadsworth.com/0534616054 for student and instructor resources, including Internet Assignments and Case Studies.

CHAPTER 3

Communication: A Critical Management Skill

Language is the picture and counterpart of thought.
—Mark Hopkins, builder of Central Pacific and Southern Pacific Railroads

Do You Know?

- What the communication process involves?
- What the KISS principle is?
- How much of a message is conveyed by body language and tone of voice rather than words?
- What the critical factors in selecting a communication channel are?
- What the weakest link in the communication process is?
- How much faster people can think and listen than they can talk?
- What active listening is?
- What barriers can hinder communication?
- What directions communication can flow?
- What four kinds of meetings are typically held?
- How to make meetings efficient and productive?
- What usually causes difficulties in dealing with the media?

Can You Define?

abstract words
active listening
agenda
body language
channels of communication
communication
communication barriers
communication enhancers
communication process
decode
downward communication
encode
external communication
feedback
gender barrier
grapevine
horizontal communication
internal communication
jargon
KISS principle
lateral communication
lines of communication
news media echo effect
nonverbal communication
perp walk
rumor mill
standard English
tone
two-way communication
upward communication
verbal channels of communication
vertical communication
written communication

INTRODUCTION

Administrators are in the communication business. Of all the skills a manager/leader/supervisor needs to be effective, skill in communicating is *the* most vital. In fact, according to Hennessy et al. (2001, p.15): "Communication is a critical part of policing. Research has shown that 93 percent of police work is one-on-one communication." Estimates vary, but all studies emphasize the importance of communication in everyday law enforcement operations.

Early law enforcement communication consisted of blowing whistles or firing weapons to attract attention. Some departments used a system of red lights on the corners of the highest structures in the community. These were turned on by the dispatcher or the local telephone operator when an officer was needed. Observing the red lights, the officer on foot or vehicle patrol then phoned the station. Officers set times to meet at certain locations on their beat to transfer information. Vehicle telecommunication and personal hand radios did not exist in those days. Technologically, law enforcement communication has come a long way.

Communication, however, is much more encompassing than messages to and from the dispatching center. Technical communications are essential to law enforcement operations, especially in emergencies. Equally important, however, are all the other kinds of communication occurring every minute.

Consider how much of a person's day is occupied with communication. Conversations, television, radio, memos, letters, e-mails, faxes, phone calls, meetings, newspapers—the list is long. McDonald (2000, p.32) notes: "By the most conservative estimates available, information is doubling every three years; that's twice as much data to deal with every 1,100 days." Even private thoughts are communication. Every waking hour, people's minds are filled with ideas and thoughts even when they do not outwardly communicate them.

Although technological advances have greatly expanded communication capabilities, the communication process has not changed. This chapter begins with a definition of communication and its importance to managers at all levels. This is followed by an examination of the communication process and its components. Next barriers and obstacles to communication are discussed, followed by a discussion of communication enhancers. Then the lines of communication are described, including both downward and upward communication. Next is a discussion of internal communication, including meetings and newsletters. This is followed by a discussion of external communication, including dealing with the media and communicating with outside agencies and the public. The chapter concludes with a discussion of communication and homeland security.

Communication Defined

Communication is the complex process through which information *and understanding* are transferred from one person to another. This process may involve written or spoken words or signs and gestures. Communication involves more than sending an idea. Successful communication occurs when the receiver's understanding of the message is the same as the sender's intent. Sounds simple enough, but often it just does not happen. People who have played the telephone game, sending a whispered message around a circle, have witnessed first hand how often messages are *not* communicated. To understand how messages can become so muddled, consider the process of communication.

The Importance of Communication Skills to Managers

As Nowicki (2001b, p.21) stresses: "The ability to effectively communicate with people is an absolute necessity for law enforcement officers."

Fulton (2000, p.130) contends: "Communication at any level is an inexact art. But misunderstood communications can have grave consequences in the 'life and death' world of police work." Lack of communication is often an obstacle to correcting problems. Without effective communication, people do not know what is expected of them or how well they are doing. Managers and subordinates may not be able to agree on the quality of services they provide. Equipment needs may not be revealed. Animosities may fester.

Consequences of not communicating well include low morale, increased union disputes, reduced work quality and quantity and sometimes even lawsuits. The list is endless.

The Communication Process

The basic parts of the communication process are the message, sender and receiver. The process, however, is much more complex than this, as illustrated in Figure 3.1.

A message originates in a sender's mind. The sender, having a unique knowledge base and set of values, must **encode** the message into words or gestures. The

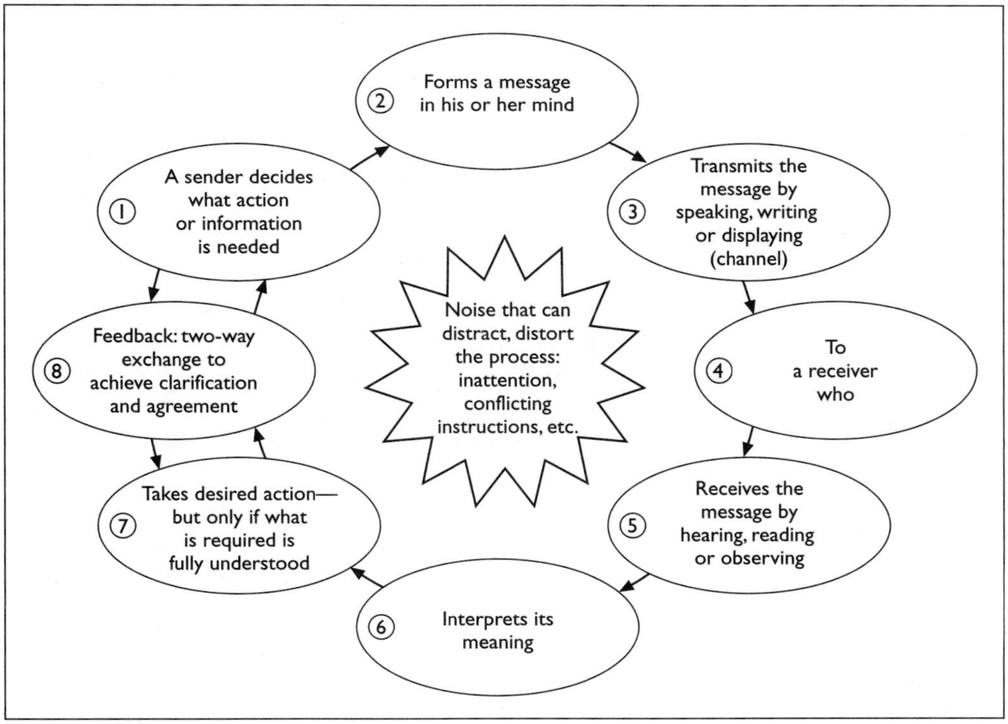

Figure 3.1
The Communication Process

code is sent through some channel (which may distort the code). A receiver, also having a unique knowledge base and set of values, must **decode** or translate the message. The receiver may or may not provide **feedback** to the sender, that is, an indication that the message is or is not understood.

Successful communication occurs only if (1) the sender can correctly encode the message, (2) the channel is free of distortion and (3) the receiver can correctly decode the message.

The **communication process** involves a message, a sender, a channel and a receiver. It may include feedback.

Often the sender is unaware that the encoding of the message may be inappropriate. For example, a physician might refer to a person using the abbreviation "S.O.B." To medical people this quite naturally means "short of breath." Laypeople, however, would likely decode it to mean something far different.

Problems that arise from encoding and decoding from one language to another can prove quite humorous. For example, several years ago Sol Linowitz, ambassador to the Organization of American States and former chairman of Xerox Corporation, met with some Central American presidents. One president asked through an interpreter what the Xerox company did, and Linowitz gave him a very brief explanation, which the interpreter translated into Spanish. Linowitz watched with concern as the listening presidents rolled their eyes, shook their heads and then suddenly became quiet, looking at him with awe. Hastily he asked the interpreter what he had told the presidents. The interpreter replied, "I told them exactly what you said—that Xerox is a company that has invented a new method of reproduction."

The problem of translating from one language to another is illustrated by the computer translation of the familiar English phrase "out of sight, out of mind" into Russian for "invisible idiot." One of the most striking examples of the devastating effects of miscommunication occurred in 1945. The Emperor of Japan and his cabinet were almost ready to accept the Allies' ultimatum to give up or be crushed. However, they wanted more time to discuss the specific terms, so they sent a message saying they were following a "mokusatsu" policy, meaning "no comment" yet. The translation, however, said that they had *ignored* the surrender demand. The result was bombs on Hiroshima and Nagasaki!

Messages do often get lost in translation. Imagine that thoughts could be color coded. You color code your thoughts blue, and the person you are talking to color codes his or her thoughts yellow. What will happen to the message? It may be a mixture of sender *and* receiver preconceptions and a totally different color—green.

In other words, effective communication takes into consideration not only the message and channel but also the sender and receiver. How effectively messages are conveyed depends on the following:

- Communication skills of the sender
- Clarity of purpose

- Effectiveness of the message itself
- Appropriateness of the channel used
- Receptivity of the receiver
- Communication skills of the receiver
- Feedback

Shared frames of reference such as language, experience and cultural heritage are extremely important in communication. The smaller the shared frames of reference, the more likely miscommunication and misunderstanding will occur.

Consider the parable of the six blind men and the elephant. Each man touched a single, different part of the animal, and each came to a very different conclusion about what an elephant was like. One man felt only the sturdy side and compared the elephant to a wall; one felt only the tusk and thought an elephant was like a spear; one felt only the trunk and believed the elephant to be like a snake; one felt only a leg and envisioned a tree trunk; one felt only an ear and thought an elephant resembled a fan; and one felt only the tail and exclaimed an elephant to be like a rope. By experiencing only an isolated part of the whole creature, each man came to a very different—and very incorrect—conclusion as to what the whole elephant appeared to be.

Another factor to consider when communicating is how to make an important message stand out from the many voices clamoring for attention in what McDonald calls the "info-glut age." He (p.32) suggests the use of three specific strategies. First, communicate rarely: "The best way to be heard above the din is to communicate less, not more." Second, communicate concisely: "For years, the joke among executives has been, 'If it's got a staple in it, it doesn't get read.' " And third, communicate with purpose: "About 80 percent of internal communication—meetings, teleconferences, presentations, e-mails, and so on—contains information that does not require action; in other words, there are no consequences if the listener ignores it." McDonald concludes: "Simplicity, in this hyperturbulent workplace, may just be the best competitive advantage you have for being heard above the noise." Keep these points in mind throughout this chapter, knowing how important communication is and that it needs to be ongoing.

Turn your attention now to the specific components making up the communication process.

The Sender of the Message

Communication begins with a person or group with a message to relay. The sender of the message will have characteristics such as age, gender, educational level and past experience that may affect the message. The purpose of the message should be clearly understood. Communication usually has one or more of the following purposes: to inform, entertain, persuade or be understood.

Once the purpose is clear, the message itself must be put into language, which may be verbal (spoken or written) or nonverbal. An effective communicator has developed the basic message "sending" skills of speaking and writing, as well as the message "receiving" skills of listening and reading. The most effective communication is a two-way exchange.

The Message

The message should be in simple, **standard English,** that is, it follows the grammatical rules of American English. Whether spoken or written, the message should avoid **jargon** (the specialized language of a field) and evasive or "impressive" language. All too often message senders attempt to avoid an issue or to *impress* rather than *express.*

Jargon from the military illustrates this tendency. Imagine yourself the receiver of the following phrases and see whether you can decode the message in each:

- Manually operated impact device
- Operate in a target-rich environment
- Controlled flight into terrain

A manually operated impact device is a hammer. Troops operating in a target-rich environment are outnumbered. Controlled flight into terrain is a plane crash.

The business world also uses such jargon. For example, employee theft is referred to as "inventory shrinkage" and losing money as having a "net profit revenue deficiency." Law enforcement, too, has its share of jargon: aforesaid, alleged perpetrator, a party later identified as John Doe, and said officer proceeded to exit his squad.

The general rule is to keep the message conversational and follow the KISS principle.

The **KISS principle** means: Keep It Short and Simple.

Use familiar words with only one or two syllables when possible. For example, use *let* rather than *afford an opportunity;* use *find out* rather than *ascertain;* use *end* rather than *terminate,* and use *use* rather than *utilize.*

Use prepositional phrases sparingly. For example, use *because* rather than *due to the fact that;* use *if* rather than *in the event that;* and use *now* rather than *at the present time.*

Omit all empty words and redundancies. For example, use *asked* rather than *asked the question;* use *blue* rather than *blue in color;* use *February* rather than *month of February;* and use *experience* rather than *past experience.*

Be especially careful in using modifiers. They can result in embarrassing statements such as the following:

> Three cars were reported stolen by our police department yesterday. (The department did not steal the cars.) This memo offers suggestions for handling obscene phone calls from the chief. (The chief did not make obscene phone calls.) Stress and anxiety can be emotionally destructive to line personnel. We must get rid of them. (Who does *them* refer to?)

Avoid words that are ambiguous or confusing. One very ambiguous word is *subsequently.* This word means "after" and also means "as a result of." This is a critical difference, especially in law enforcement, and only the sender of the message knows which meaning is intended. So use "after" or "as a result of." Other confusing terms are *bi-monthly* and *semi-monthly.* Ask a group of people what these words mean and you will see that about half will come up with the correct meaning. Much better to use *every two months* or *twice a month.*

Tone, or the emotional effect of certain words, is another factor that greatly influences the message. Some words carry negative connotations, for example, *dirt bag, snitch, soused* and *slammer.* Be aware of such words and avoid using them when communicating professionally.

Abstract words and generalities may blur messages and result in miscommunication. A department policy that prohibits *long hair,* for example, is subject to misinterpretation because it is not sufficiently specific. The sender needs to be precise. What does *at your earliest convenience* mean? It would be clearer to give the date by which you would like something done. What does *contact me* suggest? That the person write, telephone, come in for a visit, physically bump into you or perhaps try to reach you through ESP? Be as specific as possible to ensure that your meaning is communicated clearly.

Nonverbal Messages and Body Language

Nonverbal communication is how messages may be transferred without words. Mimes, for example, use facial expressions and hand and body motions to convey their messages. As Nowicki (2002, p.26) notes: "The process of effective interpersonal communications is much more than just words. The ability to pick up on the nonverbal components of interpersonal communications demonstrates much more than words. The old adage, 'It's not what you say, but how you say it' is absolutely true."

Entire books are written about **body language** and interpreting the mannerisms of other people, including eye contact or lack of it, facial expressions, leg and arm movements and so on.

The majority of communication between two people comes from body language and tone of voice.

Nowicki (2001a, p.27) reports: "Extensive research by Ray Birdwhistell showed 10 percent of the message delivered is verbal and 90 percent is nonverbal. If officers can correctly interpret what they see, they are arming themselves with a powerful tool." Interpreting eye contact, for example, is considered by many communication experts to be one of the most important skills a person can develop.

Many nonverbal messages are obvious: A frown, a smile, a shrug, a yawn, tapping fingers, rolling eyes and so forth. Consider what the following nonverbal cues tell about a person:

- Walking—fast, slow, stomping
- Posture—rigid, relaxed
- Facial expression—wink, smile, frown
- Eye contact—direct, indirect, shifting

- Gestures—nod, shrug, finger point
- Physical spacing—close, distant
- Appearance—well groomed, unkempt

Use caution, however, when interpreting body language. For example, a trial lawyer was trying to "read" the jury just before they went to deliberation and was very concerned that one man's posture—arms folded in front of him—spelled trouble for his client. However, after the verdict was read in favor of his client, the lawyer approached the juror and explained that he had expected a different response, given the man's folded arms. The juror simply replied, "I've got a big belly. A man's gotta put his arms somewhere."

Channels of Communication

Technology has expanded the **channels of communication,** or the means by which messages are conveyed.

Critical factors to consider in selecting a channel include speed and opportunity for feedback. Expense is also important.

Verbal Channels

Among the most common **verbal channels of communication** are one-on-one conversations, telephone conversations, radio dispatch, interviews, meetings, news conferences and speeches. Verbal channels are often selected because they are fast, allow for feedback and are relatively inexpensive.

One-on-one conversations are usually the most common form of communication in a law enforcement agency. Verbal communication is often used for reprimanding employees because it is more personal and allows for feedback. Such reprimands may be followed by a written memo or report.

The *telephone* is effective when feedback is needed immediately. It is a readily available, **two-way communication** with feedback occurring during the process. On the other hand, telephone conversations are usually not recorded and may involve excessive time. Further, one person may have interrupted the other. Finally, the message may be misunderstood because it is only auditory. Important visual clues are missing. Cellular phones have improved the convenience and immediate availability of verbal communication channels. As with other phone communication, however, valuable visual clues are absent.

Meetings and *seminars* also provide for two-way communication. These channels allow for an open exchange of information and ideas and for feedback. However, the timing may be bad for some, meetings and seminars may consume an inordinate amount of time, and sometimes a few individuals dominate. Conducting effective meetings is discussed later in this chapter.

A disadvantage of two-way verbal channels is that they are temporary: There is no permanent record of them. This disadvantage can be negated by taping the communication. In fact, most law enforcement agencies record all calls that come into the dispatcher.

One-way verbal communication includes audiocassettes, videos and television. Such channels are well suited to conveying information—training, for example—but are limited in that they do not allow feedback.

Written Channels

Written communication includes notes, memos, letters, e-mails, faxes, reports, manuals, bulletins, policies and the like. Written communication has the advantage of being permanent but the disadvantage of being slower and usually more expensive. The primary disadvantage of written communication, however, is lack of immediate feedback.

Reports can be prepared at the convenience of the sender, allowing time to organize and select the appropriate words. Reports can also be widely disseminated. On the other hand, they are one-way communication, impersonal, fairly expensive and may be misinterpreted.

Memos are more immediate and less expensive, provide a permanent record and can be widely disseminated. Like reports, however, they are impersonal, one-way communication.

The *fax* machine has greatly enhanced the efficiency of written communication. Fax messages are rapid, can be acknowledged and allow for feedback almost as rapidly as verbal communication.

However, faxes are less secure than other forms of communication. You don't know who is on the other end receiving the fax. Sensitive information may end up in the wrong hands this way. In addition, some organizations, including the military, do not recognize a faxed signature as being legal.

E-mail is another means of rapid communication. In fact, e-mail is quickly becoming the most popular form of communication in the business world because it enhances the lines of communication between managers and employees and between co-workers of all levels. Nimsger and Lange (2002, p.16) report: "Ninety-three percent of all corporate communication is now created electronically, with only 30 percent of that communication ever printed to paper."

E-mail is not without its perils, however, as Field (2000, p.49) cautions: "If implemented with no guiding principles or organizational agreement, electronic mail can be a potential minefield for leaders." How so? Field explains:

> Electronic mail represents a step on the path to virtual human relations. Electronic communications are seductive and will distance people from one another unless organizations assume control with specific plans and organization-based agendas. If organizations fail to preserve traditional internal communications, they risk the disappearance of critical, traditional organizational dynamics.

In addition, Fulton (2001b, p.106) cautions: "A quick, insensitive comment or an unintended or sarcastic tone may be too easy to send, or sent without thinking the wording through to be sure it means what you want it to mean. It can be the e-equivalent of speaking without thinking. Take time to read through your replies and messages, before hitting that send button." Another peril is hitting the "reply to all" and forwarding messages to unintended people. Finally, when using the global address book, people may click on the wrong name and send information to the wrong person.

Handheld computers for obtaining information on the street is another highly effective means of written communication. As Dees (2000, p.96) observes: "The promise of handheld technology in law enforcement is exciting. Palmtop-equipped officers can leave roll call for the street secure in the knowledge that they have the latest hot sheets, patrol bulletins, legal updates, personnel rosters and schedules, department policies and any other information all on their handheld. . . . The days when officers have to collect reams of paper to carry with them on patrol may be soon past us, as they can keep it all in the palms of their hands."

Another innovation is described by Miller (2002, p.68): "Wearable computers are reality, have been tested in police work, and if engineered properly, could become as widespread as cruiser laptops. Some industry experts see wearable computing as the next step in personal computing. The idea is to combine desktop computers' power, laptop and handheld computers' mobility and communications versatility into a single unit that will become as much a part of your uniform as your duty belt. . . . Wearable computers offer law enforcement hands-free capability, multiple forms of communication with others and a means of data collection."

The Receiver of the Message

A key factor in any communication is the receiver of the message. Like the sender, the receiver has certain characteristics that influence the way in which the message is interpreted, including age, gender, educational level and experiences. As Fulton (2000, p.130) notes: "Successful commanders recognize the problems of the interpretation of words and phrases, and realize that individuals will hear, read and interpret those words consistent with their own values, views and agendas. Recognizing that, and other factors, successful commanders take the steps necessary to prevent communication problems from getting out of hand."

First, consider the receiver from the sender's perspective. Who is the message for? How receptive is the receiver likely to be? What distractions might have to be overcome? Does the receiver have the necessary background and ability to understand or act on the message? What prejudices or values might hinder or enhance the communication?

Next, consider the receiver from the receiver's perspective. The most important responsibility of the receiver of a verbal message is to *listen.* Unfortunately, listening is one of the most neglected yet most important skills in communication.

Listening

Law enforcement officers need to receive information more than they need to give it. A major portion of their time is spent receiving information for forms and reports, taking action in arrests, eliciting information in interviews and interrogations and many other duties requiring careful listening. As important as listening is, many people lack good listening skills.

The weakest link in the communication process is *listening.*

It is much more difficult to listen to a recorded message than to listen to someone speaking directly to you. For example, a secretary typing a letter dictated by the chief of police began the final paragraph with the sentence: "I hardly agree with your decision." Unfortunately, what the chief had said was: "I heartily agree with your decision." Even more unfortunately, the chief did not proofread the letter but simply signed it. A totally incorrect message was delivered.

Few people have taken courses in listening. We were taught to speak, read and write, but we simply *assume* we know how to listen. Yet most people are *not* good listeners. One of the main reasons is the gap between speaking and listening rates. The average person speaks at approximately 125 words per minute but listens at about 400 words per minute. This gap lets people daydream or begin to think about other topics.

People listen and think four times faster than they talk.

Preoccupation is another common problem. People often "hear" the sounds but do not "listen" to the message; instead, they evaluate what they are hearing and concentrate on how they are going to respond. It is almost impossible to think, speak and listen at the same time. Poor listening habits are practiced and become entrenched. Other factors that affect listening include the person's attitude toward the speaker and/or the topic, the location, the time available, noise and other distractions, and lack of interest or boredom.

A Test of Listening Skills

University of Minnesota professor and listening expert Ralph Nichols suggests 10 questions to test listening skills. Answer *yes* or *no* to each of the following:

1. Do you try to make others think you are listening to them, whether you are or not?
2. Are you easily distracted from what a person is saying?
3. Do you take notes on what a person is saying?
4. Do you assess the quality of what a person will say by appearance or how the person talks?
5. We know that a person thinks four times as fast as another person talks. Do you use this excess time to think about other things, such as your reply?
6. Are you receptive to facts and figures rather than concepts and ideas in a speech?
7. Do certain words or phrases turn you off so that you cannot listen clearly to what is being said?
8. If you do not understand or are annoyed by what a speaker is saying, do you question the speaker?
9. Do you try to avoid hearing something that you decide would take too much time and trouble to figure out?
10. If you decide that a speaker is not going to say anything worthwhile, do you tune out and think about other things?

Each *no* scores 10 points. A score of 80 is excellent. Note, however, that many people disagree with the third item, thinking that taking notes is a good way to show that what is being said is important. Police officers frequently take notes as they interview and interrogate. This is a matter of personal preference and the specific circumstances involved.

Active Listening

To be an effective listener, look at the speaker. Think about the words and the implied message. Ask questions to clarify, but do not interrupt, and remain objective. In addition, as Drucker is fond of saying: "The most important thing in communication is to hear what isn't being said." It is often said that everyone talks, but few listen. The results when people do *not* listen can be disastrous.

Active listening includes concentration, full attention and thought.

Listening skills *can* be improved. Opportunities for practice occur daily. Pay attention to those with whom you are speaking, show appropriate responses to what they are saying, listen for feelings as well as the content, look at and listen to body language, and respond directly to what is being said. Active listening is hard work, but it pays off.

Recognize that in communication, receivers and senders of messages constantly switch roles. The effective communicator is skilled not only at speaking (or writing) but also at listening (and reading).

Feedback

I know that you believe that you understand what you think I said, BUT I am not sure you realize that what you heard is not what I meant! Without feedback, communication is one way. Feedback is the process by which the sender knows whether the receiver has understood the message.

Two people may talk and yet neither may understand what the other is saying. Most feedback is direct and oral. Two people discuss something, one makes a statement, and the other responds. Head nodding or shaking, smiling, grimacing, raised eyebrows, yawns—all are forms of feedback. The better the feedback, the better the communication.

Barriers to Communication

Communication barriers include:

- Time.
- Volume of information.
- Tendency to say what we think others want to hear.
- Certainty.
- Failure to select the best word.
- Prejudices (sender and/or receiver).
- Strained sender-receiver relationships.

Time is important to everyone, especially law enforcement officers and managers. Communication systems have greatly enhanced the ability to pass information from one person or organization to another. On the other hand, e-mails, faxes and other devices have deluged subordinates and managers alike with information. To cope, managers must be selective in what they personally take action on and what they delegate.

Another obstacle to communication is the tendency to say what we think others want to hear. This is especially true when the information is negative. This tendency can be dangerous because the person may form opinions or act on insufficient information. State all the facts about a situation so the receiver can correctly interpret them.

A fourth obstacle is certainty, the unwavering belief that the information a person has is accurate: "My mind's made up; don't confuse me with the facts." This is illustrated by the young man who went to see a psychiatrist to learn to cope with being dead. This young man was certain he was dead, but no one would believe him. The psychiatrist, eager to help the man, asked him, "Do dead people bleed?" When the young man answered, "Of course not," the psychiatrist asked for the young man's hand and permission to stick his finger with a pin. The young man consented and, as the psychiatrist expected, the finger bled. Amazed, the young man exclaimed, "I'll be darned. Dead people do bleed!"

Logic seldom works on those who are certain of the "facts." As an old saying astutely notes: "It ain't the things you don't know what gets you into trouble; it's the things you know for sure what ain't so."

Yet another obstacle is the varied meanings words may have. For example, the word *victim* may arouse concern and empathy, but it may also arouse annoyance and pity. Select your words carefully to convey precisely what you mean. In one department a police chief sent a memo to all officers asking for suggestions on how to improve retention. He received numerous ideas on how to help officers improve their memories. What he wanted, however, was thoughts on how to keep officers from quitting the department.

Another important obstacle to communication is prejudice. Bias against a certain race, religion, nationality, gender, sexual preference or disability can create tremendous communication barriers.

Strained sender-receiver relationships can seriously hinder communication. For example, a rookie's suggestion to a field training officer of a "better" way of searching a suspect based on the latest research is not likely to be well received. It will in fact probably be cut short with a comment such as, "Who's teaching who here?"

The Gender Barrier

Much attention is now focusing on significant differences in how men and women communicate. Such differences often create a **gender barrier.** Table 3.1 summarizes gender differences in communication.

Men and women differ not only in how they listen, but also in how they speak. Of special note is that men tend not to pause and to interrupt, while women tend to pause, allowing the male interruption. Such interruptions, even though unintentional, may create anger and tension. In addition, because men tend to speak until interrupted, they likely will dominate a conversation.

Table 3.1
Conversational Styles: Gender Tendencies

Listening	
Male	**Female**
Irregular eye contact	Uninterrupted eye contact
Infrequent nodding	Frequent nodding
Infrequent humming sounds	Frequent humming sounds
May continue another activity while speaking	Usually stops other activities while speaking
Interrupts in order to speak	Waits for pauses in order to speak
Questions are designed to analyze speaker's information	Questions are designed to elicit more information

Speaking	
Male	**Female**
Few pauses	Frequent pauses
May abruptly change topic	Connects information to previous speaker's information
Speaks until interrupted	Stops speaking when information delivered
Speaks louder than previous speaker	Uses same volume as previous speaker
Frequent use of "I" and "me"	Frequent use of "us" and "we"
Personal self-disclosure rarely included	Personal self-disclosure often included
Humor delivered as separate jokes or anecdotes	Humor interwoven into discussion content
Humor often based on kidding or making fun of others	Humor rarely based on kidding or making fun of others

Source: Peg Meier and Ellen Foley. "War of the Words." Minneapolis/St. Paul. *Star Tribune, First Sunday,* January 6, 1991. Reprinted with permission of the *Star Tribune.*

The Cultural Barrier

Hennessy et al. (2001, p.15) stress: "The ability to communicate with citizens from cultures different from one's own is critical to successful policing. The challenges for law enforcement, more so than any other governmental service profession, creates a very special need for understanding a pluralistic, multicultural society. In fact, the very success of community policing is dependent on that understanding."

If a police officer is interacting with someone who does not speak English, language translators can be of great assistance. The spoken language is not the only barrier. Jones (2002, p.21) notes: "Making a circle with the thumb and forefinger is friendly in the United States, but it means 'you're worth zero' in France and Belgium, and is a vulgar sexual invitation in Greece and Turkey." Further, according to Nowicki (2001a, p.27): "Eye contact varies with different racial and ethnic groups. For example, in the United States, Caucasians maintain eye contact while speaking about 45 percent of the time, African-Americans about 30 percent, Hispanics about 25 percent and Asians about 18 percent of the time."

Obstacles within the Process

Recall that the communication process consists of a sender, a channel, a receiver and, ideally, feedback. Problems can arise within any aspect of this process.

The *message* may be *improperly encoded.* The sender must translate or *encode* the message accurately, unambiguously and precisely, avoiding complex language.

It must get past the sender's prejudices, limitations and values. Nonverbal cues must support, not contradict, the message.

Further, the sender must not *misuse communication channels.* An obvious example is the department bulletin board, a potentially powerful communication channel. All too often, however, material is posted and left long past its effective life. Cluttered bulletin boards lose their communicating power. Other examples are dull, one-way meetings and department newsletters that do little more than report sports news and social events.

A more critical example is one-on-one communication between managers and subordinates that becomes one-way and primarily negative or disciplinary. Most one-on-one communication should be *positive.* It should not be limited to official business but also should include more personal or casual topics to let subordinates know they are important as both individuals and employees.

"Noise in the channel" may seriously interfere with communication. This may be actual physical noise, such as an airplane flying overhead, a phone ringing or more than one person talking at once. An uncomfortable room—too hot, too cold, unpleasant odors—can also detract from communication.

Written communication can be hindered by poor copy quality, messy copy with lots of cross-throughs and write-overs, illegible handwriting, faint print and so on. Such "noise" in the channel not only interferes physically with the message, but it often annoys the receiver, further hindering effective communication.

Poor timing is another common obstacle. If the receiver is upset, angry, rushed, tired, hurt, preoccupied or unprepared, the message may not be communicated.

The *message* may be *improperly decoded.* The receiver must translate or *decode* the message accurately and precisely. The encoded message must pass through not only the personality screen of the sender but also the perception screen of the receiver.

Poor *listening* habits are a prime factor in improperly decoding messages. The criticality of listening in communication has already been discussed. It bears repeating. Poor listening habits are a *major* cause of communication breakdowns. Listeners may be defensive, too emotionally involved or distracted.

Closely related to poor listening habits are *lack of trust, credibility* and *candor.* If people think they cannot believe what someone tells them, they may misinterpret or ignore messages. For example, if a manager tells subordinates that they will be getting new uniforms and they do not, the subordinates will be less likely to believe the next "promise" and question the motive behind the promise as well. Another common example is some politicians lack of credibility. What candidates say to get elected and what they actually do are often quite different.

Fulton (2001a, p.134) notes: "There are certain phrases that a police commander, at any level, should never utter during the business day: (1) 'We can't do that.' (2) 'That's the way we've always done it.' (3) 'You'll have to . . . .' (4) 'Let me get back to you on that.' (5) 'No!' and (6) 'I don't know.' " Fulton notes that if you truly don't know an answer, you should add that you'll do your best to find out. These "forbidden phrases" almost always hinder communication.

Communication Enhancers

Communication enhancers are often the opposite of actions that cause communication obstructions. To overcome the obstacle of communication overload, managers must establish priorities. Not all communications need to be available to all employees. The main criteria should be whether the employees need the information to perform assigned tasks and whether it would improve morale. Overloading employees with immaterial communications will restrict their performance and productivity.

If a message promises further information, follow through. Use and encourage free and open two-way communication whenever possible. Emphasize brevity and accuracy.

Obstacles to communication are difficult to eliminate, but many can be minimized by concentrating on what you say and write. Communicating openly and clearly reduces informal communications such as the grapevine and rumor mill. When you look at the barriers within the communication process itself, certain guidelines become obvious.

Properly encode messages. Say what you mean and mean what you say. Watch word choices. Consider the receiver of the message. Match nonverbal communication with the verbal message. Make sure messages are accurate and timely. Always be open, candid, honest and sincere. Such information can do much to eliminate rumors.

Select the best communication channel. Focus on one-on-one, face-to-face communication, which is the most powerful channel available. Although this takes more time than a bulletin or memo, it is decidedly more effective.

Be open. Investigate options rather than steadfastly clinging to *the* solution. Effective managers work together toward solutions rather than choosing up sides. In effect people agree to disagree without being disagreeable.

Internal Lines of Communication

Lines of communication are inherent in an organizational structure. Just as authority flows downward and outward, so can communication. However, communication should also flow upward.

Communication may be downward, upward (vertical) or lateral (horizontal). It may also be internal or external. Most effective communication is two way.

Downward communication includes directives from managers and supervisors, either spoken or written. When time is limited and an emergency exists, communication often *must* flow downward and one way. In such cases, subordinates must listen and act on the communication.

Top-level law enforcement managers issue orders, policies, rules and regulations, memos, orders of the day and so on. These communications are delivered primarily downward and sometimes laterally. Communication from this level filters down and is understood by receivers according to personal knowledge, training, competence and experience.

Middle-level management and the on-line supervisors also issue directives, roll-call information, explanations of directives from higher-level managers, information for department newsletters or roll-call bulletins, letters, memos and instructions. Again, such communication is distributed downward and laterally.

Upward communication includes requests from subordinates to their superiors. It should also include input on important decisions affecting subordinates. Effective managers give all subordinates a chance to contribute ideas, opinions and values as decisions are made.

Another critical form of upward communication is found in operational reports. The major portion of law enforcement operations is in the field at the lowest level of the hierarchy. Most investigations, traffic citations, arrests, form completion and other activity are at this basic level. These actions eventually travel both from the bottom up and laterally throughout the organization. Communication may take the form of reports, charts, statistics, daily summaries or logs. All are extremely important.

Downward and upward communication are also called **vertical communication. Lateral** or **horizontal communication** includes communication among managers on the same level and among subordinates on the same level. **Internal communication** includes all of the preceding as well as messages from dispatch to officers in the field—among the most important communication of any law enforcement agency.

Subordinate Communication

Communicating with subordinates is an essential managerial responsibility. Managers and supervisors accomplish organizational goals through their subordinates. Employees want to know what is going on in the organization, to be "in the know." If employees do not know what the administration expects, they cannot support organizational goals and objectives.

The Grapevine

In addition to the formal channels of communication established by an organization, informal channels also exist. Commonly referred to as the **grapevine,** these informal channels frequently hinder cooperation and teamwork.

Managers and supervisors must realize that even if they *wanted* to stop the grapevine, they could not. In fact, directing people to not talk about an issue often ensures that the word will spread more quickly. Thus it is important that managers make the grapevine work for them rather than against them.

The term **rumor mill,** commonly applied to the grapevine, suggests some of the problems associated with informal channels of communication. The grapevine is strongest in organizations in which information is not openly shared. Employees begin to guess and speculate when they do not know—hence the rumors. One way to positively influence the grapevine is to provide staff with *all* information needed to function efficiently, effectively and happily. This includes letting people know the bad as well as the good. Do not let the grapevine beat you to informing people of bad news that affects them.

Newsletters

Newsletters can be an important form of interdepartmental communication. A newsletter can address the personal side of policing. For instance, it can focus on achievements of people within the department, sworn and civilian, acknowledge and welcome new employees and cover topics such as weddings, births, deaths and community activities and contributions. They can also be educational. For example, each issue could contain a column on tips for effective report writing.

Communication at Meetings

It has been said that meetings are gatherings where minutes are kept and hours are lost. Too many meetings are held simply because they are part of the weekly routine or because other options (such as sending e-mails or memos) are ignored.

Meetings serve important functions and need not be time wasters. The keys to successful, productive meetings are planning and effective communication.

Departments typically have four types of meetings: informational, opinion seeking, problem solving and new-idea seeking.

Knowing what type of meeting to plan helps to set appropriate goals for the meeting. Every meeting should have a clearly defined purpose and anticipated outcome. Some meetings serve two or more purposes. Before scheduling a meeting, however, explore alternatives: Is group action needed? Could the desired results be accomplished by one-on-one interactions? A phone call? A memo? An e-mail?

Meeting Preparation

One key to successful meetings is a carefully prepared **agenda** or outline, usually given to participants *before* the meeting. The agenda should have a time frame, including beginning and ending. Ideally, the ending time will make it difficult to stay beyond what is scheduled, for example, the end of a shift. Schedule the most important agenda items first in case time runs out.

In addition to creating an agenda, do the following to ensure a smooth, efficient meeting:

- Schedule the meeting room.
- Prepare handouts and visual aids.
- Make name tents and arrange seating if appropriate.
- Check the room arrangement and temperature.
- Check audiovisual equipment to be used.

The meeting room should be large enough, well lit and free of distractions. Handouts and visual aids should look professional. Seating is usually most effective in a U- or an O-shape. Do not overlook the potential value of assigning seats. Name tents are especially helpful if not all participants know each other. Be sure audiovisual equipment is functioning properly. Focus the overhead projector, and be sure there is a spare bulb. Make certain flipcharts have ample paper and that colored pens are available.

Conducting the Meeting

Start on time. End on time. Starting on time is a must. People quickly learn when a manager does not begin meetings promptly and will tend to come late as a result. To counteract lateness, close the door so that those arriving late will be obvious. Some managers go so far as to lock the door.

Assign someone to take minutes or tape the meeting. At the beginning of the meeting, ask whether the agenda and schedule are acceptable. Make adjustments if necessary and then stick to the agenda and time schedule. Agree on whether to allow interruptions, including cell phone or beeper alerts, and whether to take a break.

To facilitate open communication and group participation, be aware of bad habits people may display at meetings, including speechifying, repeating the same points, interrupting, speaking without being recognized by the chair, never contributing, acting as a know-it-all or as the "we tried it and it didn't work" historian each time an idea is presented, sidetracking and changing issues.

Both the chair and participants can change such counterproductive behavior in several ways. Determine norms about how meetings will proceed. Require recognition from the chair. Outlaw personal attacks. Read the preceding list of counterproductive behaviors, and ask everyone to refrain from them. Talk to the worst disrupters before the meeting, and ask for their cooperation. Give disrupters special tasks or roles, such as taking minutes.

To facilitate discussion, comment only on behavior, never personalities. Ask the "Yes, but . . . " disrupter to give positive answers and solutions rather than objections. Stop the meeting and ask people who are engaged in side conversations to share their discussions with the entire group. Try to draw out those who do not voluntarily contribute to discussions. Smile and be reassuring.

Group-process theorists have created many models to explain group dynamics. The models explain the roles that different individuals play in making a meeting work. In these models titles are attached to the roles, such as the *initiator* who gets things started, the *harmonizer* who smoothes disputes and the *summarizer* who pulls together the pieces.

Ending the Meeting

One part of meetings that is often overlooked is the windup. Before closing a meeting, summarize the main points discussed. Review new ideas, assign tasks and set deadlines. After the meeting, prepare the minutes and distribute them as soon as practical.

Keys for effective meetings:

- Prepare in advance—have an agenda.
- Start and stop on time.
- Stick to the agenda.
- Facilitate open communication and participation.

External Communication

External communication includes all interactions with agencies and people outside the department, including the news media and citizen contacts. Law enforcement agencies must effectively interact with other components of the criminal justice system, that is, the courts and correctional services. Law enforcement agencies must also interface with other social services, as well as with other departments of the jurisdiction they serve, as noted in Chapter 2.

Every contact with the public is a public relations contact. It is critical that all members of the agency, especially those in positions of authority, present a positive image and communicate effectively. This is true no matter whether officers are giving directions or answering a call from a citizen with a raccoon in their chimney. It is true whether traffic officers are issuing a ticket or the chief of police is addressing a Rotary Club or the local PTA.

Communicating with the Media

The media can be friend or foe, depending on the effectiveness of the channels of communication. As Toohey (2001, p.43) notes: "Law enforcement and the news media need one another. It may not always be a comfortable relationship, but it is an essential one for both sides."

Difficulties in dealing with the press usually arise from the need to balance the public's right to know, the First Amendment right to freedom of the press, and the need of law enforcement agencies to protect the Sixth Amendment rights of those accused of crimes, as well as the privacy of crime victims while maintaining the integrity of an investigation.

Tyler (2001, p.48) stresses: "We must learn to work with the media and do it in an orderly, consistent and cooperative fashion or our jobs will become increasingly more difficult. . . . We should remember that the media always has the last word."

Some law enforcement agencies have a policy that line officers and supervisors are not allowed to issue statements or opinions about any activities or conditions related to their duties to newspaper reporters or radio or television stations. Such requests are referred to middle management, who may in turn refer them to a public relations department or to a public information officer (PIO). According to Arms (2001, p.10): "The PIO is an ambassador for the agency he or she represents. Through the PIO, information is conveyed to the media with credibility, accurately and in a timely manner." According to Staszak (2001, p.11): "The overwhelming search for news should warn law enforcement that the media will get their story one way or another. Cooperating with the media remains the most reasonable avenue for PIOs to take to advise the public of the department's position."

Some law enforcement executives claim that every officer is a "public information officer." Whatever approach to dealing with the media a department chooses, it should have clearly defined policies and procedures.

Policies and Procedures for Dealing with the Media

Peck (2000, p.46) suggests: "The procedures should address basic considerations such as who will be authorized to speak to the press, where and how frequently press briefings will be held, where the press will be allowed to congregate, how press movements will be controlled, and how transgressions, such as aggressive attempts by the press to get to a problem area, will be handled." No matter whether a department is small or large, it must have clearly defined policies and procedures, such as those the New York City Police Department uses (Table 3.2).

Clearly formulated policies and procedures for communicating with the media are necessary to effectively conduct agency business as well as for a sound public relations/community relations program. Toohey (p.43) stresses: "No matter what the size of your agency, one of the most important steps you can take is to adopt a written policy for dealing with the media." Further, as Zoufal (2000, p.10) notes: "As demands on municipalities for information increase, so does municipal exposure for improper release of information. Clear policies and protocols for dissemination are essential to ensuring that sensitive information is protected."

The Media and Community Policing

Behm and Teuber (2001, p.41) contend: "As law enforcement professionals, we must recognize the power of the media. In recognizing this power, we can choose to be proactive or to adopt a wait-and-see attitude." The decision seems obvious to Braunstein (2001, p.64), who comments: "As departments implement the community policing philosophy, working well with the media becomes increasingly important." Concurring, Hilte (2001, p.27) says: "The concept of 'community-oriented policing' demands that we communicate with our community. The

Table 3.2
New York City Police Department's Press Release Policy

Guidelines in Criminal Cases

The following information should be made available for publication, when and after an arrest is made:

(a) The accused's name, age, residence, employment, marital status and similar background information.

(b) The substance or text of the charge such as a complaint, indictment, information and, when appropriate, the identity of the complainant.

(c) The identity of the investigating and arresting agency and length of the investigation.

(d) The circumstances immediately surrounding the arrest, including the time and place of arrest, resistance, pursuit, possession and use of weapons and a description of items seized at the time of arrest.

NOTE: P.G. 116-22 prohibits disclosure of identity of children under 16 who are arrested or complainants. Victims of sex crimes should likewise not be identified to the press.

Pretrial disclosure of the following information may cause substantial risk of prejudice to a defendant and thereby adversely affect a case. For that reason, the following information SHOULD NOT be released without first clearing with the Public Information Division.

(a) Statements as to the character or reputation of an accused person or prospective witness.

(b) Admissions, confessions or the contents of a statement or alibi attributable to an accused person.

(c) The performance or results of tests or the refusal of the accused to take a test.

(d) Statements concerning the credibility or anticipated testimony of prospective witnesses.

(e) The possibility of a plea of guilty to the offense charged or to a lesser offense, or other disposition.

(f) Opinions concerning evidence or argument in the case, whether or not it is anticipated that such evidence or argument will be used at trial.

Source: Courtesy of the New York City Police Department.

media is our conduit to the community and can be valuable partners in that effort." Buice (2001, pp.59–60) likewise contends: "The success of community-oriented policing depends on partnerships built on trust and mutual respect from which come open and honest communication. Knowledge is power, and sharing the knowledge through the media exponentially increases that power."

Building Relationships with the Media

Rosenthal (2001, p.16) suggests: "Working with the media should begin long before any crisis hits. . . . Now is an excellent time to consider working with the media to draw up 'rules of engagement.' " Rosenthal (p.17) also suggests that larger departments should issue their own official media credentials with photos once a year. Strandberg (2000, p.90) says: "Building a partnership with the media is a first step toward improving these sometimes adversarial relationships."

Concurring, Buice (2001, p.58) stresses: "Just as the time to buy a firetruck is not on the way to the fire, the time to establish sound message management is not when the news hits the fan. Successful police chiefs and PIOs realize that effective message management is a journey, not a destination, and they understand that the journey is a long one." Buice (2002, p.16) also suggests: "Many agencies find that asking members of the media to go through Citizens Police Academies or even separate Media Academies can prevent potentially deadly blunders by reporters."

Media Guidelines

Garner (2001, p.8) reports: "Many of the most media-savvy law enforcement leaders successfully co-exist with journalists by following some relatively simple rules for survival:

- *Maintain credibility.* An earned reputation for truthfulness is law enforcement leaders' most precious asset in working with the media.
- *Stay in touch.* Media-wise police leaders take a proactive approach to working with the local media. They do not wait until a crisis has boiled over.
- *Rely on sound policies.* Fair, comprehensive and current media relations policies should be in place before a crisis erupts.
- *Have a reason.* Media-wise police leaders will be able to articulate a legitimate reason for what they must deny the media.
- *Remain modest.* The smart police leader has no problem remaining humble when he or she is in the media spotlight.
- *Impartiality is vital.* Veteran law enforcement administrators know the dangers of granting exclusives to a "pet" reporter.
- *Stay on the record.* A reporter is under no legal obligation to keep a promise made in exchange for some highly prized information.
- *Never say "no comment."* Doing so makes even the most forthright official sound like an unscrupulous politician caught with a hand in the cookie jar.

Van Blaricom (2001, p.53) cautions: "Never mislead. Regardless of the circumstances, misleading the media will never be forgiven or forgotten. The currency of trust is too valuable to squander."

Media Management in a Crisis

Rosenthal (2001, p.17) suggests: "Set up a media command post that gives journalists an on-scene vantage post and gives you a place to hold your news briefings. Be accessible. . . . Update the media as frequently as you can. This means at least every hour, if not more often. Always be straight with reporters. Give them facts, information; never speculate." Rosenthal (2000b, p.19) notes that unthinking media coverage of a critical incident can put lives at risk and seriously threaten successful resolution of the incident. He (p.20) cautions: "The media need to understand that while the public does have the right to know, there are other extremely important factors that also must be considered in making decisions about coverage of critical incidents."

Victims, Witnesses and the Media

Herman (2000, p.3) notes: "The media focus on crime isn't always good news for victims." In their attempt to get at the personal angle, reporters can be insensitive. In addition, they may print information that could hinder an investigation or jeopardize the privacy and safety of victims and witnesses. To avoid such hazards, the Fairfax County Police Department developed an information card to be given to victims and witnesses in sensitive cases. Rosenthal (2000a, p.21) describes the card, which has on the front the heading "Advisory to Crime Victims and Witnesses" and states:

> News media may wish to interview you regarding this incident. You have the right to grant or refuse interviews. If you choose to give an interview, please call one of the numbers on the reverse side. You will be given advice important to protecting your rights and the investigation, but there is no legal requirement to contact police prior to an interview.

The back of the card contains the phone numbers of the PIO and the victim services section. Guidelines for using the cards state: "These information cards are intended for distribution only in connection with serious or high profile cases, such as homicides, robberies, sex offenses and certain fatal accidents."

Sometimes media involvement alters the way law enforcement performs. For example, intense media coverage of high-profile cases may have far-reaching effects on other, more low-profile incidents and, consequently, affect how the entire criminal justice system handles such matters. This is known as the **news media echo effect,** which occurs when a highly publicized criminal case results in a shift in handling similarly charged but nonpublicized cases.

News Conferences

As Tilton (2002, p.15) notes: "According to recent surveys, many people in America rank speaking in public as one of the greatest fears of their lives. In fact, some individuals have ranked the fear of public speaking ahead of their fears of financial difficulty, illness, or even death." Many police mangers and executives

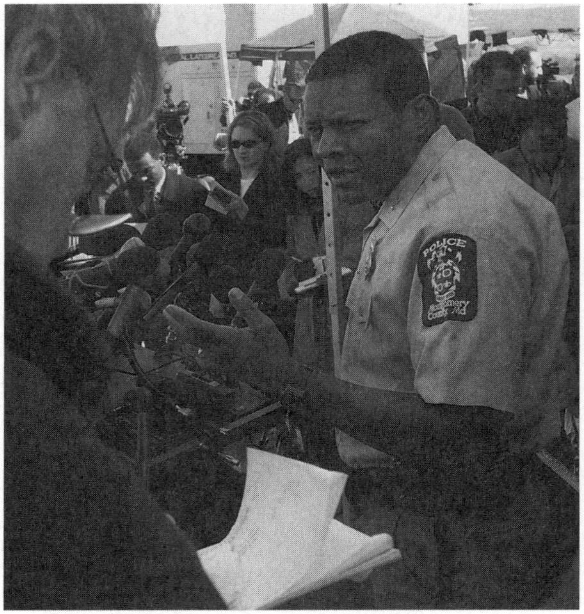

© Reuters/Brian Snyder/© Reuters NewMedia Inc./CORBIS

Montgomery County (Maryland) Chief Charles Moose answers questions from reporters at a briefing at police headquarters. In 2002, Montgomery County was the site of five shootings attributed to the Washington-area snipers.

have this same fear. However, communication during news conferences is also of vital importance to any police department. Muldoon (2001, pp.28–32) suggests five steps for a successful interview:

1. Preparation—Know what you want to say before the interview and plan to make those points during the interview. Think of the three Cs in planning your response: clarity, conciseness and conversation.
2. Attitude—Be positive. Be yourself without being too casual.
3. Appearance—On television, your facial expressions will convey most of your sincerity. The tone of your voice will carry the rest.
4. Conduct—During the interview, listen carefully to the questions that are asked. Your messages or answers to questions should be no longer than 15 to 20 seconds and should contain some element of the questions.
5. Conclusion—Remember that the camera microphone may remain on even during cutaway shots or moments of idle chatter. Keep your guard up as long as reporters are present.

Staszak (2002, p.19) comments: "Law enforcement officials can succeed in giving effective, dynamic press interviews by first arming themselves with two crucial, yet basic weapons. First, they must do their homework. Second, they must be themselves." Additional suggestions include the following: "Keep to the message. Answer in a positive manner. Reinforce the most important points. Always plan for the worst-case scenario. Personalize the messages. Project sincerity and empathy. And make a friend."

Further suggestions for giving a news conference include limiting your opening statement to 10 minutes or less and then opening the floor for questions.

Repeat each question after it is asked to help those in the audience who may not have heard it. Also make sure you understand the question before attempting to answer it. Keep your responses short and to the point, avoiding legalese and jargon. Do not allow questions that stray from the subject of the news conference; explain that you will answer extraneous questions later. Furthermore, let the audience know whether copies of your prepared statement are available. From start to finish, treat every microphone as "live" and every camera as "on." Finally, to better prepare for the next time, critique your news conferences objectively.

Using the Media

The media and law enforcement may both benefit through cooperation. In fact, in some instances, law enforcement and media collaboration is quite deliberate. Consider, for example, the **perp walk,** where suspects are paraded before the news media. However, recent criticism has fallen on this practice, and several courts across the country are considering whether perp walks may violate suspects' rights to privacy. A federal court judge in New York has already handed down a ruling forcing the NYPD to suspend its perp walks after a burglary suspect was led out of the station house in handcuffs, placed in a squad car, driven around the block and then brought back into the station, all at the request of a local news station who wanted footage of the man for their newscast.

Law enforcement may engage the media to help it accomplish its mission. Van Blaricom (p.52) notes: "Every police department has interesting stories that portray police work as a positive force for good in the community." According to Sparks and Staszak (2000, p.22): "Because the media covers issues of public interest, prudent managers should realize the importance of proactively using the media as a tool to get their department's message out to the community."

Ellis (2001, p.19) suggests that police departments remember radio: "Because news radio stations must fill anywhere from 12 to 24 hours a day with news programming, they often make large time slots available for community service programs. In Washington, DC, for example, news radio station WTOP sets aside one hour every month for a call-in program called 'Ask the Chief.' " . . . To buy that kind of radio time would cost thousands of dollars."

Some police departments are using the media in a more direct way by hosting their own television programs on the cable company's local-access channel. Jedic (2000, p.2) notes: "Law enforcement agencies rushing to embrace new technology should not overlook the old technology that continues to be the most influential and accessible of all—television. More specifically, community-access cable television. With the boom of local-access channels throughout the nation, every police agency would benefit by contacting its cable operators for scheduling and program information. Most local-access channels are free. . . . Using television is probably the most efficient way to go for relatively small departments."

Communication with the Broader Community

Police departments may communicate with the broader community through annual reports and the Internet, as well as by other means.

Annual Reports

One effective way to keep the public informed about the operations of a police department is to publish an annual report. Long recognized as effective business communication tools, annual reports can also serve law enforcement agencies. They might include the department's mission statement; a brief biographical overview of department members with names, photos, academic degrees, dates of hire, dates of most recent promotion and special duties; departmental information and statistics; a summary of projects and projected programs; a budget statement; an outline of ongoing interaction with the fire service, emergency medical care providers, scuba and rescue units, or any emergency support group in your community; and a closing, which may include statements of appreciation and remarks about the "state of the department."

The Internet

To provide criminal activity information to citizens, no tool is currently more efficient than the Internet. This type of external communication can be extremely beneficial to departments that are willing to invest the time and minimal expense to devise a Web site. As Price (2001, p.37) suggests: "A Web site can be a powerful communication tool for police and the citizens they serve. Visitors to the Web site can learn about the police department and its activities and get the latest crime data for their neighborhoods, find personal safety tips, share information on suspects, and more."

According to Snyder and Mulholland (2001, p.12): "When a law enforcement agency establishes a presence on the World Wide Web, the chief of police can have his or her own multidimensional online publication—a virtual public information officer, accessible to the public 24 hours a day, seven days a week." They suggest that a basic Web site should include the chief executive's welcome and introduction; agency structure, mission and values; agency contact information; a summary of key programs and services; answers to frequently asked questions; and links to other community and law enforcement online resources.

Bowman (2002, p.56) describes how a link on a police department's Web site allows members of the public to access more than 100,000 current records, including arrests, traffic accidents and other routine police calls.

The Internet can also help law enforcement agencies communicate more effectively with each other. Valuable information may be accessed and shared on department Web sites.

Other Modes of External Communications

Although the Internet may be the latest wave of technology to help law enforcement spread valuable information, other communication networks are also being implemented, such as emergency notification systems and faxes.

Garrett (2002, p.68) notes: "With today's technology, getting the word out is easier than it's ever been before. Computer-driven emergency notification systems allow agencies to send thousands of emergency messages within minutes to targeted groups of people to avert disaster. . . . . Flash floods, tornadoes and other quickly emerging events are not something you can send people a postcard about."

Faxes, too, can be used to communicate rapidly with a broad public. Magnotti (2002, p.5) describes FAXNetwork, a community information service

Several police departments now have their own Web sites like this one for Santa Monica. Internet communications help link law enforcement agencies with each other and the public.

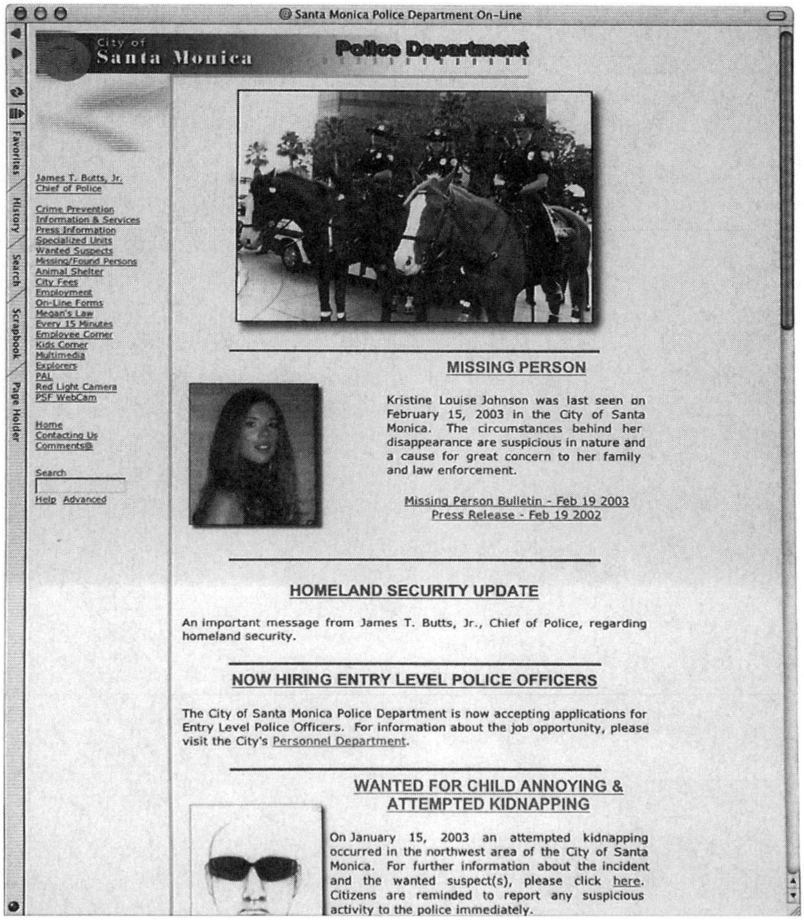

which has as its headline "Just the FAX." Says Magnotti: "I wanted the FAXNetwork to capitalize on the community's inherent interest in police work and give the community some human interest stories, portraying officers as fellow citizens engaged in interesting, albeit sometimes dangerous, work." FAXNetwork is also capable of sending out emergency notifications as well as enlisting public support in finding suspects.

Communication and Homeland Security

Roskind (2002, p.82) contends: "On September 11, 2001, the nation got its first look at a 'Class A' terrorist act, and today we are still afraid to look at the communications failure that was knowingly present and how many hundreds of lives might have been saved if communications had been fixed." According to Roskind (p.83): "The failures in communications were fully documented. The primary communications failure occurred because of information overload on the incident commander." Rogers (2002, p.48) comments: "Few can forget the chaos that was illustrated by the lack of communications at Ground Zero on September 11 in the two-hour time frame before the World Trade Center towers collapsed. In one example, an emergency official, who did not have a fire department radio, could not broadcast an alert that the north tower was in danger of collapsing. Instead, he had to send a subordinate racing across the World Trade Center plaza to hand-deliver the message to a fire chief inside. . . . Adding to the mayhem, firefighters typically use a single channel, called the fire ground channel, to communicate inside a building. On that fateful day, up to 1,000 firefighters, rather than the usual 20 or so, were attempting to communicate with each other on one congested channel." Roskind (p.82) predicts that police and fire departments will better aid in homeland defense if communications are integrated at the federal level.

Roskind (p.86) believes: "Most of the costs of creating a national system are already paid for. Computers are in most fire, police, medical and hazardous material response vehicles. The global positioning satellites are orbiting the earth. Command and control software has been developed by the military." Roskind concludes: "Coordinated computer communications is non-existent in emergency services. The lack of proper communications leads directly to loss of life and property. The federal government can double the size of the standing military, in a homeland defense role, by providing the coordination of communications infrastructure and purchasing and managing technology directed at tactical communications."

Magaw (2002, p.8) stresses: "No single government agency can alone fight the war against terrorism. No isolated piece of intelligence information can prevent another attack. We must share data as collected and analyzed by experts from every corner of the earth, and share the resulting intelligence information from that data. . . . Sharing our ideas and our information may increase the probability of identifying those who would do us harm before they strike. . . . With today's lightning-fast, highly secure and sophisticated tools of communication, we must continue to pull together and pool our ideas to create a more effective intelligence sharing policy as countries, agencies and individuals."

Summary

Effective communication is the lifeblood of a law enforcement agency, whether it is written, spoken, downward, upward, lateral, informal or formal, internal or external.

Communication is the complex process through which information is transferred from one person to another. The communication process involves a message, a sender, a channel and a receiver, and it may include feedback. Effective communication should follow the KISS principle, that is, Keep It Short and Simple. Words themselves, however, are only a small part of the message. Ninety-three percent of communication between two people comes from body language and tone of voice.

Critical factors to consider in selecting a channel include speed, opportunity for feedback and expense. The weakest link in the communication process is *lis-*

tening. People listen and think four times faster than they talk. Active listening includes concentration, full attention and thought.

Communication may be downward, upward (vertical) or lateral (horizontal). It may also be internal or external. Most effective communication is two way.

Communication barriers include time, volume of information, tendency to say what we think others want to hear, certainty, failure to select the best words, prejudices (of the sender and/or receiver) and strained sender-receiver relationships.

Communication is an important part of the law enforcement job, including meetings. Meetings may be informational, opinion seeking, problem solving or new-idea seeking. For more effective meetings: (1) prepare in advance—have an agenda, (2) start and stop on time, (3) stick to the agenda and (4) facilitate open communication and participation.

Difficulties in dealing with the press usually arise from the need to balance the public's right to know, the First Amendment right to freedom of the press, and the need of law enforcement agencies to protect the Sixth Amendment rights of those accused of crimes, as well as the privacy of crime victims while maintaining the integrity of an investigation.

Discussion Questions

1. Why is communication ability important to law enforcement managers?
2. How would you compare and contrast the various channels of communication?
3. Which is more difficult, written or spoken communication? Why? Which do you prefer?
4. What are the main obstacles to communication in your law enforcement agency?
5. What types of communication exist in your agency? What is the value of each?
6. What types of feedback are available in a typical law enforcement agency?
7. How is nonverbal communication used in law enforcement? How is such nonverbal communication depicted on television programs about law enforcement?
8. What methods do you use as an active listener?
9. What is the key role of the first-line supervisor as a communicator in a law enforcement agency?
10. What public figures do you consider to be effective communicators? What characteristics make them so?

InfoTrac College Edition Assignment

Use InfoTrac College Edition to help answer the Discussion Questions as appropriate.

Select one of the following assignments to complete. Be prepared to share your findings with the class.

- Select an area of *communication* of interest to you and research it in at least three journals, one of which should be from the criminal justice field. You might select topics such as gender differences, nonverbal communication, the impact of technology on communication or any other area you would like to know more about. Write a one- to two-page summary of your findings. Include the full reference citation for each source.
- Find and outline "Adventures in Public Speaking" by James E. Tilton.
- Find and outline "Media Trends and the Public Information Officer" by Dennis Staszak.

References

Arms, Skip. "Working with the Media in the Case of the 'Texas 7.' " *Problem-Solving Quarterly,* Spring 2001, pp.10–11.

Behm, Michael and Teuber, Terri. "Media Training for Line Officers." *The Police Chief,* April 2001, pp.34–41.

Bowman, Theron L. "Internet Database Puts Arlington Police Statistics at Public's Fingertips." *The Police Chief,* June 2002, pp.56–58.

Braunstein, Susan. "IACP's PIO Section: Helping Police Executives Meet Today's Media Challenges." *The Police Chief,* April 2001, pp.62–65.

Buice, Ed. "Leadership Principles for Effective Message Management." *The Police Chief,* April 2001, pp.58–60.

Buice, Ed. "Going the Extra Mile with the Media." *Law and Order,* April 2002, p.16.

Dees, Tim. "Handhelds on the Street." *Law and Order,* October 2000, pp.88–96.

Ellis, Andrew. "If the News Media Won't Cover Your Positive Stories, Try This . . . ." *The Police Chief,* April 2001, pp.16–20.

Field, Mark W. "Organizational Dynamics in a Technology-Driven World: The Impact of E-mail on Law Enforcement." *The Police Chief,* February 2000, pp.45–49.

Fulton, Roger. "On the Road to Good Communications." *Law Enforcement Technology,* September 2000, p.130.

Fulton, Roger. "Forbidden Phrases." *Law Enforcement Technology,* September 2001a, p.134.

Fulton, Roger. "E-Mail Management Tips." *Law Enforcement Technology,* November 2001b, p.106.

Garner, Gerald W. "Media Guidelines for the Law Enforcement Executive." *Subject to Debate,* October/November 2001, pp.8,11.

Garrett, Ronnie. "Getting the Word Out." *Law Enforcement Technology,* June 2002, pp.68–73.

Hennessy, Stephen M.; Hendricks, Cindy; and Hendricks, James. "Cultural Awareness and Communication Training: What Works and What Doesn't." *The Police Chief,* November 2001, pp.15–19.

Herman, Susan. "NCVC Provides Victims with Resources for Handling the Media." *Subject to Debate,* December 2000, p.3.

Hilte, Ken. "Preparing for the Media Mega-Event." *The Police Chief,* April 2001, pp.22–27.

Jedic, Thomas. "Rechannel Your Approach: Try Cable TV." *Community Policing Exchange,* November/December 2000, p.2.

Jones, Tony L. "Training Indigenous Personnel." *The Law Enforcement Trainer,* May/June 2002, pp.18–21.

Magaw, John W. "Communication Means More than Just Talking." *The Police Chief,* July 2002, pp.8–10.

Magnotti, Mike. "Police Fax Reports to Community." *Community Links,* May 2002, pp.5–7.

McDonald, Tom. "Plain and Simple: When It Comes to Communication, Less Is More." *Successful Meetings,* April 2000, p.32.

Miller, Christa. "Wearing Your Computer: The Hottest New Duty Gear and an Essential Tool for Officers." *Law Enforcement Technology,* August 2002, pp.68–73.

Muldoon, William J. "Five Steps to a Successful Television Interview." *The Police Chief,* April 2001, pp.28–32.

Nimsger, Kristin M. and Lange, Michele C. S. "Examining the Data." *Security Products,* May 2002, pp.16–18.

Nowicki, Ed. "Body Language." *Law and Order,* April 2001a, pp.27–28.

Nowicki, Ed. "Language and Voice Commands." *Law and Order,* May 2001b, pp.21–22.

Nowicki, Ed. "How Not to Fight." *Law and Order,* May 2002, pp.26–27.

Peck, Michael. " 'No Comment' Won't Do." *Security Management,* October 2000, pp.44–49.

Price, Cynthia. "The Police Web Site as a Community Policing Tool." *The Police Chief,* December 2001, pp.37–38.

Rogers, Donna. "Linking Communications for Interoperability: In the Wake of Large-Scale Disasters Like 9–11, Officials Strive to Improve Emergency Communications." *Law Enforcement Technology,* August 2002, pp.48–53.

Rosenthal, Rick. "Victims, Witnesses and the Media." *Law and Order,* March 2000a, pp.21–22.

Rosenthal, Rick. "Media Do's and Don't's." *Law and Order,* April 2000b, pp.19–20.

Rosenthal, Rick. "Your Critical Incident." *Law and Order,* November 2001, pp.16–17.

Roskind, Michael. "Doubling Our Defenses." *Law Enforcement Technology,* June 2002, pp.82–86.

Snyder, G. Matthew and Mulholland, David J. "Web Site Development for Smaller Police Agencies." *The Police Chief,* October 2001, p.12.

Sparks, Ancil B. and Staszak, Dennis D. "Fine Tuning Your News Briefing." *FBI Law Enforcement Bulletin,* December 2000, pp.22–24.

Staszak, Dennis. "Media Trends and the Public Information Officer." *FBI Law Enforcement Bulletin,* March 2001, pp.10–13.

Staszak, Dennis. "Making the Most of Press Interviews." *FBI Law Enforcement Bulletin,* May 2002, p.19.

Strandberg, Keith W. "Back to Basics: Media Relations 101." *Law Enforcement Technology,* August 2000, pp.90–94.

Tilton, James E. "Adventures in Public Speaking." *FBI Law Enforcement Bulletin,* February 2002, pp.15–19.

Toohey, Bill. "Tips from the Trenches: Advice from a PIO." *The Police Chief,* April 2001, pp.43–46.

Tyler, Gary K. "Four Ways to Improve Your Media Relations." *The Police Chief,* April 2001, pp.48–51.

Van Blaricom, D. P. "The Media: Enemies or Allies?" *The Police Chief,* April 2001, pp.52–56.

Zoufal, Donald R. "Legal Issues in Law Enforcement Information Sharing." *The Police Chief,* December 2000, pp.8–10.

Book-Specific Web Site

Go to the *Management and Supervision in Law Enforcement* Web site at http://info.wadsworth.com/0534616054 for student and instructor resources, including Internet Assignments and Case Studies.

CHAPTER 4

Decision Making and Problem Solving

Imagination is more important than knowledge. For knowledge is limited, whereas imagination embraces the entire world.

—Albert Einstein

Do You Know?

- What levels of decision making exist?
- What kinds of decisions managers must make?
- What functions may be served by the brain's left and right sides?
- What basic methods are commonly used to make decisions or solve problems?
- What levels of the agency benefit from group participation in decision making?
- How brainstorming can be most effective?
- What groupthink is?
- What the steps are in the seven-step problem-solving/decision-making process?
- What force-field analysis is? The nominal group technique? The Delphi Technique?
- What the SARA Model problem-solving process includes?
- What creativity is?
- What common thinking traps exist? Mental locks?
- What "killer phrases" are and how to deal with them?
- What other considerations decision making and problem solving include?

Can You Define?

Abilene Paradox
administrative decision
brainstorming
command decision
consensus decision
consultative decision
convergent thinking
creative procrastination
creativity
cross flow
cross tell
decision-making process
Delphi Technique
divergent thinking
driving forces
equilibrium
focus groups
force-field analysis (FFA)
GIGO
groupthink
innovation
intelligence
intuition
killer phrases
left-brain thinking
management information systems (MIS)
mental locks
modified Delphi Technique
nominal group technique
operational decision
participatory decision making (PDM)
problem-oriented policing (POP)
restraining forces
right-brain thinking
snap decisions
strategic decision
thinking traps
whole-brain thinking

INTRODUCTION

Decision making and problem solving are primary responsibilities of law enforcement managers at all levels. A decision is a judgment or conclusion. It is the act of making up one's mind or settling a dispute. A problem is a deviation from what is desired, a difficulty.

Most law enforcement managers developed their decision-making skills in the field as patrol officers. They made important decisions constantly, but their decisions were usually based on clear department policies and procedures. The decision to arrest someone, for example, was made many times. If something new occurred, the first-line supervisor might be directed to the scene for a decision. Even this decision was comparatively easy because standards existed and the supervisor had to consider only alternatives to the established procedure.

Because of the discretion they had as patrol officers, most law enforcement managers are comfortable making decisions as long as guidelines exist. There is little time to problem solve if someone is shooting at you. Often, however, law enforcement managers encounter unique problems that call for problem-solving decision-making skills.

This chapter begins by describing the kinds of decisions managers must make. Next the chapter examines research on how the human brain processes information and modes of thinking. Next basic methods for making decisions or solving problems are described, including participatory decision making, brainstorming, focus groups and groupthink. This is followed by descriptions of several more complex approaches to decision making, including a seven-step decision-making process, force-field analysis, the nominal group technique and the Delphi Technique. Next is a discussion of problem-oriented policing (POP) and the decisions made in this process. Then a discussion of creativity and innovation and how they help in solving problems is presented, followed by a discussion of how creativity can be hindered by thinking traps, mental locks and killer phrases and common mistakes in decision making/problem solving. The chapter concludes with a brief discussion of two other key considerations in decision making and problem solving and criteria for evaluating the decisions reached.

Kinds of Decisions

Decisions may deal with problems that are trivial or critical, short term or long term, personal or organizational. They may also be categorized by the level in the organizational hierarchy at which they are made. The executive level mainly deals with conceptual problems and alternatives, middle management most frequently makes administrative decisions and first-line supervisors most frequently make operational decisions.

Decisions may be **strategic**—executive level; **administrative**—middle-management level or **operational**—first-line level.

Decisions at all levels involve individual skills, organizational policies, different managerial styles and a certain amount of risk taking. Decisions may also be categorized by who carries them out.

Decisions may be command, consultative or consensual.

A **command decision** is one that managers make on their own, with little or no input from others. For example, the chief of police decides to give an award to an officer.

A **consultative decision,** in contrast, is one that uses input and opinions from others. The final decision is still made by the one in charge but only after considering the input of others. For example, a lieutenant in charge of organizing a Neighborhood Watch program might ask for ideas from other officers and citizens, and he may consult other agencies that already have such a program. The lieutenant then makes decisions about the program based on this input. Managers will gain greater acceptance of and support for their decisions if they seek input from all levels and weigh that input before making their final decisions.

A **consensus decision** is made democratically by a group. It is a joint decision often made by members of a committee. For example, training priorities for the year might be decided by a committee established for this purpose. This committee might operate independently or seek input from others in the organization.

Law enforcement organizations regularly make all three kinds of decisions. One key to effectiveness is that the individuals involved know what kind of decision they are making. For example, a situation in which a manager makes it very clear that he or she alone is going to decide an issue is quite different from a situation in which the manager *appears* to seek input from others but is only making a gesture. Likewise, if employees believe they are to decide an issue, but the final decision is *not* what they recommended, the entire decision-making process may be undermined.

Before looking at specific methods of decision making and problem solving, you should understand the thinking process and how it functions. Managers are expected to use their heads—their brains. Most managers have attained their present positions because of this ability, which is equated with **intelligence** or mental ability. They also have traditionally relied upon logic and reason to solve problems, but whole-brain research suggests that this may not always be the most appropriate approach.

Whole-Brain Research

The world was amazed 2,500 years ago when Hippocrates suggested that our emotions come from the head, not the heart. Twenty-five years ago another physician, Roger Sperry, reported on significant brain research establishing that the right and the left sides of the brain each have their own thoughts and memories and *process information differently.*

Left-brain thinking processes *language* and is primarily *logical.*
Right-brain thinking processes *images* and is primarily *emotional.*

According to Dr. Sperry's research, the two sides of the brain are connected by the *corpus callosum.* In brief, his research identified the division of labor between the two sides of the brain and the critical role of the corpus callosum. He received the 1981 Nobel Prize in medicine for these remarkable findings.

Brain research also indicates differences in the way each side of the brain processes information. The left side usually processes information sequentially, logically and rationally in linear fashion. The right side usually processes information spatially, intuitively, holistically and emotionally. The left side uses reasoning; the right side, imagination and creativity.

According to some researchers, people can tell which side of their brain is dominant by which hand they use. Those who use their right hand are left-brained; those who use their left hand are right-brained. According to others, however, the division is not so clear-cut. Researchers have discovered that:

1. Right-hemisphere processes add emotional and humorous overtones important for understanding the full meaning of oral and written communication.
2. Both hemispheres are involved in thinking, logic and reasoning.
3. The right hemisphere seems to play a special role in emotion. If students are emotionally engaged, both sides of the brain will participate in the educational process, regardless of subject matter.

A person's dominant mode of thinking may shift from left to right hemisphere and back again about 10 times every 24 hours. Some research even suggests that you can control which side of your brain will be dominant by switching your breathing. If you want to be more creative, you can activate the right side of your brain by forcing air through the left nostril.

Whether this is true and how distinct the functions of both sides of the brain are may be debatable. What is relatively clear, however, is that when dealing with problem-solving/decision-making situations, our educational system and our culture tend to place more value on those factors associated with the left brain: logical, rational, objective, sequential and so forth.

Our organizations, public and private, also rely heavily on rational, logical and analytical approaches to problems. Further, most effective law enforcement managers are precise, methodical and conservative. They seek to preserve the status quo—to keep things on an even keel.

The logical approach was perhaps more appropriate when organizations were less complex and change was less frequent. Our complex, rapidly changing modern society, however, requires the ability to use *both* logic and creativity in problem solving and decision making, that is, **whole-brain thinking.** The issue is not which side is better.

Modes of Thinking

Closely related to whole-brain research is research into modes of thinking. A study undertaken by the FBI Academy identified several common styles of thinking and their effects on organizational planning and management. *Pragmatists* have a short-term orientation, are concerned with the immediate, are good tacticians but lack perseverance. *Analysts* solve problems systematically and rely heavily on logic and deductive reasoning. They depend on what is historically proved and structured; they tend to lose sight of the department's mission and values, to avoid risks and to try to apply old solutions to new problems. *Realists* want to touch, hear and smell before believing. They usually solve problems quickly but tend to deal with symptoms rather than causes and often operate in a vacuum. *Synthesizers* seek change and contradictions and go beyond what is real. They question underlying assumptions and try to identify the cause of problems. *Idealists* welcome a broad range of views. They are concerned with long-range and strategic plans and the impact of decisions on employees, the law enforcement community, the public and society. They understand the big picture and tend to be good listeners and nonjudgmental.

Effective decision making and problem solving rely on both logic and creativity. Because most managers are more familiar with and reliant on logic, that's where the discussion begins.

Basic Methods for Making Decisions or Solving Problems

An important management tool is a **decision-making process,** that is, a systematic approach to solving a problem. This chapter describes several decision-making processes that you may tailor to fit specific law enforcement department problems.

Basic methods for making decisions range from using intuition and snap decisions to using a computer, with a systematic individual or group approach in between.

Intuition

Intuition is insight. It is knowing without using any rational thought process. The subconscious makes decisions based on intuition. Intuition crosses the left and right hemispheres, integrating facts and feelings.

I (author Bennett, then chief of police) recall a time when there was a series of automobile thefts from a large shopping center parking lot. Surveillance of the lot by binoculars from the shopping center rooftop, unmarked cars, special patrol in the perimeter area and other methods failed to turn up suspects. A sergeant came into my office to talk about the problem. We decided to "go take a look" and headed for a gravel pit near the shopping center. When we arrived, three people were crowded around a car in a far area of the pit. On closer examination, we saw they were spray painting the car red. We arrested the three, and that arrest cleared almost a dozen car theft cases.

It was merely a hunch to go to that location. No one had reported activity in that area. It was purely intuition. Yet, behind the decision to go to the gravel pit was the knowledge that the pit existed and that it just might be a hiding place. Some would call it sheer luck. Effective managers listen to their hunches, their gut feelings.

Snap Decisions

Closely related to intuition are **snap decisions.** Neither takes much of a manager's time. Be decisive. It is not always possible to obtain all the available information. Do not expect every decision to be perfect. Perfectionists find it difficult to make decisions because they never have sufficient information.

General Colin Powell uses what he calls the P-40-70 Rule whenever he has to be decisive. P stands for the probability of success, and the numbers indicate the percentage of information acquired. He goes with his gut feeling when he has acquired information in the 40 to 70 percent range. If time is critical, he makes the decision with only 40 percent of the information needed. According to Powell, if he waited until he had all the information, he would never make a decision; he'd always be waiting for another piece of information. It has been said that it is better to be boldly decisive and risk being wrong than to agonize at length and be right too late.

Learning to make snap decisions prudently can be extremely beneficial. Many decisions should be made on the spot, whereas some need to mature, and some need not be made at all. A not-so-great snap decision may have better results than a good decision made slowly. This is because any kind of movement often brings a new perspective that makes the right decision more obvious.

Being decisive often inspires support from subordinates and superiors. It also lets you feel in control. Having a list of 10 unsolved problems sitting on your desk can cause anxiety and stress. Many problems and decisions should be made quickly and decisively. Others can be delegated or not even made. Know when to slow down and proceed with caution, and remember that you can change your mind.

Delegating

Delegation sends the decision-making process to a subordinate. The manager is removed from the process at this point until it is time to report the results. Delegation is an excellent motivating technique and gets the job done at the level of those with firsthand knowledge of the problem. Theodore Roosevelt once said: "The best executive is the one who has enough sense to pick good people to do what he wants done, and self-restraint enough to keep from meddling with them while they do it."

When you delegate, establish a time line. Delegated tasks should be concise and clear. You must also give authority along with a level of responsibility. Effective managers make sure decisions are made at the lowest level possible. They offer assistance but encourage independence. The skills needed to delegate effectively were discussed in Chapter 2.

Not Deciding

Not to decide *is* to decide. In some instances, any decision is better than none. But in other instances, such as a life-threatening situation, a wrong decision may have disastrous results. Effective managers know when they do not have to make a decision. They use **creative procrastination**—providing time for a minor difficulty to work itself out. In other instances, the thinking trap "if it isn't broken, don't fix it" works to keep managers from getting bogged down in trivia.

Using Computers for Decision Making

A few decades ago law enforcement had limited technological assistance. Managers were truly independent decision makers with little support. The advent of computers has greatly changed this situation. A vast array of software programs is available to assist decision making at all levels.

At the operational or line level, squad cars now have computers that give patrol officers instant access to information. By tracing a license number directly from the patrol car, officers may know the history of the vehicle they are stopping before they approach it. The driver's identification and past record can also be instantly checked. This is important to personal safety and decisions about whether to arrest.

At the management level, administrative programs help with allocating personnel, budgeting, processing reports and many other functions. Computers also provide statistical information as well as analysis of this information and may even suggest implications and alternatives. Called **management information systems (MIS),** these software programs organize data to assist in decision making. They often use "what-if" analysis to project the effects of various solutions.

Hickman (2001, p.50) reports that 78 percent of the estimated 13,524 local agencies in the United States were using personal desktop computers (PCs) in administrative facilities, nearly double the percentage in 1990. He reports that among the most common types of computer files being maintained are arrests, traffic citations and stolen property/vehicles records. Other files maintained by local police agencies, in order of prevalence, are incident reports, calls for service, traffic accidents, uniform crime report (UCR) summary data, alarms, personnel, criminal histories, inventory, evidence, warrants, field interviews, UCR incident-based data, payroll, driver's license information, summonses, linked files for crime analysis and vehicle registration (p.52). Hickman (p.56) concludes: "As computer technology continues to improve, and to the extent that police agencies are able to keep up with improvements and harness new technologies, we might expect to see more efficient and effective delivery of police services."

Even with computer support, however, managers must adapt the information to current circumstances and arrive at independent decisions. Computers cannot replace experience and expertise, but they can enhance them. Anyone who works with management information systems must remember the watchword of computer users: "garbage in/garbage out," or **GIGO.**

Computer programs can also help you review goals and objectives. Based on the experience of other organizations, they can project alternatives, one or more of which may apply to a situation. From these alternatives, managers can make more informed choices. Regional information systems, or those that give more than one agency or entity access, are becoming more common. Using information systems in problem-oriented policing is discussed later in the chapter.

Participatory Decision Making (PDM)

A participatory management environment often leads to increased and better decision making. In **participatory decision making,** employees of the organization have a say in the decision-making process. Employees prefer PDM largely because decisions often directly affect them. They also bring a diversity of backgrounds and experiences to the decision making.

PDM provides more input about the number and content of alternatives because of the varied experience and background of the participants. Opportunity for innovative ideas also increases. Shared input fosters better acceptance of and commitment to the final decision. Upward and downward organizational communication also increases, as does teamwork.

The participative manager outlines the problems and leaves the development of alternatives to subordinates. This encourages creativity by the participants and improves the quality and quantity of the decisions they send to the manager. The group may obtain synergistic results when the process of working together enhances sharing and functional competition. With PDM, conflict is considered an asset, and individuals who do not "go along" are viewed as catalysts for innovative ideas and solutions.

Although obtaining consensus may be more difficult with PDM, it can be achieved if participants avoid arguing in order to win as individuals and keep their focus on reaching the best judgment of the whole group. Group members must also accept responsibility for both hearing and being heard, so that everyone's input receives a hearing. Finally group members should remember that the best results stem from a combination of information, logic and emotion—including participants' feelings about the information and decision-making process. Such participation will positively affect value judgments as well as the final decision.

An entirely participative decision-making process, however, may be difficult to establish because of lack of training on how to work together. It is difficult for officers to include themselves in the process if it has not been past practice to do so. It is even more difficult for autocratic managers to give up their decision-making authority.

If people are used to being told what to do, they may feel awkward when given a chance to participate. A certain amount of confusion and hesitancy may exist initially.

In addition, discussion and agreement are time consuming. Further, not all decisions *should* be democratic or participatory. Some decisions must be immediate, and others cannot be resolved by agreement. Sometimes, a final decision can be made only after top management considers the alternatives.

Nonetheless, if possible, decisions should involve those who will be affected by them. The synergism of the group can often produce results that a single person or even many people working independently would be unable to produce. Further, implementing the selected alternative will be easier because it is more likely to be accepted. *People tend to support what they help create.* Morale is improved, and participants feel commitment and loyalty.

All levels of the organization benefit from group participation in the decision-making process.

In any law enforcement organization, newer officers can bring fresh approaches and ideas, but these must be balanced by experience.

Although full department meetings are difficult to schedule because of multiple shifts, input from all officers can be obtained through shift discussions and a joint meeting of first-line supervisors with middle and executive management. Full department meetings should be called only for critical matters or to communicate a decision.

Although participatory leadership styles support group decision making, disadvantages might also arise, such as wasted time, shirked responsibilities, a tendency toward indecisiveness and costly delays. One very common type of participatory decision making is brainstorming.

Brainstorming

Most people are familiar with the concept of brainstorming, but the practice is often not as effective as it might be. **Brainstorming** is a method of shared problem solving in which members of a group spontaneously contribute ideas, no matter how wild, without criticism or critique. It is creative, uninhibited thinking designed to produce ideas, generate alternatives, suggest solutions and create plans. Alex Osborn, the originator of the brainstorming technique, established four rules:

1. No one is permitted to criticize an idea.
2. The wilder the idea, the better.
3. The group should concentrate on the quantity of ideas and not concern itself with the quality.
4. Participants should combine suggested ideas or build on others whenever possible.

Although brainstorming must be unfettered, it is not unstructured as many think. Participants should be prepared. They should know in advance the problem they will address. A leader should keep the ideas flowing and make sure no criticism or evaluation of ideas occurs. Group size should be limited to no more than 15 participants, and they should sit at a round or U-shaped table.

One key to an effective brainstorming session is to write all ideas on a flipchart. As pages become filled, tape them to the walls so the group will see the flow of ideas and be motivated to continue. All brainstorming sessions should have a definite ending time so a sense of urgency prevails. Most sessions should be limited to 20 to 40 minutes. Time is *not* unlimited.

During brainstorming it is critical that **divergent thinking** (right brain) occur before **convergent thinking** (left brain). Divergent thinking is free

As these officers brainstorm, they generate many creative solutions to a problem. Their ideas are as broad and radical as possible and are developed rapidly. Creativity has free rein.

flowing, creative, imaginative and uninhibited. Convergent thinking, in contrast, is evaluative, rational and objective.

To make brainstorming sessions effective:

1. Ensure that participants are prepared.
2. Write down *all* ideas.
3. Allow *no* criticizing of ideas.
4. Have a definite ending time.

After the brainstorming session, move to the critical judgment phase where ideas are reviewed, synthesized, added and subtracted, evaluated and prioritized. Brainstorming can be a powerful decision making/problem-solving tool. Another participatory approach is to use focus groups.

Focus Groups

The police/community collaboration emphasized in COPPS can be facilitated by using focus groups to help in decision making and problem solving. **Focus groups** usually consist of people from the educational community, the religious community, Neighborhood Watch groups, business groups, professional groups and ordinary citizens who express their opinions about certain issues. The groups are directed by a moderator or facilitator and are meant to collect broad information on a focused topic in an open, personal environment.

Austen (2001, p.16) identifies seven elements commonly associated with focus groups: (1) a small group of four to twelve people (2) who meet with a trained researcher/facilitator/moderator (3) for one to two hours (4) to discuss a selected topic (5) in a nonthreatening environment, (6) to explore participants' perceptions, attitudes, beliefs, ideas and (7) to encourage and use group interactions.

Although involving co-workers, citizens and outside agencies is a cornerstone of community policing, hazards do exist, one of which is *groupthink.*

Groupthink

Groupthink is the negative tendency for members of a group to submit to peer pressure and endorse the majority opinion even if it is individually unacceptable.

Groupthink is more concerned with team play and unanimity than with reaching the best solution. Group members suppress individual concerns to avoid rocking the group's boat. Groupthink is especially hazardous to law enforcement organizations because of the feeling of "family" that exists. Officers support one another, and sometimes a feeling of "them versus us" exists between law enforcement organizations and those they are hired to "serve and protect."

Even life-and-death decisions can be affected by groupthink. It can be difficult to speak up and say that safety concerns indicate that a tactical operation should be delayed, to refuse to go into a barricaded suspect incident with insufficient personnel, or wait for a back-up unit on a domestic call.

Smith and Brantner (2001, p.197) use the **Abilene Paradox** as an illustration of groupthink. Author Jerry Harvey coined the expressions *Abilene Paradox* and *a trip to Abilene* after visiting his in-laws in a small town in west Texas in the 1950s:

> On a hot afternoon during the visit, Harvey and his wife and her family decided to take a trip to Abilene, 53 miles away. They drove for an hour in a car with no air conditioning to a restaurant they didn't like, ate a meal that wasn't very good, and returned home late that afternoon, arguing about who had suggested such a bad idea in the first place.
>
> Harvey realized that while everyone had agreed to take the trip, no one had really wanted to go; they simply went along with the idea and kept their reservations to themselves. In fact, they had done the opposite of what they wanted to do, which involved sitting in the shade, drinking iced tea, and playing dominoes. Each family member felt he or she was a victim of someone else's poor decision to travel to Abilene, even though any of them could have prevented the trip by expressing an objection. The group had just experienced what he would later call the Abilene Paradox. . . .
>
> An Abilene Paradox beings innocently enough: At first, everyone in the group agrees that a particular problem exists. Later, when it comes time to discuss solutions, no one expresses a viewpoint that differs from what appears to be the group's consensus, even though many secretly disagree with it. Finally, after the solution has been implemented, group members complain privately about the plan and look for someone to blame for its development.

Smith and Brantner (p.198) give a hypothetical example of a police chief concerned about racial profiling within the department. He calls a meeting and nearly every supervisor present agrees there is a problem and each knows how he or she would handle it. The chief, however, upon receiving agreement that the problem exists, declares that the only way to deal with racial profiling is to systematically scrutinize every officer's traffic stops and other citizen contacts. Any officer detaining a disproportionate number of non-whites, regardless of the stops' validity, will automatically be subject to an internal investigation. When the chief asks for comments, no one speaks up. Each takes the others' silence to indicate approval. When the chief hears no dissenting opinions, he announces the department's new policy. The result: "Months later, many internal investigations have been opened and concluded. Citations and arrests are down. Retail theft, DUI and residential burglary are up, as are traffic accidents and citizen complaints about officer rudeness. Morale is low, line officers, supervisors, managers and commanders all express their anger and hostility about the chief's racial profiling policy—but only to one another. No one complains to the chief." This is a classic Abilene Paradox or example of groupthink. The power of positive conflict is discussed in detail in Chapter 13.

How can groupthink be avoided? It should be stressed during meetings that individual problems and concerns about a decision should be made known. Create a heterogeneous group representing a broad range of interests. Have the chief or upper management hold back opinions until others have a chance to present their ideas. Brainstorm. Beware of premature decisions—have separate meetings for identifying alternatives and making the final decision.

More Complex Decision-Making/Problem-Solving Processes

Whether decisions are made by a group or an individual, often a more complex process is used, including the seven-step decision-making/problem-solving approach, force-field analysis, the nominal group technique, the Delphi Technique or a modified form of the Delphi Technique. These approaches often include brainstorming.

The Seven-Step Decision-Making/Problem-Solving Process

Many decisions can be effectively made and many problems effectively solved through a seven-step process.

Decision making often follows these seven steps:

1. Define the specific problem.
2. Gather all facts concerning the problem.
3. Generate alternatives.
4. Analyze the alternatives.
5. Select the best alternative.
6. Implement the alternative.
7. Evaluate the decision.

Define the Problem The logical first step is to identify the problem. It must be located, defined and limited before you can seek solutions. The right answers to the wrong problem will do little to further the department's goals. The successful manager does the right things rather than simply doing things right. It makes little sense to spend valuable time solving problems that do not really matter. The problem needs to be identified *in writing.* Those involved need to agree that it is a priority problem that needs to be solved.

Take care not to confuse a problem with its *symptoms.* For example, patrol officers may be coming to work late or calling in sick more often than in the past. These could be symptoms of a deeper problem—low morale. The problem, not the symptoms, must be addressed.

Another important determination is whether the decision to be made is a large, organizational decision or a small, departmental one. If it is only a small problem, perhaps a command decision is most appropriate. Why waste the energies of top management dealing with a relatively insignificant decision? All too often myriad small decisions rob time that should be spent on more major problems.

Gather the Facts The facts and all relevant data must be obtained and reviewed. Determine existing standards, policies and rules that may affect the problem. If possible, consult everyone involved. At this stage of the decision-making process, be objective. Gather *all* facts related to the problem, not only those supporting your biases. Convert data into information. Data consist of facts and figures. Information is an analysis of these facts and figures.

Experience in dealing with identical or similar problems helps greatly. Sometimes you need to consult experts. Other times a problem may fall within department guidelines and require very little research. Rely on established department policies and practices wherever possible.

Take the time you need to be thorough. Avoid snap decisions for critical or recurring problems. Avoid crisis decisions. Usually time is available to thoroughly investigate. Seek help if needed. For example, if a problem involves your patrol vehicles' performance, seek the advice of a qualified mechanic.

Generate Alternatives Put the alternatives on a flipchart or blackboard. The following questions can generate alternatives: Is there a new way to do it? Can you give it a new twist? Do you need more of the same? Less of the same? Is there a substitute? Can you rearrange the parts? What if you do just the opposite? Can you combine the ideas? Can you borrow or adapt? The military uses the phrase **cross flow** or **cross tell** when talking about borrowing or adapting ideas. If one unit goes through an inspection, they cross tell what they learned to all the other units so those units don't make the same mistake. If they encounter a problem they have never seen before, they send out a cross flow message stating the problem and asking the other units if they have encountered the same thing and, if so, what they did about it. This helps in two ways. If other units haven't seen the problem, they can have a heads up that the problem exists. If they have encountered the problem, they can share what worked—or didn't work. There's no need to re-invent the wheel.

Motivation also has an important role in problem solving. Unless you are motivated to find a solution, you probably will not generate adequate alternatives. Some problems take time to resolve. Ideas may need to incubate, which may take a day or longer. Some of the great scientific discoveries resulted from years of study and work.

Analyze the Alternatives What are the likely consequences of each alternative? Among the many factors to consider in analyzing the alternatives are how they fit with the agency mission statement and goals, cost, personnel required, resources available, staff reaction, long-range consequences, union contract provisions, ethical considerations and problems that may arise as a result of the decision.

Time and resources may limit the alternatives. Measure present decisions with past standards.

Select the Most Appropriate Alternative Choosing the right alternative is the heart of decision making. For normal problem-solving situations, one alternative eventually appears as the best solution. For situations in which all look equal, the choice is more difficult. Most alternatives have advantages and disadvantages. Make a chart with two columns. List each alternative and its advantages and disadvantages. They may be equal in number, but assign a weight to each point. Use the total points as part of your final decision.

Determining alternatives and evaluating them is often difficult. It may require experience, knowledge, training, creativity, intuition, advice from others and even computer assistance. The more input available, the better the decision.

Implement the Alternative It does little good to decide how to solve a problem and then not implement the alternative selected. Implementation is usually the most time-consuming phase of the decision-making process. It involves several steps and should be carefully planned. Who will do the implementing? What resources will they need? When will the implementation occur?

A critical first step is communicating the decision to everyone involved. Ideally, those involved will have taken part in the decision-making process itself and will already be quite familiar with the options and the reasons a particular option was selected.

If a decision is a command or a consultative decision, such communication is vital. Effective managers keep their people in on what is happening and enlist their support from the earliest possible minute. Support those implementing the solution. Follow up to see that needed support is continually provided. Seek feedback at all stages of the implementation.

Evaluate the Decision How effective is the alternative selected? Did it accomplish the expected result? Solve the problem? Evaluation provides information for future decisions. If the solution does not prove effective, learn from the experience. It does little good to brood over solutions that do not work. It does even less good to attempt to place blame.

The primary purpose of evaluation is to improve—to learn what alternatives work and maintain and strengthen them and to learn what alternatives do not work and to change them.

The Steps Applied Assume that an organizational goal is to reduce vehicle crashes by 10 percent. The *problem* is increased traffic crashes. The major *cause* of the problem is driving behavior of the motorists. How can police action resolve the problem by reducing crashes 10 percent?

Once the problem is clearly stated, the next step is to use crash records to obtain data concerning frequency, location, day of week, time of day and causes. Computer software programs can provide data analysis and instant information.

After information is compiled, alternatives are identified. Alternative A might be to increase radar enforcement to reduce the speed of vehicles because crashes are increasing not only in frequency but also in severity. Increased speed of vehicles involved in crashes results in increased severity. Alternative B might be to station a squad car at high-crash intersections as a deterrent during the day of the week and time of day that crash occurrence is highest. Alternative C might be to add road signs to warn drivers of the crash problem. Alternative D might be to provide additional traffic patrol officers to increase enforcement of traffic violations and increase deterrent visibility. Alternative E might be to station officers in high-crash locations and have them hand out cards to motorists stopping at stop signs. The cards inform the drivers of the crash problem, locations and things they can do to help. Alternative F might be to do nothing.

Next, the alternatives must be analyzed so the best ones can be selected and implemented. Alternative A is accepted, and radar enforcement is increased in selected areas of high crash frequency. Alternative B is eliminated because of time consumption and lack of sufficient vehicles. Alternative C is accepted, and engineering is directed to install signs at the proper locations. Alternative D is eliminated because it requires funds that are not available. Alternative E is eliminated because it would take time to develop and print the card, and the officers do not think this is good use of their time. Alternative F is ruled out because measures *are* needed to reduce crashes.

The final step is evaluation, which is done six months later. It was determined that accidents were reduced by 5 percent, half the original goal. The results were disseminated to all police department members and the engineering department.

In some instances data and accurate information are not available. In such cases experience, patterns, rules, policies, regulations and personal judgment would be used.

Force-Field Analysis (FFA)

Force-field analysis (FFA) is a problem-solving technique that identifies forces that impede and others that foster goal achievement. Forces that impede goal achievement are called **restraining forces;** those that foster it are called **driving forces.** The problem itself is called **equilibrium.** In a problem situation, the equilibrium is not where you want it to be. Force-field analysis is illustrated in Figure 4.1.

Force-field analysis identifies factors that impede and enhance goal attainment. A problem exists when the equilibrium is upset because more factors are impeding goal attainment than enhancing it.

As Evers and Heenan (2002, p.16) explain: "When trying to implement a strategy, leaders often do not give enough thought to the forces that are working against implementing a strategy or miss opportunities to take advantage of forces helping to implement a strategy."

In force-field analysis, you can state the problem as an undesirable situation, then list and label each force as high, medium or low (H-M-L) to indicate the strength. The final step is to devise a plan to change the equilibrium. Select specific ways to reduce the restraining forces and other ways to increase the driving forces. The entire analysis can be put into a chart, as shown in Table 4.1.

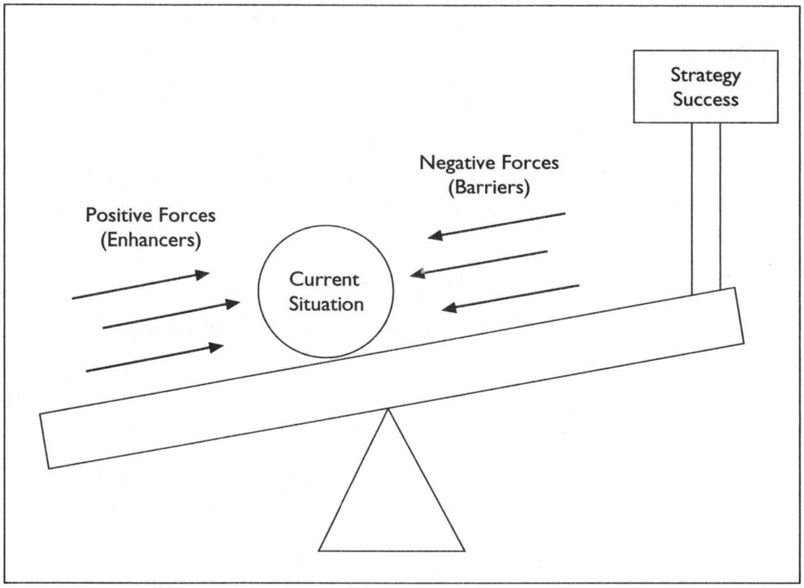

Figure 4.1
Force-Field Analysis

Source: Michael J. Evers and George Heenan. "Balancing Act: Optimizing Strategies and Projects for Success." *Minnesota Business,* March 2002, p.16.

Table 4.1
Sample Force-Field Analysis

Problem: Increasing Drug Abuse in Our Community

Restraining Forces	Driving Forces
Lack of finances	Increase in drug arrests
Lack of organization/coordination	Church groups
Lack of school cooperation	Parental concerns
Lack of church cooperation	Suicide rate
Lack of available personnel	Increase in drug use
Public apathy	Teen pregnancies
Parental drug use	Fatal accidents
Drug sales profits	

Recommended Action Plan
Create a specialized narcotics unit.
Initiate a 24-hour "hotline."
Pass an ordinance creating a drug-free zone of 1,000 feet around any school.
Conduct educational programs such as DARE in the schools.
Conduct parenting classes.
Conduct drug-free workplace programs.
Start a newsletter to be sent to all residents in the community.
Confiscate all property involved in drug arrests.
Create an Anti-Drug Abuse Council.
Hire a drug counselor for those who cannot afford one.

Source: Stan Kossen. *Supervision.* West Publishing Company, 1991.

The Nominal Group Technique

Researchers Andre Delbecq and Andrew Van de Ven found that some people work better by themselves than in a group. To take advantage of this yet capture the synergism of a team approach, they developed the nominal group technique to produce more and better ideas.

The **nominal group technique** is an objective way to achieve consensus on the most effective alternatives by ranking them.

It works like this:

1. Divide the staff or people involved into groups of six to nine.
2. Have each person write down as many ideas for solving the problem at hand as they can—without talking to anyone. Allow 5 to 15 minutes for this step.
3. Go around the group and have each person, including the leader, read one item from his or her list while the leader writes the ideas on a flipchart. No evaluation of the ideas is allowed.
4. Continue going around the room until all ideas are posted. If more than one person gives the same idea, place a tally mark behind it.

Survey on Options for Combatting the Drug Problem

As an officer on the street, you are closest to the drug problem our agency is battling. We would appreciate your suggestions on possible approaches to this problem. Please take a few minutes to answer the questions that follow. Your answers will be confidential, but all answers will be shared with all other members of the patrol division.

1. How can we increase community drug education?

____
____
____
____

2. What are the three main drug abuse problem areas?

____
____
____
____

3. What should we do to reduce the drug problem in our community?

____
____
____
____

Figure 4.2
Typical Delphi Questionnaire

5. After all the ideas are posted, allow questions to clarify the ideas but no evaluation.
6. Hand out note cards and have everyone rank the five best ideas, with "1" being the best.
7. Collect the cards and take a break. Total the rankings for each idea and divide by the number of people in the meeting. Then write on the flipchart the five ideas with the highest scores.
8. Reconvene the group and have them discuss the five ideas. Usually one best idea will emerge from this discussion.

This technique works well to obtain input from everyone, but it is also very time consuming. It should be reserved for important problems that truly require a consensus decision.

The Delphi Technique

The **Delphi Technique** was developed in the 1960s at the Rand Corporation. Like the nominal group process, the Delphi Technique is a way to have individual input result in a group effort. Rather than calling a meeting, management sends questionnaires to those who are to be involved in the decision making. Figure 4.2 illustrates a typical Delphi questionnaire.

Management then circulates the answers to all participants, who are asked to again complete the questionnaire considering the various answers. This continues until a consensus is reached. Usually, three or four cycles are enough.

The Delphi Technique uses questionnaires completed by individuals. Answers are shared, and the questionnaires are again completed until consensus is reached.

Delphi is actually a thoughtful conversation in which everyone gets a chance to *listen.* Groups often debate rather than problem-solve. The Delphi Technique removes the need for winning points or besting the opposition.

A Modified Delphi Technique

The Delphi Technique can be modified to take away the open-endedness. This **modified Delphi Technique** presents a questionnaire that contains policy statements representing key issues to be decided and a response column with three choices: Agree with, not certain but willing to try and disagree with. Those who do not agree are asked to indicate the changes they would recommend that would make the statement acceptable. This is Phase 1. Figure 4.3 shows an example of how this might look.

Phase 2 shows the number replying with each option for each statement and the choice each respondent circled. Respondents are then asked to reconsider their original responses and make any changes they want based on the responses of others. Figure 4.4 shows how this might look.

Phase 3 is a tally of the responses in Phase 2 and a summary of the actions to be taken for each item, based on those responses. Any of these decision-making methods are also appropriate for a department using problem-oriented policing.

Problem-Oriented Policing

Problem-oriented policing (POP) has become extremely popular in many departments and goes hand-in-hand with community-oriented policing. As Frazier (2000, p.11) stresses: "Police need to act as problem solvers and peacemakers in their communities. Police and citizens must work together if we are to develop

1. For each statement below, check the column that best reflects your position:
   A Agree with.
   B Not certain but willing to try for a year and evaluate.
   C Disagree with.
2. For each column where you check C, indicate in the space below the statement how you would like it amended. You may also comment if you checked A or B.

Suggested Action	A	B	C
To increase community drug education we should:			
1. Start a school DARE program. Comment:			
2. Publish in local papers a series of articles by community leaders. Comment:			
3. Highlight drug abuse literature at the library. Comment:			
To reduce the drug problem in our community we should:			
4. Increase the number of police. Comment:			
5. Begin a community-wide Anti-Drug Abuse Council. Comment:			
6. Provide stiffer penalties to drug dealers and users. Comment:			

Figure 4.3
Phase 1 of the Modified Delphi Technique

long-term solutions to crime, and if we are to enhance trust between police and the communities they serve. Problems can best be eliminated when the community and government coordinate and cooperate. For example, police may be called repeatedly to a boarded-up house to arrest trespassers. With interagency cooperation, that house could be rehabilitated and become an asset to the neighborhood, not a haven for criminal activity."

Brito and Gratto (2000, p.xiii) contend: "In the new millennium, problem-oriented policing maintains its role as a powerful tool in the policing arsenal." According to Hoover et al. (2001, p.176): "Problem solving lies at the heart of contemporary policing." The originator of problem-oriented policing, Herman Goldstein (1990, p.33), says of the approach:

> Focusing on the substantive, community problems that the police must handle is a much more radical step than it initially appears to be, for it requires the police to go beyond taking satisfaction in the smooth operation of their organization; it requires that they extend their concern to dealing effectively with the problems that justify creating a police agency in the first instance.

The approach used in problem-oriented policing is typically the SARA Model.

The SARA Model problem-solving process involves four steps (Eck and Spelman, 1987, p.xx):

1. Scanning (identifying the problem)
2. Analysis (looking at alternatives)

Following is a tally of responses to the drug questionnaire and suggested changes that we would like you to respond to. As before, for each statement and change, check the column that best reflects your position:
A Agree with.
B Not certain, but willing to try for a year and evaluate.
C Disagree with.

Suggested Action	A	B	C
To increase community drug education we should:			
1. Start a school DARE program. Change: Also have parenting classes.	5	3	3
2. Publish in local papers a series of articles by community leaders. Change: Also articles by victims and cops.	4	4	3
3. Highlight drug abuse literature at the library. Change: Distribute literature through civic groups and the schools as well.	3	3	5
To reduce the drug problem in our community we should:			
4. Increase the number of police. Change: Increase in areas known to have high rates of drug dealing.	6	5	0
5. Begin a community-wide Anti-Drug Abuse Council. Change: Members appointed by chief of police.	4	4	3
6. Provide stiffer penalties to drug dealers and users. Change: For dealers only. Counseling for users.	5	1	5

Figure 4.4
Phase 2 of the Modified Delphi Technique

3. Response (implementing an alternative)
4. Assessment (evaluating the results)

Rather than responding to isolated incidents, police focus energies on *grouping incidents into problem categories.* The scanning step incorporates the first two steps in the seven-step decision making/problem-solving process: define the specific problem and gather all facts concerning the problem. Wartell and Greenhalgh (2000, p.6) suggest: "Crime analysis units help identify problems by using information from the Records Management System (RMS) to create crime bulletins that identify similarities in locations, victims, suspects, days of the week, time of day and targets. Computer Aided Dispatch (CAD) can be used to identify locations that get repeat calls for police service. . . . Off-the-shelf software—in conjunction with CAD, RMS or other data sources—with spreadsheets, databases, charts and graphs can help identify similarities in incidents that might indicate the need for some problem solving."

Once specific problems have been identified, alternatives must be examined. The analysis phase incorporates the third, fourth and fifth steps of the seven-step process: generate alternatives; analyze the alternatives; select the best alternative. Goldstein's (p.ix) range of possible alternatives includes:

1. Concentrating attention on those who account for a disproportionate share of a problem.
2. Connecting with other government and private services.
3. Using mediation and negotiation skills.
4. Conveying information.
5. Mobilizing the community.
6. Using existing forms of social control in addition to the community.
7. Altering the physical environment to reduce opportunities for problems to recur.
8. Increasing regulation, through statutes or ordinances, of conditions that contribute to problems.
9. Developing new forms of limited authority to intervene and detain.
10. Using the criminal justice system more discriminately.
11. Using civil law to control public nuisances, offensive behavior and conditions contributing to crime.

According to Wartell and Greenhalgh (p.6): "Like scanning, basic analysis can be done with spreadsheets and databases. . . . More complex analysis can be done with a Geographic Information System (GIS). A GIS takes your database analysis one step further—into space. Using a GIS, your analysis can extend to visualizing the problem on a map, predicting where the next crime might occur, such as analyzing auto thefts in relation to auto recoveries."

The response step parallels the sixth step in the seven-step process: implement the alternative. And the assessment phase in the SARA Model parallels the seventh step of the seven-step process: evaluate the decision. In effect, the SARA Model is a streamlined version of the seven-step decision-making/problem-solving process. Grinder (2000, p.148) stresses: "Any department committed to

Table 4.2
Handling a Call vs. Solving a Problem

Handling a Call	versus	Solving a Problem
Call/case-driven response		Problem-driven response
Temporary/transient result		Longer lasting/permanent result
Less effort/energy required/expended		More effort/energy required/expended
Less imagination applied		More imagination applied
Limited results expected by officers		Less limited results expected by officers
Little collaboration with others		Much collaboration with others
Response driven by limited information		Response driven by much information

Source: Terry Eisenberg and Bruce Glasscock. "Looking Inward with Problem-Oriented Policing." *FBI Law Enforcement Bulletin*, July 2001, p.4. Reprinted by permission. Courtesy of the *FBI Law Enforcement Bulletin*.

the problem-solving process needs to understand that the first-line supervisor is the key to successful implementation."

The difference between simply handling a call and solving a problem is illustrated in Table 4.2.

The SARA Model in Action

An example of problem-oriented policing in action and the implementation of the SARA Model is seen in the 2001 winner of the Herman Goldstein Excellence in Problem-Oriented Policing Award, the California Highway Patrol (CHP), for its Corridor Safety Program. The program used the SARA Model to address a high rate of fatal accidents on an infamous stretch of rural highway in California, the roadway where actor James Dean was killed in the late 1950s, dubbed "Blood Alley."

Scanning Scanning was rigorous, with 550 qualifying roadway segments examined. Three years of collision and victim data were reviewed to minimize any statistical anomalies. To be included in the selection pool, potential corridors had to pass through or be adjacent to an urban area and fall under the jurisdiction of the CHP. Segments with fewer than five deaths in three years were also eliminated. Based on statistical rankings and input from local experts, State Routes 41/46 were selected.

Analysis The CHP formed a multi-disciplinary task force. The task force found that much of the corridor was quite remote, largely without cellular phone service and having too few call boxes. Call response times for emergency services depended on the EMS unit with jurisdiction over the area, sometimes not the closest unit. The roadway lacked adequate shoulders and medians, and existing signage was confusing and inadequate, as were existing passing and merging lanes. Being an east-west route, glare was a problem during sunrise and sunset. Various roadway curves also contributed to poor visibility.

The task force also found that the primary collision factors spoke to the presence of aggressive driving and of impatient drivers behind large, slow-moving vehicles who made unwise passing decisions. The top five collision factors were unsafe turning, driving on the wrong side of the road, improper passing, driving under the influence and unsafe speed. It also suggested that many involved in collisions were local farm workers with limited English skills who were unfamiliar with California rules-of-the-road.

Response Proposed solutions fell into four categories: enforcement, emergency services, engineering and education. Special *enforcement* operations were implemented and funded through federal traffic safety grants. Ultimately officers worked 2,922 overtime hours, offered assistance and services to motorists 2,837 times and issued 14,606 citations.

Additional *emergency* roadside call boxes were installed. A CHP helicopter was permanently assigned to the roadway, and agreements were reached with emergency service providers that the closest units should respond to collision scenes without regard to jurisdictional boundaries.

Several *engineering* changes were made in the roadway. Raised-profile thermoplastic striping was installed where passing was allowed in one direction. In no-passing zones, a widened center median with rumble strips and thermoplastic striping was installed. Outside shoulders were treated with rumble strips. Several signing, striping and maintenance projects were completed. "Stop Ahead" warning signs were posted at key intersections and chevron signs were installed to warn of impending curves.

A variety of *educational programs* and materials involved the local media, businesses, government and residents in reminding motorists to drive safely.

Assessment The efforts were quite successful with fatal collisions reduced by 10 percent and injury collisions reduced by 32 percent. Over the five years of available data, it is estimated that the safety initiatives have saved 21 lives and prevented 55 injuries.

POP and Internal Problems

Eisenberg and Glasscock (2001, p.5) note: "Since the 1980s, law enforcement agencies have applied the concept of problem-oriented policing to many community problems such as alcohol-related crimes, burglaries, graffiti, sex offenses and trespassing. While POP has become a highly visible and utilitarian policing philosophy, the use of the SARA problem-solving technique has contributed greatly to its effectiveness. . . . The application of POP to internal departmental problems . . . has occurred infrequently, yet its appropriateness appears considerable." Managers facing internal problems would be wise to consider whether applying the SARA Model might be beneficial. In addition, whether dealing with internal problems or crime and disorder community problems, the most successful decisions and problem-solving efforts will use not only logic and technology, but also creativity and innovation.

Creativity and Innovation

Brooks (2001, p.67) defines creativity as "the relating of normally unrelated elements." Creativity involves originality, uniqueness and innovation. It involves breaking with old ways of thinking.

Creativity is a process of breaking old connections and making useful new ones. It often is synonymous with **innovation.**

One strategy for law enforcement managers to develop more creativity is to increase interaction with corporate leaders and other administrators outside criminal justice. Police management has been evolving for decades and has been described as conservative and traditional. Techniques such as total quality management, team approaches and quality circles are foreign to many police managers, who need to be alert to management changes in the corporate world. Some corporate techniques cannot be adapted to the police environment, but others can. Exposure to new ideas and thoughts stimulates the mind. Brooks (p.68) offers the following suggestions for enhancing creativity:

- Think outside of the box.
- Consider every idea, no matter how crazy it might sound.
- Remember that creativity often comes from relatively unrelated concepts or ideas.
- Remember that creativity must sometimes be spontaneous.
- Look for results from your creativity activity; work toward closure and don't get bogged down in the process.
- Be patient. Let ideas percolate on their own and in their own good time.
- Be gracious and flexible when your idea isn't embraced or implemented or when it's tweaked.
- Try, try again. If one idea doesn't work, another will.

Sullivan (2001, p.68) comments: "When people talk about wanting to get out of the box and be more creative, it's good to start by understanding what is the box. . . . The box is linear, step-by-step thinking—the kind you use to do expense reports and memos." Individuals wanting to be more creative might also think about physically changing their environment.

Changing Your Environment

Arnot (2000, p.7) suggests some steps to create "sizzling mental energy":

1. **Turn up the lights.** Normal room light rarely exceeds 500–600 lux, but people need at least 1,000 lux to reap the biological benefits of light.
2. **Arrange your space.** Black and blue are good office colors. Have at least one window.
3. **Use aromatherapy.** Rosemary, peppermint and eucalyptus can boost mental energy and improve concentration.
4. **Cut the noise.** Noise demands a series of cognitive decisions. Neutralize it by turning on a fan or air conditioner.
5. **Pay attention to air quality.** Cool, dry air maintains alertness.

Some police administrators reject new programs or ideas because they did not originate with them or because the idea came from the rank-and-file. Many newspapers regularly publish excellent columns by management experts, and much of this information is adaptable to police management. In fact, many of the concepts presented in this text came from corporate America.

We are all born as potentially creative people. By the time we are adults only a very few of us have overcome all the messages that stifle individuality and creativity. Our society tends to stifle innovation and creativity. Think about school and what you were taught: Dogs cannot be colored purple; give the "right" answer; do not make a mess; do not be different; stay in line; be quiet; raise your hand if you want to talk and so on. In other words, conform. Our own habits can also stifle creativity.

Thinking Traps and Mental Locks

Thinking traps are habits people fall into without recognizing what they are doing.

Common thinking traps include:

1. Being stuck in black/white, either/or thinking.
2. Being too quick in deciding.
3. Making decisions based on your personal feelings about the proposer of an idea.
4. Being a victim of personal habits and prejudices.
5. Not using imagination.

Being stuck in black/white, either/or thinking. People caught in this trap think that if one answer is bad, the other must be good. This kind of thinking causes people to miss intermediate solutions. Brainstorming many alternatives will help overcome this trap.

Being too quick in deciding. People in this trap jump to conclusions before they hear all the facts or have all the evidence. You can avoid this trap by listing all possibilities and delaying decisions until each has been discussed.

Making decisions based on your personal feelings about the proposer of an idea. Some people tend to support only what their friends propose. To overcome this, decide that you will listen for the facts and keep your feelings out of your decision.

Being a victim of personal habits and prejudices. "We've always done it that way" thinking can keep programs from moving forward. You can avoid this trap by asking questions such as: Who else can we serve? How can we do it differently? What more might we do?

Not using imagination. People who fall into this trap are too tied to data and statistics. They do not risk using their intuition. To bypass this trap, practice brainstorming and creative thinking—think laterally, horizontally and vertically. Take the risk of going with your hunches.

To illustrate the tendency to get stuck in a thinking rut, try the "Scottish Names" game on a colleague. (Note: It is more effective if done orally because the solution is obvious when written like this.) Ask a colleague to pronounce M-A-C-T-A-V-I-S-H; then M-A-C-D-O-U-G-A-L; then M-A-C-C-A-R-T-H-Y. Finally, ask them to pronounce M-A-C-H-I-N-E-S. If they respond "MacHines," they have become a victim of preconditioned thinking, a common thinking trap.

The mind easily gets stuck in patterns. Creativity consultant von Oech (1983) calls such thinking traps *mental locks.* He suggests that sometimes we need a "whack on the side of the head" to jar ourselves out of ways of thinking that keep us from being innovative.

Mental locks that prevent innovative thinking include:

1. The right answer.
2. That's not logical.
3. Follow the rules.
4. Be practical.
5. Avoid ambiguity.
6. To err is wrong.
7. Play is frivolous.
8. That's not my area.
9. Don't be foolish.
10. I'm not creative.

The right answer. Most people will have taken in excess of 26,000 tests before they complete their education. Such tests usually focus on "right" answers. According to von Oech (p.22): "Children enter elementary school as question marks and leave as periods."

That's not logical. People need to learn to dream, create and fantasize. Both "soft" and "hard" thinking are needed. It is like making a clay pot. Clay that is not soft enough is difficult to work with. Once the pot is shaped, however, it must be fired and made hard before it will hold water. Metaphors such as this can help in problem solving as well.

Follow the rules. Parents teach their children to stay inside the lines when they color. People do rely on patterns to analyze problems, but this can be a hindrance.

Be practical. As von Oech (p.54) notes:

> Because we have the ability to symbolize our experience, our thinking is not limited to the real and the present. This capability empowers our thinking in two major ways. First, it enables us to anticipate the future. . . .
>
> Second, since our thinking is not bound by real world constraints, we can generate ideas which have no correlate in the world of experience. . . .
>
> I call the realm of the possible our "germinal seedbed." . . . Asking "what-if" is an easy way to get your imagination going.

Avoid ambiguity. A story told by von Oech involves former FBI director J. Edgar Hoover. Hoover wrote a letter to his agents, and as he was proofreading it, he decided he did not like the way it was laid out. He wrote a note on the bottom to his secretary, "Watch the borders," and asked her to retype it. She did and then sent it to all the agents. For the next few weeks, FBI agents were put on special alert along our Canadian and Mexican borders. Ambiguity should usually be avoided. When thinking creatively, however, ambiguity can help. Ask: How else might this be interpreted?

To err is wrong. This is similar to the first mental lock—that there is a "right" answer. View mistakes as learning opportunities and as a part of risk taking. If you are made of the right material, a hard fall will result in a high bounce. Mistakes or failures can be positive. Henry Ford viewed failure positively: "Failure is the opportunity to begin again more intelligently."

Play is frivolous. According to von Oech (p.97): "Necessity may be the mother of invention, but play is certainly the father." He urges that people not take themselves too seriously, especially when engaged in innovative thinking.

That's not my area. In our complex society, specialization is a fact of life. Sometimes, however, a person outside the area in which a problem exists is better able to generate possible solutions. It is not always the "experts" who come up with the best ideas.

Don't be foolish. In the Middle Ages, kings often had "fools" as part of their court. A major role these fools played was to ridicule the advice the king's counselors gave him, a forerunner of the devil's advocate role in today's society.

I'm not creative. This can become a self-fulfilling prophecy. If you think you cannot do something, you probably will not be able to. Conversely, the power of positive thinking has been proven time after time.

Killer Phrases

Closely related to thinking traps and mental locks are certain "killer phrases" people tend to use that limit the creative participation of *others* in the group.

Killer phrases are judgmental and critical and serve as put-downs. They stifle others' creativity.

Among the more common killer phrases are the following: It's not our policy. It's not our area. We don't have the time. We'll never get help. It's too much hassle. That's too radical. It won't work. Be practical. It costs too much. We've never done it that way before. Be realistic. Where did you come up with *that* idea? This isn't the time to try something like that. It's okay in theory, but I don't think we're ready for it yet. You don't really think that would work, do you? Get serious.

To handle killer phrases, recognize them, describe to the group what is happening and then challenge the group to discuss whether the killer phrases are true. Encourage the group to remain open to all ideas.

Organizations that promote creativity and innovation provide more freedom to think and act, recognize ideas and provide ample opportunities for communication as well as for private creative thinking. They also invest in research and experimentation and permit ideas from outside the organization.

Common Mistakes

Common mistakes in problem solving and decision making include spending too much energy on unimportant details, failing to resolve important issues, being secretive about true feelings, having a closed mind, making decisions while angry or excited, and not expressing ideas. Managers who reject information, suggestions and alternatives that do not fit into their comfortable past patterns can severely limit their decision-making capabilities. Inability to decide, putting decisions off to the last minute, failing to set deadlines, making decisions under pressure and using unreliable sources of information are other common errors in problem solving and decision making. Without the willingness to change, to reach out or to go farther, you cannot be creative or innovative.

Each of these common errors has an alternative, positive approach. For example, rather than making multiple decisions about the same problem, that is, reinventing the wheel, managers should establish standard operating procedures for recurring problems.

Two Key Considerations in Decision Making and Problem Solving

A decision may be logical, creative and legal, but is it ethical—morally right? Many problems facing law enforcement decision makers involve ethical issues. For example, are issues of fairness or morality involved? Who is affected? Will there be victims? What are the alternatives? Is there a law against some behavior, or does it clearly violate a moral rule? Does the decision accurately reflect the kind of person/department you are or want to be? How does it make you and your department look to the public? To other law enforcement agencies? Ethics in law enforcement is discussed in Chapter 9.

In addition, managers must weigh the risks involved against the possible benefits.

Ethical considerations and the willingness to take risks are important considerations in decision making.

What are the risks involved in deciding? In not deciding? In selecting a different alternative? In being wrong? Edison was quoted as saying he did not fail to make a storage battery 25,000 times. He simply knew 25,000 ways *not* to make one. Managers must make decisions and take risks. It comes with the job.

Evaluating Decisions

When decisions have been made, they can be evaluated against the following checklist. Is the decision:

1. Consistent with the agency's mission? Goals? Objectives?
2. A long-term solution?
3. Cost-effective?
4. Legal?
5. Ethical?
6. Practical?
7. Acceptable to those responsible for implementing it?

Thang (2001, p.15) suggests additional questions for evaluating decisions: Would your decision or action cause injury to any party? Have you been honest? Are you thinking about how the decision or action might affect others? Have you taken the time to reflect on the results of your decision or action?

Summary

Decisions may be strategic—executive level; administrative—middle management level; or operational—first-line level. Decisions may also be classified as command, consultative or consensual.

Decision making and problem solving involve thinking. Whole-brain research suggests that left-brain thinking processes *language* and is primarily *logical.* Right-brain thinking processes *images* and is primarily *emotional.* Both processes (that is, whole-brain thinking) are needed.

Basic methods for making decisions range from using intuition and snap decisions to using a computer, with a systematic individual or group approach in between.

Participatory decision making has been growing in popularity. All levels of the police department benefit from group participation in the decision-making process. Many approaches to problem solving seek solutions through brainstorming. To make brainstorming sessions effective, ensure that participants are prepared, write down *all* ideas, allow *no* criticizing of ideas and have a definite ending time.

Involving others in decision making and problem solving poses the potential problem of groupthink, the negative tendency for members of a group to submit to peer pressure and endorse the majority opinion, even if it is unacceptable to individuals.

Whether decisions are made by a group or an individual, a more complex process is often used. Among the most common systematic approaches are the seven-step approach, force-field analysis, the nominal group technique, the Delphi Technique and a modified form of the Delphi Technique.

The seven-step approach involves defining the problem, gathering the facts, generating alternatives, analyzing the alternatives, selecting the best alternative, implementing the alternative and evaluating the decision. Force-field analysis identifies forces that impede and enhance goal attainment. A problem exists when the equilibrium is upset because more forces are impeding goal attainment than enhancing it. The nominal group technique is an objective way to achieve consensus on the most effective alternatives by ranking them. The Delphi Technique uses individually completed questionnaires. Answers are shared, and the questionnaires are again completed until consensus is reached.

One popular approach to problem solving is problem-oriented policing (POP), which uses the SARA approach: scan, analyze, respond and assess. It also stresses creativity.

Creativity is a process of breaking old connections and making useful new ones. Often synonymous with innovation, creativity can be hindered by thinking traps, mental locks and killer phrases. Common thinking traps include being stuck in black/white, either/or thinking; being too quick in deciding; making decisions based on personal feelings about the proposer of an idea; being a victim of personal habits and prejudices; and not using imagination. Mental locks that prevent innovative thinking include insisting on the "right" answer and the following opinions/statements: that's not logical; follow the rules; be practical; avoid ambiguity; to err is wrong; play is frivolous; that's not my area; don't be foolish; and I'm not creative.

Killer phrases are judgmental, critical and serve as put-downs. They stifle creativity. To handle killer phrases, recognize them, describe to the group what is happening and then challenge the phrases. In addition to seeking logical yet creative solutions, managers must be concerned with ethical considerations and the risks involved.

Discussion Questions

1. Compare and contrast command, consultative and consensual decisions. Which do you prefer?
2. Do you support the findings of whole-brain research? If not, what problems do you see?
3. Can you give an example of when intuition has been important in a decision you have made?
4. Are you comfortable making snap decisions? If so, about what? If not, why not?
5. What would your model of decision making look like?
6. Who would you involve in the decision-making process?
7. How important do you think creativity and innovation are in dealing with typical problems facing law enforcement?
8. How might you engage in "creative procrastination"?
9. Of the systematic approaches to problem solving, which seems the most practical to you?
10. What is the greatest problem you think law enforcement is facing today? What approaches would you use to attack it?

InfoTrac College Edition Assignment

Use InfoTrac College Edition to help answer the Discussion Questions as appropriate.

Select one of the following assignments to complete. Be prepared to share your findings with the class.

Find a recent journal article that describes in depth how *problem solving* has been applied by a law enforcement agency. Outline the article. Then decide whether the agency used the SARA Model for problem solving. If not, what approach did they use? Be prepared to share your findings with the class.

OR

Read and outline "Looking Inward with Problem-Oriented Policing" by Terry Eisenberg and Bruce Glasscock.

References

Arnot, Bob. "Alter Your Biology to Create Sizzling Mental Energy." *USA Weekend,* January 14–16, 2000, pp.6–7.

Austen, Laurie A. "Focus Groups: A Needs Assessment Tool for Training." *The Law Enforcement Trainer,* May/June 2001, pp.16–17.

Brito, Corina Sole and Gratto, Eugenia E. *Problem Oriented Policing: Crime Specific Problems, Critical Issues and Making POP Work,* Vol. 3. Washington, DC: Police Executive Research Forum, 2000.

Brooks, Bill. "Create, Yourself." *TD,* December 2001, pp.67–69.

Eck, John E. and Spelman, William. *Problem-Solving: Problem-Oriented Policing in Newport News.* Washington, DC: Police Executive Research Forum, 1987.

Eisenberg, Terry and Glasscock, Bruce. "Looking Inward with Problem-Oriented Policing." *FBI Law Enforcement Bulletin,* July 2001, pp.1–5.

Evers, Michael J. and Heenan, George. "Balancing Act: Optimizing Strategies and Projects for Success." *Minnesota Business,* March 2002, pp.16–17.

Excellence in Problem-Oriented Policing: The 2001 Herman Goldstein Award Winners, Washington, DC: National Institute of Justice, Community Oriented Policing Services and the Police Executive Research Forum, 2001, pp.5–14.

Frazier, Thomas C. "Community Policing Efforts Offer Hope for the Future." *The Police Chief,* August 2000, p.11.

Goldstein, Herman. *Problem-Oriented Policing.* New York: McGraw-Hill Publishing Company, 1990.

Grinder, Donald. "Implementing Problem-Oriented Policing: A View from the Front Lines." In *Problem Oriented Policing: Crime Specific Problems, Critical Issues and Making POP Work,* Vol. 3, edited by Corina Sole Brito and Eugenia E.

Gratto. Washington, DC: Police Executive Research Forum, 2000, pp.141–156.

Hickman, Matthew J. "Computers and Information Systems in Local Police Departments, 1990–1999." *The Police Chief,* January 2001, pp.50–56.

Hoover, Jerry; Cleveland, Gerard; and Saville, Greg. "A New Generation of Field Training." In *Solving Crime and Disorder Problems: Current Issues, Police Strategies and Organizational Tactics,* edited by Melissa Reuland, Corina Sole Brito and Lisa Carroll. Washington, DC: Police Executive Research Forum, 2001, pp.175–190.

Smith, Dave and Brantner, Elizabeth. "Police Leadership and the Abilene Paradox." *The Police Chief,* April 2001, pp.196–200.

Sullivan, Cynthia K. "Re-Create Yourself." *Successful Meetings,* August 2001, pp.68–70.

Thang, Vo Thanh. "Six Guidelines for Decision Making." *Performance in Practice,* Spring 2001, p.15.

von Oech, Roger. *A Whack on the Side of the Head: How to Unlock Your Mind for Innovation.* New York: Warner Books, 1983.

Wartell, Julie and Greenhalgh, Fiona. "Using Technology for Problem Solving." *Problem Solving Quarterly,* Winter 2000, pp.1, 6–7.

Book-Specific Web Site

Go to the *Management and Supervision in Law Enforcement* Web site at http://info.wadsworth.com/0534616054 for student and instructor resources, including Internet Assignments and Case Studies.

CHAPTER 5

Time Management: Minute by Minute

Time management is a question not of managing the clock but of managing ourselves with respect to the clock.

—Alec Mackenzie, time management expert

Do You Know?

- What time management is?
- What the greatest management resource is?
- What is at the heart of time management?
- How the Pareto Principle applies to time management?
- How to learn where your time is actually going?
- What helps you manage time minute by minute?
- What the most common external timewasters are?
- What the learning curve principle is and how it relates to time management?
- What three words can prompt you and others to use time effectively?
- What the most common internal timewasters are?
- What creative procrastination is?
- What an effective time manager concentrates on?
- What priorities and posteriorities are?
- What the 5P Principle is?
- How to control the paper flood?
- How paperwork can be handled most efficiently?
- What the results of overdoing it might be?
- How to physically make time more productive?

Can You Define?

creative procrastination
face time
5P Principle
highlighting
learning curve principle
narrow eye span
Pareto Principle
Parkinson's Law
posteriorities
priorities
procrastination
regression
scanning
single handling
skimming
subvocalization
tickler file system
time abusers
time log
time management
Taylorism

INTRODUCTION

Voltaire, an eighteenth-century French philosopher, posed the following riddle *(Zadig: A Mystery of Fate):*

> What of all things in the world is the longest and the shortest, the swiftest and the slowest, the most divisible and the most extended, the most neglected and the most regretted, without which nothing can be done, which devours all that is little and enlivens all that is great? *The answer—time.*
>
> Nothing is longer, since it is the measure of eternity.
>
> Nothing is shorter, since it is insufficient for the accomplishment of our projects.
>
> Nothing is more slow to him that expects; nothing more rapid to him that enjoys.
>
> In greatness, it extends to infinity; in smallness, it is infinitely divisible.
>
> All men neglect it; all regret the loss of it; nothing can be done without it.
>
> It consigns to oblivion whatever is unworthy of being transmitted to posterity, and it immortalizes such actions as are truly great.

With each promotion you receive come increases in your duties and responsibilities with no increase in the number of hours in a day or extra days in the week. As Robert Frost astutely noted: "By working faithfully eight hours a day, you may eventually get to be boss and work twelve hours a day."

Frederick Winslow Taylor (1856–1915), an American engineer and efficiency expert, is best known for his time and motion studies. In these studies an efficiency expert clocked each step in a job and looked for ways to reduce the time and manpower needed. Although his system was only one of many proposed in the early 1900s, after publication of his book, *The Principles of Scientific Management* in 1911, the entire efficiency movement was often referred to as **Taylorism** (Daniels, 2002).

Time management, however, is much more than being efficient. Recall from the discussion of modes of leadership that *managers* often focus on *efficiency,* whereas *leaders* focus on *effectiveness.* Managers who are also leaders will place more emphasis on people than on tasks. However, it is helpful if they can manage their time efficiently as well as effectively.

This chapter begins with definitions of time and time management, as well as the value of time. It then discusses the importance of goals in effective time management and ways to organize your time to meet these goals. To identify how you might use time more efficiently, you should know how you are currently spending your time, so the function of time logs is described in detail. Next, the chapter discusses the importance of controlling time through use of a to-do list to make certain that priorities are set and then met through scheduling. This is followed by a look at common time abusers or unproductive time and how you might control this. One important step in managing time is controlling the paper flood and information load so common in law enforcement management. Also important is retaining what you need to remember. The chapter concludes with a discussion of how you can be most productive—without overdoing—the ultimate goal of effective time management, including the physiology of productivity.

Time Defined

Time is nature's way of keeping everything from happening all at once. On a more serious note, dictionaries define *time* as "the period between two events or during which something exists, happens or acts; measured and measurable intervals." Time is most often used in the legal sense to identify specific events. For example, "The crash occurred on January 26, 2003, at 1304 hours."

In the everyday, practical sense we measure time in years, months, weeks, days, hours, minutes and seconds. We also use many devices to measure time, the most popular of which are clocks, watches and calendars.

In spite of much conversation about time, it remains elusive, mysterious and difficult to define. Einstein determined that time is one dimension of the universe and that it is relative. (Two weeks on vacation is not the same as two weeks on a diet.) It is finite, instant, constant and, in a sense, an illusion. Your time belongs to you and no one else. How you spend your time is your decision. Once used, it can never be regained. Once you have read this paragraph, the time you took to read it is lost forever.

To realize the value of one minute, ask a person who just missed a train. To realize the value of one second, ask a person who just avoided an accident. To realize the value of one millisecond, ask the person who won a silver medal in the Olympics.

Imagine for a moment that you have a special bank account and that every morning it is credited with $1,440. Whatever amount you do not use each day, however, is taken out of the account. No balance can be carried over. Naturally you would try to use every bit of that $1,440 each day and to get the most out of it. You *do* have such a bank—a time bank. Every morning when you get up you have a 1,440-minute deposit that you can either invest wisely or squander. You cannot save it for tomorrow. Sleep does count as a wise investment.

Time Management: Planning and Organizing Time

Personal growth guru Stephen Covey contends: "Time management is really a misnomer; the challenge is not to manage time, but to manage ourselves." Morgenstern (2000/2001, p.88) suggests: "Time management is the ultimate in self-improvement. It is the foundation that will enable you to achieve your goals in every aspect of life."

It is a primary responsibility of law enforcement managers to use both their own time and employees' time productively, best accomplished through organization, planning and review. Most law enforcement managers and their subordinates work 40-hour weeks. Some departments schedule five 8-hour days, others four 10-hour days. Each officer has approximately 2,000 working hours annually (allowing for two weeks of vacation). A 20-year law enforcement career has 40,000 assigned working hours, without overtime. Organizing and planning these assigned work hours determines both personal and public benefit: "Do not count time, but make time count." Although this chapter focuses on work time, the suggestions apply to time away from the job as well.

Successful law enforcement managers at all levels get more done in less time when they develop and follow efficient techniques for using assigned time. They have a sense of time importance and a sense of timing. Managing time involves managing yourself and your daily life. It does not necessarily mean working longer or faster. Trying to do everything is not managing. Time management is committing yourself to making quality use of your time to accomplish what is important.

Time management is planning and organizing time to accomplish your most important goals in the shortest time possible.

According to Morgenstern (p.88): "Just as a closet is a limited space for objects, a schedule is a limited space for tasks. In fact, each day is simply a container, a storage unit that has a definite capacity. When you start to look at time as having borders—just like space—you'll become more realistic about how much you can accomplish."

Time management is a tool to move people from where they are to where they want to be. This means planning ahead. Jasper (2000, p.13) observes: "Most people do not plan at all. Those who do often plan from the wrong end. They list the tasks to get them through the day, then do the same thing every day of the week until the year has gone by." Jasper suggests:

> Effective planning works the opposite way. What you want to accomplish by the end of the year determines what you need to do each month.
>
> What must be done this month determines what you should do today and tomorrow. Schedule these tasks into your calendar working backward from your goals.

Time Management in a Service Organization

Many times effective time management is evaluated based on the amount of tangible product produced—this much time spent produced these results. However, service organizations such as law enforcement departments have inherent responsibilities that are time consuming yet not explicitly action-oriented and that yield few tangible results. Nonetheless, these responsibilities are vital to effective customer service, citizen satisfaction and community protection. Such tasks include consoling victims, talking with citizens, having a physical presence in high traffic accident locations, following leads in a criminal investigation in which the actual monetary loss was low and so forth. To reiterate, effective managers/leaders focus more on people than on tasks. This may appear incongruous with the focus on "tasks to be accomplished" in this chapter, but in order to have time for their people, managers need to *make* the time. This chapter focuses on ways to do so.

Value of Time

What is your time worth to you? Have you ever determined in dollars how much your time is worth? Divide your annual salary by the number of annual work hours, usually 2,080 hours. For example, if your annual salary was $50,000, your hourly rate would be $24. If you add in your fringe benefits, your total annual compensation would be much more than that. Your time is valuable and should not be squandered.

When law enforcement managers were asked if they felt they had enough time to do what their jobs demanded, the majority said they could use more hours in the workday. This is *not* a viable solution to time problems.

It is ironic that managers who exercise good time management and complete their duties are often given extra responsibilities. In this situation managers who fail to use time wisely are, in effect, rewarded.

Time is the greatest management resource.

All other resources can be increased, but time is fixed. If a person could gain 2 more productive hours a day, times 5 days per week, times 50 working weeks, that would be 500 hours or 3 extra *months* for each person in the department.

Returning to the definition of time management as "planning and organizing time to accomplish your most important goals in the shortest time possible," the logical place to begin with time management is with *goals*.

Goals and Time Management

The importance of goals has already been stressed. Goals are at the heart of efficiency and time management. It is a waste of time to do very well what you do not need to do at all.

At the heart of time management are *goals*.

Ask yourself: "What is the most valuable use of my time right now?" You can answer this only by looking at the department's goals and objectives and what you must do to accomplish them. Time management needs to be both short and long range. Think in terms of the year, the month, the week, the day and the precise moment.

Segmenting Tasks

Some time management consultants advocate setting up a **tickler file system** consisting of the following 45 files:

- 2 files, one each for the next 2 years beyond the current year.
- 12 files, one for each month of the current year.
- 31 files, one for each day of the current month.

One reason time management is so difficult is the human tendency to want to accomplish everything at once. Time management requires that time be managed, that is, organized and divided.

Some important activities may be best set aside until the following year. Simply knowing they are in the upcoming year's file clears your mind of worrying about them for the present. You may put off many activities one or more months. Put them into the appropriate monthly file.

At the end of the month, take the next month's file and divide the activities into the days available. At the end of each day—and this is a key to time management—take the next day's file and plan how to accomplish the activities slated for that day.

Goals, Objectives and the Pareto Principle

As you consider goals and objectives, the **Pareto Principle** comes into play. Alfredo Pareto was an Italian economist who observed that 20 percent of the Italian population owned 80 percent of the wealth. This and similar observations led Pareto to the conclusion that results and their causes are unequally distributed. The percentage is not always 20/80, but it is usually close. Consider the following:

- Twenty percent of your activities may produce 80 percent of your accomplishments.
- Twenty percent of your problem officers may account for 80 percent of the department's problems.
- Twenty percent of your outstanding officers may account for 80 percent of your department's successes.
- Effective leaders pay attention to the 20 percent and concentrate on improvement in those areas.

Effective time management uses the Pareto Principle to identify the 20 percent *(few) vital tasks* that will account for 80 percent of the desired results. It also identifies and places as low priority the 80 percent *(many) trivial tasks* clamoring for attention.

Figure 5.1 illustrates the Pareto Principle.

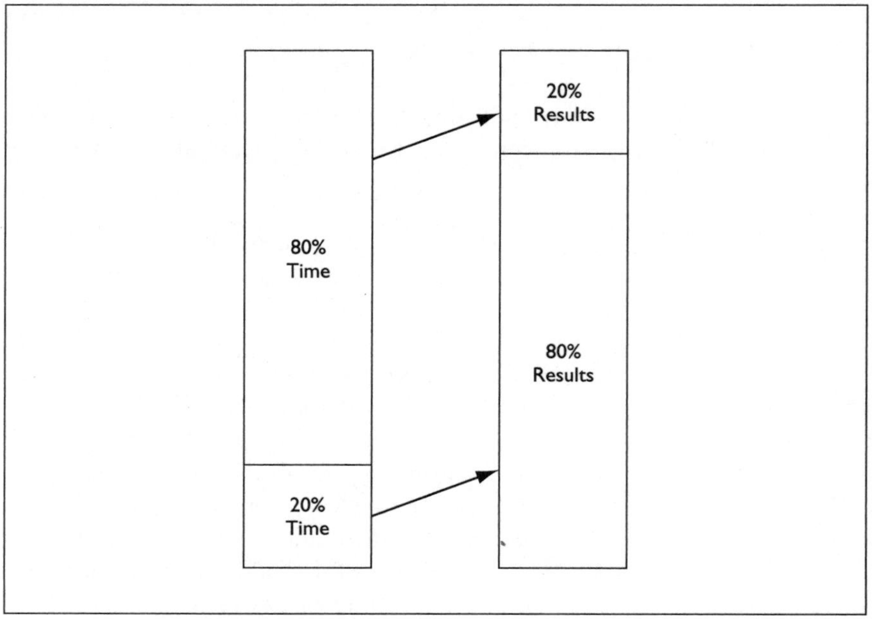

Figure 5.1
The Pareto Principle

Setting Priorities

Time is very important to police departments. In fact, response time presents an interesting time management situation. Although research shows that response time has limited effect on arrest rates, it is important for citizen satisfaction and citizens' perceptions of police performance. *Most* departments have to prioritize calls. In some cities, during certain days of the week or times of the day, there may be a backlog of five to ten calls. Field officers have to prioritize calls for service according to severity and importance. Investigators set priorities for cases to follow up, based on the information furnished by the preliminary investigation report. Field officers' and investigators' responses are reactive. They have little or no control over the types of services required on any specific shift; they have only data based on experience. As departments become more proactive, time management will become more relevant.

Morgenstern (p.88) notes: "To really tackle time, you have to look at the big picture. No matter how hectic life gets, the most successful people are able to rise above the chaos and keep their perspective because they have an overriding vision of life. If you don't have clear goals and priorities, you won't know where to spend your time. In today's fast-paced world, it's so easy to get lost in the details: the daily demands, the endless chores and tasks that make your head spin." Without goals you don't know where you are going and may end up where you don't want to be. You also need to differentiate between the urgent and the important.

Urgent vs. Important

Lyndon Johnson once noted: "The trouble with our country is that we constantly put second things first." This, unfortunately, is often true of managers as well. Managers often spend too much time on urgent things and not enough time on the important things. Gresham's Law of Time Management says: "The urgent drives out the important." The little stuff, phones, meetings, interruptions and the like keep managers from getting to the long-term tasks that need doing.

The importance of prioritizing is well illustrated by the story of the time management expert who was speaking to a group of high-powered overachievers. He set a 1-gallon Mason jar on a table along with a dozen fist-sized rocks and carefully began placing the rocks into the jar one at a time until it was filled to the top. At this point he asked, "Is the jar full?"

Everyone in the group shouted, "Yes."

The time management expert replied, "Really?" and reached under the table. He pulled out a bucket of gravel and dumped it in, shaking the jar to cause the pieces of gravel to work themselves down into the spaces between the big rocks. He asked the group once more, "Is the jar full?"

"Probably not," one of the group answered.

"Good," the expert replied, reaching under the table for a bucket of sand. He dumped the sand into the jar, and it went into all the spaces left between the rocks and gravel. Once more he asked, "Is the jar full?"

"No," the group shouted.

Again he said, "Good." Then he took a pitcher of water and began to pour it in until the jar was filled to the brim. Then he asked the group, "What is the point?"

One eager young man raised his hand and said, "No matter how full your schedule is, if you try really hard, you can always fit some more things in it."

"Sorry," the speaker replied. "That's not the point. This illustration teaches us that if you don't put the 'big rocks' in first, you'll never get them all in."

So tonight, or in the morning, when you are reflecting on this short story, ask yourself, "What are the 'big rocks' in my life?" Then put those in your jar first.

Organizing Time

Law enforcement officers can easily visualize the time available for each workday and may also plan for the week, but few officers at any level plan beyond a month. Seldom do people think of their law enforcement careers as 40,000 hours. After a career is over, it is a rare law enforcement officer who would not look back and say: "I could have accomplished a lot more."

This chapter presents several ways to organize and plan time. Select the method you like best or devise your own. The system you use does not matter, only that you do something to make your time more productive. The first step is to know how you are actually spending your time.

Time Logs and Lists

A **time log** is a detailed list of how you spend your time each day. Keeping time logs and lists will show you how you actually use your time. Maintain such logs and lists only until you see which activities actually fill your work time.

> Keeping a daily log or time list tells you how you really spend your time, as opposed to how you perceive you spend it.

Until goals are established and can be adjusted to the actual daily use of time, a great disparity often exists between what people *think* they do and what they *actually* do. Some time experts suggest that a time log be made once a year for several days to a week. When your job changes, make a new time log.

Four Sample Time-Use Logs

The chart in Figure 5.2 asks you to list your starting time for the workday and the ending time of each task you perform.

For example, if you start at 0800 and your first task is to make a to-do list, which takes 10 minutes, your task ends at 0810, and you are ready for the next task, which may be returning telephone calls. The difference between the times is the total task time.

Figure 5.3 lists goals and objectives without regard to actual time use.

Approximately 50 percent of your time should be spent on priority 1 goals, 40 percent on priority 2 goals and 10 percent on priority 3 goals. Variations of these percentages will occur with levels of manager responsibility. The executive manager may spend 60 to 65 percent of time on priority 1 goals; command or middle-level managers, 40 percent; and first-line supervisors, 30 percent.

Determine actual time use for a designated period (perhaps a week). Then review the list and make decisions regarding delegating, shortening time devoted to certain tasks or eliminating a task. If the manager position should change, keep a new time log.

DAILY USE OF TIME

DATE ________________ RANK OR POSITION ________________

ARRIVAL TIME AT WORK ________________

END TIME	TASK PERFORMED	EVALUATION

This is a task chart, not a goals chart.
List each task in detail.
Mark down time task ended.
Continue listing tasks and end time for entire day.
At end of day, review and evaluate each task as either acceptable or to be delegated, lengthened, shortened or eliminated. Notice at the end of the day the time spent on tasks that were acceptable or to be delegated.

Figure 5.2
Sample Log for Daily Use of Time

DAILY PRIORITIES AND GOAL LIST

A. Most Important—Priority 1

1 ________________ 2 ________________
3 ________________ 4 ________________
5 ________________ 6 ________________
7 ________________ 8 ________________

B. Necessary, but Less Important—Priority 2

1 ________________ 2 ________________
3 ________________ 4 ________________
5 ________________ 6 ________________
7 ________________ 8 ________________

C. Least Important—Priority 3

1 ________________ 2 ________________
3 ________________ 4 ________________
5 ________________ 6 ________________
7 ________________ 8 ________________

At the end of the day, compare this list with the time-use log. Think about what you actually did and what your priorities were. Eventually bring the two into one daily work plan.

Figure 5.3
Sample Daily Priorities and Goal List

DAILY USE OF TIME

Time	Activity	Yes	No	Del	Elim
0800–0815	______	___	___	___	___
0815–0830	______	___	___	___	___
0830–0845	______	___	___	___	___
0845–0900	______	___	___	___	___
0900–0915	______	___	___	___	___
0915–0930	______	___	___	___	___
0930–0945	______	___	___	___	___
0945–1000	______	___	___	___	___
1000–1015	______	___	___	___	___
1015–1030	______	___	___	___	___
1030–1045	______	___	___	___	___
1045–1100	______	___	___	___	___

Continue to record times for your entire workday schedule. Make a chart for your workday using whatever time intervals you desire: 5 minutes, 15 minutes, ½ hour or 1 hour. At the end of the day, decide what tasks were necessary or could be delegated or eliminated. Check the applicable column on the right side of the page for the action you took.

Figure 5.4
Sample Log for Daily Use of Time (in 15-minute Increments)

Later compare the actual time logs with the lists of goals and objectives for the position, and make adjustments to bring both lists into one actual time plan. You will need to make adjustments, but once you have learned to make a time-use plan, making changes will be easy. Figure 5.4 lists time in 15-minute periods. Otherwise, it is the same as Figure 5.2.

Figure 5.5 lists only what is considered *unproductive* time, focusing on bad habits. Most people have at least one bad work habit. Many have several. Analyze time logs to identify timewasters.

Law enforcement managers should list their five to ten top timewasters and then make a plan to overcome them. In fact, timewasters could be a training focus or the topic of a staff meeting. Changing bad time habits requires a desire to change. You must put the new habits into daily practice until they are firmly a part of your work routine and continue to practice them until the old habits disappear.

Using the Time Logs

A time log gives you an idea of what you do at work, but you do not always know if you make the most productive use of your time. This is especially true of management positions.

Patrol officers promoted to sergeant do not continue to perform the same duties; in departments where sergeants have eight or more patrol officers to manage, sergeants will find that managing the officers is a full-time occupation. In some larger departments sergeants may have up to 25 officers to manage, a severe test for the first-line supervisor. Sergeants need to know how time is actually being used.

Moving up the ladder of command, lieutenants and captains will not perform the same functions they performed as sergeants. Likewise, police executives

UNPRODUCTIVE TIME LOG

Date ______________________

Task	Approximate time spent on task

At the end of the day, determine whether a task should be: (1) eliminated from the schedule or (2) retained even though unproductive because your position requires it to meet public demand.

After several weeks review this chart with other charts for the 2-week period and determine how often the same task occurs. Is it daily, weekly, monthly or seasonal, or is there some other reason the task falls to your position when perhaps it could be performed at another level? Make the necessary adjustments.

Figure 5.5
Sample Log for Unproductive Time

(chiefs, superintendents or sheriffs) will not perform the same duties as the command level. Each level will find the time log a valuable tool for providing an accurate picture of time use.

Without a time log you do not know where time goes, how much time is spent on what duties and how frequently activities occur. Usually only a small portion of the day is uncommitted, but how is it used? A time log shows where it actually goes. After you make revisions, the time log should match the desired time allotted for specific goals and objectives. You have then achieved effective time management.

After logging your time, ask: What am I doing that I don't really have to do? What am I doing that someone else could do? What am I doing that I could do more efficiently? What activities or events are the biggest time-wasters for me? How can I eliminate them? What am I doing that wastes others' time? How can I change? When are my productivity peaks and valleys throughout each day? When do I tackle high-priority projects? How often am I interrupted? Why? Can I control or reduce the number of interruptions?

Your daily log should help you determine when you are at your peak. You can then schedule high-priority work during your peak working hours, and use your low-energy periods for low-priority work such as filing, catching up on reading and returning nonemergency phone calls.

Objections to Time Logs

The most common objection to keeping time logs is: "I don't have time." It does take time, but the payoff is worth it. Others claim that time use varies from day to day. Again true, yet patterns do exist. Some say their days are already full. Some object to putting what they do on paper. In some instances these objections are only excuses to continue with time-wasting habits.

The time log is a tool to help you determine whether a workday is full of the right tasks. If the tasks are wrong for the position, you can delegate, eliminate or otherwise change them. If all the tasks are right and the assigned work schedule is full, you have achieved good time management.

Every manager's time is broken up by diversions, unexpected distractions and interruptions of all types. It is realistic to allocate time for these. Knowing when and how frequently interruptions occur helps you reduce the time you spend on them. Also plan some time during the day for creative thinking about your job.

Controlling Time

The first step in controlling time is to ensure that you are accomplishing the tasks that must get done.

The Daily To-Do List

Although it is not necessary to continuously keep a daily log, it *is* critical to plan each day's time. This is best done the night before. Simply write down everything you should accomplish the following day. Then prioritize the items as follows:

A Acute or critical—must be done.
B Big or important—should do when A is finished.
C Can wait—nice to do if time allows.
D Delegate.
E Eliminate.

The military uses a similar approach with ! = done ASAP, A = within the next few days, B = within the next week, C = within the next month, and L = long term (anything over a month to complete).

The daily to-do list may be the single most important time management tool. It helps you manage minute by minute.

If you make a to-do list the night before, you have a jump on the next day. Sleep will come easier, and this in itself can reduce stress and tension. As Wetmore (2000, p.162) suggests: "Noting the items on paper gets them out of your head and in front of you, which helps bring them into focus, as well as prevents duplication and overlooking an important item." Do not make the list too full. Leave some time for planning and for those unexpected things that inevitably arise.

Mackenzie (1972) also describes five categories for activities:

- Important and urgent (for example, budget due next week).
- Important but not urgent (getting physically fit).
- Urgent but not important (a meeting you are expected to attend—politically important, but not task related).
- Busy work (cleaning files rather than starting on a project).
- Wasted time (sitting in traffic with no audiocassettes or cellular phone).

Of these five categories, the biggest problem is usually the important but not urgent task. Such tasks tend to be put off indefinitely. To integrate long-term tasks into your daily schedule without adding overtime, break it down into small, manageable steps and set interim deadlines on your calendar. Build in a set amount of time each day to work on the project.

Consistently write out your to-do list in one place each day. It does little good to make a list and then to lose it on a cluttered desk.

Scheduling

Morgenstern (pp.94–96) has a somewhat more detailed approach to the to-do list that not only prioritizes the items in the list but specifies when tasks will be completed and how much time they will take. She uses a *Space* formula for each item on the to-do list: "Space is an acronym that stands for Sort tasks, Purge whatever you can, Assign a time, Containerize the time needed to do the task and Equalize."

To *sort* the tasks, place an estimate of the amount of time each will take. When doing so, keep in mind the "Times Three" rule; that is, it generally takes three times longer to do something than you think. Be realistic. With a realistic time for each task, *purge* the list by determining whether someone else might be able to do the task faster or better. Noncreative, repetitive tasks and special projects can usually be easily delegated. Next *assign a time;* for example, work on a major project from 10:00 am until noon. The trick is to *containerize* the time needed; that is, start and end when you scheduled. Don't procrastinate; don't allow interruptions; and don't let it drag on. Containerizing also helps conquer the need for perfection.

The last step is to *equalize,* refine, maintain and adapt the schedule as needed. As Morgenstern (p.96) notes: "Time management is not a stagnant process. It is a constant interaction between your goals and the changing rhythms and tempos of life."

The Time Map

Morgenstern (p.92) also suggests that managers make use of time maps: "To make sure you leave enough time for the activities that support your personal big picture, you will need to draw up what I call a time map—a visual diagram of your daily, weekly, and monthly schedule. It's a powerful tool. Instead of feeling that you have to act on every request the minute it crosses your path, you can glance at your time map, determine when you have time and schedule it or skip it."

Other Methods of Organizing Time

The Franklin Day Planner is a time-management notebook used by people all over the world and an option for busy law enforcement managers. Another option is to turn your car into a training center. If you live to be 77 and drive 10,000 miles a year, you'll spend *three* years of your life in your vehicle. Yet another option is to do the least-liked tasks first. It is natural to avoid things you do not want to do. The trouble is, when you waste energy avoiding the bad things, you may lose your ability to get anything else done. One suggestion for predominantly right-brained managers is to jot each task to be accomplished on color-coded notes and stick them around the desk.

After you have identified, prioritized and scheduled the necessary tasks, the next step is to find the time to do them by identifying unproductive time.

Time Abusers: Combating Unproductive Time

Managers in law enforcement experience the same unproductive time problems found in other professions. Time abusers tend to develop into time-use monsters if not controlled.

Develop an image of time respect. Managers often contribute to their own demise by trying to solve too many problems for others when they should be solving their own. Some of this time abuse is normal and must be accepted as part of a manager's job. Generally **time abusers** can be divided into external—generated from outside—and self-generated, or internal.

External Timewasters

Among the most common outside or external timewasters are *interruptions.* Managers are interrupted approximately every eight to ten minutes. Controlling and reducing these interruptions is important not only to save time but also to maintain continuity of thought.

Among the most common external time abusers are the telephone, the e-mail chime, people who "drop in," nonessential meetings, socializing and "firefighting," or handling crises.

The Telephone

The telephone offers several advantages. You save time when you make a call instead of traveling. You also have more control over the timing of a telephone conversation than you do over a personal visit.

However, the telephone also heads the list of timewasters. Allowing too many calls, permitting conversations to last too long, failing to screen incoming calls, failing to keep conversations purposeful and allowing calls to interrupt quality creative time can be devastating to productivity. Keep a telephone time log if you find the telephone a problem.

Avoid getting caught playing telephone tag. Leave a time to receive calls and find out when individuals you are trying to call will be available. Consider leaving your e-mail address on your voice mail message. This gives you greater control of your time and eliminates small talk. In addition, you can print out your e-mail messages. When making calls, plan what you are going to talk about and stick to the subject. Eliminate as much small talk as possible, using a timer if necessary.

Screen your calls through a secretary, a receptionist, Caller ID or an answering machine that can be monitored. Always answer the phone with paper and pencil in hand. Write down the name of the person who is calling and take careful notes. This will save time later.

Always have your calls held during your most productive, creative times and during important meetings, whether they are one-on-one or in a larger group. One effective timesaver is to "batch" your calls. This relates directly to what is known as the learning curve principle.

The **learning curve principle** states that grouping similar tasks can reduce the amount of time each takes, sometimes by as much as 80 percent.

According to the learning curve, each time you repeat the same task, you become more efficient. Telephone calls are one responsibility for which the learning curve can help manage time.

Voice mail can compound the problem, however. Some managers arrive in the morning, check their voice mail and are greeted with: "You have 37 messages." Not a good way to start the day but a reality in many departments.

The secret is to reduce the disadvantages of telephones and multiply the advantages. Telephone companies have films you can use or trainers who can meet with your staff and point out the most efficient use of telephones.

The E-Mail Chime

The e-mail chime or the message "You've got mail" can also be a distraction. Most type-A personalities cannot hear the chime or message without checking to see who just e-mailed them. The chime or message can be turned off to eliminate this distraction.

Drop-In Visitors

Put limits on the visits of people who just stop in without an appointment. Be polite but firm. At times you may need to simply close your door when priorities demand that you have time alone.

Hang a "Privacy, Please" sign on your door during periods when you need uninterrupted time. Arrange specific times when others know your door is "open." Communication is, after all, critical to good management, but it also needs to be managed. Be available to others outside your own office. Then you have greater control over ending a conversation.

Stand up when someone enters your office, and conduct the conversation with both of you standing. Such conversations tend to be brief. Keep socializing to a minimum. Get to the topic that brought the drop-in visitor to your office and stick with that topic. If the person who stops by for a business reason asks,

"Got a minute?" consider looking at your watch and saying, "Actually I have exactly five minutes. What can I do for you?" The drop-in will assume you have something important to attend to and will probably respect your time.

If a drop-in visitor stays on, you might try saying, "One more thing before you go . . . ." Or you might take the person out in the hall to show him or her something—anything. Of course, you may arrange for a co-worker to interrupt you with an "emergency" if a drop-in visitor stays longer than a specified time.

Be honest. You might simply say, "I've enjoyed our talk, but I really must get *back to work.*" That simple phrase will not only be a clue to the visitor to leave but also serve as a prompt to you.

The words *back to work* will prompt you and others to keep on task.

Meetings

As much as 50 percent of managers' time may be spent in meetings, and of this, 50 percent of the time is often wasted. Think about the hourly rate of each person attending and be sure the department is getting its money's worth. Wasted time includes not only the time in the meeting but also the time spent winding up a particular task before the meeting, traveling to and from the meeting and then getting back on task.

Organizations might consider designating someone to be a "meeting attender," to go to meetings and make brief written reports. This would create more paperwork but take less time than you attending the meeting. This practice could be useful for informational meetings that do not require the manager's personal participation. Avoid nonessential meetings, and do not call them yourself.

If your sole purpose for attending a meeting is to make a presentation, find out what time the presentation is expected, arrive a few minutes before that time, make the presentation and then excuse yourself. If you find yourself at a nonproductive meeting, it can be most efficient to simply excuse yourself and leave. Use common sense, however, especially if the meeting was called by and is being chaired by your superior.

Socializing

Socializing is a factor in inefficient phone calls, encounters with drop-in visitors and meetings. Relationships are very important, and socializing is an important part of relationships. However, socializing should be confined to coffee breaks, lunch or before and after work. The phrase mentioned earlier, "I've got to get *back to work,*" reminds co-workers that you are not getting paid to socialize.

Political Game Playing

Although most managers seek to avoid politics, you cannot avoid a certain amount of political game playing. If the chief wants to talk about the grandchildren, subordinates would be wise to listen. Seek ways, however, to keep such time to a minimum.

"Firefighting"—Dealing with Crises

Law enforcement managers can expect to confront the unexpected daily. It comes with the job. Allow time in each day for these crises so you can deal with them calmly and rationally. Anticipate what might occur and have policies developed. Is the department likely to receive a bomb threat? To undergo a natural disaster? To be overrun by gang members?

If a crisis occurs for which no policy exists, get the facts, remain objective and think before acting. Then, when time permits, develop a policy for the situation should it arise again.

Internal Timewasters

Not all timewasters come from the outside. Many are self-imposed or the fault of colleagues.

Among the most common internal timewasters are procrastination, failure to set goals and objectives, failure to prioritize, failure to delegate, personal errands, indecision, failure to plan and lack of organization.

Procrastination

Procrastination is putting off until tomorrow what has already been put off until today. For some people the greatest labor-saving device is tomorrow. Do not delay things. Get them done. Get right to work on priorities.

One reason for procrastination is fear that if you do it, it will be wrong. Set a goal and think only of the goal. So what if you make a mistake? The person who makes no mistakes usually makes nothing at all! Think, "I can do it, and do it now." Motivational speaker Zig Ziglar, author of *See You at the Top,* gives members of his audiences a round piece of wood bearing the word *tuit.* He chides them that they can no longer say they will do something when they get "around to it" because they already have one.

The following techniques might help combat procrastination:

- Start with your most unpleasant task to get it out of the way.
- Set aside half an hour a day to work on a given project—schedule the time to do it.
- Do not worry about doing a task perfectly the first time through.
- Work briskly. Speed up your actions.

Another effective way to avoid procrastination is to set deadlines and let others know about them. If others are counting on you to have a task completed by a specific date, chances are you will do it. Accept 100 percent responsibility for completing tasks on time. Help others to do likewise. Finish tasks. Procrastination is one of your worst enemies.

The Air Force Academy teaches the two laws of procrastinaton. The first law: If you wait until the last minute, things take only a minute to get done. The second law: the sooner you get behind, the more time you allow yourself to catch back up.

Gleeson (2000) suggests that you realize procrastination itself is a habit. You become so used to putting things off that you keep doing so without thinking about it. The best way to break a bad habit is to replace it with a good one. "Change your 'Do it later' attitude to 'Do it now.'"

Although you want to overcome the human tendency to procrastinate, you should learn to practice *creative procrastination.*

Creative procrastination is putting off those things that do not really matter.

If you can put tasks off long enough, they probably will not have to be done. A simple example of this is sending holiday greeting cards. If you really do not feel an urgent need to send them and if you can procrastinate long enough, the holiday will pass and so will the need to send them—at least this year.

Failure to Set Goals and Objectives and to Prioritize

Too much of each day is spent by people, managers included, doing very well things they do not need to do at all.

Effective time managers concentrate on doing the right thing, rather than on doing things right.

The temptation is to clear up all the small things first so the mind is clear for the "big stuff." What often happens is that the whole day is taken up with the small stuff. Or doing the small stuff saps so much energy that little is left for the big stuff. Too many managers become bogged down in routine activities.

How do you differentiate between the trivial many and the significant few—those 20 percent described in the Pareto Principle? Consider how combat triage officers divide the wounded into three groups:

- Those who will die no matter what—make comfortable.
- Those who will live no matter what—give minimal medical attention.
- Those who will survive only with medical attention—focus attention here.

The same can be done within law enforcement agencies. Think of the consequences of what you do. Will accomplishing a given task have a positive payoff? Avoid a negative consequence? What will happen if you *do not* get a specific task done? Clearing away the trivial tasks to leave room for single-minded concentration simply does not work. It has no payoff. *You never get to the bottom of the stack.*

Effective managers set **priorities**—tasks that they must do, have a big payoff and avoid negative consequences. They also set **posteriorities**—tasks that they do *not* have to do, have a minimal payoff and very limited negative consequences.

Many managers excel at setting priorities but have no grasp of setting posteriorities. A day has only so many hours. For each new task a manager takes on, one task should be cut out. To continue to take on new responsibilities without delegating or eliminating others is courting disaster—often in the form of burnout.

Effective managers know how to say no. In fact, one of the most potent time management tools is the simple word no. When they cannot say no, effective managers know how to ask for help and to delegate.

Failure to Delegate

Many managers think that the only way something will get done right is to do it themselves. Such managers need to ask who did it before me and who will do it after me? The effective manager is one who can be gone for a few days or even weeks and everything continues smoothly during the absence. If you do not learn to delegate, there will never be another person trained to perform the work in times of crisis.

Delegate whenever possible. Train subordinates, trust them, set limited and clear expectations, provide the necessary authority for delegated tasks and give credit when they have completed the task. Delegation gives strength to the delegator and the person delegated to. It is not an abdication of responsibility.

Delegation moves organizational communication downward. Delegation must be based on mutual trust, acceptance and a spirit of cooperation between all parties. In addition, subordinates must be empowered to do the delegated tasks.

Put delegated tasks in writing with set time limits. Keep records and follow through. Do not over-delegate to the same few workers. Delegation helps people develop and spreads responsibility throughout the organization so goals and objectives are more easily attained.

Personal Errands

Only in emergencies should personal errands be attended to during on-duty time. It does not leave a good impression to see law enforcement managers on personal errands during working hours.

Indecision

Subordinates have a reasonable expectation that managers will make final decisions, especially on high-priority issues. Indecisiveness indicates a lack of self-confidence and is most frequently caused by fear of making a mistake. Approach mistakes as learning experiences; the biggest mistake may be never making a mistake. Understanding the decision-making processes described in Chapter 4 can make this managerial responsibility less threatening.

Failure to Plan

The saying goes: "Most people don't plan to fail; they simply fail to plan." Managers must learn to recognize problems and determine their causes, or time will be lost. Working the hardest or doing the most work is not necessarily the best answer if the work you choose is not of value. The average person will spend more time planning a vacation than planning a career.

The **5P Principle** states: Proper planning prevents poor performance.

Planning the use of time may save time threefold, perhaps more. If you do not take time to plan to do it right, you may have to find time to do it over.

Lack of Organization

Desk signs may *incorrectly* proclaim: "A cluttered desk is the sign of genius." If you cannot see the top of your desk, it is cluttered. Do not get rid of the clutter by putting it in the drawer. Take some action to get rid of it. Out of sight does *not* necessarily mean out of mind. Set aside time once a week to eliminate clutter. Of course, the right-brained reader might be thinking: "If a cluttered desk reflects a cluttered mind, what is an empty desk a sign of?" The following suggestions may help your office organization:

- Keep on your desk only the project you are currently working on.
- Keep reference books organized and in easy reach but off your desk.
- Keep office supplies such as paper clips in your desk.
- Set aside a certain time each day for reading.

In addition to keeping your desk and office organized and neat, keep your projects organized. Use organization charts and flowcharts to graphically portray your goals and objectives, work plans and schedules. Use tickler files to find information faster. Know where and how to find needed information.

A Caution

Remember that people are more important than schedules and plans. Put a priority on people, not on going through that pile on your desk and checking things off a to-do list.

Controlling the Paper Flood and Information Load

Knowledge is doubling every two and one-half years. One issue of the *New York Times* conveys as much information as a person living in the sixteenth century would obtain in a lifetime. The information age places tremendous demands on everyone, especially managers. Managers cannot ignore the paper flood because much of it is information vital to doing an effective job.

Control the paper flood by using single handling for most items, improving reading skills, delegating or sharing some reading tasks and adding less to the paper flood yourself.

Managers must control paperwork or it will control them. Law enforcement tasks generate extensive paperwork because of the legal requirement to document information. Reports are a large time problem. The sheer volume of reports makes them not only time consuming to read but also difficult to absorb.

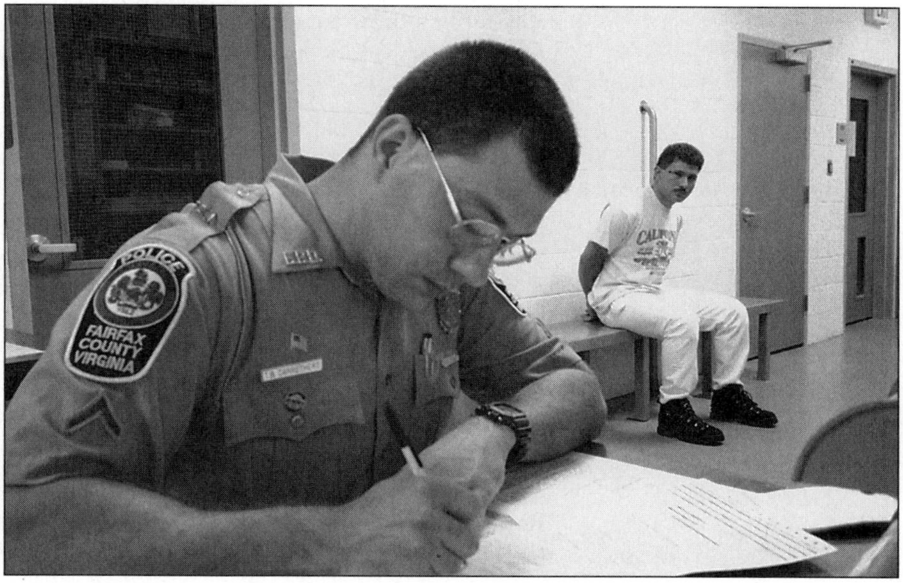

© Shepherd Sherbell/CORBIS SABA

Police administators must control paperwork, or it will control them. Here a police officer from Fairfax, VA, fills out booking paperwork on an arrest.

In addition to service and offense-related reports, managers deal with mountains of other printed information. Effective managers have a system for handling everything that lands in their "in" baskets, whether from an internal or external source. One system that works for many includes four categories:

1. Throw it away—opened or unopened depending on the return address.
2. Route it to someone else (delegate).
3. Take action on it.
4. File it for later action or reference.

This system incorporates **single handling,** that is, not picking up a piece of paper until you are ready to *do* something with it.

Handle paperwork only once—single handling increases efficiency tremendously.

Once printed information is picked up, take action: toss it, pass it on, file it or act on it. The system works best when a specific time is allotted to handle paperwork. Remember the learning curve and the efficiency in "batching" tasks, that is, doing similar tasks at the same time. Single handling also applies to e-mails. In addition, color coding e-mails helps to visually prioritize what needs to be looked at immediately. E-mails from superiors might be in red. Subfolders might be created to store e-mails relating to the same subject. E-mails can also be grouped by open issues and closed issues. Managers who receive 20, 30 or more e-mails a day need some system to keep their e-mails organized.

Organize the printed information you refer to often. Information that you use every day can be condensed on file cards; put into a Rolodex; added to personal directories, address books and calendars; written on to-do lists; or placed in action files or reference files. Use computer files or microfilm to retain information for long periods in an easily accessible, retrievable form. Prepare master indexes to locate such stored information.

Controlling the paper flood increases your decision-making capabilities, permits planning and lessens the sense of guilt when you do not complete all tasks on schedule. Have a specific place to put everything that comes into your office. Have a working file for frequently used files where they can be reached without leaving your chair.

Another way to control the paper flood is to improve reading efficiency. Learn the difference between **scanning**—reading material rapidly for specific information; **skimming**—reading information rapidly for the main ideas—and actually reading. Scan or skim most reports and publications; read only those of interest and importance. Go through your business reading pile at a quick, even pace, scanning for any time-sensitive material. Assess what you can take in quickly, what you don't need to know and what you need to read in more detail. Read in greater detail the items that are truly worth your attention. Keep and label only the clippings you want filed. Or copy them to read during downtime.

Three behaviors that slow down the reading process are subvocalization, regression and narrow eye span. **Subvocalization** is moving the lips and/or the tongue to form the words being read. Talking speed is 120–180 words per minute, which is also the speed of readers who subvocalize. Such reading needs to be speeded up. Normal reading is about 250 words per minute. Managers need to read 300–500 words per minute. Subvocalization can be stopped by keeping the lips together and placing the tongue against the back of the teeth when reading. This trains the brain to read and understand words without physically forming them.

Regression is looking back over previously read material, which slows normal reading. To eliminate regression, use the hand or finger sweep. As you read left to right, use the finger as a target to follow.

Narrow eye span occurs when a person focuses on one word at a time rather than taking in groups of words and phrases in one look. Adult eye span is between two and three words. To eliminate narrow eye span, search for your name in a magazine or a newspaper. Practice taking two lines at a time as fast as you can and searching back and forth. This is what you do when you look for a name in the phone book. It is necessary to increase not only reading speed but also reading comprehension. This comes only with practice.

Time spent taking a speed-reading course pays huge dividends because it will enhance your ability to scan information with greater comprehension. As you improve your reading skills, also improve your writing and speaking skills. Use fewer, more precise words.

Delegate reading or divide it among those who are good readers and interested in participating. It is inefficient for several people in the organization to be reading the same outside sources of information. Try having people volunteer to be responsible for a given source, such as *The Police Chief, Law and Order, Law Enforcement News, Police,* national news sources such as *Time* and *Newsweek* and local publications. The person who does the reading can highlight specific items of interest and route them to others within the department. Another way to share the information is to give brief updates at roll call or during regularly scheduled meetings.

Increase your computer skills, also. Many books and training sessions on using computers are available. Computers tremendously increase the ability to retrieve and coordinate information.

Use a Palm handheld device, and carry it with you at all times so you can record your thoughts. This is an advantage at meetings, when talking to others (including the media) and in other impromptu situations. It saves time as well as ideas.

Finally, do not add to the problem yourself. Some managers like to create paperwork because it gives a sense of personal power and fulfills a desire to influence others. Resist that impulse. Before you add to the paper flood, consider: Might a phone call work as well as a letter or memo? If you must write, is it as brief as possible? Who *really* needs copies? Can it be routed instead? Do you need copies of reports you are receiving? If not, ask to be taken off the distribution list. When you receive written material, if you foresee no further use for it or it will be available somewhere else, do not file it. Have a good reason for every contribution to the paper flood created, circulated or filed.

Retaining What You Need to Remember

Some information can be filed and retrieved when needed. Other information, however, should be retained in your mind. Forgetting has been called the relentless foe. Forgetting takes its greatest toll during the first day after learning something. To slow forgetting you must transfer the information from your short-term memory to long-term memory by *doing* something with it. This might include mentally asking yourself a question about something you have read and answering it, verbally summarizing an important concept to a colleague, highlighting the concept or taking notes on an article.

Highlighting is the memory method of choice for most college students, and it is an effective way to transfer information from short-term to long-term memory *if* it is done correctly. Unfortunately, most people simply highlight what they want to remember as they read. This is very ineffective and often results in almost the entire article being highlighted. To highlight effectively, read the entire article (or chapter) first. Then ask: "What is most important about what I have just read?" Then go back and highlight *after* you have finished thinking about what you have read. This is a highly effective way to improve retention.

Productivity—The Bottom Line

Effective managers use their time wisely to boost their productivity. Time management and productivity are integrally related. "Work smarter, not harder" is a truism. Simply putting in your time will not make you productive. In fact, the term **face time** has come into vogue in describing the time a person spends coming in early or staying late to impress their superiors. It is the classroom equivalent of "seat time." Sometimes the longer people work, the more tired and unproductive they become.

Overdoing it is not only harmful to your health but often hazardous to the quality of your work.

The most frequent complaint of law enforcement managers is that there are too many interruptions and too many duties and tasks to be performed to accomplish the higher-priority goals of the position. They are unable to control their time to the extent necessary and are constantly operating in a crisis management environment. It is mandatory, however, to establish control not only to accomplish priority tasks but also to make time for creativity, long-term planning and short-term goal innovation; to try new ideas, accept increased responsibilities and make better decisions.

Time is the most important and the scarcest resource managers possess. The organized use of your and all your personnel's time creates a productive department. Control time as you would budget dollars. How you spend time relates to how you can provide more or better law enforcement service. A capable time manager is easily recognized. Time management is one factor that moves employees up the organizational ladder.

With the future probability of fewer rather than more budget dollars, time will become even more important. Because each member of the law enforcement department is interrelated with total department time, the possibility of decreased personnel in ratio to workload will make time an even scarcer resource. This increased demand can be met only by efficient use of available time.

You cannot make time, but you *can* use available time better. Cyril Northcote Parkinson, a British humorist, summed it up neatly in his famous **Parkinson's Law:** "Work expands so as to fill the time available for its completion." Consider posting Parkinson's Law on the bulletin board for a week.

One simple way to boost your productivity (and that of your people) is to *defragment* your computer. Just as office filing cabinets get out of order from time to time, so do computer filing systems. If your computer seems sluggish, you might want to have your hard drive "defragged." Another simple time-saving method is to pack a lunch rather than going out for lunch every day. (This also saves money.) You might also consider positioning your office out of the traffic flow, reducing the chance of people poking their heads in just to say "hi."

The Physiology of Productivity

Although this chapter has focused on working smarter, not harder, that does not preclude the option to work *faster.* Pacing is a matter of habit. Many people walk slowly, talk slowly, think slowly and write slowly. You can physically take control of time and accomplish tasks within the time you have.

Speed yourself up. Walk briskly. Talk crisply. Write rapidly.

You can actually save several minutes each day by simply walking, talking, reading and writing faster. Break out of old habits. Show that time is important by making the most of it. High performance has much more to do with perspiration than with inspiration. Speeding up physically will carry over to your mental state. You will be constantly reminded that you have a finite amount of time to accomplish your goals and objectives. However, do not let time rule your life.

Summary

Time management means planning and organizing time to accomplish your most important goals in the shortest time possible. In fact, time is the greatest management resource available. At the heart of time management are goals—what you want to accomplish. Effective time management uses the Pareto Principle to identify the 20 percent (few) vital tasks that will account for 80 percent of the desired results. It also identifies and places as low priority the 80 percent (many) trivial tasks clamoring for attention.

Keeping a daily schedule tells you what you really do, as opposed to how you perceive that you spend your time. The daily to-do list may be the single most important time-management tool. It helps you manage minute by minute and control time abusers.

Among the most common external time abusers are the telephone, people who "drop in," nonessential meetings, socializing and "firefighting" or handling crises. When possible, *batch* tasks that are similar, such as making phone calls, because the learning curve principle states that if you do a group of similar tasks together, you can reduce the time they take, sometimes by as much as 80 percent. In addition, the words *back to work* can prompt you and others to keep on task.

Among the most common internal timewasters are procrastination, failure to set goals and objectives, failure to prioritize, failure to delegate, personal errands, indecision, failure to plan and lack of organization. One type of procrastination, however, may be effective: Creative procrastination—putting off those things that do not really matter. Effective time managers concentrate on doing the right thing rather than on doing things right.

Effective managers set priorities—tasks that they must do, have a big payoff and avoid negative consequences. They also set posteriorities—tasks that they do *not* have to do, have a minimal payoff and have very limited negative consequences. The 5P Principle states: Proper planning prevents poor performance. An important part of planning is devising a system to control the paper flood. Practices that you might use are single handling for most items, improving reading skills, delegating or sharing some reading tasks and adding less to the paper flood yourself. Handle paperwork only once—single handling increases efficiency tremendously.

Failure to manage time and ending up overdoing is not only harmful to your health but often is hazardous to the quality of your work. Ways to accomplish more without overdoing include speeding yourself up, walking briskly, talking crisply, and reading and writing rapidly. Minute by minute, you *can* manage your time.

Discussion Questions

1. Do you personally use some type of time list or log? A to-do list? Compare yours with those of others in the class.
2. What is the most unproductive time of your workday?
3. What are your greatest timewasters? Compare yours with those of others in the class.
4. What time management ideas presented in this chapter seem most workable to you? Least workable? Why?

5. How do you determine whether a meeting is necessary? Plan the agenda of a meeting? Control a meeting?
6. What examples of Parkinson's Law can you cite in your life or experience?
7. How much of your time is used for paperwork, including correspondence, planning, analysis, reading in-house publications and improving yourself?
8. How would you prioritize your work time?
9. How does the discretionary time of police officers working in departments using the community policing philosophy differ from those using a more traditional approach?
10. What examples of the Pareto Principle have you experienced?

InfoTrac College Edition Assignment

Use InfoTrac College Edition to help answer the Discussion Questions as appropriate.

Search for the topic of *time management.* Record how many entries you found. Then select one entry to read carefully and summarize. Be sure to include the full citation for your summary. Be prepared to share your summary with the class.

References

Daniels, George. "Taylor, Frederick, Winslow." *World Book Online Americas Edition,* October 21, 2002.

Gleeson, Kerry. *The Personal Efficiency Program: How to Get Organized to Do More Work in Less Time.* New York: John Wiley & Sons, 2000.

Jasper, Jan. "Take Back Your Time: Time Wasters . . . Time Savers—Planning Pays." *Bottom Line,* February 15, 2000, pp.13–14.

MacKenzie, R. Alec. *The Time Trap.* New York: AMACOM, 1972.

Morgenstern, Julie. "Taming the Time Monster." From *Time Management From the Inside Out.* Henry Holt and Company, 2000. Book excerpt in *Forbes Small Business,* December 2000/January 2001, pp.87–96.

Wetmore, Donald E. "Control the Free-Fall: Three Rules to Increase Productivity." *Successful Meetings,* September 2000, p.162.

Book-Specific Web Site

Go to the *Management and Supervision in Law Enforcement* Web site at http://info.wadsworth.com/05346160654 for student and instructor resources, including Internet Assignments and Case Studies.

CHAPTER 6

Budgeting and Managing Costs Creatively

Budget—a mathematical confirmation of your suspicions.
—A. Latimer

Do You Know?

- What a budget is?
- What purposes a budget serves?
- Who is responsible for preparing the budget?
- How most budgets are developed?
- Whose input is vital to any budget?
- What categories are typically included in a budget?
- What the greatest cost in a law enforcement budget usually is?
- What variance analysis is?
- What cutback budgeting involves?
- What common cost choices most organizations face?
- What the first step in managing costs is?
- Who is responsible for reducing costs?
- How subordinates might be involved in managing costs creatively?
- What are some ways a department might reduce costs? Increase revenues?
- How asset forfeiture and the Eighth Amendment are related?
- Who the lead federal funding agency is for law enforcement?

Can You Define?

accounting
accounting period
activity-based costing (ABC)
all-levels budgeting
assets
audit trail
balance sheet
block grant
bottom-line philosophy
budget
capital budget
certified public accountant (CPA)
common costs
contingency funds
cutback budgeting
depreciation
direct expenses
discretionary budget
discretionary grant
financial budget
financial statements
fiscal year
fixed costs
flexible budget
formula grant
generally accepted accounting principles (GAAPs)
indirect expenses
line items
line-item budgeting
operating budget
operating expenses
overhead
performance budgeting
petty cash fund
program budgeting
semi-variable costs
sunk cost
variable costs
variance analysis
zero-based budgeting (ZBB)

INTRODUCTION

The budget is a critical instrument in law enforcement planning, administration and operations. It is a management tool that traditionally has been used at the expense of people over profit and with not much people input. Preparing budgets is difficult because most law enforcement services are intangible. Despite these difficulties, budgets must be prepared for law enforcement agencies. Budgets are synonymous with monetary resources, which in turn are synonymous with personnel, equipment, supplies and, ultimately, the ability to provide comprehensive, continuous law enforcement services. Each agency has developed guidelines, budget forms and formats. In addition, many computer software budgeting programs are in use by law enforcement agencies at all governmental levels.

This chapter begins with a definition of budgets and a description of the purposes of budgets. Next is a listing of basic budgeting and accounting terminology. This is followed by a discussion of who is responsible for preparing the budget and the budgeting process. The chapter then focuses on budgeting systems and budget categories, followed by an explanation of how to present the budget for approval. Next is a look at monitoring the budget and the possibility of cutback budgeting. The discussion then turns to managing costs creatively including ways to reduce costs and to increase revenues. The chapter concludes with a discussion of grants: where to learn about them and how to apply for them.

Budget Defined

A **financial budget** is a plan or schedule adjusting expenses during a certain period to the estimated income for that period. Brock, et al. (1990, p.G–1) define budgeting as: "The process of planning and controlling the future operations of a business by developing a set of financial goals and evaluating performance in terms of these goals."

A budget is a working document, a tool to be used, not to be cast in stone or held in reverence. A budget, in effect, is a planning and control document, including stated financial expenditure amounts in accordance with a predetermined revenue or income. It is subject to approval by a higher authority than the person or department presenting the budget proposal.

A **budget** is a list of probable expenses and income during a given period, most often one year.

Budget can also be a verb as in, "Let's budget money for this particular project." Usually, however, it is a noun that refers to an estimate of money to be spent during a year.

Types of Budgets

Most departments have two types of budgets. The **operating budget** deals with all expenses needed to run the department: salaries, insurance, electricity and the like. The **capital budget** deals with "big ticket" items such as major equipment purchases and vehicles. Some departments also have a **discretionary budget,** which sets aside funds to be used as needed. This chapter deals with the operating budget.

Budgets are familiar tools to most people. They are used not only by law enforcement agencies, businesses and other organizations but also in personal lives. They are often viewed as negative, restrictive, something to be tolerated. But they also serve some extremely important purposes.

Purposes of Budgets

Budgets control and guide how resources are used and make those in charge of them responsible for their wise use.

Budgets serve as a plan for and a means to control resources.

Budgets establish financial parameters for department needs. The vast majority of plans and projects of the department depend on finances.

Budgets permit decision making at lower levels to work upward through the law enforcement hierarchy. First-line supervisors can present budget ideas that may ultimately be transformed into street operations. For example, the supervisor who develops an accident-prevention program and receives funding to put the program into action must be mindful of budget controls during the entire program.

Budgets also help reduce the tendency for divisions of a department to "build their own little empires" by establishing a maximum line item for each division. The detective division, the patrol division and the juvenile division may each have an allotted amount of funds. Any one division can spend only the funds approved for that division. Without budgeting, serious competition for total funds could be detrimental to the department's overall objectives.

Budgets provide an opportunity to compare expenditures with services provided. For example, the investigative division can compare personnel and other operational costs with the number of cases investigated, cases successfully closed, arrests made and property recovered.

Budgeting is a continuous process and a written commitment. Budgets are a law enforcement agency's work plan transformed into dollars, which translate into salaries, fringe benefits, equipment and special projects.

Budgets are formally approved statements of future expenses throughout the fiscal year. Expenses are constantly balanced against the approved budget allocations. Budgets control available resources and assist in their efficient use. In essence, budgets are a monetary Bible whose First Commandment is: "Thou shalt not spend more than is herein allocated."

Not less than monthly, executive managers receive itemized expenses and a statement of the balance remaining in each budget category. Some communities operate on a **bottom-line philosophy,** which permits departments to shift funds from one category to another as long as the total budget bottom line is not exceeded. Other communities consider each category as separate line items. Any shifting of funds from one category to another must be approved.

Budgets also reflect the political realities of law enforcement agencies and their jurisdictions. More effective managers are more likely to obtain approval for their programs and projects than less effective managers or those with less political clout. Before looking at who is responsible for preparing the budget and the process involved, take time to familiarize yourself with some budgeting terminology.

Budgeting and Accounting Terminology

Managers must have a working knowledge of the vocabulary of financial management. The following definitions are adapted from Brock, et al. (pp.G–1 to G–8), with the term *agency* substituted for *business* in many instances. (Reprinted by permission of Glencoe, a division of McGraw-Hill.)

Accounting is the process by which financial information about an agency is recorded, classified, summarized, interpreted and then communicated to managers and other interested parties.

Accounting period is the time covered by the income statement and other financial statements that report operating results.

Assets are items of value owned by an agency.

Audit trail is the chain of references that makes it possible to trace information about transactions through an accounting system.

Balance sheet is the financial statement that shows the financial position of an agency at a specific date by summarizing the agency's assets and liabilities.

Certified public accountant (CPA) is an accountant licensed by a state to do public accounting work.

Common costs are expenses not directly traceable to a segment of an agency such as a department or division. They might include a municipality's insurance costs.

Depreciation is the process of allocating the cost of a long-term asset to operations during its expected useful life. For example, squad cars will decrease in value as they are used.

Direct expenses are operating costs that can be identified specifically within individual departments. This would include such things as salaries and benefits.

Financial statements are periodic reports that summarize the financial affairs of an agency.

Fiscal year is the 12-month accounting period used by an agency. A calendar year, from January 1 through December 31, may or may not be the same as an agency's fiscal year.

Fixed costs are expenses that do not vary in total during a period even though the amount of service provided may be more or less than anticipated, for example, rent and insurance.

Flexible budget is a projection that contains budgeted amounts at various levels of service.

Generally accepted accounting principles (GAAPs) are the rules of accounting used by agencies in reporting their financial activities.

Indirect expenses are operating costs that cannot be easily assigned to a particular department when transactions occur and are recorded. Some indirect expenses, such as depreciation, have a meaningful relationship to individual departments and can be allocated based on this relationship. Other indirect expenses must be allocated on the most logical basis possible.

Operating expenses are those costs that arise from the normal activities of the agency.

Petty cash fund is a cash fund of a limited amount used to make small expenditures for which it is not practical to write checks.

Semi-variable costs are expenses that have characteristics of both fixed costs and variable costs. For example, utility expenses are semi-variable costs.

Sunk cost is a historical cost that has already been incurred and is thus irrelevant for decision-making purposes, for example, the purchase of a K-9. Other costs associated with the dog, however, will continue.

Variable costs are expenses that vary in total directly with the amount of service provided, for example, personnel costs including overtime.

Responsibility for Preparing the Budget

Budget preparation may be the responsibility of the records department, a financial officer assigned to planning or, in large departments, a separate division.

In smaller law enforcement agencies, executive managers may prepare the budget. In larger departments, a person of next lower rank, a staff person or a special fiscal division is assigned to prepare the details of the budget and present it to the executive manager, who then holds staff meetings or budget workshops to complete the budget.

Executive law enforcement managers should encourage managers in all divisions and at all levels to monitor budget expenditures and justify expenses within their assigned responsibilities. Such a policy encourages budget preparation participation because managers can visualize the total process.

Executive managers or assigned staff need input from all employees. Requested budget information at various levels should be in a form and language understandable to people not directly connected to preparing the final budget.

The all-levels process of budgeting preparation is becoming common in many departments. First-line supervisors know the needs of street-level law enforcement services and will include potentially overlooked items.

Managers at each level should be responsible for the budget they need, based on input from their subordinates. This results in **all-levels budgeting.**

If all levels of employees and managers have input into the budget, they will understand it and be more aware of revenue and expenditure balancing. They also become part of not only the process of budget preparation but also the goal development on which the budget is based and the subsequent budget review and possible revisions.

What people help to create, they are likely to support. The budget is one area in which support is critical. Normally the employees' most active interests will be in the areas of salaries and fringe benefits. In reality, some other budget items more severely affect their day-to-day work activities. Effective managers are able to demonstrate this to employees and ensure that subordinates do not focus solely on budget areas that directly affect them but rather on the whole picture.

Budgets will be more accurate and complete if they are prepared using a logical process beginning with the lowest levels of the department and working upward. If the total budget exceeds the amount approved for the agency, the budget must be reviewed line item by line item, and items must be eliminated that will have the least effect on total services provided. Support of all involved is needed to make such cuts without negative effects.

Typical Levels in Developing a Budget

Budget development usually starts at the level of area commands where budget requests originate. Such requests are either (1) funded within the department's base budget, (2) disapproved or (3) carried forward for review by management. At the division level, managers review the area requests, make needed adjustments and submit a consolidated request to the budget section at headquarters.

Within two to three months, the budget section identifies proposals for new funding that have department-wide impact and passes them on to the executive level. The commissioner and aides review the figures along with those from other city departments and agree on a budget to submit to the city manager.

The Budgeting Process

Sweeney (2000, p.33) stresses: "Chiefs should develop a mindset that sees budgeting as a year-round process, not just a task that occurs once a year. Throughout the year, collect and retain innovative ideas and suggestions so that these can be incorporated into the budget. It is easy to forget these suggestions, so a 'tickler file' is useful."

The budgeting process begins with the department's goals, objectives, work plans and the resources needed to carry them out. Budget preparation often includes a review of the previous year's budget. These expenditures were approved and probably apply to the new budget. Accurate figures of total costs related to successful accomplishment of past goals provide a foundation for future predictions. These figures are then adjusted to allow for increased costs due to inflation and reduced costs due to wider use, greater availability of the product or competition. The figures should be placed on a computer spreadsheet so revisions can be easily made.

The next task is to compare cost increases, line item by line item, and adjust, eliminate or add items. These changes should be based on carefully thought-out assumptions. Each year new items and programs appear, and the total amount of available funds varies, but the main budget format remains.

Most law enforcement budgets are developed by revising the previous year's budget based on logical assumptions.

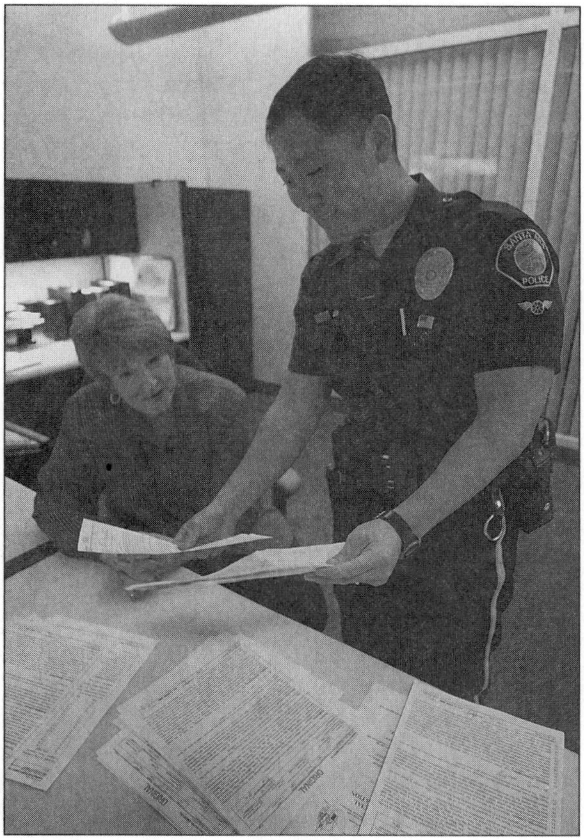

© Spencer Grant/PhotoEdit

Records help police officers identify areas where expenditures are needed. Using facts, officers can present their budget requests to their superiors. Input from all levels results in the best budget, and it helps make the budget acceptable to officers at all levels.

Most budget items are short term, that is, applicable to current-year activities. Because estimated costs are more stable over short periods, short-term expenditures are easier to plan for than long-term expenses. Carryover, or continued items or programs from previous budgets, must include inflationary costs, including cost-of-living salary increases, additional fringe-benefit costs and spin-off costs from increased vacation or sick-leave programs.

Law enforcement budget preparation is a series of events involving hearings, city council workshops, input meetings, cost estimating and a host of other technical details. The process generally involves presentation by the finance department at a governmental entity department staff meeting or by written instructions sent to the department head. Sample forms for preparing budgets are included. Dates are set for various levels of preparations, discussions and workshops.

Law enforcement agencies repeat the process with their own personnel. Any changes in procedure from previous budgets are discussed. Dates and times for different levels of completion must be established or procrastinators will be submitting at the last minute, resulting in lower-quality preparation and consideration. This may lead to omission of items important to continued effective operations.

Law enforcement agencies operate for extended periods with tasks and functions varying from day to day, month to month and year to year. It is difficult to foresee all situations that eventually must be converted into cost factors. For example, who can predict whether a squad car will be involved in an accident and "totaled"; or whether 20 inches of sleet and snow will fall, creating numerous crashes; or whether a natural disaster or a terrorist attack will occur, requiring hundreds of hours of overtime? **Contingency funds** are set aside for such unforeseen emergencies, but the precise total of allowable expenditures is difficult to ascertain.

Priorities must be weighed. Rarely are revenues sufficient to support all requests, and rarely are all requests justifiable. Justification includes the reasons the item is needed and the effect it would have on the department's operations if eliminated. Items that can be accurately cost-determined should include the source of the cost estimate. The more specific the cost and the justification, the less likely the expense is to be criticized.

Even if all requests are justifiable, final priority decisions must be based on available revenues. Tough decisions are often mandatory. Moreover, not all factors can be measured in dollars. Budgets involve intangibles, such as cost in morale and performance. In some budget preparations, the manager closest to the origin of the financial request is given the total list of requests, the estimated costs and the maximum funding available. Managers are asked to decide what to eliminate.

This prioritization often involves consultation with all employees for whom the manager is responsible. If priorities are set with employees' input, they are more acceptable. Further, employees understand the total budgeting process, which ultimately translates into their everyday operational capabilities for the budget year. Input may be given at one or several stages of the budget process.

Budget preparation should be an annual process of planning, setting goals and objectives, itemizing, obtaining input on needs and comparing the data with past budgets. Information to be used in developing the budget should be collected continuously.

All law enforcement employees should contribute ideas related to budget items as specific needs arise.

Subordinates should submit their ideas to their most immediate manager. At the proper time, managers submit summaries of these suggestions to the next level manager, and so on up to the executive manager. If such ideas are submitted during times of actual need, they will more accurately represent reality when the final budget is developed. Waiting until the last few months before budget presentation time and then rushing to obtain all the necessary information is not good budgeting procedure.

Even with this base, managers may approach budgets with reluctance and apprehension. This is partly because various internal divisions compete, and the agency's total budget competes with all other government departments for available tax revenue dollars. One way to ease the mental anguish of budgeting is to not expect perfection. Having a specific step-by-step procedure for looking at specific areas within the budget can also help lessen anxiety.

Budgeting Systems

Law enforcement budgets may take several forms. One of the most common is **line-item budgeting,** initiated in the 1900s and still popular. In this system, specific categories **(line items)** of expenses are identified and dollars allocated for each. Line-item budgets are usually based on the preceding year's budget and a comparison between it and actual expenses.

Performance budgeting allocates dollars based on productivity. Those divisions that perform most effectively are allotted a greater share of the budget. **Program budgeting** identifies the various programs an agency provides and allocates funds for each. A percentage of administrative costs, support costs and **overhead** (operating expenses exclusive of personnel) are assigned to each program. This budgeting approach requires much paperwork, and many managers feel that it is unproductive. However, it can help preserve programs in the face of budget cut pressure. **Activity-based costing (ABC)** is a modern version of the program budgeting system, except that rather than breaking down costs by program, the approach breaks down costs by activity. ABM refers to activity-based management, a logical outgrowth of this approach to analyzing costs. ABC breaks up overhead into neat little cost drivers, the factors that determine the final cost of an operation.

Zero-based budgeting (ZBB) requires justification of all expenditures, not only those that exceed the prior year's allocations. All budget lines begin at zero and are funded according to merit rather than according to the level approved for the preceding year. Zero-based budgeting requires management to articulate objectives and then identify alternative methods of accomplishing those objectives, systematically analyzing the effects of various funding levels. Such an approach to budgeting makes comparison of competing programs easier.

Budget Categories

Regardless of the budgeting system, the budget is usually divided into two classes of expenses: *variable,* which will change depending on the level of service provided, and *fixed,* or overhead, which is relatively constant. Within these two categories, subcategories of expenses can be identified.

Common budget categories include salaries and wages, services and supplies, training and travel, contractual services and other or miscellaneous.

The miscellaneous category should not be treated as a catchall but should be used for small items such as journal subscriptions or books. Budgets also often contain special one-time requests for capital equipment, such as new police vehicles or investigative equipment.

Typical Allocations to Various Categories

In most budgets, salaries and wages account for the largest expenditures, typically 80 to 85 percent. Of this amount, fringe benefits usually amount to 25 percent of the allocation.

Personnel costs usually account for at least three-fourths of the operating budget.

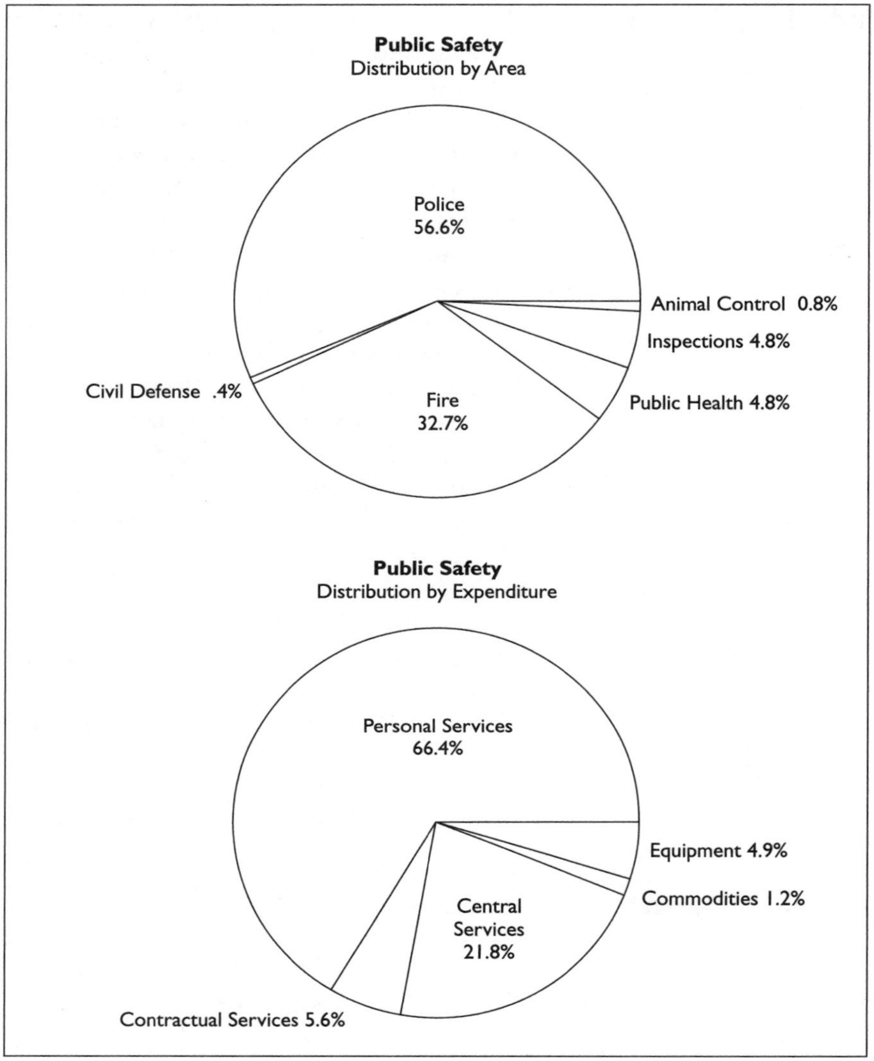

Figure 6.1
A Typical Public Safety Department's Allocation of Resources

Salaries and wages predominate primarily because of the personnel needed to provide extended-time law enforcement services.

Equipment is also used for the same extended time and consequently must be replaced more frequently. For example, a simple item such as a dispatcher's chair used 7 days a week, 24 hours a day is going to need replacement much faster than one used during a 5-day, one-shift week. Figure 6.1 shows a typical public safety department's expenditures.

Presenting the Budget for Approval

The law enforcement budget process generally culminates in presentation to the city council or city manager. Here it competes for revenues with all other departments. Many factors come into play at this point—some factual, some political.

Budget preparations should be made realistically and honestly because the law enforcement budget must be "sold" to a higher body for final approval. Political decision makers need accurate information. "Padding the budget" is often discussed, but in reality city managers, city councils and finance departments are well aware of this tactic. Managers must request funds based on needs, provide a spirit of cooperation and candor and try to avoid serious conflicts. Without factual, accurate information, decisions will likely be made based on personal contacts, innuendo, rumor and community pressure.

To increase the likelihood of budget approval, those preparing the budget should consider forming an advisory committee representative of the community and the local governing body to ensure a diversity of viewpoints and information. They might also consider surveying the community to provide back up and provide information to counter any claims by hostile officials.

After the budget is approved, it must be implemented by converting dollars and cents into law enforcement services rendered. It is the manager's responsibility to make sure these dollars are wisely used as budgeted.

Monitoring

The budget is a *tool,* not a document to be approved and then filed. After the budget is passed, the most important task is to monitor spending.

Variance analysis consists of comparing actual costs against what was budgeted and analyzing differences.

These differences should be contained in a variance report and made known to everyone who directly or indirectly influences the costs. A variance is not necessarily a sign the budget is wrong. Rather, it signals a need for control over income or expenses. Reporting budget variances is an opportunity to provide guidance to management. Variance reports should be made monthly. Problems or deviations should be identified and recommendations made for corrective action. Forms such as those in Figure 6.2 might be used to report variances and requests for budget revisions.

Budgeting is a guideline, not an infallible indicator of the future. No one can do better than an estimate, and variances *will* arise.

Cutback Budgeting

Many departments are being asked to provide more services with fewer funds. Whether called budget reduction, cutback budgeting or reduced expenditure spending, it means added frustration and anxiety for police managers.

Cutback budgeting means providing the same or more services with less funding.

According to Paynter (2000a, p.6): "Across the board, nearly every law enforcement agency in the United States wrestles with a budgetary crunch. At the same time, the demand for greater police protection is rising, but budgetary limitations make paying for it increasingly difficult." "Doing more with less" is the mandate of the future for most law enforcement agencies. Even successful

Variance Report

Account: ____________________

Date ____________________

YEAR-TO-DATE

Actual	Budget	Variance	±%

Variance Analysis

Date ____________________

	Actual Results	Budget Assumptions	Variance	%
I: Prior year-to-date				
Total				
II: Current month				
Total				

Figure 6.2
Forms for Reporting and Analyzing Variances

programs have been discontinued because of lack of funding. To a large extent, budgets control the potential and capabilities of organizations.

Causes of Cutback Budgeting

Cutbacks are caused by several factors, the most familiar being problem depletion, that is, the problem is considered solved. A second cause is erosion of the economic base, seen especially in the United States' older cities and the Northeast, in the growth of dependent populations and shifts from the Frostbelt to the Sunbelt. Other causes include inflation, taxpayer revolts and actual limits to growth. Whatever the cause, cutback management poses special challenges.

Request for Budget Revision

Account ____________ Date ________________

Year-to-date Actual $ ________

Year-to-date Budget $ ________

Variance $ ________ % ________

This variance is caused by: ______________________________

____

____

____

____

____

____

The budget should be changed to: ______________________________

____

____

______________ Effective date ______________

____

Approved ______________________________

Title ________________ Date ________________

Figure 6.2
continued

Doing More with Less

Common cost choices that management must make include whether to:

- Resist or smooth cuts.
- Make a deep gouge or small decrements.
- Share the pain or target the cuts.
- Budget for efficiency or equity.

In each case, the best choice from a management viewpoint may not make sense politically or from a team-building viewpoint. Levine presents possible solutions (p.10), such as reassigning functions to county or state governments and the following:

> Some services can be "privatized" by installing fees, user charges and contracting arrangements for special skills, and some services can be consolidated to achieve economies of scale. Services can be "civilianized" through the use of volunteers and nonsworn personnel. Some services can be reduced or eliminated by careful monitoring of the differences between citizen "needs" and citizen "wants." And expenses can be trimmed through overtime control, "downtime management," self-insurance and new pension arrangements.

"The enemies of responsible management in these difficult times," says Levine (p.10), "are complacency, convenience and wishful thinking." Compounding the problem are the "political dynamics" with "entrenched interests and neighborhood groups fight[ing] to maintain services at prevailing levels against emerging groups with new demands."

Three steps suggested by Levine might be considered by managers facing cutback budgeting (pp.11–12):

1. Assume a positive attitude toward innovation; be willing to experiment.
2. Become convinced that fiscal stress can be managed; prioritize services and projects.
3. Develop a marketing strategy to sell taxpayers on the importance and quality of public services.

Each government agency has its sources of revenues and its requirements for services. When sources of revenues do not meet the cost of requirements for services, a cutback budgeting situation develops. New revenues must be designated or services cut. Cost reductions might include cutting overtime, reducing capital outlay purchases, reducing travel, initiating hiring freezes or, in extreme instances, laying off personnel or promoting early retirement.

Seeking new revenues is another solution. A combination of cutback budgeting procedures and new revenues may be necessary.

Managers might look at how budgeting is done in the private sector, with requests for proposals and bidding an integral part of major purchases. Many businesses also use cooperative purchasing, joining together for better pricing. The same can be done in law enforcement. For example, several agencies could go together in purchasing police vehicles, thereby getting a better price.

Managing Costs Creatively

Perhaps without even realizing it, you have already learned about one of the most creative ways to manage costs—managing time. People and their time are a manager's greatest resource. The following discussion assumes that the manager is already paying careful attention to this aspect of budgeting.

Identifying Common Cost Problems

The first step in solving cost problems is to identify waste areas.

Absenteeism and turnover are major cost problems in most organizations. Managers concerned with controlling costs should have a very clear idea of just how much each subordinate is worth in dollars per day. This figure, coupled with absenteeism, is very important to managers as they look at their budgets.

Other costs managers should target are maintenance of equipment, mail, duplicating, computer and telephone. Are employees using these facilities for personal business? If so, might it make sense to establish a mechanism so they could pay for the convenience? This works well in many organizations. Meetings are another area, already mentioned, where much waste occurs. Many resource management experts suggest that at least one-fourth of all time (and dollars) spent on meetings is wasted. Paperwork is another obvious, yet frequently overlooked, area of waste. Americans create over 30 billion documents a year at a cost of $100 billion—an extremely fertile area for cost reduction.

Reducing costs is all employees' responsibility.

Employees should understand where waste is occurring and how they might help reduce it. In addition to this reactive approach to cost containment, a more proactive approach might also be used.

Employee Cost Improvement Suggestion Programs

The idea of a suggestion system is certainly not new, for such systems have been successfully operating for decades in business and industry. A typical system includes guidelines for acceptable suggestions, a mechanism for making the suggestions and rewards for those suggestions selected as feasible.

Employees can suggest ways to cut costs through an employee cost improvement suggestion program.

Successful employee suggestion programs share several common features including clearly informing all employees of the program's details and procedures, provision of fair and meaningful rewards, and continuously publicizing the program and its objectives.

Such programs are in keeping with the team concept introduced in the first section of this text and emphasized throughout. Costs must be managed if law enforcement agencies are to provide the services citizens expect and require.

Creative Ways to Reduce Costs

Reduce costs by using a regional approach or consolidating services, establishing community resource centers, contracting, using a Quartermaster system, using volunteers and privatizing.

The Regional Approach or Consolidating Services

Regional approaches to common problems allow multiple jurisdictions to pool their resources to form and share teams that are not needed on a full-time basis, for example SWAT, scuba, accident reconstruction and crime scene units. In addition, as DeFranco (2000, p.71) suggests, departments might make use of equipment from the Regional Intelligence Sharing System (RISS): "The RISS program is funded by the Department of Justice and exists to provide equipment and analytical support for law enforcement throughout the country. . . . If small agencies don't have a need for equipment on a continuous basis, or if their equipment is broken, they can borrow from one of the six regional RISS centers. . . . In general, the equipment they have access to includes night vision, audio, body-wire kits and video systems (including microwave and wireless)."

Similar to the regional approach, consolidation allows jurisdictions to share staff and services. Cities and towns with medium to small police departments might consolidate emergency services. They might also share training rooms and actual training. Many communities have a single public safety complex where police, fire and emergency medical service (EMS) personnel are located. In other communities, firefighting and EMS functions are performed by one team.

According to DeFranco (p.68): "Service and equipment sharing can be more than just a nice benefit of cooperation among agencies and between law enforcement and the private sector. It might mean the difference between getting a job done right and not being able to do it at all." DeFranco gives as an example the fact that most departments don't have the money to purchase personal watercraft (PWC), but can often obtain a free PWC from a local dealer. She reports that in 1999, Yamaha lent over 817 watercraft to more than 352 agencies.

Community Resource Centers

Another approach to reducing costs is to establish a community resource center, or more than one for large jurisdictions. Combining police services with social services can provide on-site counseling, educational tutoring, legal services, health care and after-school programs. Community-based organizations (CBOs) are provided free space to operate their programs. Stephan (2000, p.41) cites the following cost savings:

- CBO volunteers are trained in the centers' operations, minimizing the need for city personnel.
- Resource centers located in neighborhoods plagued by extremely high calls for service will reduce the cost of such calls.
- Policing costs are reduced as a result of community mobilization and improved service delivery.
- There is an immediate reduction in costs associated with vandalism and graffiti.

Stephan (p.43) concludes: "The Community Resource Center concept has demonstrated that broad-based partnerships are truly effective in dealing with community problems before they become police problems."

Contracting

Baranzini et al. (2001, p.47) suggest: "Mergers, consolidations, annexations, and the like have been a staple of the fire service for many years. . . . In the American law enforcement community, we are seeing a similar trend, as an increasing number of governmental units turn to nontraditional means of providing quality police services to their customers. One of these approaches is law enforcement services contracting—the provision of traditional law enforcement services by one governmental entity to another. . . . Sheriff's departments are providing services to adjacent cities; cities and counties are providing services to special purpose districts and other municipal corporations (such as transit authorities, airports, and part districts)."

Baranzini et al. (p.52) caution: "Let there be no doubt that contracting is hard work. There are pitfalls to being either a service provider or a customer. Costing models and price structures must be realistic, the language of the contract must be carefully drafted, and everyone in the vendor agency must own the concept."

The Quartermaster System

When examining the best way to equip a department and outfit their officers, many law enforcement administrators face a choice: provide officers with a uniform allowance or use the Quartermaster system, where the agency keeps a storehouse of uniforms. Although stocking such inventory may have some drawbacks, such as limited flexibility for special needs, the Quartermaster system has important advantages. You make a single order in quantity, providing a supply of identical stock from the same dye lot. Buying in quantity, you usually get higher quality for a lower price. Another consideration is that officers frequently are reluctant to spend their allowance on uniforms, spending it in other ways.

Volunteers

Use of volunteers is increasing in law enforcement departments across the country. According to Berger (2002, p.6): "At a time when law enforcement's limited resources are being stretched even further than usual, many agencies are turning to civilian volunteers so that police officers can serve on the front lines, working to make communities safer." Berger notes that on May 30, 2002, the Volunteers in Police Service (VIPS) initiative was announced by the U.S. Department of Justice and the International Association of Chiefs of Police (IACP). Berger contends: "Volunteers who participate in VIPS programs truly are 'very important people.' They assist departments by performing nonsworn duties such as answering phones, compiling crime data, preparing incident reports and facilitating crime prevention programs."

Berger notes that the VIPS program "is a logical outgrowth of the growing community policing trend. . . . The VIPS initiative, together with the other Citizen Corps programs, will enhance local homeland security efforts and make emergency preparedness a part of our daily lives."

The San Diego (California) Police Department had its own Volunteers in Policing before this initiative. According to the officer who heads up this program: "Last year, [volunteers] donated roughly 198,400 hours or about $2.8 million worth of unpaid labor. We would be lost without them" ("Do You Get What You Pay For? . . ." 2000, p.1).

Another example of the value of volunteers is the success of the Sun City Center Security Patrol whose volunteers have kept this retirement community's crime rate the lowest in Hillsborough County, Florida. The Hillsborough County Sheriff's Office reported that the patrol was responsible for a 60 percent drop in crime and a more than 90 percent reduction in burglaries during its first year of operation (Courter, 2002, p.42). According to Courter: "Today, the patrol has five cars and more than 1,450 volunteers who patrol 3,200 acres and 120 miles of road. The patrol operates every day of the year from six in the morning until two the next morning. . . . Typically a car carries two people, usually a husband and wife team . . . . The patrol logs 200,000 miles a year." Each member is expected to work at least one three-hour shift a month, which partially accounts for the program's success. Volunteers are not expected to do too much.

Yet another example of a successful volunteer program is the East Bay Regional Park District's bicycle patrol. The District includes 59 parks totaling 91,000 acres and 1,150 miles of sprawling trails in the San Francisco Bay area and covered by only 53 sworn officers, with sometimes as few as five officers on patrol. The Volunteer Bike Unit provides coverage in areas the sworn officers can't get to. Mallory (2001, p.80) cites the endorsement of this unit by the

District's chief: "This program fills a niche. It gives us extra bodies and hours in the field to educate the public and observe any kind of crimes or suspicious situations or hazards and report them to the police department."

Using volunteers does more than just save money—it adds value to department services and enhances community policing efforts.

Privatization

Another way to do more with less is through privatization. According to Paynter (2000a, p.6): "Privatization of policing services appears to answer some of policing's present woes. By partnering with private organizations, law enforcement may be able to address the public's calls for increased policing services and better focus on its primary function. . . . Policing functions such as general assistance, administrative support services and other tasks might be off-loaded to the private sector. A private firm could provide services such as funeral escorts, directing traffic around an accident, citing parking violations, responding to burglary alarms, etc. These services do not require police training, but can occupy up to 80 percent of an officer's time and waste an agency's limited resources."

In addition to reducing costs, managers should look for ways to increase revenues.

Increasing Revenue

Departments might increase revenue by fund raising, charging for some services, using asset forfeiture statutes to their advantage and seeking grants.

Fund Raising

The primary source of revenue for law enforcement agencies is provided by the jurisdiction served by the agency. Local police departments, for example, are supported primarily by tax dollars of that locality. Many police departments find that they are able to increase the dollars available to them by raising funds themselves. Among the methods agencies have used to raise funds are dues to a crime prevention organization and seeking support from civic groups for specific projects, such as K-9 units.

One example of a successful fundraiser is the Crown Point (Indiana) Police Department's Adopt-A-Car Program, started in 1995 when this small department needed to purchase 10 new cars but found itself $125,000 short. A lieutenant came up with the idea of asking local businesses to donate $1,500 each (tax deductible) to equip the vehicles. In return, the department painted "This vehicle equipped by (business name)" in 1 1/2-inch high letters on the back of the car. In less than two days, the department had enough sponsors to outfit its new cars and refurbish the old ones.

Contributions made by organizations or citizens are usually tax deductible. In one midwestern community, a citizen crime prevention association has an annual used book sale. Collection boxes are placed in businesses, schools and churches throughout the community, and citizens donate their used books. Each spring, space is donated by a local business, and volunteers conduct a week-long book sale. Profits are in the thousands of dollars. One purchase made with the funds was a K-9 for the police department. The officers named the dog "Books."

Weinblatt (2000, pp.55–57) describes how the Belmont (Massachusetts) Police Department secured funds from local chambers of commerce, insurance companies, civic organizations such as the Rotary Club and the Lions Club, banks and hospitals to purchase Automated External Defibrillators (AEDs) for their patrol cars. He notes that hospitals as well as the American Heart Association and the American Red Cross provided training on their use.

Charging for Services

Some agencies have begun charging for traditional services such as DUI arrests. Other departments are billing the hosts of loud parties if the police are called back to the party within 12 hours. In addition to raising revenues, some departments have noticed a 75 percent reduction in second calls about loud parties. Other departments are recouping their costs for extraordinary police services, that is, police services rendered in natural disasters, criminally caused catastrophic events such as bombings or hostage incidents, parades, athletic or timed events.

Other options for creative managers to increase revenues include charging sentenced prisoners an incarceration fee; selling department products, assets or services, for example, auction surplus equipment or unclaimed items from the property room, or providing security at sporting and entertainment events; and selling advertising rights—providing manufacturers with endorsements in exchange for compensation, products and/or services.

Additional income may be obtained from a variety of sources, such as federal and state grants, foundation funds, direct corporate giving funds, company-sponsored foundations, individual gifts of equipment or money and individual operating foundations. Departments might also charge fees for services such as reports, photographs, fingerprinting, license checks and responding to alarms.

Some agencies have found that accepting credit cards rather than insisting on cash bail has increased revenues collected. Other departments have formed special police assessment districts.

Besides collecting such fees, departments may also economize by taking advantage of the rapidly expanding electronic commerce technologies available over the Internet or via networked kiosks similar to ATMs. Such transactions might include ordering reports, issuing licenses and so on.

Asset Forfeiture

One source of additional revenue is asset forfeiture. Hartman (2001, p.4) explains: "Asset forfeiture laws at the federal level, and in most states, allow law enforcement to use proceeds of certain seizures for equipment and other needs, especially when the seized property is drug related and there are no victims to compensate." He (p.6) concludes:

> Asset forfeiture remains a powerful tool for law enforcement agencies. It remedies many of the problems that often slip through the criminal justice system, such as addressing the issue of allowing a criminal to profit from crime, and it provides a remedy for the victim. In short, asset forfeiture deprives the subject of ill-gotten gains, compensates the victim and serves the community.

According to Turner (2002, p.91): "Since the Asset Forfeiture Program was initiated, more than $2.9 billion has been shared among the agencies."

The practice of attaching guilt to objects used in committing a crime may have originated with Greek and Roman law. If, for example, a sword was used to kill a man, it was believed to possess an evil quality independent of the killer. The sword would be confiscated and sold, with the proceeds used for good deeds.

One defense of asset seizure is the Innocent Owner Defense—the assets of an owner who had no knowledge of the prohibited activity, either by act or omission, are not subject to forfeiture. The U.S. Supreme Court has ruled that asset forfeiture is governed by the Eighth Amendment and, as such, must not be so severe as to constitute cruel and unusual punishment.

The U.S. Supreme Court considers asset forfeiture to be governed by the Eighth Amendment, which forbids cruel and unusual punishment. It is up to the states to make this determination.

Grants

Numerous grant opportunities exist for law enforcement agencies at both the federal and state levels. Baker et al. (2001, p.5): note: "A police executive's ability to achieve grant financial support remains a strategic component in successful modern-day policing." As Dees (2000, p.26) suggests: "Getting grant money is something of an art form, and it's no coincidence that many of the courses and seminars in grant writing techniques are called 'grantsmanship.'" To improve the chances of receiving a grant, it is important to understand the types of grants available and which federal, state and local agencies fund such grants. There are two basic types of grants: a **formula** or **block grant,** which is awarded to states or localities based on population and crime rates and a **discretionary grant,** which is awarded based on the judgment of the awarding agency.

Federal Grant Money

According to Rogers (2000, p.18): "Billions of dollars from Washington are available to your jurisdiction—whether it's a hamlet or a huge city." Bates (2000, p.99) contends: "The key to grant hunting. . . is getting on government mailing lists for the most up-to-date information on federal grants." He points out that the federal government's fiscal year ends in September, so October is a good time to start researching new grant opportunities.

The Department of Justice's (DOJ) Office of Justice Programs (OJP) is the lead federal funding agency for law enforcement.

Eight offices within OJP make grants available to law enforcement agencies: the Bureau of Justice Assistance (BJA), the Office of Juvenile Justice and Delinquency Prevention (OJJDP), the Bureau of Justice Statistics (BJS), the Office for Victims of Crime (OVC), the National Institute of Justice (NIJ), Violence against Women, the Corrections Program Office and the COPS Office.

The BJS has three primary sources of funding. Local Law Enforcement Block Grants (LLEBG) go directly to local jurisdictions, distributing approximately $500 million per year. It is a 10 percent matching program; that is, for every $9 the government provides, the recipient must match it with $1. The Edward Byrne Formula Grant Program is based on a state's population. States receive 1/4 of 1 percent of approximately $500 million as a base proportion. After that, the grant size is based on population and crime rate. Byrne formula grants represent the single largest source of law enforcement-related funding Congress makes available to states. This is a 25 percent match program. The third program, the Edward Byrne Discretionary Grant Program, grants about $50 million to innovative programs that are within the government's high priority areas. The BJA also has a Bulletproof Vest Partnership (BVP) grant that pays up to 50 percent of the cost of NIJ-approved vests.

The COPS program, established in 1994, has been controversial, but, according to Paynter (2000b, p.27): "The COPS program already has distributed $8.8 billion dollars in grants to help fight crime in high-risk areas." Whether the program has reached its goal of 100,000 new police officers on the street depends on whose figures you use. According to Cameron (2000, p.54): "The promoted figures are fabrications . . . [and] a large proportion of COPS grants have flowed to agencies with relatively mild crime problems."

A study by the Urban Institute, *The COPS Program after Four Years* (2000), declared the COPS program a partial success, falling well short of the target of 100,000 new cops on the beat, but providing the fuel for the nationwide proliferation of community policing tactics between 1995 and 1998. The Institute also found that citizen police academies, truancy prevention programs in schools, problem-oriented policing and patrolling on foot or bike to encourage interaction between community members and police all increased as a result of COPS. COPS MORE (Making Officer Redeployment Effective) grants can be used for new technology and equipment as well as funding non-sworn personnel to free up officers assigned to administrative tasks.

The National Criminal Justice Reference Service (NCJRS) is a valuable source of information for funding available at the federal level. An agency can request to be put on the NCJRS mailing list for proposal solicitations and other information, and the agency will then receive all solicitations disseminated by OJP and the COPS office. Administrators can access the NCJRS Website at http://www.ncjrs.org or contact NCJRS by e-mail at *askncjrs@ncjrs.org.*

Kardasz (2000, p.100) describes three government programs to help law enforcement obtain specialized equipment: "The 1033 program allows the transfer, without charge, of excess U.S. Department of Defense supplies and equipment to state and local law enforcement. Agencies have received vehicles, weapons, ammunition, computer equipment, body armor, night vision equipment, radios and photographic equipment through this program." The Surplus Property Donation Program allows states to receive surplus federal property and donate it to public agencies. The 1122 program allows agencies to purchase equipment for counter-drug activities with the discounts received in federal government contracts.

State Grant Money

Funding may also be sought at the state level. Simpson (2002, p.90) stresses: "First, and perhaps most important, check with your state's single point of contact grant administrator. Some states don't have the single point of contact, but they do have someone who manages federal grant monies that are sent to the state. Usually there are matching funds required with these grants. Some lobbying with local government officials or local business owners to secure these matching funds may be required." The governor's office generally houses contact points for law enforcement-related grants. In addition, almost every state has a grant specialist in the Attorney General's Office or in the State Emergency Preparedness Office. At a minimum, each state has a contact point for the BJA's Edward Byrne Formula Grants Program.

Pekow (2002, p.87) suggests that the No Child Left Behind Act has made available a billion dollars, giving a proportional share to each state, which in turn must give 95 percent to local communities for programs that provide homework help, counseling, recreation and mentoring. This is another area law enforcement departments might want to explore at the state level, especially if they have police liaison officers in the schools.

Other Sources of Funding

Other sources of funding for law enforcement include direct corporate giving programs, usually foundations, and community-service groups such as the Rotary, Kiwanis and Elks that focus on crime prevention programs, child abuse, drug abuse, senior citizen safety and the like. The Hillsborough County (Florida) Sheriff's Office obtained a $1 million community development block grant from the U.S. Department of Housing and Urban Development (HUD). Another federal funding source is the Weed and Seed program, which weeds out crime from designated neighborhoods, moves in with a wide range of crime and drug prevention programs, and then seeds these neighborhoods with a comprehensive range of human service programs that stimulate revitalization.

The availability of discretionary grants is advertised in the *Federal Register.* This source, published Monday through Friday, also provides the application criteria and details about the grants. Most major libraries subscribe to this publication. A quick and easy way to find grant information is via the Internet. Check any of the OJP offices by indicating the office at the end of their Web address. For example, the Bureau of Justice Assistance would be found at www.ojp.usdoj.gov/BJA/. You can also call the OJP Grants Management System hotline at 888-549-9901.

The Grant Proposal

Bates (p.101) suggests: "According to successful grant recipients, the key to winning is to simply make a conscientious effort to apply." The first step in writing a grant proposal is to read the solicitation carefully and follow the instructions exactly. Where applicable, graphs and charts should be included to help communicate ideas and present data. Showing local support is also important. Rogers (2001, p.39) notes that it is often advisable to partner with a local university. Professors skilled in grant writing can lend credibility to the project.

The six components of most proposals, unless otherwise specified, are (1) a statement of need, (2) how this need can be met—the objectives of the project,

(3) who will accomplish the tasks, (4) what time line will be followed, (5) what the cost will be and (6) how the results will be evaluated.

The Environmental Protection Agency (EPA) Web site at www.epa.gov/seahome/grants/src/msieopen.htm has a step-by-step guide for writing a grant proposal, including guidance for applying for all types of grants. It also has a practice grant-writing exercise.

Sharp (2002, p.94) points out: "Grant writing is a sales job as well as a process. There is a lot of PR involved in convincing people of the need for the 'new toys,' funding, etc. An understanding of politics and the funding procedures for your jurisdiction are also helpful."

Do not be discouraged if your proposal is turned down. The key to successful grant writing is to learn from your mistakes. Many very worthwhile and successful programs were rejected repeatedly before eventually being funded. Grant seeking takes knowledge, preparation, patience and endurance. It is not easy, and the competition is keen, but the effort can be rewarding.

Summary

A budget is a list of probable expenses and income during a given period, most often one year. Budgets serve as a plan for and a means to control resources. Managers at each level should be responsible for the budget they need, based on input from their subordinates. This results in all-levels budgeting.

Most law enforcement budgets are developed by revising the previous year's budget based on logical assumptions. All law enforcement employees should contribute ideas related to budget items as specific needs arise.

Three kinds of resources must be identified: human, direct and indirect. Common budget categories include salaries and wages, services and supplies, training and travel, contractual services, and other or miscellaneous. Personnel costs usually account for at least three-fourths of the operating budget. Once the budget is developed, it should be used to monitor costs. Variance analysis consists of comparing actual costs against what was budgeted and analyzing differences.

Cutback budgeting means providing the same or more services with less funding. Managers need new strategies that involve making choices as to whether to resist or smooth cuts; to cut deeply or in small decrements; to share the pain or target the cuts and to budget for efficiency or equity. The first step in solving cost problems is to identify waste areas. All employees are responsible for reducing costs. Employees can suggest ways to cut costs through an employee cost improvement suggestion program. Costs can also be reduced by using a regional approach or consolidating services, establishing community resource centers, contracting, using a Quartermaster system, using volunteers and privatizing.

Many departments are increasing revenues, including conducting fund raisers, charging for some services, using asset forfeiture statutes to their advantage and seeking grants. The U.S. Supreme Court considers asset forfeiture to be governed by the Eighth Amendment, which forbids cruel and unusual punishment. It is up to the states to make this determination. The Office of Justice Programs (OJP) is the lead federal funding agency for law enforcement.

Discussion Questions

1. Do you have a personal budget? If so, what are your main categories?
2. Do you belong to any organizations that have a budget? If so, what are their main categories?
3. How do budgets restrict? Provide freedom?
4. What things in addition to money might a law enforcement agency budget (e.g., space)?
5. Is your law enforcement department functioning under cutback budgeting?
6. What percentage of a city's total budget goes to the law enforcement department?
7. Which department gets the largest share of the city's budget?
8. What methods might be used to raise funds for your local law enforcement agency?
9. What suggestions do you have for cutting the cost of providing law enforcement services?
10. Why must the budget be updated annually?

InfoTrac College Edition Assignments

Use InfoTrac College Edition to answer the Discussion Questions as appropriate.

Complete one of the following assignments.

- Find a recent article on *cutback budgeting in law enforcement.* Outline the suggestions. Star any that were not mentioned in the chapter. Record the full citation for the source. Be prepared to share your findings with the class.
- Read and outline "Rural and Suburban Police Leadership: Targeting External Funding" by Thomas E. Baker, Loreen Wolfer and Ralph Zezza.
- Read and outline "Implementing an Asset Forfeiture Program" by Victor E. Hartman.
- Read and outline "When Feds Say Seize and Desist" by Kelly Patricia O'Meara.

References

Baker, Thomas E.; Wolfer, Loreen; and Zezza, Ralph. "Rural and Suburban Police Leadership: Targeting External Funding." *FBI Law Enforcement Bulletin,* November 2001, pp.1–5.

Baranzini, Richard D.; Kalin, Bruce K.; and King, Jason J. "Is Law Enforcement Services Contracting in Your Future?" *The Police Chief,* December 2001, pp.47–56.

Bates, Frank. "Finding Funds for Thermal Imaging." *Law Enforcement Technology,* May 2000, pp.99–101.

Berger, William B. "Volunteers in Police Service." *The Police Chief,* July 2002, p.6.

Brock, Horace R.; Palmer, Charles E.; and Price, John Ellis. *Accounting Principles and Applications,* 6th ed. New York: Gregg Division, McGraw-Hill Publishing Company, 1990.

Cameron, Bruce. "COPS: A Political Football." *Law and Order,* October 2000, pp.54–56.

The COPS Program after Four Years—National Evaluation. Washington, DC: Urban Institute, 2000. http://www.urban.org

Courter, Eileen. "All Eyes Open: Community Volunteer Patrol." *Law and Order,* April 2002, pp.42–46.

Dees, Tim. "Grants: Resources and Opportunities Online." *Law and Order,* June 2000, pp.26–27.

DeFranco, Liz Martinez. "Share, and Share Alike." *Law Enforcement Technology,* March 2000, pp.68–72.

"Do You Get What You Pay For? San Diego Volunteers Show it Ain't Necessarily So." *Law Enforcement News,* February 29, 2000, pp.1, 9.

Hartman, Victor E. "Implementing an Asset Forfeiture Program." *FBI Law Enforcement Bulletin,* January 2001, pp.1–7.

Kardasz, Frank. "Reeling in Grant Funds." *Law Enforcement Technology,* November 2000, pp.97–100.

Levine, Charles H. "Cutback Management in an Era of Scarcity: Hard Questions for Hard Times." *Executive Police Development.* Washington, DC: Department of Justice, National Institute of Justice and the FBI, no date.

Levine, Charles H. "Cutting Back the Public Sector: Hidden Hazards of Retrenchment." *Executive Police Development.* Washington, DC: Department of Justice, National Institute of Justice and the FBI, no date.

Mallory, Jim. "Volunteer Bike Patrol Boosts Park Coverage." *Law and Order,* April 2001, pp.80–84.

Paynter, Ronnie. "Privatization: Something to Think About?" *Law Enforcement Technology,* September 2000a, p.6.

Paynter, Ronnie. "Making Cops $ Work for You." *Law Enforcement Technology,* October 2000b, pp.26–32.

Pekow, Charles. "Obtaining Federal Grants." *Law and Order,* October 2002, pp.87–89.

Rogers, Donna. "Getting a Slice of the Pie." *Law Enforcement Technology,* March 2000, pp.18–22.
Rogers, Donna. "Making Ends Meet: Tips for Snaring Grant Money." *Law Enforcement Technology,* March 2001, pp.36–40.
Sharp, Art. "Grant Writing Skills: Don't Take Them for Granted." *Law and Order,* October 2002, pp.92–94.
Simpson, Ken. "Equipment Funding." *Law and Order,* October 2002, pp.90–91.
Stephan, Michael. "Union City Community Resource Centers." *The Police Chief,* February 2000, pp.35–44.
Sweeney, Earl M. "How to Obtain Adequate Resources for Traffic Enforcement." *The Police Chief,* July 2000, pp.31–33.
Turner, David A. "Cars, Boats and Homes: Online Sales a Bonanza for U.S. Marshals Service." *The Police Chief,* August 2002, pp.89–91.
Weinblatt, Richard B. "Creative Funding: Makes AEDs a Reality in Patrol Cars." *Law and Order,* February 2000, pp.55–57.

Book-Specific Web Site

Go to the *Management and Supervision in Law Enforcement* Web site at http://info.wadsworth.com/05346160654 for student and instructor resources, including Internet Assignments and Case Studies.

CHAPTER 7

Hiring Personnel and Dealing with Unions

Nobody's perfect except when filling out a job application.

—Anonymous

Do You Know?

- What steps are involved in the selection process?
- What the most common screening methods used in the hiring process are?
- What a bona fide occupational qualification (BFOQ) is?
- What major employment legislation affects hiring for law enforcement agencies?
- What the EEOC is and how it affects hiring practices?
- What goal the Americans with Disabilities Act (ADA) seeks to guarantee?
- What kinds of inquiries or evaluations are prohibited by the ADA?
- What an affirmative action program is?
- In what areas of management EEO and affirmative action policies are important?
- What the National Labor Relations Act requires of management?
- What the National Labor Relations Board is?
- What the primary purpose of unions is?
- Why people join unions?
- What levels of negotiation are usually involved in collective bargaining?

Can You Define?

affirmative action program (AAP)
arbitration
background check
bona fide occupational qualification (BFOQ)
Civil Rights Act of 1964
closed shop
collective bargaining
delaying tactics
Equal Employment Opportunity Commission (EEOC)
Fair Labor Standards Act of 1938
Generation Xers
halo effect
Landrum-Griffin Act of 1959
mediation
National Labor Relations Act of 1935 (Wagner Act)
National Labor Relations Board (NLRB)
negligent hiring
Norris-LaGuardia Act
open discussion
rapport
reverse discrimination
right-to-work laws
special employment groups
Taft-Hartley Act of 1947
union
union shop
vicarious liability
yellow-dog contract

INTRODUCTION

Today's law enforcement agencies seek a new breed of officer—a balance of brawn and brains—one who possesses not only the physical qualities traditionally associated with policing, such as strength and endurance, but also the emotional and intellectual characteristics needed to effect public order in an ever-changing and increasingly diverse society. "People skills" have become a critical tool for law enforcement officers.

Lord and Schoeps (2000, p.172) studied the attributes considered critical by one large metropolitan police department for effective community-oriented, problem-solving (COPPS) officers. They identified 22 attributes that "emphasize problem solving; decision making; and the ability to gain new knowledge, technology, procedures and laws." In addition, according to Bratton (2001, p.32): "We need individuals who see policing as a calling, not just as a job; who see the community as a partner, not as the problem; and who can be trusted to enforce the law without violating it themselves." According to Harris and Kolkman (2000, p.63): "Rather than seeking officers locked into a simple crime-fighting mentality, agencies now want people who can think on their own, are willing to seek solutions, and engage in activities that encourage community participation in problem-solving. The officers of the 21st century are not social workers. But much more is expected of them than just 'locking up bad guys.'" Vest (2001, p.14) concurs: "Law enforcement is moving away from the 'big tough cops' in favor of candidates, regardless of size, who possess qualities that mirror the tenets of the COP [community-oriented policing] and POP [problem-oriented policing] philosophies. Also, more and more, communities want service-oriented people with interpersonal skills as their guardians of justice." Lonsway (2001, p.16) suggests: "The selection process should emphasize the skills and characteristics needed for community police officers—communication, problem solving, empathy and the ability to successfully interact with members of diverse cultures."

Knowing what attributes are desirable and finding applicants with these attributes are decidedly different. Sanow (2001, p.4) stresses: "Recruiting qualified applicants to the police force is one of today's most critical problems in law enforcement." According to Domash (2002, p.34): "Thousands of positions in law enforcement remain unfilled and agencies nationwide are seeking the answer to one scary question . . . who wants this job?" Domash (p.35) notes the large number of officers nationwide who are reaching or passing their 20-year or 25-year retirement point may result in "a potentially unprecedented crisis in law enforcement."

This chapter begins with a discussion of the critical importance of hiring well to avoid litigation from vicarious liability or negligent hiring and many other problems. The chapter then suggests steps departments can take to hire well, beginning with recruiting and continuing through the selection process: the application, testing, background checks and interviews. Next, the use of assessment centers and employment criteria departments might consider are discussed. After looking at the selection process, you will learn about laws that affect the process, including the Americans with Disabilities Act (ADA) and affirmative action. The chapter concludes with a look at how labor laws and unions affect both the selection process and the functioning of the department.

The Importance of Hiring Well

Olson (2001, p.5) stresses: "Our ability to attract and retain high quality officers at all ranks will be one of the defining issues in the coming years. The successes that we have enjoyed for the past decade could be wiped out if we fail to keep pace with our staffing needs."

The hiring process is so critical in law enforcement in part because of **vicarious liability,** which refers to the legal responsibility one person has for the acts of another. Managers, the entire agency and even the jurisdiction served may be legally responsible for the actions of a single officer. Vicarious means "taking the place of another thing or person, substituting for." Law enforcement officers have always been responsible for their individual wrongdoings, criminally or civilly. Civil liability most frequently involves violation of the Civil Rights Act, specifically Statute 42 of the U.S. Code, Section 1983, which states:

> Every person who, under color of any statute, ordinance, regulation, custom, or usage, of any State or Territory, subjects, or causes to be subjected, any citizen of the United States or other person within the jurisdiction thereof to the deprivation of any rights, privileges, or immunities secured by the Constitution and laws, shall be liable to the party injured in an action at law, suit in equity, or other proper proceeding for redress.

In other words, anyone acting under the authority of law who violates another person's constitutional rights can be sued. In 1978 in *Monell v. New York City Department of Social Services,* the court ruled that local municipalities were also liable under Section 1983 (Title 42, U.S.C.).

It is now accepted that local government may be responsible for the wrongdoing of a subordinate enforcing a local ordinance, regulation or policy. In cases in which law enforcement managers directed, ordered or participated in the acts, they are equally liable. Additionally, if upper-level managers are negligent in hiring, assigning, training, retaining, directing or entrusting, they may be liable even if they were not present.

Rostow and Davis (2002, p.101) stress: "In general, the failure to properly select an officer is a form of negligent hiring." **Negligent hiring** litigation is becoming more common. Law enforcement managers and supervisors have been held liable for negligence in hiring personnel unqualified or unsuited for law enforcement work. The majority of these cases involve failure to use an adequate selection process or to check for prior offenses or misconduct.

In one case an officer was hired on a probationary basis. During the course of patrol, the officer stopped an individual for speeding and driving while intoxicated. In making the arrest, the officer hit the driver with a blackjack with such force that the driver lost one eye. The court concluded that the city equipped the officer with a gun, a gun belt and a blackjack but had failed to check his background or provide any training.

Negligent hiring and retention have become major problems because of numerous court cases that have resulted in significant judgments. Conducting background investigations, hiring qualified personnel and then developing them into permanent employees can help reduce such lawsuits. Negligent supervision, negligent training and negligent retention are discussed later in the text.

Recruiting

As Nichols (2001, p.1) suggests: "Recruitment is one of the most difficult challenges facing police departments in the new century." Tate (2000, p.78) notes: "Finding that ideal police recruit, one who seeks a long-term career as one of society's peacekeepers, is increasingly difficult." Butterfield (2001, p.A1) reports: "Police departments in cities across the nation are facing what some call a personnel crisis, with the number of recruits at record lows." Kanable (2001, p.64) also reports: "Some agencies have seen the number of job applicants plummet by more than 50 percent in recent years." *Law Enforcement News* ("Coast to Coast . . . ," 2000, p.1) contends: "A double-edged sword hangs over police departments. While some cannot attract enough applicants to make up rates of attrition that are expected to become significant over the next few years, others are seeing their officers jump ship for what they perceive to be a better working environment."

Departments take a variety of approaches in recruiting. Traditional activities include handouts, military recruiting, advertisements (TV, radio, newspapers), job fairs and visits to colleges. National recruiting newsletters may also assist, including the National Employment Listing Service and Knights. However, according to Nichols (p.44): "The difference between departments that are able to find recruits and those that aren't is almost always tied to wages and benefits." This should be kept in mind when considering recruitment activities.

Advertising has been a staple of recruitment efforts. However, as Kanable (p.66) points out: "Advertising in two or three local papers might not be enough. Advertising in a newspaper with circulation throughout the state, ethnic newspapers and law enforcement publications or newsletters may help." Recruiting graduates of college criminal justice programs is one major source of candidates, and implementing college internships can be a valuable aid to recruitment. Research by Ross and Elechi (2002, p.297) found "tremendous support for internship programs. . . . Internships were regarded as invaluable in preparing students for criminal justice careers."

Salvatore (2001, p.50) describes how the Connecticut Police Chiefs Association has used television commercials to attract new officers. The 30-second commercial cost $23,000. "The commercial is aimed in part at high school students who, even though currently too young to join the force, will go on to college and obtain a degree. It also targets older individuals looking to make a career change."

Matthews and Kilpatrick (2002, p.32) suggest: "Creating a video presentation for use in recruitment and community presentations is an effective use of limited budgetary dollars." Another way to reach potential recruits is through a Web site. Brandon and Lippman (2000, p.41) report: "Use of the Internet is growing exponentially in this country." They quote one officer in charge of recruitment: "We can't just rely on the media to put our best foot forward; we have to do it ourselves. This Web site really serves as the department magazine and it has been very effective for us." Matthews and Kilpatrick (p.33) note: "This electronic medium can actually serve as a window through which potential applicants can view the city, its people, the department's level of professionalism, career opportunities and other features that will influence individuals' decisions." Association and commercial Web sites also offer employment listings. The IACP has a job Web site, www.iacppolicejobs.com, where departments can list job openings for a monthly fee. Job searches are free.

Another avenue in recruiting police candidates is to seek out second-career officers. For example, the Appleton (Wisconsin) Police Department actively recruits new officers from other professions, not necessarily because of their knowledge of police work but because of their maturity and stability. The impending retirement of veteran officers presents yet another recruiting opportunity for departments, recruiting reserve officers from their full-time ranks. Recruitment efforts should not overlook a department's civilian employees as well as participants in its programs such as the reserves, explorers or citizen police academies.

Recruitment efforts aimed at younger people will be most successful if they consider the characteristics of **Generation Xers,** those born during the years 1961 to 1981. According to Charrier (2000, p.46): "Knowing what motivates and concerns the next generation of officers will help law enforcement executives create more effective recruitment campaigns. . . . Fifty-four percent have attended more than one year of college. Forty percent invest in mutual funds. Sixty-three percent are dissatisfied with the way things are going in the United States." Charrier (p.47) suggests using the Web to "highlight the variety of jobs available at the officer level, from positions in tactical units like SWAT to the community-oriented jobs. Xers are looking for variety and challenges. Offer cafeteria-style benefits packages. Showcase the computer technology used by your agency. Offer a class, in or after the academy, dedicated to career development. . . . Agencies with residency requirements and rigid work schedules will likely have the greatest difficulty attracting young professionals." Charrier (p.49) also suggests: "Police agencies should consider creating non-traditional work arrangements such as part-time employment or job-sharing plans."

The Sacramento (California) Police Department is courting Generation Xers by establishing criminal justice and community-service academies associated with high schools. According to Francis (2001, p.2), the police department and the high school established the first academy in 1990. Parents and students sign a contract agreeing to the requirements of the four-year program, which includes over 50 hours of community service, exemplary citizenship and high academic standards. Says Francis: "Students wear uniforms. The college-prep courses cover ethics and law and criminal justice procedures approved by the California Commission on Peace Officer Standards. Physical fitness training is rigorous enough to prepare the students to ace the Sacramento PD's fitness exam. Students also learn conflict management, computer skills, and the setting of goals."

Campbell et al. (2000, p.27) contend that contact with a sworn officer may be the "single most important influence on people's intentions to consider a career with the agency." They recommend that: "Departments may benefit from finding ways to actively involve all sworn officers within their departments in recruiting potential candidates."

Olson (p.2) stresses: "The real challenge we are facing is not just finding the most qualified candidates, but at the same time attracting a much more diverse workforce. Having a diverse workforce is a must, and the ability to attract diverse recruits must be one of our top priorities."

Recruiting for Diversity

Streit (2001, p.70) reports: "In the U.S. there is an increasing number of women and other minority officers being sworn in. Although this number is growing, it still isn't where it should be." According to Streit (p.71): "When people within the community see a minority in uniform, it can make them more trusting of the entire department." Streit (pp.71–72) notes: "There is nothing wrong with stating in promotional materials that a certain quality is encouraged, but the wording should not discourage those who lack that quality. For example, an ad that reads: 'Seeking qualified police officer for a small department. Spanish speaking, a plus.'"

Recruiting Racial/Ethnic Minorities

According to *Law Enforcement News* ("Female, Minority Ranks . . . ," 2002, p.1), from 1990 to 2000 the percentage of full-time officers who were members of racial or ethnic minorities rose from 30 percent to 38 percent in jurisdictions of more than 250,000 residents. The largest increase was by Hispanics, whose numbers grew from 9 percent in 1990 to 14 percent in 2000. The number of black officers rose from 18 percent to 20 percent.

The Delaware State Police uses troopers from throughout the state in their recruiting efforts. They send officers into minority community centers and have developed their own job fair ("Delaware SP Reveals Secrets . . . ," 2000, p.10). Other likely places to recruit are Latino festivals, Urban leagues, NAACP meetings and minority churches.

Recruiting Women

Gold (2000, p.159) reports: "Women have sought, won and created larger roles for themselves in law enforcement—their ranks now exceed 14 percent of all sworn law enforcement positions among municipal, county and state law enforcement agencies comprised of 100 or more sworn officers." And Schulz (2002, p.25) notes that there are probably about 175 women chiefs of police in the United States. Gold also notes: "That's the good news. The bad news is that the rate of growth is painfully slow. Overall, the increase of women in law enforcement has grown a meager 5.3 percent from 1990 to 1999." This is unfortunate, because as Prussel and Lonsway (2001, pp.91–92) contend:

> Research shows not only are female officers equally as competent as their male counterparts but they also bring a number of unique advantages to law enforcement agencies. First, they often use a communication style that is consistent with the principles of community policing and can serve to de-escalate potentially violent situations. Second, they are substantially less likely to use excessive force, thus decreasing their departments' exposure to liability. Third, women often respond more sympathetically to victims of crime, especially in domestic violence situations, which represent the single largest category of calls for police service. Finally, women often provide an impetus for changes that benefit male and female officers alike, such as improvements in "family-friendly" policies governing childcare, sick leave and the assignment of light duty.

Recruiting, hiring and retaining female officers is vital to a balanced, effective department. Jones and Lonsway (2002, p.95) suggest: "To recruit and hire qualified women, perhaps the single most important thing an agency can do is to reduce the disproportionately adverse impact that current physical agility tests have on women." Lonsway (p.16) also notes: "Physical agility tests that inappropriately emphasize upper body strength often wash out qualified candidates, especially women."

Milgram (2002, p.24) contends: "The key to achieving this increase [in the female applicant pool] is implementing women-specific recruitment strategies such as having a recruiting Web page for women or sponsoring a police career orientation for women." Other women-specific strategies include revising recruiting brochures to include photos of female officers, organizing career fairs specifically for women and displaying recruiting posters in gyms, grocery stores and other places women are likely to see them. Milgram (p.26) suggests: "Police departments should reach out to women who are physically active by posting flyers in places such as gyms; locker rooms of women's sport teams; and facilities for rock climbing, karate, kickboxing, and similar activities." Maglione (2002, p.21) suggests recruiting on military bases and at women's professional basketball games.

Moore (2002, p.29) suggests recruiting women at community colleges, especially those with criminal justice and social service degree programs. Also research the community to identify and target women in female-dominated occupations such as teachers, child-care workers, social workers, clerical support personnel, civilian members of the law enforcement agency and other government agencies.

Campbell et al. (p.20) stress: "Women consistently indicated a higher level of interest in job enrichment factors such as development of knowledge and skills, intellectual stimulation, rewards for good performance, personal challenge, and opportunity for advancement." They also note: "One important strategy . . . is for police agencies to emphasize programs and policies that are designed to accommodate work-family issues."

Recruiting advertisements geared to the crime fighting, law-enforcing aspects of the profession may be ineffective. In fact, according to Lonsway (p.16) the warrior image of officers in some departments needs to be dismantled if the department is to attract women candidates. The Self-Assessment Guide, *Recruiting and Retaining Women* (no data, p.43), states: "In order to recruit more women into policing, law enforcement agencies must overcome the common perception that policing is a 'male-oriented profession' limited to duties that require only physical strength. Movies and television programs frequently show law enforcement officers in high-speed pursuits, fistfights, shoot-outs, hostage situations, and other highly dramatic situations. . . . The media stereotype of police officers contributes enormously to dissuading people who would make excellent officers under a community policing model from pursuing a career in law enforcement." In contrast, an emphasis on the helping aspects of the job might be very appealing. Departments must take care, however, not to turn off highly qualified male applicants.

If recruiting efforts are successful, the law enforcement agency will receive numerous applications from which to select those best suited for their particular agency.

The Selection Process

The selection process may be conducted by an individual or by a committee.

The selection process is based on carefully specified criteria and usually includes completing an application form, undergoing a series of tests and examinations, passing a background check and successfully completing an interview.

A typical sequence of events in the employment process is illustrated in Figure 7.1. Unfortunately, this process is sometimes lengthy, and as Solie (2000, p.20) cautions: "In today's labor market, the best-qualified candidates are not willing to wait months for your selection process to run its course. Public safety organizations must develop valid selection approaches that are also timely. Otherwise, by the time the selection process has run its course, the best-qualified candidates may have found other jobs."

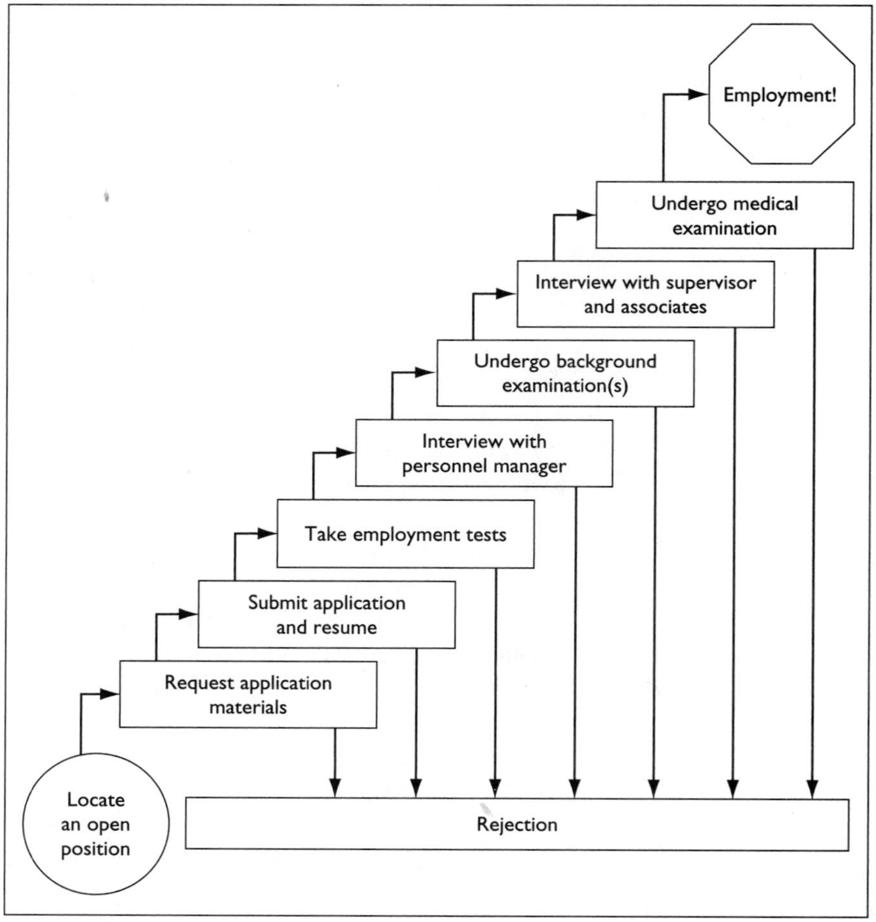

Source: J. Scott Harr and Kären M. Hess. *Seeking Employment in Criminal Justice and Related Fields,* 4th ed. Belmont, CA: Wadsworth Publishing Company, 2003, p.176.

Figure 7.1
Typical Employment Process

Hulsey and Goodwin (2001, p.8) also stress: "To remain competitive in the recruiting market for qualified employees, law enforcement agencies must develop new ways to speed the hiring process. Failure to do so will result in the law enforcement profession losing highly skilled potential employees to other occupations." They describe the "Fast Track Application Process" used by the Polk County (Florida) Sheriff's Office. They accept only complete applications submitted personally to the PCSO's Human Resources Division. Applicants are interviewed when they submit the application, and driving, credit and criminal histories are checked electronically. Candidates are informed immediately of their eligibility for employment.

The Application

The initial application is an important document to determine a candidate's competence for the job. The consent statement provides the right to verify any information on the application. The application should also have an employment-at-will provision indicating that no contract guarantees permanent employment.

Many law enforcement departments use a civil service-type application and selection process. Typically the application includes the person's name, address and length of time the person has lived there, educational background, employment record and personal experiences. It may ask whether the applicant is a U.S. citizen and, if not, whether the person has the legal right to remain permanently in the country. It may also ask whether the person has ever been convicted of a crime and, if so, when and where it took place. It may not ask whether the person has ever been arrested. A sample application is contained in Appendix A.

Other information may be asked for on a voluntary basis, including race, age, disabilities, handicapping conditions and military status. Often a statement such as the following is given: "The Anytown Police Department has an equal employment opportunity/affirmative action policy. Knowledge of your race, sex, age, handicap and medical status is necessary for monitoring the effectiveness of the program. Although you are not required to provide the information requested below, your cooperation is appreciated."

The application usually requires a date and the person's signature verifying that all the information provided is accurate. References are also usually requested.

Restricted Subjects

The following subjects are not allowed for either an application form or an employment interview: race, religion, national origin, gender, age (you may ask whether the applicant is between the ages of 18 and 70), marital status and physical capabilities. Administrators should be able to show that all questions are relevant to the position they are seeking applicants for.

Testing/Screening

Applicant testing usually progresses from the least expensive method, the written examination, to the most expensive, the background investigation, with the number of qualified recruits being narrowed at each step. Because several trips are needed to complete the process, the selection process is difficult for anyone living any distance from the hiring agency. Some agencies, such as the one in Las Vegas, have revised their selection process so that it can be completed in one trip.

The most common screening methods for selection are basic skills/written tests, medical examinations, background investigations, psychological examinations and physical fitness tests.

Other methods used with less frequency included oral boards/oral interviews, polygraphs, chief's and/or command interviews and writing tests.

Written Tests

Basic skills in math and reading can be assessed using standardized tests. Writing skills can be tested by having candidates write an autobiography or an essay explaining why they want to become a law enforcement officer. Although many conventional written test formats are available, some departments are using innovative written exam alternatives to assess not only applicants' basic skills but also their compatibility with the profession.

The National Criminal Justice Officer Selection Inventory (NCJOSI) is designed specifically to predict success for criminal justice officer positions. It includes both a cognitive (problem-solving) component and an attitude/personality component. The problem-solving component measures reading comprehension, writing and mathematics. The attitude/personality component assesses interpersonal ability, assertiveness, stress tolerance, team orientation and ethics/integrity.

Harris and Kolkman (p.64) describe a pre-employment screening test called the "Police Officer Screening Test for the 21st Century" or "POST-21." They contend: "This new applicant evaluation tool is designed to identify individuals who have the traits and attitudes most compatible with a community policing environment." The test is an "add-on exam" consisting of four parts: (1) an evaluation of the applicant's policing orientation, (2) a series of questions to test flexibility in responses, (3) an evaluation of the applicant's realistic expectations of police officer duties and (4) an essay section on problem-solving techniques.

Mahoney (2001, p.194) describes Savvy Recruiter, a battery of computer-administered and scored tests that claim to be fair, objective and culturally unbiased and that take advantage of advances in computer technology. The tests include general cognitive ability; the ability to reason in novel, unfamiliar situations; the ability to apply knowledge and skills acquired through formal training to current problems; the effects of distractibility on memory; the capacity to focus attention under stress; and the ability to read the emotions of others through voice tone and body language.

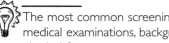

In an effort to speed the application process, the Vermont Association of Chiefs of Police initiated the first statewide test for police applicants, with the results forwarded to every police chief, sheriff and state law enforcement administrators in the state within two weeks of the test, providing a statewide pool of applicants. The chiefs reported that they got better officer candidates and that the candidates thought the test was fair ("Chiefs Cooperate in Recruiting," 2000, p.69).

The Medical Examination

The medical examination assesses overall applicant health and includes more specific tests for vision, hearing and cardiovascular fitness. Departments do allow applicants to have corrected vision with glasses or contact lenses; however, an emerging issue that many agencies are wrestling with has been whether to permit vision correction by laser surgery. The debate centers on the as yet unknown long-term effects of laser correction surgery.

Drug testing may be part of the medical examination. According to Slowik (2002, p.116): "Drug testing can be relatively inexpensive, but not very effective in identifying anyone but the most hard-core addict who cannot quit even for a few days."

Background Investigations

Candidates should undergo a thorough **background check,** usually conducted by a member of the agency. Background checks can prevent many potential problems and save the cost of training an unsuitable employee. In fact, according to Fulton (2000b, p.130): "Personnel background investigations are the single most important element of the recruitment process to avoid personnel problems in the future."

The background check includes past employers and references. The person who conducts the background check should contact every reference, employer and instructor. No final candidates should be selected until reference checks are made. Reference checks should be done from not only those who provided letters of recommendation but others as well. The same inquiries should be made for each candidate, and the questions must be job related.

The background check might also include queries regarding credit, driving record, criminal conviction, academic background and any professional license required. Candidates might be asked to sign a release and authorization statement such as that illustrated in Figure 7.2.

A request should also be made for documents such as diplomas, birth certificates, marriage licenses and driver's licenses. Applicants should be photographed and fingerprinted. Military duty should be confirmed, along with a copy of discharge papers. As Nelson (2000, p.88) stresses: "You should never shortchange the background phase of any application—if for no other reason than to prevent a wrongful hiring lawsuit in the future."

Psychological Examinations

According to Ho (2001, p.319): "Undoubtedly, psychological testing has become a crucial element in the police officer recruitment process since the President's Commission on Law Enforcement and the Administration of Justice (1967) aggressively promoted the necessity of psychologically screening police applicants' emotional stability." Nearly all departments recognize a need for psychological screening of final candidates for a police position, but because of cost or lack of

Sample Release and Authorization Statement

In connection with this request, I authorize all corporations, companies, former employers, credit agencies, educational institutions, law enforcement agencies, city, state, county and federal courts, military services, and persons to release information they may have about me to the person or company with which this form has been filed and release all parties involved from any liability and responsibility for doing so.

I also authorize the procurement of an investigative consumer report and understand that it may contain information about my background, mode of living, character, and personal reputation. This authorization, in original or copy form, shall be valid for this and any future reports or updates that may be requested. Further information may be available on written request within a reasonable period of time.

____________________ Applicant's signature

__________ Date

Figure 7.2
Sample Release and Authorization Statement

Source: © 1991 American Society for Industrial Security, 1655 North Fort Myer Dr., Suite 1200, Arlington, VA 22209. Reprinted by permission from the April 1991 issue of *Security Management*.

suitable psychologists, it may not be done. Only the leading candidates are evaluated psychologically to keep costs down.

The psychological tests often include cognitive ability, quantitative and language reasoning and the Minnesota Multiphasic Personality Inventory (MMPI), the most widely used psychological assessment test in the country. Osofsky et al. (2001, p.42) explain that clinicians' interviews focus on important criteria identified by prior research: social maturity and self-control, social tolerance, emotional stability/stress tolerance, confidence/assertiveness, personal insight, empathy, effectiveness in work relationships, conventionality and tendency to abide by rules, non-defensiveness, health and achievement/motivation.

Rostow and Davis (p.106) note that: "The expert [psychologist] should be able to forecast the chance of unacceptable conduct for each category of misconduct within a reasonable error limit. Claims of being able to identify better candidates without examinable evidence should be treated with caution." When a candidate's psychological tests indicate abnormalities, a department must consider these seriously before hiring. When testing indicates unsuitability or lack of stability, it is best not to hire.

Psychologists who work with police departments must be familiar with validity and reliability measures of tests, the legal requirements imposed by affirmative action and the ADA, as well as pertinent case law and guidelines. According to Bercaw (2002, p.132): "Ideally, the professional conducting the exam should have a close relationship to law enforcement, either through ongoing contact with the department, riding with officers on patrol, involvement with the regional academy or by being a reserve officer himself."

Polygraph Tests

According to Decicco (2000, p.5): "Approximately 56 percent of police departments use this test, based on measures of a person's respiration, heart rate and gal-

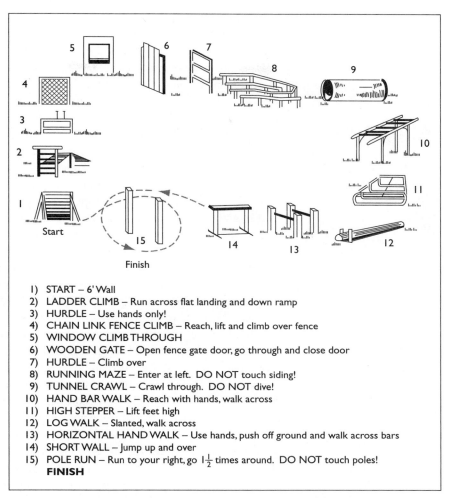

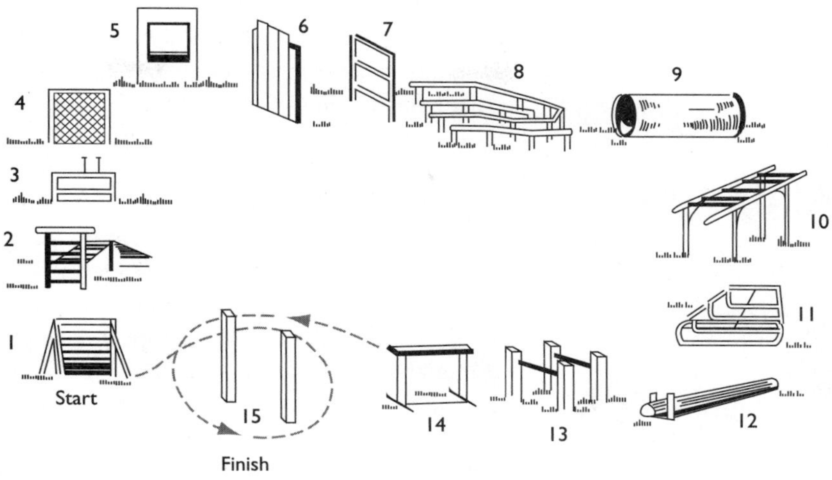

1) START – 6' Wall
2) LADDER CLIMB – Run across flat landing and down ramp
3) HURDLE – Use hands only!
4) CHAIN LINK FENCE CLIMB – Reach, lift and climb over fence
5) WINDOW CLIMB THROUGH
6) WOODEN GATE – Open fence gate door, go through and close door
7) HURDLE – Climb over
8) RUNNING MAZE – Enter at left. DO NOT touch siding!
9) TUNNEL CRAWL – Crawl through. DO NOT dive!
10) HAND BAR WALK – Reach with hands, walk across
11) HIGH STEPPER – Lift feet high
12) LOG WALK – Slanted, walk across
13) HORIZONTAL HAND WALK – Use hands, push off ground and walk across bars
14) SHORT WALL – Jump up and over
15) POLE RUN – Run to your right, go $1\frac{1}{2}$ times around. DO NOT touch poles!
FINISH

Figure 7.3
Physical-Agility Course

Source: Criminal Justice Institute, Broward Community College, Ft. Lauderdale, FL. Reprinted by permission.

vanic skin response." He suggests: "Law enforcement professionals and polygraph administrators should use the machine to deter lying, rather than to detect it."

Physical Fitness Tests

Physical-agility tests are most often of the military type and frequently include an obstacle course. The Broward Community College Criminal Justice Institute's testing center, for example, uses the physical-agility course shown in Figure 7.3.

In addition, Broward uses the following strength and endurance tests:

- Trigger pull—strong hand 18, weak hand 12
- Ten push-ups
- A standing jump based on the person's height
- Three pull-ups (from dead hang, palms facing away)
- Vehicle push—20 feet (push from rear of vehicle)
- Mile run (5 minutes maximum time)

Kenny (2000, p.58) contends: "Police work requires great endurance, strength and agility—attributes that can mean the difference between life and death." According to Schultz and Acevedo (2000, p.34): "Individual officer fitness cannot be over stressed as it can have a tremendous impact on how well a department functions. Studies have consistently demonstrated that healthy and fit officers improve work productivity, lower absenteeism rates and reduce health risks."

Rafilson (2000, p.99) notes: "There is a tremendous need in law enforcement for legally defensible physical fitness testing methods. He describes the two most common methods: "The first—generally called a fitness test—is usually based on the Cooper standards. This test measures a person's level of fitness through sit-ups, mile-and-a-half runs, bench press repetitions, etc. . . . The second model is known as job-simulation 'physical ability testing.' Candidates perform a series of linked exercises that simulate an officer's job (such as climbing a fence, dry-firing a weapon and dragging a dummy)."

According to Brooks (2001, p.31): "The law enforcement administrator who chooses to use physical fitness standards must be prepared to negotiate a veritable minefield of legal issues when those standards have the effect of discriminating against a Title VII protected class, such as women." Whether the criteria for passing should be the same for males and females is open to debate. If different standards are set, then the Civil Rights Act of 1991 might be used to claim disparate treatment. This act states: "It shall be an unlawful employment practice . . . in connection with the selection or referral of applicants or candidates for employment or promotion, to adjust the scores of, [or] use different cutoff scores . . . on the basis of race, color, religion, sex or national origin."

Moore (p.29) notes: "Entry-level physical ability tests are often outdated, are not job-related, and test for physical requirements not needed to perform the job of a modern law enforcement officer. These tests often put unnecessary emphasis on upper body strength and rely on methods of testing that eliminate large numbers of women who are, in fact, well qualified for the job. . . . The best strategy is to use a fitness model for entry-level hiring and then train recruits during the academy to reach the level of ability proven to be necessary for the job."

The Interview

In-person interviews should be held with each applicant, during which the department can explain the nature and benefits of the position to be filled. In return, the applicant can explain his or her interest in law enforcement and, specifically, your department. Provide an opportunity for the applicant to ask questions. Most applicants have questions about salary, benefits, overtime, promotions, uniform allowances and the like.

Civil Service Commission representatives or other selection board personnel usually conduct the final interview. Whether an individual or a panel conducts the interview, those responsible should be familiar with what they can and cannot ask. The same questions that were prohibited on the application are also prohibited during the interview. Interviewers should also take certain steps before, during and after the interview to make it most effective.

Before the Interview

Interviewers should review the application forms, letters of recommendation, references, notes and all other application materials. They might be asked to do a preliminary ranking of specific factors. Such materials and information should not be discussed with others in the organization and should be kept secured.

Decide the questions to ask or general areas to cover as well as who will ask each question or cover each area. Design the questions to determine the "fit" between the candidate and the position. Consider asking the following questions:

- Why do you want to become a law enforcement officer?
- What do you think you will contribute to the department?
- What do you think are the most significant trends in law enforcement?
- How have your education and experiences prepared you for this position?
- What plans do you have for self-development in the next 12 months?
- Why did you select this department/agency?

As you frame the questions, consider the following general guidelines:

- Avoid asking questions that call for yes or no answers (closed questions). Ask open-ended questions. Interviewers want to hear how candidates think and to see their ability to do so under stress.
- Avoid asking leading questions. Instead ask questions that use "why," "how," "what" and "describe" or "tell me about."
- Avoid asking about any of the prohibited information protected by the Equal Employment Opportunity Act (to be discussed shortly).
- Keep questions job related.

During the Interview

The first step is to establish **rapport,** a feeling of mutual understanding and trust. A warm greeting, friendly handshake, sincere smile and some small talk are appropriate to establish a relaxed atmosphere.

The next step is usually to explain how the interview will proceed or to set the agenda, including a general time frame. Next you can describe the job and the organization and then ask the predetermined questions.

During the question/answer portion of the interview, your listening skills are critical. Some suggest that interviewers should talk no more than 25 percent of the time. Candidates should do most of the talking. Silences should not be sources of anxiety because candidates often need time to formulate their responses. Wait patiently.

Consider tape recording the interview if you are to conduct several. This can help refresh your memory later. Candidates whose interviews you are recording should be notified of this before the interview begins. Recording all applicants and then listening to them in one sitting allows for better comparisons.

To ensure that interviews are nondiscriminatory:

- Ask the same general questions and require the same standards for all applicants.
- Treat all applicants fairly, equally and consistently.
- Be professional and consistent in addressing men and women. If using first names, do so for all candidates.
- Never indicate that you are interested in hiring a woman or minority person to improve your Affirmative Action/Equal Employment Opportunity profile. It is unlawful and insulting to apply different standards based on a candidate's gender or minority status.

Maintaining eye contact, listening carefully and taking notes are ways to show candidates you are paying attention to their responses. It is often best to take notes on a clipboard held in your lap so candidates do not see what you are writing.

Do not form an opinion early in the interview. Stay neutral throughout. Avoid the **halo effect**—the tendency to assume that candidates who are strong (or weak) in one area will also be strong (or weak) in other areas. Allow time at the end of the interview for candidates to ask questions. Conclude the interview with a thank you and an indication of when you might make a decision. Figure 7.4 summarizes obstacles to effective interviewing. Some agencies use interview rating forms such as that in Appendix B.

After the Interview

After the successful candidates are selected and notified and they accept the position, all other candidates should be notified of the decision. All selection process materials such as ratings, reference check notes and the actual application files should be returned immediately to the personnel office or other appropriate location. Successful candidates are usually required to pass a stringent medical examination before the job offer is final.

Selection is an expensive, time-consuming process for any agency. It is also a time-consuming and frustrating process for candidates. Often eligibility lists are obtained even though no actual position may be open. Elapsed time between taking an examination and obtaining a position may vary from weeks to years.

Some states have considered giving statewide examinations, permitting any participating law enforcement agency within the state to draw candidates from this list. This would eliminate much individual recruiting and selecting and also reduce costs. However, a strong desire for local testing based on local needs remains. A future consideration could be metropolitan, regional or statewide examinations, with each community making its final selections from this list.

Assessment Centers

Assessment centers are nothing new. Both the Allies and the Axis used them during World War II to train their spies. According to Cosner and Baumgart (2000, p.1): "Today, various organizations view the assessment center as a widely

OBSTACLES TO EFFECTIVE INTERVIEWING

Unfortunately, it is easy for an interviewer to make a mistake in an employment interview. Some of the common mistakes that have been detected in poorly conducted interviews are as follows:

Mistakes	Comments
Failing to establish rapport with the applicant.	As a result, the interview never gets off the ground.
Not knowing what information is needed.	Consequently, the interviewer does not know what questions to ask the applicant.
Concentrating exclusively on the applicant as a person.	The perceptive interviewer specifically attempts to compare an applicant's demonstrated abilities and experience with the actual job requirements.
Not remaining silent, or listening, long enough.	The interviewer does too much talking and fails to obtain meaningful information from the applicant.
Not allowing sufficient time to observe the applicant's responses and behavior.	The interview should not be too short and superficial. The longer the interview, the better the chances of gaining meaningful information from the applicant.
Incorrectly interpreting information obtained from the applicant.	The interviewer draws the wrong conclusion about the applicant's ability to perform.
Being unaware of or not dealing directly with biases for or against certain types of applicants (stereotyping).	This includes how you feel about hair styles, clothing, educational background, etc. ("I have never hired a good secretary from that business college.")
Being overly influenced (either favorably or unfavorably) by one characteristic or trait of that particular applicant.	This includes physical appearances, style of dress, personality, etc. ("I can't stand men who have mustaches," or "I'd hire her for this job no matter what her previous experience.")
Making a decision based only on intuition or "first impression," rather than careful insight and analytical judgment.	
Using stress techniques designed to trap or fluster the applicant.	
Conducting a poorly structured or an unstructured interview.	
Looking to see how an applicant's past life compares with the interviewer's.	This results in substantial loss of time, because more effort is spent on the "halo effect" comparison than on obtaining information relevant to the job.
Failing to control or direct the interview.	Whether out of a desire to be courteous or because the applicant is particularly dominant, the interviewer can lose control of an interview. When this happens, the interviewer must regain control skillfully—not abruptly.
Asking questions answerable by a simple "yes" or "no."	People are used to doing this because their daily business conversations are often short and to the point, but in interviewing, the interviewer must endeavor to do just the opposite—to draw the candidate out. This requires minimizing "yes" and "no" answers.
Making judgmental or leading statements.	These telegraph to the candidate desired responses. Most applicants are good enough at reading the interviewer's mind without being provided direct guidance.

Figure 7.4
Obstacles to Effective Interviewing

Source: Gary P. Scholick. "Interview Guide for Supervisors." Reprinted with permission of the College and University Personnel Association, Washington, DC.

accepted tool for recommending personnel actions in a variety of occupations, including law enforcement."

Decicco (p.5) points out the difference between an assessment center and an assessment center approach: "An assessment center is a place where a series of events or exercises will occur; however, the assessment center approach is a method that supplements the traditional assessment and selection procedures with situational exercises designed to simulate actual police officer responsibilities and working conditions."

Tinsley (2002, p.35) contends: "The assessment center method has three chief advantages: it is straightforward, it is based on common sense, and it can be applied in almost any employment context. . . . The assessment center was—and still is—one of the best methods available for selecting suitable candidates for either employment or advancement in law enforcement agencies."

Whether you use an assessment center or an internal panel, carefully evaluate personal dimensions as well in the promotional process. Conducting promotional examinations is discussed in detail in Chapter 10.

Innovations in Selection

Among the innovations being used in selection are the human resource roundtable and the candidate ride-along.

The Human Resource Roundtable

Clark et al. (2001, p.29) describe the human resource roundtable being used by the Washington State Patrol (WSP): "A roundtable is a group discussion of an applicant's employment packet before making the final hiring decision. The roundtable brings together data, insight and perspective from human resources, the department psychologist, appropriate command-level personnel and the WSP labor and risk manager (an attorney) as needed." According to Clark et al.: "The WSP has three goals during the roundtable process: (1) to hire the best applicants by decentralizing the final hiring decision from one individual to a team of professionals utilizing a multifaceted decision making employment process; (2) to reduce the agency's exposure to litigation; and (3) to continually evaluate and update the hiring process and the decision makers." They (p.35) conclude: "The roundtable is a valuable risk management tool to reduce the agency's exposure to litigation regarding hiring decisions."

The Candidate Ride-Along

Sokolove and Field (2002, p.55) explain another supplemental selection tool: "The police officer candidate ride-along readily affords qualified applicants an opportunity to observe the agency up close. . . . The police officer candidate ride-along should be viewed as a selection component designed to minimize unnecessary and time-wasting mismatches of employees and organizations." They contend: "The candidate ride-along is much like a two-way mirror. It enables the candidate to take a closer and perhaps more realistic view of the jurisdiction while also affording the prospective employer a better picture of the candidate. This creates a legitimate win-win experience for everyone."

Employment Criteria

To comply with Equal Employment Opportunity requirements and avoid legal problems, law enforcement agencies must hire personnel to meet very specific standards directly related to the job.

A **bona fide occupational qualification (BFOQ)** is one that is reasonably necessary to perform a job.

An example of a bona fide occupational qualification in law enforcement might be that the applicant has normal or correctable-to-normal hearing and vision or that the person be able to drive a vehicle.

Educational Requirements

One requirement that may pose difficulties is requiring a certain level of education. As far back as 1916 August Vollmer, father of modern policing, emphasized education for officers. Guthrie (2000, p.124) notes: "The Wickersham Commission (1937) and the President's Commission on Law Enforcement and the Administration of Justice (1967) both recommended post-secondary education for law enforcement officers." Yet many law enforcement departments require only a high-school diploma or its equivalent. According to Bowman (2002, p.11): "Only about 50 state and local police agencies nationwide require officers to have a four-year college degree." However, in 2000, 37 percent of the police departments serving cities of 250,000 or more people required new officers to meet some type of college education requirement, compared with only 19 percent a decade earlier. The percentage of departments requiring a two-year or four-year degree increased from 6 to 14 percent ("Police Education and Training . . . ," 2002, p.7). In some states, such as Minnesota, a two-year degree is required throughout the state.

Armstrong and Polk (2002, p.25) cite the advantages commonly associated with higher education: "The college experience allows for greater maturity. The individual is exposed to other cultures and lifestyles. College provides a broad base of knowledge that provides the officer with greater flexibility in the decision-making process. College educated officers are more receptive to change and new ideas. And the officer develops enhanced verbal and written communication skills."

A study conducted by Polk and Armstrong (2001, p.77) found: "Higher education reduces time required for movement in rank and assignment to specialized positions and was positively correlated to promotion into supervisory and administrative posts. Implications are that higher education will enhance an officer's probability of rising to the top regardless of whether the agency requires a college degree as a precondition of employment."

The most common reason for not requiring higher education is the fear the requirement would be challenged in court or through labor arbitration. A landmark case was *Griggs v. Duke Power Company* (1971) in which Griggs, an African-American employee, claimed that the requirement of having a high-school diploma and passing two aptitude tests discriminated against him. The court ruled that any requirements or tests used in selecting or promoting must be job related.

A similar case occurred in *Davis v. City of Dallas* (1978). The Dallas Police Department at the time required applicants to have completed 45 semester hours of college credit with a "C" average. In this case the court ruled in favor of the police department, because the city introduced evidence supporting the educational requirement. Numerous nationwide studies have examined setting education requirements for police departments with favorable conclusions.

A study by one expert relied upon factual data from two large metropolitan areas that took two years to complete, showing significantly higher performance rates by college-educated officers. A persuasive point was made that a high school diploma today does not represent the same level of achievement it represented 10 years ago.

Clearly, not everyone agrees that college education enhances patrol officer performance. The biggest objections are that there are not enough promotions to satisfy a college-educated employee, the college-educated employee would be less likely to accept authority, such a requirement would lower the pool of applicants for police positions and would be detrimental to potential minority applicants.

Still, the advantages of advanced education appear to outweigh the disadvantages. The Police Executive Research Forum (PERF) has recommended that by 2003 all entry-level law enforcement officers have completed a four-year degree.

Various recruitment and scholarship programs have been developed throughout the country to attract and educate those who are interested in criminal justice professions. One national scholarship program, the Police Corps, recruits and trains college graduates to serve as community police officers. Hoffman (2000, p.51) explains: "Future officers are hired on a tentative basis by a participating police department with the understanding they will become employees upon completion of the special Police Corps academy. The candidates agree to stay with the sponsoring department for four years in return for being fully compensated for their four-year college degree, up to an amount of $30,000."

One concern of those seeking higher education while employed as officers is how to pursue a course of study without taking time off from work. One solution is available through the Internet and distance learning, as discussed in the next chapter. A question facing applicants and administrators alike is, if a degree is sought, what *type* of degree is most beneficial? Should it be a degree in liberal arts or in criminal justice? Opinions are mixed on this issue.

Another item of contention is *how much* advanced education is recommended for officers of varying ranks. Some experts think that experience in other law enforcement agencies should substitute for education. What this ratio of experience to education should be is not clear. An officer who has both education and experience is obviously the most desirable.

Whatever the decision, a clear policy documenting that a specific level of education is a bona fide occupational qualification (BFOQ) should be established. In addition, it is becoming more common for promotion to be contingent upon a higher level of education. Fulton (2000a, p.102) suggests: "Getting your degrees, going to all kinds of training classes and getting diversified experience is the way to a successful career."

Because managers hire and promote, they must be thoroughly familiar with laws related to employment.

Laws Affecting Employment

Several laws affect employment, including the following:

- *The Equal Pay Act of 1963 (EPA)* prohibits discrimination in wages on the basis of gender for all employers.
- *Civil Rights Acts of 1964 and 1970* prohibit race discrimination in hiring, placement and continuation of employment for all private employers, unions and employment agencies.

Title VII of the **Civil Rights Act of 1964,** as amended by the *Equal Employment Opportunity Act (EEOA) of 1972,* prohibits discrimination based on race, color, religion, gender or national origin for private employers with 15 or more employees, governments, unions and employment agencies.

- *The Age Discrimination in Employment Act (ADEA) of 1967,* amended in 1978, prohibits discrimination based on age for people between the ages of 40 and 70.
- *Title IX of 1972 Education Amendments* prohibits discrimination in education benefits based on race, color, religion, gender and national origin.
- *The Rehabilitation Act of 1973,* amended in 1980, prohibits discrimination against handicapped individuals for federal contractors and the federal government.
- *The Pregnancy Discrimination Act of 1978,* an amendment to Title VII, prohibits discrimination in employment on the basis of pregnancy, childbirth and related conditions for all private employers with 15 or more employees, governments, unions and employment agencies.
- *The Civil Service Reform Act of 1978* requires a federal government "workforce reflective of the nation's diversity."
- *The Immigration Reform and Control Act of 1986* prohibits discrimination against qualified aliens or on the basis of national origin.
- *The Americans with Disabilities Act of 1990 (ADA)* prohibits discrimination based on physical or intellectual handicap for employers with 15 or more employees.

The legislation guaranteeing rights for people with disabilities provides only for fair and equal treatment in the workplace based on ability. Private employers or government agencies are not required to hire candidates for employment who are not qualified to perform essential job functions. The ADA is discussed in detail following this overview.

The **Equal Employment Opportunity Commission (EEOC)** enforces laws prohibiting job discrimination based on race, color, religion, gender, national origin, handicapping condition or age between 40 and 70.

Family and Medical Leave Act of 1993

This law requires companies of 50 or more employees to allow employees 12 weeks of unpaid leave of absence for parenting or medical reasons.

The Americans with Disabilities Act of 1990 (ADA)

The Americans with Disabilities Act (ADA) of 1990, Title I, became effective in 1992. Title II, which involves discrimination in employment practices, went into effect in 1994 and applies to all agencies with 15 or more employees.

> Law enforcement is directly affected by the ADA's goal of guaranteeing individuals with disabilities access to employment and to governmental programs, services and activities.

According to Colbridge (2000b, p.28): "For purposes of the ADA, disability means having a physical or mental impairment that substantially limits one or more major life activities, having a record of such an impairment, or being regarded as having such an impairment." Colbridge (2000a, p.30) notes: "Courts have upheld employers' decisions to not hire people with disabilities who lacked . . . qualifications . . . essential to the performance of the job." He suggests:

> The wise manager should take the time to identify the essential functions of all positions in his or her organization. For the police manager, some of the work of identifying essential functions of a police officer has been done by the courts. For example, case law has established that firing a weapon and making forcible arrests are essential functions of a police officer. Driving is also essential. As well as evidence collection. This list is obviously not exhaustive. Logically, officers must also be able to testify in court, communicate with victims and witnesses, and read and write reports. Physical functioning also is crucial to officers.

The ADA prohibits employers from discriminating against a *qualified individual with a disability (QID)* in all areas of employment, including hiring, training, promoting, terminating and compensation. It also prohibits discrimination in nonemployment areas and requires accessibility to all services and facilities of public entities.

Table 7.1 contains a brief explanation of key terms commonly used in the ADA. Notice especially the definitions for *disability* and *otherwise qualified.*

The ADA also establishes the following excluded disorders that are not caused by a physical impairment and thus are not considered disabilities: bisexuality, compulsive gambling, exhibitionism, gender-identity disorders, homosexuality, kleptomania, pedophilia, pyromania, sexual behavior disorder, transsexualism, transvestism and voyeurism.

Scuro (2001, p.31) notes: "There are still no uniform standards to be applied when addressing the daily personnel issues that are a part of the routine operations of both a public sector law enforcement agency or private sector corporation. It is this void that raises the potential for abuse by individual employees." Colbridge (2002, p.27) also notes that 12 years after the passage of the ADA: "Its meaning still is debated."

Scuro (2002, p.16) describes three Supreme Court cases decided in 1999: *Sutton v. United Air Lines, Inc.; Murphy v. United Parcel Service, Inc.;* and *Albert-*

Table 7.1
Terms Associated with the ADA

The ADA uses numerous terms to describe its requirements and the obligations of those covered by the law. Here is a brief index and short explanation of some of the key words and phrases commonly used in the ADA.

Disability	(1) A mental or physical impairment that substantially limits a major life activity; (2) a record of having such an impairment; (3) being regarded as having such an impairment.
Impairment	A physiological or mental disorder.
Substantial limitation	When compared to the average person: (1) an inability to perform a major life activity; (2) a significant restriction on how or how long the activity can be performed; or (3) a significant restriction on the ability to perform a class or broad range of jobs.
Major life activity	Basic functions that the average person in the general population can do with little or no difficulty such as walking, seeing, hearing, breathing, speaking, procreating, learning, sitting, standing, performing manual tasks, working or having intimate sexual relations.
Otherwise qualified	A person with a disability who satisfies all of the requirements of the job such as education, experience, or skill and who can perform the essential functions of the job with or without reasonable accommodation.
Essential functions	The fundamental, not marginal, duties of a job.
Reasonable accommodation	A change in the application process, work environment, or job descriptions involving marginal functions of the job, or the use of modified or auxiliary devices that enable a person with a disability to perform the essential functions of the job without causing an undue hardship or direct threat to the health and safety of herself or himself or of others.
Undue hardship	Significant difficulty or expense relative to the size and overall financial resources of the employer.
Direct threat	A significant risk of substantial harm based on valid, objective evidence and not mere speculation.

Source: Paula N. Rubin. *The Americans with Disabilities Act and Criminal Justice: An Overview.* Washington, DC: National Institute of Justice, Research in Action, September 1993, p.4.

sons, Inc. v. Kirkingburg. He reports: "In all three cases the opinions were clearly consistent with one another: the U.S. Supreme Court concluded that where a person has taken steps to overcome, adjust and adapt to an otherwise ADA protected condition or disability, that person no longer can seek protection under the act."

Employment Issues

This act has had a significant impact on the recruiting process. Most agencies have had to reorganize some of their recruiting procedures. To be in compliance, administrators should identify "essential functions" in job descriptions. Based on these, they should next develop selection criteria—ways to measure an applicant's ability to perform each essential job function.

The ADA prohibits medical inquiries or evaluations, including some psychiatric evaluations, until after a job offer has been made.

The medical examination remains an important part of the application process, however. Serious consequences could arise as a result of a police officer not having the ability to perform essential job functions. If an applicant's disability would cause a direct threat to the applicant or public safety, the risk must be identified and documented by objective medical evidence as well.

Not all psychological examinations are disallowed under the ADA. Only those tests or scales specifically designed to disclose an impairment are disallowed. The ADA does not address polygraph tests and does not consider physical agility tests to be medical examinations; therefore, such tests are not governed by the ADA. In addition, according to Colbridge (2000c, p.19): "Tests for the use of illegal drugs are not considered medical examinations for the purposes of the ADA." Applicants may be subjected to drug testing. Further, employers may hold illegal drug users and alcoholics to the same performance standards as other employees.

Reasonable Accommodations

Employers must make "reasonable accommodations" for any physical or mental limitations of a QID unless the employer can show that such accommodation would create an undue hardship or could threaten the health and safety of the QID or other employees. Reasonable accommodations might include modifying existing facilities to make them accessible, job restructuring, part-time or modified work schedules, or acquiring or modifying equipment. However, reasonable accommodations are not required when providing them causes an undue hardship for the agency.

It is unlikely that police agencies will be required to make substantial accommodations in the hiring process because the nature of police work requires some degree of fitness that can be substantiated through a job analysis. However, a reasonable accommodation goes beyond modifying job descriptions. It also means making buildings accessible to the physically disabled. Accessibility applies not only to employees but to nonemployees as well and involves parking lots, the building itself, the front desk, elevator and staff. Appendix C contains an accessibility checklist. Two government publications that provide assistance in this area are the *ADA Accessibility Guidelines* and the *Uniform Federal Accessibility Standards.*

Nonemployment Issues

The ADA regulates all services and programs provided by public entities, which includes law enforcement agencies. Police agencies report that the greatest difficulties they face when responding to people with disabilities are citizens' misunderstanding of the police role in dealing with persons with disabilities; difficulty reaching help on weekends and evenings; and mistaking disabilities for antisocial behavior. Litchford (2000, p.15) points out: "The Courts have held that the ADA does not prohibit officers from taking enforcement action, including the use of force, necessary to protect officer or public safety." Litchford (p.17) also points out: "Courts have held that the ADA requires officers, when questioning suspects at the police station, to provide auxiliary aids reasonably necessary to ensure effective communication and to delay questioning of hearing-impaired suspects or witnesses until such assistance can be provided. Unless a hearing person would be arrested without interview, a deaf person should not be arrested without provision of a qualified interpreter."

Enforcement of the ADA

The regulating agencies for the ADA are the Department of Justice (DOJ), the Architectural Transportation Compliance Board (ATCB), the Equal Employment Opportunity Commission (EEOC) and the Federal Communications Commission (FCC).

Agencies out of compliance may face civil penalties up to $50,000 for the first violation and $100,000 for subsequent violations, in addition to being ordered to modify their facilities to be in compliance.

Affirmative Action

Not only must employers avoid discrimination in the hiring process, in some instances they must actively seek out certain people and make certain they have equal opportunities to obtain jobs.

An **affirmative action program (AAP)** is a written plan to assist members of traditionally discriminated-against minority groups in employment, government contracts and education.

Affirmative action programs are mandated by several employment laws. Their intent is to undo the damage caused by past discrimination. The affirmative action policy of one agency states:

> The Anytown Police Department realizes that discrimination and the prejudice from which it results are deeply ingrained within our culture. Concentration on the mere prevention of discrimination can result in the implementation of practices that provide only superficial equality. Such practices, while possibly within the letter of the law, do not enact the full intent of the federal and state legislation, presidential and gubernatorial executive orders or the courts' interpretation of these mandates. It is, therefore, the intent of the Anytown Police Department to organize and implement policies, procedures, practices and programs that aid in overcoming the effects of past discrimination in regard to all of the protected groups.

Among the **special employment groups** included in affirmative action programs are African-Americans, Asians, the elderly, Eskimos, Hispanics, homosexuals, immigrants, individuals with AIDS, individuals with disabilities, Middle-Easterners, Native Americans, religious group members, substance abusers, war veterans, women and youth.

From this listing, one conclusion is obvious: anyone can fit into a "special employment group." Those responsible for hiring must take precautions to be fair and unbiased. They should recognize existing biases and ensure that biases do not enter into the process—a difficult task. If, for example, an affirmative action plan requires that all members of certain groups, such as minority group members, be given a personal interview, this may cause members not within this group to claim reverse discrimination. **Reverse discrimination** refers to giving women and minorities preferential treatment in hiring and promoting to the detriment of white males.

In 1978 the Supreme Court, in *Regents of University of California v. Bakke,* allowed use of race as a factor among many in admissions to achieve diversity. Alan Bakke, a 37-year-old white male engineer, was denied admission to the medical school at the University of California at Davis, although his Medical College Admission Test score and grade point average were higher than those of several of the 16 minority students admitted under a set-aside. In a 5–4 decision, the Court voted to invalidate the Cal-Davis quota system and admit Bakke to medical school. However, it endorsed affirmation action in principle.

Several court decisions have struck down affirmative action initiatives as discriminatory. In 1996 both Texas and California (Proposition 209) struck down race-based admissions policies in their universities. The Berger Court sought a middle ground regarding affirmative action, supporting the basic concept but rejecting rigid application. The Rehnquist Court has taken a more negative view of affirmative action but has not rejected the concept totally. The Supreme Court will be looking at affirmative action in 2003 when it considers whether the admission requirements of the University of Michigan are constitutional given that race is awarded 20 points while a perfect SAT score receives only 12 points.

Some departments use a form such as that contained in Appendix D to gather needed affirmative action data.

Equal employment opportunity and affirmative action policies begin with recruiting and selecting but are also important in assigning, training, promoting, disciplining and firing personnel.

Because these EEO and AA policies are important in so many areas of management, it is critical that managers understand their own policies as well as the policies and ordinances or statutes of their municipality, state and the country. Such knowledge is critical during the selection process. Possible resources are the director of personnel, the city attorney, law enforcement advisory boards, other law enforcement agencies and the International Association of Chiefs of Police.

In addition to laws related to hiring, many managers also must take into consideration restrictions imposed by unions.

Labor Laws and Unions

A **union,** in the broadest context, is any group authorized to represent the members of the law enforcement agency in negotiating matters such as wages, fringe benefits and other conditions of employment. Most states require by statute that certain conditions be met to be recognized as a union or bargaining unit. A **union shop** refers to a situation in which people must belong to or join the union to be hired.

Several laws ensure fair compensation standards as well as employees' rights to bargain collectively with management. Unions have existed in the United States for more than 200 years, beginning in 1792 when shoemakers formed a local union in Philadelphia. In 1932, the **Norris-LaGuardia Act** was passed to regulate employers' use of court injunctions against unions in preventing work stoppages. The Act also made yellow-dog contracts illegal. A **yellow-dog contract** forbids new employees to join a union. To do so would be grounds for discharge.

Another major law, sometimes called the "Magna Carta of organized labor," was enacted in 1935.

The **National Labor Relations Act of 1935 (Wagner Act)** legalized collective bargaining and required employers to bargain with the elected representatives of their employees.

This act sets forth rules and procedures for both employers and employees. Its intent was to define and protect the rights of employees and employers and to encourage collective bargaining.

The **Fair Labor Standards Act of 1938** established the 40-hour week as the basis of compensation and set a minimum wage. The **Taft-Hartley Act of 1947** was passed to balance the power of unions and management by banning several unfair labor practices, including closed shops. A **closed shop** prohibits management from hiring nonunion workers. In effect, this act allowed states to pass their own **right-to-work laws,** making it illegal to require employees to join a union. In addition, the **Landrum-Griffin Act of 1959** required regularly scheduled elections of union officers by secret ballot and regulated the handling of union funds.

The **National Labor Relations Board (NLRB)** is the principal enforcement agency for laws regulating relations between management and unions.

Strong feelings for and against unions are common in the general public and among those in law enforcement. For many law enforcement agencies, unions are a positive force; for others, they create problems and dissension; and in yet others, they are nonexistent. Even in agencies without unions, however, the possibility of employees becoming unionized is always there. Consequently, managers need to understand the current nature of unions and how they can benefit the mission of a law enforcement agency.

The primary purpose of unions is to improve employment conditions through collective bargaining.

Collective bargaining is the process whereby representatives of employees meet with representatives of management to establish a written contract that sets forth working conditions for a specific time, usually one to three years. The contract deals not only with wages and benefits but also with hours of work and overtime, grievance procedures, disciplinary procedures, health and safety,

Law enforcement unions are among the fastest-growing unions in the United States. Here a group of sheriff's deputies discusses negotiations during a union meeting.

employees' rights, seniority and contract duration. Most states have laws restricting officers from going on strike.

Law enforcement managers must recognize that officers have a right to join a union and to negotiate with management. Unions have caused administrators to re-examine their roles in negotiations, roles that have varied from remoteness to direct involvement at the bargaining table. In more recent years, both sides have engaged outside experts to represent their positions in negotiations, both at the bargaining table and during arbitration proceedings.

An estimated 66 percent of law enforcement departments in the United States work with some type of union, ranging from officially recognized discussion to representation of employees at grievance hearings, conciliation proceedings, collective bargaining or arbitration hearings. As in all other official proceedings, careful records must be retained by all individuals at all levels of the agency.

The union is obligated to protect the union employees' interests. Management is obligated to manage and control the agency. The ultimate goal of both should be excellent law enforcement services. At times the relationship develops into a struggle for power, with each assuming an adversarial position. By working together, management and unions can achieve the agency's mission to provide effective service to the community.

Types of Law Enforcement Unions

Law enforcement labor representation groups include local department benevolent associations that act on behalf of personnel, independent unions with a regional or state affiliation and nationally supported and organized labor unions such as the AFL-CIO.

Many law enforcement labor organizations simply evolved. A social group would be formed to discuss the interrelationships of a department and plan social events for the year, often including family members. Over the years these groups started discussions concerning perceived department problems and eventually grew into benevolent associations.

In the early 1960s law enforcement unions were largely local and independent. Current estimates show that 30 to 40 percent of department employees belong to local unions, 40 to 45 percent to regional or state unions, and 15 to 20 percent to national labor groups. The latter has been steadily increasing. In fact, law enforcement membership in unions is one of the fastest growing labor groups in the nation. It is estimated that in excess of 100,000 officers belong to organized labor unions in the United States.

One highly debated issue concerning union membership has been who should belong. What ranks should be included? Should managers and supervisors belong to the same union as line officers because their interests in wages and benefits are largely the same? Is there a conflict of interest?

Some studies indicate that 85 percent of law enforcement unions include both patrol officers and sergeant levels or above, which means that only 15 percent consist solely of patrol level. As long as issues are mainly concerned with wages and benefits, this is not a problem. But when issues involve taking more control of what management considers its rights, such as one-officer versus two-officer patrol cars, transfers and promotions, working-hour assignments and the like, conflict can occur. Some agencies have formed separate management-level units within the same umbrella as the rank-and-file union to overcome the objections to a single unit.

Some managers would rather not have unions. If unions are to exist, most managers would rather they be local and independent. Local union membership provides opportunity for personal, face-to-face discussions about local department problems; lower dues; more control over who is to represent the department and control over all expenditures.

On the other hand, national union representation allows national research on wages, benefits and other issues; outside representation at discussions; and greater political influence. Legal assistance is often available. Outside representation avoids union conflict issues spilling over into everyday performance and personal relationships. The main national union groups are:

- *International Union of Police Associations*—affiliated with the AFL-CIO.
- *Fraternal Order of Police*—the oldest police organization in the United States; emphasizes collective bargaining in some areas and socializing in other areas.
- *National Association of Police Officers*—consists of police unions opposed to affiliation with the AFL-CIO.
- *International Brotherhood of Police Officers*—founded in Rhode Island in 1969; emphasizes collective bargaining.
- *International Brotherhood of Teamsters*—a private union.
- *American Federation of State, County and Municipal Employees*—a union for public employees founded in 1936, affiliated with the American Federation of Labor.

Each organization decides what kind of union to have and often bases its selection on past local management/rank-and-file relationships. Attitudes toward management have often been as much a reason for union membership as other conditions of employment.

Reasons for Joining Law Enforcement Unions

A common reason for joining a union is a perceived lack of communication, inaction or deliberate disregard for the feelings and reasonable desires of the majority of employees. Other frequently mentioned reasons are lack of concern for the employees' general needs, lower wages and fewer benefits than comparable departments, peer pressure, general frustration, conditions of equipment or employment, imagined wrongs, lack of concern for legitimate grievances, badly handled personnel problems, inadequate communications, favoritism, lack of formal grievance procedures, distrust between management and the rank and file, disregard of job stress factors, past bad-faith bargaining and negotiating, lack of recognition for a job well done and a lack of leadership by management.

People join unions to ensure fair treatment, to improve their economic situation and to satisfy social needs.

Management vs. Employee Rights

Controversy between management and unions revolves largely around what is perceived as reasonable management and employee rights or demands. Managers must have specific functions reserved. On the other hand, management depends on employees to do the job. The better law enforcement tasks are performed, the better the managers and employees are perceived by the community they both serve. The better the community perception and rating of the agency, the greater the acceptance of law enforcement needs in terms of wages, benefits and general support.

The most frequently reserved management rights are determining staffing and staffing levels; determining work schedules, patrol areas and work assignments; controlling police operations; establishing standards of conduct on and off duty; establishing hiring, promoting, transferring, firing and disciplinary procedures; setting work-performance standards; establishing department goals, objectives, policies and procedures; and establishing training programs and who should attend.

Management should not have these rights unreasonably infringed upon at the bargaining table. Contracts are long-term instruments that affect not only the present regime but future managers as well. Management must possess sufficient rights to fulfill the agency's mission to the community.

The most desirable way to avoid management-employee conflict is to resolve issues at the lowest level possible. Primarily, this means between first-line supervisors and patrol officers (or equal rank). The vast majority of issues should be resolved at this level, and the first-line supervisor must have the responsibility and authority to do so.

Others perceive a more basic conflict—a distinct difference between the professional law enforcement stance and that advocated by unions. The *professional* model would be: we look to lateral entry and professional skills rather than time on the job in our selections. We want to expand the entire profession. The *union* model would be: We protect our people no matter what happens. If we have to pick between the young, educated professional and the old, established worker, we go with the old one every time.

Management, Unions and Politics

Management would like to believe that they can administer a law enforcement agency without being involved in politics. Many administrators say, "I try to stay out of politics." If this means actively supporting candidates during political campaigns, it is possible. But to remove oneself from all politics is virtually impossible. Locally elected government officials approve law enforcement budgets. Passage of desirable ordinances and statutes depends on elected officials. Gaining the respect and support of these officials after they are elected is a necessity to law enforcement administration. In some cities, unions are also very active in elections and in supporting specific candidates.

Law enforcement management involvement in politics is less likely in communities with a council/manager form of government because the chief executive officer reports directly to the city manager. The city manager is a buffer between law enforcement managers and the city's elected officials.

City management has many departments and varied personnel concerns. Even though city government may sympathize with law enforcement demands, it must balance the demands of all departments. City administration may resist binding arbitration for this reason. Final decisions are made by people not associated with the local government and who have no personal stake in how the decision may be implemented financially or managerially.

Levels of Bargaining

Bargaining may take place at various levels ranging from discussion to court settlements. At the most cooperative level, **open discussion** resolves issues and results in a win-win situation, with a contract that both sides consider fair. If discussion does not resolve all the issues, the next level may be **mediation,** bringing in a neutral third party to assist in the discussion. A mediator helps the two sides reach an agreement.

If the negotiation process stalls, the matter may be referred to **arbitration,** with the consent of all parties. Usually three arbitrators are appointed, and a majority makes the decision. Either a statute or agreement of all parties determines the method of selection. Arbitration should be a last resort. Beyond arbitration, the matter can sometimes be appealed to the courts.

> Negotiations usually proceed through these levels: discussion, mediation, arbitration and the courts.

Management and Unions Working Together

Law enforcement management/union decision making may involve mayors, councils, city managers and often outside negotiators, arbitrators, grievance committees and even the courts.

Although law enforcement officers usually do not have the right to strike, they may accomplish similar results through actions such as "blue flu" or slowdowns. Bargaining units of some type are a fact of administrators' lives. It is better to form good relationships that lead to positive results for both sides than to begin with adversarial attitudes. Working within the confines of the written contract is important at all levels of supervision and management, from sergeant to chief.

Open communication, reasonable expectations, honest cooperation, upfront presentations, a sincere desire to negotiate and common objectives—all are evidence of good-faith bargaining.

Avoid **delaying tactics** such as failing to disclose important demands until the end; deliberately withholding information; deliberately providing misinformation, untruths or distortions; providing only information that weakens the others' position; or deliberately exhibiting unwillingness to resolve the issues so as to throw the process into binding arbitration.

Successful management/union negotiations begin with a positive atmosphere within the agency during everyday activities and normal routine, for here the tone for mutual respect is established. Everyday problems have a way of developing into grievances, which may then become issues in management/union negotiations. When first-line supervisors have open dialogue and communication about problems and this continues up the hierarchy, an avenue is established for later openness in labor relations as well.

Negotiations should be entered into far ahead of budget deadlines. Timing should also avoid city and union elections. Both sides should agree on rules for negotiation procedures; maintain open channels of communication; present logical, reasonable justification for their positions; and prepare areas of agreement as well as disagreement. Areas of agreement should be disposed of as soon as possible to focus energies on differences. Both sides should recognize the emotions involved and resist overreactions. Officials on both sides should be aware that off-the-cuff, unsupportable statements can stop negotiations. Items for negotiation should not be discussed outside negotiation proceedings. No individual department head should have the authority or responsibility for final settlement. Lay the past contract and the proposed contract side by side and compare wording, additions and deletions, word for word, page by page.

The most equitable negotiations take place in an atmosphere of openness, cooperation, faith and trust. Seek fairness and focus on the main goals of both sides.

Collective Bargaining, Arbitration and the CEO

CEOs (chiefs of police, sheriffs, superintendents, directors of public safety or any other title denoting head of an agency) might take several positions in collective bargaining negotiations. At the very least, CEOs should be available to describe how a prior contract has affected the agency or how changes in the community or the agency require changes in the new contract. During negotiation stages, the CEO or the management representatives should be informed about how matters under discussion might affect their operations.

In some instances CEOs may be facilitators or advisors. In this role they can tell negotiators how specific actions would affect management's ability to administer the agency. In other instances CEOs may actively participate in the prenegotiation stages but become interested bystanders during actual negotiations, or they may actively participate in the negotiations.

In all discussions, mediations and arbitrations, retain careful records. What occurs at one level of negotiations is likely to be reviewed at the next level. In addition, what is stated at any time in the process is usually subject to appeal. After the negotiation process is complete, a contract is written containing the specific terms of the agreement. Everyone affected by the contract should receive a copy and understand its terms.

Votes of No Confidence

Berger (2002, p.6) suggests: "Police labor unions have long played an active role in the law enforcement community, and there is no argument that police officers have derived numerous benefits from belonging to unions. Nevertheless, in the past few years, a growing number of police chiefs throughout the United States have had bad personal experiences with a particular union practice—votes of no confidence." According to Berger: "When union leaders use this tactic, the ultimate goal is often to discredit and/or remove the chief. Other times, votes of no confidence are held to enhance the unions' bargaining positions in upcoming negotiations. Regardless of the motive, one thing is clear: a vote of no confidence without a proper response by the chief has the potential to undermine management's effectiveness, damage careers and negatively affect the morale of the police department." Berger suggests: "It is imperative that a chief facing a vote of no confidence, or similar attack, from union officials move quickly and aggressively to uncover the reasons for the union's actions. . . . After determining the basis for the union's actions, the chief must be prepared to address these issues in a professional and highly visible fashion with his or her municipal leaders, the media, and, most importantly, members of the community."

Summary

Selection of law enforcement personnel is a critical management function. The selection process is based on carefully specified criteria and usually includes completing an application form, undergoing a series of tests and examinations, passing a background check and successfully completing an interview. The most common screening methods for selection are basic skills/written tests, medical examinations, background investigations, psychological examinations and physical fitness tests.

Selection is often affected by laws related to equal employment, affirmative action and labor (unions). Title VII of the Civil Rights Act of 1964, as amended by the Equal Employment Opportunity Act (EEOA) of 1972, prohibits discrimination based on race, color, religion, gender or national origin for private employers with 15 or more employees, governments, unions and employment agencies. The Equal Employment Opportunity Commission enforces laws prohibiting job discrimination based on race, color, religion, gender, national origin, handicapping condition or age between 40 and 70. Law enforcement is directly affected by the ADA's goal of guaranteeing individuals with disabilities access to employment and to government programs, services and activities. The ADA prohibits medical inquiries or evaluations, including some psychiatric evaluations, until after a job offer has been made.

A bona fide occupational qualification (BFOQ) is one that is reasonably necessary to perform a job. An affirmative action program (AAP) is a written plan to assist members of traditionally discriminated against minority groups in employment, government contracts and higher education. Equal employment opportunity and affirmative action policies begin with recruiting and selecting but are also important in assigning, training, promoting, disciplining and firing personnel.

The National Labor Relations Act of 1935 (Wagner Act) legalized collective bargaining and required employers to bargain with the elected representatives of their employees. The National Labor Relations Board (NLRB) is the principal enforcement agency for laws regulating relations between management and unions.

The primary purpose of unions is to improve employment conditions through collective bargaining. People join unions to ensure fair treatment, to improve their economic situations and to satisfy social needs. Negotiations usually proceed through discussion, mediation, arbitration and the courts.

Discussion Questions

1. During which stages of the selection process is discrimination most likely to occur?
2. Compare and contrast the Equal Employment Opportunity Act and an affirmative action plan.
3. Have there been any civil suits related to law enforcement employment in your area in the past few years? In your state?
4. What is the most difficult part of the selection process?
5. What questions would you ask during an employment interview?
6. How much education should an entry-level position in law enforcement require? A management position?
7. What are other bona fide occupational requirements for an entry-level position in law enforcement? For a management position?
8. Have you ever belonged to a union? If so, what were your reactions to it?
9. Do you favor unions for law enforcement employees? What are the advantages and disadvantages for management?
10. Is the law enforcement agency in your jurisdiction unionized? How does management feel about it?

InfoTrac College Edition Assignment

Use InfoTrac College Edition to answer the Discussion Questions as appropriate.

Research one of the following topics and take a position, using specific journal references to support your view.

- Entry-level officers should/should not be required to have a college degree.
- Officers without a college degree should/should not be considered for promotion.
- Assessment centers are/are not an effective and fair way to select recruits.
- Affirmative action programs are/are not fair to white males.
- Unions are/are not usually beneficial to law enforcement agencies.

Your support may be in the form of a summary or an outline, but it should be very specific. Be prepared to discuss your views in class.

OR read and outline one of the following:

- "Closing the Recruitment Gap: A Symposium's Findings" by Gary Vest.
- "Fast Track Application Process Speeds Hiring" by Floyd S. Hulsey and Maureen Goodwin.

- "Law Enforcement Physical Fitness Standards and Title VII" by Michael E.Brooks.
- "An Effective Assessment Center Program: Essential Components" by Thurston L. Cosner and Wayne C. Baumgart.
- "Police Officer Candidate Assessment and Selection" by David A. Decicco.
- "The Americans with Disabilities Act: The Continuing Search for Meaning" by Thomas D. Colbridge.

References

Armstrong, David and Polk, O. Elmer. "College for Cops: The Fast Track to Success." *The Law Enforcement Trainer,* September/October 2002, pp.24–26.

Bercaw, George H. "Psychological Assessment." *Law and Order,* July 2002, pp.132–135.

Berger, William B. "Votes of No Confidence." *The Police Chief,* June 2002, p.6.

Bowman, Theron. "Educate to Elevate." *Community Links,* August 2002, pp.11–13.

Brandon, Harry and Lippman, Barry. "Surfing for Success: Using the Web to Improve Recruitment." *The Police Chief,* November 2000, pp.37–41.

Bratton, William J. "Recruitment Crisis Gains Momentum." *American Police Beat,* October 2001, pp.1, 32.

Brooks, Michael E. "Law Enforcement Physical Fitness Standards and Title VII." *FBI Law Enforcement Bulletin,* May 2001, pp.26–32.

Butterfield, Fox. "City Police Work Losing Its Appeal and Its Veterans: Top Jobs Going Unfilled." *The New York Times,* July 30, 2001, pp.A1, A12.

Campbell, Deborah J.; Christman, Bryon D.; and Feigelson, Melissa E. "Improving the Recruitment of Women in Policing." *The Police Chief,* November 2000, pp.18–28.

Charrier, Kim. "Marketing Strategies for Attracting and Retaining Generation X Police Officers." *The Police Chief,* December 2000, pp.45–51.

"Chiefs Cooperate in Recruiting." *Law and Order,* September 2000, p.69.

Clark, Daniel W.; Olson, Joseph W.; Porter, Lowell M.; and Leichner, Robert M. "The Human Resource Roundtable: A Recruitment and Risk Management Tool." *The Police Chief,* December 2001, pp.29–33.

"Coast to Coast, Good Police Recruits Just Keep Getting Harder to Find." *Law Enforcement News,* May 15/31 2000, pp.1,15.

Colbridge, Thomas D. "The Americans with Disabilities Act." *FBI Law Enforcement Bulletin,* September 2000a, pp.26–32.

Colbridge, Thomas D. "Defining Disability under the Americans with Disabilities Act." *FBI Law Enforcement Bulletin,* October 2000b, pp.28–32.

Colbridge, Thomas D. "Prohibited Discrimination under the Americans with Disabilities Act." *FBI Law Enforcement Bulletin,* December 2000c, pp.14–21.

Colbridge, Thomas D. "The Americans with Disabilities Act: The Continuing Search for Meaning." *FBI Law Enforcement Bulletin,* August 2002, pp.27–32.

Cosner, Thurston L. and Baumgart, Wayne C. "An Effective Assessment Center Program: Essential Components." *FBI Law Enforcement Bulletin,* June 2000, pp.1–6.

Decicco, David A. "Police Officer Candidate Assessment and Selection." *FBI Law Enforcement Bulletin,* December 2000, pp.1–6.

"Delaware SP Reveals Secrets of Its Success in Minority Recruiting." *Law Enforcement News,* February 14, 2000, pp.1, 10.

Domash, Shelly Feuer. "Who Wants This Job?" *Police,* May 2002, pp.34–39.

"Female, Minority Ranks Are Up, But It's More than Just Numbers." *Law Enforcement News,* June 15, 2002, pp.1, 8.

Francis, Stephanie B. "Ideal Candidates." *Community Links,* March 2001, pp.2–4.

Fulton, Roger. "Building Your Career." *Law Enforcement Technology,* January 2000a, p.102.

Fulton, Roger. "Recruiting and Hiring New Officers." *Law Enforcement Technology,* August 2000b, p.130.

Gold, Marion E. "The Progress of Women in Policing." *Law and Order,* June 2000, pp.159–161.

Guthrie, Edward. "Higher Learning and Police Training." *Law and Order,* December 2000, p.124.

Harris, Wesley and Kolkman, Aaron. "Selecting Community Oriented Officers." *Law and Order,* April 2000, pp.63–66.

Ho, Taiping. "The Interrelationships of Psychological Testing, Psychologists' Recommendations, and Police Departments' Recruitment Decisions." *Police Quarterly,* September 2001, pp.318–342.

Hoffmann, John. "Police Corp: An Update Two Years after the First Police Corps Graduation." *Law and Order,* January 2000, pp.50–58.

Hulsey, Floyd S. and Goodwin, Maureen. "Fast Track Application Process Speeds Hiring." *FBI Law Enforcement Bulletin,* June 2001, pp.5–8.

Jones, Sharon and Lonsway, Kimberly. "Up-Close: Recruiting and Selecting Women Officers." *Law and Order,* May 2002, pp.94–99.

Kanable, Rebecca. "Strategies for Recruiting the Nation's Finest: Help Wanted Ads May Not Be Enough." *Law Enforcement Technology,* February 2001, pp.64–68.

Kenny, Sean. " 'S.W.A.T.' for Survival." *Police,* April 2000, pp.58–59.

Litchford, Jody M. "ADA Decisions Provide Guidance for Enforcement Activities." *The Police Chief,* August 2000, pp.15–17.

Lonsway, Kimberly A. "The Role of Women in Community Policing: Dismantling the Warrior Image." *Community Links,* September 2001, pp.16–17.

Lord, Vivian B. and Schoeps, Nancy. "Identifying Psychological Attributes of Community-Oriented, Problem-Solving Police Officers." *Police Quarterly,* June 2000, pp.172–190.

Maglione, Roslyn. "Recruiting, Retaining and Promoting Women: The Success of the Charlotte-Mecklenburg Police Department's Women's Network." *The Police Chief,* March 2002, pp.19–24.

Mahoney, Mark. "Law Enforcement Recruiting Software." *Law Enforcement Technology,* October 2001, pp.194–199.

Matthews, Kurt and Kilpatrick, Tom. "Recruiting Challenges for the Smaller Department." *The Police Chief,* April 2002, pp.31–34.

Milgram, Donna. "Recruiting Women to Policing: Practical Strategies that Work." *The Police Chief,* April 2002, pp.23–29.

Moore, Margaret M. "How Effectively Does Your Police Agency Recruit and Retain Women?" *The Police Chief,* March 2002, p.29.

Nelson, Kurt R. "A Tale of Two Cities: A Comparison of Background Investigations." *Law and Order,* May 2000, pp.85–88.

Nichols, Mark. "Bucking the Trend." *American Police Beat,* February 2001, pp.1, 44.

Olson, Robert K. "Recruiting the Officers of the Future." *Subject to Debate,* August 2001, pp.2, 5.

Osofsky, Howard J.; Dralle, Penelope; Greenleaf, Wayne; and Pennington, Richard. "Developing a Partnership to Enhance Police Recruitment and Retention." *The Police Chief,* January 2001, pp.38–46.

"Police Education and Training on the Rise, But Salaries Lag." *Criminal Justice Newsletter,* May 22, 2002, p.7.

Polk, O. Elmer and Armstrong, David A. "Higher Education and Law Enforcement Career Paths: Is the Road to Success Paved by Degree?" *Journal of Criminal Justice Education,* Spring 2001, pp.77–99.

Prussel, Deborah and Lonsway, Kimberly A. "Recruiting Women Police Officers." *Law and Order,* July 2001, pp.91–96.

Rafilson, Fred M. "Candidate Physical Fitness Testing: The Need for Legally Defensible Methodologies and Outcomes." *Law and Order,* March 2000, pp.99–109.

Recruiting & Retaining Women: A Self-Assessment Guide for Law Enforcement. Washington, DC: National Center for Women & Policing, no date.

Ross, Lee E. and Elechi, Ogbonnaya Oko. "Student Attitudes towards Internship Experiences: From Theory to Practice." *Journal of Criminal Justice Education,* Fall 2002, pp.297–312.

Rostow, Cary and Davis, Robert. "Psychological Screening." *Law and Order,* May 2002, pp.101–106.

Salvatore, Anthony J., Sr. "Technology and Recruitment: Connecticut Police Chiefs Association Uses Television Commercial to Attract New Officers." *The Police Chief,* September 2001, pp.50–52.

Sanow, Ed. "Recruiting Woes? Recruit Women." *Law and Order,* July 2001, p.4.

Schultz, Ray and Acevedo, Art. "Ensuring the Physical Success of a Department." *Law and Order,* December 2000, pp.34–37.

Schulz, Dorothy M. "Law Enforcement Leaders: A Survey of Women Police Chiefs in the United States." *The Police Chief,* March 2002, pp.25–28.

Scuro, Joseph E., Jr. "The Americans with Disabilities Act in the 21st Century." *Law and Order,* February 2001, pp.31–33.

Scuro, Joseph E., Jr. "Recent U.S. Supreme Court Defines ADA Disability." *Law and Order,* May 2002, pp.16–18.

Slowik, Stanley. "Selection Systems and the Smaller Department." *Law and Order,* May 2002, pp.112–116.

Sokolove, Bruce A. and Field, Mark W. "The Law Enforcement Candidate Ride-Along: A Supplemental Selection Tool." *The Police Chief,* January 2002, pp.55–59.

Solie, Richard. "The Human Race: Speeding the Hiring Process." *APCO911 Magazine,* July 2000, pp.20–24.

Streit, Corinne. "Recruiting Minority Officers." *Law Enforcement Technology,* February 2001, pp.70–75.

Tate, Hugh. "The Recruitment Dilemma." *Law and Order,* May 2000, pp.78–82.

Tinsley, Paul N. "The Assessment Center: Lessons from the Past." *The Police Chief,* April 2002, pp.35–40.

Vest, Gary. "Closing the Recruitment Gap: A Symposium's Findings." *FBI Law Enforcement Bulletin,* November 2001, pp.13–17.

Book-Specific Web Site

Go to the *Management and Supervision in Law Enforcement* Web site at http://info.wadsworth.com/05346160654 for student and instructor resources, including Internet Assignments and Case Studies.

CHAPTER 8

Training and Beyond

The mediocre teacher tells. The good teacher explains. The superior teacher demonstrates. The great teacher inspires.
—William Arthur Ward

Do You Know?

- What the manager's single most important objective should be?
- How training and educating differ?
- What three variables affect learning?
- What the three general categories of learners or learning styles are?
- What the key is to determining the material to teach and test? What this is called?
- What three areas training can focus on?
- What principles of learning are important?
- What pitfalls to avoid in training?
- What instructional methods you can use?
- What instructional materials are available?
- What LETN is?
- Who else can assist with training?
- What a POST commission is and what it does?
- Of the training models typically used for recruits, which appears most effective?
- Where on-the-job training can occur?
- What the most common type of on-the-job training is for new recruits?
- What forms of external training there are?
- When training should be done?
- What the training cycle consists of?
- Who benefits from training?
- How the Violent Crime Control and Law Enforcement Act of 1994 affects training?

Can You Define?

andragogy
asynchronous learning
case study
coaching
content validity
counseling
demonstration
discussion
educating
environmental/instructional variables
factual questions
field training
field training officer (FTO)
hands-on learning
individual variables
information variables
in-service training
interval reinforcement
lecture
on-the-job training (OJT)
opinion-based questions
pedagogy
prerequisites
Q & A
rhetorical questions
role playing
roll call
rote learning
simulation
synchronous learning
task variables
training
videoconferencing

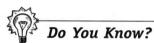

INTRODUCTION

In the first three decades of the twentieth century, law enforcement was simple. A cop often relied on physical brawn to keep the peace and political connections to keep the job. Little formal training was required. The one individual most responsible for changing that was August Vollmer, who entered law enforcement by accident in 1905 when, at the age of 29, he was elected town marshal in Berkeley, California. He soon moved to the position of chief and inherited a department that was in shambles.

Although Vollmer had little formal education, in 1908 he started the Berkeley Police School and by 1930 recruits were receiving more than 300 hours of training. This later became the University of California-Berkeley School of Criminology, providing specialized training and orientation of officers hired to be police officers. He motivated them to train others. Vollmer reached more audiences than any other officer in history. One of his protégés, O. W. Wilson, carried on his efforts to make training a priority for police officers.

Today the importance of training is recognized as a fundamental responsibility of law enforcement managers. According to Baker and Piland-Baker (2000, p.121): "Training law enforcement officers properly is one of the most significant leadership functions of the new century." Law enforcement service cannot be of high quality without training and education. The days of "handing officers a badge and a gun and putting them on the street" are long gone.

Birzer and Tannehill (2001, p.233) stress: "As we begin the 21st century, the need for more and improved police training is gathering increasing momentum. There is an obvious need for police officers to acquire knowledge of the latest legal decisions, technological advances and tactical developments in the field, and to remain proficient in a number of job-related skills." They (p.238) note: "Training is the lifeblood of the organization." Kleinman (2001, p.11) suggests: "Any competent administrator will state that, 'a dollar spent in training is worth a hundred dollars as insurance against litigation.' However, while this axiom is often heard, it is rarely followed." According to Harris (2002, p.44) suggests: "Training is absolutely essential in law enforcement but the funds to accomplish that training are not always available." When cuts need to be made, training is often one of the first targets. However, as Harris notes: "Budgetary constraints that limit training have not been considered by the courts as a valid defense in cases of failure to provide proper training."

This chapter stresses the need for continuous improvement in police professionalism. It begins with a discussion of training as a management function and liability issue and the differences between training and educating. A description of the learning process follows, including variables that affect learning, principles of learning and characteristics of effective trainers.

Next the chapter explores instructional methods and materials and looks at levels of training standards. On-the-job training can produce knowledgeable, skilled line officers, as well as supervisors and managers. The chapter then examines training at the various levels: new recruits, new sergeants, middle management and executive officers, including how external training is used. In addition to basic certification instruction, a manager must determine ongoing training needs and prioritize subjects to be included. The next discussion emphasizes the importance of ongoing training, the ideal training cycle, evaluation and the benefits of effective training programs. The chapter concludes with a brief look at the Crime Bill and its effects on law enforcement education, community-oriented policing and problem-solving (COPPS).

Training as a Management Function

Training is a major management function. A department's efficiency and effectiveness are directly related to the amount and quality of training it provides. Training not only improves productivity but also reduces liability. Training ensures that subordinates have the necessary skills to perform well, making the manager's job that much easier. For new recruits, training reduces the time they need to reach an acceptable performance level. Training also tells subordinates that the agency and the manager are interested in their welfare and development.

Failure-to-Train Litigation

Dahlinger (2001, p.53) contends: "More litigation and lawsuits are being filed against police agencies today than ever before. One common denominator that seems to occur in almost all of the cases is failure to train. The price of being the subject of just one civil liability lawsuit alleging malice can be more than some police department's entire operating budget."

The landmark case in failure to train suits is *City of Canton, Ohio v. Harris* (1989). Geraldine Harris was arrested by the Canton police and taken to the police station. When they arrived at the station, the officers found her on the floor of the patrol wagon and asked if she needed medical attention. Her reply was incoherent. While inside the station, she fell to the floor twice, so the officers left her there to avoid her falling again. No medical assistance was provided. She was released to her family, who called an ambulance. She was hospitalized for a week with severe emotional illness and received treatment for a year. She sued the city for failure to provide adequate medical attention while she was in custody. She won, with the Supreme Court ruling that a municipality might be held liable for deliberate indifference for failure to train. According to Spector (2001, p.73):

> The ramifications related to inadequate training are about to skyrocket. It is safe to say that plaintiffs' counsel will take great advantage of the Supreme Court's language in *Board of County Commissioners v. Brown,* 520 U.S. 397 (1997) (suggesting liability for failure to train a single officer), and failure to train will soon become the theory of choice in liability claims against governmental entities. It used to be that if a police department had a generally good training program, which met basic state standards, they would be safe from such claims. Now, plaintiff's attorneys will take the effort to plow through individual defendant officer's training records to find some deficiency related to their client's claimed injury and if they want to spend a few bucks, they'll hire some expert to identify these training deficiencies.

Spector (p.76) notes: "This new standard for potential liability for failing to train even a single officer leaves training officers with the daunting task of prioritizing their training."

Spector (2002, p.138) recommends: "The best way to avoid failure to train claims and to improve the quality of law enforcement is to analyze the tasks officers perform and ensure they receive quality, updated training on all topics." According to Risher (2001, p.10): "Any misstep by an officer that results in injury may lead to a failure to train claim. To avoid lawsuits based on these claims, managers must develop a training curriculum that involves every aspect of policing and carefully document the training of all officers. They also must assess the training by testing officers afterwards or by monitoring in-the-field performance evaluations."

In addition, as Dahlinger (p.54) recommends: "In order for agencies to protect themselves against claims some very basic procedures can be utilized. . . . First and foremost, a good, clear documentation of training is a must. All officers should have copies of all their training certificates and description of the training received placed both in their personnel files and in the department's training files. . . . It is also the responsibility of police departments to maintain records of the in-house training that has been conducted. . . . An effective training program can be the difference between dismissal of a suit and a serious judgment against a law enforcement agency, costing thousands of dollars."

Undoubtedly, police departments should review high-risk liability incidents and provide adequate training to avoid liability claims being upheld. Such incidents might be high-speed pursuits, detaining individuals, use of deadly force, use of nonlethal weapons, civil rights violations, firearms training and constitutional law training. Special requirements should be instituted so that no officer who has not met qualification standards may carry a weapon while on duty.

Training Philosophy

A written statement of training *philosophy* should state management's attitude toward training, the extent of resources that will be devoted to it and the training's purpose and expectations. The training philosophy should reflect that managers are essentially assigned to develop personnel, the most expensive portion of the law enforcement budget.

Developing human resources should be managers' single most important objective.

The role of law enforcement managers in training depends on the level of the manager. Executive-level managers make the final decisions as to the kind of training program needed and the groups to be involved. Middle-level management usually prepares the training program and helps determine training needs. First-line supervisors determine the needs of their officers and specialized personnel because they are closest to everyday operations.

Managers must be involved in training from determining needs through evaluation of the program. Management must be directly involved. When managers become teachers, they develop jointly with officers. It is often said that people learn best by teaching others.

Training vs. Educating

Learning theorists often make a distinction between training and educating. Some go so far as to say, "We *train* animals; we *educate* people." Training is often viewed as a lower form of learning, dealing with physical skills, the type of instruction that takes place in vocational schools and on the job in law enforcement agencies. After completing a training session, participants may be awarded a certificate or a license. For example, after receiving training in CPR, participants may be awarded a certificate by the American Red Cross.

Education, in contrast, concerns knowledge and *understanding,* the kind of instruction that takes place in colleges and universities. After completing a specific educational program, participants may be awarded a degree. Some law enforcement agencies pay employees higher salaries if they have attained specific levels of education. Some require a two-year degree, and some states, such as Minnesota and Texas, are considering legislation that would require officers to have a four-year degree before being hired.

Training generally refers to vocational instruction that takes place on the job and deals with physical skills. **Educating** generally refers to academic instruction that takes place in a college, university or seminar-type setting and deals with knowledge and understanding.

Using this distinction, a law enforcement agency might train its personnel to shoot firearms and educate them on the laws of deadly force. It might train personnel in high-speed pursuit techniques and educate them on when high-speed pursuit is to be conducted.

Usually both training and education are needed, and they often overlap. Further, in law enforcement the training may be more important, that is, the *doing* rather than *knowing.* Officers can read extensively about proper shooting techniques, but what matters is receiving expert coaching and practicing on the firing range.

Some have suggested that officers should first receive a comprehensive law enforcement education and then be trained in police work, often under the watchful guidance of a field training officer (FTO). This text does not concern itself further with the distinction between training and education. Because the term *training* is most commonly used in law enforcement—for example, organizations have training departments and a budget line item for training—this term is used throughout this text to refer to both training and education.

Variables Affecting Learning

Research on how people learn most effectively suggests that three variables are critical.

Three variables affect learning:

- Individual variables
- Task or information variables
- Environmental/instructional variables

Individual Variables

The first consideration is: *Who* is the learner? Among the important **individual variables** are the learner's age, sex, maturation, readiness, innate ability, level of motivation, personality and personal objectives. The astute supervisor will be knowledgeable about each factor in each subordinate. Questions to ask regarding individual learners include: What is the officer's current skill level? What has the officer already learned? How far, realistically, can one expect this officer to progress in a given time? How motivated is this officer?

Less (2002, p.22) observes: "The typical law enforcement agency—and, as a result, the typical in-service training classroom—is now comprised of four distinct generations. Each of these generations has its own individual defining characteristics, motivations, expectations, and learning preferences." You were introduced to Generation X in the last chapter. Table 8.1 summarizes the characteristics of these four generations.

Supervisors have limited control over individual variables, but they must be sensitive to their importance. They must also be careful of stereotyping individuals. The information in this section is meant to provide only a guide.

Learning Styles

As seen in the preceding discussion, people's preferred way of learning can differ. Some people learn more effectively by *hearing* an explanation of a concept; some learn best by *seeing* things illustrated or performed; and others learn best by *touching* or having *hands-on experience* with a new idea.

The three general categories of learners or learning styles are visual, auditory and kinesthetic.

Visual learners learn best through demonstration. They like to read and take notes. They appreciate handouts. Auditory learners learn best through lecture. They feel the need to speak and welcome classroom discussion. Kinesthetic learners want to apply what they are learning, to take a hands-on approach to learning. They appreciate role playing, scenarios and simulations.

Another way to look at learning style is to consider personality style. The 16 personality types identified by the Myers-Briggs Type Indicator (MBTI) are correlated to four learning style preferences: extrovert or introvert, sensing or intuition, thinking or feeling, and judgment or perception. Table 8.2 summarizes the basic content of each and suggests how trainers can meet the needs of officers with different learning styles.

Adult Learners

The principles of adult learning should also be considered in training programs. Research and common sense suggest that adults learn differently from children. Knowles's set forth the idea that **andragogy,** the art and science of helping adults learn, is vastly different from **pedagogy,** the science of helping children learn. Adults are not grown children; they learn differently. According to Knowles (1970, p.39):

> Andragogy is premised on at least four crucial assumptions about the characteristics of adult learners that are different from the assumptions about child learners, on which traditional pedagogy is premised. These assumptions are that, as a person matures, (1) his self-concept moves from being a directed to a self-

Table 8.1
Four Generations Compared

Generation	When Born	AKA	Defining Characteristics	Learning Preferences	Why Attracted to Career in Law Enforcement?
Generation Y	Between 1979/1980 and the late 20th century	Nexters, Echo Boomers, Net Generation	Used to being connected to the world by the Internet. Talk shows are a staple. Multiculturalism is expected. Self-confident, friendly, optimistic. Strong sense of civic duty and morality and are high achievers. Have seen first-hand horrors of school violence, Oklahoma City Bombing.	Prefer group activities and use of technology in learning. Prefer to work collectively.	Attracted to law enforcement by civic contribution, availability of training opportunities, freedom and flexibility of not being tied to a desk, chances for teamwork and mentoring.
Generation X	Between the early 1960s and late 1970s	Baby Bust, Lost Generation	Latchkey kids, often from single-parent families that grew up with MTV and computers. Raised with technology. Believe hard work is the key to success. Value education. Defining events: fall of the Berlin Wall and AIDS.	Like question and answer sessions. Enjoy games and activities. Seek creative, challenging options. Trainer must earn their respect.	Seek competitive salaries, excellent benefits to assist their families, a steady shift assignment, more time off, and a structured career path.
Baby Boomers	Between the end of WWII and the early 1960s		Grew up in front of the TV. Optimistic and involved. Driven, soul-searching. Strong work ethic. Either love or hate authority figures. May exhibit a "know-it-all" attitude. Do have much experience. Defining events include Vietnam, Civil Rights Movement, Cold War, Space Race, Women's Liberation Movement and assassinations of Martin Luther King, Jr. and two Kennedy brothers.	Like problem solving in a non-authoritarian environment.	
Veterans	Roughly between the ends of WWI and II	Traditionalists	Defined by the Great Depression, WWII, the Korean Conflict and labor unions. High degree of patriotism and reverence to the family. Raised in the age of radio and the Golden Age of Film. Dedicated, hard-working conformists. Conservative. Respect authority and adhere to rules. Often sought as mentors.	Enjoy stress-free, unhurried learning environment. Respond best to experienced instructors. Some are computer-phobic.	

Source: Data from Karen Less. "The Intergenerational Classroom in Law Enforcement Training." *The Law Enforcement Trainer,* May/June 2002, pp.20–24.

directed human being, (2) he accumulates a growing reservoir of experience that becomes an increasing resource for learning, (3) his readiness to learn becomes oriented increasingly to developmental tasks of his social roles, and (4) his time perspective changes from one of postponed application of knowledge to immediacy of application, and accordingly his orientation toward learning shifts from one of subject centeredness to one of problem centeredness.

Table 8.2
The Four Learning Styles

Learning Style		Training Suggestions
Extrovert (E) Action is the name of the game for this officer. Extroverts "think" with their mouths open, which is by thinking out loud. They will give immediate answers off the top of their heads.	*Introvert (I)* This person is most at home in the inner world of ideas and concepts. They often detach from class activities and prefer to work completely alone or in very small groups. They will likely take a while to formulate an answer.	This preference concerns from where we get our energy. Plan enough activities to keep extroverts from getting bored, yet give introverts enough time to process information internally. One way to do this is to provide optional exercises. Providing an agenda before class allows introverts to process what will be covered ahead of time, thus allowing them to participate more fully.
Sensing (S) Officers perceive their world in terms of facts, data and details. They are realistic, down to earth and practical. They live in the here and now and learn by experience. Repetition does not bother sensors. Sensors work from the bottom up—gathering details before creating the big picture. Most police officers are typed as sensors.	*Intuition (N)* Officers perceive their world in terms of possibilities, theories, ideas and relationships. They are future-oriented, imaginative and sometimes live with their heads in the clouds. Variety stimulates intuitors, who work from the top down—needing to know how everything fits together before they can learn the details.	This preference concerns how an officer will absorb information or perceive their world. Without explaining how all the pieces of subject matter fit together, you will lose the intuitors. However, if you spend too much time on the big picture, you will lose the sensors (likely most of the class). The best approach is to briefly set the stage by painting the big picture and follow with an in-depth look at each piece. When developing class exercises, give officers the option of similar exercises (repetition for sensors) or several very different exercises (variety for intuitors).
Thinking (T) Officers use a logic based on cause and effect. They prefer to do objective critiques and analyses. Problem-solving is done in terms of right versus wrong principles. These are the trainees who will ask for the reason something is done a certain way. Most police officers are typed as "thinkers."	*Feeling (F)* Officers use a logic that is subjective and personal. Decisions are made based on what is valued and not valued; problems are solved according to what is most important to the people involved—"feelers" will ask how decisions will affect people.	This preference deals with how officers evaluate the information they perceive and how they make decisions. Present class material in a systematic way (for thinkers), making sure the reasoning is logically sound. Also present material in a personal way (for feelers), and make sure you give value or meaning along with the logic. Thinkers need to have a sense of mastery and achievement during and after the class, whereas feelers need a sense of personal support and approval.
Judging (J) Officers like to come to closure. They plan ahead. Time is a resource to be managed. Judgers want structure and predictability, are more decisive than curious and do not want to waste class time with endless discussions. Their goal is to get things done, preferably early. Most police officers are typed as judgers.	*Perceiving (P)* Officers tend to be more spontaneous. They need flexibility and leave themselves open for more data and possibilities. They view time as something to be enjoyed. Their goal is the adventure of discovery; getting things done is not a priority.	This preference determines which style officers prefer to use when dealing with the outside world. Develop an agenda with time frames you can stick with so the class will begin and end on time (for judgers). However, build in some flexibility so the perceivers don't feel railroaded. You may also schedule optional time after class for perceivers to further explore the material being covered. In preparing class exercises, have one right answer for each problem so judgers will know they have reached the goal. Also be prepared to respond to perceivers who will expect to explore different angles and will always want more information.

Source: Adapted from John Sample. "Personality Type, Learning Styles and Police Training." *The Law Enforcement Trainer,* July/August 1999, pp.56–63. Reprinted by permission of John Sample.

Because of more advanced cognitive abilities, adults should not be "spoon fed" the "right" answer to a given problem but rather encouraged to think through a problem and to develop an appropriate response. As Birzer and Tannehill (p.240) suggest: "The advantages to the andragogical approach are several in that (1) it draws on the trainee's past experiences, (2) it treats trainees as adults, (3) it adapts to diverse needs and expectations of participants, and (4) it develops critical thinking, judgment and creativity in the learner."

Task or Information Variables

Task or **information variables** relate to *what* is to be learned. This might involve knowledge, skills or attitudes.

The basic curriculum for recruits must be valid and job related. The first step in validation is to conduct a job analysis defining both the tasks that constitute the job and the knowledge, skills and abilities an individual must possess to perform the job effectively. To establish **content validity,** the direct relationship between tasks performed on the job, the curriculum and the test must be established.

Job analysis is the key to determining the content to teach and test. When content relates directly to the tasks to be performed, it is considered valid. Tests that measure competence in these tasks are then also valid.

The next step is translating worker requirements into training/learning objectives. The result of these efforts is that police recruits are exposed to a curriculum that truly prepares them for a law enforcement career.

Training can focus on knowledge, skills or attitudes.

Knowledge is often equated with book learning, theory and education and includes facts, ideas and information. This is referred to as the cognitive approach. The steps involved in loading and firing a gun or in obtaining information and then writing a report are usually first presented as facts—information. Often other information, such as that related to safety or legal concerns, is included. Officers are expected to apply most of the knowledge presented to them.

Skills generally involve applying knowledge. This is referred to as the behavioral approach. Skills may be technical or motor skills, such as firing a gun, or conceptual skills, such as actually writing a good report.

According to Birzer and Tannehill (p.236): "There are some subjects in the police curricula that will benefit from behavioral and cognitive instruction. Subjects such as firearms training, defensive tactics, felony car stops, crowd control, investigative procedures, and other critical incident training will benefit from behavioral and cognitive instruction techniques." They point out a "salient paradox in the manner that a vast majority of police training is conducted. Police academies place an enormous emphasis on enforcement and the mechanical techniques of the job. The paradox here is that the reality is that police perform the crime-fighting functions a relatively small percentage of their on-duty time." They (p.237) report: "A majority of the on-duty time of police is spent on service-related functions."

Haarr (2001, p.405) reports: "Less than 3 percent of basic-training academy time is spent on cognitive and decision-making domains. . . . More than 90 percent of basic academy training time is spent on task-oriented training that instructs police recruits in the basic repetitive skills and conditioned responses associated with the reactive nature of the traditional model of policing." In Los Angeles after the Rampart corruption scandal, the city and the Department of

Justice required the LAPD to increase training in cultural diversity, duty to report misconduct, accurate report writing and Fourth Amendment issues. It also ordered interactive exercises in handling ethical dilemmas (Murphy and Gascon, 2001, p.38).

Attitudes are the most difficult to deal with through formal training. They are influenced primarily by the positive and negative examples set by managers, supervisors and others in the department. Officers may learn in training sessions that stress is a hazard of law enforcement work and that pessimism and cynicism are other occupational hazards. They may feel they are immune to stress, just as they may think they are immune to getting shot. This "it can never happen to me" syndrome so frequently attributed to law enforcement officers is not effectively dealt with through knowledge-centered training sessions.

Relevant questions about task or information variables include: How meaningful is the task or information? How difficult is it? How similar is it to tasks and information already mastered? How pleasant or unpleasant is the task? How is the instruction organized or presented?

Supervisors have great influence over this variable because they can try to ensure that the task or information being taught is seen as relevant, practical and indeed essential. They can facilitate the learning by breaking the information into small, easily mastered steps. They can relate the material to similar material that officers have already mastered. Probably the most important variable here is the last one: how the instruction is organized or presented.

Environmental/ Instructional Variables

Environmental/instructional variables refer to the *context* in which the training is provided. Common sense suggests that officers will learn better in a comfortable setting where they can see and hear what is happening and distractions are limited.

Involving students in training is more difficult and time consuming and requires more teaching skill, creativity and a greater depth of instructor knowledge. However, it is widely accepted that application is an integral part of the training process. People learn by doing. Practical applications might include case studies and role playing, small-group activities, field trips and individual student performances (discussed shortly).

Common sense also suggests that the more practice officers get with a given task, the more proficient they will become. A critical factor is that they are practicing correctly. All too often practice does *not* make perfect; it makes an incorrectly practiced procedure *permanent* and therefore counterproductive.

Knowledge of results, or feedback, also greatly enhances learning. Feedback motivates and helps ensure that the correct learning has occurred. Incentives may be related to staying alive, becoming an exemplary officer, promotions, pay raises, threats or any number of factors. Chapter 10 deals with incentives and motivation.

Implications

Given the variables affecting learning, the bottom line is: *There is no one best way to instruct.* The most effective instruction is adapted to the individual officers; the specific knowledge, skill or attitude being taught; and the setting in which the training occurs.

Principles of Learning

Familiarity with the basic principles of learning may help trainers express key concepts more effectively and enable trainees to absorb such concepts more fully. First, learning is not a spectator sport. Use active learning techniques with trainees. Second, give feedback promptly—knowing what you know and do not know sharpens learning. Third, emphasize time on task. Fourth, communicate high expectations. The more you expect, the more you will get. Finally, respect diverse talents and ways of learning. As discussed, officers will exhibit a variety of learning styles. Several principles of learning have been stated or implied in the preceding discussion. They are summarized as follows:

Principles of Learning:

- Base training on an identified need.
- Tell officers the learning objective.
- Tell officers why they need to learn the material.
- Make sure officers have the necessary background to master the skill (the **prerequisites**). Provide a way to acquire the prerequisites.
- Present the material using the most appropriate materials and methods available. When possible, use variety.
- Adapt the materials and methods to individual officers' needs.
- Allow officers to be as active and involved as possible.
- Engage as many senses as possible.
- Break complex tasks into simple, easy-to-understand steps.
- Use repetition and practice to enhance remembering.
- Give officers periodic feedback on their performance.
- Whenever possible, present the "big picture." Teach an understandable concept rather than relying on simple memorization or **rote learning.**

Retention

A key learning principle is that of interval reinforcement. **Interval reinforcement** means presenting information several times, perhaps as follows:

First time–During the introduction of a lecture.

Second time–In the middle of the lecture.

Third time–At the end of the lecture in a summary or review.

Fourth time–In a quiz a few days later, perhaps at roll call.

Fifth time–During a review session a week later.

Sixth time–In an application of the information.

Notice that the information is repeated with intervals between the repetitions. Studies have shown that if learners are presented information once, they remember only 10 percent after 30 days. If, on the other hand, they are exposed to the same information six times, they remember 90 percent after 30 days (Figure 8.1).

Adding to the retention complexity, according to Baker (2002, p.110): "Most students acquire 83 percent of their information from seeing and only 11 percent from hearing, and generally remember only 20 percent of what they

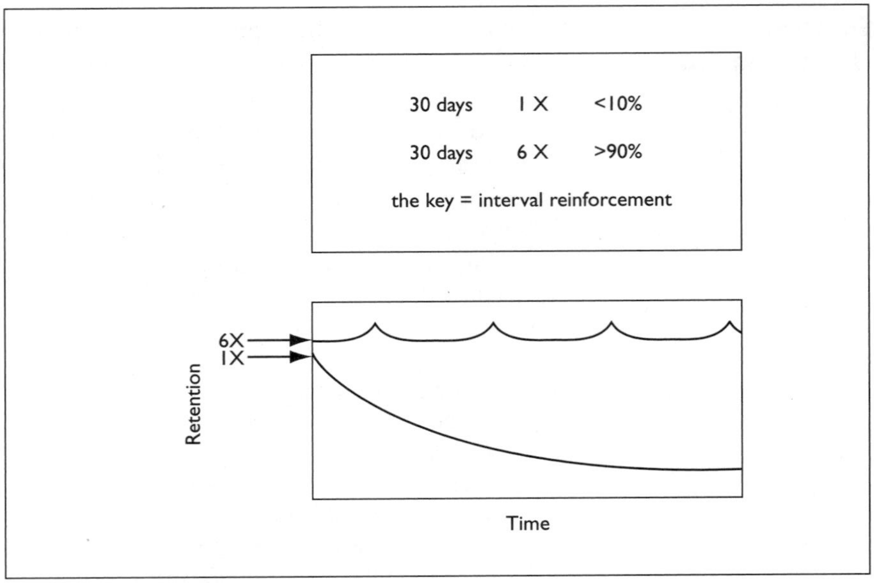

Source: Robert W. Pike. *Creative Training Techniques Handbook.* Minneapolis, MN: Lakewood Books, 1989, p.15. Used with permission of Robert W. Pike, President, Creative Training Techniques International, Inc., Eden Prairie, MN.

Figure 8.1
Interval Reinforcement

hear compared to 30 percent of what they see and 50 percent when they hear and see something."

James (2001, pp.16–17) adds another dimension to retention with two laws: "The *Law of Primacy* states that things learned first are usually *learned best.* . . . The *Law of Recency* is that things learned last are *remembered best.*" The implication is that key concepts should be presented early in the training and summarized at the conclusion of the training.

Concept vs. Rote Learning

To appreciate the value of giving officers the big picture and of organizing material into a meaningful whole, consider the following exercise.

A group of officers is told that they are about to learn a symbol system for counting to replace the traditional one through ten system. The group is divided into two subgroups. Group A is given Instructions A; Group B is given Instructions B. They have two minutes to learn the new system. After the two minutes they are given a test. Look at the two sets of instructions in Figure 8.2.

You should easily see which group will do better.

Training Tips

- Work one on one.
- Show more than you tell.
- Review often, but give time to practice as soon as possible.
- Reinforce your training with practice, positive feedback and praise.
- Always recognize improvement.

Having looked at basic principles of effective training, next consider some common mistakes trainers make.

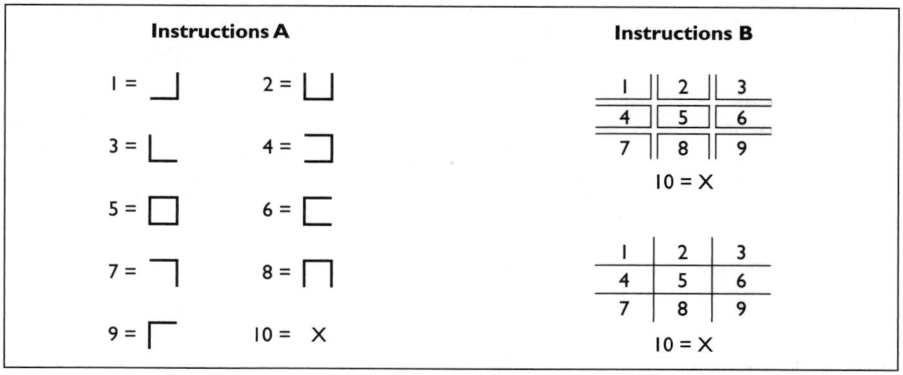

Figure 8.2
Two Sets of Instructions for Decoding a New Counting System

Training Pitfalls

Following are the most common training mistakes.

Training Pitfalls

- Ignoring individual differences, expecting everyone to learn at the same pace
- Going too fast
- Giving too much at one time
- Using tricks and gimmicks that serve no instructional purpose
- Getting too fancy
- Lecturing without showing
- Being impatient
- Not setting expectations or setting them too high
- Creating stress, often through competition
- Delegating training responsibilities without making sure the person assigned the task is qualified
- Assuming that because something was assigned or presented, it was learned
- Fearing subordinates' progress and success
- Embarrassing trainees in front of others
- Relying too heavily on "war stories"

Effective Trainers

Good trainers are hard to find. Hornburg (2000, p.59) suggests: "The best instructors are animated, personable, committed, enthusiastic and expressive." He (pp.22–24, 58) asserts that the best instructors know five secrets: (1) they know the difference between a good and a bad instructor; (2) they recognize the three types of learners in their class or audience; (3) they are self-expressive, including keeping regular eye contact; (4) they are masters of presentation technique; and (5) they are well organized.

Instructional Methods

Many training methods are available. Which to select depends on the time available, the kind and amount of training needed, how many officers need to be trained and the cost.

Instructional methods include lecture, question/answer sessions, discussion, videoconferencing, demonstration, hands-on learning and role playing.

Lecture

Lecture, direct oral presentation, is the traditional way to instruct. It is efficient, can be used with large numbers of people and is cost effective. It is well suited to conveying large amounts of information.

A lecture can successfully introduce a new subject to a group of students as well as provide supplemental information on a topic particularly to students who have little experience in that area. Because one instructor can reach a large number of students, lectures can also reduce the cost of instruction—a relevant consideration for budget-conscious training departments. Lectures are flexible and can be personalized.

Unfortunately, lecture is sometimes overused and sometimes abused. It can be boring and completely ineffective if skills are to be taught. In fact, over 40 years ago Staton (1960) defined a lecture as "a process by which facts are transmitted from the notebook of the instructor to the notebook of the student without passing through the mind of either."

Among the disadvantages of lecture are that they are passive and they cannot meet the needs of both fast and slow learners. A primary disadvantage of lecture is that it does not allow for learner participation. In addition, lecture does not provide the lecturer/trainer with feedback on how thoroughly learners are acquiring the desired information. Given these shortcomings, lectures should be short and supplemented with as many visual aids as possible, including diagrams on chalkboards, flip charts, overheads, slides and videos.

Guided lectures enable students to assimilate more material while enhancing their note taking. Provide the lecture objectives before the lecture; then encourage students to put their pens down. Use the first half of the class time to deliver the lecture, and then ask students to briefly jot down as much material as they can recall. Next, place students into small groups and have them reconstruct the lecture based on their own notes. The cooperative interaction not only generates enjoyable discussion but provides students with notes that are superior to those produced individually.

Question/Answer Sessions

Hootstein (2002, p.20) asserts: "Questioning is the heart and soul of training—the most widely used instructional strategy to facilitate learning. Questioning is the essence of effective teaching because of the numerous purposes it serves, such as motivating learning intrinsically, assessing knowledge and skills and reviewing content."

Question/answer sessions, or **Q & A** sessions, are of two basic types: Learners ask the instructor questions or the instructor asks the learners questions. Some lecturers will invite listeners to interrupt with questions that come to mind during the lecture. This is usually an effective way to break the monotony of a lecture, and it is usually the most appropriate place for the information.

Other lecturers ask that listeners hold their questions until the end to make certain they cover all the information. The disadvantages of this approach are that people often forget their questions, the questions seem irrelevant later in the lecture or people are in a hurry to leave.

A third approach, if time is limited, is to provide listeners with cards on which to write their questions. If another session is planned, the questions can be answered then. If the present session is the only one to be conducted, participants can put their name and phone number on the card and the lecturer can get the answer to them.

Instructors can encourage students to ask questions by praising good questions, repeating them and never embarrassing a student. There is no such thing as a dumb question—except perhaps the one not asked. Another approach to using questions is for the instructor to ask the students questions. Questioning helps keep the students awake and alert and provides feedback to both instructor and students.

Trainers may call on individuals to answer or wait for volunteers. Asking for volunteers creates a more comfortable atmosphere but allows some students to dominate and others to sit back and let them. It may, however, be threatening to call on individuals for answers, especially if the material is relatively difficult. Some trainers use a combination. Trainers have three basic types of questions: factual, rhetorical or opinion based.

Factual questions test students' grasp of the concepts presented, reinforcing learning through repetition. A factual question would be: "What are the elements of first-degree murder?" Instructors can move from factual questions that test *recall* to higher levels systematically: Testing *knowledge* by asking "How are. . .?" Calling for an *application:* "How could aspects of. . .?" Asking for *analysis:* "Why. . .?" Asking for *synthesis:* "If you had unlimited resources, what. . .?"

Rhetorical questions are those to which an answer is not expected, asked to get the listener thinking about a topic. For example, "What are we doing here?" The questioner does not expect an answer because it would be only speculation until more information is provided.

Opinion-based questions get students to share their personal feelings about a topic. There are no right or wrong answers, but some are more plausible than others. For example, "What type of weapon is most effective for law enforcement officers to carry?" The resulting interchange of opinions, perhaps even arguments, could lead to another instructional method—discussion.

Discussion

Discussion involves an interchange of ideas. It allows learners to be active participants and is usually motivating. Effective discussions do not just happen. They require a skilled leader, usually the supervisor or trainer, to guide the discussion, keep it on track, control the amount of time devoted to each topic, ensure balanced participation by learners and summarize the key points at the end.

Law enforcement incident reviews of how specific cases were handled make excellent topics for discussion. The strengths and weaknesses of the cases can be identified and discussed, as can other approaches that might have been equally or more effective.

Videoconferencing

Videoconferencing is simultaneous, interactive audio and video communication. Although videoconferencing has advantages, the cost of purchasing the equipment is substantial, and lengthy booking dates may be required for a multipoint hook-up. Other ways training can take place from a distance include computer-based training (CBT), satellite training and teleconferencing, simulators, electronic bulletin boards (EBBs) and online computer forums, discussed later in the chapter.

Demonstration

Many skills can be taught most effectively through *modeling* or *demonstrating* how to do something, such as how to give CPR, handcuff a suspect or frisk someone. An effective **demonstration** has the following characteristics:

- Everyone can see the demonstration.
- Each step is explained as it is slowly done.
- The purpose of the step is also explained.
- Questions are allowed along the way.
- Hazards or problems to anticipate are noted.

The demonstration is repeated at normal speed as many times as needed until everyone understands.

Hands-On Learning

Often, after a demonstration, learners are asked to do the procedure that was demonstrated. **Hands-on learning,** or actually doing what is required on the job, is an ideal form of training. It motivates learners and transfers to the real world. Whenever possible, theoretical information should be followed by some kind of actual performance. As Confucius said: "What I hear, I forget; what I see, I remember; what I do, I understand." Centuries later Aristotle said: "What we have to learn to do, we learn by doing." Some things do not change. The effect of hands-on learning on retention is clear from the curve shown in Figure 8.3.

People retain 10 percent of what they read compared to 90 percent of what they say and do. Sometimes, however, the real thing is not possible. In such instances role playing can be very useful.

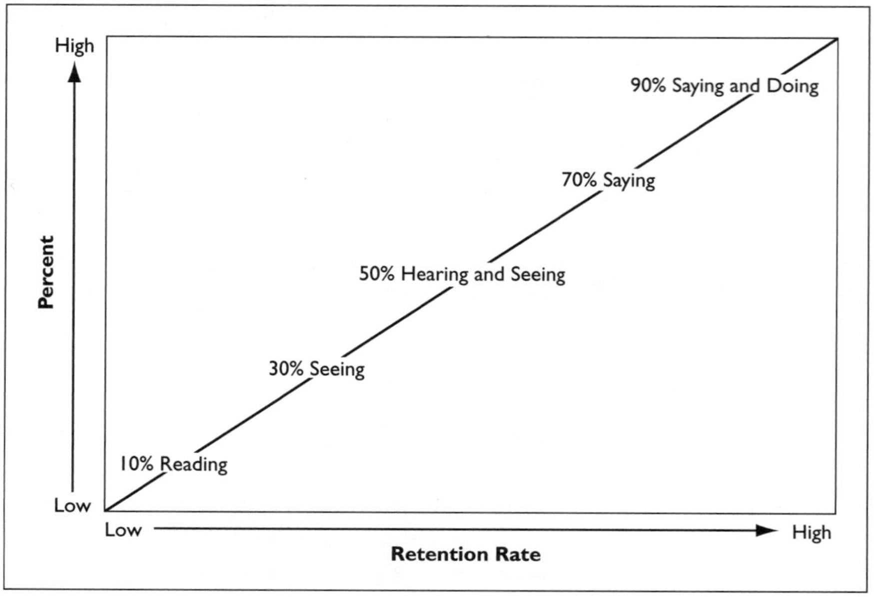

Figure 8.3
The Retention Curve

Role Playing

As the name implies, **role playing** casts people into specific parts to act out. For example, one student might take the role of an arresting officer and another that of the person being arrested. Sometimes specific scripts are provided. Other times, just the general situation is described.

In role playing the actors learn from doing and from class criticism. The watchers learn from what they see and from finding strengths and weaknesses in the performance. Role playing is especially useful in making officers more sensitive to how others feel and how their behavior affects others.

Case Studies

A **case study** is a detailed analysis of a specific incident used to instruct. Colaprete (2002, p.21) notes: "The use of case studies is not a new phenomenon in education. The most historic use is found in the medical profession." It has also been used in the legal profession and in business for decades. It is well adapted to law enforcement. He (p.22) concludes: "What case studies promote in the classroom is a student- and not instructor-centered model of instruction. This model is essential to the ever-changing demands of the law enforcement environment."

Simulations

A **simulation** or imitation of a process is yet another effective means of training. As Mason (2001, p.44) explains: "A simulation is a compressed model of an actual event. . . . A simulation can give the participants a comprehensive understanding of a complex event by revealing many of the factors and relationships that influence the outcome." He (p.46) concludes: "Training simulations are an effective and cost-efficient approach to training police officers. They offer the advantage of speeding the development of new tactics and then validating their effectiveness. Simulations provide the participants with the ability to 'experience' a critical incident and develop real life skills essential in an actual emergency. Unconventional incidents require unconventional approaches for preparation. Interactive simulations are a simple way to train for an uncertain future."

Oakes and Rengarajan (2002, p.58) contend: "Computer-based simulations have become the tools of choice for training in any field that involves interactions with a complex environment." They (p.59) note: "Simulations are becoming better at realism, incorporating sophisticated algorithms that produce virtually unlimited randomness."

According to Reintzell (2002, p.29): "Simulations borrow much from war games, as they have been used by professional military establishments around the world for many years. They provide a mechanism to practice and explore an array of potential solutions to a complex problem, while imparting skills, planning and training for virtually any eventualities."

Trevino (2000, p.56) contends: "Driving simulation improves training and saves department budgets." Other areas in which simulations are appropriate are in firearms training and use-of-force training. As Keeney (2001, p.36) notes: "Force-options simulators are becoming increasingly common in today's law enforcement training. . . . Today's simulators allow officers to use all of the various force options available to them, from voice commands to lethal force and everything in between." As Tarani (2001, p.26) suggests: "In today's extremely litigious climate an administrator would need to compare the cost of department liability versus the cost of effectively training officers to handle themselves competently in such scenarios where they would 'normally' react by using lethal force."

Combination

Usually a combination of instructional methods works best. The methods selected will depend on what is being taught.

Individual, Group or Entire Agency

Instructional methods also include whether the training should be individual, group or entire agency. Such decisions are based on similarities of officer behavior and schedules.

The individual, mentor, coach or field training officer (FTO) approach is a tradition within most local agencies and has been considered effective. Clearly, individual training is important and can be highly motivating. It is also very costly.

Group training has the advantage of giving everyone in the group the same basic knowledge and approach. Law enforcement officers must often rely on each other, sometimes without time or opportunity to discuss what action to take. Group training is more likely to produce the expected unspoken reaction. If each group member is trained to perform a specific way in a specific set of circumstances, officer safety is greatly enhanced. Group training is also more cost effective than individual training.

Some topics are important for everyone within the agency. In such instances training must be arranged to cover all shifts.

In addition to being familiar with instructional methods, trainers also need to know what instructional materials they might use.

Instructional Materials

Instructional materials include printed information, visuals, bulletin boards, audio- and videocassettes, television programs and computer programs.

As Caddell (2002, p.36) points out: "The more tools you employ, the better you will meet the learning styles of all of your students."

Printed Information

Printed materials are by far the most common and most widely used. New recruits may receive a department policy and procedure manual to memorize. New policies and procedures are distributed in print, department-wide, for all employees to learn. When new equipment is purchased, instruction books frequently accompany it. When employees enroll in more formal training programs, they may have texts to read.

In addition, professional organizations have training materials on a wide variety of topics, as do other professional law enforcement institutions throughout the country. Self-study, correspondence courses or tutorial courses are also available to help officers learn information at their own rate and convenience.

Training bulletins are ideal for low-cost training on many subjects. One authoritative source of such bulletins is the IACP, whose bulletins cover all aspects of law enforcement work at all levels. They are inexpensive and can be tailored to local department needs.

Printed materials are uniform, flexible and inexpensive. They also have disadvantages, however. They tend to be impersonal and can be boring.

Visuals

Appropriate visuals can enhance learning and help reduce barriers of time, space and language. Visuals are usually divided into two types: projected and nonprojected. Projected visuals include computer graphics, films, filmstrips, overheads, slides, videotapes and Power Point presentations. Nonprojected visuals include chalkboards, charts, diagrams, flipcharts, graphs, maps and models.

A picture is much more effective than words alone, and words and pictures together are even more effective. One reason visuals are so powerful is they fill a gap between the rate of speaking and listening, as Figure 8.4 illustrates.

Bulletin Boards

Bulletin boards can be effectively used for instruction. The key is to have someone responsible for maintaining the bulletin board and to have a long-range plan for what is to be presented each week or month. The bulletin board should be attractively arranged, uncluttered, and contain only up-to-date material. Each item posted on the board should have a removal date clearly marked in a uniform position.

Borrello (2000, p.27) suggests the bulletin board should be in a well-traveled area of the department and that it continually contain training bulletins that update and refresh the training that officers have received as well as inform them of available training courses. A separate bulletin board should be used for noneducational purposes, for example, for department members wanting to sell used guns, cars or furniture, as well as for jokes, cartoons and announcements.

Audio- and Videocassettes

These instructional media are becoming increasingly popular and affordable. They have the same advantages of printed material, that is, individual pacing and convenience of timing. They have a further advantage in that many officers learn

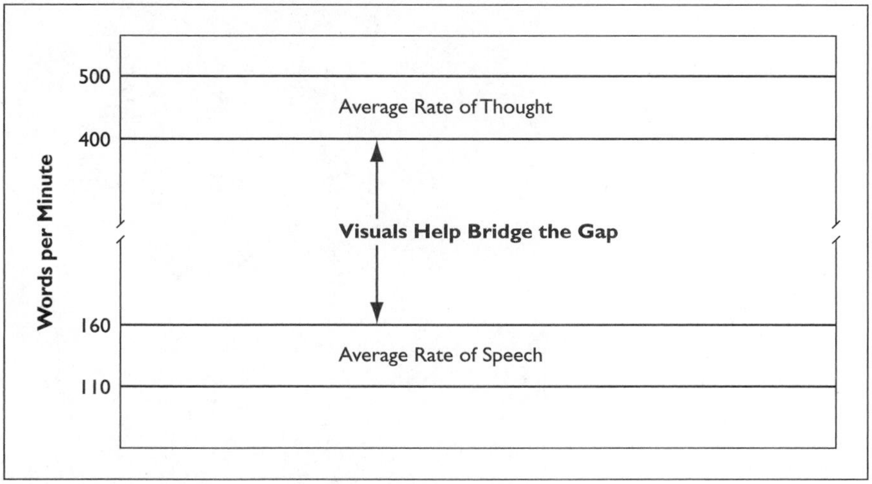

Source: Robert W. Pike. *Creative Training Technique Handbook.* Minneapolis, MN: Lakewood Books, 1989, p.34. Used with permission of Robert W. Pike, President, Creative Training Techniques International, Inc., Eden Prairie, MN.

Figure 8.4
The Power of Visuals

more easily from this method than from the more passive activity of reading. In addition, they can listen to instructional tapes while on patrol or during quiet shifts.

Departments might want to build a library of audio- and videocassettes on relevant topics. They might even include simulations and games that provide practice in problem solving and decision making as well as in manual dexterity.

Television Programs

Educational television has much to offer on general topics such as communication skills, dealing with people and cultural awareness. It is often also educational to watch popular cop shows to see what image of policing the public is watching.

The Law Enforcement Television Network (LETN) is a private satellite television system that provides current programs on a variety of law enforcement subjects; it is available through subscription.

LETN programming is planned to reach each shift with identical information, providing uniformity of training. It is difficult if not impossible for local departments to provide training on each shift unless the shift managers or supervisors do the training. This usually means it is not presented the same way to each shift.

Another televised training option is the Law Enforcement Satellite Training Network (LESTN), cosponsored by the Kansas City (Missouri) Police Department and the FBI. LESTN broadcasts teleconferences on current topics. Viewers can call in questions and talk with experts at no charge.

Computer Programs

Learners using computer programs are more active than when simply reading, listening to or viewing materials. The programs allow learners to proceed at their

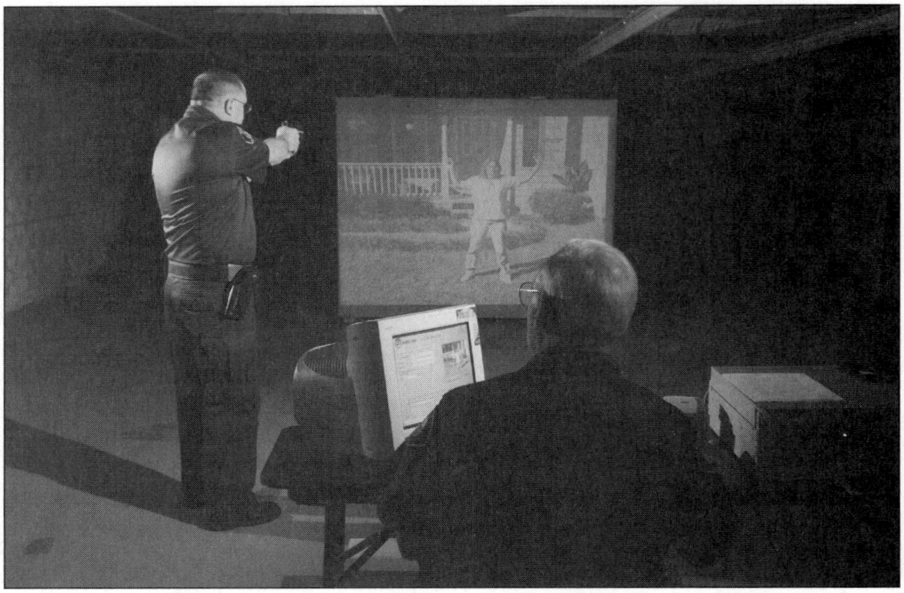

New multimedia technology is used in the continued training of law enforcement officers. Here one officer takes target practice using a simulator while another officer operates the computer to conduct the exercise.

own pace, and most provide immediate feedback on the accuracy of responses. Many programs allow learners to skip material they can show they already know.

Distance or E-Learning

Distance learning and training (DLT) has been around for many decades, beginning with the correspondence courses popular in the 1950s and 1960s. Distance learning has come a long way since then. As Cone and Robinson (2001, p.34) suggest: "Whether it's online learning, e-learning, distance education—whatever you choose to call it—technology-enabled learning solutions are integral to most training departments these days." Because this type of learning may not be as familiar to managers as the other types, a more detailed discussion is presented here.

According to Austen-Kern (2001, p.28): "A program is considered to be in the distance learning area when the instructor and student(s) are not at the same location during the majority of the instructional period."

Morrison (2000, p.98) reports: "The distance-learning products on the market today cover a variety of topics and methods of instruction. Everything from CPR, first responder and EMT training to hostage negotiations and emergency vehicle operations is available outside the classroom." Smith et al. (2002, p.82) point out: "E-learning is becoming a rich, integrated multimedia, multidiscipline experience." Among the advantages they cite are accessibility, flexibility, quality and cost-effectiveness. They (p.84) suggest: "In 10 years it is estimated that 80 percent of all adult on-the-job training will occur online."

Spranza (2001, p.83) notes: "A well-designed distance learning experience will incorporate a balance between the academic materials to be learned and a degree of interactivity." One consideration in selecting distance learning courses is whether they provide synchronous learning or asynchronous learning. **Synchronous learning** is real-time, instructor-led online learning in which all participants are logged on at the same time and communicate directly with each other. **Asynchronous learning,** in contrast, is learning in which interaction between teachers and students occurs intermittently with a time delay.

According to Larson (2000, p.103): "Online training is expected to provide a tremendous savings to taxpayers. The online training also is expected to save time by providing training in any location across the state; improve training efficiency; save money by eliminating employee travel costs; ensure consistency of training content and delivery; ensure effectiveness; and constantly evolve the curriculum." Another key advantage according to Kenner (2001, p.116) is that certain subject matter is retained as much as 250 percent more than when the information is presented in an e-learning format rather than in a classroom-based setting.

E-learning does have its downside. Zenger and Uehlein (2001, p.57) point out: "Centuries of experience have shown the power of people coming together to learn." They contend: "People prefer to learn in a social situation. There's accountability in a classroom that's missing in e-learning. Learning occurs casually and indirectly when individuals interact. And instructor-led sessions remove people from their daily work responsibilities, so participants can focus on learning. There's no such protection when using e-learning methods."

Grimm (2001, p.9) also points out: "Despite current software being relatively 'user friendly,' computer illiteracy and 'technofear' among employees can impede learning." In addition, according to Dees (2000, p.13): "Students enrolled in distance learning courses need to be self-directed, highly disciplined learners."

Other Training Options

Other organizations available to assist with training include the American Society of Law Enforcement Trainers (ASLET), the National Association of Field Training Officers (NAFTO), the Federal Law Enforcement Training Center (FLETC), the National Center for State and Local Training, the FBI National Police Academy and the FBI.

The American Society of Law Enforcement Trainers (ASLET), founded in 1987, has approximately 2,500 members. The National Association of Field Training Officers (NAFTO) was chartered in 1991 to advance the interests of field training officers in all areas of criminal justice.

The Federal Law Enforcement Training Center (FLETC) seeks to provide high-quality, state-of-the-art law enforcement training for a broad spectrum of participating agencies in a cooperative, interagency manner. According to Adams and Loberg (2001, p.48): "FLETC . . . delivers basic and advanced training to 27,000 federal law enforcement students annually." The National Center for State and Local Training is a component of the Federal Law Enforcement Training Center established in 1982 to provide training in advanced topics and develop specialized law enforcement skills.

A major training program is the FBI National Police Academy. The FBI sustains all costs for sessions. The Academy started in 1935 and is located on the U.S. Marine Base at Quantico, Virginia. The Academy lasts 11 weeks and is offered four times a year. Each session includes 250 selected personnel. In addition, the FBI holds schools ranging from one hour to three weeks for local and state law enforcement officers.

Further, as Harris (p.45) suggests, departments can use local resources such as health professionals for training on stress, AIDS and the like; English teachers for assistance in report writing; and local prosecutors for updates on new laws. He also suggests departments consider assistance from the Federal Emergency Management Agency (FEMA) for courses on terrorism, disaster response and similar topics. In addition, smaller departments should consider the Small Town and Rural Training (STAR) Program, which presents free training programs at selected sites throughout the United States.

Training Standards

Standards for police training, how much and what it should consist of, have been controversial since the early 1800s when Peel set forth his principles of reform. Compared to other professions, law enforcement does not require extensive formal training. Attorneys receive over 9,000 hours of instruction and doctors over 11,000 hours. Officers receive 400 to 800 hours of instruction.

In 1967 the President's Commission on Law Enforcement and the Administration of Justice recommended that Peace Officer Standards and Training (POST) commissions be established in every state. These boards were to set mandatory minimum requirements and provide financial aid to governmental units to implement the standards.

Peace Officer Standards and Training (POST) commissions exist in every state to set requirements for becoming licensed as a law enforcement officer.

Among the specific charges of the POST commissions were:

- Establishing mandatory minimum training standards (at both the recruit and in-service levels), with the authority to determine and approve curricula, identify required preparation for instructors and approve facilities acceptable for police training.
- Certifying police officers who have acquired various levels of education, training and experience necessary to adequately perform the duties of the police service.

Table 8.3 provides a recommended basic training curriculum, as well as the specific subjects included in each topic.

Table 8.3
Recommended Basic Training Curriculum

Topic*	Number of Hours	Percent of Total Course
Introduction to the Criminal Justice System	32	8
Law	40	10
Human Values and Problems	88	22
Patrol and Investigation Procedures	132	33
Police Proficiency	72	18
Administration	36	9
TOTAL	400	100

*The specific subjects included in each topic were as follows:

Introduction to the Criminal Justice System: An examination of the foundation and functions to the criminal justice system with specific attention to the role of the police in the system and government;

Law: An introduction to the development, philosophy, and types of law; criminal law; criminal procedure and rules of evidence; discretionary justice; application of the U.S. Constitution; court systems and procedures; and related civil law;

Human Values and Problems: Public service and noncriminal policing; cultural awareness; changing role of the police; human behavior and conflict management; psychology as it relates to the police function; causes of crime and delinquency; and police-public relations;

Patrol and Investigation Procedures: The fundamentals of the patrol function including traffic, juvenile, and preliminary investigation; reporting and communication; arrest and detention procedures; interviewing; criminal investigation and case preparation; equipment and facility use; and other day-to-day responsibilities;

Patrol Proficiency: The philosophy of when to use force and the appropriate determination of the degree necessary; armed and unarmed defense; crowd, riot, and prisoner control; physical conditioning; emergency medical services; and driver training;

Administration: Evaluation, examination, and counseling processes; department policies, rules, regulations, organization, and personnel procedures.

Source: *Report on Police* (1973). Standard 16.3. p.394.

Source: Terry D. Edwards. "State Police Basic Training Programs: An Assessment of Course Content and Instructional Methodology." *American Journal of Police,* Vol. 12, No. 4, 1993, p.27.

Basic Certification Instruction

Some agencies require a certificate or license before they will hire an individual. Others prefer to do the training themselves. In some instances state statutes specify a certain level of education and training before a person can become a law enforcement officer. One such state is Minnesota, whose Peace Officer Standards and Training (POST) Board accredits colleges to provide the academic subjects (education) and a skills program.

The *academic* learning objectives cover administration of justice, state statutes, criminal procedure, human behavior, juvenile justice, operations and procedures, and cultural awareness. The *clinical skills* learning objectives cover techniques of criminal investigation and testifying, patrol functions, traffic law enforcement, firearms and defensive tactics.

Academy Training for New Recruits

The type of people who are becoming officers has changed. Fewer have military backgrounds—more have college educations. The boot-camp approach using stress in academy training may make officers question their self-worth and willingness to follow orders blindly. When modern adult learning principles and self-image psychology are examined, it is revealed that the application of pressure to create a stressful response prior to training is *counterproductive.* Applying extreme pressure before training is as ineffective as giving new recruits handguns and expecting them to qualify prior to firearms training.

According to Guthrie (2000, p.124): "Typically, academy training is rigid, authoritarian and does not lend itself to higher order thinking. It is conducted in a paramilitary setting, with discipline the mainstay of daily activities. . . . Law enforcement needs to incorporate more use of cognitive skills and problem solving in entry-level training."

The traditional high-stress boot-camp model flies in the face of what is known about how adults learn. The academic model, in contrast, trains recruits in the necessary knowledge and skill areas. They have little or no staff contact outside the formal training. A weakness of this model is that it fails to indoctrinate recruits into the law enforcement culture, an important part of their overall training.

Another approach, the individual development model, maximizes adult learning principles (discussed earlier in the chapter), avoids personally derogatory practices and reflects the agency's values.

Of the training models typically used for law enforcement recruits, experts recommend a blend of the paramilitary and the academic.

On-the-Job Training

The most common and frequent training in law enforcement agencies is on-the-job training.

On-the-job training (OJT) may occur during field training, in-house training sessions or roll call.

Field Training

Field training may take several forms. It might consist of *rotation,* which provides opportunity for additional knowledge and increased competence in a specialized area. Rotating through various specialties provides opportunity for more of the total-person approach to learning.

The most common type of on-the-job training for new recruits is done by the **field training officer,** or **FTO.**

Rookie officers are assigned to a field training officer who teaches them "the ropes." Not all law enforcement officers make good FTOs, however. All FTOs should be carefully selected and then thoroughly trained before instructing others.

Coaching or **counseling,** both forms of one-on-one field training, can also take place on the job as the need arises. Cottrell and Layton (2002, p.15) explain: " 'To coach' comes from the root meaning, 'to bring a person from where they are to where they want to be.' " Counseling is usually presented by staff or the personnel department in a wide variety of areas. Jones (2000, p.118) notes: "Coaching is a valuable supervisory tool to obtain or maintain desired officer performance."

Subbing, another form of field training, takes place when individuals must be absent from their jobs for some reason. A law enforcement supervisor might be ill, and a senior patrol officer might take charge. Or the supervisor may be gone to a conference, and a subordinate may be left in charge. Supervisors should train their subordinates to the point that one could assume their job. This *does not* constitute a shirking of duties by the supervisor but is simply another step in developing better officers.

Training can take place in the field when experienced officers, who have been through the same situations as new officers, can share information, provide solid instructions and give constructive criticism for the new recruits.

In-House Training Sessions

In-house training sessions, also called **in-service training,** are frequently used in local law enforcement departments. Specific portions of a shift may be set aside for training and repeated for each shift. Instruction may be by the supervisor, by someone else within the department or by an instructor brought in from another department or from outside the law enforcement field. In-house training sessions should be based on the department's needs. Their length will depend on the instructor, the material to cover and the time available.

Consultants are not used more often, primarily because of the expense. Consultants are used mainly for their expertise and ability to look at problems without local bias or obligations. In areas where several law enforcement departments exist in proximity, it is sometimes cost effective to share training. One department, for example, might be known for its outstanding work on community relations. Another might be known for its expertise in investigating gang-related criminal activity. Yet another might be known for its work with juveniles. These three departments might share their expertise during in-service training sessions.

Relationships might also be established with local, state and federal agencies to exchange instructors and perhaps materials on special problem areas such as drug investigations. They might also include prosecutors and courts, the coroner's office, private security consultants and social services personnel.

Roll Call

Roll call, the brief period before each shift when officers check in and receive their briefing before going on duty, can be a popular, economical time to provide training. The time must be used wisely because roll call generally lasts only 10 to 15 minutes. Nonetheless, training in short bursts is much more effective than long sessions for some subjects. Roll call is well suited to short topics of specific, immediate interest to the on-line officer, and that interest increases training success. Nowicki (2002, p.12) points out: "With a careful budgeting of time, virtually every law enforcement agency that conducts a daily roll call can have an extra forty hours or more each year to train law enforcement officers." He suggests that roll call can be used to test officers on concepts introduced during training. They can practice patterns of movement or the interview stance during roll call. As Nowicki stresses: "Record keeping is important and, without a good system, it can be extremely confusing as to which officer received what training and when."

Remedial Training

One of the most unpleasant tasks a manager faces is dealing with unsatisfactory performance. But as Phelan (2000, p.48) suggests: "Practical and procedural support when managing unsatisfactory behavior is likely to promote proper skills development as well as an effective training environment." Phelan (p.50) describes four essential components of the remedial process:

1. Performance review: Explain precisely what error/omission occurred.
2. Demonstration/explanation: Tell/show the proper procedure.
3. Resource acquisition: Inform the member what resources are required to correct/modify the behavior.
4. Compliance time line: Give a defined period of time in which to correct the problem.

Schennum (2000, p.67) stresses: "When an officer starts to display problems, the FTO must bring them to the officer's attention immediately, both verbally and written." Together they should develop an action plan to improve the problem behavior. Dealing with problem behaviors is discussed in detail in Chapter 11.

Becoming a Sergeant

Of particular importance is effective training for newly promoted sergeants. This promotion is a critical and challenging adjustment for the officer who for the first time must supervise others. Unfortunately, as Goolsby (2001, p.82) contends: "The training of supervisors has long been neglected by police organizations. Most agencies still use a system that applies the sink-or-swim philosophy. Preparation for the job usually consists of little more than attendance at a supervisory school some time within the first year of promotion."

Fulton (2002a, p.102) reports that new supervisors learn in many different ways: observing their supervisors, studying policy and procedure manuals, taking formal training courses and through trial and error. Of trial and error, Fulton suggests: "This method of learning is the new supervisor's least favorite way to learn. The 'trial' part causes them stress and the 'error' part causes them even more stress. When things go wrong, they can go very wrong, very quickly. Using this learning method, it can take years to climb the learning curve, and forcing them to do this is setting them up for failure. Police commanders should do everything they can to help their new supervisors learn the skills required before promoting them."

This is exactly what is being done in Coppell, Texas. Goolsby (p.83) describes the Coppell Approach: "Using the FTO model, the department developed a supervisor development program or SDP. The program identifies certain tasks and subjects that new supervisors must know before they can perform as supervisors without assistance." The categories included in the seven-week, four-phase program are directing subordinates; decision making (stress and non-stress conditions); scheduling; self-initiated activity; officer safety issues; verbal skills with employees and with citizens; radio monitoring; writing; timeliness; follow-up; arrest review/probable cause; assertiveness; problem solving; interpersonal skills; written directives; knowledge of the law, of city policy and of liability issues; acceptance of feedback; attitude toward department and management; relationship with the public, with ethnic groups and with supervisors; and general appearance. Proficiency in all areas must be documented before the actual promotion takes place.

The Alabama Department of Public Safety, described by Mahaney (2000, p.10), uses three phases of training for new sergeants. The first phase includes organization theory, leadership principles, management of police organizations, organizational goals, media relations, problem solving/decision making, time management, stress management, ethics and integrity and effective communications. The second phase includes the yearly operational budget/fiscal management, the hiring process, the training process, measuring productivity, employee evaluations, police discipline, special problems in personnel issues, legal aspects of discipline and termination, public relations and public interaction, motivation and effective public speaking. The third phase includes laws of public order, civil liability, use of force and escalation principles, contingency planning, tactical operations exercise, intelligence preparation, logistical support for operations, communications and reporting, psychological aspects of critical incidents, critical incident debriefing and a review of critical incidents.

While the content may vary, the importance of effective training is stressed by Harrison (2001, p.151): "Although some may minimize the impact of the sergeant's role, it is the most important level of management; they are the ones who implement philosophy and turn intent into reality. Their work will either motivate or discourage those around them. The success of the chief or sheriff rests in their hands."

Fulton (2002b, p.142) lists the most common, and serious, mistakes made by new supervisors:

- Immediately made drastic changes in discipline or procedures.
- Failed to take charge.
- Tried to be "one of the guys."
- Gave no positive reinforcement.
- Failed to listen.
- Failed to effectively use time.
- Limited knowledge of labor laws, contracts or procedures.

He urges: "A reasonable and prudent, newly promoted police commander at any rank would try to avoid these common mistakes."

Training at the Management Level

Management on-the-job training can consist of using actual past department problems and requesting managers to offer solutions. These problems are related to the department in which the manager operates.

Technical skill development can take place through reviewing the total law enforcement experience, then evaluating what was done and deciding how it could be done better. Managers can improve their human-relations skills by attending seminars, workshops, conferences or courses at colleges and universities.

A number of approaches to management training are available. Some departments rotate the manager through divisions. Job rotation, although sometimes painful, gives the police manager a total department experience. Other departments do not use rotation, and once managers are appointed, they remain in that position until their next promotion or retirement. Stagnation often reigns in such agencies. New managers may be assigned to experienced managers who act as mentors.

Large city departments provide their own management training, tailored to their special problems and needs. Smaller agencies use a combination of methods: lecturers from federal, state and local law enforcement agencies or special management seminars. Smaller departments may band together in training groups to share resources.

Management and supervisory training is available externally at the federal, state and local levels. The FBI, Northwestern Traffic Institute and Southern Police Institute are among the agencies providing training for qualified officers nationally.

External law enforcement management courses are available through the International City Managers Association, the International Association of Chiefs of Police and the American Management Association. They are also available through local universities and colleges. External management training offers interaction with people from other agencies in identical positions. This sometimes establishes a long-term relationship for future exchange of information. These seminars also expose managers to new ideas and programs.

Opportunities for self-development are also available through correspondence courses, as well as individual management courses offered by universities, colleges and other agencies. Such courses are valuable for their content as well as for the self-discipline required to complete them independently.

External Training

Attendance at training sessions and seminars outside the department is costly, but it introduces officers to new ideas and subjects not available locally. External training provides the opportunity to meet officers from other departments, to share and appreciate the universal nature of some law enforcement problems. Possibilities for external training include local college courses; the Federal Bureau of Investigation; the Northwestern Traffic Institute; the International Association of Chiefs of Police; the Bureau of Alcohol, Tobacco and Firearms; the Drug Enforcement Agency; and the U.S. military branches of service.

Officers should document in writing their participation in such external training.

External training may take the form of college classes, seminars, conferences, workshops and independent study.

College Classes

Colleges and universities offer a wide variety of courses on subjects not taught by law enforcement departments. The department may pay for the tuition, fees, books and other costs, or officers may pay for them. In either case, such training usually takes place during officers' off-duty hours.

Some departments have incentive programs that permit officers who attend college courses for credit to receive extra pay. The increase in availability of college-level courses has had a tremendous impact on raising the level of police education.

Ironically, some college-educated officers find varying degrees of acceptance by older officers on the department. Resentment is beginning to be minimized by the many candidates today with degrees in criminal justice and the number obtaining degrees while working. The debate surrounding the educational requirements for officers was discussed in Chapter 7.

Seminars, Conferences and Workshops

Pick up any law enforcement journal and the opportunities available for training through seminars, conferences and workshops become immediately apparent. In a single month, for example, the IACP offers the following training programs: Administering a Small Law Enforcement Agency; Police Records Management; Innovative Approaches to the Public Information Process; Progressive Patrol Administration; Police Planning, Research and Implementation; and Criminal Investigations Management Symposium.

Costs for seminars, workshops and conferences vary greatly, ranging from free (not very common) to hundreds of dollars per participant. Travel costs are also often involved. Nevertheless, this is sometimes the most effective alternative for obtaining needed expertise in a given topic. Many service clubs, such as Rotary, Kiwanis and Optimist, will financially assist law enforcement agencies with such educational opportunities.

Conferences for professional law enforcement organizations also offer sessions on a wide variety of topics and have the added advantage of allowing for the interchange of ideas among professionals from around the country. If budgets allow, attendance at state-level and even national conferences should be a part of the training program.

Who to send is often a key question. One way to decide is to consider who would make the best in-service instructor. Officers who attend conferences, workshops or seminars should be expected to share the information gained. Usually the officer who attends puts on a training session. This sharing improves the instructor officer's self-esteem and professional reputation, which is valuable in establishing credibility in court as an expert witness. Most of all it enhances the agency's reputation as one that employs quality people and trains them well.

Even if the budget will not allow officers to attend conferences and conventions, the information from them is often available through publications of professional organizations.

Independent Study

Some departments have limited opportunity for external training. Most officers in such departments, however, will have access to a public library where they can set their own pace for education. Another avenue of independent study is the variety of distance learning and training (DLT) courses now available online, as discussed.

Ongoing Training—Lifelong Learning

Before getting the job, as a rookie, upon promotion to sergeant and beyond—throughout a law enforcement career—training should be ongoing. Regardless of the methods used, training must be continuous because people fail to remember a high percentage of what they learned. New subjects continually arise that must be learned, including new laws and court decisions.

Officers' training should be ongoing—lifelong learning.

Fulton (2002c, p.154) contends: "Those police managers who develop a pattern of lifelong learning will not only gain promotions, they will gain the respect of their peers, subordinates and supervisors. As a result of their knowledge, professional supervisors find it easier to do their jobs, and people in their department find it easier to trust them as a commander. . . . Choosing a pattern of lifelong learning through reading, classes and college can put you far ahead of other officers for promotions, respect and a bright future."

The Training Cycle

Because effective training is ongoing, it can be viewed as a cycle, as Figure 8.5 illustrates.

The training cycle consists of need identification, goal setting, program development, program implementation, program evaluation and back, full circle, to assessment of need based on the evaluation.

Need Identification

Training programs must emphasize actual individual and department goals. Needs come to light from officers' conversations, supervisors' and managers' observations, complaints, officers' suggestions and other sources.

Training needs of officers at various levels of experience can be determined in a number of ways. Among the most common are:

- Reviewing new statutes that affect police operations and investigations.
- Taking department surveys.

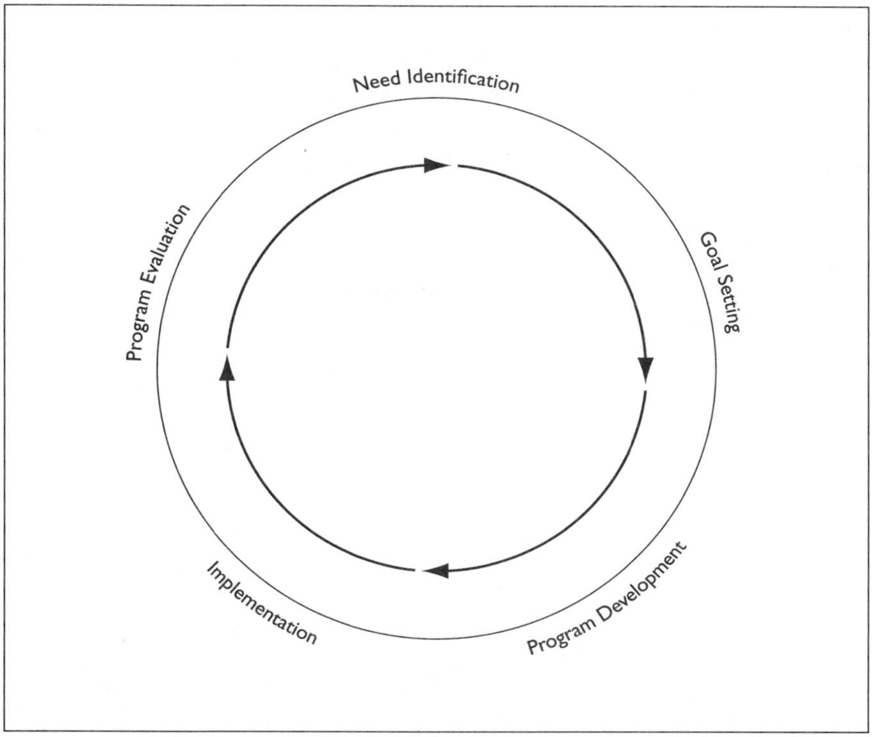

Figure 8.5
The Training Cycle

- Reviewing reports and noting deficiencies.
- Reviewing internal and external complaints.
- Reviewing lawsuits against the agency.
- Analyzing specific law enforcement functions.
- Interviewing line officers and detectives.
- Interviewing managers and supervisors.
- Getting input from other agencies and the community.

These various methods of identifying training needs are likely to indicate which subjects are considered priorities, as well as various types and levels of training needed in any given department. Police officers in the field are an excellent information source for training needs. They see the practical application and value of training, and they bear the initial responsibility when a liability suit is filed against the department. Police management bears the overall responsibility for failure to train.

Goal Setting

As with any type of goal setting, training goals should reflect specific training objectives that:

- Are specific and observable.
- Are measurable with a set criteria.
- Have a clear time line for achievement.

Program Development

After the needs have been identified and goals and objectives specified, the actual training program must be developed or, for existing programs, revised based on the needs assessment. Usually the following steps are taken:

- Determine subject matter and objectives based on identified needs.
- Prepare the training.
- Select the most appropriate method(s).
- Select/write materials, audiovisual aids and tests.
- Select the instructor.
- Schedule the training.
- Reserve the facility.
- Present the training.
- Evaluate.
- Learners apply new knowledge on the job.
- Evaluate.

Who should provide the training? Managers, by their position, should be constantly providing individual, on-the-job training, helping subordinates grow and develop. Managers may also schedule more formal training sessions and present information themselves. They may seek assistance from an expert within the department. Or they may bring in someone from outside the department. Whether managers do the actual training or not, they are responsible for ensuring it is effective and meets their subordinates' needs. The ultimate responsibility is theirs.

Cost The amount of money budgeted for training varies greatly from department to department. In addition to the costs for instructors and materials, the cost of officers' salaries during training should also be factored in. Training costs can be cut by sharing resources with other departments, co-hosting training, using FBI programs, seeking scholarships for officers to attend training and seeking sponsors for officers.

Facilities The type of training, method of instruction and audiovisuals will affect the physical facilities needed. The facility should be conducive to learning and to two-way communication. It should be well lit and well ventilated, contain adequate seating and writing surfaces and have good acoustics. Depending on the size of the group, a microphone may be necessary. If so, the most effective type is a small, wireless microphone.

Program Evaluation

Like training, evaluation should be continuous. The officers' grasp of the material should be tested in the classroom and on the job. Such evaluation will help determine whether further training is needed in a specific area.

One effective nontest way to evaluate training effectiveness is to compare officers' performance before and after training. Other before-and-after information that might reflect the effectiveness of training can be obtained from records of complaints, grievances, absenteeism, turnover and the like.

Trainers should consider having the trainees complete an evaluation of the session, including responding to such questions as these:

- How effective was the instructor?
- How interesting was the session?
- How relevant was the material?
- How was the pacing of the session?
- What did you like most about the training?
- What could be improved?

These questions could be posed during interviews or through more formal questionnaires such as that illustrated in Figure 8.6.

Benefits of Effective Training Programs

Borello and Fraser (2001, p.26) state: "Training in law enforcement can certainly be considered a defining characteristic of professionalism. The benefits of training can be many. Officer safety tops the list."

Evaluation Form Skill Development Workshop

Items below evaluated on a 1 to 10 scale. Please circle number that indicates your evaluation. (10 represents the most positive reaction; 1 the least positive)

1. How well did the training program hold your interest?	10	9	8	7	6	5	4	3	2	1
2. How would you evaluate the leader's knowledge of the topics?	10	9	8	7	6	5	4	3	2	1
3. How effective was the leader's presentation?	10	9	8	7	6	5	4	3	2	1
4. How useful were the notebook/handouts?	10	9	8	7	6	5	4	3	2	1
5. How useful was the group participation?	10	9	8	7	6	5	4	3	2	1
6. How useful were the audio/visuals?	10	9	8	7	6	5	4	3	2	1
7. What overall rating would you give the program?	10	9	8	7	6	5	4	3	2	1

8. How would you evaluate your participation in the program? (check one)

Overall workload	Too heavy ______ Too light ______	Just right ______
Classroom demands	Too heavy ______ Too light ______	Just right ______
Homework assignments	Too heavy ______ Too light ______	Just right ______

9. If asked by a co-worker to describe the workshop and its value to you, what would you say?

10. In what specific ways could this program be improved?

Figure 8.6
Sample Evaluation Form

Source: Stan Kossen. *Supervision,* 2nd ed. St. Paul, MN: West Publishing Company, 1991. p.285.

Training programs can benefit individual officers, supervisors, managers, the entire department and the community.

Benefits for Individual Officers

Benefits for individual officers include improved chances for career success, increased motivation, improved morale, increased productivity, greater feelings of self-worth, reduced chances of injury on the job, greater confidence, pride, improved work attitudes and increased job satisfaction.

Benefits for Supervisors and Managers

Among the many benefits supervisors of those trained might enjoy are getting to know officers better, furthering their own advancement and career, gaining more time, establishing better human relations, increased confidence in officers' abilities, increased flexibility, increased creativity, fewer discipline problems and mistakes, and improved discipline.

Benefits for the Entire Department and Community

Many benefits enjoyed by individual managers also benefit the entire agency. In addition, the organization and ultimately the community benefit from training in more efficient, effective officers; increased quantity and quality of work; reduced turnover, absenteeism, waste, complaints and grievances; greater public support; and increased departmental pride.

Clearly, training is an important function of the effective manager/supervisor at all levels of the department. Borello and Fraser introduce a "Best Practices

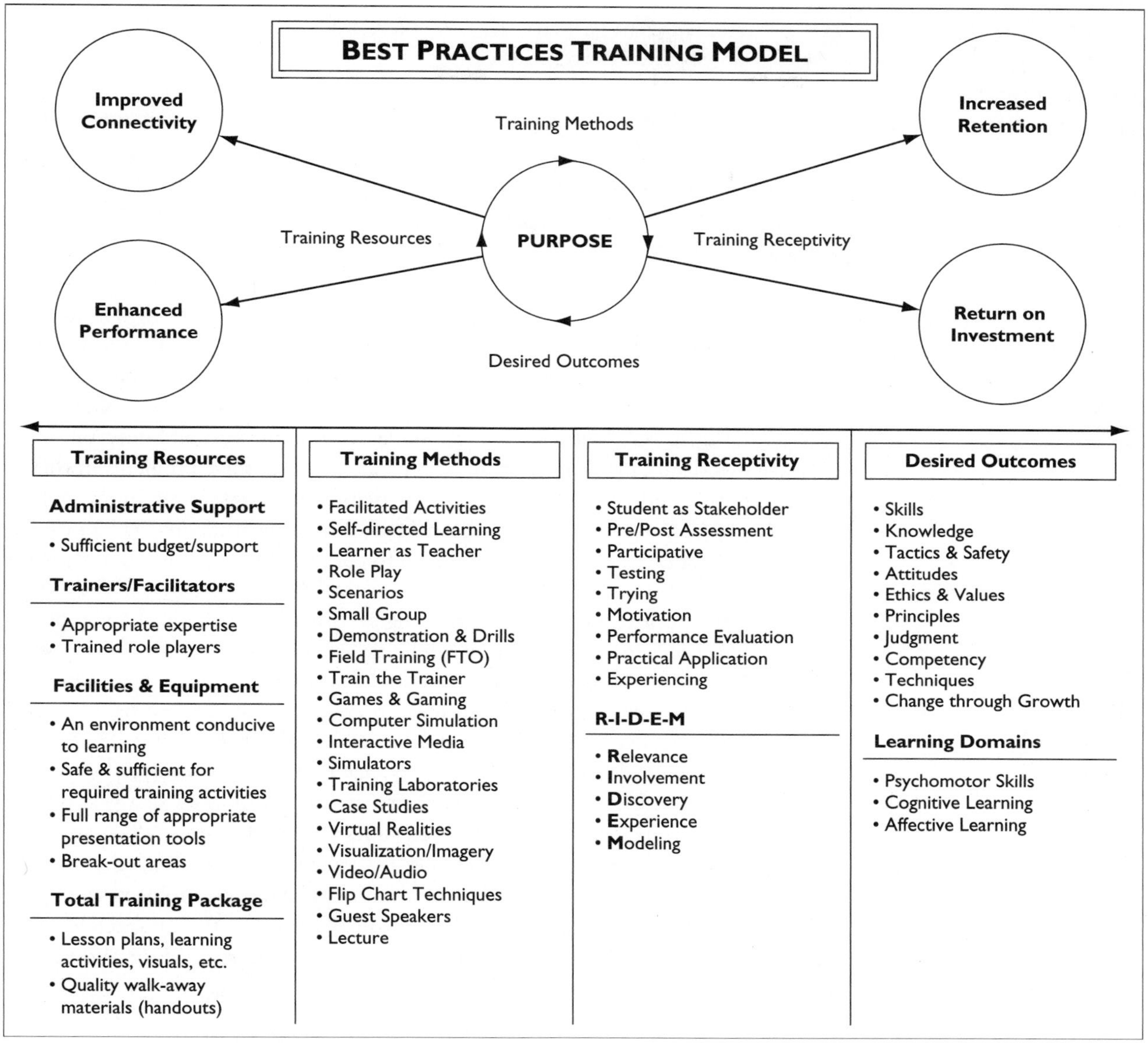
BEST PRACTICES TRAINING MODEL
Improved Connectivity
Increased Retention
Training Methods
Training Resources
PURPOSE
Training Receptivity
Enhanced Performance
Return on Investment
Desired Outcomes
Training Resources
Administrative Support
• Sufficient budget/support
Trainers/Facilitators
• Appropriate expertise
• Trained role players
Facilities & Equipment
• An environment conducive to learning
• Safe & sufficient for required training activities
• Full range of appropriate presentation tools
• Break-out areas
Total Training Package
• Lesson plans, learning activities, visuals, etc.
• Quality walk-away materials (handouts)
Training Methods
• Facilitated Activities
• Self-directed Learning
• Learner as Teacher
• Role Play
• Scenarios
• Small Group
• Demonstration & Drills
• Field Training (FTO)
• Train the Trainer
• Games & Gaming
• Computer Simulation
• Interactive Media
• Simulators
• Training Laboratories
• Case Studies
• Virtual Realities
• Visualization/Imagery
• Video/Audio
• Flip Chart Techniques
• Guest Speakers
• Lecture
Training Receptivity
• Student as Stakeholder
• Pre/Post Assessment
• Participative
• Testing
• Trying
• Motivation
• Performance Evaluation
• Practical Application
• Experiencing
R-I-D-E-M
• Relevance
• Involvement
• Discovery
• Experience
• Modeling
Desired Outcomes
• Skills
• Knowledge
• Tactics & Safety
• Attitudes
• Ethics & Values
• Principles
• Judgment
• Competency
• Techniques
• Change through Growth
Learning Domains
• Psychomotor Skills
• Cognitive Learning
• Affective Learning

Figure 8.7
Best Practices Training Model

Source: Andrew Borrello and Jim Fraser. "The Best Practices Training Model." *The Law Enforcement Trainer,* September/October 2001, p.28. Reprinted by permission.

Training Model," which nicely summarizes the main concepts presented in this chapter (see Figure 8.7). They (p.29) contend: "The Best Practices Training Model was created as a review tool for trainers to deliver a very valuable gift—the gift of growth through learning—and to deliver that gift in the most effective, blended and connective way possible."

The Violent Crime Control and Law Enforcement Act of 1994

The Violent Crime Control and Law Enforcement Act of 1994 authorizes major funding for law enforcement training.

The federal crime bill's Police Corps and in-service scholarship programs represent the largest federal investment in education for law enforcement personnel since the Law Enforcement Education Program in the late 1960s and 1970s. The act also puts hundreds more officers on the street in an effort to bolster community policing.

Training and COPPS

As more agencies nationwide adopt a community-oriented policing and problem solving (COPPS) philosophy, training of recruits must incorporate these shifts in principles and practices. Birzer and Tannehill (p.233) suggest: "There is an urgent need for police officers who are skilled communicators and decision makers, who are capable of helping citizens identify and solve problems in their communities, and who possess effective mediation and conflict-resolution skills."

Haarr (p.413) reports that a regional police training academy "had a positive impact on police recruits' attitudes related to community policing, public–police relations, problem-solving policing, as well as traditional policing. . . . Unfortunately, the positive gains that the training academy had made in shaping police recruits' attitudes toward community policing and problem-solving policing were lost by the end of the field-training process. In particular, at the end of field training, police recruits believed that fewer resources should be devoted to community policing, expressed less favorable views toward community policing and its effectiveness, and felt less qualified to engage in problem-solving tasks related to the SARA model." Haarr further reports: "By the end of their first year on the job, police recruits held more negative attitudes toward community policing and problem-solving policing. . . . The positive gains the training academy made in increasing police recruit support for community policing and problem-solving policing were not sustained once police recruits returned to their respective police agencies." These findings have important implications for supervisors and managers at all levels.

Summary

Developing human resources should be managers' single most important objective. This objective requires providing both training and education. Training generally refers to vocational instruction that takes place on the job and deals with physical skills. Education generally refers to academic instruction that takes place in a college, university or seminar-type setting and deals with knowledge and understanding. Both training and education are needed for effective learning.

Three variables that affect learning are individual variables, task/information variables and environmental/instructional variables. The three general categories of learners or learning styles are visual, auditory and kinesthetic. Training can focus on knowledge, skills or attitudes.

Job analysis is the key to determining the content to teach and test. When content relates directly to the tasks to be performed, it is considered valid. Tests that measure competence in these tasks are then also valid.

Important learning principles include the following: base training on an identified need; tell officers what the learning objective is; tell officers why they need to learn the material; make sure officers have the necessary background to master the skill (the prerequisites); present the material using the most appropriate materials and methods available; when possible use variety; adapt the materials and methods to individual officers' needs; allow officers to be as active and involved as possible during training; engage as many of the senses as possible during training; break complex tasks into simple, easy-to-understand steps; use repetition and practice to enhance remembering; and give officers periodic feedback on how they are performing. Whenever possible, present the "big picture"—teach an understandable concept rather than relying on simple memorization.

Training pitfalls to avoid include ignoring individual differences; expecting everyone to learn at the same pace; going too fast; giving too much at one time; using gimmicks that serve no instructional purpose; getting too fancy; lecturing without showing; being impatient; not setting expectations or setting them too high; creating stress, often through competition; delegating training responsibilities without making sure the assigned person is qualified; assuming that because something was assigned or presented that it was learned; fearing subordinates' progress and success; embarrassing trainees in front of others; and relying too heavily on "war stories."

Effective learning depends on intelligent selection of methods and materials. Instructional methods include lecture, question/answer sessions, discussion, demonstration, hands-on learning and role playing. Instructional materials include printed information, visuals, bulletin boards, audio- and videocassettes, television programs and computer programs. The Law Enforcement Television Network (LETN) is a private satellite television system that provides current programs on a variety of law enforcement subjects, available through subscription.

Other organizations available to assist with training include the American Society of Law Enforcement Trainers (ASLET), the National Association of Field Training Officers (NAFTO), the Federal Law Enforcement Training Center (FLETC), the National Center for State and Local Training, the FBI National Police Academy and the FBI itself. Peace Officer Standards and Training (POST) commissions exist in every state to set requirements for becoming licensed as a law enforcement officer.

Of the models of training typically used for law enforcement recruits, experts recommend a blending of the paramilitary and the academic. The most common training is on-the-job training. It may occur during field training, in-house training sessions or roll call. The most common type for new recruits is that done by the field training officer, or FTO. External training may take the form of college classes, seminars, conferences, workshops and independent study.

Officers' training should be ongoing. This results in a training cycle consisting of needs identification, goal setting, program development, program implementation, program evaluation and back, full circle, to assessment of needs based on the evaluation. Training programs can benefit individual officers, supervisors, managers and the entire department and community.

The Violent Crime Control and Law Enforcement Act of 1994 authorizes major funding for law enforcement training.

Discussion Questions

1. How would you compare and contrast training and education?
2. Which instructional methods do you think are most effective? Least effective?
3. Which instructional materials do you think are most effective? Least effective?
4. What is the role of the employee in self-development?
5. When would you use a group or conference method of training?
6. When would you use external training programs?
7. What are the major considerations in developing a law enforcement training program?
8. What would you include in a law enforcement training philosophy statement?
9. What five subjects do you consider most essential for a management development training program?
10. What training could be conducted during a cutback budgeting period and still provide reasonable training?

InfoTrac College Edition Assignment

Use InfoTrac College Edition to answer the Discussion Questions as appropriate.

Research the topic of *distance learning in law enforcement* in at least two journals. List the advantages and disadvantages according to your sources. Be sure to give the full references for each source. Be prepared to share your findings with the class.

OR

Read and outline "Management Training for Police Supervisors: A Cost-Effective Approach" by Patrick Mahaney.

References

Adams, Malcolm and Loberg, Gary. "Training America's Finest." *The Police Chief,* November 2001, p.48.

Austen-Kern, Laurie. "Distance Learning: A Primer for the Training Manager." *The Law Enforcement Trainer,* May/June 2001, pp.28–30, 43.

Baker, Thomas. "Computer Technology in Police Academy Training." *Law and Order,* August 2002, pp.107–110.

Baker, Thomas E. and Piland-Baker, Jane. "Police Training in Cyberspace." *Law and Order,* May 2000, pp.121–124.

Birzer, Michael L. and Tannehill, Ronald. "A More Effective Training Approach for Contemporary Policing." *Police Quarterly,* June 2001, pp.233–252.

Borrello, Andrew. "Tips to Enhance and Reinforce Police Training." *Police,* January 2000, p.27.

Borrello, Andrew and Fraser, Jim. "The Best Practices Training Model." *The Law Enforcement Trainer,* September/October 2001, pp.26–29.

Caddell, Alan. "Constructing Effective Instruction: You Need the Right Tools." *The Law Enforcement Trainer,* March/April 2002, p.36.

Colaprete, Frank A. "Case Studies: An Underused Resource in the Police Training Process." *The Law Enforcement Trainer,* September/October 2002, pp.20–23.

Cone, John W. and Robinson, Dana G. "The Power of E-Performance." *TD,* August 2001, pp.33–41.

Cottrell, David and Layton, Mark C. *The Manager's Coaching Handbook: A Practical Guide to Improve Performance.* Dallas, TX: CornerStone Leadership Institute, 2002.

Dahlinger, Charles. "The Consequences of Not Adequately Training or Reviewing Departmental Policy." *Law and Order,* December 2001, pp.53–54.

Dees, Tim. "Distance Learning Pitfalls." *Law and Order,* May 2000, pp.13–14.

Fulton, Roger. "Learning Supervisory Skills." *Law Enforcement Technology,* February 2002a, p.102.

Fulton, Roger. "Common Mistakes That Should Be Avoided." *Law Enforcement Technology,* June 2002b, p.142.

Fulton, Roger. "Lifelong Learning." *Law Enforcement Technology,* July 2002c, p.154.

Goolsby, Wade. "Developing Supervisors: The Coppell Approach." *The Police Chief,* August 2001, pp.82–85.
Grimm, Eric. "Advantages and Disadvantages of Online Learning." *Performance in Practice,* Spring 2001, pp.9–10.
Guthrie, Edward. "Higher Learning and Police Training." *Law and Order,* December 2000, p.124.
Haarr, Robin N. "The Making of a Community Policing Officer: The Impact of Basic Training and Occupational Socialization on Police Recruits." *Police Quarterly,* December 2001, pp.402–433.
Harris, Wesley. "Cost Effective Training Strategies." *Law and Order,* June 2002, pp.44–46.
Harrison, Bob. "Policy and Procedure: What New Sergeants Need to Know." *Law and Order,* October 2001, pp.151–153.
Hootstein, Ed. "The Art of Questioning: How to Ask to Get the Best Learning." *TD,* December 2002, pp.20–21.
Hornburg, James P. "5 Secrets of the Best Instructors." *The Law Enforcement Trainer,* April 2000, pp.22–24, 58–59.
James, Gary W. "Take the ID Road to Success." *Training & Development,* April 2001, pp.16–17.
Jones, Tony L. "Coaching for Performance." *Law Enforcement Technology,* July 2000, pp.116–122.
Keeney, Mark A. "Force-Options Simulations: Are They the Answer?" *Police,* July 2001, pp.36–39.
Kenner, Brian. "Delivering Life-Saving Information to First Responders." *Law Enforcement Technology,* September 2001, pp.114–118.
Kleinman, David. "More Bang for Your Training Buck." *The Law Enforcement Trainer,* May/June 2001, pp.10–12.
Knowles, M. S. *The Modern Practice of Adult Education: Andragogy vs. Pedagogy.* New York: Association Press, 1970.
Larson, David. "Training Comes to the Patrol Car." *Law Enforcement Technology,* September 2000, pp.102–105.
Less, Karen. "The Intergenerational Classroom in Law Enforcement Training." *The Law Enforcement Trainer,* May/June 2002, pp.22–27.
Mahaney, Patrick. "Management Training for Police Supervisors: A Cost-Effective Approach." *FBI Law Enforcement Bulletin,* July 2000, pp.7–11.
Mason, Roger. "Using Simulations as a Training Tool." *The Police Chief,* November 2001, pp.44–46.
Morrison, Richard D. "Interactive Training." *Law Enforcement Technology,* January 2000, pp.97–98.
Murphy, William A. and Gascon, George. "New Training Program Helps LAPD Meet Training Standards." *The Police Chief,* November 2001, pp.38–42.
Nowicki, Ed. "Roll Call Training." *Law and Order,* August 2002, p.12.
Oakes, Kevin and Rengarajan, Raghavan. "E-Learning: Practice Makes Perfect." *TD,* November 2002, pp.58–60.
Phelan, Regis Leo. "Use a Systematic Approach in Remedial Training to Modify, Improve Job Performance." *Police,* January 2000, pp.48–50.
Reintzell, John F. "Crisis on Demand: Simulation Training for Emergency Management." *The Law Enforcement Trainer,* September/October 2002, pp.28–32.
Risher, Julie A. "Police Liability for Failure to Train." *The Police Chief,* July 2001, p.10.
Schennum, Tim. "The Action Plan as an FTO Tool." *Law and Order,* December 2000, pp.67–69.
Smith, Gerald; Debenham, Jerry; and Mays, Carroll. "Get Smart: E-Learning for Police." *Law Enforcement Technology,* January 2002, pp.82–84.
Spector, Elliot. "Emerging Legal Standards for Failure to Train." *Law and Order,* October 2001, pp.73–77.
Spector, Elliot. "Failure to Train." *Law and Order,* June 2002, pp.136–138.
Spranza, Francis. "Intro to Distance Learning: The Hows and Whys of Bringing Distance Learning to Law Enforcement." *Law Enforcement Technology,* November 2001, pp.82–86.
Staton, Thomas F. *How to Instruct Successfully: Modern Teaching Methods in Adult Education.* New York: McGraw-Hill Book Company, 1960.
Tarani, Steve. "Force Options Training: Delivery and Balance." *FBI NAA,* March/April 2001, pp.20–26.
Trevino, Ernest C. "Driving Simulation Improves Training, Saves Department Budgets." *The Police Chief,* November 2000, pp.56–58.
Zenger, Jack and Uehlein, Curt. "Why Blended Will Win." *TD,* August 2001, pp.54–60.

Book-Specific Web site

Go to the *Management and Supervision in Law Enforcement* Web site at http://info.wadsworth.com/05346160654 for student and instructor resources, including Internet Assignments and Case Studies.

CHAPTER 9

Promoting Growth and Development

None of us is as good as all of us.
—Ray Kroc, founder of McDonalds

Do You Know?

- What the workplace culture is?
- What norms are and why they are important?
- Where an officer's first loyalty must lie?
- How managers can shape the workplace culture?
- What the Johari Window describes?
- What a necessary first step for growth and development is?
- What personal goals specify and what areas they should include?
- What touchstone values and daily values are and how they are related?
- What a balanced performer manager is?
- What stages of growth people typically go through?
- What mentoring is?
- How someone might develop a positive image?
- In what areas of cultural awareness law enforcement officers need development?
- What ethics entail and how to develop ethical behavior?
- What the key elements of corrupt behavior are?
- Why it is important to help officers grow and develop?

Can You Define?

balanced performer managers
balancing
blind self
code of silence
cultural awareness
daily values
dependent
ethical behavior
ethics
ghosting
gratuity
hidden self
holistic personal goals
independent
integrity
interdependent
job description
Johari Window
key result areas
majority worldview
mentor
minority worldview
norms
open self
police culture
racial profiling
subconscious self
supernorms
synergy
touchstone values
undiscovered self
workplace culture

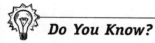

INTRODUCTION

Law enforcement managers have two obligations as developers: developing themselves and developing their subordinates. Both are normally accomplished simultaneously.

Because managing is getting work done through others, you will get the best from subordinates by developing their abilities. This is not always accomplished by being the "good guy." It is pleasant to have good interpersonal relationships with all workers, but it is not always possible. There are times for praise and times for discipline.

This chapter begins by discussing job descriptions and the workplace culture. Next it describes the importance of developing positive interpersonal relationships and of goal setting. This is followed by a look at balanced performer managers and how they might empower those who report to them. Next you will learn the stages of growth employees go through, the important managerial role of mentors, and approaches to developing positive attitudes, a positive image, cultural awareness and a sense of ethics and integrity. The chapter concludes with a discussion of the long-range importance of developing personnel, how managers can be motivators for change and how they might evaluate the workplace climate for growth, development and change within their department.

Job Descriptions

A **job description** is a detailed, formally stated summary of duties and responsibilities for a position. It usually contains the position title, supervisor, education and experience required, salary, duties, responsibilities and job details.

Job details make a specific position different from all others in an organization. Patrol officers' duties are different from those of detectives. Likewise, the duties of sergeants, lieutenants and chiefs differ.

Job descriptions are not limiting or restrictive. They are simply minimum requirements, and the job description should make this clear. Employees who can expand these tasks or do them differently and better should be encouraged to do so. Job descriptions provide the basis not only for getting work done but also for setting expectations and standards for evaluation.

Tasks must be broadly stated and leave room for growth, change and expansion. They should also be reviewed at least annually, when some tasks may be eliminated and others added. For example, recently resources have shifted from the war on drugs to the war on terrorism in many departments. Law enforcement managers must respond to that national interest.

All law enforcement personnel have opportunities to expand their tasks and perform them better. Any law enforcement task can be done better, with greater total effect. Managers need to use every available resource to develop the best in each individual and the team. One key is a positive work culture.

The Workplace Culture

The workplace culture is evident in any organization. Visit an engineering firm, and you are likely to encounter a well-dressed staff who greets you quite formally. Visit the local newspaper, and you are likely to encounter a casually dressed staff who greets you quite informally. Further, within many workplace cultures, subcultures exist. Within an advertising agency, for example, the sales force may dress up, whereas the creative staff may favor T-shirts and blue jeans. Each workplace develops its own culture.

The **workplace culture** is the sum of the beliefs and values shared by those within the organization, serving to formally and informally communicate its expectations.

These beliefs and values are a type of "collective conscience" by which those within the group judge each other.

The Socialization Process

Sherman (1999, p.301) explains:

> Every occupation has a learning process (usually called "socialization") to which its new members are subjected. The socialization process functions to make most "rookies" in the occupation adopt the prevailing rules, values, and attitudes of their senior colleagues in the occupation. Very often, some of the existing informal rules and attitudes are at odds with the formal rules and attitudes society as a whole expects members of the occupation to follow. This puts rookies in a moral dilemma: should the rookies follow the formal rules of society, or the informal rules of their senior colleagues?

He (p.302) also states: "There are four major stages in the career of anyone joining a new occupation: (1) The *choice* of the occupation, (2) the *introduction* to the occupation, (3) the first *encounter* with doing the occupation's work and (4) the *metamorphosis* into a full-fledged member of the occupation." The transformation of the police officer's identity and self-image may be more radical than in many other fields. Sherman (p.304) further explains:

> In the encounter stage, the rookie gets the major reality shock in the entire process of becoming a police officer. The rookie discovers that police work is more social work than crime fighting, more arbitration of minor disputes than investigations of major crimes, more patching of holes in the social fabric than weaving of webs to catch the big time crooks. . . .
>
> The result of those encounters is usually a complete change, a total adaptation of the new role and self-concept as a "cop." And with that transformation comes a stark awareness of the interdependence cops share with all other cops. . . . They are totally and utterly dependent on other police to save their lives, to respond to a call of an officer in trouble or need of assistance.

This perspective is a defining element of the police culture.

The Police Culture

Click (2002, p.64) states: "Call it 'The Blue Wall,' 'The Thin Blue Line,' 'the Brotherhood' or any other name, it all means the same thing. . . . If you carry a badge, then you're family." The **police culture** has been extensively written about and is often described as isolationist, elitist and authoritarian.

Paoline et al. (2000, p.576) report: "According to the conventional wisdom, the police culture consists of a set of values, attitudes and norms that are widely shared among officers, who find in the culture a way to cope with the strains of their working environment. Some research implies that the conventional wisdom is overdrawn, and recent research has begun to question it more directly. Changes in the composition (i.e., the race, sex and education of police personnel), as well as philosophical and organizational changes associated with community policing, could be expected to further fragment police culture and to shift the distribution of police attitudes."

Within some departments there is no clear mission statement and conflict occurs between officers who see themselves as crime fighters and those who prefer the social-service role emphasized in community policing.

Management consultant Fulton (2002, p.154) notes that when he is hired to conduct management training, he arrives a day early to get a feel for the community and its police officers. He seeks out one or more police officers and asks for directions to his hotel: "Those brief encounters tell me a great deal about the culture of that department. They help tell me whether I have a progressive, citizen-oriented police force, or an occupying army with an 'us vs. them' mentality." Fulton considers five components to be primary in evaluating a department's culture: (1) attitude, (2) appearance, (3) conduct, (4) professionalism and (5) public confidence. He asks:

> Do your officers look, act and perform like professional police officers? Do they project the image of well-trained, educated and disciplined protectors of the public? Are they courteous and helpful to all classes of citizens? Are they unbiased and nondiscriminatory in all of their actions and interactions with the public?

An important part of any culture is its norms.

Norms

What is important within any department is expressed as norms.

Norms are the attitudes and beliefs held by the members of a group.

Norms are, in effect, what is "normal." Most people do not want to be considered "abnormal," so they do and say what others expect of them, for example:

- Do the job the way you're told.
- It's okay to be late.
- Never give so many citations you make your colleagues look bad.

These norms are enforced by putting pressure on those who do not conform. Norms can hurt or help managers. Negative work norms can destroy morale and decrease performance; positive norms can heighten morale and improve performance. Two norms common in many police departments are a fierce loyalty to one another and the accompanying **code of silence,** the unwillingness to reveal any misconduct by fellow officers. Trautman (2002, p.19) contends: "The development of loyalty and the code of silence among officers is a totally natural phenomenon among people who spend significant time together."

Trautman (2001, p.68) reports on a study of 1,116 officers in which 46 percent of those responding stated they had witnessed misconduct by another officer but took no action. He (p.69) also reports that: "Of those who committed the misconduct, 47 percent advised they had felt pressure to take part in the code of silence from the officers who committed the misconduct." The officers in the study rated their organization's level of the code of silence by separate work groups on a scale of one to ten, with one being nonexistent, ten being severe. Patrol was rated worst at 4.3, followed by supervisors 3.9, investigators 3.7, administrators 3.6 and civilians 2.2.

Trautman (p.71) suggests: "The Us vs. Them mentality is usually present within the minds of those who participate in the code of silence. The code of silence and the Us vs. Them Phenomenon often bond together." The result is intense loyalty, which is a very positive feature of the police culture. Dees (2001, p.214) suggests: "Loyalty and faithfulness to one's fellow officer is a good thing, but only when that loyalty advances the mission of criminal justice to enforce the law and maintain order while respecting the rights and protections afforded the individual."

An officer's first loyalty must be to defend the Constitution and laws of the United States, his or her state constitution and laws, and local laws.

According to McErlain (2001, p.87): "Those who would suggest that some law enforcement officers today no longer hide behind the banner of loyalty are either naïve or concealing reality, contributing to the problem and enabling others to do the same. Some progress has been made in tearing down this age-old problem, but in many ways a police culture that exalts loyalty over integrity still exists."

Changing the Workplace Culture

Trautman (2001, p.75) recommends: "The most powerful means for transforming the organizational culture of a law enforcement agency into an atmosphere that is consistent with employees embracing loyalty to principle above all else is a combination of leadership, role modeling and training."

Managers can shape the workplace culture by doing the following:

1. Identify existing norms.
2. Evaluate the norms—do they work for or against the department's mission?
3. Encourage positive norms and try to eliminate negative ones through modeling and training.

Shaping the workplace culture requires the type of participatory management discussed earlier. Recognize, however, that when shaping the workplace culture, you can expect to encounter a kind of "Catch-22" in the form of **supernorms,** that is, overriding expectations of a given work group; for example, never volunteer information or do not criticize. Many of the communication skills discussed in Chapter 4 will help you deal with these supernorms and change those that are counterproductive.

You might also find the best subculture in your organization and hold it up as an example from which others can learn. Do not expect change overnight—it may take several years. Perhaps most important, live the culture you want. Walk the talk.

Within the workplace culture you and your people can grow and develop personally and professionally. The culture must expect, encourage and reward growth. Establishing a nurturing workplace culture depends on developing positive interpersonal relationships.

Developing Positive Interpersonal Relationships

Developing good manager–subordinate relations requires fairness, trust and confidence on everyone's part. It is not always the formal relationships, important as they are, that establish a rapport between manager and subordinate. It is a two-way feeling of respect, regard and trust.

Consider the employee who says, "I would do anything for the boss I have now. He demands a lot, but he is fair, and I trust that he will do what he says." More than likely this employee's manager has emotional maturity, displays confidence without being overbearing, knows his and the subordinate's job, would not ask the subordinate to do anything he would not do, expresses confidence in the subordinate and deals with the subordinate with compassion. Mutual respect develops when both manager and subordinate deal with each other in the same way.

Self-Disclosure and Feedback

An important part of developing relationships is for managers to get to know each member of the work unit better and, in the process, get to know themselves better. A model termed the **Johari Window** (named after the authors Joe and Harry) illustrates how people can learn more about others and themselves. The model is based on the premise that everyone has four parts to their identity, as Figure 9.1 illustrates.

Your **open self** is what you know about yourself and what you show to others. Your **hidden self** is the secret part that you do not share with others. Your **blind self** is the part of you that others can see but you do not know about yourself. Your **undiscovered** or **subconscious self** is the part of you that neither you nor others have yet discovered.

The Johari Window describes four parts of identity:

- The open self
- The hidden self
- The blind self
- The subconscious self

According to this model, through the process of self-disclosure and feedback—that is, honest interaction with others—you can widen the area of openness, reduce the hidden and blind parts and learn something about your undiscovered self.

Honest, open interaction with subordinates can help *everyone* within the workplace culture grow and develop. The direction this growth and development takes depends on the goals that are set.

Goal Setting

The importance of organizational goals has been discussed. Within organizational goals, managers should include growth and development, both individual

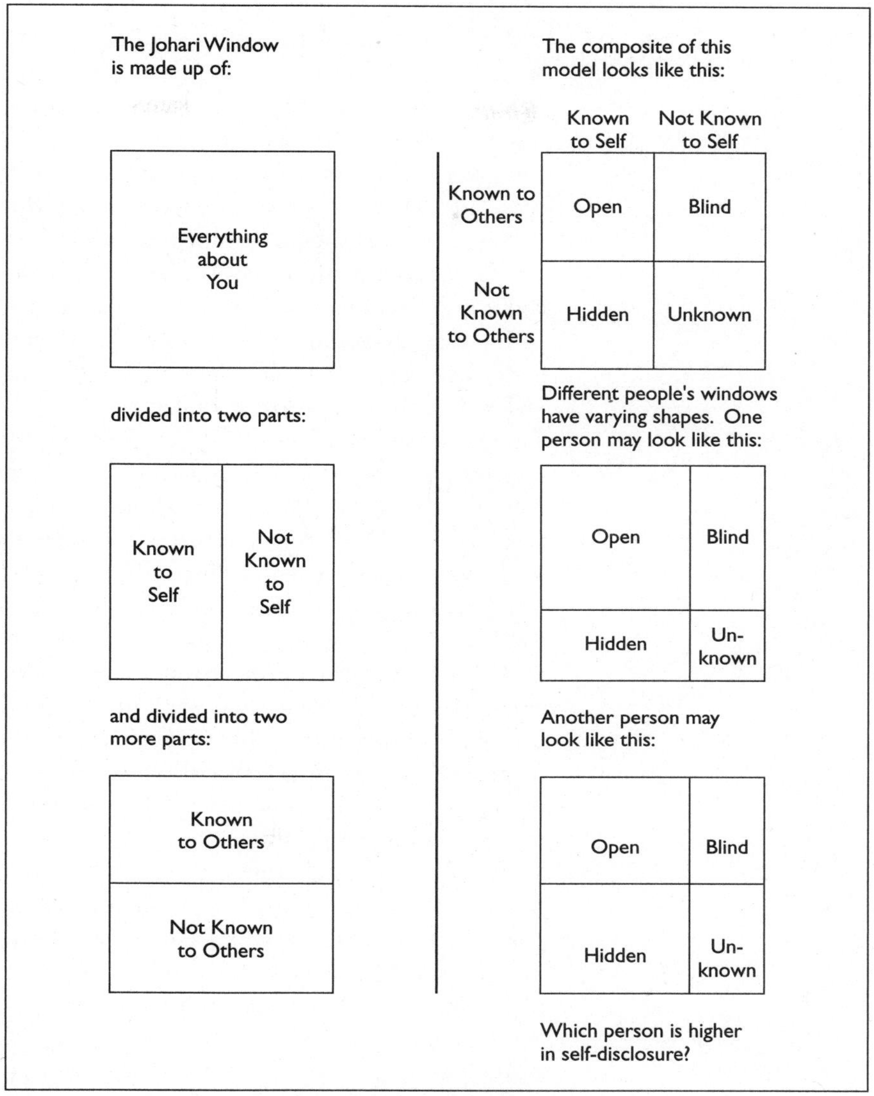

Figure 9.1
The Johari Window

Source: Paul R. Timm. *Supervision,* 2nd ed. St. Paul, MN: West Publishing Company, 1992, p.52.

and organizational. Remember that goals are targets: specific, measurable outcomes with a time line.

Personal and organizational goals are a necessary first step for growth and development.

Goals should be (1) stated positively, (2) realistic and attainable and (3) personally important.

A personal goal states what, when and how much.

The *what* is the specific result to achieve. The *when* is the target date by which the goal will be reached. The *how much* is, whenever possible, a quantifiable measure. Effective goals meet several of the following criteria: They are specific and realistic, action oriented, consistent with ability and authority and measurable. They should also include "stretch" and have a set deadline.

Law enforcement managers may set a goal of "talking to their subordinates about organizational and personal problems." They may help subordinates set their goals, which should be discussed and then written down. A specific time period should be established to accomplish the goals, and progress should be reviewed at the end of that period.

Goals should be specific. Vague, general goals are rarely accomplished. Saying you are going to "reduce crashes by 10 percent" is not necessarily a goal that you can achieve, desirable as it might be. You have no control over many variables associated with the goal, so select a realistic goal. Law enforcement officers in the field may set a goal of "increasing contacts with traffic violators by 10 contacts per day." This *would* be both realistic and achievable.

In the same vein, goals should not be excessively difficult. Excessively high goals destroy the chance for personal achievement. Goals must be attainable. If employees can help determine goals, they are more likely to achieve them. These goals may be higher than if managers establish them. An example of an unrealistic goal would be that all officers become expert sharpshooters. Varied levels of shooting ability exist. A more realistic goal would be that all officers take firearms range practice and qualify.

Goal setting, goal achievement and ultimate performance are directly related. It is exciting to realize that few people use more than 20 to 30 percent of their potential. People have few limits except those they impose on themselves. The 4-minute mile was considered impossible—until Roger Bannister ran it. The 7-foot high jump, the 17-foot pole vault—the impossible achieved.

Untapped potential exists in you and your people. The task is to create an exciting workplace in which people want to grow and develop and are helped to do so.

Holistic Goal Setting

Although managers are not technically responsible for their subordinates' off-the-job activities and aspirations, people have much more to them than their jobs. Indeed, a common problem of law enforcement officers is that their jobs become all-encompassing, overshadowing other important aspects of life. Effective managers consider themselves and those they manage as "total" people. **Holistic personal goals** should include not only the job/career, but also any other areas of importance such as financial, social, avocational and the like.

Managers will naturally be most concerned with the career/job-related goals such as learning new skills, but the other areas are also important. Managers should take care not to foster a lopsided workplace culture, focused entirely on

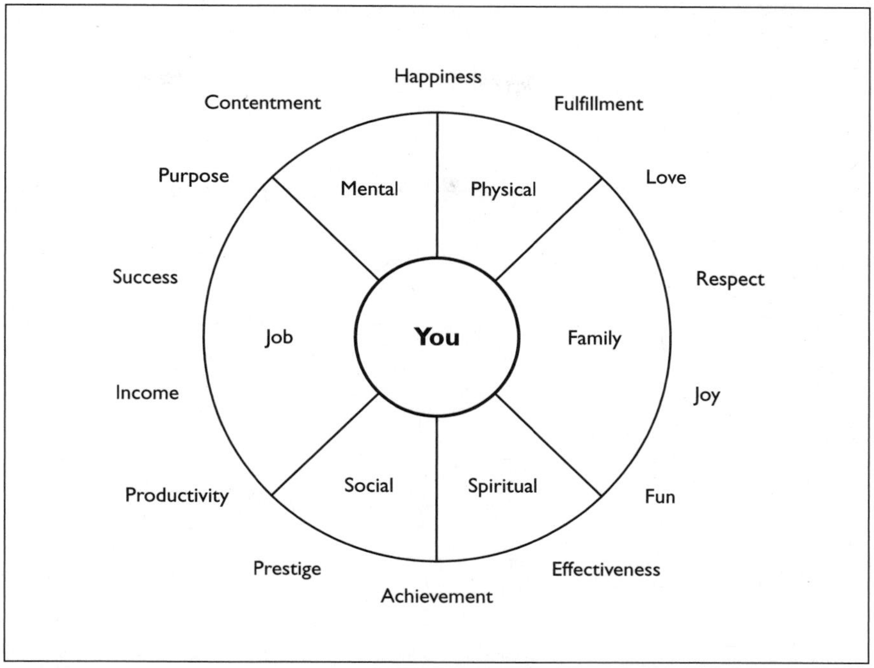

Figure 9.2
Life's Circle

Source: Stephen R. Covey. *The 7 Habits of Highly Effective People.* New York: Simon and Schuster, 1989, p.270. Copyright © 1989 by Stephen R. Covey. Reprinted by permission of Franklin Covey Co.

career/job goals. Figure 9.2 illustrates the various aspects of each individual that might be part of any growth and development program.

Goals and Values

Closely related to goals are the values you hold—what is important to you. What are your **key result areas**—broad categories people often talk about as important? Figure 9.3 lists 20 key result areas commonly identified.

Rank from 1 to 10 (1 being the most important) what you want. These are your **touchstone values.** Then rank how you actually spend the majority of your time, energy and money day to day. These are your **daily values.** How do the rankings compare?

Touchstone values, what people say is important to them, and *daily values,* how people actually spend their time and energy, need to correlate.

Often what people value and what they spend the majority of their time on conflict. For example, a person may have family as his or her Number 1 touchstone value, yet have work as the Number 1 daily value. Managers and those they manage need to examine their touchstone and daily values and seek a closer correlation between them.

Figure 9.3
Touchstone and Daily Values in Key Result Areas

Touchstone Values	Daily Values	Key Result Areas
________	________	Achievement (sense of accomplishment)
________	________	Work (paying own way)
________	________	Adventure (exploration, risks, excitement)
________	________	Personal freedom (independence, choices)
________	________	Authenticity (being frank and genuinely myself)
________	________	Expertness (being excellent at something)
________	________	Service (contribute to satisfaction of others)
________	________	Leadership (having influence and authority)
________	________	Money (plenty of money for things I want)
________	________	Spirituality (my religious beliefs/experiences)
________	________	Physical health (attractiveness and vitality)
________	________	Emotional health (handle inner conflicts)
________	________	Meaningful work (relevant/purposeful job)
________	________	Affection (warmth, giving/receiving love)
________	________	Pleasure (enjoyment, satisfaction, fun)
________	________	Wisdom (mature understanding, insight)
________	________	Family (happy/contented living situation)
________	________	Recognition (being well known; prestige)
________	________	Security (having a secure, stable future)
________	________	Self-growth (continuing development)

Source: David G. Lee, Senior Consultant with Personal Decisions, Inc., of Minneapolis, MN. Reprinted with permission.

Balanced Performer Managers and Empowerment

It cannot be repeated often enough: The most effective managers are those who accomplish priority tasks through their people. Managers who do everything themselves, no matter how well the tasks are done, are *not* effective managers, as Figure 9.4 illustrates.

Managers who concentrate on excelling themselves, on climbing up through the ranks rather than helping their subordinates to excel, are not balanced performers. Nor are the managers who do little or nothing themselves, relying on subordinates to carry the load but without providing an example for them to follow.

Managers who contribute their efforts to accomplishing department goals while simultaneously developing their subordinates into top performers are superior **balanced performer managers** who empower others.

Managers who empower allow subordinates to grow to their fullest potential.

Stages of Growth

The stages of growth in a manager–employee relationship can be compared to that of a parent and child.

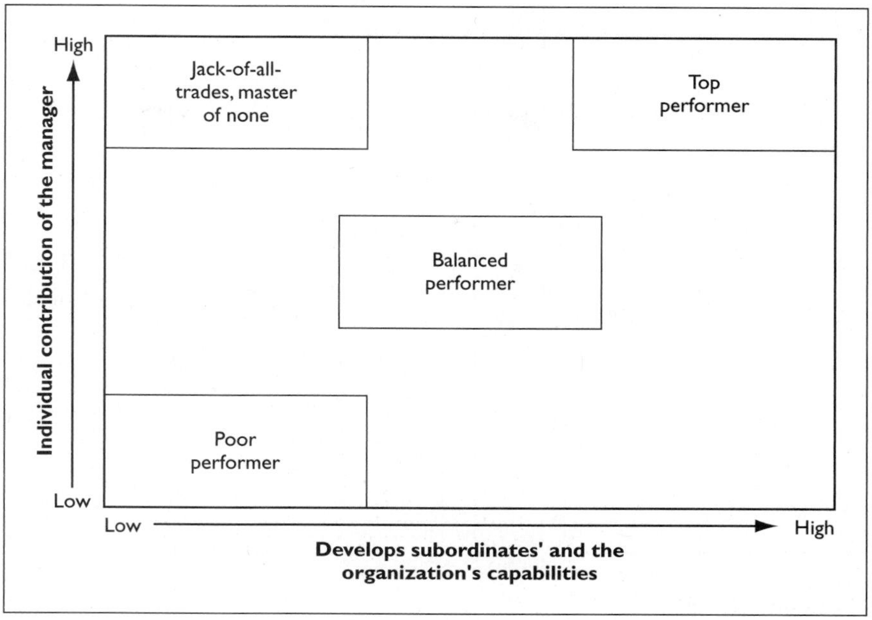

Figure 9.4
Balanced Performer

The three stages of growth are dependent, independent and interdependent.

The first stage is the **dependent** stage. Rookies are initially learning the job and are very dependent on others. They watch, follow and need direction. The manager's role at this stage is usually to *tell* them what to do.

As officers grow, develop and gain confidence, they become more **independent,** just as adolescents learn to be less dependent on their parents. The manager's role at this point is to allow more freedom and give more responsibility. Traditionally, managers who brought their people to this level felt they had done their job—moving their subordinates from dependence to independence.

More progressive managers, those who use participative leadership approaches, take their subordinates one step further, moving them to being **interdependent.** The role of the manager shifts to that of a collaborator—similar to the relationship of a parent to an adult son or daughter. In such a relationship levels of trust, cooperation and communication are high, producing **synergy,** where the whole is greater than the sum of its parts. For example, it is the effect produced by a finely tuned orchestra. The relationship is illustrated in Figure 9.5.

One major problem for supervisors is adjusting techniques for handling personnel on the same shift who have diverse experience. Supervising an officer with 10 years of experience demands different approaches than would be used with a new recruit. Veteran officers have knowledge, experience and self-confidence that rookies lack. Supervisors should seek input on decisions from these veteran officers, giving credit where merited, praising good work and mentoring rather than managing. Supervisors should not unknowingly punish veteran officers by overloading them because of their experience.

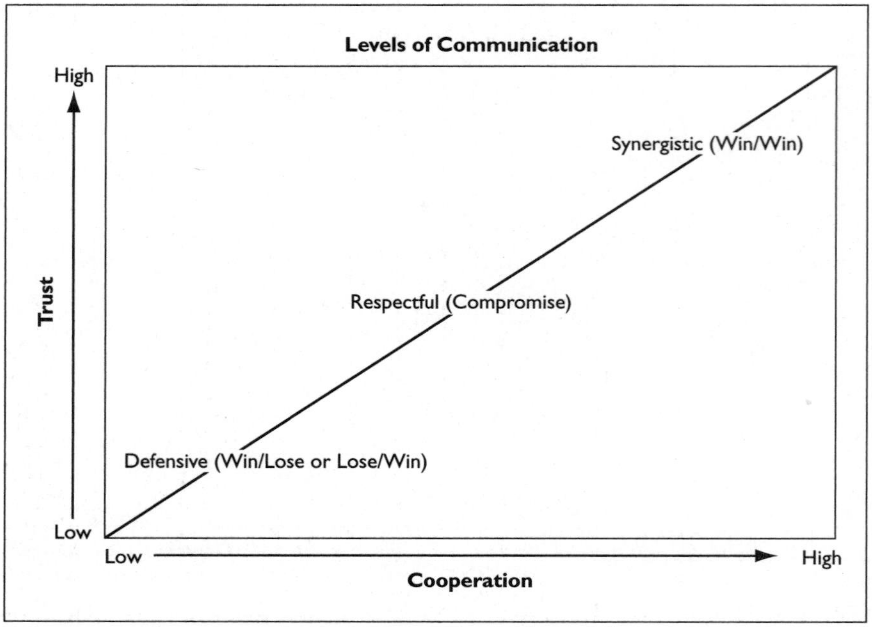

Source: Stephen R. Covey. *The 7 Habits of Highly Effective People.* New York: Simon and Schuster, 1989, p.270. Copyright © 1989 by Stephen R. Covey. Reprinted by permission of Franklin Covey Co. www.FranklinCovey.com.

Figure 9.5
The Interaction of Cooperation, Trust and Open Communication to Produce Synergism

Education is one important way to move employees from dependence to independence and finally to interdependence. All members of the police department should be encouraged to continue their education through special seminars, undergraduate and graduate courses, in-service training, research, writing and teaching, as discussed in Chapter 8.

Managers as Mentors

Mentoring involves teaching, coaching, counseling and guiding. McDonald (2002, p.21) suggests: "Mentoring is about recognizing how good people already are and agreeing to work together to make them even better." Every law enforcement organization has employees who need help to be better people and better employees. Managers can make that difference by assuming the role of mentor.

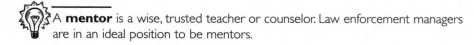

A **mentor** is a wise, trusted teacher or counselor. Law enforcement managers are in an ideal position to be mentors.

Usually a mentor is a person of senior status who counsels a younger person, but sometimes mentors are of equal seniority. In fact, two people may be mentors to each other in different areas of work. Mentors help further the right type of education, express confidence in the other person, correct actions that, if continued, could be detrimental to advancement and foster the right attitudes.

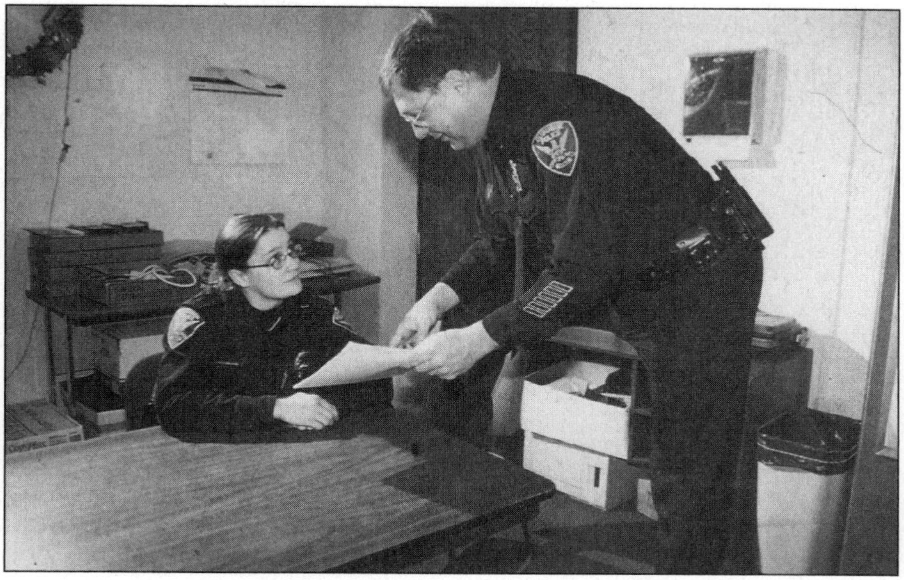

Mentors can play a vital role in developing employees, offering them their knowledge and skills and giving them encouragement and support.

© Jim Shaffer

The purpose of mentoring is to help mentees reach their full potential. Most law enforcement officers who have worked their way to the top of the organization have had mentors along the way. As Williams (2000, p.19) points out: "The probationary period can be a stressful time for police recruits. . . . This may prove particularly true for women and minorities." She (p.20) reports: "Research has found that a mentor may prove crucial to a new hire's successful transition into an organization and, furthermore, that mentoring benefits protégés, mentors and organizations alike." She (p.21) contends: "The enthusiasm, camaraderie, and professionalism mentoring programs achieve affect the entire culture of an organization. . . . Mentors provide both practical and emotional support, both knowledge and understanding."

Swope (2001b) suggests that it is not just recruits who can benefit from mentoring: "The managers and leaders in the police department have a responsibility to the new supervisor to reduce the number of mediocre and failing supervisors. They can do this by having an established and competent lieutenant or captain coach and mentor the newly promoted sergeant." In addition, Swope (p.146) suggests: "Mentoring and coaching applies not just to sergeants but can be helpful and effective as an officer moves to each higher level of responsibility."

Holloway (2001, p.85) cautions: "The mere presence of a mentor is not enough. . . . To be effective, mentoring programs need focus and structure. . . . Prospective mentors should participate in professional development to learn about the mentoring process and what is expected of them before assuming their duties."

Developing Positive Attitudes

"Attitude," says Pederson (2000, p.120): "It makes all the difference to any environment when the attitude that prevails is positive. Each police force administration, by its attitude alone, may influence individual branches of service more than one might think." Effective managers are upbeat and positive. They see opportunities in setbacks. They encourage risk taking and are supportive when mistakes happen. And they encourage these attitudes in their subordinates.

Personality problems can be more devastating to employees than poor work performance. Managers must help certain employees to develop—those who are loners, who are sarcastic, who talk incessantly about themselves, who constantly complain or who have other personality problems. Directing them to outside counseling may be necessary. Managers have a responsibility to deal with problems in employee attitudes. Dealing with problem behaviors is the focus of Chapter 11.

Attitudes are not something managers can take away from someone. They are intangible. What people say and do and how they behave determine how others perceive them. Working with employees on specific negative attitudes can be an important part of their growth and development. British psychiatrist J. A. Hadfield illustrates the power of a person's mental attitude in his book, *The Psychology of Power.* He describes having three people test the effect of mental suggestion on their strength, as measured by gripping a dynamometer. Hadfield first tested them for a baseline, giving no suggestions. The average grip was 101 pounds. He then hypnotized them and suggested they were very weak. Their average grip dropped to 29 pounds. He next suggested they were very strong, and the average grip jumped to 142 pounds.

Officers' attitudes are important personally, but they are also crucial to the public's perception of officers in general and the department they represent.

Developing a Positive Image

How people see themselves is their self-image. How others see them is their public image. The two often differ, as the Johari Window illustrated earlier.

A critical part of a subordinate's development is creating a positive public image. As Will Rogers noted: "You never get a second chance to make a good first impression." This is particularly true for law enforcement officers, who often have only one contact with individual citizens. Officers in a large city who make a traffic stop, for example, are unlikely to ever see that particular driver again. How they approach the driver, what they say and do, is the image the driver will retain of the officer. It may also become the image that person has of the entire law enforcement organization.

Managers must help subordinates learn to make favorable impressions whenever and wherever possible. Because law enforcement officers are so visible, they leave an impression even when they make no contact, merely by the way they patrol, their appearance, their manner and their attitude.

Their uniforms, their badges, their guns—all smack of authority. Add mirrored sunglasses, handcuff tie tacks and a swaggering walk, and a negative image is likely to be conveyed. Law enforcement officers should be encouraged to consider how they look, how they walk and how they talk to the public, especially when in uniform. According to Johnson (2001, p.27): "The police officer's uniform has a profound psychological impact on others. . . . It conveys power and authority." Officers should soften this image by considering the public as their "customers" or "clients" and treating them with respect.

Law enforcement officers who have a good appearance and act with competence and courtesy will leave a favorable impression with the majority of the public.

A positive image will be greatly enhanced by treating all citizens fairly and equally. This often requires officers to recognize their personal biases and to deal with them.

According to the *Sourcebook of Criminal Justice Statistics 2001,* 25 percent of those polled reported a "great deal" of confidence in police, 41 percent reported "quite a lot" of confidence in the police; 27 percent reported "not much" confidence; and 6 percent reported "no" confidence in the police. This is greatly improved from 20 years ago. In 1981 only 15 percent reported "a great deal" of confidence in police; 34 percent reported "quite a lot"; 42 percent reported "not much"; and 8 percent reported "none."

Much of an officer's image will be shaped by how he or she treats those who are different from themselves, be it a gender, racial or economic difference.

Developing Cultural Awareness and Sensitivity

Cultural awareness is another critical area of development for law enforcement personnel.

Cultural awareness means understanding the diversity of the United States, the dynamics of minority–majority relationships, the dynamics of sexism and racism and the issues of nationalism and separatism.

According to Coderoni (2002, p.16): "Police in mainstream America often deal with situations that lead to miscommunication and, inadvertently, tragic consequences if the police are not trained to recognize and understand citizen reactions based on differing cultural norms. As the United States quickly becomes one of the most culturally diverse nations, law enforcement agencies must train their officers to understand and be understood by those with whom they differ in areas other than merely language." He (p.18) notes: "The dynamics of society demonstrate that cultural and racial divisions are becoming more prevalent and the basic social and economic disparities that have caused many problems in America have not, and will not, disappear anytime soon. The same conditions that exist in society today were present more than 25 years ago when this country literally was tearing itself apart racially. As long as the rift between cultures continues and so many people perceive that they have no legitimate means to achieve the American dream, racial clashes will continue to occur."

Officers need to appreciate diversity both within their departments and in their communities. Most people understand and accept that our society is multicultural. Although the United States is a melting pot of people from all parts of the world, some enjoy majority status, whereas others are viewed as minorities.

Members of the majority often view things quite differently from those in the minority. Elements of majority and minority worldviews have been outlined by the Minnesota Peace Officer Standards and Training (POST) Board. The **majority worldview** includes the following:

- The majority views its philosophy and ideas as being the most legitimate and valid.
- Minority viewpoints, although their expression may be tolerated, lack the force and power of the majority and therefore are less valid than and secondary to the majority viewpoint.
- Minority members have the option of leaving society if they cannot abide by majority rule.
- Alternative viewpoints are often disruptive or disloyal.
- Power, status and wealth are the result of hard work and/or genetics.

The **minority worldview** includes the following:

- Minorities must perform better to be accepted as average.
- Majority groups have power and control major institutions.
- Minority groups lack the power to control their own destiny.
- The minority views fairness as more valid than power, status and wealth.
- The minority views success as achievable only by working through the rules set by the majority.
- The minority world views the criminal justice system as biased against minorities.

In addition to members of minority groups who are U.S. citizens, the United States is faced with thousands of illegal immigrants of different races, ethnic groups, religions and cultures. Citizenship is an important issue for arresting officers because, under Vienna Convention rights, officers must notify noncitizens of their right to contact their consulate before making any postarrest statements.

Many immigrants may become victims, but because they come from cultures in which law enforcement officers are feared rather than seen as protectors, they are unlikely to cooperate with officers or to report when they are victimized.

In a sense, law enforcement officers are in a better position than many to understand minority status because they often view *themselves* as being in the minority, isolated from the mainstream of society. As law enforcement officers become aware of their own culture and as community-oriented policing gains ground, officers may seek to reduce this view of themselves as a minority, to interact more with the public and to see themselves as part of the mainstream.

Another aspect of cultural awareness is understanding and respecting differences in sex as well as differences in sexual preference. Cultural awareness also means identifying and respecting the rights of specific separatist/nationalist groups currently active in American society, including the Ku Klux Klan, the American Nazi Party, neo-Nazi skinheads, the Aryan Brotherhood/White

Cultural awareness is a critical area of development for law enforcement personnel. Officers must appreciate the cultural diversity that exists within their communities. One way is for local patrol officers to interact with the people of their neighborhoods, like this officer who takes time to talk with a business owner who is an immigrant from the Philippines.

Supremacists, Posse Commitatus, the National Socialist Party, the Black Muslim Movement, the American Indian Movement (AIM) and the Jewish Defense League (JDL). When such groups engage in terrorist activity, such as the 1995 bombing of Oklahoma City's Murrah Federal Building, it may be difficult to remain objective. When hate groups' words translate into criminal actions, they have gone well beyond exercising their civil rights.

Another challenge regarding immigrants is that they often settle in poor neighborhoods that have high crime rates and may therefore be associated with crime. Law enforcement personnel must guard against stereotyping such immigrants as criminals simply because they live in crime-infested neighborhoods. Such stereotyping may lead to racial profiling.

Racial Profiling

"Racial profiling," according to Ramirez et al. (2000, p.3), "is defined as any police-initiated action that relies on the race, ethnicity or national origin rather than the behavior of an individual or information that leads the police to a particular individual who has been identified as being or having been engaged in criminal activity." Fridell (2001, p.1) explains: "The term 'racial profiling' is a new label for a longstanding concern that policing is not practiced impartially.

And while there is no way to absolutely measure to what extent allegations are true or merely perceived, in fact, in some ways it doesn't matter. Both biased policing and the perceptions of biased policing are critical issues that agency executives need to address."

Fridell et al. (2001, p.1) note: "American policing is facing a tremendous challenge—a wide-spread perception that the police are routinely guilty of bias in how they treat racial minorities." As Meek (2001, p.92) points out: "Perceptions, whether real or imagined, have the force of reality and must be treated as such." He (p.91) contends: "Racial profiling continues to be one of the most critical issues facing law enforcement."

Ramirez et al. (p.4) report: "National surveys have confirmed that most Americans, regardless of race, believe that racial profiling is a significant social problem." And some data supports this contention. Smith and Petrocelli (2001, p.4) analyzed traffic stop data from the Richmond (Virginia) Police Department and found: "Minority citizens in general, and African-Americans in particular, were disproportionately stopped compared with their percentage in the driver-eligible population. However, they were searched no more frequently than Whites; in fact, Whites were significantly more likely than minorities to be the subject of consent searches. . . . Minority drivers were more likely to be warned; whereas Whites were more likely to be ticketed or arrested."

Gist (2000, p.iii) stresses: "The guarantee to all persons of equal protection under the law is one of the most fundamental principles of our democratic society." As Schott (2001, p.28) points out: "Officers who detain or arrest someone solely on the basis of race have violated the Fourth Amendment of the Constitution." He (p.30) makes the common-sense observation: "Seizures of people should be based on what they do and not who they are." Kruger (2002, p.8) cautions: "Officers who base their *Terry* stops or other investigative activities on a suspect's race alone violate the law and are guilty of misconduct that very well may be sufficient to terminate their employment." However, according to a police legal trainer: "It may be borderline incompetence to not use race if intelligence information points to a particular race. Race may be a factor, and it would be ludicrous to ignore the obvious" (Nowicki, 2002, p.16).

The problem of racial profiling has, at its center, the fact that *profiling* has been a valuable tool in policing for decades. As Sharpe (2002, p.9) notes: "Criminal profiling is easy to understand. If 90 percent of all murders were committed by clowns, is it not fair to say that the first likely suspect in a murder case would have a rubber nose?" In a similar vein, Huntington (2001, p.18) asks: "In the wake of the WTC and Pentagon attacks, has it become 'okay' to profile certain kinds of criminals? . . . Indeed, should police stand firm and not be afraid to admit that profiling can be a powerful tool in apprehending criminals . . . and terrorists?" Huntington (p.20) notes: "With the recent terrorist attacks profiling has once again become a hot issue. How 'correct' is it for cops to use profiling (just like the DEA, FBI and other agencies use it) to watch for potential terrorists? At airports, law enforcement and security personnel are taught to watch for certain traits—paying for a ticket in cash, no luggage, Middle Eastern descent, nervousness, etc.—to alert them to potential terrorists. Why is this suddenly approved conduct for law enforcement but using the same tactics to profile a drug dealer is not appropriate?" He suggests renaming "profiling" to "building a case." And race is part of most descriptions of suspects.

The courts are generally supportive of race being included as one of several factors in identifying suspects. In *United States v. Weaver,* a DEA officer stopped and questioned Arthur Weaver because he was a roughly dressed, young black male on a direct flight from Los Angeles who walked rapidly from the airport toward a cab, had two carry-on bags and no checked luggage, and appeared nervous. Weaver was carrying drugs and was arrested, but he challenged the legality of the officer's intervention. The Eighth Circuit Court of Appeals upheld the officer's conduct, explaining:

> Facts are not to be ignored simply because they may be unpleasant—and the unpleasant fact in this case is that he [DEA agent] had knowledge, based upon his own experience and upon the intelligence reports he had received from Los Angeles authorities, that young male members of the African-American Los Angeles gangs were flooding the Kansas City area with cocaine. To that extent then, race, when coupled with the other factors [the agent] relied upon, was a factor in the decision to approach and ultimately detain [the suspect]. We wish it were otherwise, but we take the facts as they are presented to us, not as we would wish them to be.

Despite such court support, officers must be educated on how to avoid unintentional racial profiling based on personal bias. According to Huntington (p.19): "Some agencies have responded to the profiling wars by simply ceasing to encourage or endorse any kind of profiling information. Just don't say it. Don't notice it, don't teach it, and don't train it." Obviously, this is not the answer. Fridell et al. (p.3) suggest avoiding the term *racial profiling,* because profiling has a legitimate place in law enforcement, and replacing it with *racially biased policing,* which has no place in law enforcement.

One approach to identifying if racially biased policing is occurring is to collect data on police-initiated stops of citizens. Most frequently this deals with traffic stops. In 1999 Connecticut was the first state to pass legislation requiring every municipal police agency and the state police to collect data on race for every police-initiated traffic stop. However, as Cox (2001, p.61) contends: "A major concern voiced by critics of racial profiling legislation is that police officers will stop making traffic stops altogether out of fear of looking unfair or biased." Buerger (2002, p.380) describes some of the supervisory challenges arising from racial profiling legislation:

> New responsibilities and difficulties can be expected in six main areas: (1) equipping officers to deal with new public expectations (and misunderstandings) about racial profiling, (2) dealing with instances of "monkey-wrenching" resistance, (3) mediating disputes and citizen complaints, (4) handling cases of discipline and morale problems, (5) selling the program to subordinates (perhaps the most important duty of all) and (6) "managing up" within the organization to provide appropriate resources.

Buerger (p.392) notes that resistance against racial profiling legislation mandating data collection may result in **balancing,** unfairly stopping unoffending motorists to protect officers from the "statistical microscope" individually or collectively. Buerger suggests: "To them [officers], the issue is reduced to simple terms: 'If I stop a Black guy, I have to stop X number of White guys to make the numbers come out right.'" This results in a great deal of unproductive work and may generate citizen complaints. **Ghosting,** falsifying patrol logs, might also occur to "make the numbers come out right."

Buerger (pp.389–390) cautions: "Work slowdowns, various forms of defiance designed to thwart the requirements of the law, 'going underground' while making stops, 'balancing' or 'ghosting' and behavior problems collectively summed as 'badmouthing' are all harbingers of future problems. It will fall to the supervisors to look for, identify, and correct these deviations before they reach the point of formal complaints against the department." Buerger (p.403) concludes: "Police supervisors face an enormous burden to maintain morale in the face of a law regarded as an insult and to maintain productivity while ensuring compliance with the law."

Rivera (2001, p.85) notes another issue related to data collection: "The broader issue with data collection is one that is often missed: collection is simply a process focusing on a symptom and not a solution to the problem. Data collection is a first step in the right direction. He recommends nine ways to prevent racial profiling: (1) agency review, (2) citizen feedback review, (3) data collection, (4) violator surveys, (5) profile prevention training, (6) human diversity and sensitivity training, (7) community outreach, (8) implementation of the training and (9) evaluation of the results.

In addition to helping subordinates develop a positive attitude, a positive image and cultural awareness and sensitivity, managers should foster a strong sense of integrity and ethical behavior.

Developing a Sense of Ethics and Integrity

Ruby Ridge, Waco, O. J. Simpson, Rodney King, Abner Louima—these names and others have had the law enforcement community reeling from attacks on its integrity and ethical standards. **Ethics** refers to the rules or standards of fair, honest conduct. Ethics has become a primary focus in almost every profession and is the topic of countless articles, seminars and workshops. **Integrity** refers to steadfast adherence to an ethical code.

Ethical behavior is that which is "moral" and "right." Law enforcement personnel must develop high ethical standards both on and off duty.

Conditt (2001, p.19) notes: "Every organization has an official, or formal, code of conduct that sets forth the responsibilities of its employees and the rules and regulations governing employee conduct. . . . The informal code of conduct is an organization's unwritten, generally accepted, standard of conduct." In addition, according to Klockars (1983, p.427): "Some areas of human conduct develop their own distinct ethics while others do not." He suggests that special codes of ethics are developed if the area:

- Has some special features making it difficult to bring under the domain of general, conventional ethics. Police, for example, can use force, even deadly force, and may lie and deceive people in their work.

- Involves issues of concern not just to those who practice them, but also to others. They involve moral controversy.
- Involves certain types of misconduct that cannot or perhaps should not be controlled by other means.

Law enforcement fits all three conditions, partly because of its great discretionary power.

A multitude of personal, departmental and external forces shape the dynamics of police integrity that ultimately affect each police officer's career. Personal forces that affect police personnel include economy/personal finances, diversity issues in the department, family values/moral literacy, experience with aggressive police tactics, the police subculture, community response to police activities and presence, frustration with the criminal justice system, peer influence and alcohol/drug abuse. Departmental forces that affect police personnel include the promotion system, leadership, reward structures, departmental values/policies, the accountability system, the quality of supervision, the disciplinary system, in-service training, entry-level training and the selection/hiring process. These departmental forces are influenced in part by external forces that affect the entire agency, such as civilian complaint boards, news media, political influences, community demands and other sectors of the criminal justice system (courts and corrections). (See Figure 9.6.)

To clarify the expectations regarding officer ethics and integrity, most law enforcement departments have a formal code of ethics, often framed and hanging on the wall. Such codes usually have at least three important themes:

- Justice or fairness is the dominant theme. Officers are not to take advantage of people or accept gratuities.
- Because of the importance of the law and the officer as tools of the Constitution, law enforcement behavior must be totally within the bounds set by the law.
- At all times, law enforcement officers must uphold a standard of behavior consistent with their public position.

The Law Enforcement Code of Ethics of the International Association of Chiefs of Police (IACP) (Figure 9.7) is an example of such a standard.

A code of ethics helps officers make decisions lawfully, humanely and fairly. However, ethics isn't about what we say; it's about what we do. To determine whether an action is ethical, consider the following questions: Is it legal? Is it the best solution for the greatest number of people? How would you feel if it were made public? Does it follow the Golden Rule? Would you like such a decision directed at you? Is it the right thing to do?

McNeff (2001, p.10) observes: "In today's police environment, the incorporation of ethics into all aspects of police agency training and operations may yield wide-ranging benefits, including reduced exposure to liability." According to Josephson (2002, p.36): "Police chiefs and other law enforcement executives must take special care to ensure that the men and women entrusted to protect

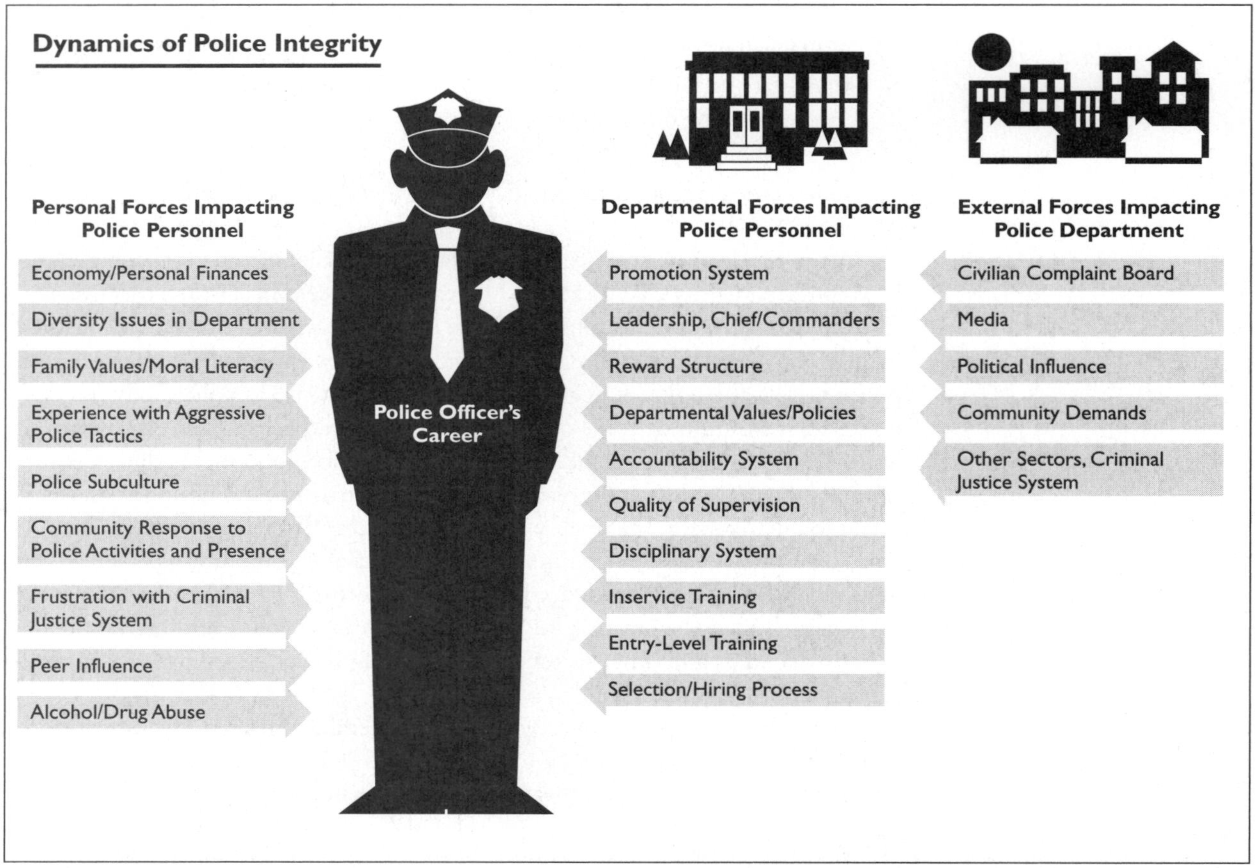

Figure 9.6
Dynamics of Police Integrity

Source: Stephen J. Gaffigan and Phyllis P. McDonald. *Police Intergrity. Public Service with Honor.* U.S. Department of Justice. January 1997, p.92. (NCJ 163811)

the public do so with the utmost competence and integrity." He (pp.36–37) cautions: "If one is not vigilant, it is hard to avoid the distortion of attitude that can come from dealing with disproportionate numbers of violent, disrespectful, and dishonest people, many of whom do not hesitate to bait and taunt police officers. And, in addition to regular doses of human frailties and flaws, officers often witness the failings of an imperfect criminal justice system. In this setting, the officers face four tough ethical challenges:

1. To be constantly and scrupulously honest—on reports, testimony, affidavits, and even overtime records—even when the results are undesirable or even unfair.
2. To put loyalty to the badge and the public above loyalty to all else, including misbehaving colleagues, who will pressure the good officer to look the other way or otherwise tolerate unprofessional or illegal conduct.

Law Enforcement Code of Ethics*

All law enforcement officers must be fully aware of the ethical responsibilities of their position and must strive constantly to live up to the highest possible standards of professional policing.

The International Association of Chiefs of Police believes it is important that police officers have clear advice and counsel available to assist them in performing their duties consistent with these standards and has adopted the following ethical mandates as guidelines to meet these ends.**

Primary Responsibilities of a Police Officer

A police officer acts as an official representative of government who is required and trusted to work within the law. The officer's powers and duties are conferred by statute. The fundamental duties of a police officer include serving the community; safeguarding lives and property; protecting the innocent; keeping the peace; and ensuring the rights of all to liberty, equality and justice.

Performance of the Duties of a Police Officer

A police officer shall perform all duties impartially, without favor or affection or ill will and without regard to status, sex, race, religion, political belief or aspiration. All citizens will be treated equally with courtesy, consideration and dignity.

Officers will never allow personal feelings, animosities or friendships to influence official conduct. Laws will be enforced appropriately and courteously and, in carrying out their responsibilities, officers will strive to obtain maximum cooperation from the public. They will conduct themselves in appearance and deportment in such a manner as to inspire confidence and respect for the position of public trust they hold.

Discretion

A police officer will use responsibly the discretion vested in the position and exercise it within the law. The principle of reasonableness will guide the officer's determinations and the officer will consider all surrounding circumstances in determining whether any legal action shall be taken.

Consistent and wise use of discretion, based on professional policing competence, will do much to preserve good relationships and retain the confidence of the public. There can be difficulty in choosing between conflicting courses of action. It is important to remember that a timely word of advice rather than arrest—which may be correct in appropriate circumstances—can be a more effective means of achieving a desired end.

Use of Force

A police officer will never employ unnecessary force or violence and will use only such force in the discharge of duty as is reasonable in all circumstances.

Force should be used only with the greatest restraint and only after discussion, negotiation and persuasion have been found to be inappropriate or ineffective. While the use of force is occasionally unavoidable, every police officer will refrain from applying the unnecessary infliction of pain or suffering and will never engage in cruel, degrading or inhuman treatment of any person.

Confidentiality

Whatever a police officer sees, hears or learns of, which is of a confidential nature, will be kept secret unless the performance of duty or legal provision requires otherwise.

Members of the public have a right to security and privacy, and information obtained about them must not be improperly divulged.

Integrity

A police officer will not engage in acts of corruption or bribery, nor will an officer condone such acts by other police officers.

The public demands that the integrity of police officers be above reproach. Police officers must, therefore, avoid any conduct that might compromise integrity and thus undercut the public confidence in a law enforcement agency. Officers will refuse to accept any gifts, presents, subscriptions, favors, gratuities or promises that could be interpreted as seeking to cause the officer to refrain from performing official responsibilities honestly and within the law. Police officers must not receive private or special advantage from their official status. Respect from the public cannot be bought; it can only be earned and cultivated.

**Adopted by the Executive Committee of the International Association of Chiefs of Police on October 17, 1989, during its 96th Annual Conference in Louisville, Kentucky, to replace the 1957 code of ethics adopted at the 64th Annual IACP Conference.*

***The IACP gratefully acknowledges the assistance of Sir John C. Hermon, former chief constable of the Royal Ulster Constabulary, who gave full license to the association to freely use the language and concepts presented in the RUC's "Professional Policing Ethics," Appendix I of the Chief Constable's Annual Report, 1988, presented to the Police Authority for Northern Ireland, for the preparation of this code.*

Continued

Figure 9.7
Law Enforcement Code of Ethics

Cooperation with Other Officers and Agencies
Police officers will cooperate with all legally authorized agencies and their representatives in the pursuit of justice.

An officer or agency may be one among many organizations that may provide law enforcement services to a jurisdiction. It is imperative that a police officer assist colleagues fully and completely with respect and consideration at all times.

Personal/Professional Capabilities
Police officers will be responsible for their own standard of professional performance and will take every reasonable opportunity to enhance and improve their level of knowledge and competence.

Through study and experience, a police officer can acquire the high level of knowledge and competence that is essential for the efficient and effective performance of duty. The acquisition of knowledge is a never-ending process of personal and professional development that should be pursued constantly.

Private Life
Police officers will behave in a manner that does not bring discredit to their agencies or themselves.

A police officer's character and conduct while off duty must always be exemplary, thus maintaining a position of respect in the community in which he or she lives and serves. The officer's personal behavior must be beyond reproach.

Figure 9.7
continued

3. To avoid the arrogance, alienation or anger that can result in disrespectful or physically abusive conduct.
4. To avoid callousness or cynicism that weakens commitment and performance."

Fair or not, the conduct of law enforcement personnel is expected to be above reproach. Fuller (2001, p.6) notes: "The police service in this country is more closely scrutinized and subject to more uninformed, biased criticism than any other occupational group, with the possible exception of presidential candidates. The average street cop is expected to conduct his or her personal and professional life with more integrity and decorum than most other citizens, however unrealistic and difficult that may seem at times." One area in which officer conduct may be called into question is in whether or not they accept gratuities.

Accepting Gratuities

Whether it is ethical for officers to accept gratuities is controversial. A **gratuity** is defined as a favor or gift, usually in the form of money, given in return for service; for example a tip given to a waiter in a restaurant. As White (2002, p.22) suggests: "Differentiating between gratuities and corruption is not a clear concept." He (p.23) notes: "Departmental policies on gratuities vary among agencies, and officers may question exactly what constitutes a gratuity. To eliminate confusion, departments should ensure that their policies clearly distinguish what is acceptable." White (p.21) presents the most common arguments for and against gratuities.

Allowing Gratuities

Gratuities help create a bond between officers and the public, thus fostering community policing goals. They represent a nonwritten form of appreciation and usually are given with no expectation of anything in return. Most gratuities are too small to be a significant motivator of actions. The practice is so deeply entrenched that efforts to root it out will be ineffective and cause unnecessary violations of the rules. A complete ban makes officers appear as though they cannot distinguish between a friendly gesture and a bribe. Finally, some businesses and restaurants insist on giving gratuities.

Many contend that accepting gratuities is often the first step in officers' engaging in unethical behavior and from there into actual corruption.

Banning Gratuities

Accepting gratuities violates most departments' policies and the law enforcement code of ethics. Even the smallest gifts create a sense of obligation. Even if nothing is expected in return, the gratuity may create an appearance of impropriety. Although most officers can discern between friendly gestures and bribes, some may not. Gratuities create an unfair distribution of services to those who can afford them, voluntary taxing or private funding of a private service. Finally, it is unprofessional.

Unethical Behavior and Corruption

The Knapp Commission, the Mollen Commission Report, the Christopher Commission, the Rampart Board of Inquiry—all found extensive unethical behavior and corruptions in the police departments investigated. Monahan (2000, p.79) notes: "Corruption is not unique to policing, but perhaps no other profession is more adversely affected by corruption than law enforcement. An accusation can devastate a police department and the ensuing scandal can demoralize the entire profession." Unethical behavior may include taking overlong breaks, abusing sick time, arriving late for work, falsifying time sheets, lying, tampering with evidence, compromising an investigation, being disrespectful to the public, drinking on the job and the like. Corruption goes beyond unethical behavior in that it is done for personal gain.

The key elements of corrupt behavior are that the conduct (1) is prohibited by law or rule, (2) involves misuse of position and (3) involves a reward or personal gain for the officer.

As Rothlein (2000, p.68) cautions: "Corruption is a corrosive element that will spread like rust if it is not contained and eliminated. Addressing unethical behavior and corruption has become a top priority and major challenge for police administrators. The causes of corruption are complex. Many factors can contribute to corruption, including greed; personal motivators such as ego, sex, or the exercise of power; tolerance of the behavior by the community; socialization from peers and/or the organization; inadequate supervision and monitoring of behavior; lack of clear accountability of employees' behavior; and no real threat of discipline or sanctions."

The Slippery Slope

Sherman's Slippery Slope of Corruption posits that police corruption begins with a lowering of ethical expectations and values to attain a gratuity of minor value, for example, accepting a free cup of coffee. Although this action in itself is most likely harmless and inconsequential as a corrupting force, it may over time produce a snowball effect, leading an officer to accept gratuities of larger magnitude.

Furthermore, such practices often lead those providing the "freebies" to expect preferential treatment by recipient officers. Strandberg (2000, p.100) notes: "Corruption takes on many forms, and something seemingly insignificant can put an officer on a slippery slope, leading to major crimes." Trautman (2000, p.65) notes: "Research repeatedly confirms that most scandals start with one employee doing relatively small unethical acts and grow to whatever level the leadership allows."

Noble Cause and Ends vs. Means

Another facet of unethical behavior concerns the noble cause corruption dilemma, in which officers believe unlawful means are justified when the result is the protection of human life or some other noble cause. Unquestionably, law enforcement officers face difficult decisions daily.

Adcox (2000, p.19) notes: "The tendency of police officers to place ends over means is not new. There is ample historical evidence to suggest that similar police values, beliefs and practices have existed since the inauguration of modern policing in the United States. History has shown that some police officers have come to value results over duty and principle, and the standard measurement of good police work has become goal achievement, with all else being secondary." Adcox (p.27) concludes: "As the only governmental entity granted awesome coercive authority, it is imperative that police officers exercise their power responsibly and ethically. The cynicism and stress caused by the many conflicting loyalties and expectations of modern policing can, however, cloud the honorable intentions of even the best police officer. When officers are confronted with the really 'bad guys,' there are strong temptations to take advantage of the powers entrusted and the discretion granted. . . . It takes individual moral courage and strong ethical principles to resist the 'ends justifying means' pitfall."

Above the Law

Thompson (2001, p.77) suggests: "The American public readily understands and recognizes that the police are entitled to special privileges and exceptions relative to obeying the laws. Police officers are allowed to exceed the speed limits and violate traffic controls in the interest of law enforcement. They are allowed to carry concealed weapons, and they often own or have access to weaponry that is prohibited or at least greatly restricted to private citizens." He notes: "Early in the indoctrination into policing, some officers receive the message that they are special and they are above the law. He (p.79) cautions: "Equality under the law is the foundation of American criminal justice. If law enforcement officers believe they are above the law, then this subverts the very essence of law enforcement and criminal justice in our society."

Bad Apples or a Bad Barrel?

Often the argument is heard that just as a few "bad apples" can ruin the entire barrel, so a few bad cops can ruin the entire department. Trautman (2000, p.65) contends: "The 'rotten apple' theory that some administrators propose as the cause of their demise is usually nothing more than a self-serving, superficial facade, intended to draw attention away from their own failures." Swope (2001a, p.80) believes: "It is the unethical breeding environment of the barrel that generates the major difficulties. It is the barrel, the culture of the police organization, that can cause the root shaking scandals that periodically face some police organizations." Swope (p.83) also believes: "An officer's behavior is influenced more directly by the actions or lack of actions in response to ethical shortcomings of his superiors than by the stated directives or written ethical code of an organization."

Perry (2001, p.24), likewise, suggests examining the barrel: "The rotten-apple theory won't work any longer. Corrupt police officers are not natural-born criminals. . . . The task of corruption control is to examine the barrel, not just the apples, the organization, not just the individuals in it, because corrupt police are made, not born."

Perry (p.25) contends: "Those who serve the public must be held to a higher standard of honesty and care for the public good than the general citizenry. A higher standard is not a double standard. Persons accepting positions of public trust take on new obligations and are free not to accept them if they do not want to live up to the higher standard." Managers must examine their department and find ways to promote integrity and ethical behavior that adheres to this higher standard.

Promoting Ethical Behavior and Integrity

A good starting point, according to Pedersen (2001, p.138), is to eliminate the code of silence: "The code of silence encourages people not to speak up when they see another officer doing something wrong." Fulton (2000, p.250) stresses: "Police commanders must exemplify the honesty and integrity they seek in their subordinates." In addition: "Ethical mentoring and role modeling should be consistent, frequent and visible" ("Achieving and Maintaining High Ethical Standards," 2002, p.66).

As a symbolic statement of commitment to ethical behavior, the IACP has recommended a Law Enforcement Oath of Honor:

> On my honor,
> I will never betray my badge,
> my integrity, my character,
> or the public trust.
> I will always have
> the courage to hold myself
> and others accountable for our actions.
> I will always uphold the constitution
> and community I serve.

"A public affirmation of adherence to ethical conduct is a powerful way to demonstrate commitment to ethical standards" ("Achieving and Maintaining High Ethical Standards"). In addition to the oath, numerous departmental policies and procedures have been identified as helping foster an environment of ethical behavior and officer integrity.

Rothlein (p.70) recommends that to successfully institute an anti-corruption policing strategy, both short- and long-term goals are needed. He suggests that short-term goals might include changing behavior by heightening the risk of detection and reducing opportunity and temptation. Long-term goals might include developing a value system and high ethical standards within the agency and managing the culture of the department.

McCarthy (2000, pp.36–43) presents seven steps that can help prevent unethical behavior: "(1) Recruit with great care. (2) Establish appropriate policies and put them in writing. (3) Adopt a good employee evaluation process. (4) Make sure your sergeants share management's values and philosophies. (5) Develop operational controls. (6) Perform regular anti-corruption inspections and audits. And (7) implement ethics and integrity training into every training activity."

Josephson (p.39) suggests: "Train officers to think more rigorously about the ethical dimensions of their choices. This can be accomplished if all phases of career development—recruiting, training, evaluation and discipline—promote two vital ethical qualities: (1) ethical discernment, the ability to distinguish right from wrong and make hard decisions where there is no clear cut right answer, and (2) ethical discipline, the moral strength to do the right thing even when it is difficult and costly to do so."

Schafer (2002, p.17) notes: "Ethical dilemmas challenge the intellect because of the conflicting answers to the questions, 'What should I do?' and 'What will I do?' If a person must choose between two options that do not oppose one another, selecting an option becomes a matter of choice and not a decision between right and wrong. In most cases, choosing right over wrong takes courage because people who make ethical choices often subject themselves to social and professional ridicule. Ethical decisions build personal character, but not without pain."

As discussed in previous chapters, training and encouraging officers to make ethical decisions is a vital element in promoting community-oriented policing and problem solving.

Ethical Considerations in Community-Oriented Policing and Problem Solving

Ethical behavior and integrity are critical to the successful implementation of community-oriented policing and problem solving (COPPS). Paynter (2000, p.63) notes: "With the advent and implementation of community policing, it's important that the police profession be viewed as the guardians of the Constitution and civil rights."

The Long-Range Importance of Developing Personnel

Developing individuals and team players is important because most future law enforcement managers will come from the lower levels of the organization.

If officers are not self-developed or developed by managers at all levels, where will future executives come from?

Managers as Motivators for Change

Law enforcement organizations are similar to all other organizations. They constantly change. If they are to flourish, they must embrace change and make it work for them. Sometimes change occurs in a revolutionary manner, but most

Evaluate Your Organization

1. Inflexible: discourages the new and unusual	1	2	3	4	5	6	7	Open to new ideas; receptive	______
2. Focused on present or past	1	2	3	4	5	6	7	Future oriented; anticipates future	______
3. No way to train further or develop new skills	1	2	3	4	5	6	7	Many opportunities to learn new skills	______
4. Individual effort more important than group effort	1	2	3	4	5	6	7	Cooperative efforts, participation in group is important	______
5. Little planning and communication	1	2	3	4	5	6	7	Active planning, with involvement of others	______
TOTAL									______

If your organization scored between 5 and 19, it is *not* conducive to growth and development. If your organization scored between 20 and 29, the growth and development environment is positive but needs improvement. A score of 30 and above indicates that your organization values growth and development.

Figure 9.8
Evaluate Your Organization Survey

often it is evolutionary. Law enforcement managers at all levels play a significant role in this process, which may involve change in the organizational structure, its goals and objectives; its members or in the community it serves. Change involves alteration of attitudes and work behavior as individuals, as team members and as members of the department.

Swope (2002, p.135) contends: "The groups of people that have the most ability to create an organizational culture based on integrity are the corporals, sergeants and lieutenants. True, a sergeant may not be able to change the department but he can change his squad; a lieutenant may not be able to change the department but he can change his platoon. At some point these sergeants and lieutenants will be their departments' captains and majors, where they may be able to change the department."

Evaluating the Climate for Growth, Development and Change

Law enforcement managers who want to evaluate their workplace culture and its conduciveness to growth, development and change can use the brief survey in Figure 9.8.

Summary

The workplace culture is the sum of the beliefs and values shared by those within the organization, serving to formally and informally communicate its expectations. These group attitudes and beliefs are called norms. An officer's first loyalty must be to defend the Constitution of the United States, his or her state constitution and laws, and local laws.

To shape the workplace culture, managers should identify existing norms, evaluate them and then encourage positive norms and try to eliminate negative ones through modeling and training. A positive workplace culture promotes good interpersonal relationships. Such relationships must be built on self-understanding.

A model, the Johari Window, shows how people can learn more about themselves and others. The Johari Window describes four parts of a person's identity: the open self, the hidden self, the blind self and the subconscious self.

Personal and organizational goals are a necessary first step for growth and development. A personal goal states what, when and how much. Holistic goal setting should include career/job, financial, personal, family/relationships and spiritual/service. Goals should also consider values. Touchstone values, what people say is important to them, and daily values, how people actually spend their time and energy, need to correlate.

Managers who contribute to accomplishing department goals while simultaneously developing their subordinates into top performers are superior balanced performer managers who empower others. As managers help their people grow and develop, they should be aware of the three stages of growth. Employees initially are dependent. As they grow and develop they become independent and finally interdependent. Managers can often help their people through these stages by mentoring. A mentor is a wise, trusted teacher or counselor. Law enforcement managers are in an ideal position to be mentors. As mentors, managers should help their subordinates develop positive attitudes, a positive image, cultural awareness and a strong sense of ethics.

Law enforcement officers who have a good appearance and act with competence and courtesy will leave a favorable impression with the majority of the public. To create such positive impressions, law enforcement personnel must develop cultural awareness and sensitivity. They must understand the diversity of the United States, the dynamics of minority–majority relationships, the dynamics of sexism and racism and the issues of nationalism and separatism.

Another important area for growth and development is in ethics. Ethical behavior is that which is "moral" and "right." Law enforcement personnel must develop high ethical standards both on and off duty. The key elements of corrupt behavior are that the conduct (1) is prohibited by law or rule, (2) involves misuse of position and (3) involves a reward or personal gain for the officer. Developing individuals and team players is important because most future law enforcement managers will come from the lower levels of the organization.

Discussion Questions

1. How would you describe an ethical person? Who might be role models in our society?
2. What would you include in a job description for a law enforcement officer? A sergeant? A chief or sheriff?
3. What norms would you like to see in the law enforcement agency you work for?
4. What do you consider the five most important touchstone values listed in Table 9.1?
5. What are your three most important touchstone values? Your three most important daily values? Do they correlate? If not, what should you do?
6. What ethical problems have you faced in your life?
7. Have you had any mentors in your life? Been a mentor to someone else? If so, what seemed to enhance the experience?
8. Do you consider Andy Sipowitz of *NYPD Blue* a good cop? Why or why not? (If you have not seen this program, try to watch it so you can contribute to the discussion.)
9. Should officers accept gratuities? If so, what is acceptable?
10. What skills would you like to further develop? How important would this be to your law enforcement career?

InfoTrac College Edition Assignment

Use InfoTrac College Edition to answer the Discussion Questions as appropriate.

Select one of the topics introduced in this chapter to study in more depth. Find a recent article related to it and either summarize or outline the article. You may use more than one article if you want. Be sure to give the full reference citation. Be prepared to discuss your findings with the class.

OR

Read and outline one of these articles:

- "Mentoring for Law Enforcement" by Julie Williams.
- "The Psychological Influence of the Police Uniform" by Richard R. Johnson.
- "The Role of Race in Law Enforcement: Racial Profiling or Legitimate Use?" by Richard G. Schott.
- "Collecting Statistics in Response to Racial Profiling Allegations" by Karen J. Kruger.
- "Institutional Integrity: The Four Elements of Self-Policing" by John H. Conditt, Jr.
- "The Problem with Gratuities" by Mike White.
- "Making Ethical Decisions: A Practical Model" by John R. Schafer.
- "Repairing Broken Windows: Preventing Corruption within Our Ranks" by Frank L. Perry.
- "The Relationship between Multicultural Training for Police and Effective Law Enforcement" by Gary R. Coderoni.

References

"Achieving and Maintaining High Ethical Standards: IACP's Four Universal Ethical Documents." *The Police Chief,* October 2002, pp.64–70.

Adcox, Ken. "Doing Bad Things for Good Reasons." *The Police Chief,* January 2000, pp.16–28.

Buerger, Michael E. "Supervisory Challenges Arising from Racial Profiling Legislation." *Police Quarterly,* September 2002, pp.380–408.

Click, Steven M. "The Brotherhood." *Police,* May 2002, p.64.

Coderoni, Gary R. "The Relationship between Multicultural Training for Police and Effective Law Enforcement." *FBI Law Enforcement Bulletin,* November 2002, pp.16–18.

Conditt, John H., Jr. "Institutional Integrity: The Four Elements of Self-Policing." *FBI Law Enforcement Bulletin,* November 2001, pp.18–22.

Cox, Stephen M. "Refuting Concerns about Collecting Race Data on Traffic Stops." *Law and Order,* October 2001, pp.61–65.

Dees, Tim. "First Loyalty." *Law and Order,* October 2001, pp.213–214.

Fridell, Lorie. "New PERF Report Addresses 'Racial Profiling.'" *Subject to Debate,* June 2001, pp.1, 10.

Fridell, Lorie; Lunney, Robert; Diamond, Drew; Kubu, Bruce; Scott, Michael; and Laing, Colleen. *Racially Biased Policing: A Principled Response.* Washington, DC: Police Executive Research Forum, 2001.

Fuller, John J. "Street Cop Ethics." *The Law Enforcement Trainer,* May/June 2001, pp.6–8.

Fulton, Roger. "Preventing Corruption." *Law Enforcement Technology,* December 2000, p.250.

Fulton, Roger. "Departmental Culture—What's Yours Like?" *Law Enforcement Technology,* April 2002, p.154.

Gist, Nancy E. "Foreword." In *A Resource Guide on Racial Profiling Data Collection Systems: Promising Practices and Lessons Learned* edited by Deborah Ramirez, Jack McDevitt and Amy Farrell. Washington, DC: National Institute of Justice, 2000, pp.iii–iv. (NCJ 184768)

Holloway, John H. "The Benefits of Mentoring." *Educational Leadership,* May 2001, pp.85–86.

Huntington, Roy. "Profiling: Suddenly Politically Correct?" *Police,* December 2001, pp.18–20.

Johnson, Richard R. "The Psychological Influence of the Police Uniform." *FBI Law Enforcement Bulletin,* March 2001, pp.27–32.

Josephson, Michael. "Character Counts: Now More than Ever." *The Police Chief,* September 2002, pp.36–39.

Klockars, Carl B. *Thinking about Police: Contemporary Readings.* New York: McGraw-Hill, 1983.

Kruger, Karen J. "Collecting Statistics in Response to Racial Profiling Allegations." *FBI Law Enforcement Bulletin,* May 2002, pp.8–12.

McCarthy, Robert. "Steps Chiefs Can Take to Prevent Unethical Behavior." *The Police Chief,* October 2000, pp.36–43.

McDonald, Tom. "Training Day." *Successful Meetings,* December 2002, p.21.

McErlain, Ed. "Acknowledging the Code of Silence." *Law and Order,* January 2001, p.87.

McNeff, Michael. "One Agency's Effort to Reduce Liability Risk through Emphasis on Ethics." *The Police Chief,* August 2001, p.10.

Meek, James G. "Confronting Biased Enforcement Claims." *Law and Order,* October 2001, pp.91–96.

Monahan, Francis J. "Investigative Commissions: Implemented Reforms Prove Ephemeral." *The Police Chief,* October 2000, pp.79–84.

Nowicki, Ed. "Racial Profiling Problems and Solutions." *Law and Order,* October 2002, pp.16–18.

Paoline, Eugene A., III; Myers, Stephanie M.; and Worden, Robert E. "Police Culture, Individualism and Community Policing: Evidence from Two Police Departments." *Justice Quarterly,* September 2000, pp.575–605.

Paynter, Ronnie L. "Protecting All the People." *Law Enforcement Technology,* April 2000, pp.62–66.

Pedersen, Dorothy. "Attitude CAN Make a Difference." *Law Enforcement Technology,* August 2000, pp.120–122.

Pedersen, Dorothy. "Rising above Corruption: How to Put Integrity at the Forefront in Your Department." *Law Enforcement Technology,* October 2001, pp.136–142.

Perry, Frank L. "Repairing Broken Windows: Preventing Corruption within Our Ranks." *FBI Law Enforcement Bulletin,* February 2001, pp.23–26.

Ramirez, Deborah; McDevitt, Jack; and Farrell, Amy. *A Resource Guide on Racial Profiling Data Collecting Systems: Promising Practices and Lessons Learned.* Washington, DC: National Institute of Justice, 2000. (NCJ 184768)

Rivera, Richard G. "Nine Ways to Prevent Racial Profiling." *Law and Order,* October 2001, pp.85–88.

Rothlein, Steve. "Fostering Integrity in Policing: A Corruption Prevention Strategy." *The Police Chief,* October 2000, pp.68–76.

Schafer, John R. "Making Ethical Decisions: A Practical Model." *FBI Law Enforcement Bulletin,* May 2002, pp.14–18.

Schott, Richard G. "The Role of Race in Law Enforcement: Racial Profiling or Legitimate Use?" *FBI Law Enforcement Bulletin,* November 2001, pp.24–32.

Sharpe, R. E. "Practicing Realism, Not Racism." *Law Enforcement News,* June 15, 2002, pp.9, 11.

Sherman, Lawrence. "Learning Police Ethics." In *Policing Perspectives,* edited by Larry Gaines and Gary Cordner. Los Angeles: Roxbury Publishing Company, 1999, pp.301–310.

Smith, Michael R. and Petrocelli, Matthew. "Racial Profiling? A Multivariate Analysis of Police Traffic Stop Data." *Police Quarterly,* March 2001, pp.4–27.

Sourcebook of Criminal Justice Statistics—2001. Washington, DC: Bureau of Justice Statistics, 2002.

Strandberg, Keith W. "Light Dawns on the Dark Side: Corruption." *Law Enforcement Technology,* July 2000, pp.98–104.

Swope, Ross. "Bad Apples or Bad Barrel?" *Law and Order,* January 2001a, pp.80–85.

Swope, Ross. "Mentor the First Line Supervisor." *Law and Order,* October 2001b, pp.145–150.

Swope, Ross. "The Ethical Gatekeeper." *Law and Order,* June 2002, pp.132–135.

Thompson, David. "Above the Law?" *Law and Order,* January 2001, pp.77–79.

Trautman, Neal E. "How Organizations Become Corrupt: The Corruption Continuum." *Law and Order,* May 2000, pp.65–68.

Trautman, Neal E. "Truth about Police Code of Silence Revealed." *Law and Order,* January 2001, pp.68–76.

Trautman, Neal E. "The Code of Silence Antidote." *The Law Enforcement Trainer,* March/April 2002, pp.18–21.

White, John. "The Problem with Gratuities." *FBI Law Enforcement Bulletin,* July 2002, pp.20–23.

Williams, Julie. "Mentoring for Law Enforcement." *FBI Law Enforcement Bulletin,* March 2000, pp.19–25.

Book-Specific Web Site

Go to the *Management and Supervision in Law Enforcement* Web site at http://info.wadsworth.com/05346160654 for student and instructor resources, including Internet Assignments and Case Studies.

CHAPTER 10

Motivation and Morale

The convict's stroke of the pick is not the same as the prospector's.
—Antoine de Saint-Exupéry

You can buy a man's time; you can buy his physical presence at a given place; you can even buy a measured number of his skilled muscular motions per hour. But you cannot buy enthusiasm . . . you cannot buy loyalty . . . you cannot buy the devotion of hearts, minds, or souls. You must earn these.
—Clarence Francis

Do You Know?

- What motivation is?
- What theories of motivation have been proposed by Maslow? Herzberg? Skinner? Vroom? Morse and Lorsch?
- Which kind of reinforcement is more effective?
- When reinforcement should occur?
- What the most common external motivators are?
- What internal motivators include?
- How you can make the law enforcement job more interesting?
- What morale is?
- What factors might indicate a morale problem?
- What factors might be responsible for morale problems?
- Who is most able to improve or damage individual and department morale?
- How you might improve morale?
- What you should base promotions on?
- What three phases an assessment center typically uses for law enforcement personnel?
- Whether promotions should be from without or within?

Can You Define?

assessment center
contingency theory
expectancy theory
external motivators
hierarchy of needs
hygiene factors
incentive programs
intangible rewards
internal motivators
job enlargement
job enrichment
job rotation
morale
motivation
motivator factors
negative reinforcement
perception
perks
positive reinforcement
Pygmalian Effect
reinforcement theory
self-actualization
self-fulfilling prophecy
self-motivation
tangible rewards
two-factor theory

INTRODUCTION

Why do some law enforcement officers arrive at work ahead of time, eager to perform? Why do others arrive just in the nick of time? Why do some perform at a high level without direction and others need constant direction? Why are some upbeat and others chronic complainers? What motivates such behavior?

Consider the following conversation between two officers, one who had just completed an especially frustrating shift. This officer asked the other, "Why do we come here day after day and put up with this crap?" The other officer thought for a moment and then answered, "I don't know. I think it has something to do with house payments." Most people do need to work to survive. What will make them also enjoy their work and do their best? What will motivate them?

This chapter begins with an examination of the turnover problem in law enforcement. The remainder of the chapter looks at motivation and morale, two keys to officer retention. First motivation and self-motivation are defined. Next the motivational theories of Maslow, Herzberg, Skinner, Vroom, and Morse and Lorsch are discussed. This theoretical discussion leads into a more practical examination of the causes and symptoms of an unmotivated work force followed by a discussion of external, tangible motivators and internal, intangible motivators. Next is the critical question that managers at all levels ask: "What really motivates employees?" The chapter then looks at the law enforcement career as a motivator and the benefits of motivated personnel.

The discussion then turns to morale and its definitions, both individual and organizational. Next indicators of morale problems are presented, along with a discussion of some reasons for such problems. Specific suggestions for building morale are then outlined, followed by a discussion of the relationship between promotions and morale. The chapter concludes with an example of one innovative program geared to improve morale inexpensively.

Officer Retention, Motivation and Morale

According to Orrick (2002, p.100): "In recent years, police agencies nationwide have experienced increasing levels of staff turnover." He suggests that a contributing factor is the introduction of new generations of officers, Generations X and Y. These officers are well-educated, but "prone to change jobs more frequently than previous recruits. . . . This was illustrated by a recent survey of police academy recruits revealing that 40 percent planned to leave their current agency within three years of graduation." He also notes: "The skills and abilities required of police officers, including good judgment, oral and written communication skills, and problem-solving abilities, make them attractive candidates for many private businesses."

He (p.102) estimates the costs for replacing an officer, including separation costs, recruitment, selecting, new employee training and on-going training costs, to be $58,900. In addition to these costs, Orrick (p.100) notes: "Over time, agencies with higher turnover and less experienced officers often suffer reduced productivity, lower quality of service delivery, more frequent complaints and liability risks."

Warrell (2000, p.59) suggests: "For the most part, [turnover] is the result of four issues: training, wages, equipment and working conditions." These issues are directly related to motivation and morale, the focus of this chapter. Lonsway and Campbell (2002, p.108) note: "One of the major forces undermining the retention of women in policing is the occurrence of discrimination or harassment." This is addressed in Chapter 11. In addition, motivators for women officers are somewhat different than those for men, as discussed later. Consider now, motivation up close.

Motivation Defined

Motivation is an inner or outer drive to meet a need or goal.

Self-motivation is derived from within an individual. Outer motivation is provided from external sources to influence an individual or to furnish a reason for another person to do a desired act in a desired way. A *motive* is an impetus, an impulse, an intention that causes a person to act, individually or collectively, in a directed manner.

Motivation and *morale* are terms often used in management but not easily defined or understood. Lack of motivation is often the reason for low morale. Research psychologists have outlined factors that affect motivation and morale. Incentives must be worthwhile to employees; they must be reasonably attainable; and employees must feel a sense of responsibility to achieve them. In modern police terms, employees must be empowered. Motivation requires a sense of well-being, self-confidence and accomplishment. To keep levels of motivation and morale high, managers must give recognition.

Can managers motivate their subordinates? According to some, motivation can come only from within. A story from business helps illustrate the point. A young salesperson was disappointed because he had lost an important sale. Discussing it with the sales manager, the man lamented, "I guess it just proves you can lead a horse to water, but you can't make him drink." To which the sales manager replied, "Let me give you a little advice. Your job isn't to make him drink. It's to make him thirsty."

Managers can, however, create an environment that will motivate people by creating opportunities for success and recognizing accomplishments.

Self-Motivation

When employees know an agency's goals and choose to help meet them, this is **self-motivation.** Fortunately for management, most employees want to do a good job. It is management's job to help and to provide additional motivation when needed. For example, an officer who works long after the shift is over to make certain a victim is adequately taken care of may be rewarded by being given time off during the next shift. Many incentives other than monetary ones encourage employees and cost nothing. They take little time, yet are seldom used. Most employees have pride in their work. They want to satisfy themselves and their employers.

Self-motivated law enforcement officers work for personal job satisfaction. Law enforcement work gives them a sense of accomplishment and personal value. Self-motivated officers are dedicated to their work and make every hour on the job count.

Job satisfaction remains a basic reward of working, even though not many employees would mention it as a benefit. Recreation and time for home life, children and rest are equally important. Self-motivated employees are more apt to work toward organizational as well as personal goals because the melding of both provides even more job satisfaction.

Not all jobs provide an enjoyable environment. Many people work only to make a living, to provide security for their families and to supply the funds to enjoy the other things in life. Many work at jobs they do not like. Not all law enforcement officers like their work. In these situations managers need to be motivators.

Many theories of motivation have been developed based on extensive research of employees in the work environment. These studies reveal that although monetary rewards are a necessary part of jobs, money is *not* the major consideration as long as it is basically adequate for living.

Motivational Theories

Each individual has needs even though that person may not have a list of needs or even have consciously thought about them. These needs make each of us what we are and cause us to do what we do. Each individual takes action to meet these needs.

The 1960s saw the development of many theories about motivation. Knowledge of these theories helps us understand what people can do for themselves and what managers can do for employees. The results of studies by human-behavior researchers apply as much to law enforcement as to any other profession.

The Hierarchy of Needs—Abraham Maslow

One of the best-known studies of human needs was conducted by Abraham Maslow in 1962. He concluded that every human has five basic needs, which he assembled into a hierarchy, as Figure 10.1 illustrates.

Maslow's **hierarchy of needs** is, in the order they need to be met, physiological, safety and security, social, esteem and self-actualization.

At the base of the hierarchy are *physiological needs:* air, food, water, sleep, shelter and sex. It is mandatory that at least air, food, water and sleep be satisfied, or a person could not function or proceed to the next level. Some segments of the world's population live their entire lives just trying to satisfy this level of need. Shelter could be added to the list because it is more than merely a place to sleep; it is protection from the elements.

The second level, *safety and security,* includes protection from serious injury and death, freedom from fear and a clear authority structure. Humans function better in an environment free from fear. It has long been known that children need a set of standards even though they tend to rebel against them. Adults also need a set of standards, an authority structure, even though they, too, sometimes rebel. People want a level of certainty, to know where they stand. This translates

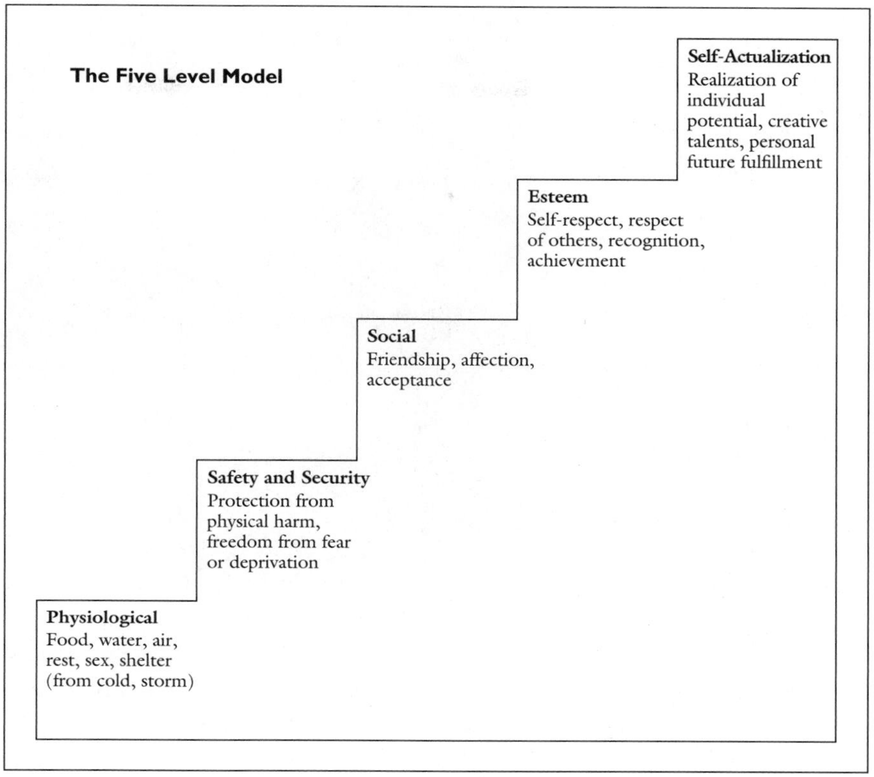

Figure 10.1
Maslow's Hierarchy of Needs

at work to safety from accidents, a reasonable promise of job security and an opportunity for increases in pay and promotions.

The third level, *social,* includes friendship, love, affection and group and team belonging. These are important needs for everyone. Workers want peer acceptance, approval, sharing and friendship.

The fourth level, *esteem,* includes self-respect, respect and recognition from others, status, a title, added responsibility, independence and recognition for job performance.

The fifth level, *self-actualization,* refers to achievement, meeting individual goals and fulfilling one's potential. **Self-actualization** is what you do when all the other needs are satisfied. It is fostered by the chance to be creative and innovative and by having the opportunity to maximize skills and knowledge.

According to Maslow's theory, people's wants are always increasing and changing. Once an individual's basic (primary) needs have been satisfied, other needs take their place. The satisfied need no longer acts as a motivating force. If a number of needs are unsatisfied at any given time, an individual will try to satisfy the most pressing one first. Maslow believed that all levels of needs probably exist to some degree for individuals most of the time. Rarely is any one need completely satisfied, at least for long. Hunger, for example, may be satisfied after eating, but it emerges again later.

Maslow's theory of needs is popular because it makes sense. People can identify these needs in their own lives. In addition, the needs can be seen operating on the job. In many jobs, including law enforcement jobs, the first two levels of

© Spencer Grant/PhotoEdit

Social interaction among officers—friendships and a sense of teamwork—contributes to job satisfaction and motivation.

needs are automatically provided. Safety, for example, is extremely important in law enforcement. The law enforcement organization must do everything possible to ensure its officers' safety—and the officers should know what steps have been taken.

Satisfied needs do not necessarily become inactive needs. If law enforcement officers receive salary increases, they may raise their standard of living and then another salary increase is as welcome as the first.

Law enforcement organizations may meet the needs of the group but not of individuals. For example, with a minimal number of promotions, other means of satisfying the need for recognition must be found. Managers can play an important role in providing on-the-job authority structure. They can provide respect through praise and recognition for tasks well done.

Managers can help subordinates meet even the highest goals, fulfilling individual potential through training and on-the-job educational opportunities. Officers seek challenging opportunities to provide service to the community. If their performance is good, they expect fair compensation and rewards. The agency should provide clear goals that have been mutually agreed upon, and officers should expect to meet those goals, both individually and as a group. Maslow's five levels of needs and their translation into specific job-related factors are illustrated in Figure 10.2.

Two-Factor Hygiene/Motivator Theory—Herzberg

Another behavioral psychologist, Frederick Herzberg, developed the **two-factor theory,** or the hygiene/motivator theory. Herzberg's theory divides needs that require satisfaction through work into two classes: hygiene factors and motivator factors.

Herzberg's **hygiene factors** are **tangible rewards** that can cause *dissatisfaction* if lacking. **Motivator factors** are **intangible rewards** that can create *satisfaction.*

Complex	Self-actualization	Challenging job
		Creativity
		Achievement in work
		Advancement
		Involvement in planning
		Chances for growth and development
	Esteem	Merit pay raises
		Titles
		Status symbols/awards
		Recognition (peer/boss)
		Job itself
		Responsibility
		Sharing in decisions
	Social	Quality supervision
		Compatible co-workers
		Professional friendships
		Department pride/spirit
	Safety/Security	Safe working conditions
		Fringe benefits
		Seniority
		Proper supervision
		Sound department policies
		Protective equipment
		General salary increases
		Job security
		Feeling of competence
Basic	Physiological	Heat/air conditioning
		Base salary
		Cafeteria/vending machine
		Working conditions
		Rest periods
		Efficient work methods
		Labor-saving devices
		Comfortable uniform

Figure 10.2
Maslow's Levels of Needs and Job Factors

Dissatisfaction and satisfaction are not two ends of a continuum, because people can experience lack of dissatisfaction without necessarily being satisfied.

Tangible rewards pertaining basically to the hygiene factors do *not* provide satisfaction. They simply prevent dissatisfaction. Having officers who perform only because they are not dissatisfied is seldom conducive to high performance. Providing more tangible rewards is highly unlikely to accomplish better results.

The hygiene factors are similar to Maslow's lower-level needs. People assume these factors will be met. If they are not, people will be dissatisfied. Company policies, job security, supervision, a basic salary and safe working conditions are extrinsic factors that do not necessarily motivate people to do better work. They are expected.

Herzberg's hygiene factors help to explain why many people stick with jobs they do not like. They stay because they are not dissatisfied with the tangible rewards such as the pay and the retirement plan even though they are definitely not satisfied with the work itself.

Industry found that when many of the wage increases, fringe benefits, seniority and security programs were initiated, they did not substantially reduce the basic problems of low productivity, high turnover, absenteeism and grievances.

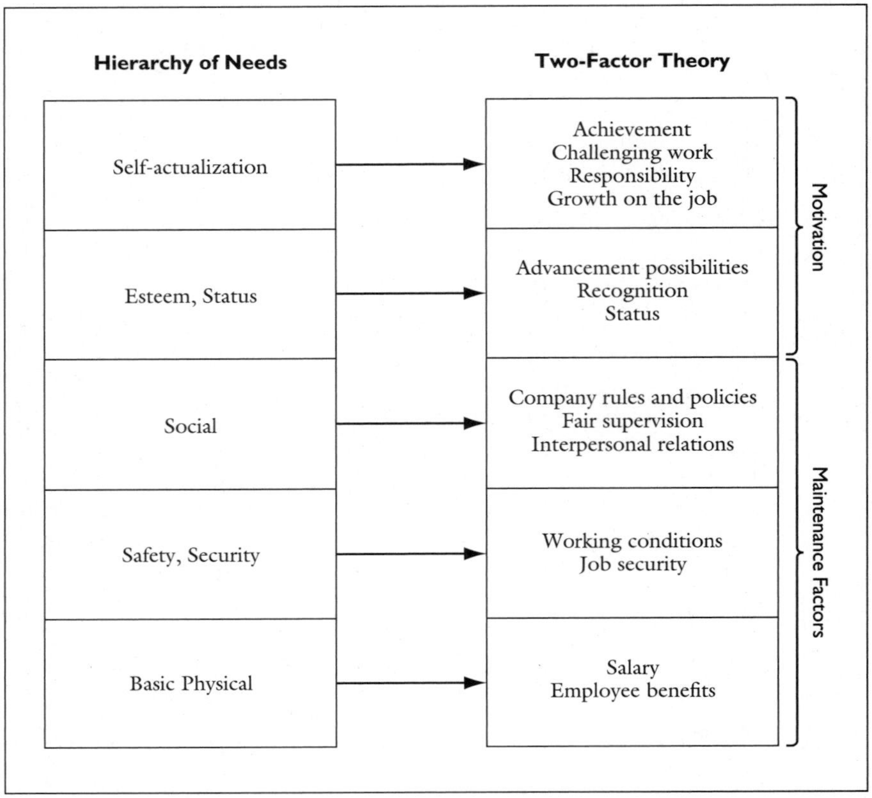

Figure 10.3
Comparison of Maslow and Herzberg

Source: Stan Kossen. *Supervision,* 2nd ed. St. Paul, MN: West Publishing Company, 1991, p. 278.

Herzberg claimed that approach was wrong. Instead, jobs should provide greater control over outcomes of work, have clearly established goals and have more to do rather than less. Figure 10.3 shows the relationship between Maslow's hierarchy of needs theory and Herzberg's two-factor theory.

As Herzberg (1978, p.49) pointed out: "A man whose work possesses no contentment in terms of self-fulfillment, but exists exclusively to fulfill the purposes of the enterprise or a social organization, is a man doomed to a life of human frustration, despite a return of animal contentment. You do not inspire employees by giving them higher wages, more benefits, or new status symbols. It is the successful achievement of a challenging task which fulfills the urge to create. . . . The employer's task is not to motivate his people to get them to achieve; he should provide opportunities for people to achieve so they will become motivated."

Herzberg's theory, like Maslow's, does not consider differences in people, for the same motivators will not motivate everyone. Law enforcement managers, for example, will find that not all patrol officers are motivated by the same needs. Managers have to adjust motivational approaches to the individual.

Most employees still believe that satisfying work is more important than increased salary and advancement, *if* the basic salary is adequate. The job itself—

law enforcement work—is a good example: The work is satisfying because what officers do is meaningful to them and to the community they serve. Most law enforcement officers are *not* in it for the money.

Reinforcement Theory—Skinner

Extremely influential writings by B. F. Skinner suggest that behavior can be shaped and modified using positive and negative reinforcement. Skinner's pioneering work in behavior modification was first described in his book *The Behavior of Organisms,* published in 1938 and expanded in *Walden Two,* published in 1948. A key conclusion of Skinner's research is that behavior is a function of its consequences. The ethics behind modifying behavior became highly controversial in the 1960s. Nonetheless, Skinner's theories *are* still relevant to managers, are implicit in the motivational theories just discussed and seem to be simple common sense.

In reinforcement theory employees are rewarded for good behavior. They repeat the behavior to achieve the reward, and it becomes a learned behavior. Employees are punished for bad behavior. They stop the punished behavior to avoid future punishment. Rewards are called **positive reinforcement;** punishments, **negative reinforcement.**

Skinner's **reinforcement theory** suggests that positive reinforcement increases a given behavior and negative reinforcement decreases a given behavior.

Use of both positive and negative reinforcement is readily seen on the job. Often both are used, and both make sense. Other principles of reinforcement theory also have relevance for managers.

Positive reinforcement is more effective than negative reinforcement. The closer in time to the behavior, the more effective the reinforcement will be.

What is the problem with punishment? With a history as old as the human race, it is the belief that the harsher the punishment, the greater its effectiveness in changing behavior. Many managers, including those in penology, still adhere to this belief.

The means to inflict punishment have changed, with the whip, the rack and the stock falling into disfavor. Today's punishments are more subtle but have the same effect. Punishment-oriented managers might use techniques such as criticizing or ridiculing someone in public, ignoring a job well done, withholding needed information or avoiding discussion on an expected promotion or raise.

Although the punishments have changed, the problems associated with using a punishment-oriented management style have not. First, and perhaps most important, punishment can cause a get-even attitude. This can take the form of "fight"—where the employees cause problems by what they say or do. Or it can take the form of "flight," where the workers "quit but stay." They simply put in the required time and do as little as possible.

A second problem is that managers have to be constantly watching over employees. If vigilance is relaxed, the negative behavior is likely to recur.

A third problem is that subordinates may come to associate punishment with the manager's presence and may dread seeing the manager coming around. They may become defensive every time the manager appears.

Yet another problem with punishment is that sometimes any kind of attention, even punishment, is considered more positive than being ignored. Teachers are well aware of this phenomenon with "problem" students who act up merely for the attention they get when they do. Law enforcement officers who crave acknowledgment of their existence by their superiors may feel that criticism is preferable to being totally ignored.

The other principle of the reinforcement theory that managers need to consider is the time factor. Many incentives once thought to be powerful motivators are delayed—and scheduled. A good example is the paycheck. A law enforcement officer may conduct an excellent investigation on the first of the month but not be paid until the fifteenth of that month. In such cases, the paycheck is not seen as related to the investigation.

That is why incentives such as praise and recognition, given *immediately,* can be powerful motivators. Positive reinforcement can be highly motivating, but the theory also has some disadvantages. It does not consider human needs and tends to simplify behavior and rewards. It does not consider that employees may be motivated by the job itself, may be self-motivated or may consider rewards as manipulation, which they will eventually reject. Failing to reward can lead to decreased production, and failing to punish poor performance can reinforce that behavior.

The Expectancy Theory—Vroom

Victor H. Vroom's expectancy theory looks at options employees have on the job. It combines some features of the preceding theories and advances the ideas that employees believe good work on the job will lead to high job performance and that high job performance will lead to job rewards.

Regardless of the chief individual motivating factors, if employees believe that performance will lead to satisfying motivational needs, they will work hard. Naturally, employees must be able to perform. According to Vroom's theory of motivation, employees become motivated to take action when the following three-step process takes place:

1. A motivating factor—a need to satisfy or goal to achieve—exists that is important to the employee.
2. The employee believes that by putting in the required or requested effort, the job can be performed.
3. The employee believes that by successfully performing the job as requested, the need will be satisfied or the goal will be achieved.

Employees have an effort expectancy and a performance expectancy. If managers clearly define the tasks and help employees with direction and skill training to perform the job, effort expectancy will rise. Managers can help achieve performance expectancy by providing means of satisfying individual needs.

Managers must know what opportunities specific jobs offer before they can use them as motivational opportunities for employees. These may be money, opportunity for educational or job growth, praise or peer recognition. Expectancies vary even with individuals doing the same job. Expectancy theory integrates ideas about employee motivation.

Vroom's **expectancy theory** suggests that employees will choose the level of effort that matches the performance opportunity for reward.

For example, if a law enforcement officer investigating a crash that happened one-half hour before shift change realizes that completing the investigation will take an hour, he or she can complete it, ask another officer to take over the investigation or do a poor job by leaving the investigation before obtaining the needed information.

The officer knows doing the complete job will receive recognition by the sergeant. He or she knows asking someone else to complete the investigation will lead to complications in obtaining facts and completing reports. He or she knows that leaving the scene without information for proper reporting will be reason for reprimand. The officer will probably choose to put in the extra time and complete the report because the rewards are a better expectancy than a reprimand. It will also look better on his or her record. The officer should also understand that making repeated comments to those involved in the crash that "this is on my own time" are negative and may result in a complaint. On the other hand, the satisfaction of a job well done and the good inner feeling that results may be motivating in themselves.

Contingency Theory—Morse and Lorsch

Closely related to the expectancy theory is the contingency theory developed by John J. Morse and Jay W. Lorsch. They built on McGregor's Theory X/Theory Y (Chapter 2) and Herzberg's motivation and maintenance factors in their research on how an organizational task *fit* affects and is affected by task performance and employees' feelings of *competence.* The four key components of the contingency theory are the following:

- People have a basic need to feel competent.
- How people fill this need varies and will depend on how the need interacts with other needs and the strengths of those needs.
- Competence motivation is most likely to exist when task and organization "fit."
- Feeling competent continues to be motivating even after competence is achieved.

Morse and Lorsch's **contingency theory** suggests fitting tasks, officers and the agency's goals so that officers can feel competent.

Contingency theory further suggests that highly structured tasks might be performed better in highly structured organizations that have a management structure that resembles McGregor's Theory X approach. Conversely, highly unstructured tasks might be performed better in more flexible organizations whose management structure resembles the Theory Y approach. In law enforcement work, both kinds of tasks occur. Consequently, flexibility in management style becomes very important.

Motivational theory has important implications for law enforcement managers and supervisors. No matter which theories they believe have the most credence, managers must understand that certain external, tangible motivators and certain internal, intangible motivators are important in accomplishing goals through others.

Causes and Symptoms of an Unmotivated Work Force

Causes of an unmotivated work force might include overwork, downsizing, endless restructuring, boredom, frustration and promotions—who gets them and why—work conditions and the court system.

Symptoms of an unmotivated officer include absenteeism, constant complaining, lack of care for equipment, lack of respect for other officers, lack of respect for rules and regulations, low morale, sleeping or loafing on duty, slovenly appearance and tardiness. Dealing with these symptoms is the focus of the next section. In addition to recognizing the causes and symptoms of lack of motivation, managers must also understand and know how to use the knowledge that certain external, tangible motivators and certain internal, intangible motivators are important in accomplishing goals through others.

External, Tangible Motivators

Although external motivators no longer have the power they once had, they are expected. As Herzberg's theory states, basic needs must be met or dissatisfaction will result. This is not to say that lack of dissatisfaction will be motivating. It is likely, however, to keep people on the job and to keep them from counterproductive behavior.

Among the most common **external motivators,** or tangible rewards, are salary, bonuses, insurance, retirement plans, favorable working conditions, paid vacation and holidays, titles and adequate equipment.

The Compensation Package

The law enforcement profession is not known for its great salaries. Nonetheless, money is important to most employees. They want and need enough salary to be comfortable and to meet their basic financial responsibilities. Some officers work two jobs until they have the amount of money they consider necessary. It is true that money talks. What managers must remember, however, is that it says different things to different people.

Although pay in the law enforcement profession is not at the top of the scale, the entire compensation package is usually competitive. One important factor is an equitable procedure for raises. In a well-managed department, employees would not have to ask for raises. They would know what to expect—and when—in return for their performance and dedication. Given the hazardous nature of law enforcement work, the compensation package should include health, disability and life insurance.

McDonald (2000, p.25) notes: "Most employees simply do not understand or appreciate the value of their benefit packages, which traditionally amount to between 25 to 28 percent of their cash compensation. Items such as profit sharing, medical and dental plans, life insurance and 401(k) contributions—not to speak of small things like flu shots and parking fees—all add up. You need to make sure your workers both know and value what they're getting." Johnson (2001, p.68) suggests: "Be sure to analyze needs and offer a mix of options, even if some benefits are purchased by employees and handled as convenient, payroll deductions (known as voluntary benefits), such as auto and homeowners' insurance."

Perks

Perks, or tangible rewards, can be as large as a luxury cruise for the "training suggestion of the year" or as small as a reserved parking spot. Little extras can contribute much to making jobs more attractive. Some perks cost nothing, and others are relatively inexpensive. Consider the following:

- Cards or small gifts for special occasions such as birthdays or service anniversaries
- Tickets to sporting events and shows for outstanding performance
- Free coffee and snacks
- Facilities and equipment for heating meals, such as microwave ovens
- Daily newspaper and magazines, including professional journals
- Personal notes for achievements—on the job and off
- Support for league teams such as softball and bowling
- Smiles

Incentive Programs

Incentive programs can also be used to motivate; however, according to McDonald (p.25): "Traditional salary and bonus programs alone no longer motivate people. . . . Probably the biggest challenge we have in motivation today has to do with the [younger generations in the workforce]. The prospect of a 30-year career of 40-hour weeks crowned with a solid pension plan does not motivate these people. For them, time is compressed; they want what they want now. Items like fast-track career paths, flexible work hours, ongoing training, spot bonuses, unique merchandise and travel incentive programs are some of the desires, as well as anything that makes balancing work and personal life easier; dry cleaning, child-care allowances, fitness membership—the more creative the better."

Working Conditions and Schedules

Employees expect adequate heat, light, ventilation and working hours. They also expect a well-maintained squad car and up-to-date equipment. Having a desk or a private office can also be rewarding. Inadequacies in working conditions can cause great dissatisfaction.

The work environment can have a great impact on morale. People appreciate working in a clean, attractive and healthy environment. A local florist might be approached to donate some plants to brighten up the offices. Seasonal decorations can help add to appropriate holiday spirit. Attractive artwork can liven up otherwise drab hallways. Interested employees might want to form a committee, organize a garage sale to raise money and decorate certain areas of the department according to a planned schedule. The options are limitless.

In addition, flexible hours and job sharing opportunities, when possible, are attractive motivators to many officers, especially those trying to balance the job with family life.

Security

Although this may seem like an internal reward—or motivator—many aspects of security are indeed external, tangible and expected. Among them are fair work rules, adequate grievance procedures, reasonable department policies and discipline and seniority privileges. Some aspects of the compensation package such as insurance and retirement plans also meet basic security needs.

Social

Like the need for security, employees' social needs can fall within the external, tangible category when such things as parties, picnics, breaks and social gatherings are considered. Opportunities to mix with one's peers and superiors, sometimes including spouses, may be very rewarding.

Status

The need for status can also be partially met by external, tangible rewards such as privileges, titles, private offices, awards and other symbols of rank and position. These external, tangible factors are sometimes called *maintenance* factors. Provided in adequate quantity and quality, they merely prevent dissatisfaction. The best managers can hope for is a "fair day's work for a fair day's pay." To get subordinates to truly perform, managers usually need to provide internal, intangible motivators as well.

Internal, Intangible Motivators

Internal, intangible motivators can spark employees to give their best effort to accomplish individual and department goals.

Internal motivators, or intangible rewards, include goals, achievement, recognition, self-respect, opportunity for advancement, opportunity to make a contribution and belief in individual and departmental goals.

Goals and Expectations

Goals need to be set and met. Specific goal setting results in greater accomplishment. Goals should make officers reach to their levels of competence. Different goals are often needed for individual officers. The reason some students fail in school is because goals are too easy and they become bored. On the other hand, the same goals may be too high for other students to achieve and they become frustrated. Students who achieve to their level of competence will be motivated.

The highly touted management by objectives, or MBO, relies on clear, meaningful goals, both for individual officers and for the organization. Goals establish future direction of effort. Accomplishing goals provides room for creativity, innovation, diversity and a sense of accomplishment.

Operational goals should be set by first-line and middle managers, with the participation of patrol officers. Goals should be consistent and communicated.

Realistic goals, proper resources to do the job, employee communication and a personal and organizational sense of accomplishment all play a major role in law enforcement motivation. Closely related to goals are expectations. To illustrate the importance of expectations, recognize the **Pygmalion Effect:** What managers and supervisors expect of their officers and how they treat them largely determine their performance and career progress. It is a type of self-fulfilling prophecy.

Achievement, Recognition, Growth and Advancement

Achievement is a motivator. It can be a series of small accomplishments or one accomplishment that ultimately grows to a larger one. It can be a task done well for the first time, something done better than before, a higher score or committing fewer errors.

Recognition is also a motivator, whether it comes from peers or managers. Recognition is most effective if it can be related to a person's personal qualities rather than to the performance itself. For example, rather than saying "Good job on solving the XYZ case," emphasize the personal qualities involved, such as, "I admire your determination to keep working on the XYZ case until you got it solved."

Recognize accomplishment. Too often managers fail to use this reward that costs nothing. Recognition of something well done, offered at the time of accomplishment, is a powerful motivator: "Thank you for working overtime to get that report to me." "I have just reviewed your case report. It is excellent and reflects a lot of thought." Some employees report that their managers have never complimented or praised them in an entire year. Some managers cannot bring themselves to praise subordinates either because it is not in their nature or they are too busy.

In addition to recognition, employees want growth and advancement in their jobs. Orrick (p.103) contends: "Studies have repeatedly found that employees are more concerned with opportunities for advanced training and career development programs than salary alone." It does not have to be promotions or pay raises. It can even be little things: being given personal responsibility for a task, a title, concern for employees' health and welfare, a little risk taking for excitement or deserved praise for a not-so-important task done well. All can contribute to a critical motivator: self-esteem.

Self-Esteem

Self-esteem involves self-confidence, a feeling of self-worth. As individual tasks are successfully accomplished, self-esteem builds. A sincere compliment by another person on your ability to perform a task also builds self-esteem. It is law enforcement managers' responsibility to build self-esteem in their team. The more self-esteem individuals in the agency have, the higher the organizational esteem will be. Recall Maslow's hierarchy of needs and, specifically, the fourth level labeled "esteem."

Officers with low self-esteem will perform low-level work. If they have been told they are incompetent, they probably will not perform well. This has been referred to as **self-fulfilling prophecy.** People tend to behave and eventually become what they think others expect of them. Law enforcement managers need to apply the implications of the self-fulfilling prophecy to everyday employee/law enforcement task performance. As one poster reads: "Every job is a self-portrait of the person who did it. Autograph your work with excellence."

Officers' perceptions of themselves and other people directly influence how the officers conduct themselves in public. This is important because law enforcement is a "people" profession. Officers' attitudes directly influence how they handle other people. Officers with low self-esteem are overly concerned with themselves because they fear failure and know they are not functioning as well as they should.

Managers can build individual self-esteem in the following ways:

- Do not embarrass subordinates, especially in front of others.
- Recognize and build on individual accomplishments.
- Give praise for things done well at the same time as you give criticism for things not well done.
- Give personal attention.
- Ask employees' opinions on problems.
- If an employee gives an opinion or suggestion, act on it in some way. Do not ignore it.
- Help individuals develop to their potential.
- Give employees breathing room for ideas, creativity and innovation.
- Give special task assignments.
- Get to know employees as individuals.
- Give certificates of appreciation when deserved.
- Truly listen.
- If employees express ideas, write them down in their presence.
- If someone has complimented an officer, pass it on.
- Assign part of the next departmental meeting to different officers.
- Share important information. Let everyone be "in the know."
- Acquire a piece of equipment that will help officers do a better job.

A Feeling of Importance

Managers must let their subordinates know they count. One manager used the following memo to let his employees know how valuable they were:

> "You Arx A Kxy Pxrson" Xvxn though my typxwritxr is an old modxl, it works vxry wxll—xxcxpt for onx kxy. You would think that with all thx othxr kxys functioning propxrly, onx kxy not working would hardly bx noticxd; but just onx kxy out of whack sxxms to ruin thx wholx xffort.
>
> You may say to yoursxlf—"Wxll I'm only onx pxrson. No onx will noticx if I don't do my bxst." But it doxs makx a diffxrxncx bxcausx to bx xffxctivx an organization nxxds activx participation by xvxryonx to thx bxst of his or hxr ability.
>
> So thx nxxt timx you think you arx not important, rxmxmbxr my old typxwritxr. You arx a kxy pxrson.
>
> (*Pasadena Weekly Journal of Business,* 155 S. El Molino Ave., Suite 101, Pasadena, CA 91101. Reprinted by permission.)

One of the best ways managers and supervisors can let their people know they are important is to *listen* to them. Chapter 3 emphasized the role listening plays in communication. Law enforcement managers who truly listen to their subordinates will learn a great deal about their needs and feelings. The more managers know about their officers and their needs, the more they can help them meet those needs.

The more managers concentrate on the person talking to them, the more they show how much they value that person. Psychiatrists usually spend most of a patient's time listening. They understand this primary need of the patient to unburden, to let it all out. At the same time they learn a tremendous amount of information about the patient.

Effective listening is an *active* form of communication. You must work at it. Physically show your attentiveness. Ask questions. Clarify. Take notes. Maintain eye contact. If you do not believe that listening is active, the next time someone tries to tell you something, do not pay attention, excuse yourself and start to make a phone call, or simply look away from the person, in no way encouraging them to continue the conversation. The person will immediately be able to tell that you are not interested.

Being Involved, Included and "In" on Things

The importance of participative management has been discussed. The more employees feel a part of a department, the harder—and better—they will work. To establish and maintain involvement, use a team approach and encourage suggestions.

What Is Really Motivational?

Fulton (2001, p.226) stresses: "By properly observing, listening and talking with each individual in your unit, you can find out what will motivate them to do a good job. Some employees need constant praise, while others want to be left alone to do their jobs." He suggests that most employees can be motivated to do a good job by meeting a combination of needs: the need for power, for equity, for recognition, for freedom and for affiliation. The important thing is to recognize that what is motivational for one officer may not be for others.

Dr. Douglas Heath, professor at Haverford College, looked at motivators beyond those provided by the job in what he called "Whole Person" motivation. Dr. Heath has surveyed thousands of people across the country about the most commonly held hopes, goals and achievements. He has his audiences rate from 1 to 12 the following hopes and goals adults have for their lives:

- Leadership/power
- Happy marital relationship
- High income
- Being a competent parent
- Psychological maturity
- Self-fulfillment/happiness
- Ethical sensitivity/idealism
- Fulfilling sexual mate

- Competence in a satisfying vocation
- Contributing citizen to community/nation
- A close, same-sex friend
- Good physical health

You may want to rate them yourself before reading the results of Heath's research.

According to Heath, the seven highest goals are, from most to least important: self-fulfillment/happiness, good physical health, psychological maturity, happy marital relationship, ethical sensitivity/idealism, competence in a satisfying vocation and satisfaction in being a competent parent. Clearly, managers should be concerned with more than strictly job-related factors when considering what will motivate their subordinates.

Managers need to know what might be motivational for their employees or "what makes a person tick."

The Law Enforcement Career as a Motivator

Law enforcement work itself can be a motivator. Many officers find that law enforcement tasks, in and of themselves, are a basis for self-motivation. When a law enforcement applicant appears before an interviewing board and is asked, "Why do you want to be a law enforcement officer?" the answer is invariably a variation of "Because I like to work with people," or "I want to provide a service, and I think law enforcement work is an opportunity to do that."

Herzberg identified several factors that could lead to dissatisfaction on the job, including inadequate pay, difficult work schedules, inadequate benefits, poor working conditions and the like. Brody et al. (2002, p.187) note: "Two important known job dissatisfiers are the presence of all-inclusive policies and established procedures, and a rigid adherence to existing rules."

Herzberg also noted that job satisfaction is primarily a reflection of personal growth factors in one's workplace assignment. He identified three primary sources of job satisfaction: (1) the importance of the work itself, (2) the sense of responsibility while doing the work and (3) the feeling of recognition for that work.

Van Brocklin (2001, p.79) points out: "Like the military, law enforcement cannot compete with the private sector when it comes to tangibles such as pay, benefits, flex time, entrepreneurial opportunities, or profit sharing. It shouldn't try to. When it does, it misses its strongest selling point. Studs Terkel, one of the greatest oral historians of our time and a Pulitzer Prize-winning author of numerous bestsellers, observed, 'Most of us have jobs that are too small for our spirits.' "

Law enforcement entails a great variety of skills: handling an automobile, using weapons, conversing with all types of people, interviewing and interrogating, using computers and computerized information, setting up case investigations and so on. Everything law enforcement officers do provides task significance. They have a high degree of autonomy in their decisions and actions. Decisions are often instantaneous and permanent. In addition, their actions are highly visible because of their uniforms. This visibility should provide motivation to do the best possible job at all times.

Personal growth can be achieved by providing opportunities for departmental training, seminars, college classes or public talks to civic organizations and youth groups. These types of job enrichment opportunities can also provide a higher degree of self-motivation and self-control in performing law enforcement tasks in emergencies, without close manager control.

The law enforcement job is generally not perceived as boring and routine. If it becomes that way, it is generally the officer's fault because ample opportunities exist to make it more exciting. Even routine foot and vehicle patrol should not be boring. Many exciting things happen on a shift or at least have the potential for happening.

The importance of interesting work is illustrated by the story of a man visiting Mexico who found in a little shop a very comfortable, attractive, reasonably priced handcrafted chair. Extremely pleased, the tourist asked the shop manager if he could make him a dozen chairs just like it. The Mexican nodded and, obviously displeased, said, "But the señor knows that I must charge much more for each such chair."

The tourist, astonished, exclaimed, "More? In the United States if you buy in quantity, you pay less. Why do you want to charge me more?"

The reply, "Because it is so dull to make twelve chairs all the same."

Managers should make the law enforcement job itself more interesting and challenging for officers, provide goals, make challenges out of routine work and make contests among employees. Law enforcement tasks can be studied and made more interesting. Assignments can be made more efficiently and with greater variety to make the total job more satisfying. COPPS certainly offers the opportunity to make a difference.

Giving more responsibility, providing opportunity for employees to perform the job without being directly told what to do, treating each employee according to his or her own needs—these actions are motivating.

Law enforcement work can be made more interesting and motivating in three important ways:

- Job rotation
- Job enlargement
- Job enrichment

Job Rotation

Job rotation can make the job more challenging. Job rotation also serves as a training opportunity and provides variety—an opportunity to understand the total law enforcement job. Different things happen on the day shift than on the night shift or middle shift. Job tasks are different in the patrol, detective, juvenile, narcotics and administrative divisions.

Job rotation is often done on a temporary basis. Such cross-training not only provides a better understanding of the total law enforcement effort but also gives supervisors more flexibility to deal with absences and requests for vacations. Job rotation also prepares officers for promotions and can serve as a motivator as such officers begin to feel competent doing new and different tasks.

Job Enlargement

Giving additional responsibilities, such as making a survey of vehicle licenses to determine the number of outsiders in the community, can provide helpful information for the department, other departments or the community. Increasing the number of tasks may be perceived as a threat. Given the right training and tools, officers should perceive **job enlargement** as motivating, giving them renewed interest in and enthusiasm for law enforcement work.

Building on Herzberg's work, Hackman and Oldham (1976) set forth their theory of job enrichment, specifying five core job characteristics underlying job satisfaction: task identity, task significance, skill variety, job feedback and autonomy. Certainly all of these can be provided through police work.

Job Enrichment

Job enrichment is similar to job enlargement, except that in job enrichment the focus is the quality of the new jobs assigned rather than the quantity. Job enrichment emphasizes adding variety, deeper personal interest and involvement, increased responsibility and greater autonomy. Job enrichment is appropriate for any highly routine job.

For some officers, however, job enrichment might also be perceived as threatening. Some officers do not want enrichment. They do not need more challenges because they may already be working to capacity. They may be comfortable in their routine, or they may be burned out.

Not all officers will want to do all law enforcement tasks. Maybe they are satisfied with routine tasks. The lower level of tasks may satisfy their needs of security, money and group belonging. Even if given the opportunity, they may prefer one division over another. Not all officers want promotions. They would rather be responsible for only what they do, not for getting results from other people.

Job Satisfaction and Community Policing and Problem Solving

One benefit often attributed to community-oriented policing and problem solving is that officers are more motivated and morale is heightened. This is a result of officers feeling they are indeed making a significant difference in the community. Officers in departments embracing COPPS report greater job satisfaction. Some officers, however, find this approach to policing to be "soft on crime" and see officers committed to COPPS as social workers rather than crime fighters. This can lead to problems within the department and needs to be addressed.

Sherwood (2000, p.191) studied the effect of community policing on job satisfaction and found: "Officers from the department that was observed to be more advanced in implementing community policing reported significantly higher scores for skill variety, task identity, task significance and autonomy." In addition, he (p.208) reports: "The data do suggest that departments that make changes in their structure and function toward a more community-based system of policing are better positioned to bring about job enrichment." Furthermore (p.209): "Allowing officers to work regularly with neighborhood residents creates a natural work unit that will increase skill variety and task identity. . . . By granting police officers the increased responsibility and authority to engage in proactive problem solving, managers enhance the vertical loading of the job and increase autonomy."

Brody et al. (p.181) studied the effect of implementing community-oriented policing on police personnel job satisfaction. They found that in some departments the changes produced uncertainty and insecurity in police agencies; however, in other agencies adopting community policing has had a positive effective on job satisfaction. They also found COPPS emphasis on problem-solving and the SARA Model is especially satisfying to most officers and that "both the small and large successes accomplished through problem-solving efforts will be broadly celebrated as officer, staff and community accomplishments."

Benefits of Motivated Personnel

The benefits of having highly motivated personnel are numerous—less sick leave, better coverage, more arrests and better investigations. In fact, most of the numerous benefits listed in Chapter 9 as resulting from an effective training program would also result from effective motivation. With both effective training and motivational programs, these benefits are highly probable. The price of not paying attention to motivation is often low morale and a generally negative environment.

Morale: An Overview

An office poster designed to inspire employees to greater efforts read: "You can—if you will!" Beneath it, someone had scrawled, "And you're canned if you won't!" Both sayings relate directly to morale and employees' attitudes toward their jobs.

Morale can make or break an individual or an organization. As Napoleon observed, referring to his army: "An army's effectiveness depends on its size, training, experience and morale . . . and morale is worth more than all the other factors combined."

Morale is *always* present. It might be high, low or on an even keel, but it exists perpetually. Management's responsibility is to keep morale as high as possible and to be alert to signs that it may be dropping. The morale of individuals, work units and an entire agency concerns managers and supervisors.

Achieving high morale is a complex challenge, with different problems depending on the size of the department and the leadership style. Even within the same agency, morale, as it relates to job satisfaction, can differ from one position to another.

Morale is somewhat elusive and difficult to define. Individuals and organizations differ greatly, and what would induce high or low morale in one might be the opposite in another. Good or poor morale is generally attributed to individuals, whereas high or low morale characterizes the entire organization.

Morale is a person's or group's state of mind, level of enthusiasm and amount of involvement with work and with life.

Good or high morale is a *can-do* attitude. As Admiral Ben Morrell says: "Morale is when your hands and feet keep on working when your head says it can't be done." The right kind of persistence *does* pay. Coaches stress the importance of that "second effort" in winning games. The willingness to make another try when the first one fails distinguishes the average player and employee from the star. A Chinese proverb proclaims: "The person who says it cannot be done should not interrupt the person doing it."

Douglas MacArthur, the general so instrumental in helping win World War II, might never have gained his status without persistence. When he applied for admission to West Point, he was turned down, not once but twice. He persisted, however, applied a third time, was accepted and marched into history.

Morale can be measured by observing the actions and statements of employees. Are they positive and upbeat? Do people take pride in their work? Are they supportive? Or are they negative? The quality of officers' work will be affected as much by their morale as by their skills. Effective managers know that people's job performance is directly related to how they feel about the job, themselves, their peers, their managers and their agency.

Although improved morale will not always increase employees' effectiveness and productivity, it puts employees in the frame of mind to be productive. Given good supervision and good working conditions, employees with high morale will be extremely effective. As Andy Granatelli noted: "When you are making a success of something, it's not work. It's a way of life. You enjoy yourself because you are making your contribution to the world."

Indicators of Morale Problems

Good managers are always alert for changes in work attitudes that may indicate trouble. They might notice sullenness, irritability, indifference, tardiness or increased absenteeism. Among the most common indicators of morale problems are noticeably less positive attitude, loss of interest and enthusiasm, negativism and lack of respect. Other indicators are excessive absenteeism, sick leave and turnover; excessive sick leaves, longer lunch hours and/or breaks and coming in late and leaving early. Still other indicators include low productivity, less attention to personal appearance, many grievances and complaints and many accidents.

Indicators of low morale include lack of productivity, enthusiasm and cooperation; absenteeism; tardiness; grievances; complaints; and excessive turnover.

Managers may recognize these red flags in individual officers, or they may be pervasive throughout the department. In the latter case, the manager faces a much greater challenge. A first step is to identify *why* morale might be low. Seldom is the answer simple or singular.

To identify causes of morale problems, some managers distribute a survey that includes questions such as the following (to which respondents answer: strongly disagree, disagree, uncertain, agree or strongly agree):

1. This is a good department to work for.
2. My supervisor understands me.
3. My supervisor listens to my concerns.
4. I have the training I need to do a good job.

5. I have the equipment I need to do a good job.
6. I am proud to be a member of this department.

Such a survey not only helps identify areas that might be causing morale problems but also lets employees communicate their feelings and know that these feelings are important to the department. However, the results of the survey must be *used.* Employees who think the department is insensitive might use a lack of follow-through to support their contention.

Surveys are not the only way to identify factors contributing to a morale problem. Managers who communicate well with their subordinates can often discover problems simply by having an open-door policy and listening to what people say. The closer managers are to their employees, the easier it will be for them to recognize a change in morale before it becomes disruptive.

Reasons for Morale Problems

The underlying causes of morale problems are not always easy to determine. Individual morale can be low and the organizational morale high, or the reverse can be true. Some people point out that morale is related to happiness and well-being. Others say it is more related to work benefits. Still others believe it is a philosophical problem of self-fulfillment. In general, employees who work toward organizational goals are deemed to have high morale, and those who do not are deemed to have low morale.

If a law enforcement agency has inadequate, nonequitable salaries and fringe benefits, lacks modern equipment and does not provide adequate resources, morale is likely to be low. Measures must be taken to correct these inadequacies. If all these factors *are* met and morale is still low, the problem is probably centered in individual needs.

Causes for low morale include job dissatisfaction and failure to meet important individual needs.

One important cause of low morale is job dissatisfaction. Among the job-related factors contributing to low morale are lack of administrative support; ineffective supervision; lack of necessary equipment or training to perform effectively; lack of promotion opportunities; political interference; corruption within the department; the criminal justice system itself, which may appear to be a revolving door for criminals; and the image of the police frequently portrayed by the media.

In addition, police wages and salaries have never been high, although the total benefit package and sense of job security have always made the job desirable. Given that police endure a high level of stress, most certainly face an abnormal risk of injury or death on the job and have a higher rate of burnout than most workers, police positions are underpaid.

When individual morale is low, employees should first examine themselves. Mental attitudes toward superiors, fellow workers and the public have a great deal to do with job satisfaction.

Table 10.1
Worker and Supervisor Ratings Compared

Job Conditions	Worker Rating	Supervisor Rating
Full appreciation of work done	1	8
Feeling "in" on things	2	10
Sympathetic help on personal problems	3	9
Job security	4	2
Good wages	5	1
Work that keeps you interested	6	5
Promotion and growth in company	7	3
Personal loyalty to workers	8	6
Good working conditions	9	4
Tactful disciplining	10	7

Source: William B. Melincoe and John P. Peper. *Supervisory Personnel Development.* California State Police Officers Training Series, #76, Sacramento, CA, p. 87.

Perception, the angle from which people view things, makes a tremendous difference in what they see. For example, the difference between a cute little mischief-maker and a juvenile delinquent is whether the child is yours or someone else's.

A story about a young couple who opened a salmon cannery in Alaska also illustrates this point. They were having a hard time selling their salmon, despite an extensive advertising campaign. The problem was that their salmon was grey, not the pink salmon customers were used to. They pondered the problem for several days and then had a brainstorm. They changed the can's label, putting in bold letters right under the brand name "The only salmon guaranteed not to turn pink in the can." It worked.

A similar situation exists in how subordinates rate certain job factors and how managers rate the same factors. Consider the survey results summarized in Table 10.1. Full appreciation of work done and feeling "in" on things led the workers' list. These same factors were at the bottom of the supervisors' ratings. Similarly, good wages were at the top of the supervisors' list and in the middle of the workers' list. Such information is critical for managers to know.

For those who firmly believe in Abraham Maslow's hierarchy of needs, it may be time to check the employees' needs for affiliation, achievement and self-actualization.

Building Morale

The individual most able to raise or lower individual and department morale is the manager/supervisor.

Improving morale requires certain attitudes on the manager's part. First, managers must believe that subordinates *can* grow and change—they can improve their attitudes/morale given the right circumstances. Managers must be like the tailor, who, according to George Bernard Shaw, is the "only person who behaves sensibly because he takes new measurements every time he sees me."

Second, managers must be open and honest with their subordinates, treat them with respect and seek to understand them. Finally, managers must understand themselves. They must recognize their own prejudices, their own strengths and weaknesses, their own obstacles to high morale and their critical role as a model for others.

The story is told of the Reverend Billy Graham visiting a small town and asking a young boy how to get to the post office. After receiving directions, Dr. Graham invited the lad to come to the church and hear him explain to the townsfolk how to get to heaven. The boy declined, saying, "I don't think so. You don't even know how to get to the post office."

Credibility is crucial. Managers who seek to build morale must exhibit high morale themselves. Only then can they hope to raise the work unit's morale. Several options for morale building are available to managers and supervisors.

Options for building morale include:

- Being positive and upbeat.
- Setting clear, meaningful goals and objectives.
- Setting appropriate standards.
- Being fair.
- Making no promises that cannot be kept.
- Providing the necessary resources.
- Developing organizational and personal pride.
- Providing a sense of participation—teamwork.
- Treating each person as an individual.
- Giving deserved recognition.
- Criticizing tactfully.
- Avoiding the "boss" attitude.
- Communicating effectively.

People enjoy working with a boss who is cheerful and optimistic. Like magnets, people are drawn to the positive and repelled by the negative. An upbeat attitude is contagious—as is a negative attitude. A shoe manufacturer recently ran an ad for slippers that read: "Keeps your feet from getting cold." The ad was a total flop. When the copy was changed to read "Keeps your feet warm and comfortable," sales doubled.

You have heard it before, but goals and objectives are at the heart of most management areas, and this certainly includes morale. Companies with the least employee turnover and the highest morale are those that have successfully communicated the company's mission and goals. Law enforcement executive managers should set department goals and objectives with the input of their subordinates—and this includes the line officers. The moment officers get the feeling they are not sharing in the department's goals, in what is going on, morale will drop, productivity will decrease and serious problems will arise.

Reasonable, clear, fair employee standards for conduct and behavior also should be established, published and made known. Employees expect this, and the law enforcement organization cannot function without these standards. As obvious as it may sound, it is critical that managers be fair in all aspects of the job. Most employees do not mind reasonably strict rules and procedures if they make sense and apply equally to everyone. Fairness is a common denominator for increased employee morale.

Likewise, managers should never promise things they cannot deliver. They should not be overly optimistic, trying to please their subordinates or telling them what they want to hear simply to keep them happy. It is very tempting to do so and to hope that things will work out for the best, but this can lead to problems.

Law enforcement employees need resources to do a good job and to feel good about themselves and what they do. Training is essential. All employees need to feel competent in the tasks for which they are responsible. Training also needs to be ongoing so officers are up to date. Their equipment should also be current and in good working condition.

The appearance of the station, the squad cars, the insignia on the squad car door, identification or name signs on each room in the station, desk name signs, uniforms that leave a favorable impression—all reflect morale. Many of these do not cost lots of money, but they can make a significant difference in how officers feel about themselves and their organization.

Organizational and personal pride are closely related. Employees like to work for an organization they can be proud of. All law enforcement organizations have individual identities based largely on management goals and objectives. Bring up the subject of department and personal pride at staff and department meetings. Do not just think you are the best; really work at being the best. Often, competing in intradepartmental competitions such as sharp-shooting, physical fitness or intradepartmental sports can contribute to a feeling of pride. These can also foster a sense of participation, another factor contributing to high morale.

Employees like to be in on things. They like to think that what they do counts. They want to be part of the action. Participation does not mean a brainstorming session or a debate every time change is needed, but there should be opportunity for employee input. If employees express good ideas, praise them. If an idea is not workable, explain why. Do not ask for input and then be negative about the ideas expressed.

Despite an emphasis on teamwork, every employee is an individual and must be recognized as such. Call them by the name they prefer to be called, including nicknames in appropriate situations. Take an interest in their problems. Employees who have problems at home cannot function at full efficiency on the job. Although managers cannot usually *do* anything about such problems, they can lend a sympathetic ear.

Too many law enforcement managers criticize when things go wrong but fail to praise when things go right. This is illustrated in the story about the first month of World War I, when generals were handling huge armies under unprecedented circumstances. On the Western Front, the Battle of the Marne ended the German advance, stabilized the front and saved France. Leading the French armies was Marshal Joffre, a soldier viewed by most as unimaginative. Years later when the battle was analyzed, military commentators tried to decide who should receive credit for this decisive victory. The commentators could come to no agreement other than that surely some general had made a crucial move at the correct moment. They decided to ask Marshal Joffre who was responsible. Joffre's reply was: "I really don't know who ought to get credit for the victory at the Marne. I know only one thing. If we had been defeated, everyone would have agreed at once that the fault was mine."

Show judgment in giving credit and praise. It can be carried to extremes so that subordinates come to rely on it for every task they complete. Such people are like the little boy who said to his dad, "Let's play darts. I'll throw and you say 'Wonderful.'"

A wise manager once said, "That criticism is best which sounds like an explanation." It is easy to be critical. The real management challenge is to come up with constructive alternatives. Several other considerations are important when criticism is necessary.

- Be certain of the facts. Do not make mountains out of molehills.
- Correct in private; praise in public.
- Be objective and impersonal. Do not compare one officer unfavorably to another.
- Ask questions; do not accuse. Allow those you are correcting to explain themselves.
- Focus on the action that needs correcting, not on the individual officer. Emphasize what is to be done, not what is wrong.

The legitimate purpose of criticism is *not* to humiliate but to help subordinates do better next time. Remember that criticism is seldom as effective as praise in changing behavior. Before managers give a person a "kick in the pants," no matter how much it is deserved, they should raise their sights and *try* to give a pat on the back instead.

Managers should also avoid the "boss" attitude, striving to be friendly yet businesslike, and to think of "We" instead of "I." When appropriate, they should smile and be enthusiastic.

Finally, managers should communicate effectively. Communication builds morale. Employees want to know what is going on and how they are doing. Employees cannot act or react in a vacuum. Department newsletters, letters of commendation, constructive criticism, news releases, department bulletin boards, personal conversations, department or staff meetings—all are forms of communication.

It is demoralizing for officers to hear inside information from news media rather than from their superiors. It is essential that police administrators keep their officers informed. Among the ways to do this are newsletters, attending roll call, going on ride-alongs and simply walking around the department, sometimes referred to as Management by Walking Around (MBWA). Administrators who take this approach should be prepared to hear negative comments, especially at first.

Promotions and Morale

Management positions within the law enforcement profession are more limited than in almost any other profession. This can cause severe morale problems. The promotion process must be fair, and those who want promotions must be helped in their quest.

Not everyone is management material. Those who are not should be guided into seeking satisfaction on the job in other ways, perhaps in developing a specialty the agency needs. The future of law enforcement agencies rests in making the best use of personnel. Those who are best suited for management—who have leadership qualities and communication skills—are those who should be promoted.

Promotions must be fair and based on management qualities, not on technical skills or seniority.

According to Lunney (2002, p.1): "The promotion process in a well-administered police service is based on performance and potential, with the best decisions made in a spirit of objectivity and equity. There remains, however, a constant tension between objectivity on one hand and the inescapable influence of personal relationships on the other."

Written examinations have been the most frequently used technique to make promotional selections of mid- to lower-level police positions. Any examination should be validated for the type and size of the agency using it. Written examinations, oral examinations and on-the-job performance ratings can be used for promotional decisions.

Most law enforcement agencies use a civil service examination, both written and oral. It is common to require minimum or maximum ages, terms of service, specific types of experience and other criteria for eligibility to take the examination. Most merit systems provide similar examinations. Final selection of the top three candidates (or any pre-established number) is made from the written and oral examinations. The Civil Service Commission, the city manager, the mayor with the city council's approval or the law enforcement chief executive officer then makes the choice.

According to Booth (2002, p.71): "In any competition, success depends upon the knowledge, skills and abilities contestants have developed and practiced over time. . . . The very best candidates emerge from a point where three factors converge. The first factor is how well the candidate knows himself or herself. . . . The second convergent element is an understanding of the expectations of the organization. . . . The third element is an understanding of the problem being addressed. The candidate who has given some thought to the kinds of problems he or she will be confronted with once he or she is promoted will have a much better chance of success than the candidate who is being hit cold with these types of issues during a promotional testing process."

Kroecker (2000, p.67) recommends that an effective approach to responding to an aging management workforce is: "to link the promotional process and training and development efforts in a way that raises the overall capabilities of the staff while also identifying the most qualified individuals for positions."

Assessment Centers

A trend is to use an **assessment center** to select those eligible for promotion, especially at the upper levels. As Hilgenfeldt (2000, p.237) explains: "An assessment center is quite different from the traditional forms of testing since it utilizes multiple instruments to measure and evaluate a candidate's performance in a variety of exercises and scenarios."

Hurley (2001, p.175) notes: "Assessment centers offer police managers a 'snapshot' of any candidate's performance at a higher rank. Candidates for promotion are assessed by an independent organization that is detached from the police agency and local politics. This is key: it removes personality conflicts, friendship and influences from the promotional process, a frequent complaint of those who are passed over for promotions." Examples of the methods used in assessment centers are contained in Table 10.2.

The total assessment typically is organized into three phases.

Assessment centers use three phases:

1. Testing: written examination, verbal screening and psychological testing
2. Oral board interview, situational testing, leaderless group discussion and individual psychological interview
3. Polygraph examination, background check, physical examination and officer/staff interviews

Table 10.2
Typical Management Assessment Center Methods

Method	Description	Example Traits Analyzed
Management game or simulation	Participants perform in a simulated setting, sometimes with a computer simulation, make necessary decisions and analyze the results.	Organizing ability, financial aptitude, decision making, efficiency under stress, adaptability and leadership capacity
Leaderless group discussions	Participants in a group with no formally appointed leader are asked to solve a business problem.	Aggressiveness, persuasiveness, verbal skills, flexibility and self-confidence
In-basket exercise	A mail in-basket for an ill executive is given to the participants to analyze, to set priorities and to take action on.	Organizing ability, decision making under stress, conceptual skills, ability to delegate and concern for others
Role playing	Participants are asked to take the roles of hypothetical employees, as in a performance evaluation interview.	Insight, empathy to others, human and technical skills and sensitivity to others
Psychological testing	A series of pencil-and-paper instruments is completed by the participants.	Reasoning, interests, aptitudes, communication tendencies, leadership and group styles, motivation profile and the like
Case analysis	Participants are given a case to analyze individually and present to a group of evaluators.	Verbal ability, diagnostic skills, conceptual skills, technical skills and so on
In-depth interviews	Participants are interviewed by raters—usually after some of the above exercises have been completed—regarding a variety of personal interests, skills and aptitudes.	Verbal ability, self-confidence, managerial skills, commitment to career and so on

Source: International City Managers Association, 1120 G Street, NW, Washington, DC, p. 253. Reprinted by permission.

During the second phase, candidates confront hypothetical problems that managers typically encounter. At the end of the second phase, candidates are ranked using the information from the first two phases. A predetermined number are selected in rank order to complete the third phase.

Whether an assessment center is used or the promotions are done in-house, whenever possible it is usually best to promote from within the agency. This is not always easy. Sometimes this decision is not up to the immediate supervisor or manager. But studies and common sense show that passing over qualified personnel to bring in an outsider almost invariably erodes morale.

When possible, promote from within.

Seeing colleagues receive a promotion can be highly motivating for those who also want to be promoted.

Strategic Career Planning

Arnold (2000, p.63) points out: "Few police officers plan their careers. Most do not focus on promotion possibilities early enough, and have not prepared enough—either through formal education or assignment selection—to equip themselves for leadership roles. Strategic career planning can be a kind of road map to professional success."

According to Fulton (2000, p.118): "Preparation is the key to getting promoted." He suggests 10 steps to promotion: (1) Start early. (2) Learn from others. (3) Avoid problems. (4) Be committed. (5) Prepare, prepare, prepare. (6) Make your intentions known. (7) Get a mentor. (8) Learn the rules. (9) Get the resources you need. And (10) Do your best. He concludes: "Your best chance for getting promoted is to be a professional at every rank you hold, prepare for the next rank, and always do the best you can."

Police/Family Programs

The police career is difficult to keep separate from officers' personal lives. Tasks and experiences are often intermixed with family well-being. Job stress is often family stress. Traumatic experiences do not end with the termination of the shift or on arrival home. Incidents that result in shooting a suspect or end with an officer being injured or killed on duty are endured by the family as well as by the officer. Police family members often have no more understanding of the police job than the average layperson. To compound the problem, police spouses often have careers in addition to family responsibilities. The officers' daily interactions with the seamy side of life and with problem people may cause a distorted, unbalanced view of society. In severe cases this can lead to alcoholism, drug abuse, separation, divorce or even suicide.

To cope with these problems, a number of police departments have experimented with police-spouse seminars to explain work shifts, police jargon, salaries, fringe benefits, types of police incidents, types of people police come in contact with, police equipment, police training and panel discussions on selected subjects, with the panel consisting of officers, spouses and experts on the subject. Expectations and fears of officers and their spouses are discussed freely. Spouses often form support groups that meet regularly or when a crisis arises.

An Innovative Program for Maintaining Veteran Officers' Morale

Promotions are extremely hard to come by in law enforcement, and many officers do not want them, preferring to drive a squad car rather than sit behind a desk. Administrators are often faced with the difficult task of keeping morale high for patrol officers who have been on the job for several years. One innovative approach to this challenge was developed by the Pierce County Sheriff's Department in Tacoma, Washington—the Master Patrol Officer program (MPO). This program has three distinct phases: the Entry level, the Advanced Patrol Officer level and the Master Patrol Officer level. Table 10.3 describes the requirements for each.

The Master Patrol Officer point system gives credit for education, experience and involvement in law enforcement service or in the community. Table 10.4 gives the highlights of the Master Patrol Officer point system. Physical recognition of Master Patrol Officer status is provided by double chevrons or corporal stripes worn by MPOs.

Summary

Motivation is an inner or outer drive to meet a need or goal. Researchers who have studied motivation and proposed theories about it include Maslow, Herzberg, Skinner, Vroom, and Morse and Lorsch.

Maslow's hierarchy of needs is, in the ascending order they need to be met, physiological, safety and security, social, esteem and self-actualization. Herzberg's hygiene factors are tangible rewards that can cause dissatisfaction if lacking. Motivator factors are intangible rewards that can create satisfaction.

Skinner's reinforcement theory suggests that positive reinforcement increases a given behavior and negative reinforcement decreases a given behavior. Positive reinforcement is more effective than negative reinforcement. In addition, the closer in time to the behavior, the more effective the reinforcement will be.

Vroom's expectancy theory suggests that employees will choose the level of effort that matches the performance opportunity for reward. Morse and Lorsch's contingency theory suggests fitting tasks, officers and the agency's goals so that officers can feel competent.

No matter what theory or combination of theories law enforcement managers subscribe to, external and internal rewards are important. Among the most common external motivators or tangible rewards are salary, bonuses, insurance, retirement plans, favorable working conditions, paid vacation and holidays, titles and adequacy of equipment. Internal motivators or intangible rewards include goals, achievement, recognition, self-respect, opportunity for advancement, opportunity to make a contribution and belief in individual and departmental goals. Law enforcement work can be made more interesting and motivating in three important ways: job rotation, job enlargement and job enrichment.

Morale is a person's or group's state of mind, level of enthusiasm and amount of involvement with work and life. Indicators of low morale include lack of productivity, enthusiasm and cooperation; absenteeism; tardiness; grievances; complaints and excessive turnover. Causes of low morale include job dissatisfaction and failure to meet important individual needs.

The individual most able to raise or lower individual and department morale is the manager/supervisor. Options for building morale include being positive

Table 10.3
MPO Requirements of the Pierce County Sheriff's Department (Tacoma, Washington)

Phase I

Entry Level Requirements

1. Three years as a Deputy Sheriff with the Pierce County Sheriff's Department.
2. Last two evaluations must have a total score of 70 or better. A current evaluation from within the last 12 months must be provided.
3. Candidates must apply with a typewritten letter which must be endorsed by his/her immediate supervisor.

Phase II

Advanced Patrol Officer Requirements

1. A total of six years with the department, 50 percent of which must have been spent in the field force.
2. Upon completion of the sixth year, a candidate's last two evaluations must be 80 or above with no individual factor below 70.
3. An average shooting score of expert or better while in this phase.
4. At least four points accumulated as an accident-free driver (entry-level time included).
5. Three years to complete this phase.

Education:

Sixteen points total required with a minimum of eight points from any approved law enforcement training classes. Points may be accumulated for higher learning achieved prior to coming into the department.

Experience:

Fifteen points total with a minimum of six from specialized support assignments from within the department.

Major involvement:

No points necessary for this segment. However, points may be earned for use in Phase III.

Phase III

Master Patrol Officer Requirements

1. A total of ten years minimum with the department, 70 percent of which must have been spent in field force patrol (3 years advanced and 4 years master phase).
2. Accumulate a total of seven years of accident-free driving points.
3. Shooting scores shall average expert or better during this 4-year phase.
4. Typewritten letter requesting consideration as an MPO and showing that all requirements have been met.
5. Evaluations must be 80 percent or above with no individual factor below 70 percent.

Education:

Eight additional points accumulated from law enforcement training classes.

Experience:

Twelve points total with three points required from specialized support assignments within the department.

Major involvement:

Six points total.

Source: Paul D. Thrash. "An Incentive Program: Boosting Morale of Veteran Officers." *Law Enforcement Technology,* October 1992, p. 53. © PTN Publishing Co. *Law Enforcement Technology,* October 1992. Reprinted by permission.

Table 10.4
The MPO Point System

Education		Major Involvement	
AA degree or 90 quarter hours	*4 pts*	In House participation or service on:	
BA degree	*6 pts*	Board of Professional Standards	*2 pts per year*
MA degree	*8 pts*	FTO Advisory Board	*2 pts per year*
PhD degree	*10 pts*	Accident Review Board	*2 pts per year*
Approved law enforcement classes	*1 pt per 8 hr class*	Radio Users Committee	*2 pts per year*
Mandatory or refresher classes do not receive points. A maximum of four points for a one-week school and eight points for a two-week school.		Special Project Boards or Committee	*1 pt per project*
		Publish an article in a law enforcement-related magazine or journal	*1 pt per article*

Experience	
Accident-free driving record	*1 pt per year*
Master shooter (96 percent and above)	*2 pts*
No sick leave usage	*0.5 pt per year*
Medal/awards	*3 pts per year*
Specialized support assignments (K-9, Juvenile, Civil, Traffic, DARE, Warrants, etc.)	*3 pts per year (maximum 6 pts)*
Field Training Officer (FTO)	*5 pts per year (maximum of 10)*
Assigned responsibilities (SWAT, Bomb Squad, Dive Team, Search/Rescue)	*2 pts per year (maximum of 6)*

Community Involvement	
Involvement in any community service project or social service project as a leader or board member. a) sports b) other civilian non-profit organization c) Military Reserve Service	*2 pts per project*
Involvement as an officer (1-year minimum) a) union/guild b) law enforcement c) any statewide or national law enforcement support group approved by the MPO board.	*2 pts per project*
Serves as president of any of the above organizations for a minimum of one year	*3 pts per office*

Source: Paul D. Thrash. "An Incentive Program: Boosting Morale of Veteran Officers." *Law Enforcement Technology,* October 1992, p. 56. © PTN Publishing Co. *Law Enforcement Technology,* October 1992. Reprinted by permission.

and upbeat; setting clear, meaningful goals and objectives; setting appropriate standards; being fair; making no promises that cannot be kept; providing necessary resources; developing organizational and personal pride; providing a sense of participation—teamwork; treating each person as an individual; giving deserved recognition; criticizing tactfully; avoiding the "boss" attitude; communicating effectively; and accepting what cannot be changed.

One important factor affecting morale is promotions. Promotions must be fair and based on management qualities, not on technical skills or seniority. Some law enforcement agencies use assessment centers to determine promotions. Such centers typically involve three phases: (1) testing: written examination, verbal screening and psychological testing; (2) oral board interview, situational testing, leaderless group discussion and individual psychological interview and (3) polygraph examination, background check, physical examination and officer/staff interviews. When possible, law enforcement administrators should promote from within to improve overall morale.

Discussion Questions

1. What motivates you?
2. What do you consider your basic needs? Write down the top five.
3. What are five motivators that make you do better work?
4. What would not motivate you?
5. Do you agree or disagree with the following statement: "It is not possible to motivate anyone." Why?
6. What makes *your* on-the-job morale go down? Go up?
7. What are some ways to give personal recognition for a job well done?
8. What job conditions make you feel best?
9. How do morale and motivation interact?
10. If you could make one change in your life that would improve your morale, what would that change be?

InfoTrac College Edition Assignment

Use InfoTrac College Edition to answer the Discussion Questions as appropriate.

Search for a recent article on *what is motivational on the job*—either in the business world or in law enforcement. Outline your findings and give the full source. Be prepared to share your findings with the class.

OR

Read and outline "The Work Itself as a Motivator" by John L. White.

References

Arnold, Jon. "Strategic Planning for Career Development." *The Police Chief,* April 2000, pp.61–63, 196.

Booth, Walter S. "Three Common Factors of Successful Promotion Candidates." *The Police Chief,* July 2002, pp.71–75.

Brody, David C.; DeMarco, Christianne; and Lovrich, Nicholas P. "Community Policing and Job Satisfaction: Suggestive Evidence of Positive Workforce Effects from a Multijurisdictional Comparison in Washington State." *Police Quarterly,* June 2002, pp.181–205.

Fulton, Roger. "10 Steps to a Promotion." *Law Enforcement Technology,* May 2000, p.118.

Fulton, Roger. "Motivate Your Officers." *Law Enforcement Technology,* October 2001, p.226.

Hackman, J.R. and Oldham, G.R. "Development of the Job Diagnostic Survey." *Journal of Applied Psychology,* 1976, pp.153–170.

Herzberg, Frederick. "The Human Need for Work." *Industry Week,* July 24, 1978, pp.49–52.

Hilgenfeldt, Keith M. "Promotional Assessment Centers." *Law and Order,* 2000, pp.237–239.
Hurley, James J. "Assessment Centers: Judging Promotability without Conflict." *Law and Order,* October 2001, pp.175–176.
Johnson, Tami L. "Attracting and Retaining Employees." *Minnesota Business,* February 2001, pp.68–69.
Kroecker, Timothy. "Developing Future Leaders: Making the Link to the Promotional Process." *The Police Chief,* March 2000, pp.64–69.
Lonsway, Kimberly and Campbell, Deborah. "Retaining Women Officers." *Law and Order,* May 2002, pp.107–111.
Lunney, Robert. "Puzzling through the Politics." *Subject to Debate,* January 2002, pp.1, 4–5.
McDonald, Tom. "Eyes on the Prize? The Old Incentives Don't Work." *Successful Meetings,* July 2000, p.25.
Orrick, W. Dwayne. "Calculating the Cost of Police Turnover." *The Police Chief,* October 2002, pp.100–103.
Sherwood, Charles W. "Job Design, Community Policing, and Higher Education: A Tale of Two Cities." *Police Quarterly,* June 2000, pp.191–212.
Van Brocklin, Valerie. "Reawakening the Spirit of Policing." *The Police Chief,* August 2001, pp.78–81.
Warrell, George III. "Turnover: A Small Agency Nightmare." *Law and Order,* September 2000, pp.59–61.

Book-Specific Web Site

Go to the *Management and Supervision in Law Enforcement* Web site at http://info.wadsworth.com/05346160654 for student and instructor resources, including Internet assignments and case studies.

CHAPTER 11

Discipline and Problem Behaviors

I would rather try to persuade a man to go along, because once I have persuaded him, he will stick. If I scare him, he will stay just as long as he is scared, and then he is gone.

—Dwight D. Eisenhower

Do You Know?

- What discipline is?
- How morale and discipline differ?
- What the purpose of discipline is?
- What the foundation for most disciplinary actions is?
- What a fundamental management right is?
- What a primary rule for the timing of discipline is?
- What to consider when assessing penalties?
- What steps are usually involved in progressive discipline?
- What balance of consequences analysis is?
- What consequences are most powerful?
- How managers can use the balance of consequences?
- What the PRICE Method consists of?
- How much time effective praise and reprimands require?
- What ratio of praise to blame is usually needed?
- What strokes managers can use?

Can You Define?

appeal
balance of consequences analysis
comprehensive discipline
demotion
disciplinary actions
discipline
dismissal
gunnysack approach
insubordination
just cause
negative discipline
negligent retention
one-minute managing
positive discipline
PRICE Method
progressive discipline
reprimand
self-discipline
stroke approach
summary discipline
summary punishment
suspension
termination

INTRODUCTION

Managers are challenged in the area of discipline as in no other. Values have changed, and court decisions have supported more liberal views of discipline over the past decades. The days of autocratic, despotic discipline are gone.

Imposing some form of discipline is almost sure to be a part of law enforcement managers' responsibilities during their careers. Managers must be prepared to exercise this responsibility when necessary. Most people assume that when discipline is discussed, it refers to punishment in its various forms. But discipline is far broader than punishment.

This chapter begins with a definition of discipline, followed by a description of positive, constructive self-discipline and a look at the typical rules and regulations for law enforcement departments. Of importance when considering discipline is the tension between clarity of role and creativity, as well as common problem behaviors you can anticipate.

Next, the need for managers to accept that positive discipline is not always effective and to recognize the need for negative discipline/punishment is examined, including guidelines for administering negative discipline, for using progressive discipline, for using summary punishment and for providing a process to appeal and important legal considerations. This is followed by a discussion of comprehensive discipline, including such systems as the balance of consequences analysis, the PRICE Method, one-minute managing and the stroke approach. The chapter concludes with a brief description of an effective disciplinary system.

Discipline Defined

Discipline is training expected to produce a desired behavior—controlled behavior.

Discipline should never be an end in itself. It should be used to develop highly trained, efficient law enforcement officers. Those officers with the highest performance have a high level of determination, pride, confidence and self-discipline. **Self-discipline** is a set of self-imposed rules governing a person's self-control. Leaders throughout the world set degrees of discipline, as do religions. Discipline can be a form of voluntary obedience to instructions, commands or expected demeanor.

Anderson (2001, p.78) describes Sir Robert Peel's emphasis on discipline: "With an understanding that discipline built effective performance, once selected, officers were bound by what has been referred to as an Iron Discipline. Peel's reforms, particularly in regards to discipline, were not only intended to promote and preserve the public peace, but to promote and preserve the public trust." Anderson contends: "As providence would have it, the iron discipline that Sir Robert Peel advocated still remains an effective remedy against the arduous nature of the profession, both on a personal and organizational front."

Discipline is closely related to morale. As discussed in Chapter 10, morale is a state of mind, an employee's attitude. Discipline, in contrast, is a state of affairs, or how employees act.

Morale is how a person feels; discipline is how a person acts.

Morale and discipline are closely related because the level of morale affects employees' conduct. The higher the morale, the fewer the discipline problems. Conversely, the lower the morale, the more likely discipline problems will erupt.

The purpose of discipline is to promote desired behavior, which may be done by encouraging acceptable behavior or punishing unacceptable behavior.

Positive, Constructive Self-Discipline

Positive, constructive self-discipline, like self-motivation, is usually most effective. **Positive discipline** uses training to foster compliance with rules and regulations and performance at peak efficiency. Miraglia (2000, p.69) suggests: "The instructional purpose of discipline in basic training is to provide experience in self-confidence and courage." He (p.70) also suggests: "Police officers need to learn to act independently and as a part of a cohesive disciplined unit."

Maintaining Positive Discipline

It is to law enforcement managers' advantage to maintain a high degree of self-discipline within subordinates. They might begin by exercising self-discipline as an example.

When employees willingly follow the department's rules and regulations and put forth full effort to accomplish their individual and departmental goals, positive discipline prevails. The Navy would call this a "taut ship." But officers need to know the rules and what is expected of them.

Knowledge of Rules, Regulations and Expected Behaviors

Everybody should understand what they can and cannot do. The more employees know, the more able they are to conduct themselves as expected. To inform employees, managers might post rules on bulletin boards, distribute Standard Operating Procedure manuals and discuss the rules at meetings.

An agency's policy and procedure manual is the foundation on which most discipline must be based.

Martin (2002, p.114) suggests that policy and procedure manuals "must reflect reality, practicality and the underlying philosophy that accomplishing the departmental mission is more important than detail-oriented rules." He (p.116) also suggests: "If a procedures manual is to have any credibility, it must be easy to comply with and easy to understand. . . . Short and concise documents are more likely to be read and understood than lengthy ones."

According to Carpenter (2000, p.1): "A well-written policy and procedure manual serves as the foundation of a professional law enforcement agency." Fulton (2001a, p.118) suggests that, at minimum, the policy and procedure manual should cover sexual harassment prevention, pursuit, relief of duties and use of force. He also recommends regular review of such policies.

Officers should have input on rules. If they have a voice in establishing the rules, they are more likely to support them. Having a few rules that everyone supports is better than having many rules that are violated.

Typical Rules and Regulations for Law Enforcement Departments

Rules and regulations are often established by civil service boards and will vary with each department. Officers should be aware of all rules and regulations, and all members of the agency are subject to disciplinary action if they violate these.

General Conduct

Officers are expected to report for duty at the designated time and place. They must not engage in disorderly conduct or accept gifts from suspects, prisoners or defendants. Officers must refrain from using unnecessary force on any person. Officers must object and refuse to obey an immoral or illegal order.

Performance of Duty

Officers must preserve the law, protect life and property and enforce federal statutes, state laws and county and city ordinances. Officers are required to discharge their duties calmly and firmly, to act together and to assist and protect each other to maintain law and order. Any officer who fails to comply, by act or omission, with any order, procedure, rule or regulation of the department or who acts in the performance of official duties in a way that could discredit himself or herself, the department or any other member of the department may be considered in neglect of duty. Officers must be courteous and respectful in dealing with the public and respond promptly to all calls for assistance from citizens or other officers.

Prohibited Acts while on Duty

Officers should not congregate in the dispatch area or engage in horseplay or loud, boisterous conversations in public view or hearing. They should keep their quarters, lockers, vehicles and desks neat, clean and orderly. Officers should not smoke while in contact with or serving the public or loiter in cafes, drive-ins, service stations or other public places.

Other Restrictions on Behavior

Officers must not knowingly make a false report, either oral or written. For unionized law enforcement organizations, relevant provisions of the labor agreement must be considered. Some supervisors fear that with a union contract they cannot make discipline stick. This is *not* true. No union contract protects workers from discipline when a valid work rule is violated.

Maintaining discipline is a fundamental management right.

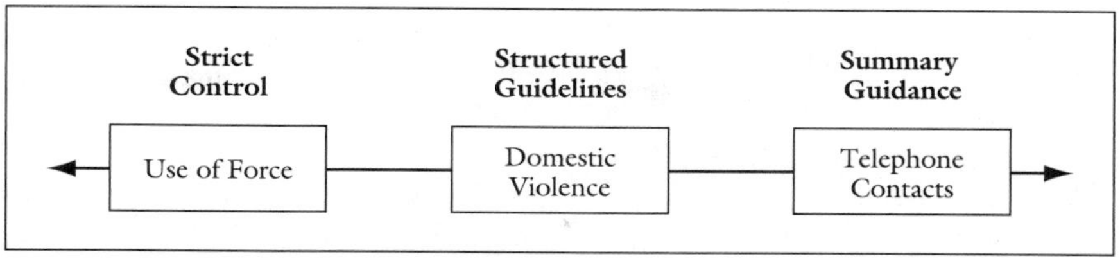

Figure 11.1
The Continuum of Policy: Levels and Examples

Source: Geoffrey P. Alpert and William C. Smith. "Developing Police Policy: An Evaluation of the Control Principle." *American Journal of Police*, 1994, p.9. Reprinted by permission.

Policy vs. Discretion

Although clear policies and procedures are necessary, they can be overdone. Too often the policy and procedure manual collects dust on the shelf because it is just too big. Effective managers recognize when control is necessary and when discretion should be allowed. Policies should be made to cover high-risk, low-frequency police functions, for example, use of deadly force and high-speed pursuits. Other police functions, such as most domestic dispute calls, require discretion within guidelines. Yet other functions, such as telephone contacts with citizens, may actually be hindered by controlling policies. Figure 11.1 shows a continuum on which control and discretion may be viewed.

Clarity of Role vs. Creativity

Specific rules and regulations leave little doubt as to what is expected of officers. This emphasis on formal rules is the result of three developments: the need for due process in discipline; protection against civil litigation; and the accreditation movement. Despite this emphasis on rules and regulations, the question arises: Do such written directives help officers learn the correct way to do law enforcement work and motivate them to do so, or do they send a message to officers that they are not trusted?

An excessive number of rules may discourage innovation, risk taking, imagination and commitment to the department's mission. The trend in business is just the opposite. Control is achieved not through formal, written rules and regulations but by developing team spirit and a commitment to shared values.

The administrator's challenge is to lead by instilling the desired values and culture within the organization. This might include gearing recruiting, selecting and socializing toward basic departmental values and basing assignments, promotions and other rewards on these basic values. They must also sometimes deal with problem behaviors.

Common Problem Behaviors

In local law enforcement agencies, the most frequent charges are intoxication on the job, insubordination, frequent tardiness, negligence, prohibited moonlighting, incompetence or unsatisfactory performance, improper handling of evidence, violation of a municipal ordinance, conduct unbecoming an officer, use of abusive/racial/ethnic language, failure to report for duty or leaving duty without permission, abusive actions against prisoners or people under arrest and careless operation of a vehicle. Among the most challenging and serious problem behaviors are substance abuse, use of excessive force, corruption, sexual harassment and insubordination.

Substance Abuse in the Workplace

Telltale signs of substance abuse in the workplace include an increase in absenteeism, employee grievances, employee theft, accidental injuries and workers' compensation claims. Other signs include a decrease in job interest, productivity and quality of work.

Managers should recognize the symptoms of alcohol or drug abuse. If they suspect an employee is abusing alcohol or drugs, they should never accuse the employee of doing so because this could open the manager and the department to a slander or defamation of character lawsuit. Rather, focus on job deficiencies and corrective action. Show a genuine concern for the employee's problem and attempt to refer him or her to a qualified specialist. Give officers ample opportunity to seek assistance. Follow up if an employee enters a treatment program.

Use of Excessive Force

Use of excessive force has always been difficult, resulting in numerous lawsuits. Use of force is sometimes a necessary part of the job, but determining what is reasonable is highly subjective. According to Rogers (2001, p.82): "Use of force vs. excessive use of force affects every American police department in the country."

The landmark case in use of force is *Graham v. Connor* (1989) in which the Court held: "The calculus of reasonableness must embody allowance for the fact that police officers are often forced to make split-second judgments—in circumstances that are tense, uncertain, and rapidly evolving—about the amount of force that is necessary in a particular situation." As Nowicki (2002b, p.20) explains: "The standard, according to this decision, is the 'reasonably objective officer.'"

Bob Boyle, secretary of the Boston Police Patrolmen's Association, and Jamarhl Crawford, Boston chairman of the New Black Panther Party, discuss recent police shootings of citizens, September 12, 2002. Discussions such as these help create and maintain clear policies regarding the use of force.

AP Photo/Angela Rowlings

The IACP use of force project (*Police Use of Force in America 2001,* p.1) defines *force* as "that amount of effort required by police to compel compliance from an unwilling subject." This includes physical, chemical, impact, electronic and firearm force. The IACP defines *excessive use of force* as "the application of an amount and/or frequency of force greater than that required to compel compliance from a willing or unwilling subject."

According to the study (p.i) police used force at a rate of 3.61 times per 10,000 calls for service. In other words, police did *not* use force 99.9639 percent of the time. Physical force was the most common force used, followed by chemical force and then impact. Arrests were the most frequent circumstance of use of force (39 percent), followed by disturbances (21 percent), traffic stops (14 percent), domestics (11 percent), drunk/disorderly (9 percent) and investigation (6 percent). Forty-six percent of all use-of-force incidents occurred when the subject was intoxicated or under the influence of drugs.

Between 1994 and 2000, of the 7,495 force-related complaints reported, 750 were sustained; that is, excessive force was used 0.42 percent of the time. In other words, excessive force was *not* used in 99.583 percent of all reported cases.

Lathrop (2000, p.17) cautions: "Officers must use only the level and amount of force reasonably necessary to accomplish a law enforcement objective." He recommends: "Many different types of a force option continuum exist. Every law enforcement agency should establish one that fits their needs and use it as part of the review process."

Use-of-force expert Nowicki (2001a, p.35) describes the Use of Force Model used by the Federal Law Enforcement Training Center (FLETC). This model has five levels. Level One is the Compliant Level where no use of force is usually reasonable. Level Two is the Resistive (Passive) Level where the subject does not follow the officer's commands. Force options here include guiding or directing the subject through hands-on techniques. Level Three is the Resistive (Active) Level, which occurs when a subject actively resists arrest. Level Three force options include joint manipulation or restraints, leverage techniques, pressure points or even OC (pepper) spray, with a warning given first under proper circumstances. Level Four is the Assaultive (bodily harm) Level, a direct physical attack on an officer or others. Appropriate force options at this level include strikes with hands, fists, elbows or knees; kicks; baton strikes; and forcefully directing the subject to the ground. Level Five is the Assaultive (serious bodily harm or death) Level, where the appropriate response would be deadly force.

Despite the popularity of use-of-force continuums, Williams (2002, p.14) cautions: "Force continuums often represent an unrealistic, almost wishful ideal." He (p.15) notes: "Self-imposed requirements of a force continuum can cause various consequences. While sincerely attempting to adhere to the policies and training that they have received about employing force continuums, officers can encounter threats to their personal safety and can face departmental, as well as civil, liability." Williams (p.18) concludes: "While use of force stands as a difficult issue for all law enforcement agencies, force continuums often represent an additional obstacle in the overall debate. Policies that require officers to strictly adhere to force continuums can cause problems not only for the officers but also for the public they serve."

Petrowski (2002, p.24) stresses: "It is not prudent to use an escalating force continuum when training officers to use force in defense of life. Force continua perpetuate hesitation and exacerbate the natural reluctance of officers to apply significant force even when faced with a serious threat." He suggests that officers be trained to differentiate between the two circumstances giving rise to use of force: (1) an imminent threat of harm and (2) effecting the seizure of a *non-threatening* subject who is resisting or attempting to escape. Petrowski (p.25) asserts: "The cornerstone of use-of-force training should be threat assessment."

Rosenbaum (2001, p.71) suggests: "There are tools available to police managers who want to be proactive in the area of use of force in order to help guide officer behavior, to teach proper use of force, to correct it when it is on the borderline, to deal with it through discipline when it crosses over that line. One of these tools is clear policies regarding use of force."

Use of force policies should be brief and follow state and federal laws governing officers' action. Grossi (2002, p.20) contends: "A policy that is tactically sound allows for contingencies. As most officers know, police use of force is a reactive process. We react to a suspect's actions. So a good use of force policy has built-in contingencies." He suggests that force policies must also be tactically sound and administratively feasible.

One way to reduce the force needed might be using K-9s as suggested by Smith (2000, p.36): "In light of several court decisions around the country, consider using law enforcement-trained K-9s as an alternative—and safer—means of applying force."

According to Nowicki (2001b, p.31): "Even the most professional law enforcement agencies may occasionally be sued through a 1983 action involving use of force." He (2002a, p.6) stresses: "Police officers cannot sacrifice their personal safety for the sake of avoiding possible litigation." He notes: "Many officers would rather face a snarling Neanderthal with a gun than a slick attorney wearing a three-piece suit and armed with a subpoena." Nowicki (2002a, p.6) says: "There are three rules relating to use of force by any officer. Rule number one is you go home the same way as when you went to work: *Alive.* Rule number two is you don't go to prison. Rule number three is you keep your job. If your use of force is reasonable, you protect yourself, your agency, the community and even the assailant. But when in doubt, always remember rule number one."

The death of Amadou Diallo resulting from officers firing 41 shots, 19 of which hit him, is a case in point. As Fyfe (2000, p.1) points out: "Under the circumstances they faced, any reasonable cop would have feared imminent death." As Messina (2000, p.9) explains, four plainclothes officers observed Diallo duck into a doorway as they approached. Officer McMellon, with his shield hanging in front of him from a chain, said to Diallo: "Police Department, City of New York. We'd like to have a word with you." Diallo backed into the doorway, and McMellon told Diallo to stay where he was and keep his hands where they could see them, but Diallo turned toward the officers while pulling a black object from his pocket and going into what appeared to be a shooting stance. Officer Carroll yelled "Gun" and both officers fired. McMellon, trying to retreat, fell backward down the stairs, and the other two officers thought he had been shot, so they opened fire. In an experiment after the incident, 20 officers tried to get down the steps quickly in reverse, and 18 of them fell. The two who didn't were small female officers with little feet.

Fyfe (p.4) suggests: "The police assaults on Rodney King and Abner Louima were crimes—we should not confuse the Diallo tragedy with them. Neither the beating of King nor the beastial assault on Louima involved professionals trying to do properly what they were trained and expected to accomplish. Instead, the cops who went to jail for those offenses were thugs, who simply tried to teach 'troublesome' black men a lesson, and then lied about what they had done. That distinguishes these cases from what those four Bronx cops were attempting to do when they mistook Diallo's wallet for a gun; these four were acquitted not because the jury was manipulated, but because they had committed no crime."

Corruption

The problem of corruption was discussed in detail in Chapter 9 and is only briefly reviewed here. Corruption is of concern because officers in the field are exposed to numerous opportunities to benefit personally from actions they take against criminals. They may be offered bribes or come across huge amounts of drugs or cash. They may feel overworked, underpaid and therefore entitled to take what they consider just compensation for the risks they face on the job. Yet, whenever one member of a police department is found to be corrupt, the hundreds of thousands of honest, hardworking officers suffer. The problem of police corruption affects agencies of all sizes, in all areas of the country.

Sexual Harassment

Sexual harassment has increased in visibility during the past decade and has also resulted in numerous lawsuits. Sexual harassment is a type of sex discrimination prohibited by Title VII in federal law, as well as by most state laws. The federal government defines sexual harassment as "unwelcome sexual advances, requests for sexual favors, and other verbal or physical conduct of a sexual nature" ("Preventing Sexual Harassment," n.d., p.1).

There are basically two types of sexual harassment. The first type, quid pro quo harassment, involves a supervisor's demand for sexual favors from an employee in return for a job benefit. The second type, hostile-environment harassment, as the name implies, involves a hostile environment (whether created by co-employees or by supervisors). Pedersen (2001, p.130) reports: "The most common offenses, according to surveys of female officers are jokes, comments, cartoons, calendars and verbal harassment." She also reports: "A Florida study of 3,000 policewomen indicated that 69 percent claimed to have been sexually harassed on the job. Forty percent reported it occurred on a daily basis."

The police environment may be more conducive than others to sexual harassment because of the nature of the work, for example, investigating sex crimes and pornography rings. Some evidence also suggests that sexual harassment is significantly higher in male-dominated occupations. Women who report sexual harassment run the risk of the situation getting worse, of other officers refusing to talk to her or to cover her when she calls for backup. Says Pedersen (pp.120–121): "Breaking the code of silence can mean everyone will be against you, so some people quit and don't even make a report."

To prevent charges of sexual harassment, departments need a clear policy that identifies conduct that may constitute sexual harassment. The policy should also include a statement that such conduct will not be tolerated and that those found guilty of prohibited conduct will be subject to appropriate disciplinary action. According to Carlan and Byxbe (2000, p.124): "The failure to adopt a proactive and aggressive policy to eliminate sexual harassment is clearly a liability gamble."

However, as Fuss and Snowden (2000, p.65) caution: "Merely having a written policy is not enough. The policy must be disseminated, training sessions on applying the policy need to be held, and the policy needs to provide methods for reporting incidents. If an employee is harassed by his or her immediate supervisor, an alternative reporting system is needed." They (p.67) note: "A brief, easily administered survey can yield meaningful management results to help chiefs assess and monitor perceived sexual harassment in their departments."

Insubordination

Policing has traditionally followed a quasi-military structure, with higher-ranking officers authorized to give lawful orders to lower-ranking officers that must be obeyed, whether they personally agree with them or not. Failure to carry out such lawful orders can expose an officer to discipline for **insubordination.** Fulton (2000, p.150) says: "In law enforcement, insubordination is defined as a failure to obey a lawful and direct order from a supervisor."

Fulton notes: "Most cases of insubordination do not address clear-cut life or death public safety situations. Most insubordination cases brought before these bodies involve routine, day-to-day supervisor/subordinate relations that are rule, policy or procedural violations." He recommends: "Choose battles carefully. . . . Keep in mind that most insubordinate cases do not ultimately result in termination. That means that you may get that employee back again after the lengthy disciplinary process has only fined, suspended or reinstated that employee. That can be when the battle really begins. For this reason it's wise to choose your battles carefully."

Negative Discipline/ Punishment

Law enforcement managers at all levels will sometimes find it necessary to use negative discipline. **Negative discipline** uses reprimands and punishments for wrong behavior in an effort to compel expected behavior. In nonemergency situations, managers should make reasonable efforts to gain voluntary compliance. If that fails, managers must exercise the disciplinary responsibilities of their position.

Iris (2002, p.135) contends: "For minor deviations from departmental policies, counseling of an officer or retraining to address some perceived area of substandard performance may be appropriate. But for more serious or repeated infractions, the ability of a police chief to suspend or discharge an officer is a crucial tool." He (p.136) stresses: "The ability to impose discipline as necessary is vital to police executives. It is a crucial means to ensure that officers in their commands do the right thing—or at least, do not do the wrong thing."

Harris and Gilmartin (2000, pp.20–21) suggest: "Supervisors have a choice: pay now or pay later. The amount of time they spend preventing and dealing with problems early on is almost always insignificant compared to the time required to deal with problems after they have gotten out of control."

Fulton (2001b, p.170) offers guidelines for when a manager needs to point out a problem behavior to an officer. First, get the facts. Then criticize the conduct, not the person. Be specific and ask for an explanation. Assess whether the behavior can be changed. Try to say something positive to reinforce the overall worth of the officer to the department. Don't belabor the point. Make clear what you expect and reaffirm your support. Heller (2002, p.77) asks: "What better way to get the best from people than to let them know that you care about them?"

It is also crucial to document the meeting. Harris and Gilmartin (p.24) note: "Lack of documentation is one of the major reasons courts and less formal adjudicators have overturned disciplinary actions."

The purpose of negative discipline is to help offenders correct behavior and to send a message to others that such behavior is not acceptable. The ultimate decision to bring a disciplinary action may arise because an employee commits a number of minor violations or an obviously serious one. Those being disciplined must fully understand what they are being disciplined for and why. Managers must have the authority to exercise discipline and be willing to proceed through hearings and appeals if necessary. The discipline recommended should fit the offense and be neither excessively harsh nor lenient.

A primary rule of effective discipline is that it should be carried out as close to the time of the violation as possible.

Delays cause further problems. Witnesses may have left employment, different versions may be manufactured, or facts may be forgotten.

Disciplinary actions should be carried out in private to avoid embarrassment and defensiveness. One exception to the privacy rule is if an employee openly confronts a manager in front of others. In such cases the manager must take immediate, decisive action to maintain respect and control of the department.

Initial disciplinary action should be *corrective.* Only when corrective discipline, training and counseling have little or no effect should disciplinary action be punitive. Punishment has the disadvantage of showing what should not be done, rather than reinforcing what should be done.

Supervisors first need to identify which officers, through their actions or lack thereof, deserve punishment or other disciplinary action. They must then determine which action is most appropriate and how to administer it.

Identifying the Problem Performer—Early Warning Systems

Although the majority of officers in a department readily cooperate with supervisors and their performance requests, some resist supervisory requests by repeatedly challenging and questioning orders, and still others outright fail to perform. According to Walker et al. (2001, p.1): "It has become a truism among police chiefs that 10 percent of their officers cause 90 percent of the problems."

What is needed is a way to identify these problem officers early. Walker et al. (2000, p.132) suggest: "Early warning (EW) systems are data-driven management tools for identifying police officers with performance problems and for providing some intervention to correct those problems. EW systems have emerged as popular tools for enhancing police accountability." According to Arnold (2001, pp.80–81): "Early Warning Systems (EWS) were developed as proactive tools and have been utilized by some law enforcement agencies for over a decade with beneficial results. These systems have, to a limited degree, provided a 'heads up' regarding behavioral problems with police officers and afford the agency an opportunity to implement remedial action." However, as Rhyons and Brewster (2002, p.33) caution: "An early warning system is not a substitute for good supervision. Instead, it is a tool designed to help good supervisors become better." They (p.36) stress: "The buy-in of employees and employee groups or unions is critical to the success of any early warning system."

Green (2002, p.96) cautions: "Everyone may have a bad day, but if lack of performance continues it can become habitual and worsen." He (p.97) suggests: "Supervisors can set up their own early warning systems just by being observant of their employees and creating a working file to review. Careful notes on their observations can help link together seemingly minor occurrences and identify potential problems, such as officer-involved collisions, use of force, officer injuries, sick leave abuse, tardiness, poor appearance, complaints, productivity or anything that is felt to be important."

Schennum (2000, p.67) recommends: "When an officer starts to display problems, the FTO must bring them to the officer's attention immediately, both verbally and written." After problem officers have been identified, no matter at what stage in their employment, Schennum recommends that an Action Plan or a Performance Plan be developed to improve the deficient behavior. The goal is to successfully overcome the problem behavior.

According to Jones (2000, p.118): "A performance plan helps officers understand a department's performance standards. . . . If work is not up to par, the supervisors should discuss the causes of these performance problems with the officer and try to help the officer correct them." If the behavior does not improve, Jones (p.122) recommends a performance contract: "Performance contracts are used as a last resort before termination and are designed to keep the termination process legal and fair."

Managers need to be aware that problem performers are often master manipulators who use a variety of strategies, including diverting a supervisor's attention, blaming others, using humor, seeking pity, apologizing, agreeing with the supervisor or arguing with the supervisor.

Determining Penalties

Many variables enter into penalty determination; for example, is it a first offense or a repeated offense? Are there extenuating circumstances? Each case must be tried on its own facts, and penalties must be assessed in the same way. No single penalty will do justice to every set of circumstances. The penalty should have a legal and moral basis and should include an appeal process. Penalties should also be reasonable. If they are viewed as too lenient, they probably will not be enforced because it is not worth the effort. If they are too harsh, they may not be enforced because they are too severe.

The offense and offender, how the offense was committed and the offender's attitude and past performance are important considerations in assessing penalties.

Most law enforcement departments have either departmental or civil service rules and regulations that define which behaviors are violations and the penalty for each. Punishments vary from warnings to termination of employment. Some departments use a table of offenses, penalties and application of appropriate disciplinary actions. Appendix E contains a sample of such a table. Such tables are not to be used automatically. Supervisors must consider the specific circumstances carefully when evaluating offenses and penalties, including the employee's work history, contribution to the agency and probability of rehabilitation. *Each case must be considered individually.*

The most frequent **disciplinary actions** in municipal law enforcement employment are oral or written reprimands, efficiency rating demerits, summary punishment for minor offenses, withholding part or all of an officer's salary for a specified time, decrease of seniority rights, a fine, suspension, demotion in rank or dismissal.

Progressive Discipline

Many departments operate under the concept of progressive discipline. Employees are usually given a light penalty for the first infraction of a rule, a more severe penalty for the next infraction and so on. The primary objective of progressive discipline is to give employees a chance to voluntarily improve their performance and to clearly inform employees that stronger disciplinary actions will be taken if they do not correct the behavior.

Progressive discipline uses disciplinary steps based on the severity of the offense. The steps usually are:

- Oral reprimand.
- Written reprimand.
- Suspension/demotion.
- Discharge/termination.

The most frequent type of penalty is an oral or a written *warning* or **reprimand.** An *oral reprimand* is a conversation between a supervisor and an employee about a specific aspect of the employee's performance. It informs employees that continued behavior or level of performance will result in more serious action. The supervisor must provide specifics. Employees should know what to correct and how, and they must have sufficient time to make the correction before other action is taken. Normally employees cooperate and problem behavior is eliminated.

If the warning is important, the supervisor should make a written record and place it in the personnel file. A *written reprimand* is a formal written notice to the employee regarding significant misconduct, specific inadequate performance or repeated offenses for which the employee has received an oral reprimand. The same conditions apply as for a warning. The violation should be stated in detail, along with what actions will correct the behavior, a time limit, whether there have been previous oral warnings for the same conduct and what will occur if the employee does not correct the violation. A written reprimand is usually recommended for a violation that must be corrected immediately. It should be given by at least a first-line supervisor and perhaps a middle-line manager, with the supervisor as a witness. The employee should receive a copy of the written reprimand.

A warning or a reprimand sends a signal to employees that management has disapproved. It is best to handle all employee penalty matters in person. The procedure may permit the employee to state his or her position before management takes final action.

A **suspension,** being barred from a position, is the next most serious punishment. Suspensions may be with or without pay. Normally, suspensions are given after consultation with the middle manager and the executive manager. Suspensions with pay normally are given to provide time for management to investigate a situation. It is not in any way a finding of wrongdoing. For example, an officer who shoots and kills a suspect may be suspended with pay while the matter is investigated. A coroner's jury will probably convene, and management will consider its findings in making a final decision. If the officer's action was justified, the officer is returned to duty as though no action had been taken.

Suspensions may usually be appealed to the executive manager, city manager, civil service board or a special board. They may also be a matter for union support or denial.

The most serious forms of punishment are *demotion* and *dismissal* or *termination.* These actions are taken by the head of the law enforcement department or the government jurisdiction and are also subject to appeal. These actions are end-of-the-road punishments, administered in very serious first offenses or in situations in which the employees have disregarded other warnings, reprimands and suspensions.

A **demotion** places an employee in a position of lower rank and pay and can seriously impede the remainder of the employee's career. **Dismissal** or **termination** is the most serious penalty. It is used when management decides strong action must be taken in the best interests of the organization and its other employees. Termination is necessary when employees do not respond to attempts to correct behavior that violates written rules and regulations and of which the employees were provided proper notice. Incompetence and inability to get along with other employees are two major reasons for termination. Other major reasons are dishonesty or lying and insubordination.

Technically, dismissal and termination are slightly different. *Dismissal* is an action taken by a hiring and firing authority. It is not voluntary on the part of the employee. It is, in effect, a discharge or firing. *Termination* is also an end to employment, but it may be voluntary or involuntary. Employees may terminate employment due to reasons such as illness or accepting a different job. The differences are basically a matter of semantics.

Terminations are costly to the organization. Replacement selection costs are high, and training is a long-term commitment. Unfortunately, in some situations termination is the only recourse. Most managers will say that firing an officer is one of their most distasteful responsibilities.

Although firing someone is seldom easy, it is almost always easier than keeping them. Normally termination occurs only after a serious offense, after repeated offenses by the same employee or after a series of the same type of offense where warnings, oral and written reprimands, suspension or similar previous dispositions of a disciplinary action went unheeded.

Wrongful termination lawsuits have been rising in the past decade. These actions arise from the due process clause of the Fourteenth Amendment of the Constitution, which prohibits persons acting as agents or employees of the state or its political subdivisions from depriving a person of property or liberty without due process. A person has the right not to be terminated from employment except for good or just cause. Title 42, U.S.C., Section 1983, provides a procedure by which a person employed by a state, county or municipal government can bring suit against a department or supervisor for violating the person's constitutional rights in the termination process. Due process requires a valid reason for termination, procedural action, notification of the person to be terminated and an opportunity for a hearing.

Difficult as termination is for police managers, it remains their responsibility. Failure to exercise it when justified results in the ultimate failure of manager effectiveness. Should a manager fail to terminate an officer when justified, and the officer does anything "wrong" in the public's eyes, the manager and the entire department could be sued for **negligent retention.**

Discharge should be presented so employees can retain self-esteem, if possible. They should be told whether they can expect references for what they did well while on the job, when the termination takes effect, how the announcement will be made and whether they can resign voluntarily for the record. Any actions taken should center on the behavior or offense rather than on the individual.

Summary Punishment

Not all disciplinary actions fall within the realm of progressive discipline. Managers must have the authority to exercise *summary* discipline when certain infractions occur. **Summary discipline,** or **summary punishment,** is discretionary authority used when a supervisor thinks an officer is not fit for duty or when, for any reason, the supervisor thinks immediate action is needed.

Summary punishment may require officers to work a day or two without pay or may excuse them from duty for a day without pay. Officers who receive summary punishment have a right to a hearing.

Guidelines for Administering Negative Discipline

When you use negative discipline, what you do *not* do is often more important than what you do. Officers may become defensive and less concerned with listening than defending themselves. Communication skills and tact are essential in these situations. The following guidelines apply when using negative discipline:

- Get the facts first. Consider the circumstances. Was the misbehavior accidental? Did the person know the rules? Was this the first offense? Keep adequate records.
- Be calm. Allow tempers to settle. Avoid sarcasm. Do not threaten, argue or show anger.
- Know your powers as outlined in your job description.
- Check on precedents for similar offenses.
- Suit the disciplinary action to the individual and the situation. Know each subordinate and his or her record. The severity of the discipline should match the seriousness of the offense.

- Focus on the behavior, not on the person. Be sure the behavior is something the person has control over or can change.
- Do not ascribe intent to the behavior or imply it was done on purpose. Focus only on the behavior.
- Be sure the person is attentive and emotionally ready to listen.
- Be clear, specific and objective. Use actual examples of problem behavior.
- Check for understanding by asking questions. How is the person taking the criticism?
- Respect the employee's dignity.
- End with expectations for changed behavior.
- Follow up.

Effective discipline is more easily maintained with a written set of guidelines such as the preceding. Managers should coordinate their disciplinary efforts. Every manager should enforce every rule, regulation and policy equally. Rules that are unenforced or unenforceable should be changed or cancelled. Further, managers should set the example, letting their subordinates know they mean what they say.

Supervisors should avoid the **gunnysack approach** to discipline. This occurs when managers or supervisors accumulate negative behaviors of a subordinate and then dump them all on the officer at the same time rather than correcting them as they occur. Accumulated, they may be serious enough to warrant dismissal. However, handled one at a time, the officer might have had a chance to change.

Steps in Administering Negative Discipline

To apply discipline, write down your main goal in taking disciplinary action—change the employee's behavior and reduce the chances of the behavior happening again. Write down the violation and what conduct was involved, much the same procedure used in making a charge against a citizen. State the reason for the action, specifically, what has been violated and how. Show how the behavior creates a problem. State how you feel about it.

Listen to the employee's explanation. Remember that to err is human. To blame somebody else is even more human. Anticipate this and help employees sort out their responsibilities. Also recognize that if an excuse is good enough, it becomes a reason. Managers and supervisors cannot know everything. They, too, can make mistakes. If this happens, managers must openly admit their mistake and offer a sincere apology for the *misunderstanding.*

Suggest corrective action and, if possible, involve the person in the suggestion. Be firm but fair. Fairness does not mean treating everyone equally. A rookie will make mistakes that might not be tolerated if made by a veteran officer. State exactly what action you are going to take and explain that further violations will bring more severe results. Offer assistance in resolving the present problem. Describe how you value the person as an individual and as an important part of the work group and the entire department. Secure a commitment to future positive behavior.

McGregor (Theory X/Theory Y) says the lessons learned from a hot stove should be present in effective discipline. When a person touches a hot stove (violates a rule or regulation), the burn (punishment) is immediate, consistent (it happens every time) and impartial (it is the same for everyone). Further, the severity of the burn depends on the length of time the stove and victim remain in contact and the heat of the stove. The burned individual may initially feel anger at the stove, but in reality, the anger is an indictment of oneself and the carelessness causing the burn. The anger will lessen, and the victim will have a healthy respect for the stove in the future.

The final step is to tell the individual how to appeal the decision. The right to appeal should be inherent in any disciplinary action.

Appeal

An **appeal** is a request for a decision to be reviewed by someone higher in command. The most frequent appeals are to a review board or department disciplinary board. Appeals can also be made to a civil service board review, a district or high court and, in some cases, a management–labor board. Many departments use an internal review procedure, including the following steps.

Step One

The employee requests a face-to-face meeting with the immediate supervisor within five working days. The supervisor and employee meet, and the supervisor decides to withdraw or stand by the disciplinary action.

Step Two

An employee who is not satisfied with the results of Step One presents the written reasons for dissatisfaction to the department head within five days. The department head sustains or rescinds the disciplinary action within three working days.

Step Three

An employee who is not satisfied with the results of Step Two presents the written reasons for dissatisfaction with the department head's response to the top-level manager of the jurisdiction. Within five days the manager or representative either sustains or rescinds the disciplinary action. This is the final step.

Departments may also have a process for employees to appeal disciplinary actions to a civil service commission. This process usually involves the employee appearing for a hearing before a board that rules in the matter. Such hearings may be closed to the public. The decision and findings of the commission are in writing and are considered final.

Legal Considerations

The terms *just, good* or *sufficient cause* appear in many discipline cases. Black's Law Dictionary refers to **just cause** as "a reasonable cause which must be based on reasonable grounds, and there must be a fair and honest cause or reason, regulated by good faith."

Just cause requires a statement of the charge or charges, a procedure for answering the charges and a process of review. Due process also applies, which means every employee is entitled to certain rights. Federal laws prohibit firing employees on the basis of race, religion, sex, age, national origin, union memberships or activities or because of work missed due to jury service.

Disciplinary actions are subject to specific procedures as established by the civil service or department rules and regulations. If an officer is charged with a criminal offense, the legal procedure is the same as for any citizen. In these cases, violation of civil service rules and regulations of the law enforcement department would, in all probability, await the outcome of the criminal action even though they are completely separate actions.

If the situation involves the arrest of an officer, the input of the local district attorney's office should be obtained as early in the investigation as possible. The criminal violation is more than likely a joint violation of department rules and regulations but must be charged and tried separately. Each case may proceed differently, depending on the local court process. Criminal charges are involved in very few of the total violations of rules and regulations cases. The officer may be suspended, with or without pay, pending the outcome.

In general, violations of department rules and regulations are investigated using the same basic procedures as those accorded criminal violations. All facts must be carefully documented. Search warrants should be obtained when legally required to secure evidence. Gathering evidence, taking statements, seeking witnesses and adhering to legal procedures of handling evidence are all important.

Civil service hearings are similar to criminal hearings. Legal procedures vary, but the charges are read in an open hearing, witnesses are called and the employee is present. Employees may or may not testify because they are not required to give incriminating evidence against themselves.

Past personnel records may be introduced into evidence if relevant. Proper, detailed documentation of the facts supporting any violation of department rules and regulations is the key to justice. Most disciplinary action cases overturned by the courts have involved situations in which proper documentation was lacking, prejudice was involved, the violation was based on an action deemed a discretionary matter on the officer's part, evidence was based on polygraph examinations or violations of due process procedures were involved.

Comprehensive Discipline

Comprehensive discipline uses both positive and negative discipline to achieve individual and organizational goals. Several specific approaches to comprehensive discipline have been developed, including the balance of consequences analysis, the PRICE method, the one-minute management approach and the stroke approach.

The Balance of Consequences Analysis—Wilson Learning Corporation

Building on Skinner's reinforcement theory and Vroom's expectancy theory, Wilson Learning Corporation developed the **balance of consequences analysis.** This process uses a grid such as that shown in Figure 11.2 to analyze problem behavior.

For example, Officer Jones is a popular foot patrol officer. He spends lots of time chatting with citizens on his beat, having made friends with shopkeepers and owners of business establishments as well as residents in the area. The problem is that he is always late with his incident reports. Investigators complain that

Behavior	
Undesired (current)	Desired
Positive Consequences	Positive Consequences
Negative Consequences	Negative Consequences

Figure 11.2
Balance of Consequences Analysis

Source: Steve Buchholz. *The Positive Manager.* p. 125. Copyright © 1985 by John Wiley and Sons, Inc., New York. Reprinted by permission.

they do not have the reports when they need them. Further, Jones often has to put in unpaid overtime to get his paperwork done.

His sergeant does not want to lose him because he is a skilled officer, and his friendliness and popularity are an asset to the department. But the lateness of his reports is causing problems. The sergeant analyzes the consequences operating in this situation.

First, what are the rewards Jones receives from socializing?

- Pleasant visits with citizens
- Satisfaction from knowing people like him
- Praise from peers and superiors for being people oriented

Against this list, the negative consequences of the behavior must be looked at. These include:

- Complaints from the investigators.
- Overtime (unpaid).
- Reduced chances for promotion.

Next consider what positive results would occur if Jones stopped socializing and got his reports done on time:

- Investigators would stop complaining.
- Unpaid overtime would stop.
- Chances for promotion will increase.

On the other hand, what negative consequences might result?

- Miss the good times socializing
- Miss the praise for being people oriented
- More actual work to do

BEHAVIOR	
Undesired (current)	**Desired**
Late reports	Reports on time
Positive Consequences	**Positive Consequences**
Pleasant visits	Less criticism
Satisfaction	Less overtime
Praise	Promotion more likely
Negative Consequences	**Negative Consequences**
Criticism	No pleasant visits
Overtime	Less praise
Promotion less likely	More work

Figure 11.3
Officer Jones' Balance of Consequences Analysis

The balance of consequences grid would look like Figure 11.3.

The balance of consequences analysis considers behavior in terms of what positive and negative results the behavior produces and then focuses on those results.

A final piece of information is needed to complete the analysis, that is, the strength of the consequences. Consequences fall into one of three either/or categories. Every consequence is either:

- Personal or organizational (P or O).
- Immediate or delayed (I or D).
- Certain or uncertain (C or U).

Personal, immediate and certain (PIC) consequences are stronger than organizational, delayed or uncertain (ODU) consequences.

Look at Jones' positive consequences for the undesirable behavior:

- Pleasant visits with citizens—personal, immediate, certain (PIC)
- Satisfaction from knowing people like him—personal, immediate, certain (PIC)
- Praise from peers and superiors for being people oriented—personal, delayed, certain (PDC)

Compare this with the positive consequences if he should do less socializing and get his paperwork done on time:

- Investigators would stop complaining—personal, delayed, certain (PDC).
- Overtime (unpaid) would stop—personal, delayed, certain (PDC).
- Chances for promotion will increase—personal, delayed, uncertain (PDU).

Clearly, the positive consequences for the *undesirable behavior* are stronger than those for the desirable behavior. The same is true for the negative consequences. The negative consequences associated with the undesirable behavior are delayed and uncertain. The negative consequences for less socializing are immediate and certain. The message for management:

Change the balance of consequences so that employees are rewarded for desired behavior and punished for undesired behavior—not vice versa.

Managers can change the balance of consequences by:

- Adding positive consequences for desired behaviors.
- Adding negative consequences for undesired behaviors.
- Removing negative consequences for desired behaviors.
- Removing positive consequences for undesired behaviors.
- Changing the strength of the consequences, that is, changing an organizational consequence to a personal one, a delayed consequence to an immediate one or an uncertain consequence to a certain one.

Consider the following situation: A law enforcement department is doing an analysis of its efficiency and has asked all officers to complete time sheets at the end of their shifts. One shift sergeant is having difficulty getting her officers to turn in their sheets. The officers see the sheets as busywork, interfering with efficiency rather than helping to improve it, so they often leave work without completing them. The sergeant then has to track them down the next day to get them to fill them in. As a solution to the problem, the sergeant gets on the P.A. system at the beginning of the shift, reads the names of those who did not complete their time study and asks them to report to the front desk to fill them in. Examine the following list of consequences of the described behavior.

- Filling out the sheets takes a few minutes past quitting time.
- This results in getting caught in a traffic jam.
- Officers may get chewed out by the sergeant if they do not fill in the sheet.
- Officers are given time at the beginning of their next shift to fill in the sheets.
- Officers get their names read over the P.A. system.
- Colleagues clap and cheer when the names are read.

BEHAVIOR	
Undesired (current) Not filling in time sheets	**Desired** Filling in time sheets
Positive Consequences Get time next shift (PIC) Get name announced (PIC) Colleagues cheer (PIC)	**Positive Consequences** NONE
Negative Consequences Make supervisor unhappy (ODC) Unreliable survey results (ODU)	**Negative Consequences** Caught in traffic (PIC) Name will not be read (PIC)

Figure 11.4
Balance of Consequences Analysis—Time Sheet Problem

- The efficiency study will not be reliable if all officers do not complete the time sheets.
- The sergeant has to spend time getting officers to comply with the request.

This problem can be looked at using the balance of consequences analysis. A key to using this tool is to look at the behavior through the eyes of the beholder—in this instance, the problem officers. The analysis will look like the chart in Figure 11.4.

In this case it is obvious that reading the names over the P.A. system is positively reinforcing the undesired behavior, not punishing it. Peer pressure might be brought to bear on those who do not participate. Or those who turn their sheets in as desired could be rewarded in some way.

The PRICE Method

The PRICE Method, developed by Blanchard (1989, p.18), is a five-step approach to employee performance problems such as attendance.

The **PRICE method** consists of five steps:

- **P**inpoint
- **R**ecord
- **I**nvolve
- **C**oach
- **E**valuate

The five steps are applicable to most problem behaviors. The first step is to *pinpoint* the problem behavior and make certain the employee knows about it. Say, for example, an officer frequently uses profanity in public. This unacceptable behavior needs to be changed. Exactly what constitutes profanity must be specified.

The second step is to *record* how often and when the problem behavior occurs. Under what circumstances does the officer use the profanity? Who else is usually present? What triggers it? How often does it happen? At any certain time of day? This record establishes the behavior as problematic and also provides a baseline from which to work.

Third, *involve* the officer in setting a goal to eliminate the problem behavior and deciding on specific strategies to meet this goal. The strategies should include a specific time line as well as incentives for specific accomplishments toward goal achievement.

Fourth, *coach* the officer regularly and consistently. According to Blanchard: "This is the most critical part of the plan. It is also the step where managers most frequently stumble." Provide positive reinforcement whenever the officer substitutes an acceptable word for what would normally elicit a profanity. Enlist the aid of other officers to help provide positive reinforcement. Make certain others do not use profanity without being criticized. Double standards will undermine the PRICE Method.

Finally, *evaluate* the performance according to a predetermined schedule to monitor progress.

One-Minute Managing

The One Minute Manager, for which Blanchard is perhaps best known, suggests that managers can use **one-minute managing,** including both praise and reprimands, to get their subordinates to perform at peak efficiency with high morale.

Both praise and reprimands can be effectively accomplished in one minute.

Blanchard and Johnson (1981, p.44) suggest that *one-minute praising* works well when managers:

1. Tell people *up front* that you are going to let them know how they are doing.
2. Praise people immediately.
3. Tell people what they did right—be specific.
4. Tell people how good you feel about what they did right and how it helps the organization and the other people who work there.
5. Stop for a moment of silence to let them "feel" how good you feel.
6. Encourage them to do more of the same.
7. Shake hands or touch people in a way that makes it clear that you support their success in the organization. (Any such physical contact should be done in a way that could never be construed as sexual harassment.)

Blanchard and Johnson (p.59) suggest that *one-minute reprimands* work well when managers:

1. Tell people *beforehand* that you are going to let them know how they are doing in specific terms.

The first half of the reprimand:

2. Reprimand people immediately.
3. Tell people what they did wrong—be specific.
4. Tell people how you feel about what they did wrong—in specific terms.
5. Stop for a few seconds of uncomfortable silence to let them *feel* how you feel.

The second half of the reprimand:

6. Shake hands or touch them in a way that lets them know you are honestly on their side. (Again, with any physical contact, avoid any appearance of sexual harassment.)
7. Remind them how much you value them.
8. Reaffirm that you think well of them but not of their performance in this situation.
9. Realize that when the reprimand is over, it's over.

Figure 11.5 illustrates how one-minute praisings and reprimands constitute a comprehensive disciplinary approach.

Blanchard cautions that simply knowing the secrets of one-minute praising and reprimanding is not enough:

> To use these tools well, you must understand some specific management techniques. . . .
>
> Giving an equal amount of praise and criticism may not be enough to save you from being thought of as a bad boss. In most groups, there's a need for four times as many positive interactions—that is, praising—as negative interactions.

A reprimand has such a powerful effect that it takes four positive words to balance one negative word.

An effective manager usually gives four times more praise than blame.

Blanchard describes a corporation he worked with where criticism and praise were approximately equal. The employees thought their relationship with their boss was "totally negative." Even when the ratio was changed to two praisings for every one reprimand, people still thought their boss was "all over them." Only when the ratio became four praisings to one criticism did the employees feel they had a "good relationship" with their boss.

The Stroke Approach

The Better Than Money Corporation is founded on the principle that management has available to it several options that are "better than money" to motivate employees. This principle carries over into the corporation's main business, consulting on excellence in customer service. Its **stroke approach** includes five kinds of strokes:

- Positive—any sincere, positive comment or expression. Clearly a warm fuzzy.

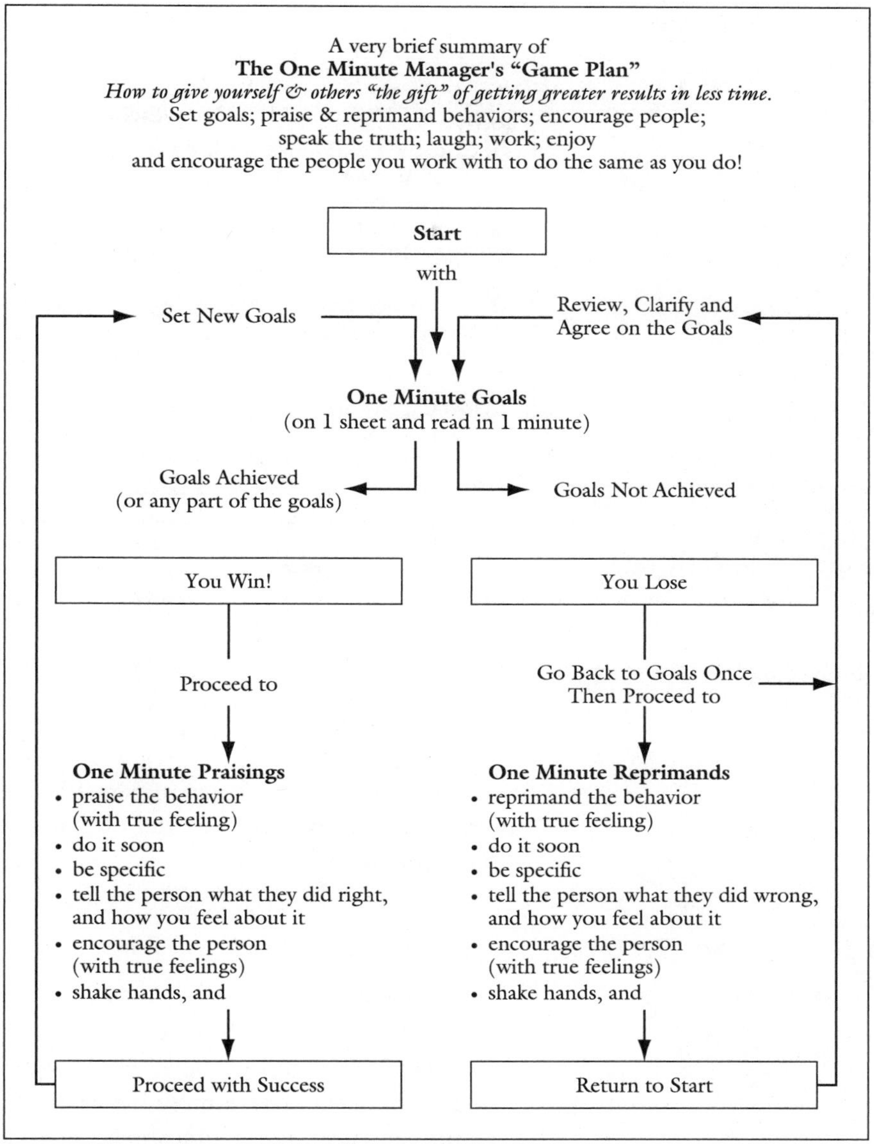

Figure 11.5
The One Minute Manager's "Game Plan"

Source: Kenneth Blanchard and Spencer Johnson. *The One Minute Manager.* p.101. Copyright © 1981 by William Morrow and Co. Used by permission of William Morrow and Company, Inc., Publishers, New York.

- Negative—any negative action or word that is clearly a cold prickly.
- Absent—lack of any word or recognition.
- Crooked—a positive stroke followed by a negative one, for example, "That's a beautiful dress you have on. I wonder when it will be in style."
- Plastic—a comment given as a ritual, for example, "How are things going?"

STROKING OBJECTIVE FOR:

Date: ____________________

1. Give out two Positive Strokes per day.
   - Genuine
   - Sincere
   - Specific
   - Timely

2. Identify one top performer in your work group.
   Name ____________________
   Give two Positive Strokes per week. (Do not combine with #1).

3. Identify one marginal performer in your work group.
   Name ____________________
   Give two Positive Strokes per week. (Do not combine with #1).
   ____

Figure 11.6
Using Strokes to Discipline Positively

Source: Copyright © 1980 by John Tschohl, Better Than Money Corporation. Courtesy of Service Quality Institute, Minneapolis, MN. Reprinted by permission.

Managers can give strokes that are positive, negative, absent, crooked or plastic. They should focus on positive strokes.

To use strokes effectively, managers should concentrate on the positive strokes as much as possible. Figure 11.6 shows how a manager might set "stroking objectives" each day.

A Disciplinary System

A fair, equitable disciplinary system has the following characteristics:

- Reasonable and necessary policies, procedures and rules to govern employees' conduct at work and promote both individual and organizational goals. Regular review of these standards.
- Effective communication of these policies, procedures and rules as well as the consequences for noncompliance.
- Immediate, impartial and consistent enforcement of the policies, procedures and rules.
- An appeals procedure.

Summary

Discipline is training expected to produce a desired behavior—controlled behavior. Discipline and morale are closely related. Morale is how a person feels; discipline is how a person acts. The purpose of discipline is to promote desired behavior. This may be done by encouraging acceptable behavior or punishing unacceptable behavior. An agency's policy and procedure manual is the foundation upon which most discipline must be based.

A primary rule of effective discipline is that it should be carried out as close to the time of the violation as possible. Progressive discipline uses disciplinary steps based on the severity of the offense. The steps are usually (1) oral reprimand, (2) written reprimand, (3) suspension/demotion and (4) discharge. The offense and offender, how the offense was committed and the offender's attitude and past performance are important considerations in assigning penalties.

Discipline, either positive or negative, depends on the use of consequences. The balance of consequences analysis considers behavior in terms of what positive and negative results the behavior produces and then focuses on those results. Personal, immediate and certain (PIC) consequences are stronger than organizational, delayed or uncertain (ODU) consequences. Managers should change the balance of consequences so that employees are rewarded for desired behavior and punished for undesired behavior—not vice versa.

The PRICE Method consists of five steps: (1) pinpoint, (2) record, (3) involve, (4) coach and (5) evaluate. Both praise and reprimands can be effectively accomplished in one minute. An effective manager usually gives four times more praise than blame. Managers can also give strokes. These strokes might be positive, negative, absent, crooked or plastic. The focus should be on positive strokes.

Discussion Questions

1. Why is discipline a broader term than punishment?
2. What level of law enforcement manager should investigate the majority of discipline problems?
3. What is constructive discipline?
4. Do you think written departmental rules and regulations are necessary? For what areas?
5. What behaviors would be severe enough violations to warrant termination?
6. What would be a constructive law enforcement department philosophy for discipline?
7. Are there too many departmental rules and regulations? Not enough? What are the most important ones?
8. Why is discipline necessary for individual functioning? For organizational functioning?
9. Choose a problem behavior you would like to change and do a balance of consequences analysis. Are there changes you can make to help change the problem behavior?
10. As a manager, what types of positive and negative discipline would you be inclined to use?

InfoTrac College Edition Assignment

Use InfoTrac College Edition to answer the Discussion Questions as appropriate.

Select one of the following topics and find a recent article about it:

- Progressive discipline
- Excessive use of force
- Sexual harassment on the job
- Police corruption

Summarize the main points of the article and give the full reference. Be prepared to share your findings with the class.

OR read and outline one of the following articles:

- "Put It in Writing: The Police Policy Manual" by Michael Carpenter
- "Reviewing Use of Force: A Systematic Approach" by Sam W. Lathrop
- "Force Continuums: A Liability to Law Enforcement?" by George T. Williams
- "Use-of-Force Policies and Training: A Reasoned Approach (Part Two)" by Thomas D. Petrowski

References

Anderson, Jonathan. "Iron Discipline: Then and Now." *Law and Order,* August 2001, pp.77–78.

Arnold, Jon. "Early Misconduct Detection." *Law and Order,* August 2001, pp.80–86.

Blanchard, Kenneth. "A PRICE That Makes Sense." *Today's Office,* September 1989, p.18.

Blanchard, Kenneth and Johnson, Spencer. *The One Minute Manager.* New York: William Morrow and Company, 1981.

Carlan, Philip E. and Byxbe, Ferris R. "Managing Sexual Harassment Liability: A Guide for Police Administrators." *The Police Chief,* October 2000, pp.124–129.

Carpenter, Michael. "Put It in Writing: The Police Policy Manual." *FBI Law Enforcement Bulletin,* October 2000, pp.1–5.

Fulton, Roger. "Preventing Insubordination." *Law Enforcement Technology,* June 2000, p.150.

Fulton, Roger. "Policy and Procedure Update." *Law Enforcement Technology,* March 2001a, p.118.

Fulton, Roger. "How to Criticize Effectively." *Law Enforcement Technology,* July 2001b, p.170.

Fuss, Timothy L. and Snowden, Lynne L. "Surveying Sexual Harassment in the Law Enforcement Workplace." *The Police Chief,* June 2000, pp.65–72.

Fyfe, James J. "Reflections on the Diallo Case." *Subject to Debate,* April 2000, pp.1, 3–4.

Green, Don. "Problem Employees in Smaller Agencies." *Law and Order,* October 2002, pp.96–99.

Grossi, Dave. "Use of Force Policy and Procedure: Tactically Sound, Administratively Feasible?" *The Law Enforcement Trainer,* January/February 2002, pp.20–21.

Harris, John J. (Jack) and Gilmartin, Kevin M. "Malcontent and Disgruntled Employees: What Is a Supervisor to Do?" *The Police Chief,* December 2000, pp.19–24.

Heller, Daniel A. "The Power of Gentleness." *Educational Leadership,* May 2002, pp.76–83.

Iris, Mark. "Police Discipline in Houston: The Arbitration Experience." *Police Quarterly,* June 2002, pp.132–151.

Jones, Tony L. "Coaching for Performance." *Law Enforcement Technology,* July 2000, pp.118–122.

Lathrop, Sam W. "Reviewing Use of Force: A Systematic Approach." *FBI Law Enforcement Bulletin,* October 2000, pp.16–20.

Martin, Jeff. "Revising Departmental Policy and Procedure Manuals." *Law and Order,* July 2002, pp.114–116.

Messina, Phil. "Dissecting the Diallo Shooting: Four Seconds to Hell." *The Law Enforcement Trainer,* July/August 2000, pp.8–10, 30–33, 46.

Miraglia, Greg. "The Role of Discipline in Basic Training." *The Police Chief,* May 2000, pp.69–70.

Nowicki, Ed. "Use of Force Options." *Law and Order,* February 2001a, pp.35–37.

Nowicki, Ed. "Use of Force: Dealing with Litigation." *Law and Order,* April 2001b, pp.29–31.

Nowicki, Ed. "(Un)Reasonable Force." *Police,* March 2002a, p.6.

Nowicki, Ed. "Excessive Force Investigations." *Law and Order,* April 2002b, pp.20–21.

Pedersen, Dorothy. "Sexual Harassment: Is the Atmosphere Right for It in Your Precinct?" *Law Enforcement Technology,* October 2001, pp.128–134.

Petrowski, Thomas D. "Use-of-Force Policies and Training. A Reasoned Approach (Part Two)." *FBI Law Enforcement Bulletin,* November 2002, pp.24–32.

Police Use of Force in America 2001. Alexandria, VA: International Association of Chiefs of Police.

"Preventing Sexual Harassment." St. Paul, MN: Equal Opportunity Division, Department of Employee Relations, no date.

Rhyons, Lori and Brewster, David. "Employee Early Warning Systems: Helping Supervisors Protect Citizens, Officers and Agencies." *The Police Chief,* November 2002, pp.32–36.

Rogers, Donna. "Use of Force: Agencies Need to Have a Continuum and Officers Need to Be Able to Articulate It." *Law Enforcement Technology,* March 2001, pp.82–86.

Rosenbaum, Steven H. "Patterns and Practices of Police Misconduct." *Law and Order,* October 2001, pp.67–71.

Schennum, Tim. "The Action Plan as an FTO Tool." *Law and Order,* December 2000, pp.67–69.

Smith, Brad. "Police Service Dogs: The Unheralded Training Tool." *Police,* January 2000, pp.36–39.

Walker, Samuel; Alpert, Geoffrey P.; and Kenney, Dennis J. "Early Warning Systems for Police: Concept, History and Issues." *Police Quarterly,* June 2000, pp.132–152.

Walker, Samuel; Alpert, Geoffrey P.; and Kenney, Dennis J. *Early Warning Systems: Responding to the Problem Police Officer.* Washington, DC: National Institute of Justice Research in Brief, July 2001. (NCJ 188565)

Williams, George T. "Force Continuums: A Liability to Law Enforcement?" *FBI Law Enforcement Bulletin,* June 2002, pp.14–19.

Book-Specific Web Site

Go to the *Management and Supervision in Law Enforcement* Web site at http://info.wadsworth.com/05346160654 for student and instructor resources, including Internet Assignments and Case Studies.

CHAPTER 12

Complaints and Grievances

A complaint is an opportunity to prove the kind of stuff you and your department are made of, a chance to cement a relationship so solidly it will last for years. That's much more important than who's right and who's wrong.
—Anonymous

Do You Know?

- How a complaint and a grievance differ?
- Who may register a complaint?
- What categories of law enforcement misconduct are often included in external complaints?
- How complaints might be avoided?
- What the most common causes of internal complaints are?
- How job satisfaction, communication and performance are related?
- What the Pinch Model illustrates?
- When complaints do not need to be taken seriously?
- What two functions are served by a careful complaint investigation?
- How officers may protect themselves legally when under investigation?
- What the majority of grievances concern?
- What the outcome of a complaint or grievance might be?

Can You Define?

arbitration
civilian review boards
complainant
complaint
crunch
exonerated
external complaints
Garrity protection
grievance
grievant
internal complaints
mediation
not sustained
ombudsman
pinch
Pinch Model
sustained
unfounded

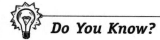

INTRODUCTION

Chapter 11 discussed problem behaviors perceived by managers. This chapter reverses the perspective and looks at problems perceived by subordinates and by those outside the law enforcement organization. These perceived problems may result in complaints or grievances.

It is an organizational fact of life that most law enforcement supervisors must deal with complaints as part of their responsibilities. How supervisors react to complaints will directly affect the organization's ability to function effectively. If complaints are not dealt with promptly, thoroughly and fairly, the result will be serious negative consequences for the entire organization.

This chapter begins with definitions that differentiate between complaints and grievances. It then examines the difference between external and internal complaints, as well as complaint policies and how complaints are handled and investigated, including the role of internal affairs investigations and the civilian review board. Next, grievances are discussed, including their causes and resolutions, mediation and arbitration, followed by an examination of the disposition of complaints and grievances. The chapter concludes with discussions of how to handle the chronic complainer and the legal rights and procedures for officers named in disciplinary actions.

Definitions

By definition, a complaint and a grievance are basically synonymous. Either can be described as a criticism, charge, accusation, offense or finding of fault. Complaints and grievances may also be described as circumstances or conditions thought to be unjust, whether real or imagined.

A **complaint** is a statement of a problem. A **grievance** is a formally registered complaint.

A complaint or grievance is an initial action taken by someone against a person or an organization for a perceived wrong. Whether real or imagined, the wrong is sufficient in the mind of the person complaining that the matter must be brought to the attention of the proper authority. The action taken may be an oral criticism, a written statement, a listing of wrongs, a civil service procedure, a meeting demand, a hearing demand or formal legal action.

Complaints

Complaints are an unavoidable part of being a manager. Even the most efficient managers get their share of complaints—justified or unjustified.

A complaint may be made by the general public, by people arrested or by employees of the law enforcement department, including peers or managers. The person or group filing the complaint is called the **complainant.**

Complaints may be external or internal.

External Complaints

Law enforcement departments exist to serve their communities. With this basic premise, citizens can be thought of as consumers of law enforcement services and, like any business, departments should "aim to please." Research suggests that customers who have bad experiences tell approximately 11 people about it; those with good experiences tell just 6. Managers should recognize that it is impossible to please everyone all the time. Some citizens, rightly or wrongly, will perceive a problem and register a complaint.

External complaints are those made by citizens against a law enforcement officer or officers, a supervisor, support staff and/or the entire department. The complaint may be made by an individual or a group. It may be as "trivial" as a citizen receiving what he or she perceives to be an unjustified parking ticket or as serious as a charge of brutality or racism.

Studies have found that complaints are not filed evenly by people across demographic parameters. A complainant profile generated by such studies shows that nonwhite, unmarried, low-income males under age 30 are most likely to complain about the police. In fact, nearly 75 percent of all complaints against officers come from this segment of society.

The studies also revealed that the officers most likely to receive complaints against them were those under age 30 assigned to uniformed patrol duties with fewer than 5 years of police experience and only a high school education.

People who call in complaints without leaving a name are generally not as credible as those who identify themselves. This does not mean, however, that anonymous complaints should be ignored. With the drug problem as serious as it has become, with intimidation, injuries and in some cases death threatening those who provide information, it is understandable that people may not want to give their names.

An employee who receives a complaint should obtain all possible information about the incident. Sometimes the complainant may be under the influence of alcohol or other drugs and, if interviewed later, may give a considerably different story. Many departments have dispatcher complaint forms. Others automatically record all calls into and out of the department.

The motive for the complaint should be determined. The author recalls a series of complaints from one person concerning a local judge's driving. It developed that the complainant had been before the judge on a DUI, charged and sentenced. Since then he had been following the judge when the judge was driving and reporting every minute infraction of traffic laws, even one mile over the speed limit. He never wanted to sign a complaint or appear as a witness, just to make nuisance reports that took up law enforcement time. After a personal interview, the calls stopped.

The Police Executive Research Forum has published a model policy statement for handling citizen complaints. The intent of the policy statement is to provide precise guidelines to ensure fairness to officers and civilians alike. It seeks to improve the quality of services in three ways: (1) by increasing citizen confidence in the integrity of law enforcement actions, (2) by permitting law enforcement officials to monitor officers' compliance with department procedures and (3) by clarifying rights and ensuring due process protection to both citizens and officers.

Research by Worrall (2002) found that when law enforcement agencies made improvements in their citizen complaint review procedures, the number of complaints increased. Worrall (pp.356–357) explains: "To understand why more complaints may be filed when complaint review procedures are improved, it is first necessary to give attention to the characteristics of complaints and the relative levels of 'success' they have traditionally had by complaining. To the extent that traditional complaint review mechanisms are (or were) hostile to certain individuals, it makes sense that complaints have not always been filed as frequently as they otherwise would be."

Causes of External Complaints

Specific categories of misconduct subject to disciplinary action need to be clearly defined.

Categories of officer misconduct often included in external complaints are crime, excessive force, false arrest, improper entry, unlawful search, harassment, offensive demeanor and rule infractions.

The annual report of a large urban police department included information about complaints, including the types of complaints processed and their disposition, as summarized in Table 12.1.

Table 12.1
Disposition of Allegations against the Police

	Exonerated	Unfounded	Not Sustained	Sustained	Totals
Excessive force	55	1	14	3	73
Attitude/Language	8	6	31	11	56
Conduct unbecoming a police officer	13	5	22	38	78
Attn. to duty (Substandard performance)	1	0	0	0	1
Lack of police service					
Violations regarding reports	1	1	0	0	2
Other	17	1	36	65	119
Totals*	95	14	103	117	329

Summary of Disciplinary Actions Taken in Response to Sustained Allegations	
Dismissed from the department	1
Suspended	25
Written reprimand	32
Oral reprimand	2
Referred to training	10
Counseling	23
Psychological evaluation	5
Off-duty employment ban	1
Officers resigned	3
Total	102

*There are 25 cases pending disposition.

The most common complaint in this department, and also the most frequently sustained complaint, was conduct unbecoming an officer. The most common disciplinary action taken was written reprimand. Interestingly, the second most frequent allegation, and the most frequently exonerated, was excessive force. Suspension and counseling were other frequently used disciplinary actions. Such reports tell the public that police agencies do not take officer wrongdoings lightly and support the fact that police departments have in-house procedures to investigate public and individual complaints about officer conduct and actions.

Reducing External Complaints

Preventing misconduct is a primary way to reduce complaints. Agencies should make every effort to eliminate organizational conditions that may foster, permit or encourage improper behavior by officers.

Complaints can be reduced through effective recruitment and selection, training, policy and procedures manuals, effective supervision, community outreach and data collection and analysis.

Data collection and analysis might reveal problem behavior before complaints are registered. In one department, for example, an officer had a fine record on traffic enforcement, but analysis revealed that he was giving tickets to men and warnings to women, with seven women warned for each man given a ticket.

Internal Complaints

Complaints by officers are generally brought to the attention of the next highest manager. If the complaint is against a manager, it is brought before the next highest manager. If the complaint is against the head of the department, it is brought before the city manager or other head of local government, following the chain of command.

When investigating internal complaints against specific employees, the primary purpose should be to correct the behavior and make the employee a contributing member of the department. Employees are a tremendous investment. Everything reasonable should be done to reach a conclusion satisfactory to management and the employee.

The following guidelines might assist in handling internal complaints: always be available, listen carefully and gather all the facts. Address the problem, and if an apology is called for, do so immediately. Explain your decision and why it was made as well as how it can be appealed.

A manager's attitude toward complaints can mean the difference between a temporarily rocky road and a permanent dead end. Recall that many complaints may be symptomatic of low morale or of problems with employees' feelings of self-worth.

Causes of Internal Complaints

Law enforcement officers are not known to be "cry babies." They usually pride themselves on being tough, disciplined and able to take whatever they need to. They may, however, be harboring feelings of dissatisfaction that manifest themselves in observable behaviors. A number of conditions can cause officers to complain.

Most **internal complaints** are related to working conditions or management style.

Officers may be dissatisfied with safety conditions, condition of vehicles, lack of equipment needed to do the job or other work conditions. They may also think their managers are too strict or too lenient, have too high or too low standards, over- or undersupervise, give too little credit and too much criticism, will not accept suggestions, show favoritism or make unfair job assignments. The discussion of motivation and morale in Chapter 10 includes signs that officers are unmotivated and/or experiencing low morale—instances in which complaints and grievances are likely to appear.

Reducing Internal Complaints

When signs of employee dissatisfaction appear, preventive action is needed. When managers sense that "things are not going right," it may be time to set up a personal talk or a shift or department meeting. Determine the type of discontentment and the cause. Pay special attention to what employees are saying in small groups. Talk with individual officers about things in general. Make it known that you are available to discuss matters formally or informally. As noted by Buchholz and Roth (1987, pp.70–71):

> For many years researchers have looked for a correlation between satisfaction and performance. They have researched satisfaction about self, job, peers, management and organizations. They found that a person could be satisfied with all of these and still not perform well.
>
> The breakthrough came when satisfaction was correlated to *communication.* The results of this research can be summarized as follows:

Satisfaction	Communication	Performance
high	high	highest
low	high	high
high	low	low
low	low	lowest

From this research you can conclude that employees who were satisfied and talked about it performed the best; employees who were dissatisfied and did not talk about it performed the worst. They probably used their energy to remain hidden. These are findings you might expect. Surprisingly, however, those who were satisfied but did not talk about it were ranked lower in overall performance than those who were dissatisfied but talked about it. What does this mean? Even people who may not be fully satisfied but have an environment where they can *communicate* about their dissatisfaction perform better than those who may be satisfied but are in a climate that lacks open communication.

Communication is directly related to job performance. Those who are dissatisfied on the job and communicate perform better than those who are satisfied and do not communicate.

Let subordinates be "in the know." Communicate and encourage two-way conversations, with *listening* to employees the most important part. Such communication will not only help employees be more satisfied but also help identify problems before they become major. This is illustrated in the **Pinch Model,** Figure 12.1, which illustrates the importance of open communication and the likely consequences of its absence.

A **pinch** is a small problem between individuals, a situation in which an individual or individuals feel something is wrong. It's not a full-blown problem—yet. Pinches result from such things as the supervisor changing the rules, changing the schedule, failing to provide expected support or feedback or failing to keep a promise. They can also result from misunderstandings and failure to clarify expectations on the job. If small problems are handled effectively,

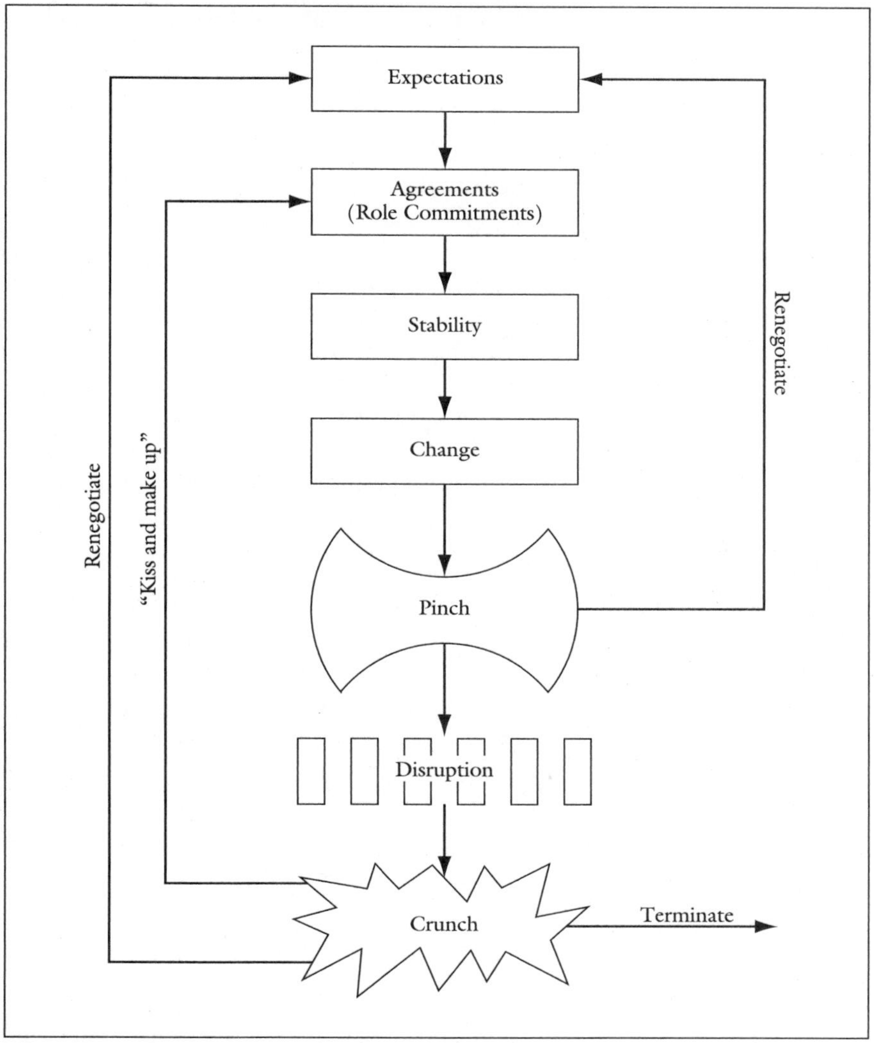

Figure 12.1
The Pinch Model

Source: Steve Buchholz and Thomas Roth. *Creating the High Performance Team.* p.73.

©Tom Carter/PhotoEdit

The lines of communication within a department must be kept open. Encouraging communication can help keep a pinch from becoming a crunch.

major problems can be avoided. If they are *not* dealt with, they may accumulate and disrupt performance and relationships, usually leading to a major confrontation, or **crunch.**

A crunch occurs when the problem becomes serious. It is marked by strong emotional reactions from both sides. This may be a heated argument or total avoidance. At this point two alternatives often exist. First, those involved in the crunch may "kiss and make up" but without dealing with the root problem. This results in a vicious cycle, with pinches leading to crunches and more confrontation. Or it may result in transfer or termination. The Pinch Model suggests that when pinches or crunches occur, manager and subordinate need to renegotiate, starting with an open discussion of expectations.

The Pinch Model illustrates the importance of communication in dealing with complaints and the consequences of not communicating effectively.

In addition to keeping lines of communication open and encouraging subordinates to express their concerns, managers can help reduce complaints in other ways. They can help employees improve their education and their work conditions; inspect and improve equipment and determine what additional equipment can be requested in the next budget; give praise when it is deserved. And when criticism is deserved, make it constructive criticism delivered in private.

Often people with complaints have tunnel vision and have not considered points on the other side. A complaint is usually nothing personal. Regard it as a chance for successful change. Be positive rather than negative. Surprisingly, most complaints can be worked out if they are not allowed to proceed too far. Complaints handled inappropriately often become grievances.

Complaint Policies

Any manager who wants to operate efficiently and maintain high morale must take every complaint seriously. No matter how trivial or unreasonable a complaint may seem to managers, it does not appear that way to the person making it.

A basic rule: *Never* take a complaint lightly.

Every police department should have a written complaint review policy explaining procedures used to investigate complaints, the roles and responsibilities of the supervisors and the officer complained against, the function of internal affairs, possible dispositions and the appeal process. The IACP Model Policy for Investigating Officer Misconduct (2000, p.44) states: "Establishment of procedures for investigating complaints and allegations of employee misconduct is crucial to demonstrate and protect this agency's integrity. This agency shall accept and investigate fairly and impartially all complaints of employee misconduct to determine the validity of allegations and to impose any disciplinary actions that may be justified in a timely and consistent manner."

It is essential that citizens support and have confidence in the police department. A complaint policy not only establishes a plan but also states the department's philosophy regarding public complaints. Police administrators know that police–civilian encounters will inevitably cause problems. Police have unique authority in the community, as well as considerable discretionary power. The agency, community, employee and complainant all benefit from a fair, open investigation policy of complaints against the police.

Regardless of its origination, whether external or internal, the complaint must be investigated and resolved.

Handling and Investigating Complaints

Complaints can be received from any source, in person, by mail or by phone. Even complaints from juveniles, anonymous sources and arrestees should be accepted if the facts warrant.

Making a complaint should be easily accomplished. A clearly marked, easily accessible office should be open from early morning until evening. Often this is the office of internal affairs. Phone complaints should be accepted any time.

Whenever possible, complaints should be in writing. If this is not possible, the department should complete a complaint description form and send it to the complainant to be reviewed, signed and returned to the agency.

A complaint against an officer, support staff or the entire department must be investigated thoroughly, following the same principles as in a criminal investigation. This is true whether the complaint is from someone outside or within the department. The investigation and adjudication of complaints will depend on the specific charge and on the past record of the officer involved. The investigation process should have a definite time limit, such as 120 days, with a onetime, 30-day extension possible.

A careful investigation of a complaint instills confidence in management's fairness and protects those accused of wrongdoing.

Complaints require mandatory action. In some cases the basis for the complaint is readily discernible and easily verified. In other cases, however, the facts are not as clear or even in dispute. These matters are considerably more difficult to resolve. In yet other situations the complaint is completely irrational, but it has to be dealt with rationally.

Most complaints about minor infractions such as discourtesy or sarcasm can be investigated by the accused officer's first-line supervisor. More serious allegations should be assigned to the department's Internal Affairs (IA) department, discussed shortly.

In dealing with complaints, determine the exact nature of the complaint. What specifically occurred that caused the complainant to take action? An investigation must support the specifics and must involve the person complained against.

If a police officer is charged with a violation of rules and regulations and thinks the charge is unjust, the officer can request a hearing. If the charge is upheld at the hearing, the appeal procedure will vary from department to department. The hearing may be with the city manager, city council, police complaint board or civil service commission. If upheld by one of these hearing authorities, it may be possible to appeal to the District Court. Officers' rights regarding complaints and grievances are discussed later in the chapter.

The person assigned to the investigation must be able to draw a conclusion from the specifics of the complaint. All complaints against law enforcement employees must be investigated within the constraints of the legal process. Inquiries must be objective. Conclusions and final decisions should be avoided until all facts are available. In spite of their seemingly minor nature, complaints may have a major impact on department morale if not investigated properly. It is necessary to investigate complaints to clear the person complained against as well as to serve the interests of justice. Considerations in the investigation include investigating immediately and collecting both positive and negative facts, interviewing those complained against as well as the complainant, and taking written statements, if necessary, checking personnel records of those accused as well as previous complaints of the person accusing and then conducting a fair hearing.

Good complaint investigations not only protect the reputation of the department and any accused employee but also provide an opportunity for the complainant to be heard and the public to be notified of the results. Immediate disposition of such incidents builds public confidence, law enforcement morale and a general sense of justice.

A department's rules and regulations or grievance procedures established by union contracts often define actions to be taken, punishable offenses and employees' status until complaints are thoroughly investigated.

Actions to be taken, offenses deemed to be wrongs, the status of the employee until the case is decided and other matters are often defined in the department rules and regulations or grievance procedures established by union contracts.

Internal Affairs Investigations

Lober (2002, p.57) notes: "Internal affairs can impact the cultural values and the core values of your department in several ways." He suggests that how seriously complaints about such things as sexual harassment or misconduct, use of force and the like are investigated sends a loud, clear message as to what is acceptable conduct. Lober also recommends: "A police department should not measure the effectiveness of its internal affairs unit by the number of sustained cases but by the conformance of the department's officers to the standards of conduct."

Thurnauer (2002, p.73) contends: "A simple declaration that all complaints against any member of the police department will be received and investigated leaves little room for dispute." He recommends: "The officer who is the subject of the complaint should know the circumstances of the complaint immediately unless a criminal investigation prohibits it." He (p.78) notes: "Immediately after the complaint is received, the person assigned to investigate will usually be able to tell whether or not there is a criminal element to the case. . . . If there is even a hint that there is criminal behavior on the part of the employee, then the first steps should be to separate the matter into both a criminal investigation and an administrative investigation." The criminal investigation should be conducted first, including the *Miranda* warning if applicable. This is followed by the administrative investigation, including a *Garrity* warning if applicable.

The first step is to review all pieces of evidence. Carefully examine all documents, statements and photographs submitted by the complainant. Next, obtain copies of all associated elements of the case. These can include a copy of the crime or arrest report, a computer printout of the call-for-service, a copy of radio transmissions and any other retrievable items. A fundamental component of most investigations is interviewing all involved parties.

Officers' Rights and Legal Procedures

The nature of police work makes officers vulnerable to a variety of legal actions. In October 1990 the National Law Enforcement Rights Center was formed. This center, an offshoot of the National Association of Police Organizations (NAPO), provides legal resources to police defendants and their attorneys. The center was established to protect officers' legal and constitutional rights, attempting to put police officers on a level playing field with everybody else.

A variety of legislation has also been proposed throughout the past decade to protect due process rights of officers involved in disciplinary hearings and other court actions.

In fact, several states have enacted Law Enforcement Officers' Bills of Rights (LEOBR). The Violent Crime Control and Law Enforcement Act of 1991 contains proposed federal legislation concerning mandated due process rights afforded peace officers who are the subject of internal investigations that could lead to disciplinary action. In other jurisdictions, contracts resulting from collective bargaining provisions may affect the investigative process where police officers are involved.

In general, a Police Officers' Bill of Rights gives law enforcement officers, sheriffs and correctional officers the right to be notified of any pending disciplinary action within a reasonable time prior to the action taking effect, to be treated with a specific minimum standard of fairness while under investigation, to request a hearing if an investigation results in a recommendation of disciplinary action, and to advance review and comment on any adverse material being placed in the officer's personnel file.

Brooks (2002, p.26) reminds managers: "The self-incrimination clause of the Fifth Amendment to the U.S. Constitution prohibits forcing individuals to provide evidence against themselves in a criminal matter. The due process clause of the Fourteenth Amendment makes this requirement applicable to the states. . . . The U.S. Supreme Court ruled in *Garrity v. New Jersey* [1967] that a violation of the Fourteenth Amendment occurs when the government uses a police officer's statement in a criminal trial against that officer." Says Brooks (p.27): "The Garrity ruling imposes significant restraints on law enforcement administrators investigating misconduct allegations within an agency." However, he (p.28) notes: "Nothing in Garrity prohibits forcing cooperation by law enforcement employees with internal investigators." Officers accused of misconduct can be threatened with loss of their jobs if they do not cooperate with an internal investigation. Officers can protect themselves by getting in writing a **Garrity protection,** a written notification that they are making their statement or report involuntarily:

> On (date) at (time) at (place), I was ordered to submit this report (give this statement) by (name and rank). Consequently, I submit this report (statement) involuntarily and only because of that order as a condition of continued employment.
>
> I believe the department requires this report (statement) exclusively for internal purposes and will not release it to any other agency or authority.
>
> I hereby specifically reserve my constitutional rights to remain silent under the Fifth and Fourteenth Amendments. Further, I rely specifically upon the protection afforded to me under the doctrines set forth in *Garrity vs. New Jersey* (1967).

This protects the officer should the matter become a criminal issue. The statement or report could not be used against the officer. It might also help break the code of silence.

While under investigation, officers may find legal protection from a Law Enforcement Officer Bill of Rights (LEOBR), if one has been enacted in that state, and under the Garrity protection.

Civilian Review Boards

In some communities, **civilian review boards** have been designated to investigate and dispose of complaints against law enforcement officers. According to Finn (2000a, pp.22–23) most citizen review or oversight boards fall into four main types: "(1) Citizens investigate allegations of police misconduct and recommend a finding to the head of the agency. (2) Officers investigate allegations and develop findings. Then citizens review and recommend that the head of the agency approve or reject the finding. (3) Complainants may appeal findings established by the agency to citizens who review them and make recommendations to the head of the agency. (4) An auditor investigates the process the agency uses to accept and investigate complaints and reports to the agency and the community the thoroughness and fairness of the process."

A police chief meets with concerned citizens to address local issues. External complaints from citizens should be taken seriously and investigated thoroughly.

© Jim Shaffer

Law enforcement agencies usually have opposed such civilian review boards on the grounds that they erode the authority of the responsible law enforcement manager. In addition, according to Finn (p.23): "Most agencies have opposed citizen oversight because they feel that oversight procedures represent outside interference, oversight staff lack experience with and understanding of police work, and oversight processes are unfair."

At the heart of the debate regarding the civilian review boards is the question of whether police possess the ability, the structure and the will to police themselves. Those in favor of review boards think they take pressure off the police to investigate their own and help reduce public belief that the police will whitewash wrongdoing within the agency. Further, because the review board is an external agency, it can be more independent in its investigation. In addition, review board membership can represent more elements of a diverse community.

Police, on the other hand, believe that the department can police its own, that it has its own complaint-handling procedures through existing department policies and that the police have governed themselves in the past and will continue to do so. Many police executives think that civilian review boards substantially reduce the effectiveness of the police agency administration. Accountability is the essence of the issue. Police believe they have accountability through the existing structure of first-line supervisor, middle manager, upper-level manager and, finally, chief of police.

Finn (p.26) also notes, however: "Despite serious reservations about citizen oversight, many law enforcement administrators have identified several ways that such systems can benefit police agencies. These include bettering an agency's image with the community, enhancing an agency's ability to police itself, and most important, improving an agency's policies and procedures." He (p.27) concludes: "If both sides make a sincere and sustained effort to work together, citizen oversight can help law enforcement administrators perform their jobs more effectively and with increased public support."

Despite the controversy, many larger cities have civilian review boards. According to one account, approximately 100 municipalities throughout the country use civilian panels to investigate complaints.

A case can be made for either side. However, the agency assumption is that the organization should investigate and dispose of its own matters. If there is a serious fault in the final disposition of a complaint, the appointing authority can take action against the responsible manager, but managers should have authority to deal with matters within their own departments. Other remedies such as civil or criminal actions or hearings before civil service boards are also usually available.

Civilian review boards typically have the power only to make recommendations to the police chief executive, not to impose discipline. Some, however, are advocating a modification in the nature of such boards, from a strictly reactive body to one more involved in preventing incidents leading to complaints.

It is conceivable that citizens might expect more sympathy from a panel of other civilians, yet such findings support the notion that civilian review boards are capable of making fair, objective, unbiased decisions regarding complaints, not automatically and disproportionately siding with the citizen complainant to the detriment of the officer or the department. An alternative to civilian review boards is the civilian ombudsman.

The Civilian Ombudsman

Boatman (2001, p.219) explains that a civilian **ombudsman** is "a new office intended to deal with complaints about police officers' actions, provide a liaison between police and residents and make policy recommendations to the police, mayor and city council." Some departments find this a better solution than a "politicized civilian review board operating behind closed doors." According to Boatman (p.220): "The presence of a community ombudsman has seen minor complaints against police officers nearly double, but serious complaints have been cut in half. . . . For the review process to work, it can be neither window dressing nor adversarial. Both the independence of the ombudsman and the ultimate responsibility and authority of the chief must be preserved."

Grievances

Grievances are as much a part of law enforcement managers' responsibilities as complaints. Grievances can come only from law enforcement employees, not from the public. A grievance is a claim by an employee that a rule or policy has been misapplied or misinterpreted to the employee's detriment. The person filing the grievance is known as the **grievant.**

Grievances are a right of employees. Formal grievance procedures are not provided to cause problems but rather to promote a more harmonious, cooperative relationship between employees and management.

Managers' decisions are not always correct. Different interpretations can be put on rules, regulations, policies and procedures. The grievance procedure provides a means of arriving at decisions concerning these varied interpretations. In most instances the final decision may be more satisfactory to all parties involved because it involves input from a number of sources and is not just one person's opinion. Law enforcement managers should not treat employees who file grievances any differently from any other employee.

Causes

Dissatisfaction with physical working conditions and equipment causes the majority of grievances. Almost a third are caused by dissatisfaction with management's actions.

Vehicle condition, quality and timeliness of repair, equipment used in emergencies, lighting conditions, office space, excessive reports, type of acceptable firearm, protective equipment such as armored vests and tear gas and other physical items are the subject of much debate and dissatisfaction. Law enforcement supervisors need to discuss these matters at staff meetings because they are generally budget items that depend on decisions made by higher-level managers.

Roughly 30 percent of grievances result from some management behavior or action. This includes plural standards of conduct, failure to recognize good work, obstinate dealing with subordinates, failure to use procedures uniformly and fairly, use of obscene language, discrimination and other types of objectionable manager behavior.

Grievances concerning rules, regulations, policies and procedures center primarily on violations of civil rights. In the early years of policing, requirements were harsh concerning hairstyle, facial hair and off-duty employment. Employees realize some rules and regulations are necessary for the common good of management, employees and the community. They object, however, to what they consider over-regulation. Many also object to off-duty conduct regulations. They believe that stricter regulations should not apply to officers simply because of their profession.

Law enforcement organizations generally have standard policies for vehicle operation, physical use of force and when to use firearms. Even so, some objections arise on grounds that officers should be able to use individual discretion. Civil and criminal actions against law enforcement officers have tended to force standardized procedures in these areas. In general, objections are low if the rules and regulations are communicated to the entire department and a two-way discussion is held concerning limitations and reasons.

The failure of management to do what employees expect also causes employee dissatisfaction. Employees, in general, want to do a good job and resent too many impediments. Among perceived impediments are:

- Failure to communicate and to train employees to do the job effectively.
- Failure to explain procedures and then blaming employees for not doing it right.
- Failure to praise when it is deserved.
- Managers' failure to set a good example for subordinates.

Managers should not penalize employees for actions not directly related to performance of duty or to the best interest or safety of other department employees and not specifically in the rules, regulations, policies or procedures.

Resolving Grievances

Most noncontractual grievances are resolved at the first-line supervisor level. These are matters not associated with salaries, fringe benefits or conditions negotiated by the labor union or an employee group representative. The first-line manager talks to the grievant or the group filing the grievance. Through two-way communication, an objective approach by both sides, common sense, fair play and discussion of all issues and alternatives, the matter may be resolved at this level.

If the matter is not resolved at the first level, a formal grievance is filed and forwarded to the next level manager. If not resolved at this level, it proceeds to the head of the department. If it fails to be resolved at this level, the matter proceeds to voluntary arbitration, civil service board proceedings or other assigned hearing boards. Figure 12.2 illustrates the chain of command a grievance may go through.

Many law enforcement departments have ordinances, statutes or formal procedures for handling grievances. Following is an example of a grievance ordinance.

> *Informal Grievance Procedure.* Any employee or group of employees having a grievance should first discuss the grievance with their immediate supervisor within

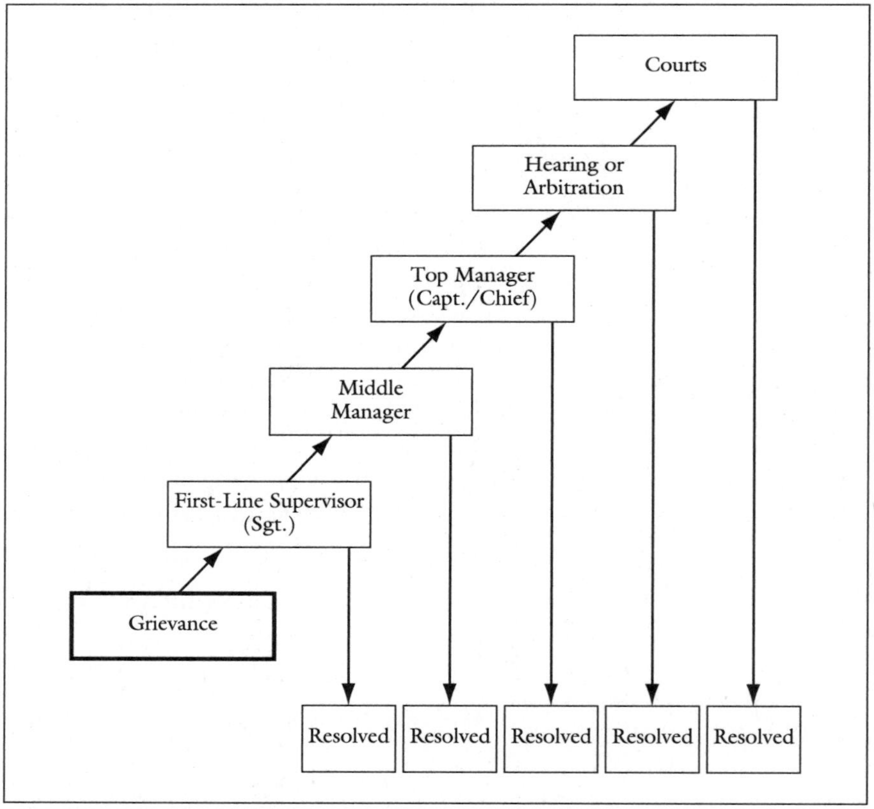

Source: "Conflict Management and the Law Enforcement Professional in the 1990s." *Law and Order,* May 1994. Reprinted by permission of the publisher.

Figure 12.2
Grievance Chain of Command

five working days of the occurrence that caused the grievance. Within five working days, the supervisor should reply. If the supervisor's answer does not satisfactorily adjust the grievance, the employee should follow, within five working days, the formal grievance procedure outlined in the next section.

Formal Grievance Procedure. The following steps are used in the formal grievance procedure.

Step 1. The grievance is submitted in writing to the employee's immediate supervisor. The supervisor meets and discusses the grievance with the employee and/or their representative, if any, and replies in writing to the employee within five working days.

Step 2. If a settlement is not reached, the written grievance will be presented within five working days to the next level of supervision. The second level supervisor or their representative has five working days to investigate and render a written decision.

The procedure continues in this fashion, going up the hierarchy to the department head, the city manager and finally the civil service commission.

The ordinance provides employees an opportunity and right to bring dissatisfactions to management. It does not necessarily mean the grievance is justified, but it provides a procedure for having the matter heard and decided. It is an orderly procedure that applies to all employees equally and is free from interference, restraint, coercion or reprisal. The intent is to make grievances an aboveboard matter for discussion rather than a behind-the-back approach to problems.

The ordinance's wording makes it clear that employees have a chance to be heard. Grievance procedures are provided to avoid having problems fester, grow and become unmanageable. The results of such a procedure are most often positive for employees, management and the organization.

Mediation and Arbitration

Sometimes mediation or arbitration is used to settle grievances. **Mediation** brings in a neutral outside third party who tries to reconcile the two sides after hearing both and recommending a solution, which is not binding on either party. Finn (2000b, p.74) suggests: "Mediation benefits are most likely to occur when misunderstandings, miscommunication, or lack of communication are the primary factors in the dispute." Finn (p.79) observes: "Because mediation is almost always held in private and the results are confidential, some police administrators may regard it as having less 'teeth,' and therefore less of a deterrent effect, than an internal affairs investigation." Nonetheless, Finn (p.80) says: "The costs of mediation are low and offset by the increased time internal affairs units can devote to more serious citizen (and internal) complaints." Cooper (2000, p.8) observes: "The key to successful mediation, whether formal or informal, lies in allowing the participants to fashion their own agreement."

Arbitration also brings in a neutral outside third party who, like the mediator, listens to both sides. The arbitration hearings may be informal or formal. After hearing both sides, the arbitrator recommends a solution. Unlike the mediator's recommendation, however, the recommendation of the arbitration *is* often binding.

Disposition of Complaints and Grievances

A complaint or grievance investigation usually results in one of four findings: sustained, not sustained, exonerated or unfounded.

A **sustained** complaint or grievance is one in which the investigative facts support the charge. If the investigative facts are insufficient, that is, the evidence does not support the accusations, the complaint or grievance is **not sustained.** An **exonerated** complaint or grievance is one in which the investigation determines that the matter did occur but was proper and legal. An **unfounded** complaint or grievance is one in which either the act did not occur or the complaint was false.

Whatever the outcome, the officers and department are "marked." The complainant or grievant, the person against whom the accusation was made, superiors and the press (if the matter had been previously publicized) should be notified of the findings and outcome.

Most cases are disposed of in a relatively short time, either as sustained or not sustained. A surprisingly small number have little basis for further action. If a complaint or grievance is sustained against an individual, progressive discipline such as that discussed in Chapter 11 is recommended. If corrective measures are necessary, they must be executed as soon as possible. At a set future time, the matter must be rechecked to determine whether further action is needed.

The Chronic Complainer

There is a story about a hound sitting in a country store in the Ozarks, howling. A stranger comes into the store and asks the storekeeper, "What's the matter with the dog?"

"He's sitting on a cocklebur."

"Why doesn't he get off?"

"He'd rather holler."

Some people are basically negative about everything. Griping has become a habit—a chronically dismal way of looking at one's department, supervisor and fellow officers. Some people just are not happy unless they are complaining. As Harris and Gilmartin (2000, p.19) note: "Although these people represent only a small percentage of an organization's personnel, they demand the largest amount of supervisory time." They (p.20) contend: "When organizations do a good job of selecting and a poor job of maintaining employees, they can expect to see some of their hard-working, dedicated and productive employees become angry, cynical malcontents. . . . With practical skills, supervisors can develop the 'courage to confront,' which is essential if supervisors hope to become more effective and confident when dealing with malcontent and disgruntled employees."

Managers who have such subordinates should recognize the problem and make a concerted effort to at least not let the negative attitude affect others. Among the tactics managers might use are the following:

- Do not overreact to the negativism. When possible, ignore it.
- Relax tension. Negative people often make those around them feel stressed. Do not let that happen. Break the tension with a little humor.

- Promptly undo any damage. Negative workers often stir up their peers and disrupt the department or work group. If this happens, send the negative person out of the common work area and get everyone else back on track.
- Make your expectations clear. Have a heart-to-heart talk with the negative person. Try to find out why he or she is so negative. Let the person know you expect the negativism to be kept out of the department.
- Set an example. Be as optimistic and upbeat as possible. Encourage your subordinates to act positively, too.

Summary

A *complaint* is a statement of a problem, whereas a *grievance* is a formally registered complaint. A complaint may be made by the general public, by people arrested or by employees of the law enforcement department, including peers or managers. The person or group filing the complaint is called the complainant.

Complaints may originate externally or internally. External complaints are those made by citizens against a law enforcement officer or officers, a supervisor, support staff and/or the entire department. Categories of officer misconduct included in external complaints are crime, excessive force, false arrest, improper entry, unlawful search, harassment, offensive demeanor and rule infractions. External complaints can be reduced through effective recruitment and selection, training, written directives, manuals, supervisory responsibility, community outreach and data collection and analysis.

Most internal complaints are related to working conditions or management style. Many could be avoided if communication were improved. Communication is directly related to job performance. Those who are dissatisfied on the job and communicate their discontent perform better than those who are satisfied and do not communicate. The Pinch Model illustrates the importance of communication in dealing with complaints and the consequences of not communicating effectively.

A basic rule is to *never* take a complaint lightly. A careful investigation of a complaint instills confidence in management's fairness and protects those accused of wrongdoing. While under investigation, officers may find legal protection from a Law Enforcement Officer Bill of Rights (LEOBR), if one has been enacted in that state, and under the Garrity protection.

A grievance is a claim by an employee that a rule or policy has been misapplied or misinterpreted to the employee's detriment. The person filing the grievance is known as the grievant. Dissatisfaction with physical working conditions and equipment causes the majority of grievances. Almost a third are caused by dissatisfaction with management's actions.

Mediation and arbitration bring in a neutral outside third party to intervene in grievance proceedings. A complaint or grievance investigation usually results in one of four findings: sustained, not sustained, exonerated or unfounded.

Discussion Questions

1. How are complaints and grievances similar? Different?
2. Why is it important to investigate complaints immediately?
3. How would you investigate a complaint from a person who does not want to give a name?
4. What is your position on civilian review boards?
5. Can you think of an example of some pinches in your work? Crunches?
6. What changes would you suggest in the grievance procedure?
7. How would you reduce the frequency of grievances within a law enforcement organization?
8. Which would you prefer to settle a grievance: mediation or arbitration? Why?
9. Do you know of any grievances filed in your local law enforcement agency? If so, what was the problem and how was it resolved?
10. Have you ever been involved in a complaint or grievance, either as the one being charged or the one making the charge?

InfoTrac College Edition Assignment

Use InfoTrac College Edition to help answer the Discussion Questions as appropriate.

Once you have taken a position on civilian review boards (see Discussion Question 4), find a recent journal article to support that position. Outline the main points supporting your position. Be sure to include the full reference cite. Be prepared to discuss your position and support with the class.

OR

Read and outline one of the following articles:

- "Statements Compelled from Law Enforcement Employees" by Michael E. Brooks
- "Getting Along with Citizen Oversight" by Peter Finn

References

Boatman, Robert. "Monitoring the Police: The Civilian Ombudsman as a Community Liaison." *Law and Order,* October 2001, pp.219–220.

Brooks, Michael E. "Statements Compelled from Law Enforcement Employees." *FBI Law Enforcement Bulletin,* June 2002, pp.26–31.

Buchholz, Steve and Roth, Thomas. *Creating the High-Performance Team.* New York: John Wiley and Sons, 1987.

Cooper, Christopher. "Training Patrol Officers to Mediate Disputes." *FBI Law Enforcement Bulletin,* February 2000, pp.7–10.

Finn, Peter. "Getting Along with Citizen Oversight." *FBI Law Enforcement Bulletin,* August 2000a, pp.22–27.

Finn, Peter. "Two Mediation Systems Help Manage Citizen Complaints." *The Police Chief,* August 2000b, pp.67–80.

Harris, John J. (Jack) and Gilmartin, Kevin M. "Malcontent and Disgruntled Employees: What Is a Supervisor to Do?" *The Police Chief,* December 2000, pp.19–24.

International Association of Chiefs of Police. "Model Policy Offers Guidance on Investigating Officer Misconduct." *The Police Chief,* October 2000, pp.44–50.

Lober, Richard E. "Value-Based Leadership and the Role of Internal Affairs." *The Police Chief,* May 2002, pp.54–57.

Thurnauer, Beau. "Internal Affairs: Practice and Policy Review for Smaller Departments." *The Police Chief,* October 2002, pp.73–82.

Worrall, John L. "If You Build It, They Will Come: Consequences of Improved Citizen Complaint Review Procedures." *Crime & Delinquency,* July 2002, pp.355–379.

Book-Specific Web Site

Go to the *Management and Supervision in Law Enforcement* Web site at http://info.wadsworth.com/05346160654 for student and instructor resources, including Internet Assignments and Case Studies.

CHAPTER 13

Conflict—It's Inevitable

Parties in conflict must be able to disagree without being disagreeable.

—Anonymous

Do You Know?

- Whether conflict must be negative?
- What possible benefits conflict might generate?
- What major sources of conflict exist in the law enforcement organization?
- What the 10/80/10 principle is?
- What management's responsibility is as far as conflict is concerned?
- How conflicts that arise during crises should be dealt with?
- How a problem employee is characterized?
- What types of personalities might be likely to result in conflict?
- How managers can deal with problem people?
- What the confrontation technique is and what to expect from it?
- What healthy conflict does?
- What the keys to maintaining healthy conflict are?
- What the intersubjectivity approach to resolving conflict involves?

Can You Define?

approach-approach conflict
approach-avoidance conflict
avoidance-avoidance conflict
avoiders
bullies
complainers
conflict
confrontation technique
exploders
healthy conflict
intersubjectivity
intersubjectivity approach
know-it-alls
marginal performer
negative conflict
nonactor liability
ombud
passives
pessimists
positive conflict
principled negotiation
problem employee
snipers
yes people

INTRODUCTION

Most people agree that death and taxes are inevitable. Add *conflict* to the list of inevitables for managers, especially within a law enforcement organization. McCaffery (2001, p.26) says: "Facing conflict and confrontation is inevitable for anyone in law enforcement." One reason is that our society has become increasingly complex. Choices used to be simpler. Coffee, tea or milk? Vanilla, chocolate or strawberry ice cream? Think about the number of choices *within* choices. What kind of Coke? With or without calories? Caffeine? What kind of weapons? Squad cars? Uniforms? Investigative equipment?

Another reason conflict is inevitable is that managers deal with people, and within the law enforcement agency people have strong egos and are used to speaking their minds and getting their way. But they are also people who depend on each other to get results—sometimes to stay alive.

A third reason conflict is inevitable is that resources are limited, and the law enforcement organization is no exception. Choices must be made as to allocation of human resources (who is assigned to what shift) and monetary resources (salaries, perks).

Indeed, all organizations, including law enforcement, will have conflict. Individual and organizational goals; differences in employee lifestyles and individual needs; varied interpretations of rules and regulations; physical, social and psychological differences; and variations in viewpoints all exist and contribute to disagreement and conflict.

This chapter takes a closer look at the conflicts law enforcement managers must deal with, including some conflicting views of conflict, sources of conflict and the responsibility of managers to reduce negative conflict and make positive conflict work for the benefit of the organization. This is followed by a discussion of how to recognize and acknowledge conflict, how to manage crisis conflict and how to deal with problem employees, including problem behaviors and difficult people. Next the probability of role conflict within the organization is examined, followed by a look at external conflicts and politics, both internal and external. The chapter concludes with a discussion of how to maintain healthy conflict and the importance of conflict resolution skills.

Conflict Defined

Conflict is a struggle, a mental or physical fight, a controversy, a disagreement or a clash. Conflict can range from an internal struggle within a person over whether to smoke a cigarette or take a drink to armed combat between nations over boundaries or religious beliefs.

Conflict includes controversy. As Fulton (2000b, p.118) notes: "The ability to handle controversy is critical to the success of any police commander, at any rank. The problem may be internal to your police department, such as disagreements over who is getting promoted or allegations of selective discipline. Or the controversy may involve disagreements over external issues such as police policies or tactics and how they are implemented in your community. Controversy is inevitable. Understanding that controversy is a part of policing, and accepting the fact that you must handle it, puts you in a good position to handle it effectively."

Controversy and conflict can be fleeting or prolonged, conscious or subconscious, destructive or constructive. Conflict may be:

- **Approach–approach conflict**—selecting one of two positive alternatives.
- **Approach–avoidance conflict**—selecting one positive alternative that will also produce a negative consequence.
- **Avoidance–avoidance conflict**—selecting one of two negatives, commonly referred to as "the lesser of two evils."

Because conflict is inevitable for managers and supervisors, they must have the skills to manage it effectively.

Conflicting Views of Conflict

Conflict has always existed between people and organizations. As McDonald (2002, p.27) observes: "Conflict is not the same as violence. Conflict simply means difference between two or more people in ideas, personalities or whatever." The first reaction to conflict is that it is bad and should not exist. However, considering the tension that exists within individuals and the competition between people and organizations, it is reasonable to expect disagreements created by everyday interactions.

Law enforcement organizations are no different. Officers as individuals have all the personal problems of other employees. Law enforcement organizations consist of a number of divisions and a hierarchy of command. Most requests for law enforcement service and contacts involve conflicts. Citizens call the police when they have problems they cannot resolve.

Most people believe conflict is always negative because they see the destructive results of conflict in wars, in marriages, in organizations and among individuals. Law enforcement departments also have traditionally regarded conflict as inherently bad. Administrators note its damaging effects. Morale decline, lower productivity, lack of creativity, poor performance and many other ills have been blamed on **negative conflict.** The prevailing attitudes are to avoid or eliminate conflict by adding more and more rules and regulations. Law enforcement agencies where conflict reigns are regarded as poorly administered. In departments in which conflict is poorly handled, it *is* a destructive force. Excessive conflict without resolution *is* negative and can lead to disunity in individual and organizational purpose, decreased morale and lower productivity.

This need *not* be the case, however. Conflict does not have to be destructive. If it is recognized for what it is, conflict can be a positive influence because it can bring attention to problems that need to be resolved. **Positive conflict** can result in personal or organizational growth.

How managers approach conflict determines whether it is a negative or a positive force within the organization.

Although organizations with badly managed conflict are hamstrung with dissension, those with *no* conflict are in an equally unproductive situation.

Organizations with no conflict are dormant, static, unimaginative, unable to change and in danger of becoming obsolete.

A healthy amount of conflict, properly handled, motivates individuals and organizations. It exposes problems, defines causes, obtains input from those involved toward constructive solutions and may develop new outlooks.

Conflict is constructive if it:

- Encourages better decision making and/or change.
- Makes life more interesting.
- Reduces irritation.
- Enriches a relationship.
- Increases motivation to deal with problems.
- Is stimulating.

Conflict can be agitating and exciting, indicating organizational vigor. It can keep a groove from turning into a rut.

Conflict that opposes without antagonizing can be extremely beneficial to a law enforcement organization, keeping it innovative and responsive to change.

It is usually not disagreement that creates anger and hostility; rather, it is the manner in which the disagreement is handled. As George Bernard Shaw noted: "The test of breeding is how people behave in a quarrel." The challenge to managers is not to suppress conflict but to minimize its destructiveness and to transform the anger often associated with it into positive, creative forces.

Sources of Conflict

Conflict originates from several sources. In law enforcement organizations the most common forms of conflict are internal, between two or more individuals, between organization and officer, between groups within the organization or between officers and other agencies and the public.

Conflict may come from individual, interpersonal or job-related sources as well as from sources outside the organization. Change is a major source of conflict.

Individual Sources

Parks (2000, p.83) notes: "Employee conflict causes an enormous loss of effectiveness and productivity. Many times the unresolved conflicts fester, negatively impacting morale and harmony in the workplace." Individual, internal conflict exists because of uncertainty, lack of knowledge, criticism, pressures of superiors or the organization, differing opinions on organizational goals or the fear of doing something wrong.

Many law enforcement personnel hearings involve actions such as conduct while off duty, failure to cooperate, insubordination, excessive use of force, violation of duty requirements, excessive use of alcohol, the filing of false reports or other violations of rules and regulations. In most instances, some internal conflict is at the heart of the problem and manifests itself in a conflict with other officers or with management.

Personal problems at home can be brought to the workplace, for example, problems with children, financial matters, one's spouse and the like.

Interpersonal Sources

Interpersonal sources of conflict result because personnel come from different cultures, have different backgrounds and have different dominant needs. Many conflicts arise because of personality differences and may be the result of prejudices or biases or of different perceptions and values. Much conflict results from the various ways people view the world—ways that reflect the individual's upbringing, culture, race, socioeconomic class, experience and education. Such conflict is often expressed this way: "He has never done anything to me, but I just can't stand him."

Sometimes a large group is dissatisfied, usually as a result of factors such as low pay, inadequate benefits, poor working conditions or exceptionally strict discipline. Frequently, whole group dissatisfaction arises during contract negotiations, and management must communicate openly during such times.

Small group dissatisfaction illustrates the management theory referred to as the 10/80/10 principle, which divides members of a department into three categories:

- Ten percent who are self-motivated high achievers
- Eighty percent, the core group, who do average work
- The bottom 10 percent who cause management 90 percent of their problems

The 10/80/10 principle divides the work force into three categories: 10 percent who are high achievers, 80 percent who are average achievers and 10 percent who are unmotivated troublemakers and cause 90 percent of management's problems.

Job-Related Sources

Job-related conflicts usually involve organizational and administrative objectives, goals, rules and regulations; the hierarchy structure; differences on how to use resources and conflicts between personnel and groups. Conflict may arise from differences over facts, methods or basic philosophies on such matters as use of force.

Groups within the organization may be promoting self-interests ahead of organizational interests. Internally, departments such as administration, dispatch, juvenile, investigation and patrol compete for allocated budget funds.

Competition also adds to conflict. Most officers seek recognition and promotion, which may result in extremely destructive interpersonal conflicts. Conflict may arise when an officer of less seniority is promoted over an officer of more seniority, when a patrol officer turns over a case to an investigator and never hears anything more about the case, or when one officer does the work and the shift manager takes the credit. Conflict may also arise when a senior patrol officer gets a smaller salary than a starting detective, when a senior officer is assigned to patrol in a new squad car or when officers are given preferential shift assignments.

Use of Force: A Major Source of Conflict

Excessive use of force has been a major issue for police and a hot political issue in many cities, as discussed in Chapter 11. Several chiefs of police in major cities have lost their positions as a result of wrongful use-of-force incidents under their administration.

The majority of excessive force claims are filed against police officers and agencies under Section 1983. Claims arise in three major areas: arrests and seizures of criminal suspects, postarrest or pretrial detention and postconviction confinement.

In one use-of-force complaint, a father and son appeared at a police station, the son showing serious cuts and bruises to his face and head. The father claimed police had beaten his son during a traffic stop, one officer holding the boy's arms back while the other struck him repeatedly, all prior to a formal arrest. During the complaint investigation, the supervisor located several photographs taken at the county jail, two hours after the boy's arrest, clearly showing the young man's face and head free of injury. When the supervisor confronted the father and son with the time-and-date-stamped photos, they demanded to speak to their attorney. Apparently the father had beaten the son for getting arrested and then plotted to sue the police department for monetary damages. In this case basic investigatory processes revealed a false use-of-force complaint.

Perhaps the best known use-of-force case is that of *Rodney King v. Los Angeles.* Both the city and the officers involved were sued under Section 1983. Additionally, other officers who stood by and did nothing to prevent the alleged wrongful acts were involved under the **nonactor liability** provisions. That is, officers who were present at a scene at which use of force was in question or where force was obviously excessive yet did nothing to prevent it have also been held liable by the courts.

A frequently cited precedent case is *Byrd v. Brishke* (1972). In this case the plaintiff was surrounded by a dozen officers and repeatedly struck. Because he could not identify the officers who beat him, he filed on the theory that the officers not involved in the beating should be held liable for negligently or intentionally failing to protect him from others who violated his rights by beating him. The court established a clear duty to act on the part of both supervisors and peer officers who observe other officers committing unconstitutional acts.

Harassment: Another Major Source of Conflict

In recent years the number of cases of alleged harassment has increased substantially. According to the Equal Employment Opportunity Commission (EEOC): "Sexual harassment is unwelcome sexual attention, whether verbal or physical, that affects an employee's job conditions or creates a hostile working environment." Although this seems a simple definition, it has initiated complex, unsettling lawsuits with substantial risks for both plaintiff and defendant. One standard is what a reasonable person would think is out of bounds or would interfere with work.

As noted in Chapter 11, law enforcement agencies must have a clear written policy forbidding harassment of any form, including sexual or racial harassment. The policy should state its purpose, describe the prohibited activities or conduct, outline employees' and supervisors' responsibilities and detail the complaint procedure. Although the majority of sexual harassment complaints are initiated by women, the same conditions apply to men.

Sources of Conflict External to the Law Enforcement Organization

Municipalities have limited resources to operate the total city government. The law enforcement organization is one agency competing for a share of these resources. If law enforcement personnel perceive they are not obtaining sufficient resources for reasonable operation, conflict will arise. If, for example, the fire department receives more money than the law enforcement department or vice versa, heated disagreement is likely.

Change—Yet Another Major Source

Change is constant in most people's lives, both at home and at work, and people tend to resist it. Change threatens the status quo and the basic need for security. People like what is familiar to continue, but change means dealing with an unknown.

In law enforcement work, change is constant. Technological advances have introduced a variety of equipment. Laws and court decisions are constantly in dispute and changing. When change occurs in administration or operations, managers tend to be more involved with the organizational aspects of the change than with human relations. The organization changes, but the organization is people. It is how people react to change that is important.

Change affects individuals in a law enforcement organization because it requires new learning and new approaches and introduces fear of the unknown. A change of shift, assignment to a new manager, change of patrol partner, placing computers in the squad cars and many other changes affect officers.

The first reaction to change is usually reluctance to accept it or fear it will not work. Management must explain changes and provide training so personnel can make a successful transition. Failure to explain change will bring resistance. Managers should explain not only that a change will be made but also that input from employees is desired and that there will be a follow-up and assessment.

Responsibility for Conflict Management

Law enforcement agencies have a number of levels at which conflict may be resolved. Supervisors are the front line to resolve conflict at its source and are directly responsible for most personnel. Yet personnel are the most frequent source of conflict, and personnel conflicts should be resolved at this level when possible.

Supervisors are also essential to conflict management because they are usually the first to know that conflict exists in the ranks. It is their responsibility to mediate these conflicts unless they believe the conflicts are deeper and more involved than the shift level of management can handle.

Group conflicts may have to proceed to middle or upper management. Using higher-level authority sometimes resolves a situation temporarily but may not always identify the problem.

If there is conflict in the relationships of manager and subordinates, such as a past problem or personal prejudices, the matter should be sent to the next management level. If conflicts exist between supervisors, responsibility shifts to middle-management level. All conflicts could potentially shift to the executive manager, city manager, civil service proceedings or the courts. Resolution at the lowest level is preferable.

Recognizing and Acknowledging Conflict

Regardless of the level of intervention, the best method to resolve conflict is usually to deal directly with those involved, determine the cause of the conflict and seek a solution. Delaying the inevitable only increases the probability of a worse problem.

Avoiding is a decision to "leave it to someone else." Managers who accept responsibility have choices of actions to minimize or eliminate the conflict and in many cases to rise to new levels of performance and productivity because of it. Often managers wish a problem would simply go away. They would like to have officers who all agree with their opinions. They dislike officers who disagree with them and may even consider them insubordinate. Such managers would rather use the power of their position to resolve conflict than to resolve it through input and cooperation.

Traditionally, most managers have thought that expressing anger or opposing the majority opinion is not professional. But simply because a feeling is not expressed does not mean it will go away. It often remains and influences a person, whether it is recognized or not. A statement such as, "My sergeant and I just don't see things the same way" often really means, "I don't like my sergeant."

In addition, even if a feeling or an idea is not spoken, it may still be expressed through facial expressions, finger-pointing and standing too close to someone as conflict escalates. The result of such action is that the conflict is still there, but because it has not come out into the open or been put into words, it cannot be resolved.

A manager's responsibility is to recognize conflict when it occurs, have a system for reporting conflict and take action as soon as possible.

Evading an issue does not resolve the conflict. Transferring or isolating individuals does not identify a conflict either and may interfere with the entire organization's operation. Some managers avoid conflict by seeking out employees who are not apt to "rock the boat," using the authority of their position autocratically, increasing feelings of agreement but never actually agreeing, or stalling for time, hoping the problem will go away. Willingness to do battle when necessary is a form of honesty and is expected of managers and supervisors.

Managing Crisis Conflict

Conflict is a constant concern of management. Usually it is best handled through discussion, exploration of causes and alternatives and participatory leadership. In crises, however, such conflict management is not possible.

Conflicts that arise during crises must be managed by following established procedures and the chain of command.

Fulton (2000a, p.94) stresses: "Any good commander recognizes that reasonable people can disagree—even in critical situations. However, somebody must assume the leadership role and be in charge. . . . In critical situations, there can be only brief internal strife. You must make the decision to either assume the leadership role or commit your unit to the mission established by one of your peers who has chosen to assume that role. You cannot hesitate in critical situations—to do so may endanger the mission as well as the safety of your personnel. Disagreement and indecision are the materials that injuries and lawsuits are made of in police work."

Fulton (2001, p.142) further notes: "How you handle the crisis may be more important than the actual outcome. During critical situations, others are looking to you for guidance, command and leadership. You must be perceived as a decisive part of the solution if you are to gain the respect of all who are involved. Your future may depend upon your performance under pressure in any given situation."

Crisis management is usually reactive rather than proactive. Procedures must be established to minimize conflicts and to resolve those that occur during a crisis. The following guidelines might assist:

- Anticipate the kinds of conflict and who might be involved. Establish precedents.
- Make certain one person is clearly in charge.
- Make certain all officers know what they are responsible for doing.
- Let no one shirk assigned responsibilities.
- Keep lines of communication open. Keep everyone involved informed, including your superior, but also control the flow of information.
- Make decisions that allow the most options.
- If the crisis is prolonged, be sure personnel get rest and can attend to personal needs.
- If the crisis is prolonged, put someone in charge of routine duties that still must be performed while the crisis continues.
- As the crisis winds down, expect delayed stress reactions (depression, irritability, irrational outbursts). Hold debriefings.
- Return to normal operations as soon as possible.
- Evaluate performance and identify conflicts that should have been avoided or handled differently.

Dealing with Problem Employees

Employees have many reasons for exhibiting objectionable behavior. A formerly excellent employee may change behavior due to physical illness or emotional or mental breakdown. This may not be exhibited violently or suddenly but subtly and over a long period. A change in behavior may also occur in response to disruptive and objectionable changes in department rules or regulations.

According to Feltgen (2001, p.41): "In a government setting, where strong union contracts provide for job protection and complex disciplinary review boards, managers may have an extremely difficult time effectively taking on and terminating unproductive employees." However: "If management holds firm to its position of terminating unproductive employees, it will discover that underperforming employees will show remarkable improvement during the first phase of retraining" (Feltgen, p.45).

A key question is: Are problem employees too costly to retain, or is it wiser to change their behavior? Changing behavior is usually more cost-effective than replacing employees, so managers must learn more about employee assistance programs (EAP) and their underlying philosophy. Many law enforcement agencies operate their own EAPs. Others contract with outside agencies to provide services such as counseling and peer support, as discussed in the next chapter.

A **problem employee** exhibits abnormal behavior to the extent that the behavior is detrimental to organizational needs and goals as well as the needs and goals of other law enforcement personnel.

Such behavior reduces the department's effectiveness and the desired professional level of law enforcement service to the community and results in numerous conflicts.

A **marginal performer** is an employee who has demonstrated ability to perform but does just enough to get by.

Often employees themselves are responsible for their problems: their mental attitude, physical condition and emotional well-being. The manifestations of such problems are laziness, moodiness, resistance to change, complacency, absence or tardiness and disorganization. These problems could probably be altered with changes in attitude, physical condition or emotional well-being.

Many factors affect employees and determine their behavior. New law enforcement employees enter the field with expectations of becoming professionals already having some college education or a college degree. In addition, new officers expect law enforcement education courses more directly related to their career while on the job. Many of today's officers plan to attend college-level criminal justice courses after employment. With education comes higher expectations of special tasks, promotions, specialized assignments and higher salaries.

Dealing with Difficult People

Personality problems such as hostility, excessive sensitivity or bad attitudes can disrupt a law enforcement organization. In severe cases it may be necessary to refer an employee to outside counseling or assistance. With hostile employees it is best to listen and make arrangements to discuss the matter later when emotions have subsided. During later discussion managers should make it clear that the behavior is unacceptable because of its effect on other employees and operations.

Conflict often results from personality clashes. Personality types can be placed on a continuum ranging from those who are always in total agreement to those who are always in total disagreement. In the middle are those who are noncommittal, never taking one side or the other (see Figure 13.1).

Difficult people include yes people, passives, avoiders, pessimists, complainers, know-it-alls, exploders, bullies and snipers.

Yes people are vocally supportive in your presence but rarely follow through. They smile, nod and do nothing. They always have excuses when a deadline rolls around. Yes people have a high need for acceptance and usually avoid open conflict. They tell you what they think you want to hear.

Tactfully confront the no-action behavior. When you make an initial request, give them time to say no. If they do not, have them put the commitment in writing or say exactly when they will complete the project. Do not allow them to make unrealistic promises. Build incremental steps, deadlines and checkpoints. Follow up and monitor the expected results. Show your approval when the promised action is taken.

Passives are silent, unresponsive people who seldom offer their own ideas or opinions, keeping their thoughts to themselves. Their responses are usually short and noncommittal. Some will put in writing what they will not say. Working with passives can be frustrating. The major coping strategy is to get them to open up and talk to you. Comment on their quietness. Help reduce their tension. Ask open-ended questions and wait for them to answer, and then thank them for their ideas.

Avoiders put things off; they procrastinate or physically absent themselves to avoid getting involved. To deal with indecisive avoiders, find out why they are stalling. Probe. Question. Listen. Move away from vagueness toward specificity. Express the value of decisiveness. Explore alternatives. Help them make decisions, and then give support after they have made a decision.

Figure 13.1
Personality Types

Pessimists always say "no," are inflexible and resist change. Structure their work relationships so they have little contact with other workers.

Closely related to pessimists are **complainers**—those who find fault with everything and everyone. These people continually gripe but take no personal responsibility for anything. Confront them, interrupt the complaining and have them detail the problem. Acknowledge and understand the complaint, but do not agree with it, argue about it or accept blame for it. Discuss the realities of the situation and focus on solving it.

Know-it-alls are highly opinionated, speak with great authority, are sure of themselves, have all the right answers (or think they do) and are impatient with others. Know-it-alls have a strong need for order and structure, to be right (or at least to never be wrong), to be seen as competent and to be admired and respected. Use the know-it-alls' expertise and at the same time be sure your ideas are fully considered and used. Acknowledge their expertise, but help them see their effect on others. Show them how their ideas are helpful and yet not necessarily the only way to view an issue. Avoid being a counter-expert, but do your homework and know your facts. Raise questions without confrontation. Let them save face.

Exploders yell and scream. They are overemotional and sometimes even hysterical. Because you cannot talk to people who are yelling and screaming, first disarm the anger. Stand up and face them squarely. Do not let them go on for more than 30 seconds, but do not tell them to calm down. Put your hand out to stop them. Call them by name and keep repeating the name until they stop yelling. Validate their feelings: "I understand you are angry. I want to work with you but not this way." Help them regain self-control. Let them cool off. Ask, "What do you need right now?" As a last resort, simply walk away from them.

Bullies attack verbally or physically, using threats and demands to get their way. They are like steamrollers, using unrelenting, hammering arguments to push people to back down. They have a high need to be correct and are impatient with others. Stand your ground without being aggressive, and avoid a head-on fight. Do not argue or worry about being polite. Use low-key persistence. Do not let them interrupt. Establish eye contact, call them by name and be clear about what you do and do not want.

Snipers are hostile, aggressive people who do not attack openly like the exploder and bully but rather engage in guerrilla warfare, using subtle digs, cheap shots and innuendos. Like exploders and bullies, snipers have a strong judgmental view of how others should think and act, but they choose to stay hidden and attack covertly. Neutralize sniping without escalation into open warfare. Meet in private and avoid countersniping. Bring them out into the open while avoiding a direct confrontation by saying things such as, "Are you trying to make a point?" "What are you trying to say?"

To deal with problem people, get their attention, identify the problem behavior, point out the consequences, ask questions, listen and explain expectations. Avoid defensiveness.

In addition, as Meany (2001, p.72) suggests, take a good look at the problem employee: "You may discover this: You're so focused on yourself that the problem is not with Person X, it's with you."

Handling Personal Attacks

Smith and Brantner (2000, p.108) note: "Understand and accept that you can control yourself, but you cannot control others." They (p.109) suggest: "Monitor your self-talk: Do you talk like someone who expects good things to happen? Do you do things that show you are helpless, or show that you are in charge?" Personal attacks normally arouse anger in the person who is attacked. Do *not* become angry. An angry exchange of words seldom accomplishes anything except damage. Instead, analyze the behavior and the attacker's charges. Take a deep breath and concentrate on remaining calm. The longer you remain calm and in control, the more likely you are to take positive steps toward resolving the conflict. Recognize that no one can make you angry but yourself. You are in sole control of how you react. Do not relinquish this control to others. At the same time, accept the right of others to disagree with your views.

If you find that you are becoming angry, acknowledge it out loud: "This is starting to really irritate me." This gives the other person fair warning that you may blow up and is another way to buy time while you maintain control. *Respond* to the person rather than *reacting*. Listen to what the person is asserting. Could it be right? Ask clarifying questions. State your own position clearly.

Defuse the other person's anger. Get on the same level physically, that is, sit if the person is sitting; stand if the person is standing. Be quiet and allow the person to vent. Empathize by saying something such as: "I can see how you might feel that way." But do not patronize.

Focus on the present and the future, on resolving the conflict rather than on placing blame. It takes two people to make a conflict. Open the lines of communication and keep them open, but do not exceed your level of authority. Make only promises that you can keep.

If the person continues to be angry and confrontational, ask, "What do you expect me to do?" or "What do you want?" Such statements may disarm a vindictive troublemaker. They may also help you discover a person's genuine concerns. If the person asks for something you cannot deliver, say so.

If all the preceding fail, accept that this person must want the conflict to continue for some reason. At this point seek intervention from a higher level of authority or suggest that the attacker get help from another source. Distance yourself from people who seem intent on making your job more difficult, and limit their access to you.

It is probably a truism that no one truly "wins" an argument. This is illustrated by the law enforcement lieutenant who was hardworking, conscientious and highly skilled but had not received a promotion in 10 years. Asked to explain his failure to advance, he replied, "Several years ago I had an argument with the chief. I won."

Handling Disagreements between Others in the Department

The first step in handling disagreements between two subordinates is to decide whether intervention is wise. Some conflicts are truly personality clashes rather than problem centered. In such cases it is fruitless to intervene and will only weaken your leadership when conflicts involve true problems rather than simply personalities. Some managers rely on the confrontation technique to handle such disputes.

The **confrontation technique,** insisting that two disputing people or groups meet face-to-face to resolve their differences, may effectively resolve conflicts or it may make them worse.

Sometimes those in conflict will resolve their differences themselves. Often, however, the differences intensify, positions harden, people become angry and defensive and logic gives way to personal attacks. Those in conflict refuse to back down on any points. The adversaries bluff, not wanting to show their true feelings.

Managers might intervene in conflicts if employees cannot reach a solution or the solution does not end the conflict. They should intervene if the conflict is disrupting the department. Once you decide it would be beneficial to intervene, meet with each person privately to discuss issues and to confirm the willingness of both parties to resolve the conflict. Then select a neutral meeting location.

If the conflict is truly disruptive, consider using the power of your position and issue an ultimatum to stop the bickering: "Come to an agreement by the end of the shift, or I'll come up with one for you that neither of you will probably like." At other times one subordinate may be clearly in the right on a given issue. In such instances an effective manager will serve as a mediator between the conflicting employees to resolve the conflict as rapidly as possible.

Most often, however, both subordinates are partially right and partially wrong. In such instances, the following guidelines may be helpful:

- Listen to both sides to understand the issues.
- Do not take sides.
- Separate the issue from personalities.
- Do not speak for one to the other.
- Get the parties to talk with each other and to listen.
- Point out areas of misunderstanding, but place no blame.
- Get the parties to reverse roles to see the other's point of view.
- Search for areas of agreement.
- Allow both to save face in any solution reached.
- Stress the importance of resolving the conflict.
- Monitor any solution agreed upon.
- If no solution can be reached, suggest a third-party mediator or negotiator.

Helping Employees Get Along

Although conflict can be healthy, it can also be destructive. You cannot row a boat in two directions at the same time. Law enforcement employees have to pull together to accomplish their goals and objectives. It is management's job to see that they do so most of the time.

Conflicts between groups or divisions generally involve dispatch and patrol, patrol and investigation, line and manager or line and communications. Most law enforcement departments have a regulation that states: "Officers and employees of the department shall conduct themselves in a manner that will foster the greatest harmony and cooperation between each other and organizational units of the department." Violations of this rule generally occur due to lack of cooperation, lack of understanding of the others' duties, lack of two-way communication or personality differences.

Employee conflicts may also arise from the constant internal struggle for recognition and authority, from one division feeling that another division is slacking off or from one shift thinking the other shifts are "dumping" on them.

When this type of conflict is not resolved, employees tend to choose sides, leading to more serious group as well as individual confrontations. Organizational goals will take a back seat to individual bickering. Hassles develop in the squad room. Officers meet over coffee or park in out-of-the-way areas of the community, talking to each other from squad car windows, discussing the latest developments. Managers who look the other way let the problem become worse.

Managers should call all parties involved in the conflict to determine the main issues. The earlier this takes place, the better the chances of resolution. As in any conflict, this should be done in private. All parties should have a chance to tell their side of the problem. Until the causes of the problem can be determined, there is no chance for solution. Ask for a frank statement of the problem as each individual sees it.

No one should be allowed to interrupt another person unless the person being interrupted is out of reasonable control. Merely providing an outlet for frank discussion sometimes brings about a better feeling.

After all sides have been presented, go over the total problem and point out differences. Ask whether anyone has ideas about how the differences can be eliminated. Point out strengths and weaknesses of the varied positions. Be firm that the matter must be resolved, and then find points on which the parties can agree. As Lewis (2001, p.245) notes: "The greatest trick is to get people to see the answer for themselves so they take ownership of the solution and work to solve it." He (p.243) suggests that communication is the "ultimate problem solving tool."

Employees can do more than they think about their own problems by just getting together, listening to the other side and calmly discussing the problem. When serious personal conflicts develop that are beyond the manager's training and skills, it may be necessary to call in a specialist or to temporarily transfer employees to another shift or other duties. If necessary, take the matter to a higher level of management. Prepare a written report covering the details, parties to the dispute and actions taken and ask for a date for further discussion.

The Role Conflict of Sergeants

Sergeants find themselves in a position filled with potential role conflict. One basic issue is that of loyalty. Do sergeants owe first allegiance to their patrol officers or to their superiors? An IACP survey showed that patrol officers and lieutenants each felt that sergeants owed their first allegiance to them; sergeants were generally uncertain.

Fulton (2002, p.106) describes some common mistakes committed by supervisors who have not had previous supervisory experience: unclear policies, lack of direction, micromanagement by superiors and preconceived notions vs. reality. Explaining preconceived notions vs. reality, Fulton says: "When commanders take over their new command, they get hit with a heavy dose of reality. Their people don't necessarily respond to those management theories. Subordinates don't know, understand or care about the policy or procedure manual." Another problem is failure to take charge, preferring to be "one of the guys."

To make the transition from patrol officer to supervisor less stressful, managers should provide sergeants with a clear, concise, written job description and training. Ideally, veteran sergeants might serve as mentors to newly promoted sergeants.

Using Ombuds

Parks (p.84) describes an **ombud** as "a designated neutral or impartial dispute resolution practitioner whose major function is to provide confidential and informal assistance to managers and employees." He explains: "History has shown that employees who make complaints against other employees often suffer retaliation. When an employee informs a supervisor of the conflict, a formal process is inevitably introduced, resulting in rumors, people taking sides and a negative impact on morale. The end result is that both the accuser and the accused suffer when all they wanted was for the issue to be resolved. Given these drawbacks, many employees elect to ignore the problem, hoping it will go away. When it does not, the tension becomes too great, and the employee finally comes forward. The result is that everything the employees previously feared becomes a reality."

Parks (p.87) describes the Alternative Dispute Resolution (ADR) program being used by the Los Angeles Police Department in which ombuds are an integral part: "By providing an effective conflict resolution alternative for employees, the ADR program reduces the potential for employee-generated lawsuits."

Dealing with External Conflicts

External conflicts can be with other agencies or with the public.

Conflicts with Other Agencies

External conflict may exist between law enforcement organizations at municipal, county, state and federal levels, as well as with private police and security agencies. Disagreements over jurisdictional authority, powers of arrest, who is in charge at the scene of an incident involving several jurisdictions, specialized and technological duties at the scene of a crime and many other issues cause conflict. Often it is the same basic conflict that exists internally within a law enforcement organization, that is, a lack of understanding and communication that deteriorates into a personality conflict. The goal of providing the best possible public service is lost.

Conflicts with the Public

Law enforcement personnel often come into conflict with angry citizens with complaints, people being arrested or given a citation or citizens angry about a general law enforcement situation they have heard about.

The potential for conflict between officers and the public exists because officers' perception of their duties may differ from the public's. Officers on traffic patrol may enforce speeding laws. Offenders given citations may ask, "Why are you picking on me for going 5 miles over the speed limit on this open stretch of road? I'm not hurting anyone. Why aren't you over by the school where you could do some good?" Or "Why aren't you picking up criminals?" Officers rarely see vehicle crashes happen, but they are expected to determine who is in the wrong—a potential for conflict of opinion.

Dispatchers or desk personnel are often on the receiving end of such complaints. How they handle them may be important to present and future public relations. Over the years a number of approaches for handling angry complainants have been developed.

People involved in these conflicts have learned that the first stages are important to defusing the situation. Except when the complainant is intoxicated or emotionally or mentally disturbed, the defusing phase takes from one to five

Law enforcement personnel often come into conflict with angry citizens and must try to diffuse the situation. New York City Police officers block a wall of angry anti-war protesters near the UN Headquarters on Feb. 5, 2003.

AP Photo/Diane Bondareff

minutes. Things have either calmed down by that time or the complainant is not going to be satisfied with anything you try to do.

During the first few seconds of the conflict, look directly at the complainant, maintaining eye contact when possible. Move to a position on the same level as the complainant (standing or sitting), make sure you provide direct attention and show concern for the person's problem. Use an unemotional tone and start a sympathetic approach by giving a corroborative response to the problem. This helps take them off the defensive. If the person is shouting or excessively abusive, take him or her into another room. The person may enjoy a sense of importance by telling you off in front of others. If the abuse continues, tell the person the acceptable limitations and that he or she could be charged with disorderly conduct (if your local judges support such arrests).

When the person has calmed down, get further information about the complaint itself. Take notes. This shows the complainant you are interested enough to record the information and by itself may calm some people down.

Follow the monologue and, if necessary, interrupt with questions to stop a prepared harangue by causing the complainant to think about something less emotional. Determine what, if any, action you can take. Consider alternatives mentally. Explain what you can do for the complainant. If you cannot resolve the problem, explain why and refer it to the proper sources. Take action at your level if you can. You are selling a service to the public.

Mediation and Community Policing

Cooper (2000, p.10) notes: "When departments use mediation to resolve conflicts in their communities, they empower residents to take responsibility for their actions and to resolve their own problems, not just in arguments with their neighbors but in other areas of their lives as well. Thus, when officers take the time to mediate disputes, they help citizens exercise their constitutional rights while freeing themselves to solve other problems instead of answering repeat calls for service. In the end, a little extra attention goes a long way."

Dealing with Internal and External Politics

Dealing with conflicts, internal or external, can be hazardous to managers, even if they are not directly involved. Intra- and interagency conflicts inevitably involve politics. People take sides; battle lines are drawn. Managers who attempt to stay out of conflict may be perceived as wishy-washy or fence sitters. In the midst of the conflict, managers have to keep their employees functioning efficiently.

To do so, managers should first separate their responsibility from the political games going on, focusing on the tasks to be accomplished. They should refrain from discussing any politically sensitive situation with subordinates. This is quite a different matter from keeping your people "in the know." Managers should also respect the chain of command even if they tend to side with the position taken by someone lower in the hierarchy. In addition, managers should say the same thing to everyone involved. They must remain honest and objective and not simply tell people what they want to hear. Finally, when the conflict ends, as it inevitably will, managers must help smooth the return to normalcy. When it's over, it's over.

Police chiefs should become politically active in supporting political issues affecting delivery of law enforcement services.

Maintaining Healthy Conflict

Law enforcement managers seek to control destructive conflict, but at the same time they should maintain healthy conflict to improve performance and productivity.

Healthy conflict challenges the status quo and offers constructive alternatives.

Healthy conflict breeds change and improvement. In fact, bringing conflict into the open is often one of the healthiest things you can do because it clarifies issues, reduces stress, clears the air, stimulates decision making and brings things to a forum where they can be dealt with, enabling relationships to continue to grow.

Managers should also provide a healthy state of conflict in their relations with their superiors because they need challenges as much as subordinates. Healthy conflict induces creative alternatives and innovative approaches to ideas and problems.

Law enforcement managers who ignore or put down subordinates' opinions, who think only their ideas are of value or who constantly remind employees of what they have not accomplished do not foster healthy conflict.

Managers should encourage subordinates to make suggestions. It is healthy to receive input from others because their ideas and creativity can be valuable to the organization. Guidelines for competition must be established to keep it within healthy boundaries. Such opposition is a help. Kites rise against the wind, not with it.

Keys to maintaining healthy conflict include open, two-way communication, receptivity to new ways of doing things and encouragement of risk taking.

Healthy conflict in law enforcement organizations may include:

- Competition between patrol zones, shifts and patrol and investigative units.
- Brainstorming sessions to develop new techniques for patrol and investigations.
- Contests for creative and innovative ideas on law enforcement projects and programs.
- Idea-developing sessions for improving task performance.

An organization that has too little conflict is no better than one that has too much. One is dormant, the other paralyzed. The secret in organizational conflict is establishing a balance between none and too much. Law enforcement departments with a balance of conflict are active, progressive organizations.

Managers can help create constructive conflict by encouraging subordinates to disagree and to question the status quo and rewarding them when they do. If they suspect subordinates are afraid to voice disagreement, they should assure them that their ideas are needed and welcomed.

Avoiding the Suppression of Conflict

Some managers avoid conflict, preferring instead to always act as peacemakers. This is certainly appropriate in many instances, but sometimes it may result in delaying the resolution of arguments or finding the best solution to problems. Recall the discussion of the Abilene Paradox in Chapter 4 and groupthink. Smith and Brantner (2001, p.198) suggest: "Chiefs must test their ideas by giving their advisors an opportunity to disagree." To avoid suppressing conflict that may result in beneficial change, consider the following guidelines:

- Allow all sides to be heard. Encourage participation. Explain why the debate must continue.
- Recognize that some people are threatened by conflict and want disputes resolved as quickly as possible. Help them feel less threatened.
- Make it clear that conflicts are to be expected and that they serve a valuable purpose. Encourage those who disagree in a healthy manner, who are innovative and who have suggestions for doing things differently.

Understanding

A key to positive conflict is to pursue agreement with understanding. Those involved should agree to agree or agree to disagree, but understanding is a must. The classic failure in interpersonal communications is the failure to recognize the other person's right to believe in the good sense of his or her point of view. A problem-solving approach to conflict would include the following:

- Understand each party's views.
- Identify underlying needs and concerns.
- Search for potential solutions.
- Enumerate probable consequences.
- Select manageable alternatives that satisfy all parties.
- Develop mechanisms to monitor and adjust.

Learning more about each other and about the task required of those involved in a conflict is helpful. Lack of understanding of each other's jobs increases conflict. Some departments rotate officers between shifts and patrol zones to provide a broader understanding of the total problems of the community. This also applies to divisions. For example, transferring some patrol personnel to investigations may help patrol understand problems of the investigating division.

Another solution is to have each person or group state what they would do if they were the other person or group in the conflict. In other words, force them to perceive the issue from the other side. It is much the same approach as having others state how they perceive you and comparing this with how you perceive yourself. Such an approach can be very revealing.

Another approach to solving group conflict is **intersubjectivity.** This refers to people's mutually understanding and respecting each others' viewpoints, a kind of reciprocal empathy. In this approach, each person's most important ideas about the problem and its solution are recorded on separate 3-by-5-inch cards. From the total set of cards, about 40 are chosen to represent all contributions.

The group involved in the conflict meets, and each person is given a set of cards and asked to organize them in a meaningful way. Most people arrange their cards on the table in plain view, and discussion arises as to how each is sorting and arranging. The power of the exercise is not in what each person does with the cards but in the discussion it produces. This provides a basis for deepening mutual understanding and for the eventual merging of different perspectives.

The **intersubjectivity approach** uses 3-by-5-inch cards as a means to get people in conflict to share their most important ideas about a problem and to come to a mutual understanding of and respect for each other's viewpoints.

The goal of conflict negotiation is not total solution but a manageable level of conflict.

Conflict Resolution Skills

Conflict is inevitable, so managers must learn to deal with it effectively and manage it positively. Conflict resolution skills should be part of every officer's training because it will be invaluable on the streets as well as in interactions within the organization. Conflict can result in one of three situations: win-lose, lose-lose and win-win.

In *win-lose situations,* the supervisor uses command/control authority, giving orders and expecting them to be carried out. The subordinate must either obey or face disciplinary action. This is how conflicts have traditionally been managed within law enforcement organizations. Win-lose can produce frustration.

In *lose-lose situations,* a conflict is settled through an ineffective compromise, with neither side feeling they have accomplished their purpose. The underlying philosophy is that "something is better than nothing" and that direct confrontation should be avoided. Such short-term solutions may result in even greater conflict in the future.

In *win-win situations* the focus is on the basic merits of each side rather than on interpersonal haggling. Research from the Harvard Negotiating Project has resulted in a method known as **principled negotiation,** a higher-level approach to effective mediation that focuses on mutually satisfying options. One key is separating the people from the problem. The participants should see themselves as working together to solve a particular problem. Diener (2000, p.132) explains it this way:

> Two kids squabble over the last orange in the fridge. Their father hears the ruckus, enters the kitchen and, without a word, thinks of a solution: He slices the fruit in equal halves and gives one to each child. Yet they're each disappointed. Why? Because one kid wanted to eat the pulp, and the other just wanted to bake with the rind!

Principled negotiation proceeds in four basic steps, each involving both theory and practice, as Figure 13.2 illustrates.

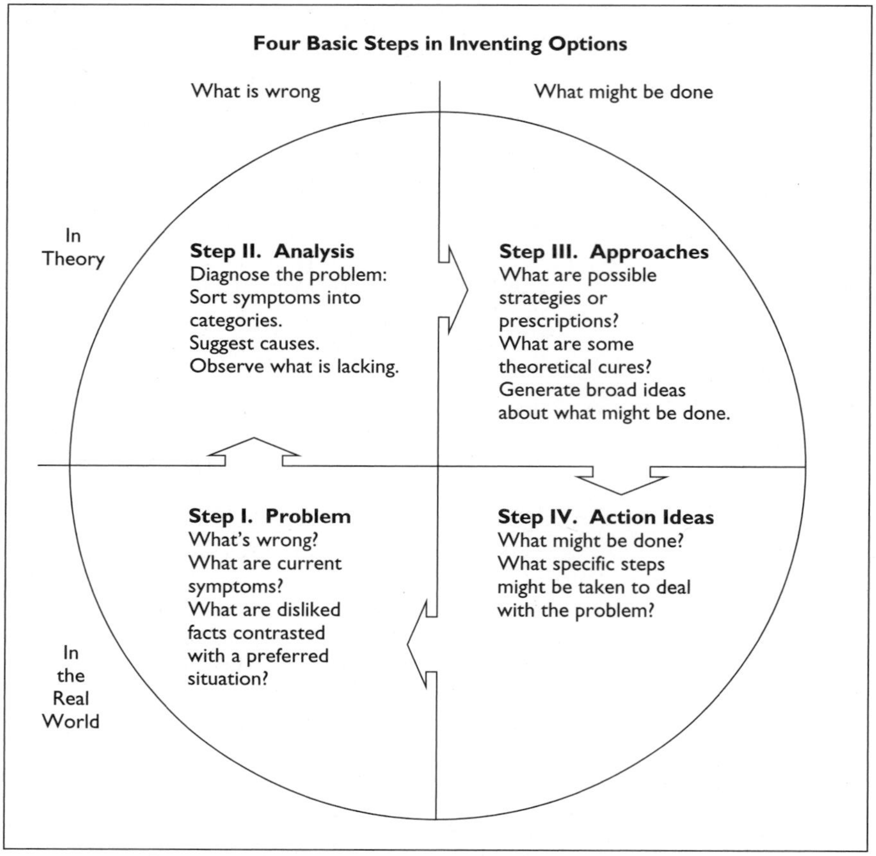

Figure 13.2
The Steps in Principled Negotiations

Source: Joseph Billy, Jr. and Ronald J. Stupak. "Conflict Management and the Law Enforcement Professional in the 1990s." *Law and Order,* May 1994, p.39. Reprinted by permission of *Law and Order.*

First, clearly identify the problem. Is the problem actually the heart of the conflict or merely a symptom of a deeper problem? Once you have identified the problem, analyze it to determine its underlying causes. The third step is to discuss alternative approaches to resolving the conflict. Fourth, reduce these alternative approaches to action ideas—steps that you can implement to resolve the conflict.

How to approach mediation often depends on the specific circumstances. Table 13.1 provides basic approaches to mediation and when each might be appropriate.

Summary

How managers approach conflict determines whether it is a negative or a positive force within the organization. A healthy amount of conflict, properly handled, motivates individuals and organizations. It exposes problems and may create a forum in which people can define the problem's causes. Those involved can provide input that leads to constructive solutions and developing new outlooks. Conflict that opposes without antagonizing can be extremely beneficial to law enforcement organizations, keeping them innovative and responsive to change.

Table 13.1
Mediation

Approach	When to Use
Ask employees to pinpoint the root of the problem	To build cooperation To pave the way for yielding to an employee's suggestion To maintain harmony and good will
Take charge of the situation	In an emergency were quick action is vital To implement unpopular ideas To enforce rules or discipline (Use sparingly.)
Work toward a reasonable compromise	When other methods aren't working To establish a middle ground To get quick group agreement
Integrate all parties into a creative solution	To benefit from merging insights of people with different perspectives To get long-term commitment from everyone involved
Step back from the whole situation	An issue is trivial Someone else can be more effective The issue is part of a bigger problem that must be solved separately

Source: Adapted from Dorothy Simoneli, "War of the Workers," IB (*Independent Business,* May–June 1994 pp.72–73. Copyright 1994 by Group IV Communications, Inc., 125 Auburn Court, Suite 100, Thousand Oaks, CA 91362.

Conflict may come from individual, interpersonal or job-related sources as well as from sources outside the organization. The 10/80/10 principle divides the workforce into three categories: 10 percent who are high achievers, 80 percent who are average achievers and 10 percent who are unmotivated troublemakers and cause 90 percent of management's problems.

The manager's responsibility is to recognize conflict when it occurs, have a system for reporting conflict and take action as soon as possible. Conflicts that arise during crises must be managed by following established procedures and the chain of command.

A problem employee exhibits abnormal behavior to the extent that the behavior is detrimental to organizational needs and goals as well as the needs and goals of other department personnel. In addition to problem employees, law enforcement managers must also be able to deal with people who, although not technically "problem" employees, are extremely difficult to work with. These include yes people, passives, avoiders, pessimists, complainers, know-it-alls, exploders, bullies and snipers. To deal with problem people, get their attention, identify the problem behavior, point out the consequences, ask questions, listen and explain expectations. Avoid defensiveness.

Conflict need not be negative. To bring conflict into the open, some managers use the confrontation technique, which brings two disputing people or groups face-to-face to resolve their differences. It may either effectively resolve conflicts or make them worse. Healthy conflict challenges the status quo and offers constructive alternatives. Keys to maintaining healthy conflict include open, two-way communication, receptivity to new ways of doing things and encouragement of risk taking. One way to foster healthy conflict is the intersubjectivity approach, which uses 3-by-5-inch cards as a means to get disputing parties to share their most important ideas about a problem and to come to a mutual understanding of and respect for each others' viewpoints. Managing conflict is a great responsibility.

Discussion Questions

1. What is the supervisor's role in managing conflict?
2. What are some steps to reduce conflict?
3. What are examples of destructive conflict? Constructive conflict?
4. What are sources of conflict among law enforcement agencies at different levels of government?
5. What are possible sources of conflict between the police and the public?
6. What are signs of conflict between law enforcement employees?
7. How would you recommend reducing, controlling or preventing conflict?
8. Can you identify "difficult people" you know who fit the categories described in this chapter?
9. What are the biggest changes law enforcement has faced in the past decade that might cause problems for personnel?
10. Do you know of instances in which conflict has produced positive results? Would these results have been accomplished without conflict?

InfoTrac College Edition Assignment

Use InfoTrac College Edition to answer the Discussion Questions as appropriate.

Conflict is a very broad topic. Search this topic to find a subtopic of interest to you. Read at least one recent article on it and outline the main points. Include the full reference citation. Be prepared to discuss your findings with the class.

OR

Read and outline "Training Patrol Officers to Mediate Disputes" by Christopher Cooper.

References

Cooper, Christopher. "Training Patrol Officers to Mediate Disputes." *FBI Law Enforcement Bulletin,* February 2000, pp.7–10.

Diener, Marc. "Realdeal: Follow Your Nos." *Entrepreneur,* July 2000, pp.132–133.

Feltgen, John W. "Conflict Management: Taking on Deadwood in Law Enforcement." *The Police Chief,* December 2001, pp.41–45.

Fulton, Roger. "Working with Other Commanders." *Law Enforcement Technology,* February 2000a, p.94.

Fulton, Roger. "Handling Controversy." *Law Enforcement Technology,* April 2000b, p.118.

Fulton, Roger. "Earning Respect." *Law Enforcement Technology,* April 2001, p.142.

Fulton, Roger. *Law Enforcement Technology,* June 2002, p.106.

Lewis, Scott. "Conflict Resolution: Communication as the Ultimate Problem Solving Tool." *Law and Order,* October 2001, pp.243–245.

McCaffery, Kevin. "Using Persuasion Tactics to Manage Conflict." *Police,* January 2001, pp.26–27.

McDonald, Tom. "Brand-New Key: Locking Horns with Co-Workers? Two Ways to Turn Foes into Friends." *Successful Meetings,* March 2002, p.27.

Meany, Rebecca. "What a Pain!" *Successful Meetings,* February 2001, p.72.

Parks, Bernard C. "Ombuds Office Provides Simpler Method of Reducing Conflict among Employees." *The Police Chief,* August 2000, pp.83–89.

Smith, Dave and Brantner, Elizabeth. "Mental Preparation." *Law and Order,* May 2000, pp.107–109.

Smith, Dave and Brantner, Elizabeth. "Police Leadership and the Abilene Paradox." *The Police Chief,* April 2001, pp.196–200.

Book-Specific Web Site

Go to the *Management and Supervision in Law Enforcement* Web site at http://info.wadsworth.com/05346160654 for student and instructor resources, including Internet Assignments and Case Studies.

CHAPTER 14

Stress

Your day-by-day—sometimes minute-by-minute—contact with criminals, complainants and citizens alike who are crying, cursing, bleeding, puking, yelling, spitting . . . and just plain crazy subjects your system to repeated onslaughts of disturbance.

—Charles Remsberg, *The Tactical Edge*

Do You Know?

- Whether stress must always be negative?
- What common sources of stress are?
- What may be a major source of stress?
- What the four categories of stress are?
- Which law enforcement employees face stress from additional sources?
- How stress can affect people?
- What physical problems stress is related to?
- What percentage of illness is stress related?
- What the symptoms of burnout are?
- How managers can help prevent burnout?
- What post-traumatic stress disorder (PTSD) is? Who is most at risk for PTSD?
- What negative coping mechanisms may be used?
- How stress can be reduced?
- How alcohol, drugs and smoking relate to stress?
- What programs can reduce stress?
- What departments can provide to help officers?

Can You Define?

acute stress
afterburn
blue flame
burnout
burst stress
chronic stress
circadian system
critical incident
critical incident stress debriefing (CISD)
cumulative stress
desynchronization
disequilibrium
distress
diurnal
employee assistance program (EAP)
eustress
external stress
homeostasis
operational stress
organizational stress
personal stress
post-traumatic stress disorder (PTSD)
psychological hardiness
stress
traumatic stress
type A personality
type B personality

INTRODUCTION

Hans Selye, MD (1907–1982), the father of the stress field, originally defined *stress* as the body's nonspecific response to any demand placed on it. He later said stress was simply the wear and tear caused by living.

Stress, like conflict, has both a positive and a negative aspect. In ancient China the symbol for stress included two written characters—one for opportunity and one for danger.

Stress can be helpful (eustress) or harmful (distress), depending on its intensity and frequency as well as how it is mediated.

Eustress is positive stress that enables people to function and accomplish goals. It allows law enforcement officers to react instantaneously in life-threatening situations, to feel the excitement, the energy and the heightening of the senses. **Distress,** in contrast, is negative stress that can lead to a variety of diseases including depression.

Although stress can be positive, most people equate stress with distress. The remainder of this chapter will use the term in this sense because it is the negative stress that managers must try to manage effectively. Lost hours, illness and reduced performance are costly to any organization. Law enforcement workers' compensation claims have increased substantially due to stress-related disorders. In activities at home and at work, too many high-stress incidents are occurring with no chance to "come back to normal" between incidents. Stress can become overpowering.

Reese (2001, p.14) notes: "Contemporary law enforcement officers must function as counselors, social workers, psychologists, negotiators and investigators, as well as traditional police officers. Their work alternates from dull and boring to moments of sheer panic, when life and death decisions have to be made in a matter of seconds. These combinations of factors in police work, dealing with terrible situations and traumatized victims, and working under the threat of physical danger result in overwhelming stress."

This chapter begins by defining stress and identifying some major sources of stress, including general sources, personality factors and job-related sources. This is followed by a look at stressors in police work, including death notifications; shift work, overtime and fatigue; critical incidents; and line-of-duty deaths. How these might affect officers' families is also discussed. Next is an in-depth discussion of reactions to stress or the symptoms likely to be present, including physical, psychological, behavioral and on-the-job. Levels of stress, including the most extreme—burnout—are identified. The results of excessive levels of stress are then described, including post-traumatic stress disorder, depression and suicide. Next, the chapter examines ways to cope with stress and how stress levels can be reduced. The chapter concludes with descriptions of how organizations can reduce stress, effective programs to manage stress and an examination of the manager's/supervisor's role in minimizing the negative effects of stress.

Stress Defined

Stress means different things to different people. To a mechanical engineer, it means the point at which objects break or deteriorate from excessive pressures or physical tension. Stress is not that different in humans. A single high-stress incident or recurring minor stress can cause the mind or physical body to deteriorate or break down completely. **Stress** is generally thought of as tension, anxiety, strain or pressure. It is the body's internal response to a situation a person perceives as threatening. Volpe (2000, p.183) says: "Stress is a physical, chemical or emotional factor that causes bodily or mental tension resulting from factors that tend to alter an existing equilibrium."

The biological concept of homeostasis helps explain how stress occurs. **Homeostasis** is the process that keeps all bodily functions, such as breathing and blood circulation, in balance. To see homeostasis at work, run in place for a few minutes and then sit down. The running mildly stresses your body, temporarily putting it out of balance. After you rest, however, your body returns to normal. The same thing happens in acute stress, illustrated in Figure 14.1.

Acute stress is severe, extremely intense distress that lasts a limited time and then the person returns to normal. It is sometimes called **traumatic stress.** Volpe (p.183) suggests: "Acute stress is temporary stress that creates peak performance. . . . Acute stress can be good for leaders in small doses. It keeps us alert, challenged and assured all our systems are responding. It can actually improve our leadership performance as it takes us out of our 'comfort zone' and forces us to adapt to the new stimulus."

The stress response is a survival tool built into humans from their beginnings, an instinctive physical response that prepares a person to either fight or run to safety. Volpe (pp.183–184) explains: "Physically, blood rushes to the

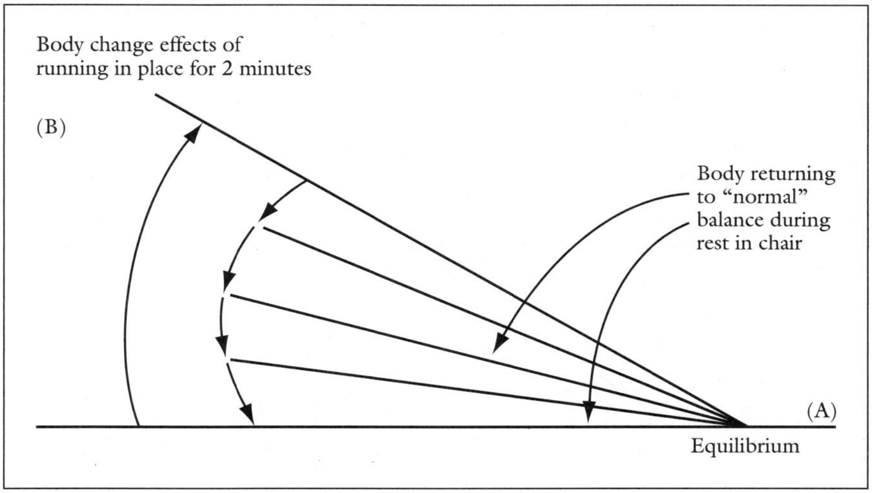

Source: Lynn Hunt Monahan and Richard E. Farmer. *Stress and the Police: A Manual for Prevention.* Pacific Palisades, CA: Palisades Publishers, 1980, p.6. Reprinted by permission.

Figure 14.1
Acute Stress and Homeostasis

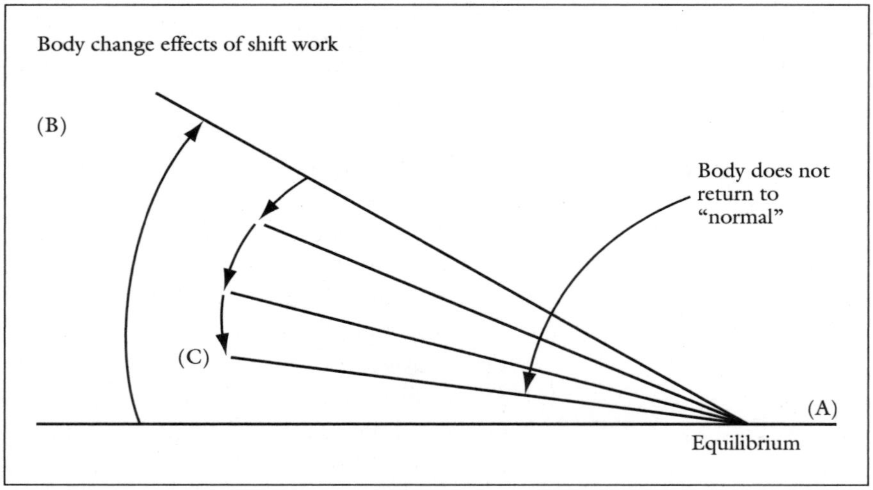

Figure 14.2
Chronic Stress and Disequilibrium

Source: Lynn Hunt Monahan and Richard E. Farmer. *Stress and the Police: A Manual for Prevention.* Pacific Palisades, CA: Palisades Publisher, 1980, p.7. Reprinted by permission.

brain, breathing increases, blood pressure goes up and our senses become finely tuned to the surrounding environment. The body releases large amounts of Adrenaline and Cortisone, the body's primary 'stress fighting' hormones. . . . Psychologically, we focus on specific problems better and think more clearly because the brain gets more blood and oxygen."

Chronic stress, in contrast, is less intense but continues and eventually becomes debilitating. It is sometimes called **cumulative stress.** A person suffering from chronic stress does not return to normal but remains in a state of **disequilibrium,** as illustrated in Figure 14.2.

Volpe (p.184) notes: "Chronic stress can have a critical impact on the ability to make competent, principle-based decisions. In this mode, our bodies are in a 'continuous state of siege.' A serious lawsuit, a lengthy internal disciplinary investigation, or supervising a problem officer over a long period of time may cause a chronic stress reaction."

Sources of Stress

Stress comes from several sources, many work related.

Stress commonly arises from uncertainty, lack of control and pressure.

Uncertainty is an unavoidable part of life and of law enforcement. Officers responding to a call often have no idea what awaits. They may be unsure of who they can trust or believe. Uncertainty is also associated with change, going from the known to the unknown. Major changes in a person's life such as getting married, having children or having someone close to you die are all stressful.

Lack of control may be seen when law enforcement officers apprehend suspects they believe to be guilty and see these suspects not prosecuted or found not guilty. Officers must work with assigned partners they did not select. They must be polite to surly citizens.

Pressure is also abundant in law enforcement, with work overloads, paperwork, sometimes-unrealistic expectations from the public and the responsibility to protect life and property and to preserve "the peace."

In addition to these three general categories of stressors, sources of stress can also be found by looking at a person's lifestyle, personality and job.

Sources of stress can be found in a person's daily living, personality and job.

Daily Living or General Sources of Stress

Some common stress producers of daily living are changing relationships, a lifestyle inconsistent with values (too committed), money problems (credit-card debt, poor investments), loss of self-esteem (falling behind professionally, accepting others' expectations), and fatigue or illness (poor diet, lack of sleep or lack of exercise).

Personality as a Source of Stress

Psychologists often divide individuals into two types: **type A personality,** an aggressive, hyperactive "driver" who tends to be a workaholic; and **type B personality,** who has the opposite characteristics. The type A person is more likely to experience high stress levels.

Job-Related Sources of Stress

Stress is often caused by the department and the job itself. Among the stressors are mandatory overtime, severe consequences for making a mistake, varied workloads, the need to react quickly and effectively to rapidly changing conditions, personal conflicts, limited opportunities for advancement, a flood of paperwork, inadequate equipment, pay below the going rate, rotating shifts, isolation from other officers, lack of privacy, unpredictable meal breaks and work that alternates between being sedentary and physically exhausting.

Reese (p.16) adds to the list: paramilitary structure, lack of input into policy and decision making, lack of adequate training or supervision, lack of reward/recognition for efforts, role conflict, pressure to prove oneself, court rulings perceived as too lenient on offenders or as too restrictive on methods of criminal suppression and investigation, anxiety over the responsibility to protect others and fear of doing something against regulations or being second-guessed.

A major source of employee stress may be upper-level management.

Some top police managers must accept responsibility for causing stress among their employees by their management style. Autocratic managers who seek no input from employees or fail to keep them informed increase stress.

Law Enforcement-Related Sources of Stress

The Society for Police and Criminal Psychology lists on their Web site (www.heavybadge.com) 10 reasons cops are different and how this impacts on their stress, noting: "The badge is not just pinned on a chest, it is pinned on a lifestyle. (1) Law enforcement officers are seen as authority figures. People deal with them differently and treat them differently. (2) They are isolated. Wearing a badge, uniform and gun makes a law officer separate from society. (3) Law enforcement officers work in a quasi-military, structured institution. (4) Shift work is not normal. (5) Camaraderie can be a two-edged sword in that it can create an 'us vs. them' view of the world. (6) Officers have a different kind of stress, called **burst stress,** in that they go from complete calm to high activity and pressure in one 'burst.' (7) They need to be in constant emotional control. (8) Officers work in a fact-based world with everything compared to written law. (9) The 'at work' world of officers is very negative, which can cause cynicism. (10) The children of officers have a more difficult adjustment."

Law enforcement is a high-stress profession. When officers receive a call to proceed to an armed robbery in progress, a domestic disturbance involving shooting, a murder or a crash involving deaths, it is traumatic. According to Aaron (2000, p.438): "Unlike members of most other professions, police officers encounter experiences of physical danger, including the threat of serious injury or death to themselves, and exposure to others who have been seriously injured, killed, or otherwise traumatized." Law enforcement officers *do* have periods of boredom, but they also have periods of high anxiety, similar to those experienced during war. Officers know their lives may be in danger, often at the most unexpected times.

Doing routine tasks and then suddenly being thrown into a traumatic situation is exceptionally stressful.

Officers are on the alert immediately upon being notified of a call. They go from passivity to action in moments. Their bodies become pumped with energy. The adrenaline flows. The heart and pulse rates jump. Breathing is rapid. When they arrive, they know they have to decide what action to take. A single instance is normally not overwhelming, but continued similar incidents over extended periods accompanied by changes in health, stamina and age eventually take a toll.

Everyday confrontations with crime victims and those who commit crimes are also stressful.

When people request law enforcement services, it generally means problems, conflict and stress. Officers are well aware of these probabilities when they enter law enforcement. What they are often not aware of is the total effect of stress-inducing incidents over time. Harpold and Feemster (2002, p.3) note: "The day-to-day stress of dealing with people and their problems . . . can traumatize officers and poison their spirits."

Many officers make it a personal responsibility to work on certain special-interest cases and work overtime on their own. Even when not physically working overtime, they are doing so mentally and emotionally.

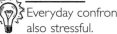

Police are often under sudden and excessive stress, and frequently investigate incidents involving confrontation and violence. Little Rock, Arkansas, police officers comfort Tory Kennedy, 10, center, after he was held hostage in a Little Rock neighborhood in 2002. The child, one of four, escaped through a window before three others were released by the man holding them.

AP Photo/Danny Johnston

Officers also investigate incidents involving confrontation and violence. These incidents create stress equal to or higher than that in most occupations. Many participants in these incidents have been involved in violence before the officers arrive, and often the violence continues after they arrive. Domestic disputes, disorderly conduct, rape and gang activities are examples of such confrontations.

Officers seldom have a chance to discuss events during emergencies. They receive orders and act on them. The quasi-military nature of law enforcement structure prevents them from questioning orders. Although officers have legal authority and responsibility to carry out their duties, they often have to repress how they feel when dealing with the public. For example, drunks often verbally abuse officers, and although the officers may make an arrest, they normally accept such verbal abuse as part of the job.

Officers have an opportunity to take control in various situations, and this does release stress. Officers can also make independent decisions, which normally increases confidence, self-assurance and self-esteem. Because most of these situational feelings can be discussed only with other officers, police officers tend to become isolated from society in varying degrees, and this can produce stress.

Another source of stress for officers is fear of legal action against them and their agency. Every arrest is a possible basis for a lawsuit. Once publicized, a lawsuit suggests that the officer was wrong even though the suit may have no legal basis.

It is difficult to preassess the total effect of going from boredom to high stress, dealing with conflict and confrontation, coping with the criminal element, facing the adversity of courtroom tactics, dealing with the spin-off effects on family members, writing tedious reports, handling criticism by managers and many other everyday pressures of the job.

Four categories of law enforcement stress are external, operational, organizational and personal.

External stress is produced by real threats and dangers, for example entering a dark and unfamiliar building, responding to a "man with a gun" alarm and high-speed pursuit. **Operational stress** is daily confrontation with tragedy, deceit, immorality, brutality and danger.

Organizational stress is produced by elements inherent in paramilitary organizations such as changing schedules, odd hours, and detailed rules, policies and procedures. Hawkins (2001, p.347) describes four factors within organizations that cause stress: (1) an authoritarian structure, (2) lack of participation in decisions affecting daily work tasks, (3) lack of administrative support and (4) unfair discipline. Zhao et al. (2002, p.59) suggest other organizational causes of stress: excessive workloads; inadequate equipment/technology; staff, policies/procedures, budget resources, and supervision/direction; poor working conditions; and too much red tape. Sewell (2002, p.15) notes that organizational changes occurring in departments across the country can also be stressful and recommends: "The most important step in dealing with the stress of organizational change is an awareness that it exists."

Personal stress may be generated by an officer's race or gender or in adjusting to the police culture's values.

Law Enforcement Personnel with Additional Stressors

Some officers are placed in high-stress assignments such as narcotics, undercover and fugitive squad units. Stress levels vary tremendously depending on the assignment, the area and the shift.

Additional stress is often experienced by women officers, minority officers, investigators and managers.

Women Officers

In addition to the stress experienced because of the job they have selected, female officers have some stressors not faced by their male counterparts, for example, male chauvinism, lack of respect and support, higher rate of turnover, citizen negativism and sexual harassment. Reese (p.16) suggests additional stress for females is caused by lack of acceptance by predominantly white, male forces with subsequent denial of information, alliances and protection as well as a lack of role models and mentors.

Women currently constitute about 14.3 percent of all sworn law enforcement officers nationwide, a relatively small increase over the past 25 years

("Despite Some Gains . . .," 2000, p.1). Gold (2000b, p.160) contends: "Recruiting and retaining qualified women will remain obstacles until we change the way society sees women in law enforcement, how women officers see themselves, and how women are perceived by their male colleagues." According to Strandberg (2000, p.80): "There still are many male officers who don't think policing is a job for a woman." Gold (2000a, p.12) reports: "To compete with male officers for scarce promotional opportunities, women still have to withstand teasing, intimidation, even harassment. Some women see this as too high a price."

Recruiting and Retaining Women: A Self-Assessment Guide for Law Enforcement notes: "The military model, which places value on strict, unquestioning adherence to rules, is not only contrary to the skills desired in community policing officers, it is a culture foreign to most female recruits." And when hazing, shunning and humiliation are considered acceptable techniques to tear recruits down before building them up, "it is very easy for sexual harassment to join that acceptable list."

Another stressor on female officers, seemingly more so than for males, includes personal issues related to home life and the issue of who is expected to care for family members.

Minority Officers

Minority police officers may experience more stress than majority police officers because they are expected to be more tolerant of community problems within their minority population, yet are also expected to enforce the law impartially. They may also be expected to join a minority organization within the department, separating them from the majority of the force. And, like their female counterparts, according to Reese, minority officers face the additional stress of lack of acceptance by a predominately white force with subsequent denial of information, alliances and protection as well as a lack of role models and mentors. In addition, plainclothes minority officers are at greater risk of being mistaken for criminals by other officers in large departments, where officers in one precinct do not necessarily know officers in another precinct.

Investigators

Several stressors accompany the responsibilities of being a criminal investigator. They may have to investigate several cases at once, often within short timeframes, because suspects can be incarcerated for only a short time without sufficient evidence. Many investigators work long hours, often on their own time, which can lead to fatigue and eventually burnout. They may also become frustrated with the court system and the perception of a revolving door criminal justice system. In addition, they may be under constant scrutiny of citizens who expect cases to be solved rapidly. Investigators may not get needed backup or may have less sophisticated equipment than the criminals they are investigating. Finally, they may question society's values as they deal with horrible, inhumane crimes.

Managers/Supervisors

When officers are promoted, they assume the added stress of being managers. Promotion often involves managing officers who formerly were peers. Sometimes these relationships are difficult because of close, even social friendships, or prior antagonistic relationships. Most officers, however, understand what is required of the law enforcement manager position. They know that managers have to discipline and correct.

The amount of stress managers face varies with the position, level and assigned duties. First-line supervisors often work in the field with the officers, performing the same duties, especially in smaller departments. In addition, they have the problems of managing others.

The higher the level of law enforcement manager, the more stress there is in developing programs, preparing budgets, making speeches, settling personnel grievances and complaints, resolving citizen complaints and many other duties. Top managers have more control over their work and less stress from lack of control. Middle and first-line managers generally have more stress because of lack of control over their work.

Death Notification

One very stressful responsibility for law enforcement officers is notifying family members of a death, either accidental or caused by a criminal action. According to Johnson (2000, p.180): "Most police officers will have to make a death notification at some point in their career, but few have been trained how to handle this type of emotionally charged duty." He outlines five steps in making an appropriate death notification.

Officers should first *prepare for the call* mentally and emotionally. This includes obtaining all the facts including where the deceased's body is and how the family can collect it and the deceased's property. Next they should *set the stage* as they appear in person to make the notification. "Setting the stage involves developing nonverbal cues to tip off the family about what is coming, gradually softening the blow of the words the officer must say. . . . Some nonverbal cues an officer can use are a slow walk to the door, a sad frown, slumped shoulders and holding the uniform hat in the hand rather than wearing it" (p.178). The third step is to *deliver the message*: "Delivery of the message should begin with, 'I have some bad news,' or 'There has been an accident.' The next sentence should be that the person is dead. It is important to use the word 'dead' because it is clear, to the point, but yet is not offensive."

The fourth step is to *handle the reactions.* Johnson (pp.179–180) describes the range of emotional responses officers should be prepared for: "The family members may appear calm. . . . They may become hysterical, screaming and crying loudly. A person may faint, or, if they have a heart ailment, they might go into a heart attack. . . . Some people will react with anger. . . . Some may also experience survivor's guilt. . . . The officer should be prepared as these feelings of guilt or anger might be turned toward him."

The fifth step is to *disengage,* leaving the grieving family members in the hands of another qualified person after providing them with information on the administrative things that will need to be dealt with. Johnson (p.180) concludes: "The most important thing the officer should remember while performing this difficult duty is the Golden Rule. The officer should think about how he would want his own family notified if he were killed."

Another stressful aspect for many officers is working irregular hours.

Shift Work, Overtime and Fatigue

Humans are naturally day-oriented **(diurnal)** in their activity patterns. They are equipped with a complex biological timekeeping system (the **circadian system**). This system's major function is to prepare the body for restful sleep at night and active wakefulness during the day. The circadian system has a resetting mechanism that realigns it, but that mechanism is designed to cope with a "fine tuning" of *only* one hour or so per day. It is *not* designed to cope with the gross changes characteristic of moves to and from night work.

The brain relies on outside influences to keep its circadian rhythm functioning effectively. The most obvious influence is daylight. Other influences are sleep, social contact and regular meal times. When these timekeeping clues are altered through shift work, the body's circadian rhythm is negatively affected and results in **desynchronization** (deviation from the night-sleep, day-wake pattern). Cochrane (2001, p.22) explains: "Shift work upsets the intricate network of interrelated clocks and schedules that keep the human body functioning efficiently." This can cause insomnia, infertility, stomach problems and cardiovascular illness. As a result, performance wanes, accident rates rise, attentiveness decreases.

Others also note the hazards of fatigue. Vila (2002, p.45) contends: "Fatigue tends to impair decision making, increase irritability, cause greater impulsiveness and aggression, slow reflexes and decrease attentiveness. . . . Tired cops can't manage people as well, they can't observe as well, make decisions as well, communicate as well, drive as well or do any of the other job tasks as well that require complex interactions between thinking, feeling and acting." He (p.44) also says that fatigue diminishes the ability of officers to learn: "On top of tired officers' tendency to fall asleep during training—at least unless weapons are being fired—they're much less likely to retain what they did manage to absorb and add it to their stock of expertise unless they get sufficient good quality sleep that same day."

Vila et al. (2001, p.191) note: "Inadequate sleep can lead to chronic problems on the job, on the highway, in social situations, and at home as well as sleep disorders and heart and gastrointestinal disease." They (p.189) describes fatigue-related problems identified by scientists at Walter Reed Army Institute of Research:

> Sleep deprivation degrades the higher, more complex mental processes. Soldiers lose battlefield awareness. They lose the ability to integrate information into a coherent and accurate representation of the tactical situation. In contrast, simple mental processes are unaffected. This disparity between the effects of sleep deprivation on simple and complex mental abilities helps explain friendly fire incidents. In the sleep-deprived state, soldiers can still put the cross-hairs on a target and fire rounds accurately down range, but their orientation to the terrain and tactical situation degrades. They can shoot and shoot accurately but no longer can distinguish friend from foe.

According to Vila et al.: "We arguably should be even more concerned about overly fatigued police officers because they tend to have more individual discretion than soldiers on a battlefield and because their duties in the community often are more complex and ambiguous than combat confrontations."

Domash (2000) reports on a study by the Chicago Police Department which found: "If there is any conclusion that can be drawn from this study, it is that shift work is deleterious to the physical and psychological health of the individual and to the well being of the organization."

Vila et al. (2002, p.4) point out: "Fatigue among police patrol officers arising from departmental policies and practices may degrade individuals' abilities and hence the performance of organizations." Vila and Kenney (2002) suggest: "Weary from overtime assignments, shift work, night school, endless hours spent waiting to testify and the emotional and physical demands of the job—not to mention trying to patch together a family and social life during irregular breaks in off-duty time—police officers fend off fatigue with coffee and hard-bitten humor. . . . It is well known that impulsiveness, aggression, irritability and angry outbursts are associated with sleep deprivation."

According to Pedersen (2001, p.130): "Getting enough sleep needs to be treated as a safety issue just like firearm safety." She (p.131) stresses: "The dangers associated with lack of sleep are astounding. Fatigue is strongly associated with traffic accidents. . . . One of the things that makes fatigue so dangerous is our inability to judge if we're tired, and if so, how tired." She (p.132) also notes: "Twenty-four hours without sleep proved equivalent to a 0.1 percent blood alcohol level, or 'legally drunk' just about anywhere in North America." Vila et al. (p.193), likewise, stress: "Officers should be educated about the hazards of fatigue and encouraged to consider alertness an important aspect of being fit for duty."

Fatigue may wear down the body's defenses, thus magnifying the effects of other stressful events. Among the most stressful events encountered in police work are critical incidents.

Critical Incidents

A **critical incident** is any event that elicits an overwhelming emotional response from those witnessing it and whose emotional impact goes beyond the person's coping abilities. According to Berger (2002, p.6): "Studies show that as many as three-fourths of officers involved in a critical incident leave the force within five years." In one study of stressors, several dealt with critical incidents, including harming/killing another person or another police officer or seeing another police officer killed. The rank order of 14 stressor variables from this study is shown in Table 14.1.

Officer-involved shootings have been identified in numerous studies as critical incidents that cause considerable stress in officers. As Douglas (2002, p.45) notes: "Active shooting incidents are characterized by confusion and anxiety, and friendly fire accidents are a very real danger." Officers involved in shooting incidents may experience a wide range of effects, including perceptual disturbances such as tunnel vision, sense of time slowing down or speeding up, sense of sounds diminishing or increasing in volume and memory loss. Muscular control may also be affected. Leg muscles can tremble or lock, hands can shake and muscles in the upper back and shoulders can go into spasm.

Artwohl (2002, p.18) contends: "People have two distinctly different modes of processing information. One, the rational-thinking mode, happens during low emotional arousal states, whereas the second, the experiential-thinking mode,

Table 14.1
Rank Order of 14 Stressor Variables (N = 415) (5 = highest; 1 = lowest)

Stressor	Mean
Child Beaten/Abused	4.39
Harming/Killing Innocent Person	3.93
Conflict with Regulations	3.90
Harming/Killing Another Police Officer	3.89
Domestic Violence Calls	3.89
Another Officer Killed	3.71
Hate Groups/Terrorists	3.67
Poor Supervisor Support	3.64
Riot Control	3.43
Public Disrespect	3.41
Barricaded Subjects	3.28
Shift Work	3.08
Another Officer Hurt	3.08
Hostage-Takers	2.96

Source: Dennis J. Stevens. "Police Officer Stress." *Law and Order,* September 1999, p.79. Reprinted by permission.

occurs during states of high stress and emotional arousal, such as would occur during an officer-involved shooting." He explains: "Experiential thinking represents a system that automatically, rapidly, effortlessly and efficiently processes information, an obvious advantage in a life-threatening situation demanding an immediate response." In Artwohl's study, 21 percent of the officers saw, heard or experienced something during that event that later was found to have not really happened or happened very differently than how it was remembered. In addition, 74 percent of the officers surveyed reported that they responded automatically to the perceived threat, giving little or no conscious thought to their actions (p.23).

Especially traumatic for officers are "suicide by cop" (SBC) incidents. Honig (2001, p.89) suggests: "As any officer can attest, confrontation with a suicidal person is often dangerous and can frequently turn deadly." According to Honig (p.90): "Overall, 98 percent of the precipitators were male. Additionally, 48 percent of the weapons chosen by the precipitators were firearms. . . . 58 percent asked police to kill them; 63 percent had a psychiatric history; 38 percent had previous suicide attempts; 65 percent had a history of alcohol or drug abuse; and 39 percent had a history of domestic violence. In 24 percent of the situations, law enforcement officers initially used less-than-lethal weapons . . . which were unsuccessful in preventing the subsequent shooting by a law enforcement officer."

Paynter (2000, p.44) reports: "Verbal dissuasion, consisting of commands to drop the weapon, was used in 95.7 percent of the cases reviewed and had little success in defusing the situation." Says Paynter (p.40): "Academics call the phenomenon victim-precipitated homicide, officers on the street call it suicide by cop. Whatever it's named, the results are the same—the suspect ends up injured or dead and the cop carries a bag full of emotions ranging from shock and remorse to shame, anger and powerlessness."

Praet (2002, p.14) suggests that departments differentiate suicide by cop from death by indifference: "Many otherwise seemingly nonviolent people engage in self-destructive conduct with no apparent regard for the consequences of their actions. Many officers have been confronted by the hallucinating family member whose drug-induced paranoia causes him or her to act out violently toward innocent relatives in the presence of officers. These situations simply do not fit the classic definition of suicide by cop since there will rarely, if ever, be any immediate or prior evidence of suicidal behavior. . . . What is actually occurring in these situations is the person is throwing caution to the wind and proceeding with his or her conduct in spite of the likelihood that officers will be forced to intervene with deadly force. . . . Generally, this abhorrent behavior is associated with some superseding factor such as drugs, alcohol or mental illness."

Whether it is suicide by cop or death by indifference, the officer who pulls the trigger is likely to experience tremendous stress that can haunt the officer for a long time. Another source of tremendous stress is the death of a fellow officer.

Line-of-Duty Deaths

As Thrash (2000, p.64) contends: "Few citizens are unaware of what it means to see police cars with their emergency lights and headlights on, slowly following one another for blocks and sometimes for miles. For the more than 700,000 sworn law officers in America today, for whom the possibility of being killed in the line of duty has always been a known job hazard, it is a somber and moving experience."

Carpenter (2001, p.119) notes: "Between January 1900 and December 2000, 14,294 enforcement officers were killed in the line of duty—an average of 143 officers killed each year, 12 killed each month or one killed every two and a half days." More than 230 police officers across the nation were killed in the line of duty during 2001, including the 70 officers who died at the World Trade Center on September 11. As Floyd (2002, p.52) points out: "No matter how routine the assignment might seem, a police officer's life is often at risk."

According to Fridell and Pate (2001, p.643): "Over 97 percent of the slain officers were male and 86.8 percent were white. Just over one-quarter of the officers were between the ages of 25 and 30, and a full two-thirds were 40 years of age or younger." They (p.644) also report: "Two-thirds of the officers were on one- or two-officer vehicle patrol, 14.6 percent were on special assignment; 14.1 percent were off duty and 4 percent each were working undercover or as detectives."

Pinizzotto et al. (2002, p.8) note that since 1998 the number of accidental line-of-duty deaths surpassed the number of officers killed by felons. Of the 344 accidental deaths occurring from 1996 to 2000, 197 were due to automobile accidents. They (p.10) note that the officers were typically in their mid-30s with about 10 years of experience who worked hard, took risks and possessed a sense of invincibility. They (p.13) suggest: "Supervisors need to become more alert to the dangers in which officers sometimes place themselves by improperly using their vehicles."

Line-of-duty deaths place a tremendous strain on any department. According to Wade (2001, p.13): "One of the most dreaded, traumatic events any law enforcement agency can experience, line-of-duty deaths, creates chaos within any organization, impacting every sworn officer and civilian employee." She stresses: "The timely and compassionate notification of the fallen officer's family must remain the highest overall priority. No one deserves to get that kind of gut-wrenching, life-shattering information from a television news bulletin."

Although any line-of-duty death will affect an agency, the death of a partner can be especially devastating. Any department might experience such a tragedy, and each should be prepared to properly handle the situation. Written policies should detail how to notify the family, assist with funeral arrangements, help the family complete paperwork required to receive benefits and provide continuing support to the survivors. Officers should understand the Public Safety Officers' Benefits (PSOB) program, which was "designed to offer peace of mind to men and women seeking careers in public safety and to make a strong statement about the value American society places on the contributions of those who serve their communities in potentially dangerous circumstances" (*Public Safety Officers' Benefits Program,* 2001, p.1). The program awards death, disability and education assistance benefits to the survivors of law enforcement officers killed or permanently and totally disabled in the line of duty.

In 1998 Congress created the Public Safety Officers' Educational Assistance (PSOEA) Program, which also makes benefits available to spouses and children of public safety officers killed or permanently and totally disabled in the line of duty. Another resource is Concerns of Police Survivors (COPS), Inc., a national support group founded in 1984 for spouses and children of officers killed in the line of duty. As Schmitt (2000, p.156) notes: "The stated mission of COPS is to 'provide resources to assist in the rebuilding of the lives of families of law enforcement officers killed in the line of duty as determined by federal criteria.'" In addition to providing support groups, COPS sends approximately eight mailings a year to its members. Regular mailings are also sent to the 4,000 agencies in its database.

Peer support and support groups are helpful in many ways. Veteran members may advise new members on available financial benefits and can shepherd them through the complex paperwork and procedures. They can make referrals for local services for everything from a funeral home to a counselor. Support groups may hold regular meetings during which problems and issues can be discussed.

The effects of critical incidents can be far reaching, including causing problems within the family.

Victimized Families

The aftermath of a stressful incident can greatly affect an officer's family and leave damaging emotional scars, a phenomenon identified as **afterburn.** Risk factors that make a police family vulnerable to stress include limited knowledge of police work among family members, a conflict between job and family priorities, and isolation felt by the officer and spouse. Protective factors that may help police families better handle the stress of police work include an awareness of job-related stress factors, a negotiated family structure with clear roles and responsibilities, conflict resolution skills and a social support system.

Reactions to Stress/Symptoms

Stress demands a response, which may range from minimal to serious.

Stress affects people in numerous ways: physical, emotional and psychological.

Law enforcement managers need to recognize signs of stress in their subordinates and in themselves. Symptoms of stress appear differently in different people.

Physical

Medical reports have indicated that as many as 60 percent of patients have indications of stress that negatively affect their health.

Stress is related to heart problems, hypertension, cancer, ulcers, diabetes, chronic headaches, anxiety-related disorders, asthma, excessive eating, decreased sex drive, fatigue, dizziness, muscle aches and tics, backaches and frequent urinating.

Stress can cause these medical conditions, or the conditions can be prolonged, increased in severity or aggravated by stress. Living in our complex, fast-paced society results in many stress-related diseases.

An estimated 85 percent of all illnesses are stress related.

According to the American Medical Association, approximately 23 million prescriptions are written each year for stress-related illnesses. Physical symptoms of stress include abdominal pains, diarrhea, fatigue, headaches, increased pulse rate/pounding heart, overeating or hunger for something sweet, sleep problems, stomach upsets and weight increase or decrease. If these symptoms persist, the person should have a medical examination.

Psychological

Psychological symptoms of stress include boredom, defensiveness, delusions, depression, apathy, emotional illness, hostility, loneliness, nervousness, paranoia, sudden mood changes and tension.

Behavioral

Behavioral symptoms of stress include accident-proneness, anger, argumentativeness, blaming others, drug and/or alcohol abuse, excessive violence, irritability, inability to concentrate, lack of control, neurotic behavior, nail biting, obsession with work, rage, rapid behavior changes, uncontrollable urges to cry and withdrawal.

One person, after reading about the common symptoms of stress just discussed, commented, "I've had all these symptoms." This is probably true of most people. It is only when the symptoms appear in excess or several appear simultaneously that problems arise.

On the Job

Stress reactions found among police officers include repression of emotion, displacement of anger, isolation and unspoken fears. In addition, police officers may behave inappropriately under stress, for example, becoming verbally or physically abusive, looking for any excuse to call in sick, arguing with other officers, placing themselves in danger or engaging in "choir practice" (heavy drinking with peers). They may argue with supervisors, criticize the actions of fellow officers and supervisors, lose interest in the job or sleep on duty.

Levels of Stress

Comments of people in various stages of stress include the following: "I'm tired all the time." "My stomach feels like it has a thousand butterflies." "I just can't concentrate on anything anymore." "I'm really tense, but I feel better after a couple of beers."

Stress can progress through escalating stages such as emotional distancing, denial, isolation, agitation, irritability, depression, anger, blaming others, changing relationships, overreacting or underreacting on the job and taking excessive risks.

Excessive stress usually develops over time. Initially one or more symptoms appear in a mild form. Sleep may be affected, drinking may increase or imagined illnesses may appear. At this level some actions mentioned later in the chapter should be considered.

In the next level the signs of stress are more aggravated but not so much so that the person cannot maintain acceptable work patterns or comparatively normal behavior. The person may experience singular or infrequent occurrences of mild outbursts, crying, withdrawal or impulsiveness.

In the final level of stress, people become nonfunctional. They exhibit easily recognized abnormal behavior at home and on the job. The symptoms in the preceding level become more aggravated and frequent or even constant. Depression or anxiety appears, and a feeling of hopelessness develops. People at this level may think they will never get better. For them, life has little purpose. Work performance decreases drastically, and the person takes frequent days off due to illness. Employees may not be able to go to work or, if they do, they cannot concentrate and experience great difficulty making decisions. According to Mulroy (2000, p.67): "Long-term stress is not only destructive, but may be fatal in police work." The quiz in Table 14.2 allows you to evaluate your stress level.

Stress at its most advanced stage is often called burnout.

Burnout

Burnout occurs when someone is exhausted or listless because of overwork. Burnout results from long-term, unmediated stress. Hawkins (p.343) says: "Burnout is a syndrome of emotional exhaustion, depersonalization and reduced personal accomplishment." A once-motivated, committed employee experiences physical and emotional exhaustion on the job brought about by unrelieved demands.

Symptoms of burnout include lack of enthusiasm and interest, decreased job performance, temper flare-ups and a loss of will, motivation or commitment.

Table 14.2
Stress Level Quiz

Take this simple quiz to evaluate your own stress level. The "Social Readjustment Rating Scale," as it is called, was designed by social scientists Thomas Holmes and Richard H. Rahe on the premise that health and survival are based on the body's ability to maintain a balance of all its physical and mental processes. Too much change in our lives can overtax our adaptive resources, causing illnes. The forty-one positive and negative life events listed here are valued according to the amount of adjustment needed to cope with each.

Directions: Add up the indicated points for every life event or change that you have experienced during the past year.

Life Event	Life-Change Units
Death of spouse	100
Divorce	73
Marital separation	65
Imprisonment	63
Death of close family member	63
Personal injury or illness	53
Marriage	50
Dismissal from work	47
Marital reconciliation	45
Retirement	45
Change in health of family member	44
Pregnancy	40
Sexual difficulties	39
Addition of new family member	39
Business readjustment	39
Change in financial state	38
Change in number of spousal arguments	35
Major mortgage	32
Foreclosure of mortgage or loan	30
Change in responsibilities at work	29
Son or daughter leaving home	29
Trouble with in-laws	29
Outstanding personal achievement	28
Spouse begins or stops work	26
Begin or end school	26
Change in living conditions	25
Revision of personal habits	24
Trouble with boss	23
Change in work hours or conditions	20
Change in residence	20
Change in schools	20
Change in recreation	19
Change in church activities	19
Change in social activities	18
Minor mortgage or loan	17
Change in sleeping habits	16
Change in number of family reunions	15
Change in eating habits	15
Vacation	13
Christmas	12
Minor violation of the law	11
YOUR TOTAL	—

Scoring: Accumulating more than 300 stress points in one year greatly increases the risk of illness. From 150 to 299 points, the risk is reduced by 30 percent. A total of fewer than 150 points involves a low risk.

Source: Adapted from *The Book of Stress Survival* by Alix Krista. Copyright © 1986 Gaia Books Limited. Reprinted with permission of Gaia Books Limited. U.S. edition published by Fireside, Simon and Schuster, Inc.

Those most likely to experience burnout are those who are initially most committed. You cannot burn out if you have never been on fire. To those in police work, the **blue flame** is the symbol of a law enforcement officer who wants to make a difference in the world. The enthusiasm shown by rookie officers as they recover their first occupied stolen vehicle or make their first collar is like a torch being lit. The key is knowing how to keep the flame burning throughout the many stresses of an entire law enforcement career.

Burned out employees can often be helped by a change—something to motivate them. Sometimes changes in the job itself help—adding new dimensions to old tasks. Expert assistance is usually needed at this level, and counseling may be necessary.

To avoid burnout, keep the work interesting, give recognition, provide R and R (rest and relaxation), avoid "other duties" and limit the assignment.

Other extremely serious consequences of stress include post-traumatic stress disorder, depression and suicide.

Post-Traumatic Stress Disorder (PTSD)

As they wage war on crime and violence, law enforcement personnel may have a problem similar to that experienced by military combat personnel. During World War I, soldiers were *shell-shocked.* In World War II, they suffered from *combat fatigue* and *battle stress.* Psychologists gradually came to realize that civilians involved in major catastrophes such as earthquakes, fires and rapes experienced similar stress disorders. Symptoms included diminished responsiveness to their environment, apathy, disinterest, pessimism and diminished sex drive.

Law enforcement officers may experience **post-traumatic stress disorder (PTSD),** a clinical name associated with a debilitating condition suffered by Vietnam War veterans.

Traumatic events (1) are likely to be sudden and unexpected, (2) threaten officers' lives, (3) often include loss (partner, physical ability or position) and (4) may abruptly change officers' values and self-confidence.

The first phase after the incident, the initial impact phase, may last a few minutes or a few days. Attention is on the present, with the officer stunned or bewildered and having difficulty coping with normal situations.

This phase may be followed by the recoil phase of wanting to retell the experience and attempt to overcome it through this retelling. The need is for support from fellow officers. Personal reactions may be withdrawal, anxiety, hopelessness, insomnia and nightmares. Other reported symptoms commonly experienced are flashbacks, depression, sexual dysfunction, obsessive behavior (particularly with alcohol and drugs) and fear. According to Kinchin (2000, p.65): "Research indicates that most [officers] will be traumatized briefly, and around 15 percent will be traumatized enough to lead them to suffer from post-traumatic stress disorder. Some may have to retire as a direct result."

Kates (2001, p.30) contends: "PTSD does not mean mental illness. It is a normal reaction to an abnormal amount of stress." Kureczka (2002, p.21) recalls: "While it took strength, courage and the will to live to survive my physical battle [being shot by and then fatally shooting a bank robber], it took far more moral fortitude and emotional resolve to survive the aftermath. If anything could be construed as brave or heroic as a result of my incident, it would be that I broke through the 'image armor' and triumphed over tragedy by honestly confronting and resolving my psychological battle, the ultimate test."

Those who can be of greatest assistance are fellow officers, immediate supervisors, unit commanders, peer counselors, chaplains, mental health professionals, the officer's family and, in some cases, the media and citizens. Those who assist should be good listeners, show empathy and concern, offer reassurances and support and provide group grief sharing.

Officers in larger law enforcement departments and those assigned to more difficult and violent tasks, such as murders, SWAT teams or narcotics teams, are the most likely candidates for PTSD.

In addition, as Heiskell (2000a, p.10) suggests: "Because PTSD is an anxiety disorder in which the victim is left jittery and tense, the practice of exercise and relaxation techniques is extremely valuable. Massage therapy has also proved to be effective in lowering anxiety and stress for some individuals. Acupuncture has been shown also to ease excessive fear reactions and can reduce traumatic dreams." Untreated PTSD can lead to depression.

Depression

Hoofnagle (2002, p.84) points out: "Although depression may be regarded as a character weakness or personality flaw by some, it is actually a serious and life-threatening illness. Anyone can be affected, and police officers are no exception." "Bringing Depression into the Light" (2002, pp.2–3) explains:

> If you've ever had major depression, you will recognize its hallmarks. You feel constantly sad or burdened, you lose interest in all activities, even those you used to enjoy. Work, school, relationships and other aspects of your life get derailed or put on hold indefinitely because you just don't have the energy for them. . . . Trying to "snap out" of a severe depression is like trying to talk yourself out of a heart attack. . . .
>
> Depression and alcohol abuse often go hand-in-hand. Occasionally, drinking excessively is a symptom of severe clinical depression. More often, depression results from excessive drinking. Prolonged alcohol abuse and alcoholism can lead to prolonged periods of depression. It becomes a vicious circle of suffering. . . .
>
> Because depression involves a biochemical imbalance in the brain, medications that restore the balance can be an important tool in your recovery. More than 70 percent of people with depression improve with medication therapy. . . .
>
> For some people with depression, talk therapy—alone or with medication—can help.

One of the most tragic results of untreated depression is suicide.

Suicide

Czarnecki et al. (2002, p.22) declare: "Suicide is the quiet killer in law enforcement." Honig and White (2000, p.156) note that "nearly twice as many police officers die by their own hand as are killed in the line of duty." They (p.159) also report: "Owning a firearm results in a five-fold increase in suicide rates among the general population. . . . Compared to other occupations that involve shift work or danger, police officers have a significantly higher suicide rate. Other job-related concerns, such as being under investigation, being suspended or experiencing a significant professional failure were also identified as precipitants for suicide. . . . Officers experiencing martial problems were five times more likely to commit suicide, while officers facing suspension were seven times more likely to commit suicide. A final contributing factor is retirement. Retired officers were ten times more likely to commit suicide than their peers were."

In addition, alcohol played a role in an estimated 35 percent of officer suicides. According to Heiskell (2000b, p.62): "Nearly 100,000 Americans die each year as a result of alcohol abuse. Alcohol is a factor in more than half of the nation's homicides, suicides and traffic accidents."

Steo (2002, p.44), an officer who attempted suicide with his police service pistol, describes how depression affected him and what he learned: "Depression is a silent killer when you are in its grasp. You cannot think right. Your logic is skewed. Depression wears away at you with a terrible pain. The one thing I learned about depression and suicide is that I did not want to die. I just wanted the pain to stop. I didn't look at suicide as dying, but just relieving the pain. . . . Denying this illness only puts you at risk. Just remember what Tom Hanks said in *Cast Away,* 'You have to make it to tomorrow, because you don't know what good things the tide will bring in.'"

Coping with Stress

No one escapes stress. How people *deal with* it determines whether they cope and develop or deteriorate. Stress in its more severe stages can be totally devastating. The severity of stress must be taken into account when considering how best to reduce its effects to a tolerable, manageable level.

Negative coping mechanisms commonly used by law enforcement officers include cynicism, secrecy and deviance.

Take definite steps to reduce stress. Most people need to work to earn a living but may need to change their attitudes about their work or about the people they work with. The symptoms of stress are often obvious, but its cause is more difficult to determine and even more difficult to change. Unfortunately, we tend to treat the symptoms rather than reduce the causes of stress. A story told by Saul Alinsky illustrates this point:

> A man jumps into a river to rescue a drowning man. He saves the first victim but has to jump into the river again to save a second and then a third. After a fourth rescue he rushes from the scene. When an onlooker asks where he is going, he responds, "Upstream to stop whoever is pushing these guys into the river!"

Although the rescuer's decision seems reasonable, it is not likely to be appreciated by the fifth and sixth drowning victims. Managers must pay attention not only to the victims of stress but also to the conditions that created it. In law enforcement the source may be an incident, a citizen, a manager, a fellow officer or other sources. Having identified the source of the stress, study all methods of relieving stress and determine what might work best.

Reducing Stress Levels

Stress levels can be reduced through physical exercise, relaxation techniques, good nutrition, taking time for oneself, making friends, learning to say no, staying within the law, changing one's mental attitude, keeping things in perspective and seeking help when it is needed.

Physical exercise improves the body's stamina to deal with stress and provides time away from work temporarily, which is also healthy.

Relaxation techniques are often helpful. Most consist of removing all distractions, closing your eyes, imagining yourself in a peaceful setting and breathing slowly and deeply for 10 to 20 minutes. Courses on relaxation are often offered through community health programs. Some people meditate as a relaxation technique.

Good nutrition also helps reduce stress. A diet that improves general health will help reduce stress. Information on diets is available from physicians, community health programs or libraries. Reducing cholesterol levels requires one type of diet, whereas losing weight or dealing with a specific physical condition may require another type of diet.

Take time for yourself. Take vacations. Try to keep your mind off job-related matters when not on duty. Develop hobbies and outside interests; volunteer. Some officers write poetry to relieve stress. Take walks, listen to music, or go window-shopping. You will accomplish more at work if you are mentally and physically recharged by some time off.

Make friends both within and outside the department. Get active in a club or civic group. Problems and worries become smaller if you have others to share them with.

Learn to say no. Do not be taken advantage of. A sweatshirt bears the message: "*Stress*—what happens when your gut says 'no' and your mouth says 'Of course, I'd be glad to.' " Do not volunteer for more than you can reasonably carry.

Stay within the law, no matter what temptations arise. Yes, law enforcement officers can and do perform illegal acts, and this adds to job tension. Consider what you do not only from a legal but also from an ethical standpoint. Doing "right" things reduces stress; doing "wrong" things increases stress. There is no "right" way to do a "wrong" thing.

A *change in mental attitude* can provide release from stress. As the adage says, "Accept what you cannot change." The power of the mind is strong. Positive attitudes provide a new outlook on life and your cause of stress. Negative attitudes can be self-defeating.

Keep things in perspective. If you think something is threatening, it is almost as dangerous as if it were. Do not blow things out of proportion. Be realistic. Your mistakes almost never last in others' minds as long as they do in your own.

Seek help if you need it. Law enforcement officers deal with life-threatening situations as part of their job. If you need help coping with the job's dangers, seek counseling. Talk about the problem with other officers and see how they deal with it. It is as real to them as to you. Mental stress is often more difficult to deal with than physical stress.

Other ways to reduce stress include getting plenty of sleep, setting personal goals, making a "to-do" list and taking things one at a time, smiling and laughing to lighten your day, saying positive things to yourself, taking time to recharge by taking mini-timeouts, volunteering or helping others. Finally, *do NOT smoke,* and if you drink, *drink in moderation. AVOID drugs* to control stress unless recommended by a qualified physician.

Alcohol, drugs and smoking increase stress over time and can also seriously affect physical health.

Especially important is assuming responsibility for your own well-being. As Harpold and Feemster (p.6) stress: "Choosing to be healthy is the best weapon against the negative influences of stress. Once a commitment is made to fight back against the negative factors of stress, life becomes healthier and more enjoyable. Fighting back includes the deliberate adoption and implementation of stress reduction techniques and the vigilance of the law enforcement community to protect its members from the effects of negative stress as vigorously as officers protect society from lawlessness."

Stressful situations are not necessarily permanent. Situations change, as do levels of stress. You have a role to play in determining what happens. Develop a personal strategy for dealing with your stress. Reexamine your personal goals. Maybe you have set them too low or too high or need to change them completely. If necessary, change your lifestyle. Get plenty of rest and eat right. And don't take yourself too seriously. Confront situations, deal with them and put the unknown behind you. You will be better able to get on with the important things.

How the Organization Can Reduce Stress

The law enforcement administration can do much to reduce employee stress.

Testing and Selection

Administrators can continue the strong testing already in use to select candidates most likely to cope well with stress by being physically fit, mentally stable and emotionally well balanced. Law enforcement employees who start healthy have a good foundation for remaining healthy during their careers. Administrators need to demand tests designed specifically for the needs of law enforcement personnel selection.

Law enforcement budgets provide training, weapons and vehicles, and they should provide funds for keeping fit. As in the medical profession, those in law enforcement must sometimes cope with emergency situations that demand immediate yet highly analytical responses. In both professions life may depend on the actions taken. Psychological testing and interviews can help screen out mentally and emotionally weak or unstable applicants. Doing so is not only good for the department but is also best for the candidates, even though they may not believe so at the time. The department benefits by less sick leave and absenteeism, greater productivity, better employee relationships, fewer resignations, fewer new hirings (with the associated costs) and more work hours available due to less new officer training time. Potential employees are saved from attempting a career likely to fail, loss of time spent in the wrong vocation or possible public humiliation in a critical situation.

In one instance a finalist for an entry-level law enforcement position was at the top of the eligible list. After the interview the board agreed he was the best selection from approximately 125 applicants. He proceeded to the psychological test, and the resulting report stated that the candidate had bipolar disorder (manic depression), so much so that he might be suicidal. Because the board could not assume the risk, the candidate was turned down. What would have happened without the psychological test, especially when this officer would be carrying a weapon? No one will know because he was not hired, but the case shows the importance of psychological screening for law enforcement officers.

Ongoing Psychological Support

Periodic psychological fitness-for-duty evaluations are also important. Psychological reviews should be available for employees who have developed mental or emotional problems after employment. They should also have psychological assistance available after a killing or other severely traumatic event while on duty.

Some agencies have full-time police psychologists. Others have regular access to confidential psychological services. Many agencies are now using self-help groups for police who are plagued with problems such as alcoholism and post-traumatic stress disorder. In addition some areas have treatment centers for law enforcement personnel with job-related stress disorders and other types of psychological problems. Some agencies use a psychologist jointly with the county or state. Smaller departments may obtain the assistance of a retired psychologist in the community as a volunteer or on a small retainer.

Be aware that officers may resist psychiatric help because they view it as a sign of weakness. They may be reluctant to admit they have stress-related problems for fear of losing their co-workers' respect or lessening their chances for promotion. Brown (2000, p.89) points out: "In many jurisdictions, the psychologist is viewed as an outsider because of the perception that an officer needing that kind of help is frowned upon by peers and is clinically dysfunctional. Many psychologists are relegated to a wait-and-see role and as a result officers who need to release pent-up frustrations have no outlet and either cause harm to themselves or others. By expanding the role of police psychologists, departments would take more of a proactive stance in meeting the needs of officers." For example, the New York Police Department has mandated that 55,000 NYPD personnel undergo mandatory counseling to address emotional fallout from the World Trade Center disaster ("Can We Talk? . . .," 2001, p.1).

© Michael Newman/PhotoEdit

Police departments nationwide have implemented peer support groups to help officers deal with problems. Officers are more willing to confide in their colleagues because they share the same set of stresses.

Programs to Prevent/Reduce Stress

The business world has implemented stress-reduction programs such as athletic club memberships, physical activities, flex time, free time and company gripe sessions. Some of these programs might be options for law enforcement organizations. Other programs include peer support groups, critical incident stress debriefing, organizational consultant programs and chaplain programs.

Peer Support Groups

Peer support groups are a particularly effective type of stress-reduction program.

Police departments of all sizes are implementing peer support programs to help officers deal with stress and emotional difficulties.

A peer support group was started in New York by Detective Richard Pastorella. In 1982 Pastorella was left blind, half deaf and missing a hand from a failed attempt to disarm a terrorist bomb. As he lay recuperating in his hospital bed, alone, depressed, feeling utterly worthless, he decided other officers in similar circumstances should not have to suffer alone as he was. Three months after his discharge from the hospital he started the Police Self-Support Group. The group's membership included officers wounded by criminal violence, injured in traffic or other accidents, or traumatized by seeing a fellow officer go down. Almost all suffered from post-traumatic stress disorder.

No amount of police machismo can deflect the cold, hard reality of PTSD. Like a relentlessly corrosive force if left unattended, PTSD can gnaw away at one's psychological bridges until they collapse. A similar type of program aimed at alleviating stress, particularly PTSD, is critical incident stress debriefing.

Critical Incident Stress Debriefing

Critical incident stress debriefing (CISD) is another effective way to prevent or reduce stress. In CISD, officers who experience a critical incident such as a mass disaster, a crash with multiple deaths or a particularly grizzly murder are brought together as a group for a psychological debriefing soon after the event. A trained mental health professional leads the group members as they discuss their emotions and reactions. This allows officers to vent and to realize they are not going crazy but are responding normally to a very abnormal situation.

A CISD should take place within 24 to 72 hours after a critical incident. Earlier is usually too soon for full emotional impact to have occurred. If only one officer is involved in the critical incident, he should be joined in the CISD by volunteers from the department who have experienced a similar incident or have been trained in PTSD.

To overcome officers' reluctance to participate in a mental health program, attendance at a CISD should be mandatory. A CISD should not become an operational critique. The groups should be small and everything said kept confidential.

Law enforcement departments should include an **employee assistance program (EAP)** or provide referrals to outside agencies for psychological and counseling services and to assist officers with stress, marital or chemical dependency problems.

The Organizational Consultant Program

Yachnik and Honig (2000, p.104) describe the organizational consultant program developed and implemented by the Los Angeles County Sheriff's Department: "The program alleviates officer stress by training supervisors in prevention and early intervention. The idea is to help the supervisors help their officers. The two components of the program, education and mentoring, are designed as proactive intervention."

Chaplain Corps

When troubled or stressed, many people turn to their faith for guidance and solace. Some departments make chaplains available to officers who need a place to turn in times of stress. Streit (2000, p.88) suggests: "Chaplains open their arms and ears to officers and departments in need of their services." Says Streit (p.90): "The most important thing a chaplain does is serve as a confidential listener for police officers."

Roberts (2001, p.52) describes the police pastor program used by the Shreveport (Louisiana) Police Department. In this program 20 local ministers go on patrol with officers. In addition to serving as eyes and ears for the police, the pastors assist with death notifications, calming hostile crowds and providing assistance to citizens in a non-law enforcement capacity.

Other Stress Management Programs

Health programs and stress management seminars are another means to help law enforcement officers prevent destructive stress or at least reduce it.

Health programs include medical and psychological services and fitness programs. Law enforcement administration can also provide in-service health and fitness training and weight control classes.

Law enforcement management should provide an opportunity for employees to attend stress management seminars. All personnel, including dispatchers, should attend. A distinct benefit from attending such seminars is a better understanding of the nature of stress and ways to prevent, cope with or reduce its effects. The FBI has all new agents complete a Stress Management in Law Enforcement (SMILE) course to help them better understand the stress they may encounter on the job. Through such exposure they become more aware of the emotional and psychological dangers of the job, beyond the physical ones most expect to find in law enforcement.

Individuals who can successfully cope with stress have what psychology has termed **psychological hardiness.** Such individuals believe they can influence and control their lives and accept change as normal and positive.

The Role of the Manager/Supervisor

Law enforcement managers have an important role in minimizing the effects of stress in themselves and their subordinates. First-line supervisors are in daily contact with shift officers, need to work with them to reduce stress and have concern for their problems.

Establishing rapport with all officers is essential to reducing stress. Law enforcement managers can provide both positive reinforcement and constructive criticism if there is a foundation of respect and communication. They should keep in close touch with their subordinates and recognize the symptoms of stress. If an officer shows such symptoms, the manager should be ready to assist and reduce to whatever level possible the degree of stress. Sometimes just having someone to talk to is the most helpful. If counseling or psychological assistance is needed, it should be provided or information furnished regarding local sources of assistance.

Stress may seem overwhelming, but the good news is that you can do a lot to minimize the stress in your life and in the lives of your officers. You are in charge.

Summary

Stress can be helpful (eustress) or harmful (distress), depending on its intensity and frequency as well as how it is mediated. Stress often arises from uncertainty, lack of control and pressure. Sources of stress can occur in a person's daily living, personality and job.

A major source of employee stress may be upper-level management. Doing routine tasks and suddenly being thrown into a traumatic situation is exceptionally stressful. Everyday confrontations with crime victims and those who commit crimes are also stressful. Four categories of law enforcement stress are external, operational, organizational and personal. Additional stress is also often experienced by women officers, minority officers, investigators and managers.

Stress affects people in numerous ways: mental, physical, emotional and psychological. Stress is related to heart problems, hypertension, cancer, ulcers, diabetes, chronic headaches, depression, anxiety-related disorders, asthma, excessive eating from nervous tension, decreased sex drive, fatigue, dizziness, muscle aches and tics, backaches and frequent urinating. An estimated 85 percent of all illnesses are stress related.

Symptoms of burnout include lack of enthusiasm and interest, decreased job performance, temper flare-ups and a loss of will, motivation or commitment. To avoid burnout, keep the work interesting, give recognition, provide R and R (Rest and Relaxation), avoid "other duties" and limit the assignment.

Law enforcement officers may experience post-traumatic stress disorder (PTSD), a clinical term associated with a debilitating condition suffered by Vietnam War veterans. Officers in larger departments and those assigned to the more difficult and violent tasks, such as murders, SWAT teams or narcotics teams, appear to be the most likely candidates for PTSD.

Negative coping mechanisms commonly used by law enforcement officers include cynicism, secrecy and deviance. Stress levels can be reduced through physical exercise, relaxation techniques, good nutrition, taking time for oneself, making friends, learning to say no, staying within the law, changing one's mental attitude, keeping things in perspective and seeking help when needed. Alcohol, drugs and smoking increase stress over time and also can seriously affect physical health.

Support groups are one particularly effective type of stress-reduction program. Critical incident stress debriefing (CISD) is another effective way to prevent or reduce stress. Law enforcement departments should include employee assistance programs (EAP) or provide referrals to outside agencies for psychological and counseling services and assistance for officers with stress, marital or chemical dependency problems. Health programs and stress management seminars are other means to help officers prevent destructive stress or at least reduce it.

Discussion Questions

1. What do you consider the five most stressful aspects of work in law enforcement?
2. What are major stressors in your life right now?
3. How would you reduce your level of on-the-job stress?
4. Has your level of stress changed with job changes? Age changes? Changes due to a singular incident? Changes due to a series of similar incidents?
5. Have you taken any psychological tests? Which ones?
6. Are you a type A or a type B personality? What significance does that have to your work in law enforcement?
7. Have you ever participated in a support group? How effective was the experience?
8. Do you know anyone who has burned out? Can you explain why?
9. How does stress at the management level differ from that at the line level?
10. Does your local law enforcement agency have an EAP or other forms of employee support to reduce stress?

InfoTrac College Edition Assignment

Use InfoTrac College Edition to help answer the Discussion Questions.

Select a topic related to *stress in law enforcement* and find a recent article dealing with the topic. Summarize the main ideas of the article and include the full reference citation. Be prepared to share your summary with the class.

OR

Read and outline one of the following articles:

- "The Effects of Sleep Deprivation" by Glory Cochrane.
- "Perceptual and Memory Distortion during Officer-Involved Shootings" by Alexis Artwohl.
- "Accidentally Dead: Accidental Line-of-Duty Deaths of Law Enforcement Officers" by Anthony J. Pinizzotto, Edward F. Davis and Charles E. Miller, III.
- "Line-of-Duty Police Death Notifications: Planning for the Unthinkable" by Donna J. Wade.
- "Surviving Assaults: After the Physical Battle Ends, the Psychological Battle Begins" by Arthur W. Kureczka.
- "Managing the Stress of Organizational Change" by James D. Sewell.
- "Negative Influences of Police Stress" by Joseph A. Harpold and Samuel L. Feemster.

References

Aaron, Jeffrey D. K. "Stress and Coping in Police Officers." *Police Quarterly,* December 2000, pp.438–450.

Artwohl, Alexis. "Perceptual and Memory Distortion during Officer-Involved Shootings." *FBI Law Enforcement Bulletin,* October 2002, pp.18–24.

Berger, William B. "Agency Response to Line-of-Duty Deaths." *The Police Chief,* May 2002, p.6.

"Bringing Depression into the Light." *Discover,* Spring 2002.

Brown, Ed. "Transitioning the Role of Police Psychologists." *Law and Order,* May 2000, pp.89–90.

"Can We Talk? Officials Take Steps to Head Off 9/11 Post-Traumatic Stress." *Law Enforcement News,* November 30, 2001, pp.1, 8.

Carpenter, David. "Police with Families; States with Obligations." *Law and Order,* May 2001, p.119.

Cochrane, Glory. "The Effects of Sleep Deprivation." *FBI Law Enforcement Bulletin,* July 2001, pp.22–25.

Czarnecki, Fabrice; Kasanof, Adam; and Trautman, Neal. "Preventing Police Suicide: What *You* Can Do to Help." *The Law Enforcement Trainer,* January/February 2002, pp.22–25.

"Despite Some Gains, Female Cops Still Find Too Few Cracks in the Glass Ceiling." *Law Enforcement News,* June 15, 2000, pp.1, 9.

Domash, Shelly Feuer. " 'Steady Tours': Can They Benefit Officers, Agencies?" *Police,* April 2000, pp.46–49.

Douglas, Dave. "Jumping into the Fire." *Police,* October 2002, pp.44–48.

Floyd, Craig W. "For Law Enforcement, 2001 Was Deadly." *American Police Beat,* May 2002, pp.52–59.

Fridell, Lorie A. and Pate, Antony M. "The Other Side of Deadly Force: Felonious Killings of Law Enforcement Officers." In *Critical Issues in Policing: Contemporary Readings,* 4th ed. Edited by Roger G. Dunham and Geoffrey R. Alpert. Prospect Heights, IL: Waveland Press, Inc., 2001, pp.636–663.

Gold, Marion E. "Blasting through the Glass Ceiling." *Law Enforcement News,* May 15/31, 2000a, pp.12, 14.

Gold, Marion E. "The Progress of Women in Policing." *Law and Order,* June 2000b, pp.159–161.

Harpold, Joseph A. and Feemster, Samuel. "Negative Influences of Police Stress." *FBI Law Enforcement Bulletin,* September 2002, pp.1–7.

Hawkins, Homer C. "Police Officer Burnout: A Partial Replication of Maslach's Burnout Inventory." *Police Quarterly,* September 2001, pp.343–360.

Heiskell, Lawrence. "Post-Traumatic Stress Disorder." *Police,* March 2000a, p.10.

Heiskell, Lawrence. "Alcoholism: Equal Opportunity Disease." *Police,* June 2000b, p.62.

Honig, Audrey L. "Police-Assisted Suicide: Identification, Intervention, and Investigation." *The Police Chief,* October 2001, pp.89–93.

Honig, Audrey L. and White, Elizabeth K. "By Their Own Hand: Suicide among Law Enforcement Personnel." *The Police Chief,* October 2000, pp.156–160.

Hoofnagle, Laura. "Recognizing Depression and Raising Awareness among Law Enforcement Professionals." *The Police Chief,* February 2002, pp.84–89.

Johnson, Richard. "Making Death Notifications." *Law and Order,* October 2000, pp.177–180.

Kates, Allen R. "Post-Traumatic Stress Disorder: Hoax? Or Reality?" *The Associate,* January/February 2001, pp.29–31.

Kinchin, David. "The Trauma of Police Work." *Law and Order,* March 2000, pp.63–65.

Kureczka, Arthur W. "Surviving Assaults: After the Physical Battle Ends, the Psychological Battle Begins." *FBI Law Enforcement Bulletin,* January 2002, pp.18–21.

Mulroy, Darrell E. "Stress: How It Contributes to Poor Performance." *Law and Order,* September 2000, pp.67–68.

Paynter, Ronnie L. "Suicide by Cop." *Law Enforcement Technology,* June 2000, pp.40–44.

Pedersen, Dorothy. "Sleepy Heads on Patrol." *Law Enforcement Technology,* July 2001, pp.130–138.

Pinizzotto, Anthony J.; Davis, Edward F.; and Miller, Charles E., III. "Accidentally Dead: Accidental Line-of-Duty Deaths of Law Enforcement Officers." *FBI Law Enforcement Bulletin,* July 2002, pp.8–13.

Praet, Bruce D. "Suicide by Cop or Death by Indifference?" *The Police Chief,* July 2002, p.14.

Public Safety Officers' Benefits Program. Washington, DC: Bureau of Justice Assistance Fact Sheet, July 2001. (FS 000271)

Recruiting & Retaining Women: A Self-Assessment Guide for Law Enforcement. Los Angeles, CA: National Center for Women & Policing, no date.

Reese, James T. "6 Keys to Stress-Free Living." *The Associate,* January/February 2001, pp.14–17.

Roberts, James N., Jr. "Police Pastor Program Puts Religious Leaders in the Squad Cars." *The Police Chief,* February 2001, pp.52–54.

Schmitt, Sheila. "C.O.P.S. Helps Families Cope." *Law and Order,* October 2000, pp.156–158.

Sewell, James D. "Managing the Stress of Organizational Change." *FBI Law Enforcement Bulletin,* March 2002, pp.14–20.

Steo, Dominick. "Police Officers, Depression and Suicide." *American Police Beat,* April 2002, p.44.

Strandberg, Keith. "Breaking through the 'Brass' Ceiling." *Law Enforcement Technology,* June 2000, pp.76–82.

Streit, Corrine. "Someone Officers Can Trust." *Law Enforcement Technology,* September 2000, pp.88–93.

"Ten Reasons Cops Are Different." www.heavybadge.com.

Thrash, Paul. "Saying Goodbye." *Police,* May 2000, p.64.

Vila, Bryan. "Cops: Learn You're A, B, Zzzzzzs." *The Law Enforcement Trainer,* September/October 2002, pp.44–47.

Vila, Bryan and Kenney, Dennis Jay. *Tired Cops: The Prevalence and Potential Consequences of Police Fatigue.* Washington, DC: National Criminal Justice Reference Service, 2002. (NCJ 190634)

Vila, Bryan; Kenney, Dennis Jay; and Morrison, Gregory B. "The Importance of Managing Police Fatigue." *The Police Chief,* April 2001, pp.188–193.

Vila, Bryan; Morrison, Gregory B.; and Kenney, Dennis J. "Improving Shift Schedule and Work-Hour Policies and Practices to Increase Police Officer Performance, Health, and Safety." *Police Quarterly,* March 2002, pp.4–24.

Volpe, J. F. "A Guide to Effective Stress Management." *Law and Order,* October 2000, pp.183–188.

Wade, Donna J. "Line-of-Duty Police Death Notifications: Planning for the Unthinkable." *FBI Law Enforcement Bulletin,* April 2001, pp.13–17.

Yachnik, Michael and Honig, Audrey L. "Organizational Consultant Program Takes Aim at Officers' Stress." *The Police Chief,* August 2000, pp.104–106.

Zhao, Jihong "Solomon"; He, Ni; and Lovrich, Nicholas. "Predicting Five Dimensions of Police Officer Stress: Looking More Deeply into Organizational Settings for Sources of Police Stress." *Police Quarterly,* March 2002, pp.43–62.

Book-Specific Web Site

Go to the *Management and Supervision in Law Enforcement* Web site at http://info.wadsworth.com/05346160654 for student and instructor resources, including Internet Assignments and Case Studies.

CHAPTER 15

Deploying Law Enforcement Resources and Improving Productivity

The deployment of police strength both by time and area is essential.
—Basic Tenet of the Peelian Reform Act of 1829

Do You Know?

- How to measure law enforcement productivity?
- How law enforcement productivity has traditionally been measured?
- What function police logs serve?
- What the largest law enforcement division is?
- How area assignments are determined?
- How patrol size is determined?
- Why rapid response is important?
- What basic premise underlies random patrol?
- What the Kansas City study of preventive patrol found?
- What methods of patrol might be used?
- Whether one- or two-officer patrol units are more effective?
- What civilianization is and how it affects personnel deployment?
- What predisaster plans should include?
- What the crime triangle is?
- How to most effectively channel resources to fight crime?
- How community policing affects deployment?
- How to improve law enforcement productivity?
- What a management information system (MIS) is?
- What key ingredients ensure a successful quality circle?
- What the single most important factor in high productivity and morale is?

Can You Define?

aggressive patrol
civilianization
cone of resolution
crime triangle
dog shift
hot spots
incivilities
lag time
management information system (MIS)
police logs
productivity
proportionate assignment
quality circle
quota
random patrol
shift
technophobia
watch

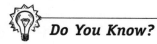

INTRODUCTION

As Hudson (2000, p.26) stresses: "The supervisor's primary job is getting the work done and maintaining productive relations with employees." Law enforcement agencies exist for a purpose—to fulfill a specific mission. Management, in conjunction with line personnel, sets forth this mission and the requirements for accomplishing it. Missions mean little without action, and in most businesses, including law enforcement, that means schedules. The link between mission and schedules is illustrated in Figure 15.1.

The characteristic that distinguishes law enforcement personnel allocation from most business and industrial situations is the manner in which tasks are generated. In most nonlaw enforcement situations, the tasks to be performed are known in advance, and the number of people required to complete them is easily determined. For example, if a shoe manufacturing plant needs to produce 10,000 pairs of shoes next week to meet orders, the tasks to perform and the number of people needed to perform them can be determined with some precision.

Some law enforcement tasks are also predictable. For example, escorting distinguished visitors or maintaining order along a parade route are services known ahead of time. Personnel requirements can be determined and allocated well in advance of the event. Most law enforcement tasks, however, can be predicted only in terms of the likelihood of their occurring at a specific time and place. Such tasks make up the bulk of law enforcement work and are the basis of the personnel allocation problem. To understand the problem in this context, it is helpful to view each law enforcement task that occurs as having two coordinates: (1) the time at which the event occurs and (2) where it occurs.

Each time a call is received, one objective of most law enforcement departments has been to move a patrol unit to the scene as quickly as possible. How quickly the patrol unit arrives depends on its location relative to the location of the call. Law enforcement executive managers have always been faced with the

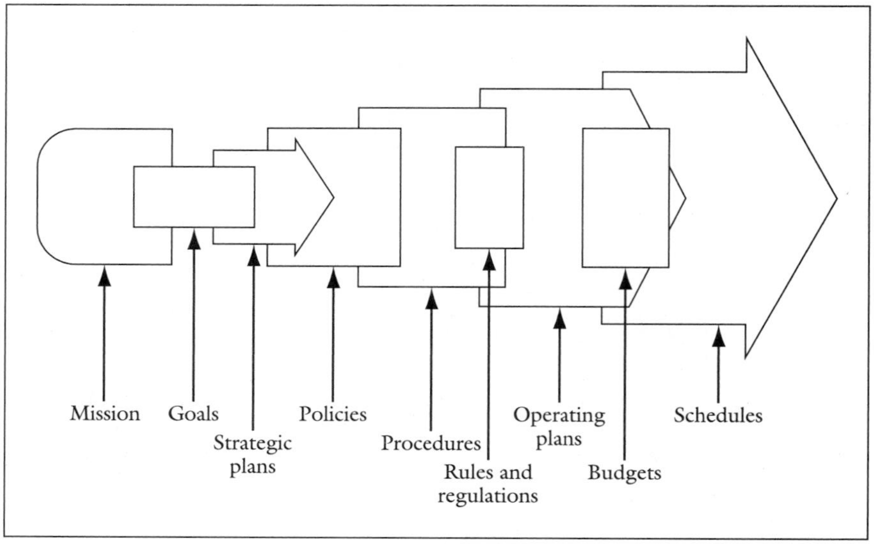

Figure 15.1
How Plans Interlock: From Missions to Schedules

Source: Lester R. Bittel. *The McGraw-Hill 36-Hour Management Course.* New York: McGraw-Hill Publishing Company, 1989, p.77. Reprinted by permission.

challenge of providing satisfactory levels of services with a fixed number of personnel and resources. Recently many have been faced with providing *more* services with *fewer* personnel. This requires budget cutbacks and increased emphasis on deployment of existing personnel.

Many departments can answer only actual requests for services, with no time available for preventive patrol. Some departments must establish priorities for answering service requests. For them, not only is preventive patrol time nonexistent, but also requests for service are backlogged. A burglary in progress call would be answered, but a barking dog complaint would be deferred or not answered at all.

This chapter begins by examining law enforcement productivity and ways that managers and supervisors can improve productivity through those they oversee. A definition of productivity is presented as well as a look at how it has traditionally been measured. The chapter then examines the key management function of deploying personnel, including how they have traditionally been deployed, factors affecting deployment, assignment rotation, overtime and research findings about deployment and response time. Next is a look at differentiated response and random patrol, including the results of the Kansas City Preventive Patrol Experiment, followed by a presentation of the methods of patrol currently in use. This is followed by a look at other ways the law enforcement personnel pool might be expanded, including involving citizens through citizen police academies, citizen patrols and reserve units; using departmental volunteers and civilianizing departmental positions. Next is a discussion of the deploying of resources during emergencies, the traditional goal of deploying resources to fight crime and how community policing affects the deployment of personnel.

Next is an examination of some symptoms of productivity problems and how such problems might be addressed. Among the most promising ways to enhance productivity are to use computers and other recently developed technologies. The discussion then focuses on specific approaches that have proved successful, including the use of quality circles, followed by a look at how to promote productive work teams. The chapter concludes with a return to previous discussions of leadership, discipline, motivation and morale as they relate to productivity.

Law Enforcement Productivity

Productivity from the law enforcement department, one of the most costly municipal services, is expected. Managers' effectiveness is judged by the results they obtain using the available resources, and today's police administrator is pressured to provide more services with fewer resources.

Jokes about productivity are common in the workplace. For example, when one man was asked how long he had been working for his company, he answered, "Ever since they threatened to fire me." Or the supervisor who when asked how many people worked for him replied, "Oh, about half." Lack of productivity is no joke.

Productivity Defined

Productivity is converting resources to achieve results efficiently and effectively. Productivity measures results gained from a specific amount of effort. An efficient use of resources alone may not be effective or meet a desired need. An effective use of resources may not be efficient or sufficient in overall impact. Productivity planning helps to strike a balance between efficiency and effectiveness guided by an overall desire for value.

Measuring Law Enforcement Productivity

Law enforcement services are not as measurable as production-line efforts. Production lines measure productivity in units manufactured; businesses measure it in profits.

> Law enforcement productivity is measured by the quality and quantity of services provided.

Increased productivity is a high-priority. A balance between management and worker expectations has to be achieved without abandoning the concept that work must be productive. Reasonable standards must be determined. Desired management productivity and employee performance capability must be balanced. Once this balance is determined, employees have a standard against which management can measure them. If accurate records are kept, employees will know where they stand in relation to what is expected and to all other employees who perform the same functions.

> Law enforcement productivity has traditionally been measured by arrests, stops, traffic citations, the value of recovered property and reduction of crashes and crime.

The main concern with these productivity measurements is that law enforcement officers may not have much control over them. Reduction in crashes or crime may be short term, or there may be no reduction at all, but this does not necessarily mean that officers are not productive.

Quotas vs. Performance Standards

Productivity normally involves setting minimum standards, which, in law enforcement, brings up the question of quotas. A **quota** is a specific number or proportional share that each is expected to contribute or receive. It is difficult not to use arrests, tickets issued, number of service calls answered and number of reports and activities initiated by officers as a basis for productivity because these are what officers do. But also important are how these tasks are executed, the quality of the reports and the public's perception of the officers.

Traditional Means of Deploying Personnel

Managers must prepare a plan before assigning personnel to perform tasks. A good operational plan based on facts is the manager's defense against pressure groups, which generally make demands based on politics, emotions or personal opinions. Managers should review, evaluate and revise plans as necessary to meet changing needs and goals. They can do this by measuring productivity and reviewing various reports.

Police Logs

One way to determine needs and time requirements is to have each officer complete time logs and then analyze tasks.

Police logs provide data for better deployment of personnel.

The logs need not be complicated. They can simply list requests for services, time, nature of the request and time the incident was completed, as Figure 15.2 illustrates.

Such logs provide information for studying the types of incidents that occur, the best ways to investigate them and how to assign personnel where they are needed most. The logs need not be completed every day but over enough time to determine basic information and to revise them to reflect changes in the community. Table 15.1 illustrates data collected in a community of approximately 12,000.

Such data indicate the various breakdowns to meet the needs for law enforcement services. Many departments use computers and special software programs to analyze these needs.

Computer Scheduling

Dees (2002, p.68) notes: "Of all the duties of a police supervisor, few are more thankless than making out the duty roster. The job is tedious, easy to mess up and no matter how it's done, someone is probably going to be unhappy with it." DeFranco (2000, p.80) also points out: "Creating a workable schedule is one of the toughest tasks challenging law enforcement managers." She suggests: "Not only must the department's shifts be taken into account, but individual officers' time-off needs and agency requirements for officer training that leave holes in the schedule have to be factored in. Officer seniority and shift preferences also have to be considered. What often emerges is a chart that makes no one happy."

Streit (2001, p.126) suggests: "Scheduling officers doesn't have to be a difficult and time-consuming task. There are various software systems on the market that are developed to make scheduling easier and require fewer man-hours." In addition, according to Rogers (2001, p.98): "Officers can now schedule vacation time, check comp time or arrange shift swaps just by making an ordinary Internet connection." Some software even allows the local district attorney's office and law enforcement agencies to coordinate the subpoenaing of officers to court.

June 24, 20–– Officer James Jones		
Reported for duty: 1500 hours		
1500 report of accident	1545	45 min.
1545 patrol	1555	10 min.
1555 domestic	1620	25 min.

Figure 15.2
Sample Log

Table 15.1
Sample Data Derived from Police Logs

Anytown Police Department
Police Incident Analysis
July 20--

INCIDENTS by DAY of WEEK		
Sunday	114	18.0%
Monday	78	12.3
Tuesday	72	11.4
Wednesday	75	11.8
Thursday	78	12.3
Friday	116	18.3
Saturday	100	15.8

INCIDENTS by SHIFT		
Day Shift	191	30.2%
Swing Shift	265	41.9
Graveyard Shift	177	28.0

INCIDENTS by RESPONSE TIME-ZERO RESPONSE	
Zone 1	4
Zone 2	0
Zone 3	2
Zone 4	1
Zone 5	1
Zone 6	1
Zone 7	0
Zone 8	0
Zone 9	3
Zone 10	1
Zone 11	0
Zone 12	0
Zone 13	0
Zone 14	0

INCIDENTS by RESPONSE TIME	
Day Shift	4.50 minutes
Swing Shift	3.88 minutes
Graveyard Shift	3.06 minutes

INCIDENTS by ZONE	
Zone 1	61
Zone 2	35
Zone 3	78
Zone 4	26
Zone 5	73
Zone 6	34
Zone 7	28
Zone 8	42
Zone 9	113
Zone 10	44
Zone 11	18
Zone 12	20
Zone 13	10
Zone 14	42

Table 15.1
continued

INCIDENTS by TYPE of SERVICE	
Suspicion	114
Crimes-Arrests	50
DOC	30
Assault	0
DUI-DWI	15
Assists	77
Emergencies	71
Accidents	21
Traffic	58
Juvenile	34
Animal	20
Vandalism	22
Suicide	0
Domestics	18
Alarms	35
Miscellaneous	67

INCIDENTS by TIME of DAY	
0000-0100	26
0100-0200	29
0200-0300	24
0300-0400	12
0400-0500	14
0500-0600	5
0600-0700	16
0700-0800	20
0800-0900	19
0900-1000	28
1000-1100	18
1100-1200	32
1200-1300	31
1300-1400	21
1400-1500	35
1500-1600	28
1600-1700	30
1700-1800	26
1800-1900	35
1900-2000	27
2000-2100	39
2100-2200	40
2200-2300	25
2300-2400	35

Factors Considered in Employee Deployment

A law enforcement agency has a specific number of fixed positions. The only way these can be reduced is to adopt a "flattened" organization, for example, reducing the number of middle-level managers, using joint dispatching with another community or using joint jail services with the county or a neighboring community. With the rising cost of jail services to meet federal standards, it is increasingly popular to use joint jail services.

After the fixed positions are filled, the remaining personnel are assigned to uniformed patrol, investigative, juvenile or other specialized divisions.

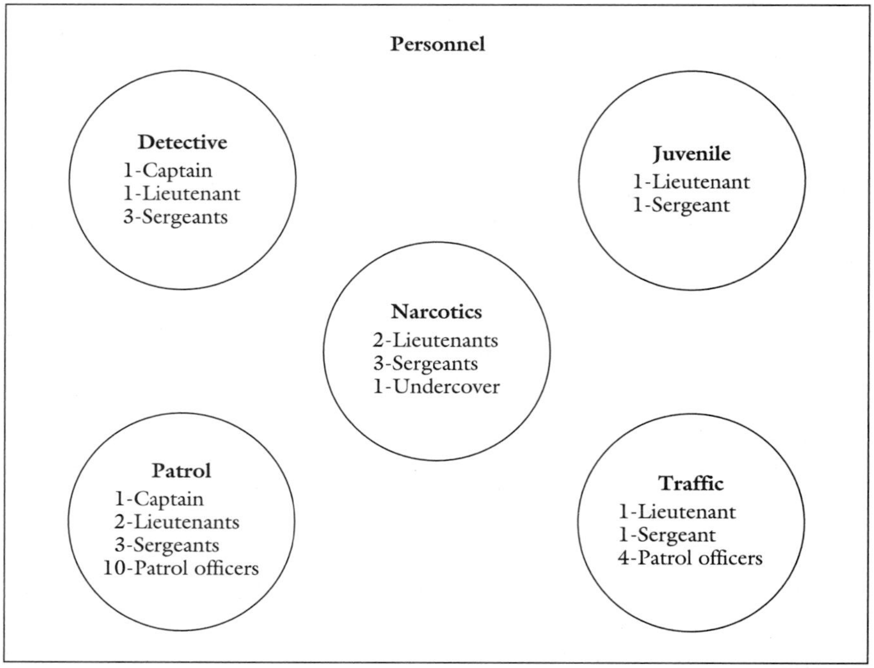

Figure 15.3
Division of Personnel

The largest division is the uniformed patrol unit, which provides services 24/7.

Other specialized divisions have fewer officers and often provide services for only portions of the day. Specialized personnel are assigned by demand based on frequency of incidents and cases requiring a specific service. A typical division of personnel is illustrated in Figure 15.3.

If law enforcement managers examine the service call data, they will readily observe variations in all areas. Personnel assignment should match those variations as much as possible.

The teams should usually be under the leadership of a local commander. As Anemone and Spangenberg (2000, p.23) state: "There is no one more capable of determining the best way to solve local problems than the man or woman who commands the precinct." Although community policing emphasizes the importance of allowing the patrol officer to problem solve and use discretion, Anemone and Spangenberg point out: "Most officers on patrol lack the expertise, authority or network of connections necessary to handle problems on their own." They (p.24) suggest four requirements for a successful commander: (1) accurate and timely intelligence, (2) rapid deployment, (3) effective tactics and (4) relentless follow-up and assessment.

Shifts

Shift work has increased since the invention of the electric light bulb, and with the increase has come problems (described in Chapter 14) for those working the night shift. Patrol shifts traditionally have three eight-hour shifts, five days a week, with two days off. A **shift** is simply the time span to which personnel are assigned. Some departments call it a **watch.** One common division is 7 a.m. to 3 p.m.; 3 p.m. to 11 p.m.; and 11 p.m. to 7 a.m. (the **dog shift**).

Shift assignments should be based on data. Regular assignments, split shift assignments or overlapping shift assignments can be considered. Some departments simply divide personnel into three equal shifts, but this is seldom effective. Rarely should personnel be equal on all shifts. Assignment of personnel by day of week and determination of days off are also based on data. Assignments must maintain a balance between actual needs and the effects of some assignments on morale. Because computers allow rapid statistical data to be developed, personnel changes can be made at any time from one area to the other.

In recent years 10- and 12-hour shifts have become common and have frequently resulted in higher officer satisfaction and easier scheduling. In a typical 3/12 shift plan, an officer works three 12-hour shifts, three days a week for three weeks. The fourth week generally involves four 12-hour shifts, and then it is back to three days a week for three weeks, and so on. Such shift formats appear popular with officers and citizens alike. In addition to being economical, the format improves officer morale and productivity. However, Vila et al. (2002, p.14) found that: "The 12-hour workday seems more likely to leave officers more fatigued by the shift's end, especially during the third or fourth consecutive 12-hour shift. Longer shifts also tend to magnify the impact of any overtime."

Many departments rotate shifts and area assignments or both. According to Vila et al. (pp.114–115): "There are three general shift rotation options: nonrotating, 'forward' (with the clock), and 'backward' (against the clock). Not rotating remains the best scheme, because almost any change in our daily sleep routines tends to increase fatigue over the short run by running afoul of circadian rhythms. . . . Among the shift change or rotation options, backward shift rotation is the hardest to adapt to biologically because the body's circadian rhythm interval is slightly predisposed to rotating forward, that is, from day to evening shifts."

Other departments, especially those using community policing, assign permanent shifts, areas or both, believing this allows officers to become more familiar with their assignment and therefore more effective. Still others have experimented with and implemented alternative scheduling formats. Figure 15.4 shows an alternate team-staffing schedule.

The 12 1/2-hour team is broken up into three shifts; day (0600–1830), swing (1300–0130) and graveyard (1800–0630). This places the maximum number of officers on the street when needed most—the overlap between swing and graveyard shifts from 1800 hours until 0130 hours. Similarly, the 10-hour team is broken into the same three shifts, with different hours. Day shift is from 0630–1630 hours, swing is from 1500–0100, and graveyard is from 2100–0700. This provides an overlap of officers from 2100–0100.

The Elk Grove (Illinois) Police Department has enhanced its organizational efficiency through an alternative scheduling program based on equal workloads for allocated personnel, that is, based on calls for service (CFS). The program is

January

Sunday	Monday	Tuesday	Wednesday	Thursday	Friday	Saturday
1 12½ OFF *10 WORK*	**2** 12½ OFF *10 WORK*	**3** *12½ WORK* 10 OFF	**4** *12½ WORK* 10 OFF	**5** *12½ WORK* 10 OFF	**6** 12½ OFF *10 WORK*	**7** 12½ OFF *10 WORK*
8 12½ OFF *10 WORK*	**9** 12½ OFF *10 WORK*	**10** *12½ WORK* 10 OFF	**11** *12½ WORK* 10 OFF	**12** *12½ WORK* 10 OFF	**13** 12½ OFF *10 WORK*	**14** 12½ OFF *10 WORK*
15 12½ OFF *10 WORK*	**16** 12½ OFF *10 WORK*	**17** *12½ WORK* 10 OFF	**18** *12½ WORK* 10 OFF	**19** *12½ WORK* 10 OFF	**20** 12½ OFF *10 WORK*	**21** 12½ OFF *10 WORK*
22 12½ OFF *10 WORK*	**23** *12½ WORK* *10 WORK*	**24** *12½ WORK* 10 OFF	**25** *12½ WORK* 10 OFF	**26** *12½ WORK* 10 OFF	**27** 12½ OFF *10 WORK*	**28** 12½ OFF *10 WORK*
29 12½ OFF *10 WORK*	**30** 12½ OFF *10 WORK*	**31** *12½ WORK* 10 OFF				

**January 23 would be the Training Day for the 10-hour team and "Payback" day for the 12½ hour team.*

April

Sunday	Monday	Tuesday	Wednesday	Thursday	Friday	Saturday
1 12½ OFF *10 WORK*	**2** 12½ OFF *10 WORK*	**3** *12½ WORK* 10 OFF	**4** *12½ WORK* 10 OFF	**5** *12½ WORK* 10 OFF	**6** 12½ OFF *10 WORK*	**7** 12½ OFF *10 WORK*
8 12½ OFF *10 WORK*	**9** 12½ OFF *10 WORK*	**10** *12½ WORK* 10 OFF	**11** *12½ WORK* 10 OFF	**12** *12½ WORK* 10 OFF	**13** 12½ OFF *10 WORK*	**14** 12½ OFF *10 WORK*
15 12½ OFF *10 WORK*	**16** *12½ WORK* 10 OFF	**17** *12½ WORK* 10 OFF	**18** 12½ OFF *10 WORK*	**19** 12½ OFF *10 WORK*	**20** *12½ WORK* 10 OFF	**21** *12½ WORK* *10 WORK*
22 *12½ WORK* 10 OFF	**23** 12½ OFF *10 WORK*	**24** 12½ OFF *10 WORK*	**25** 12½ OFF *10 WORK*	**26** 12½ OFF *10 WORK*	**27** *12½ WORK* 10 OFF	**28** *12½ WORK* 10 OFF
29 *12½ WORK* 10 OFF	**30** 12½ OFF *10 WORK*					

**If the changeover occurred in April, this is the way it would look. The actual changeover is the week of the 15th. The 10-hour team had changed to having weekends off. The only concern for scheduling should be requests for time off, as some officers do not like to work during this somewhat confusing period.*

Source: Ron Allgower and Michael P. Henry. "Alternate Team Staffing Concept Offers Benefits to Officers and Management." *Law and Order,* August 1998, p.88. Reprinted by permission.

Figure 15.4
The Alternate Team Staffing Concept

limited to patrol and is based on voluntary selection of permanent shifts. The program is structured around three shifts:

- 11 p.m. to 7 a.m.—a permanent first shift
- 7 a.m. to 3 p.m.—the second shift, which rotates with the third shift
- 3 p.m. to 11 p.m.—the third shift, which rotates with the second shift. Some officers are permanently assigned to this shift at their own request.

The Nassau County (New York) Police Department conducted a pilot program using *steady tours.* As Domash (2000, p.47) explains, the steady tours consisted of a 12-day cycle of 12-hour shifts with two days on, three days off, three days on, four days off. There were also a number of 10-hour tours from 7 p.m. to 5 a.m. with four days on and four days off. These schedules left 32 hours of make-up time for the 12-hour tours and 36 make-up hours for the 10-hour tours based on their contract of working 1,856 hours per year. Two studies of the steady tour scheduling were "extremely positive" with overtime and sick time both decreasing.

Careful consideration must be given to shift scheduling. Shift work can be directly related to disasters, creating a vulnerable window from about 1 a.m. to 6 a.m. It was during this time that the Exxon Valdez, Three-Mile Island and Chernobyl incidents occurred. In one study more than half the officers surveyed had moderate to severe problems with poor-quality sleep. Further, almost 80 percent of those on the night shift fell asleep while on duty.

Different shift systems work best in different departments. Simpson and Richbell (2000, p.21) suggest: "Managers . . . should experiment with different shift systems to find the one that works best for their departments." In addition, as Vila et al. (p.16) recommend: "Employee involvement in scheduling and shift assignment decisions also is critical because an officer's attitude and overall level of emotional stress affect his or her ability to deal with fatigue."

Proportionate Assignment

Area assignments are determined by requests for services based on available data. This is called **proportionate assignment.** No area should be larger than the time it takes a car to respond to emergency calls in a reasonable time.

Area boundaries should be primary arteries, if possible, to provide faster access. Car assignments generally follow the size of the areas to be patrolled and the frequency of requests for services in those areas. If personnel are not sufficient to provide the level of services the community needs or demands, additional personnel must be requested. If this cannot be provided, explore using law enforcement reserves or other methods.

A number of factors determine proportionate assignment. A first step is to list those items requiring time and to weight the importance of each. For example, felonies are generally weighted heavier than misdemeanors. In recent years drug offenses and related problems have required specialized personnel and increased training of regular officers. Even more recently homeland security efforts have become a priority.

To determine patrol area size, consider square miles, street miles, amount of crime and disorder and response time.

Job Rotation

Assignment rotation is another aspect of deploying law enforcement resources, although it is somewhat controversial. In assignment rotation, patrol officers receive training and gain experience and competence in another area such as investigation while detectives are rotated back to patrol. Patrol officers would see such rotation as positive in most instances; however, the same may not be true of the detective assigned to patrol. In addition, as opponents of rotation argue, even if personnel understand and support the theory of staff cross training and the generalization and diversification of job responsibilities, criminal investigation remains a highly specialized function requiring ongoing, uninterrupted development and application of skills. Further, from a training standpoint, it is not cost effective. Perhaps the strongest argument against job rotation in the investigation division is seen in the handling of the Jon-Benet Ramsey investigation in Boulder, Colorado. The chief, a proponent of rotation, mandated that every two years personnel assigned to investigations be routinely transferred back to patrol. The department had no experienced investigators to process the crime.

Overtime

Police departments across the country vary considerably in the attention paid to overtime management and the data about it. Overtime can be controlled through a combination of analysis, record keeping, management and supervision. Records should be kept of work done on paid overtime and on unpaid, or compensatory, overtime. Records should include the department's total payments for overtime, overtime payments to individual officers and commands and the purpose or circumstance requiring overtime (shift extensions, holidays, court appearances, emergency mobilizations, special events, briefings and roll calls, etc.).

Managers must recognize that overtime is often influenced by a contract that mandates uses and rates. In addition, Chamberlain (2001, p.42) points out: "The Fair Labor Standards Act (FLSA) governs overtime pay. It requires that 'nonexempt' employees receive overtime pay at time-and-a-half their regular rates when and if they actually work more than a prescribed number of hours in a prescribed work period." Overtime should be viewed, within limits, as an unavoidable cost of policing due to inevitable shift extensions, court appearances, unpredictable events and contract requirements.

Kammerer (2000, p.34) suggests that departments consider reducing court overtime by creating a full-time court liaison sergeant (CLS) position. The Torrance (California) Police Department did so and saw an immediate increase in savings. The sergeant worked with the district attorney's office to determine which officers were really required to testify. In one case the district attorney's office had subpoenaed 17 officers for a preliminary hearing. When the CLS called and questioned the necessity of so many officers, the district attorney told him the case was being continued and no officers would need to appear. The CLS asked the district attorney to review the case to determine which officers were absolutely necessary before resubpoenaing. The district attorney called back the next day to say only six officers needed to appear. In this case alone the Torrance Police Department saved approximately $2,525 in court overtime.

Response Time

Most statistical breakdowns provide information on patrol areas and response times. A federal study released in the 1960s stated that a response time of one minute or less was needed to increase arrests at crime scenes. Few law enforcement departments can guarantee a response time of less than three minutes on all calls for service. Reasons other than on-scene arrests, however, also require rapid response.

A response as rapidly yet as safely as possible builds public confidence in law enforcement capabilities and competence. It also places officers at the scene to protect evidence before people or the elements destroy it. It increases the chances of locating witnesses and making arrests. Further, it increases the chances of providing lifesaving emergency first aid to crime victims.

Other considerations in response time are barriers to patrol such as ditches, hills, water, number of officers available, total patrol area size, number of subpatrol areas, types of offenses and types and quantity of service requests. Safety is of utmost importance. The response should not pose a more significant threat to society than the incident to be investigated.

An even more important factor than police response time is the time between the occurrence of the incident and the report to the police, commonly referred to as **lag time,** over which police have no control. Another time factor important to total response is the time between when the dispatcher receives the call and dispatches it to a patrol car. Perhaps the most important factor, however, is citizen expectation.

The Kansas City Response Time Analysis study found that a large proportion of crimes were not discovered until some time after they occurred and were therefore unaffected by rapid police response. The Police Executive Research Forum (PERF) replicated the Kansas City study over three years and confirmed the findings.

Differentiated Response

It is only logical that the type of call influences the response. After a literature review and a survey of over 200 police departments serving jurisdictions of more than 100,000, a group of police practitioners and researchers were charged with developing a model for police response to citizen calls for service. The result was the Differential Police Response Strategies Model, which consists of three key components:

- A set of characteristics to define a type of incident
- A time factor to identify the relationship between the time the incident occurred and the time the police received the call

Table 15.2
General Differential Response Model

			Type of Incident/Time of Occurrence																							
			Major Personal Injury			Major Property Damage/Loss			Potential Personal Injury			Potential Property Damage/Loss			Minor Personal Injury			Minor Property Damage/Loss			Other Minor Crime			Other Minor Noncrime		
			In-Progress	Proximate	Cold	In-Progress	Proximate	Cold	In-Progress	Proximate	Cold	In-Progress	Proximate	Cold	In-Progress	Proximate	Cold	In-Progress	Proximate	Cold	In-Progress	Proximate	Cold	In-Progress	Proximate	Cold
Response Alternatives	Sworn	Immediate																								
		Expedite																								
		Routine																								
		Appointment																								
	Nonsworn	Immediate																								
		Expedite																								
		Routine																								
		Appointment																								
	Nonmobile	Telephone																								
		Walk-In																								
		Mail-In																								
		Referral																								
		No Response																								

Source: Raymond O. Sumrall et al. *Differential Police Response Strategies.* Washington, DC: Police Executive Research Forum, 1981, p.9. Reprinted by permission.

- A full range of response strategies, ranging from an immediate response by a sworn officer to no response, with numerous alternatives in between as shown in Table 15.2.

Operation Bullseye

One precinct of the Phoenix (Arizona) Police Department has developed a special form of response called Operation Bullseye, whose basic idea is containment. When an emergency call involving a felony comes in and the felony has occurred within five minutes of the call and a subject and vehicle description is available, two units respond to the scene. All other available units go to major intersections and observe traffic moving away from the scene. The crime scene is the bullseye, with concentric rings representing time and distance from the scene.

Random Patrol

During preventive patrol, officers frequently establish a pattern, which can become known to criminals and used to their advantage. To overcome this potential problem, many departments use **random patrol,** that is, patrol by random number selection.

One type of random patrol uses a computer to select random numbers. Officers going on duty are provided an envelope with these numbers, which they select at random. Officers then patrol the area designated by that number for no longer than 10 minutes and then select another number. Criminals cannot know where officers will patrol because the officers themselves do not know until they reach in the envelope for the area number.

> The basic premise of random patrol is to place officers closer to any potential incident or request for service before it happens, based on data provided by experience. Goals are to reduce response time and erase set patrol pattern habits.

If patrol areas are assigned to cars on a purely random basis, probability theory predicts that patrol cars will be closer to the point of need when they are requested than under any other system of patrol assignment.

The Kansas City Preventive Patrol Experiment

Although the Kansas City Preventive Patrol Experiment was conducted more than 30 years ago (1972), it remains the most comprehensive study of preventive patrol. The experiment divided 15 beats in Kansas City into three groups, each having five beats:

Group 1—Reactive beats: no preventive patrol, responding only to calls for service

Group 2—Control beats: maintained their normal level of preventive patrol

Group 3—Proactive beats: doubled or tripled the level of preventive patrol

Given the large amount of data collected and the extremely diverse sources used, the overwhelming evidence is that decreasing or increasing preventive patrol within the range tested in this experiment had no effect on crime, citizen fear of crime, community attitudes toward the police on the delivery of police services, police response time or traffic accidents (Klockars, 1983, p.160).

> The Kansas City Preventive Patrol Experiment found that increasing or decreasing routine preventive patrol had no effect on crime, citizen fear of crime, community attitudes toward the police on delivery of police services, police response time or traffic accidents.

Klockars (p.130) commented on the results of the Kansas City experiment: "It makes about as much sense to have police patrol routinely in cars to fight crime as it does to have firemen patrol routinely in fire trucks to fight fire." However, Manus (2000, p.8) cautions: "The misinterpreted Kansas City preventive patrol study has been reduced to one regrettable sound byte. The oversimplified sound byte 'random patrol brings random results' has inhibited meaningful analysis of police performance." Says Manus (p.10): "Statistical studies and analysis may tell the police administrator that response times are not important, but attendance at a typical community meeting sends a different message to the police practioner."

Aggressive Patrol

Aggressive patrol, or proactive patrol, focuses on preventing and detecting crime by investigating suspicious activity. The premise behind aggressive patrol is that through purposeful contact with individuals, officers will build an intelligence base of information regarding who lives and works on their beat.

Another application of such patrol is aggressive traffic enforcement of suspicious vehicles (those driving at night without headlights, speeding or weaving through traffic), which often leads to arrests. Aggressive patrol also fits well with community policing.

Methods of Patrol

Given the wide range of circumstances encountered during patrol, a variety of patrol methods have been devised. The most common remains automobile patrol.

> Common methods of patrol include automobile, bicycle, motorcycle, foot and air patrol. Other methods include mounted, water and special-terrain patrol.

Table 15.3 provides a summary of patrol methods.

Automobile Patrol

Numerous factors make automobile patrol the preferred patrol method for the majority of departments because they can respond rapidly to a scene, carry multiple passengers and types of equipment and work well in a variety of weather situations. However, as Bellah (2001, p.76) points out: "The automobile has its disadvantages: It cannot go everywhere and it has a tendency to isolate the officer from the citizenry." There remains some controversy, however, regarding whether one- or two-officer patrol units work better.

One-Officer vs. Two-Officer Patrol Units

Officer safety is at the core of the argument favoring two-officer patrol units, which also make a shift less boring and provide a chance for officers to develop working relationships. However, officer productivity and operational efficiency are increased using one-officer patrol units. If two officers are needed, two squads can be sent on a call.

Using one-officer units with appropriate delay procedures for another car to arrive at a scene is an effective administrative and budgeting procedure. The use of electronic patrol car locators can enhance officer safety in a one-officer unit. Such locators are also of great value in deploying patrol personnel. According to Wrobleski and Hess (2003, p.177):

> The one-officer unit offers several advantages, including cost-effectiveness in that the same number of officers can patrol twice the area, with twice the mobility, and with twice the power of observation. In addition, officers working alone are generally more cautious in dangerous situations, recognizing that they have no backup. Officers working alone also are generally more attentive to patrol duties

Table 15.3
Summary of Patrol Methods

Method	Uses	Advantages	Disadvantages
Foot	Highly congested areas Burglary, robbery, theft, purse snatching, mugging	Close citizen contact High visibility Develop informants	Relatively expensive Limited mobility
Automobile	Respond to service calls Provide traffic control Transport individuals, documents and equipment	Most economical Greatest mobility and flexibility Offers means of communication Provides means of transporting people, documents and equipment	Limited access to certain areas Limited citizen contact
Motorcycle	Same as automobile, except that it can't be used for transporting individuals and has limited equipment	Maneuverability in congested areas and areas restricted to automobiles	Inability to transport much equipment Not used during bad weather Hazardous to operator
Bicycle	Stakeouts Parks and beaches Congested areas	Quiet and unobtrusive	Limited speed
Mounted	Parks and bridle paths Crowd control Traffic control	Size and maneuverability of horse	Expensive
Air	Surveillance Traffic control Searches and rescues	Covers large areas easily	Expensive
Water	Deter smuggling Water traffic control Rescues	Access to activities occurring on water	Expensive
Special-terrain	Patrol unique areas inaccessible to other forms Rescue operations	Access to normally inaccessible areas	Limited use in some instances

Source: Henry M. Wrobleski and Kären M. Hess. *Introduction to Law Enforcement and Criminal Justice,* 7th edition. Belmont, CA: Wadsworth Publishing Company, 2003, p.183.

because they do not have a conversational partner. The expense of two cars compared to one, however, is a factor.

Experiments by the Police Foundation using both types of unit staffing in a large city police department revealed that officers in two-officer units were more likely to be assaulted by a citizen, be injured in the line of duty and have a suspect resist arrest. Studies that have looked at the frequency of assaults and injuries to patrol officers have upheld these findings that single-officer units tend to be safer.

Whether a one- or two-officer patrol unit is used should be determined by individual circumstances.

Some districts may require two-officer units and, under specific instances and for short periods, more than two. Sometimes union contracts dictate that two-officer units be used, which can seriously hinder management as it plans for the most effective deployment of its personnel.

Bicycle patrol and foot patrol are methods that have become more popular with the adoption of community policing.

Bicycle Patrol

Bicycle patrols are reported to be more effective than automobile patrols in certain instances. Officers on bicycles can cover larger sections of the community and are especially effective for night patrol. In addition, bikes are very maneuverable and can go places vehicles cannot. They can go over curbs, down steps and into otherwise inaccessible places. Particularly effective in enforcing drug laws, they are visible, mobile and responsive to citizens and have been excellent public relations tools. According to Strandberg (2001a, p.102): "Bike patrols are on the cutting edge of community policing. Many cities have instituted these patrols, and their communities are the better for it."

Schons (2000, p.79) further notes: "A bicycle patrol officer establishes a high profile image and provides a positive role model for bicyclists of all ages. Used as a community-policing tool, the uniformed officer on bicycle patrol demonstrates bicycle safety and enforces the rules, leading by direct example." Davala (2002, p.91) notes that since the inception of bike patrol by the Maryland State Police, crime numbers have dropped: "They have dropped because the bike officers have become more involved with schools, church groups and other members of the community, seeking out ways to address their needs and concerns. . . . The bike patrol allows officers to be approached with community problems. It helps build safe neighborhoods, and it is a source of great personal satisfaction for the officer who gains the trust and friendship of the citizens he serves."

Vonk (2002, p.92) contends: "The effectiveness of officers on bicycles in community policing roles has long been established. . . . Beyond community

Bicycle patrols are reported to be more effective than automobile patrols in certain instances. Officers on bicycles can cover larger sections of the community, and bikes can go places vehicles cannot go and are very maneuverable.

policing there exist reactive policing and proactive policing, including surveillance, night operations and traffic enforcement, all of which are being performed by bike officers across the country." In addition, according to Hudson (2002, p.97): "Several agencies around the country have recently begun employing bikes for crowd management and crowd control." The LAPD, for example, has a bicycle rapid response team that debuted at the Democratic National Convention in 2000 and has since been called into action for many situations requiring crowd control management in downtown LA.

Goetz (2002, p.103) describes how the Seattle Police Department uses police bicycles in crowd control situations: "Bicycle use in a crowd control situation can be broken down into two types: static and moving. The most effective use requires a careful blending of both." He (p.104) suggests: "Although the police bike squad works extremely well with other units on the front lines, it also works well on the periphery. The speed and mobility of the squad allows it to quickly outflank a crowd if it moves in an undesirable direction. . . . In addition, the strong flanking presence provided by the bikes can discourage people on the outskirts from joining the main group."

Woods (2002, p.83) recommends that a department develop standard operating procedures when starting a bike unit. The SOP should include a broad policy statement defining the purpose and scope of the bike patrol, a description of the bike officer profile and selection process, duties, hours of operation, adverse weather prohibitions, special assignments and maintenance requirements.

Mroz (2001, p.44), an officer with 40 years of biking experience, suggests that he had much to learn about policing on a bike. For example: "Riding down stairs is a critical skill for police bicycle officers. It's not as hard as it seems, but the first time is an act of faith." He also described a test in which officers were to dump their bikes after a hard bike sprint and run to handcuff a "suspect." Every officer either nearly collapsed or fell as they started to run: "The change in muscle groups from biking to running, especially after the bicycle sprint, was the cause. Better not to learn this on the street."

Mountain Bikes

Mountain bikes for patrol are becoming increasingly popular in departments around the country. According to Cook (2001, p.50): "Mountain bicycles are best suited to the rigors and abuse of police work." Vonk (2000, p.28) stresses: "The mountain bike officer has many unique considerations and should be trained properly. . . . An officer on a bike must be able to maneuver safely and legally in heavy traffic while patrolling as well as while responding to emergency calls."

Electric Bikes

Because bicycle patrol can be a physically challenging duty, many departments are using electric bicycles, which officers pedal most of the time and switch on an electric motor when they want an assist climbing a hill or a burst of speed. Officers can use both the motors and their legs when in a hot pursuit. Or just before arriving at a crime scene, officers can let the motor do the pedaling while resting a moment to catch their breath. According to Siuru (2000, p.47) over 30,000 e-bikes are being used in the United States.

Motorcycles

Another type of popular two-wheeled patrol vehicle is the motorcycle. As Polan (2000, p.71) notes: "Police motorcycle officers (PMOs) have patrolled our streets to enforce our traffic regulations since their introduction in Pittsburgh, Pa., almost 100 years ago." He (p.73) suggests: "With urban areas becoming more congested, the mobility and effectiveness of the police motorcycle provide administrators with an excellent resource. The low operating cost (low fuel consumption) in combination with the psychological impact on traffic reduction is only one of motorcycles' many advantages."

According to Cichello (2001, p.77): "Law enforcement motorcycles come in many flavors; the most common is the standard Harley Davidson or Kawasaki police special. These bikes are big, street-going monsters capable of highway speeds and serve in departments all across America." Despite the maneuverability and cost-effectiveness, motorcycle patrol is vulnerable to the weather.

All-Terrain Vehicles (ATVs)

Another valuable law enforcement patrol vehicle is the all-terrain vehicle. Karlya (2000, p.38) suggests: "ATVs are best suited to use in the dirt. With their flat, low-pressure, flotation-type tires, they're practically unstoppable, whether deep sand or gumbo mud lies ahead. Smaller fallen trees or hills that would block normal police bikes—to say nothing of cruisers—are child's play for an ATV. These qualities allow ATV-mounted officers to patrol and respond quickly in rugged terrain that might otherwise demand helicopters or horses. The racks on ATVs can carry a substantial amount of support equipment as well." Although law enforcement agencies have numerous options for methods of patrolling, many departments are also incorporating foot patrol into their policing strategies.

Foot Patrol

Foot patrol, the oldest form of patrol, has many of the same advantages as bike patrol and is making a comeback in many jurisdictions. Foot patrol is an excellent means to develop rapport between the beat officer and citizens. Foot patrol officers can instruct citizens in crime prevention techniques and refer them to available governmental services.

Foot patrol is *proactive* rather than reactive, seeking to handle neighborhood problems before they become crimes. However, foot patrol does have disadvantages. It is relatively expensive and limits officers' ability to respond rapidly to calls for service in another area.

Many studies show that increasing the number of officers on foot patrol may not reduce crime but will increase citizens' feelings of safety. Foot patrol is also an important component of community policing. Community policing, in turn, is part of a trend to bolster personnel available to law enforcement by enlisting the aid of citizens, either as volunteers or as employees.

Air Patrol

The patrol function is further enhanced by the availability of airborne law enforcement units. Strandberg (2001b, p.20) contends: "Two officers in a helicopter can do the work of 10 to 15 officers on the ground." Swager (2000, p.42) notes: "Our pilots seem to have the knack of being in the right place at the right time—monitoring patrol channels for the area they're in and maintaining really good working relationships with other units. You can ask the deputy on the street how he feels when he hears those rotors coming."

One disadvantage of air patrol is the high cost. To combat the often prohibitively high operation and maintenance costs associated with airborne units, some departments have begun using gyroplanes as a more cost-effective alternative aircraft.

Water Patrol

In many areas water patrol is an important addition to peace keeping. Weiss and Dresser (2000, p.75) suggest: "Tactical operations in and around water and floating crime targets present a unique set of challenges for law enforcement." They list several issues, including the weight of the equipment, how to perform teammate rescues if submerged, water approaches and tactics for dealing with boats, ships and other floating structures. They (p.77) conclude: "Tactical water training for law enforcement officers is increasingly important because more and more departments are looking at the water as a new avenue to help them in their fight against crime."

Expanding the Law Enforcement Personnel Pool

Agencies have expanded their personnel pool through the use of citizen police academies, citizen patrols, reserves and volunteers within the department—frequently, retired individuals, including retired police officers. Another trend is the civilianization of certain law enforcement functions.

Citizen Police Academies

Several police departments seeking to implement community policing have started citizen police academies (CPAs). Since the organization of the first recorded U.S. citizen police academy in Orlando, Florida, in 1985, many communities have developed their own academies, each with its own unique focus. According to Aryani et al. (2000, p.16): "CPAs provide the public with a working knowledge of their law enforcement agency's mission, operation, policies and personnel. They also create mutual trust and cooperation between the police and residents." Shafer and Bonello (2001, p.435) explain: "CPAs are designed to provide the participant with a basic understanding of crime and the associated police response within a community. Using a variety of teaching mediums (lectures, discussions, role-playing, simulations, demonstrations and field observations) agencies endeavor to provide participants with an inside perspective on the organization and people protecting their community."

According to one participant: "This program is a vital source of information about community policing. I am ready to go out and spread the word about law enforcement" (Caddell, 2002, p.1). Many academies also include ride-along programs for participants.

Citizens on Patrol

In many jurisdictions community policing strategies include citizen patrols. One such citizen patrol, operating in Fort Worth, Texas, encouraged community residents to patrol their own neighborhoods and be directly responsible for reducing crime. The program currently has over 2,000 patrollers, representing more than 87 neighborhoods in the city.

In Delray Beach, Florida, a city with a population of 50,000, the police department's largest volunteer project is the Citizens Observer Patrol (COP), whose three primary goals are to:

- Effectively reduce crime and disorder in selected communities.
- Establish a working relationship between the Delray Beach police and its citizenry.
- Empower people to take ownership of their communities to reduce crime.

The Delray Beach Citizens Observer Patrol has 850 members in 21 sectors. Crime has markedly diminished in every area.

Courter (2002, p.42) describes the Sun City (Arizona) Center Security Patrol consisting of five cars and more than 1,450 volunteers who patrol 3,200 acres and 120 miles of road. According to the Hillsborough County Sheriff's Office, the patrol was responsible for a 60 percent drop in crime and a more than 90 percent reduction in burglaries during its first year of operation. A car typically carries two people, often a husband and wife team. The patrol logs 200,000 miles a year and is funded completely by donations. The sheriff credits the security patrol and its coordination with his office as the major reason Sun City Center has the lowest crime rate of any area in the county.

Mallory (2001, p.80) describes another type of citizen patrol being used in the East Bay Regional Park District in the San Francisco Bay area. The Volunteer Bike Unit provides coverage in areas the sworn officers can't get to: "This program fills a niche. It gives us extra bodies and hours in the field to educate the public and observe any kind of crimes or suspicious situations or hazards and report them to the police department. . . . Bike patrollers perform a variety of tasks. They hand out brochures and maps to park users, provide traffic control at special events, explain the park rules that allow dog owners, bicyclists and hikers to peacefully co-exist in the park district's varied facilities that include fishing, swimming, hiking, picnicking and nature programs."

Reserves

Reserve officers, sometimes called part-timers, auxiliaries, specials or supernumeraries, are valuable assets to police departments in the effort to expand law enforcement resources. Reserve officer programs vary considerably from department to department. According to Weinblatt (2000b, p.28): "The activities undertaken by reserves range from general law enforcement to those that fall under the guise of special events and traffic control duties." Weinblatt (2001a, p.24) notes that in many departments the reserves are required to complete the same basic academy training as full-timers. Weinblatt (2001b, p.24) describes the contribution of the reserve program of the Wasilla (Alaska) Police Department: "From May 1999 to May 2000, the Wasilla reserves donated 3,361 total hours. That's over $100,000 in police manpower on the city's streets."

In some jurisdictions reserve officers have powers of arrest and wear the same uniform as law enforcement officers except for the badge, which says "reserve." They may even purchase their own firearm and ballistics vest and drive their personally owned vehicles during operations.

Some jurisdictions recruit reserves from those retiring from their full-time ranks. Many reserve units function in specialized roles, for example, search-and-rescue operations.

Issues exist regarding the use of reserves, particularly in labor and liability concerns. To allay labor concerns, some departments have a contract with full-time officers stating that reserves are used only if a regular officer turns down the overtime or wants to take "comp" time off. To address liability issues, most agencies require reserves to complete rigorous training courses. Some, in fact, require reserves to go through the full basic academy, not accepting the reserve academy training as adequate.

As Bair (2000, p.66), a reserve officer, says: "Reserve officers really want to be the best that they can be, but we can only be as good as the training that we are given." Kinsey (2002, p.229) cautions: "Reserve officers must be compensated for all time worked if an employee relationship has been established." He (p.230) explains: "It is important to establish if a reserve officer is an employee or a volunteer. The FLSA expressly excludes volunteers from the definition of employees covered by the act. The FLSA prohibits employees from volunteering time to the employer. It is vital for the law enforcement officials to understand that the provisions of the FLSA cannot be waived by an agreement with an employee."

Volunteers

The three groups of law enforcement personnel just discussed—citizen police academy participants, citizen patrols and reservists—consist primarily, if not solely in many jurisdictions, of volunteers. And their numbers are increasing. San Diego, for example, has nearly 1,100 volunteers who donated about 198,400 hours, providing $2.8 million worth of unpaid labor ("Do You Get What You Pay For? . . . ," 2000, p.1).

One innovative program uses volunteers to assist in a private/public sector partnership—state safety teams. Weinblatt (2000a, p.19) describes the team established by the North Carolina Transportation Association, which has counterparts nationwide. The association has 50 designated safety officers, of which 19 are active in road safety patrol. Other activities include public and law enforcement training endeavors geared toward drug interdiction, commercial vehicle inspection and accident investigation.

In 2002, the Volunteers in Police Service (VIPS) initiative was created as a joint effort of the U.S. Department of Justice and the International Association of Chiefs of Police. According to Berger (2002, p.6): "VIPS is designed to bring together law enforcement volunteer programs nationwide to share resources and support each other's efforts. This national initiative helps state and local law enforcement agencies by increasing the number of law enforcement volunteers, expanding or improving various components of existing programs and aiding agencies in establishing new VIPS programs." Their Web site is www.policevolunteers.org.

As with the concern over using reserves, some paid, full-time officers are hesitant to embrace volunteers. To overcome staff resistance to volunteer programs, managers should emphasize that volunteers are used to make officers' jobs easier, not to take work away from them. Keeping officers on the streets is what a volunteer program is about.

Explorers

Yet another way to expand and or support sworn officers' efforts is through an Explorer program. Boertien (2001, p.127) explains: "The Explorer programs are actually intended to allow youth to explore certain career fields." Most departments provide extensive training in personal conduct, first aid, police procedures, weapons familiarization, crime scene investigation, traffic control, interpersonal communication, criminal law and specialized police duties. Giordano (2001, p.148) describes how one community recruited local teens already involved in the Explorer program to help curb speeding and other traffic problems through an effort called CAN ID (Cadets Assisting Neighborhoods to Identify Driving Violations):

> After a brief training in traffic monitoring practices, including the use of handheld digital radar detectors, the students or cadets who sign up for CAN ID take to the streets in teams of two to watch for moving violations, which range from "people who blow through stop signs" to those who ignore pedestrians in crosswalks. . . .
>
> The cadets, however, don't hand out tickets to delinquent drivers. Instead, they take their logs back to the department, where with the help of police officers, they run the plate numbers to identify the drivers. A warning letter is sent out to each of the motorists . . . [advising that] future violations will be documented.

Civilianization

Civilianization refers to hiring citizens to perform certain tasks for the law enforcement department.

Civilianization is a cost-effective way to make use of the numerous and varied capabilities of citizens, while at the same time freeing up law enforcement personnel to concentrate their efforts on tasks they have been specifically trained for. Many routine functions performed by officers do not require their expertise nor their special authority and arrest powers. Animal-control officers, dispatchers, jailers and others might be civilians, rather than sworn peace officers.

As Rams (2000, p.35) suggests: "Nowadays, police chiefs and sheriffs say, departments opt not to send specialists, such as the public information officer or the records manager through the police academy because those people don't need to know how to make a car stop or read Miranda rights. The cost savings to law enforcement agencies is significant."

Citizens and agencies within a jurisdiction are also of extreme importance when management is faced with deploying resources during an emergency.

Deploying Resources in Emergencies

During normal deployment, law enforcement managers have time to use statistics and studied judgment to determine allocation requirements, but during emergencies, present circumstances and experience largely dictate which personnel are deployed. Results depend on what managers in the field decide during those first minutes at the scene.

Law enforcement managers must be trained in emergency procedures, including medical emergencies, earthquakes, tornados, hurricanes, flooding, radioactive waste accidents, hostage taking, bomb threats, terrorist attacks, aircraft crashes, large fires, gas leaks, riots or other large crowd disturbances and snipers. They must be familiar with Civil Emergency Preparedness plans and the availability of assistance locally and from other agencies. They must be aware of the availability of emergency equipment and the location of area hospitals and rescue squads. This information should be condensed into written predisaster plans.

Predisaster plans should include the following:

- Which emergencies to prepare for
- What must be done in advance (supplies on hand, agreements with other agencies, etc.)
- What specific functions must be performed during the emergency and who is responsible for performing them, including outside organizations and agencies that might help
- What steps need to be taken to restore order after an emergency has ended
- How to evaluate a response

The plan should be made by top management in conjunction with those who would be involved in implementing it, including government officials, fire department personnel, health care personnel and so on.

Many jurisdictions use a three-level approach, with *Level 1* for minor events that can usually be handled by on-duty personnel. *Level 2* is for moderate to severe situations requiring aid from other agencies and perhaps other jurisdictions. *Level 3* is for catastrophes in which a state of emergency is proclaimed and county, state and perhaps federal assistance is requested. In such instances the National Guard may be called. The emergency plan should identify the levels of emergencies that might occur and the level of response required. Increasingly, law enforcement agencies across the country are devising and implementing Incident Command Systems (ICSs) to coordinate their emergency response. Ruff (2000, p.52) suggests: "There must be a firm commitment to the principle that the first responding police officer is the initial incident commander." He contends that: "ICS is designed as a standard system allowing personnel from diverse agencies to meld into a common and unified emergency management structure."

Unfortunately, many managers place emergency planning as a low priority, thinking that such emergencies are unlikely to happen in their jurisdiction. But they could, and when they do, most citizens expect their law enforcement agencies to alert them, deal with it and keep them informed.

Managers should not only have predisaster plans and *practice* them but also be familiar with establishing command posts, furnishing information to the press and obtaining intelligence information on which they can make decisions. Accurate information is needed to know whether to evacuate, provide extra security, treat injured people, prevent looting, put up barricades or redirect traffic. Most law enforcement departments have experienced managers who have been involved in similar incidents. No fixed rules will serve in every situation, but there are guidelines. A great deal of independent decision making occurs in these moments. Law enforcement decision makers must be prepared for short, intense incidents or long-term sieges involving many hours. Douglas (2001, p.33) recommends that a Unified Command structure include all departments within the jurisdiction responsible for critical services, including law enforcement, fire, emergency medical services, power and gas, streets or highways departments, water services, sewer, the city manager and the media.

According to Cardwell and Cooney (2000, p.15): "Terrorist attacks, transportation accidents, natural disasters and political and sporting events bring unseen burdens to public safety agencies. These incidents can cause agencies to flounder or succeed based on the amount of preparedness and cooperation among the various entities called upon to deal with such crises." Rohen (2001, p.148) also stresses: "Command and control of a terrorist threat or incident is a critical emergency management function that demands an integrated and unified framework for the preparation and execution of plans and orders."

The first law enforcement manager at the scene must take control, regardless of rank. Stalling for a manager of higher rank to take over could be fatal to people who need evacuation or rescue or to people being threatened. Normally, time is on the side of law enforcement in criminal or hostage situations. Subterfuge to gain time is important. Direct confrontation should be avoided unless it is the last resort. Each incident of this type has individual elements to consider, and no matter how many incidents an officer has been called on to resolve, a surprise element usually requires a considered, different decision.

Technological Aids

A variety of technological devices are helping law enforcement better cope with resource deployment during and following emergencies. For example, in the hurricane-vulnerable region of the Florida Keys, rugged PC mobile laptop computers were used by sheriff's deputies during an evacuation to help with radio time, security sensitive data and prioritizing who needed to be evacuated from the barrier island chain first.

Miller (2002a, p.46) notes that personal digital assistants (PDAs) can put everything officers need in the palms of their hands, including computer aided dispatch information, while away from their cruisers.

Emergency call boxes have been used in the United States since the early 1900s, but their use and popularity waned after WWII, when two-way radio communications became available to law enforcement. Recently, however, emergency call boxes have seen a resurgence.

Another technological aid that helps law enforcement handle medical emergencies is the automated external defibrillator (AED). Because medical research has shown that up to half of all sudden cardiac arrest (SCA) deaths could be prevented with early defibrillation and officers commonly arrive on the scene of an SCA before paramedics or other personnel, many departments believe it makes sense to have AEDs and officers trained in their use. Rhodes (2001, p.95)

Computers and other technological advances have made the job of patrol officers more efficient and safer. They can enter license numbers and addresses to find out almost instantly whether they are dealing with a wanted person. Maryland State Police sergeant demonstrates the capabilities of voice activation technology in December 2002.

Gail Burton/AP Wide World

explains: "Defibrillation is the process of stopping a fatal heart rhythm with a controlled electrical shock. It may be the only hope for victims of sudden cardiac arrest." The American Heart Association (AHA) says that first responders must administer care to a person within eight minutes of a sudden cardiac arrest for them to have more than a 4 percent chance of survival (Paynter, 2001, p.94).

Deploying Resources to "Fight Crime"

Many individuals in law enforcement and probably the majority of the citizens they serve consider crime fighting as a primary responsibility of their agency. It is. Doing so has become more difficult, however, given shrinking resources and the advanced technology many criminals use. However, as Miller (2002b, p.94) explains, crime statistics analysis software covers a broad spectrum of tactical, strategic and administrative needs, including crime mapping. Forsythe and Fisher (2000, p.70) note: "Fighting crime in the digital age means outfitting investigators with the best possible tools for collaborating, sifting through evidence and building a case." According to Meyer and Morgan (2000, p.1) computers can be used to develop analytical time lines associated with crime. They (p.2) contend: "Time line analysis can help law enforcement investigators record and analyze large amounts of data, prepare for witness interviews and write affidavits." In addition (p.5): "Time line analysis can provide investigators with a method of quickly tracking and retrieving information that they may have spent many hours developing."

The Crime Triangle

One tool to help law enforcement tackle crime through problem solving is the crime triangle, shown in Figure 15.5.

The basis for the crime triangle is Cohen and Felson's Routine Activities Theory, which proposes that crime occurs during the intersection, in time and space, of motivated offenders and suitable victims (or targets), under

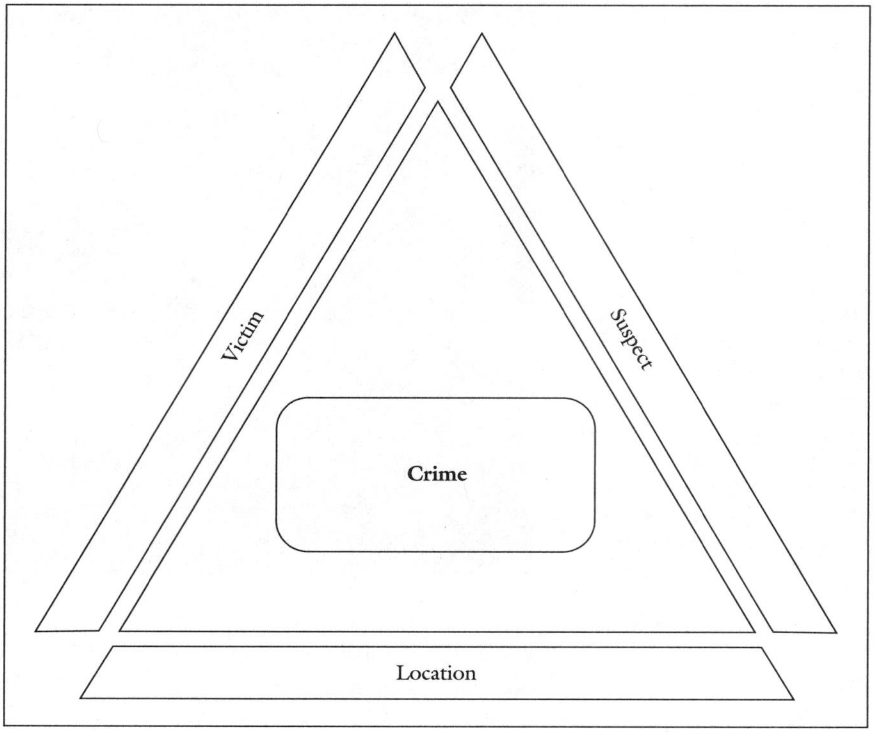

Figure 15.5
The Crime Triangle

Source: Ralph B. Taylor. "Crime and Small-Scale Places: What We Know, What We Can Prevent, and What Else We Need to Know." In Taylor et al. *Crime and Place: Plenary Papers of the 1997 Conference on Criminal Justice Research and Evaluation,* July 1998, p.2.

circumstances of absent or inadequate guardianship. Crime is presumed amenable to suppression if any of the three legs of the triangle is removed or neutralized.

The **crime triangle** is a model that illustrates how all three elements—motivated suspect, suitable victim and adequate location—are required for a crime to occur.

One side of the crime triangle, the suspect, is most often the focus of crime-fighting efforts.

Focus on Criminals

Just as managers are beginning to tap into the resources of their community, they are also beginning to do more partnering with other agencies to apprehend criminals. A prime example of such a partnership is that between the Metro-Dade Police Department in Miami and the Bureau of Alcohol, Tobacco and Firearms (ATF), Miami District Office. The program is called Project Achilles because they target career criminals who are known to possess firearms. This possession of firearms makes them vulnerable, putting them within both the state and the federal criminal justice system. The program grew out of studies that indicate that 6 percent of the criminals arrested commit up to 70 percent of all serious crime.

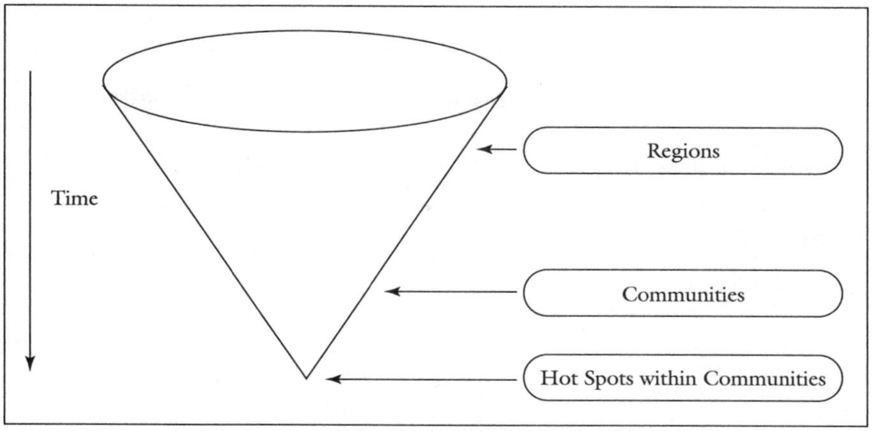

Figure 15.6
The Cone of Resolution

Source: Ralph B. Taylor. "Crime and Small-Scale Places: What We Know, What We Can Prevent, and What Else We Need to Know." In Taylor et al. *Crime and Place: Plenary Papers of the 1997 Conference on Criminal Justice Research and Evaluation,* July 1998, p.2.

Focusing on career criminals is a logical approach to fighting crime. Equally promising in crime-fighting efforts is a focus on high-crime locations.

Focus on Location

In the crime triangle, location is a critical element. Some criminal justice researchers and practitioners have begun to focus on *places* where offenses occur, identifying hot spots, a term borrowed from geology to designate a region of potentially volatile geologic, or volcanic, activity. **Hot spots** are specific locations with high crime rates. A hot spot can be a single address, a cluster of addresses, part of a block, an entire block or two or an intersection. To organize data about crime over time at various levels of analysis, criminologists have applied the concept of the **cone of resolution** (Figure 15.6), this time borrowing from geography.

Borrowing another concept, this time from ecology, Braiden (1998, p.8) suggests another way to view the significance of location—"the hunt and the habitat":

> I can't think of two special-interest groups more philosophically opposed to each other than hunters and animal rights activists, yet there are two things they totally agree upon: The species will survive the hunt; it will not survive loss of its habitat.
>
> What can policing learn from this basic principle of nature? Well, if the ultimate goal is to eliminate the criminal species forever, surely the best way to do that is to eliminate the habitat that spawns and sustains that species. Structured as it is, the criminal justice system puts 95 percent of its resources into the hunt while the habitat is left almost untouched. We can never win working that way, because the habitat never stops supplying new customers for the hunt.

Another way of viewing the role of habitat or location as an element of crime causation is to consider **incivilities,** or signs of disorder. Wilson and Kelling's classic "broken windows" theory suggested that such incivilities lead to higher crime rates, victimization rates and residents' perception of the fear of crime.

A focus on the third side of the crime triangle—the victims and reducing their suitability as targets—brings community policing into the scene.

Community Policing and Deployment of Personnel

Community policing assigns officers to specific neighborhoods and actively involves them in helping the neighborhood solve its problems and avoid victimization. This proactive approach usually includes increased emphasis on foot patrol.

Miller and Hess (2002, p.xix) note:

> Community policing offers one avenue for making neighborhoods safer. Community policing is not a program or a series of programs. It is a philosophy, a belief that working together, the police and the community can accomplish what neither can accomplish alone. The *synergy* that results from community policing can be powerful. It is like the power of a finely tuned athletic team, with each member contributing to the total effort. Occasionally heroes may emerge, but victory depends on a team effort.

Restructuring of an organization typically includes a decentralization of authority, a flattening of hierarchical layers, the use of teams and the implementation of civilianization. In addition, new management styles require more coaching, mentoring and empowerment of subordinates.

Another element of community policing requires assigning officers permanently to defined beats, allowing them the benefit of "owning" their neighborhood beats. This further enables officers to participate in community-based problem solving and to balance reactive responses to crime incidents and emergencies with a proactive focus on preventing problems before they occur or escalate.

In fact, community policing is an ideal way to increase productivity. As Bauman (2000, p.32) suggests: "Police productivity is a state of the mind, an approach to the job." He offers some tried-and-true suggestions for making good use of down time:

- Concentrate on problem areas—talk to neighbors. One problem solved today might prevent 10 calls next month.
- Consider "knock and talks"—knocking on a door, engaging occupants of a problem location in conversation and looking around for any plain-view evidence, perhaps even asking for consent to search.
- Hide and watch—using binoculars in a problem area.
- Working traffic—can be very productive even if you are not inclined to write lots of tickets. Big criminals often commit little crimes.
- Engaging in building and bar checks—you might find an open door before a burglar does, surprise a burglar or encounter someone making a drug deal.

Appendix G contains sample goals, daily routines, methods, responsibilities and duties of a community policing officer.

Citizen Involvement

DiIulio (1993, p.9) suggests that citizens must become "co-producers of justice": "Citizens in a democracy must begin by holding themselves and their neighbors accountable for public affairs. A democratic vision of the justice system, therefore, is anything but a sop to public frustrations with crime and disorder. Citizens who expect judges, police and other justice officials to solve society's crime problems are unrealistic; citizens should not expect the officials to succeed without the active cooperation and support of the community."

Bonello and Schafer (2002, p.19) note: "In the past two decades, citizen police academies (CPAs) have become increasingly popular among American police agencies of all sizes." They (p.23) note: "CPAs can further community policing goals by increasing understanding, trust and dialogue with members of the community who historically have been at odds with the police. CPA programs represent one mechanism that agencies can use to realize their community policing objectives." Garrett (2002, p.6) likewise notes: "A citizen's police academy is an effective way to bring law enforcement and the public together."

According to Skogan et al. (2000, p.1): "An important feature of many community policing initiatives is that they provide new avenues for citizen involvement in partnerships with police. Residents may be called upon to help identify and prioritize neighborhood problems for action, to become involved in problem-solving efforts, and to help shape police policies and operations. The commitment to responsiveness and information sharing that many police agencies make as they adopt community policing ideally must be matched on the civilian side with an enthusiastically involved representative segment of a concerned public."

One example of a joint activity between police and members of the community was a one-day cleanup campaign of an area in a Florida community, which resulted in collecting more than 100 tons of garbage, 10 tons of rusted-out appliances and junk and over 50 abandoned vehicles. The waste management department furnished the hauling equipment. Departments might start a DARE program in a school, an Operation Identification program or a Neighborhood Watch Program.

They might also conduct monthly meetings for police, residents and business people to discuss mutual problems, possible causes and viable solutions or begin foot patrol, bicycle patrol or mounted patrol in high-crime areas.

Citizen input on perceived officer effectiveness and efficiency will help managers assess departmental productivity. Police are effective when they produce the perception that crime is under control. Managers need to find out how the public perceives the police department's efforts. This is often very different from what those within the department think.

Productivity Problems

Symptoms of productivity problems are similar to those of motivation/morale problems: high absenteeism and turnover, high levels of waste, high accident rates and unreasonable complaints and grievances. According to Cohen (2000, p.44): "The Internet is the office's biggest time waster since the coffee break." He (p.46) suggests: "Server logs record all the Internet activity on a network, telling you who visited what Web site, how long they stayed, what they looked at, what they searched for and where they went next." Examination of server logs can reveal whether employees are less productive because of time spent on nonwork-related Internet activities.

Improving Productivity

Often the difference between promising ideas and productive results is a good manager. Productivity is directed from the top and accomplished at the bottom of the organizational hierarchy. Such productivity can be improved by:

- Clearly explaining organizational goals.
- Permitting more decisions to be made at the "doing" level.
- Supporting creativity and innovation.
- Increasing individual control over the tasks for which officers are responsible.

Furthermore, managers and supervisors at all levels must set performance expectations and then insist that those they oversee meet these expectations. Each department level must hold the next level accountable.

Law enforcement productivity can be improved by:
- Training and experience.
- Rewards and incentives.
- Improved equipment.
- Technology.

Training and experience can improve productivity by helping people do tasks more efficiently. Productivity can also be increased through a reward system. Deserved praise, commendations and personal recognition are rewards. Monetary rewards, although effective, may not be as effective as personal rewards that build self-esteem and self-worth. All the concepts in Chapter 10 related to motivating employees are relevant.

In addition, improved law enforcement productivity can be accomplished by introducing improved equipment. An up-to-date communications and computer center can assist officers; however, the equipment should be procured based on a realistic cost assessment in relation to expected benefit. Many smaller, less costly pieces of equipment can increase patrol productivity. For example, cell phones for each unit, radar installed in most beat cars, a car desk or lighted clipboard for report writing are small items that can increase productivity.

Implementing mobile computing systems has several benefits including higher crime-solution rates, greatly reduced clerical costs and, most important, increased officer safety. Such systems are excellent examples of ways in which technology can increase productivity.

Technology

Productivity can be increased without adding employees by using technology presently available and soon to become available. Taping reports to be recorded later by clerk typists, using computers, installing improved 911 and computer-assisted dispatch (CAD) systems, superhighway police information systems and a host of other future technologies will vastly enhance police productivity.

Computers can be used in a variety of ways to enhance productivity, for example, record keeping, data analysis, word processing, investigating, inventorying property rooms and maintaining stolen-property files. One way computers are improving departments' productivity is by facilitating the organization of data through a management information system (MIS). Figure 15.7 illustrates the components of a management information system.

MIS procedures include collecting, analyzing and reporting past, present and projected information from within and outside the organization.

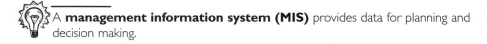

A **management information system (MIS)** provides data for planning and decision making.

Integrated justice systems are improving not only the productivity of law enforcement but also that of the entire criminal justice system. The goal is to have the original information, collected by the officer on the street, flow into every other application used by every other step in the justice system.

Faced with an endless barrage of technical advances and innovations, managers might become overwhelmed and intimidated. They must strive to avoid technical obsolescence by preventing employees and themselves from succumbing to **technophobia,** the fear of using technology because of unfamiliarity or uncertainty as to how it works.

To keep up with technology, managers might use the National Aeronautics and Space Administration's (NASA) Technology Utilization Program, established

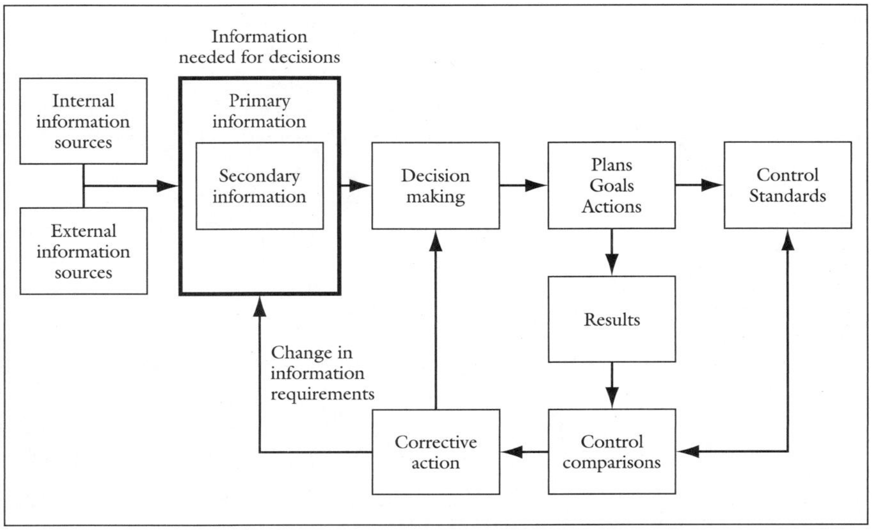

Source: Lester R. Bittel. *The McGraw-Hill 36-Hour Management Course.* New York: McGraw-Hill Publishing Company, 1989, p.234. Reprinted by permission.

Figure 15.7
Components of a Management Information System (MIS)

in the early 1960s by congressional mandate to promote the transfer of aerospace technology to other areas. For example, a Pennsylvania police department called upon NASA's ability to enhance ATM films so the images were sufficiently sharpened to identify a car and driver, resulting in the arrest of a kidnapper/murderer.

In addition to capitalizing on technological advances to enhance productivity, some agencies are taking approaches successfully used in business to reorganize the way officers within the agency work together. An example is the quality circles approach to productivity.

Quality Circles Approach

A **quality circle** is a group of five to ten employees with common interests and common work hours who volunteer to meet to solve problems in their workplace. Quality circles began in the early 1960s in Japan, as management sought to improve productivity by raising worker satisfaction. In the 1970s Lockheed and Honeywell used quality circles with great success. During the 1980s quality circles expanded into the private and public service sectors.

Recall that such abstract motivational theories as McGregor's Theory Y and Maslow's Hierarchy of Needs contend that employees, if allowed to influence job-related decisions, tend to take more personal interest and pride in their work. This results in increased productivity and a more effective organization. Participation in a quality circle increases workers' job satisfaction, allowing them to satisfy their needs for personal achievement, recognition and increased self-esteem. Stevens (2000, p.204) describes some of the core principles of TQM:

> The organization must address both internal and external customers (police personnel and residents).
>
> Most individual performance measures are counter-productive because they invite conflict and competition rather than cooperation. Moreover, individual performance measures do not measure customer needs; instead they focus on organizational expectations (arrest, service calls and dollar amounts of confiscated property and contraband).
>
> The organization should have a constancy of purpose subscribed to by all employees and the desire to constantly improve service rather than be satisfied with what has been accomplished so far. . . .
>
> All organizational members must be goal-driven and participate in goal-attainment, not personal achievements within the organization.

Team members should receive training in brainstorming, problem definition, data collection and analysis.

Key ingredients for successful quality circles include in-depth training, management participation, feedback and publication of circle achievements.

The quality circle *coordinator* is responsible for establishing and monitoring the program. The coordinator also trains the facilitators and provides materials the circles need. The organization of typical quality circles is illustrated in Figure 15.8.

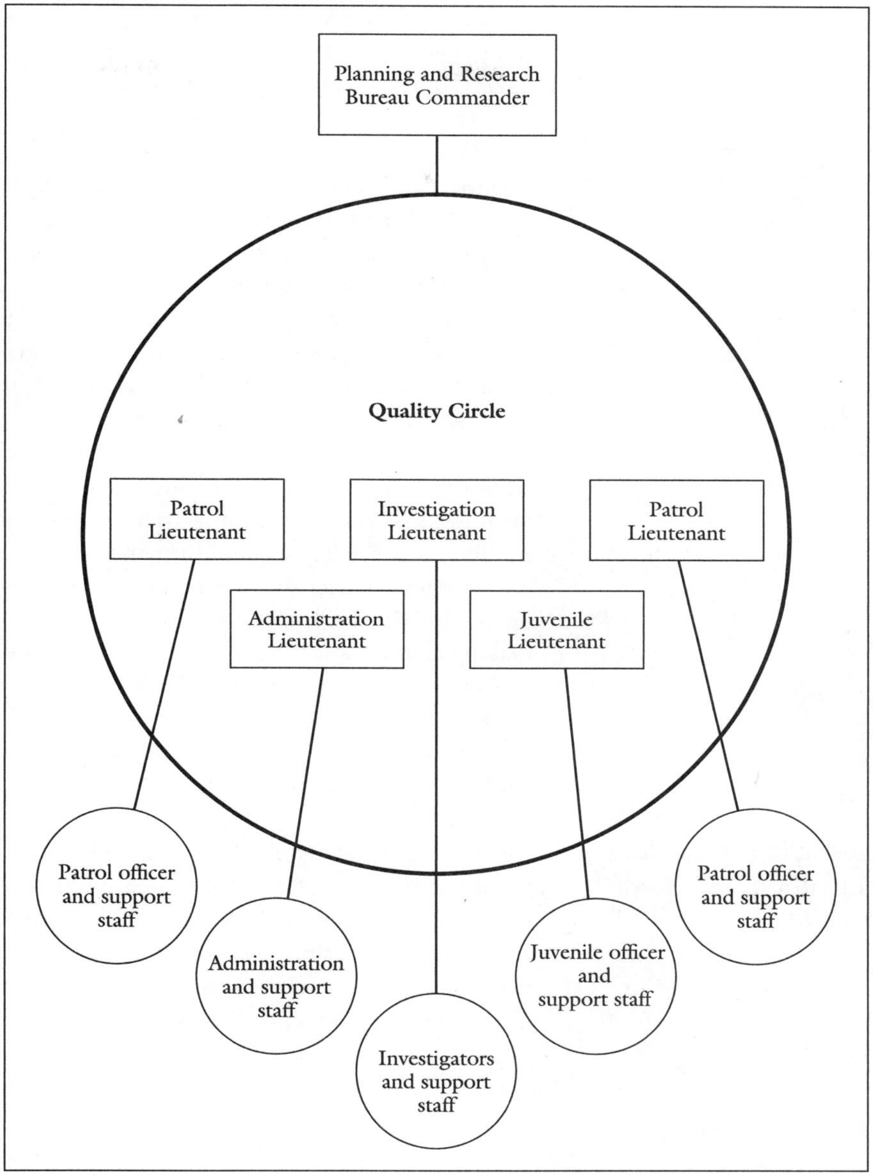

Figure 15.8
Typical Quality Circle Organization

Productive Work Teams

Productive work teams have several characteristics, most of which have already been discussed in other contexts. In a productive team, members work toward common goals that everyone knows, understands and accepts. The goals not only serve the organization but also give team members opportunities to develop professionally. Members know their individual responsibilities and priorities and how they relate to those of other members. Policies that govern team interaction are fair, consistently applied and subject to change. Obsolete policies are replaced with ones appropriate to the team's current circumstances.

The work atmosphere is informal, comfortable and fairly tension free, but still dynamic. Work discussions are numerous and always pertinent to the team's tasks. Communication lines are open. During discussions all members are free to express their ideas and opinions. Members not only speak their minds and relay information about team assignments and procedures but also listen to each other. Members are comfortable asking questions if they do not understand. Criticism is acceptable and is delivered frequently, frankly and constructively. The team is comfortable with conflict. Members recognize disagreements and work fairly and intelligently toward resolving them.

Members have a great amount of trust in one another. They cooperate rather than compete. They are eager to help each other with tasks and with developing to the fullest professional potential. They encourage one another to achieve at high levels but do so without setting unrealistic expectations.

Team morale and productivity are high. Members' enthusiasm prompts them to work hard. They attend to details, follow through on intentions and perform to the best of their ability. Members take pride in their achievements and readily accept feedback on performance.

The team leader shows interest in each team member's achievement and regularly provides feedback on performance. The leader consults members before making changes affecting the team. The leader does not dominate, nor do members defer unduly to the leader. When work circumstances do not call for participative leadership, members are comfortable with the leader assuming control. The team operates without power struggles; the issue is not who controls but what is the best way to do the job.

Leadership, Discipline, Motivation and Morale Revisited

An anonymous quote reads: "Interest and attention are just as important to people as grease and oil are to a machine. Without it they don't run smoothly, never reach top speed and break down more frequently."

Developing a spirit to perform is one of management's jobs. Law enforcement managers use four motivating techniques: redesigning the law enforcement job; providing productive work and an opportunity for achievement and recognition; stating clear, concise and achievable goals; and providing some form of reward and enticement system for excellent performance. Intrinsic as well as extrinsic rewards can be used.

> The quality of management in the organization is the single most important factor for high productivity and morale. They are integrally related.

Let officers know what is expected of them and follow up to see that they meet expectations. Law enforcement work provides a high potential for individual performance based on individual competence.

All employees should know what is expected on the job. They should know how their performance will be judged and receive feedback on how well they accomplished it. The relationship between job performance and expected results should be clear.

Summary

Law enforcement productivity is measured by the quality and quantity of services provided. It has traditionally been measured by arrests, traffic citations, value of recovered property and reduction of crashes and crime. Police logs provide data for better deployment of personnel. The largest division is the uniformed patrol unit, which provides services 24/7.

Area assignments are determined by requests for services based on available data. This is called proportionate assignment. No area should be larger than the time it takes a car to respond to emergency calls in a reasonable time. To determine patrol area size, consider square miles, street miles, the amount of crime and disorder and response time. Although rapid response may not deter crime or increase the apprehension of criminals, it *is* important because fast response builds public confidence in law enforcement capabilities and competence. It also places officers at a scene to protect evidence before people or the elements destroy it. It increases the chances of locating witnesses and making arrests. Further, it increases the chances of providing lifesaving emergency first aid to victims of crimes.

Most law enforcement departments use some form of random patrol, the basic premise of which is to place officers closer to a potential incident or request for service before it happens, based on data from experience. Goals are to reduce response time and erase set patrol pattern habits. However, the Kansas City Preventive Patrol Experiment found that increasing or decreasing preventive patrol had no effect on crime, citizen fear of crime, community attitudes toward the police on delivery of police services, police response time or traffic accidents.

Common methods of patrol include automobile, bicycle, motorcycle, foot and air patrol. Other methods use mounted, water and special-terrain patrol. A consideration related to automobile patrol is whether one- or two-officer units should be used, which should be determined by individual circumstances.

Many managers, in an attempt to expand their employee base, have begun using alternative personnel resources, including citizen patrols, reserves and volunteers, in addition to civilianizing some law enforcement functions. Civilianization refers to hiring citizens to perform certain tasks for the law enforcement department.

Managers also must be prepared to deploy resources during times of emergency and, therefore, should have carefully formulated predisaster plans. These plans should include, at minimum:

- Which emergencies to prepare for.
- What needs to be done in advance (supplies on hand, agreements with other agencies, etc.).
- What specific functions must be performed during the emergency and who is responsible for performing them, including outside organizations and agencies who might help.
- What steps need to be taken to restore order after the emergency has ended.
- How the response is to be evaluated.

Managers are also expected to fulfill their responsibility to deploy resources to fight crime. The crime triangle is a model illustrating how all three elements—motivated suspect, suitable victim and adequate location—are required for crime to occur. Focusing on career criminals (suspects) is one logical approach to fighting crime. Focusing on specific locations with high crime rates, areas known as hot spots, is another approach. Focusing on victims brings community policing into the crime-fighting scene.

Community policing assigns officers to specific neighborhoods and actively involves them in helping the neighborhood solve its problems and avoid victimization. This proactive approach usually includes increased emphasis on foot patrol. It often incorporates problem-oriented policing, which is also proactive rather than reactive, seeking out problems and their solutions instead of attempting to solve crimes after they have occurred.

Law enforcement productivity can be improved by training and experience, rewards and incentives, improved equipment and technology. One means to improve productivity is through a management information system (MIS), which provides data for planning and decision making.

Quality circles can help enhance productivity. A quality circle is a group of five to ten employees with common goals and hours who volunteer to meet to solve problems in their workplace. Key ingredients for successful quality circles include in-depth training, management participation, feedback and publication of team achievements.

The quality of management in the organization is the single most important factor for high productivity and morale. They are integrally related.

Discussion Questions

1. What factors should be considered in determining personnel assignment to shifts?
2. What is your opinion of the random patrol method of deploying law enforcement personnel?
3. Do you favor one- or two-officer patrol units? Why?
4. Does your law enforcement agency use civilianization? If so, for what positions? Could this be expanded?
5. What emergencies should be planned for in your jurisdiction?
6. Have you ever been involved in a disaster or emergency that required law enforcement officers? If so, how effectively did they perform?
7. What proportion of resources do you feel should be allocated to "fighting crime"?
8. What innovative ideas can you think of to increase effectiveness and productivity?
9. How does your law enforcement agency use computers?
10. When are you highly productive? What factors are present during those times?

InfoTrac College Edition Assignment

- Use InfoTrac College Edition to answer the Discussion Questions as appropriate.
- Research two *methods of patrol* that are of interest to you. Outline the main characteristics of each as well as any other information you find interesting. Include the full reference citations. Be prepared to share your findings with the class.

OR

- Read and outline one of the following articles:

- "British Policing and the Ottawa Shift System" by Mike Simpson and Suzanne Richbell.
- "The Citizen Police Academy" by Giant Abutalebi Aryani, Terry D. Garrett and Carl L. Alsabrook.
- "Citizen Police Academies: Do They Just Entertain?" by Elizabeth M. Bonello and Joseph A. Schafer.
- "Nationwide Application of the Incident Command System" by Michael D. Cardwell and Patrick T. Cooney.
- "Investigative Uses of Computers" by Craig W. Meyer and Gary M. Morgan.

References

Anemone, Louis R. and Spangenberg, Francis E. "Building on Success: TrafficStat Takes the NYPD's CompStat Method in a New Direction." *The Police Chief,* February 2000, pp.23–28.

Aryani, Giant Abutalebi; Garrett, Terry D.; and Alsabrook, Carl L. "The Citizen Police Academy: Success through Community Partnerships." *FBI Law Enforcement Bulletin,* May 2000, pp.16–21.

Bair, John M. "Just a Reserve? The Contributions Can Be Many." *Police,* March 2000, p.66.

Bauman, Michael P. "Police Productivity: A State of Mind, An Approach to the Job." *Police,* January 2000, pp.32–34.

Bellah, John. "Low-Speed Ahead." *Law Enforcement Technology,* October 2001, pp.76–82.

Berger, William B. "Volunteers in Police Service." *The Police Chief,* July 2002, p.6.

Boertien, Robert. "Multnomah County Volunteers." *Law and Order,* October 2001, pp.127–131.

Bonello, Elizabeth M. and Schafer, Joseph A. "Citizen Police Academies: Do They Just Entertain?" *FBI Law Enforcement Bulletin,* November 2002, pp.19–23.

Braiden, Chris. "Policing—The Hunt and the Habitat." *Law Enforcement News,* October 31, 1998, pp.8, 10.

Caddell, Alan. "Citizen Academy: Hands." *Community Links,* August 2002, pp.1–2.

Cardwell, Michael D. and Cooney, Patrick T. "Nationwide Application of the Incident Command System." *FBI Law Enforcement Bulletin,* October 2000, pp.10–15.

Chamberlain, Jeffrey. "Doing Comp Time." *Police,* January 2001, pp.42–43.

Cichello, Dan. "Road Warriors of the Desert." *Law and Order,* April 2001, pp.76–79.

Cohen, Alan. "No Web for You." *FSB,* October 2000, pp.44–56.

Cook, Paul. "Bicycle Patrol: The Fiscal Perspective." *The Police Chief,* November 2001, pp.49–54.

Courter, Eillen. "All Eyes Open: Community Volunteer Patrol." *Law and Order,* April 2002, pp.42–46.

Davala, Christopher. "Pedaling into Community Policing." *Law and Order,* April 2002, pp.88–91.

Dees, Tim. "Scheduling Software." *Law and Order,* February 2002, pp.68–72.

DeFranco, Liz. "Computer Scheduling." *Law Enforcement Technology,* January 2000, pp.80–82.

DiIulio, John J., Jr. "Rethinking the Criminal Justice System: Toward a New Paradigm." In *Performance Measures for the Criminal Justice System.* Bureau of Justice Statistics and Princeton University, October 1993, pp.1–18.

"Do You Get What You Pay For? San Diego Volunteers Show it Ain't Necessarily So." *Law Enforcement News,* February 29, 2000, pp.1, 9.

Domash, Shelly Feuer. " 'Steady Tours': Can They Benefit Officers, Agencies?" *Police,* April 2000, pp.46–49.

Douglas, Dave. "Emergency Management and Emergency Operations Centers." *Police,* November 2001, pp.32–36.

Forsythe, David and Fisher, Beth. "Online Case Management." *Law Enforcement Technology,* February 2000, pp.66–71.

Garrett, Ronnie L. "Citizens: A Valuable Resource." *Law Enforcement Technology,* December 2002, p.6.

Giordano, Alice. "Teen Drivers Turn into Speed Busters." *Law and Order,* July 2001, pp.148–149.

Goetz, Mike. "Police Bicycle Use in Crowd Control Situations." *Law and Order,* April 2002, pp.102–104.

Hudson, David. "Assuring Police Officer Performance: Whose Job Is It?" *The Police Chief,* December 2000, pp.26–27.

Hudson, Don. "LAPD's Bicycle Rapid Response Team." *Law and Order,* April 2002, pp.97–99.

Kammerer, Robert K. "Become a Master, Not a Slave, to Your Court Overtime." *The Police Chief,* January 2000, pp.34–37.

Karlya, Mark. "Rough Riding on an ATV." *Law Enforcement Technology,* September 2000, pp.38–42.

Kinsey, James M. "The FLSA and Reserve Officers." *Law and Order,* September 2002, pp.229–232.

Klockars, Carl B. *Thinking about Police: Contemporary Readings.* New York: McGraw-Hill, 1983.

Mallory, Jim. "Volunteer Bike Patrol Boosts Park Coverage." *Law and Order,* April 2001, pp.80–84.

Manus, Raymond P. "Random Thoughts on the KC Patrol Study." *Law Enforcement News,* November 30, 2000, pp.8, 10.

Meyer, Craig W. and Morgan, Gary M. "Investigative Uses of Computers: Analytical Time Lines." *FBI Law Enforcement Bulletin,* August 2000, pp.1–5.

Miller, Christa. "Everything You Need in the Palm of Your Hand." *Law Enforcement Technology,* April 2002a, pp.46–50.

Miller, Christa. "The Numbers Behind the Maps." *Law Enforcement Technology,* July 2002b, pp.94–99.

Miller, Linda S. and Hess, Kären M. *The Police in the Community: Strategies for the 21st Century,* 3rd ed. Belmont, CA: West/Wadsworth Publishing Company, 2002.

Mroz, Mike. "Cops on Bikes." *Police,* December 2001, pp.41–45.

Paynter, Ronnie L. "Unique Partnership Brings Lifesaving AEDs to County." *Law Enforcement Technology,* February 2001, pp.94–96.

Polan, Jim. "Motorcycle Operations Require Training." *Law and Order,* July 2000, pp.71–73.

Rams, Bill. "The Civilianization of Sworn Positions: But What about the Families Benefits?" *The Law Enforcement Trainer,* May/June 2000, pp.34–37.

Rhodes, David. "Automatic External Defibrillators." *Law and Order,* August 2001, pp.95–99.

Rogers, Donna. "Keeping Time on the Internet." *Law Enforcement Technology,* August 2001, pp.98–103.

Rohen, Gary J. "WMD: Integrating the Joint Operations Center and Incident Command System." *The Police Chief,* October 2001, pp.148–163.

Ruff, Gary W. "Using Routine Incidents to Develop Effective Incident Command System Skill." *The Police Chief,* January 2000, pp.52–54.

Schafer, Joseph A. and Bonello, Elizabeth M. "The Citizen Police Academy: Measuring Outcomes." *Police Quarterly,* December 2001, pp.434–448.

Schons, Carl R. "Special Report: Bike Patrol." *Law and Order,* April 2000, pp.79–80.

Simpson, Mike and Richbell, Suzanne. "British Policing and the Ottawa Shift System: Easing the Stress of Rotating Shifts." *FBI Law Enforcement Bulletin,* January 2000, pp.19–26.

Siuru, Bill. "What's New in E-Bikes." *Law and Order,* February 2000, pp.47–48.

Skogan, Wesley G.; Hartnett, Susan M.; DuBois, Jill; Comey, Jennifer T.; Twedt-Ball, Karla; and Gudell, Erik. *Public Involvement: Community Policing in Chicago.* Chicago, IL: Institute for Policy Research, Northwestern University, September 2000. (NCJ 179557)

Stevens, Dennis J. "Improving Community Policing: Using Managerial Style and Total Quality Management." *Law and Order,* October 2000, pp.197–204.

Strandberg, Keith. "E-Bike Makes Biking a Breeze." *Law Enforcement Technology,* June 2001a, pp.102–107.

Strandberg, Keith. "Setting Up an Air Unit." *Law Enforcement Technology,* September 2001b, pp.20–25.

Streit, Corinne. "Scheduling Your Time as Well as Your Officers." *Law Enforcement Technology,* April 2001, pp.126–130.

Swager, Brent. "Aviation Unit: Sheriff's Office Benefits from Extended Coverage." *Law and Order,* May 2000, pp.40–42.

Vila, Bryan; Morrison, Gregory B.; and Kenney, Dennis J. "Improving Shift Schedules and Work-Hour Policies and Practices to Increase Police Officer Performance, Health and Safety." *Police Quarterly,* March 2002, pp.4–24.

Vonk, Kathleen. "Riding a Mountain Bike on Patrol: A Training Issue?" *The Law Enforcement Trainer,* September/October 2000, pp.28–38.

Vonk, Kathleen. "Beyond Community Policing: The Crime Fighting Effectiveness of the Police Cyclist." *Law and Order,* April 2002, pp.92–96.

Weinblatt, Richard B. "Volunteers Assist in Private/Public Sector Partnerships." *Law and Order,* January 2000a, pp.19–20.

Weinblatt, Richard B. "Reserve Applicant Screening." *Law and Order,* August 2000b, pp.28–30.

Weinblatt, Richard B. "Honolulu Reserves Shine in the Sun." *Law and Order,* March 2001a, pp.24–26.

Weinblatt, Richard B. "Alaska's Reserves Brave the Elements." *Law and Order,* May 2001b, pp.24–25.

Weiss, Jim and Dresser, Mary. "Police Go Waterborne: Tactical Training in a Nautical Environment." *Law and Order,* January 2000, pp.74–77.

Woods, Tom. "Special Report: Bike Patrol." *Law and Order* April 2002, pp.78–85.

Wrobleski, Henry M. and Hess, Kären M. *Introduction to Law Enforcement and Criminal Justice,* 7th ed. Belmont, CA: Wadsworth Publishing Company, 2003.

Book-Specific Web Site

Go to the *Management and Supervision in Law Enforcement* Web site at http://info.wadsworth.com/05346160654 for student and instructor resources, including Internet Assignments and Case Studies.

CHAPTER 16

Performance Appraisals and Evaluation

Excellence is not a standard; it is a frame of reference, a state of mind.

—Anonymous

Do You Know?

- What two basic types of evaluation exist?
- Who can be evaluated?
- What is crucial in a successful evaluation?
- Who should conduct an evaluation?
- What purposes are served by evaluation?
- What evaluation's main purpose should be?
- What function job standards serve? In what areas they may be established?
- What a by-the-numbers evaluation is?
- What consequences evaluation should have?
- What common types of performance evaluation are?
- What the main purpose of a performance interview is?
- How frequently to evaluate performance?
- What problems may occur in evaluations?
- What legal requirements performance appraisals must meet?
- What the four levels in the Kirkpatrick Model of training evaluation are?
- How to evaluate the entire organization?
- What accreditation is and who does it?

Can You Define?

accreditation
automated performance evaluation
behaviorally anchored rating scales (BARS)
by-the-numbers evaluation
descriptive statistics
evaluate
evaluation
formal evaluation
halo effect
horn effect
inferential statistics
informal evaluation
performance appraisal
performance interviews
pre-evaluation
promotability/assignment factors
standards
valid

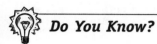

INTRODUCTION

We are constantly evaluating others and being evaluated ourselves. People evaluate, in varying degrees, every time they meet someone. The opinion they form of others, even in a social situation, is an informal evaluation. People in romantic situations evaluate each other as future partners. In the business world, people are evaluated as potential customers. People who wager on racing evaluate the horse and the jockey before they bet. At election time, people evaluate the candidates for office. Law enforcement is no exception.

This chapter defines evaluation and distinguishes between informal and formal evaluation. Next the chapter discusses the importance of evaluation on the job as well as specific purposes of evaluation and the criticality of performance criteria or standards that are clearly job related. This is followed by a discussion of recognizing value in policing and what might be assessed. Next the chapter examines a variety of surveys and rating forms and the type of information sought during evaluations as well as common types of performance evaluations. The discussion then turns to performance interviews, guidelines for evaluating and problems to anticipate during evaluations, as well as a brief look at automated performance evaluation and the legal requirements involved. This discussion is followed by a look at the benefits of evaluation and the evaluation cycle. The chapter then examines evaluating the teams within a department, evaluation training, evaluating the entire department and the potential role of accreditation in evaluation. The chapter concludes with a look at evaluation and research.

Evaluation Defined

Appraisal and *evaluation* are synonyms. Both refer to measuring on-the-job performance. Decisions should be based on a standardized, objective and structured set of criteria. Appraisals and evaluations are used for both on-the-job performance and promotions. Some jurisdictions use evaluations for step or salary increases. To **evaluate** means to determine the worth of, to find the amount or value of, or to appraise. All these definitions apply to people as well as to objects.

Informal vs. Formal Evaluation

A field training officer provides continuous informal evaluation while helping rookies learn to perform tasks efficiently. The time comes, however, when the rookies will have to pass a test—a formal evaluation of their skills. Both types of evaluation are necessary.

Evaluation can be informal or formal.

Informal evaluation is thought by some experts to be better than formal evaluation. They do not believe that evaluating on a precise date is truly how to evaluate. It is better to make judgments whenever necessary. Thus, evaluation should be continuous. They also point out that evaluating at the time behavior occurs is more apt to consider the behavior rather than personality. Informal evaluation also saves time because it does not require extensive records.

Formal evaluation systems are called efficiency ratings, employee appraisals, service ratings, progress reports, performance appraisal, employee performance review, merit ratings or appraisal interview. Regardless of what it is called, evaluation is arduous.

Specialists or law enforcement managers devise formal rating forms, and managers at all levels administer them. Employees answer standard questions for individual evaluation and for comparison with other employees. There are various ways of measuring performance: quality of task performance, productivity measurements, attendance records or individual and group testing.

Basically, managers want to know what subordinates are doing, how well they are doing it and how strong performance can be continued and weak areas improved. Evaluation helps law enforcement managers measure past performance, identify important performance areas and set the stage for future development. Of all the methods, seniority alone is probably the least likely to indicate good performance. Regardless of the rating form selected, law enforcement managers must observe subordinates performing their assigned tasks and conduct a **performance appraisal.** They must find some form of comparison and measurement and assess employees' development. However, as Seiler (2000, p.107) suggests: "Performance appraisals often are anticipated with about as much enthusiasm as a trip to the dentist by both supervisors and employees alike."

Groups and organizations, as well as individuals, are evaluated.

Law enforcement employees are judged both as individuals and as a group or department. Employees are evaluated by managers and also by the public as they perform community tasks. The public evaluates the law enforcement organization based on personal contacts, how well it suppresses crime or prevents crashes, personal and equipment appearance, local news stories, rumors and other people's opinions and experiences.

Evaluation on the Job

Evaluation exists in every law enforcement organization in some form. Managers must select which form of evaluation to use and who will conduct it. They evaluate subordinates, and they evaluate their own managers. Most informal evaluation is done mentally, without written record, on the spot during a crisis situation and based on reports, opinions of others or other more immediate factors.

Regardless of managers' opinions of performance appraisals, it is their direct responsibility in most law enforcement organizations. Many managers dislike the formal evaluation process. Putting in writing their opinions of their subordinates is not appealing. Martin (2002, p.49) stresses: "Vague and incomplete appraisals have consequences. Some officers are not appropriately recognized for their good work while others are rated higher than they should be." He notes: "Appraisals present a tremendous opportunity to officially recognize the good work by officers and make it clear that their career goals are important."

Law enforcement managers' attitudes toward evaluation and their ability to evaluate are critical factors for a successful evaluation system.

The importance and usefulness of evaluation depend on which performance appraisals are used. Evaluations are generally done every six months (or more frequently for probationary employees). The formal process should not be so frequent that it becomes burdensome for managers or employees.

Decide how employees will be rated: as individuals, in comparison with other employees doing similar tasks, or by national standards. Make sure that employees are aware of this.

Managers who provide the most immediate direction of subordinates should do the evaluation.

They can most directly observe employee behavior at the level at which the majority of required tasks are performed. In most cases, the police sergeant evaluates patrol officers, the first-line supervisor for other divisions. The administrative sergeant or lieutenant evaluates dispatch personnel. The investigative sergeant or lieutenant evaluates investigative personnel.

If employees are transferred during a rating period, each responsible manager should put in writing the evaluation for the period of responsibility. A system to establish time periods for evaluation and reminders should be devised, often based on the hiring anniversary date. Some type of immediate follow-up and feedback should be provided between formal ratings as needed. Law enforcement managers are motivators, and motivation is one reason for evaluation.

Purposes of Evaluation

Evaluation helps to validate the selection process, satisfy liability and EEO requirements, provide feedback and provide a basis for retention/termination decisions.

Purposes of evaluation include promoting common understanding of individual performance levels, needs, work objectives and standards; providing feedback and suggesting specific courses of action to improve, including trainings; and setting objectives for future performance. Evaluation may also be used to identify department-wide training needs and to make decisions about promotions, reassignments, disciplinary actions and terminations.

Performance appraisals are not intended to cause undue burdens to managers but rather to provide consistent criteria for improving employee performance. When employees understand how they are doing, know that what they are doing contributes to the organization and know what they are doing correctly, performance levels will justify the evaluation effort.

Some managers claim that evaluations take too much time, that employees resent it or that to do an evaluation is a "pain." The truth is, managers must evaluate employees—either by means of formal rating systems or informally. If managers correct employees on the job, they are in fact evaluating task performance. If they fail to correct a situation that needs correcting, they are not accepting responsibility.

Performance appraisals help managers and employees evaluate work behavior and assess effectiveness and productivity. Most law enforcement organizations use some form of performance evaluation. The criteria for performance evaluation must be related to the required tasks. The job description should be carefully reviewed, and the evaluation should directly relate performance to the functions listed in the job description.

The main purpose of performance evaluation is to improve employee performance.

Some other uses of evaluation are to inform employees where they stand individually and in comparison with the work group, document information against lawsuits and assist managers in assigning and planning human resources use.

Performance Criteria/Standards

Performance appraisals must be based on clearly stated job descriptions and clearly stated performance standards. If job descriptions change, evaluations must reflect these changes. Evaluation forms and standards MUST fit the job. What tasks are rated? What level of performance is required? As many criteria as possible should be written. A humorous, exaggerated example is presented in Table 16.1.

Generally, evaluators must consider what is to be accomplished, the quantity and quality of tasks to be performed and the level of performance required. Regardless of the standards used to evaluate performance, evaluation requires time, effort and money. Figure 16.1 presents a simple *Sergeant's Checklist,* which might be used to evaluate officers' on-the-job performance.

Table 16.1
Guide to Employee Performance Appraisal

Performance Factors	Far Exceeds Job Requirements	Exceeds Job Requirements	Meets Job Requirements	Needs Some Improvement	Does Not Meet Minimum Requirements
Quality	Leaps tall buildings with a single bound	Must take running start to leap over tall buildings	Can leap over short buildings only	Crashes into buildings when attempting to jump over them	Cannot recognize buildings at all
Timeliness	Is faster than a speeding bullet	Is as fast as a speeding bullet	Not quite as fast as a speeding bullet	Would you believe a slow bullet?	Wounds self with bullet when attempting to shoot
Initiative	Is stronger than a locomotive	Is stronger than a bull elephant	Is stronger than a bull	Shoots the bull	Smells like a bull
Adaptability	Walks on water consistently	Walks on water in emergencies	Washes with water	Drinks water	Passes water in emergencies
Communication	Talks with God	Talks with the angels	Talks to himself	Argues with himself	Loses those arguments

Source: Paul R.Timm. *Supervision,* 2nd ed. St. Paul, MN: West Publishing Company, 1992, p.39.

Sergeant's Checklist*

Date ____________

Officer Checked ____________

Sergeant ____________

Time: From ____________ To ____________

If answer is Yes, place check mark after statement.

1. ATTITUDE

- Is he a willing worker . . . . ______
- Is he interested in his job . . . . ______
- Is he satisfied with his assignment . . . . ______
- Is he a clock watcher . . . . ______
- Does he have confidence in himself . . . . ______

2. PERSONAL APPEARANCE

- Are his shoes shined . . . . ______
- Is his brass polished . . . . ______
- Is he neat and clean . . . . ______
- Is his equipment in good shape . . . . ______

3. HOW DOES HE APPROACH AND CONTACT THE PUBLIC

- Is he courteous . . . . ______
- Does he take personal affront at violators . . . . ______
- Is he positive in his approach . . . . ______
- Does he use an impersonal business approach . . . . ______

4. DRIVING HABITS

- Does he drive defensively . . . . ______
- Does he observe all regulations . . . . ______
- Does he check his vehicle at start of shift . . . . ______
- Does he handle car as if it were his own . . . . ______

5. OBSERVATION

- Does he have good habits of observation . . . . ______
- Does he recognize crime situations . . . . ______
- Is he on the alert for traffic hazards . . . . ______
- Does he check his beat thoroughly . . . . ______

6. BEAT KNOWLEDGE

- Does he know his beat and stay on it . . . . ______
- Does he know the people on his beat . . . . ______
- Do the people on his beat know him . . . . ______
- Does he recognize trouble areas of his beat . . . . ______

7. TREATMENT OF PRISONERS

- Is he polite and courteous when he makes an arrest . . . . ______
- Is he firm yet kind to prisoners . . . . ______
- Is he rude and inconsiderate . . . . ______
- Is he friendly and impersonal . . . . ______

8. TRAFFIC CONSCIOUSNESS

- Does he engage in enforcement activity . . . . ______
- Is he prone to overlook violations . . . . ______
- Does he warn as well as cite . . . . ______
- Is he interested in traffic issues . . . . ______

9. MISCELLANEOUS

- Does this officer have a sense of humor . . . . ______
- Does he need more experience . . . . ______
- Does he possess and use common sense . . . . ______
- Does he want to be a police officer . . . . ______

*This checklist might be adapted to use inclusive language (e.g., eliminate male pronouns).

Source: *Police Supervision.* International Association of Chiefs of Police, 1985, pp. 112–113. Reprinted by permission.

Figure 16.1
Sergeant's Checklist

Evaluation information should be related to the standards required of the position and to specific task behavior, not personality. If employees are at a zero level of performance, pay should not increase, but opportunity to improve and assistance from the manager should be available. If this does not improve performance, employees should be terminated.

Gather information on improvements as well as failures. The manager's job is to help everyone achieve their level of competence. Although some evaluation systems rank order employees, usually they should not be rated on a curve but individually. It is possible to have all excellent employees or the reverse. Employees who meet established standards at the required level should be provided an acceptable rating regardless of how other employees perform. That is why standards or performance criteria are important to successful evaluation. Evaluation should be positive—not negative.

Standards may involve quality of performance, quantity and meeting established limits, such as time, level of performance, public relations effect or manner of performance. In law enforcement work, quality rather than quantity is often important. Competence and courtesy in handling requests for service are important factors. Without performance standards supervisors may be inconsistent and unfair in promotions, awards and discipline. Performance standards allow supervisors to be consistent and fair in these matters.

Performance standards should be mission related, measurable, attainable and practical to monitor. Such standards let officers know what to expect, remove personality from ratings and provide a basis for objective appraisal with a minimum of inconsistencies.

Job standards make it easier for employees to meet requirements and for managers to determine whether they have been met.

Obviously, numerical or quantity standards are easier to meet and evaluate, but many law enforcement tasks do not lend themselves to quantitative standards.

When standards are established, they must be made known to employees so employees know what is expected. Managers must accompany subordinates in the field periodically to know what they are doing and how well. They cannot do this from behind a desk.

Reports also measure performance. Activity reports indicate types and numbers of tasks performed. The number of citizen complaints or commendations are also indicators of performance quality.

Standards may include areas such as physical energy to perform and emotional stability while performing law enforcement tasks; individual judgment; reliability; loyalty and ability to get along with the public, fellow employees and managers; creativeness and innovation; attitude; knowledge of tasks; competence; and amount of required management.

Standards vary considerably among federal, state, county and municipal organizations.

Recognizing Value in Policing

Before looking at ways to actually measure the performance of individual officers, work teams and the entire department, consider what Moore et al. (2002, p.132) say are valuable goals of policing and measures associated with them:

- Reduce criminal victimization—reported crime rates; victimization rates.
- Call offenders to account—clearance rates; conviction rates.
- Reduce fear and enhance personal security—reported change in levels of fear; reported changes in self-defense measures.
- Guarantee safety in public spaces—traffic fatalities, injuries and damage; increased use of parks and other public spaces; increased property values.
- Use financial resources fairly, efficiently and effectively—cost per citizen; deployment efficiency/fairness; scheduling efficiency; budget compliance; overtime expenditures; civilianization.
- Use force and authority fairly, efficiently and effectively—citizen complaints; settlements in liability suits; police shootings.
- Satisfy customer demands/achieve legitimacy with those policed—satisfaction with police services; response times; citizen perceptions of fairness.

They (p.71) stress: "If some important values go unmeasured, the police will produce less of that value than is desirable." They (p.171) conclude:

> Citizens need high-quality measures of police performance to determine whether their police department is performing well. As "owners" of the police, they need to see the extent to which the police department is producing results that matter to them, and whether the organization is positioning itself for even better performance in the future.
>
> At the moment police departments are being driven by performance measures that capture only a portion of the value they can contribute to their local communities. The systems can describe levels of reported crime, and efforts the police have made to respond to crimes with both arrests, and threats of arrest. They can describe the extent to which the police have been successful in calling offenders to account for their crimes.
>
> Missing from these measures is the contribution the police make to many other important purposes. These include preventing crime through means other than arrest, reducing fear, enhancing safety and security in public spaces, and providing responsive, high-quality services to citizens. . . .
>
> To improve the system [of assessing police performance], three conceptual steps must be taken.
>
> First, we must recognize the wide variety of valuable contributions that police departments make to their communities, and treat all of these valuable effects as important, interlocking components of the police mission.
>
> Second, we must recognize that we are interested in economizing on the use of force and authority, as well as money, and that the police must be evaluated in terms of the quality of justice they produce as well as the amount of safety and security. . . .
>
> Third, we must recognize our interest in helping police departments strengthen their capabilities for the future, as well as perform well in the present.

Hopefully, the suggestions of Moore et al. are reflected in the pages that follow, considering the total police job and the values that are important to officers, managers and citizens alike.

Surveys and Rating Forms

Whether a department creates its own assessment instrument or adopts one from another department, the survey should be objective, comprehensive, reliable and current.

The Redondo Beach (California) Police Department extensively reviews both sworn and nonsworn personnel. The form for sworn personnel uses 23 dimensions ranging from knowledge of legal codes and procedures to attitude toward law enforcement work. Five additional dimensions are established for the ranks of officer and agent—driving skills, firearms, interview techniques, investigative skills and radio procedures. Eight additional dimensions are established for sworn supervisory personnel: approachability, budgetary management, delegation, disciplinary control, evaluation of employees' performance, fairness and impartiality, training and instruction and supportiveness of policy and procedure (see Figure 16.2).

A separate nonsworn evaluation form contains general performance factors as well as specific tasks related to the job: police services officers, police services specialists, parking enforcement officers, crime prevention specialists and animal-control officers.

By-the-numbers evaluation makes evaluation more objective by using a numerical scale for each dimension.

The Redondo Beach evaluation forms, for example, go from 1 (least proficient) through 7 (most proficient). The values of 1, 4 and 7 are designated as "anchors" with 1 representing *unacceptable*, 4 *acceptable* and 7 *outstanding*. Raters need not comment on any factor unless it is rated 7 or less than 3. **Promotability/assignment factors** attempt to make the evaluation "count for something."

Evaluation should have consequences. Those who rate in the acceptable range might be considered for promotions, special assignments or pay raises. Those who rate below the acceptable range might be given counseling, training, a demotion, salary reduction, probation or, in extreme cases, termination.

In the Redondo Beach Police Department, a simple mathematical formula is used based on the individual ratings assigned to each factor. The rating counts toward 25 percent of the promotional process and 50 percent of the selection process for special assignments. In addition, the evaluation has other consequences, with those having acceptable or higher overall ratings being considered for special training.

In Redondo Beach, two weeks before their formal evaluation, those being evaluated are given a pre-evaluation form, as shown in Figure 16.3.

Pre-Evaluation is a procedure that allows those being evaluated to have input by completing a form outlining their accomplishments. The Redondo Beach Evaluation Manual (p.17) notes:

> The prime factor in obtaining the best results of the performance evaluation is the supervisor's fair, impartial and sincere desire to help the employee grow and advance. *The performance evaluation process can either be the key link in the*

REDONDO BEACH POLICE DEPARTMENT
PEACE OFFICER PERFORMANCE EVALUATION

NAME (LAST, FIRST, INITIAL) JOB CLASSIFICATION SERIAL NUMBER
ASSIGNMENT/DIVISION
EVALUATION TYPE
( ) PROBATION ( ) SEMI-ANNUAL ( ) OTHER (SPECIFY)

EVALUATION PERIOD: FROM: __________ TO: __________
RATING INSTRUCTIONS: Rate observed behavior with reference to the scale below by using the numeric value definitions contained in the evaluation program guidelines. Specific comments are required for all ratings of 3 or less or 7.

DIMENSIONS RATED	*GENERAL PERFORMANCE FACTORS*	*LEVELS OF PROFICIENCY*
JOB SKILLS		
	01. KNOWLEDGE OF LEGAL CODES AND PROCEDURES	1 2 3 4 5 6 7
	02. NEATNESS OF WORK PRODUCT, SPELLING, GRAMMAR	1 2 3 4 5 6 7
	03. ORAL EXPRESSION	1 2 3 4 5 6 7
	04. PLANNING AND ORGANIZING WORK	1 2 3 4 5 6 7
	05. PROBLEM SOLVING/DECISION MAKING	1 2 3 4 5 6 7
	06. THOROUGHNESS AND ACCURACY	1 2 3 4 5 6 7
	07. WRITTEN EXPRESSION	1 2 3 4 5 6 7
PRODUCTIVITY		
	08. ACCEPTANCE OF RESPONSIBILITY	1 2 3 4 5 6 7
	09. INITIATIVE, RESOURCEFULNESS, AND OBSERVATION SKILLS	1 2 3 4 5 6 7
	10. QUANTITY OF WORK	1 2 3 4 5 6 7
	11. SEEKS TRAINING TO ENHANCE ABILITIES	1 2 3 4 5 6 7
WORK CONDUCT		
	12. ABILITY TO FOLLOW INSTRUCTIONS	1 2 3 4 5 6 7
	13. ATTENDANCE	1 2 3 4 5 6 7
	14. CARE OF EQUIPMENT	1 2 3 4 5 6 7
	15. DEALING WITH CO-WORKERS	1 2 3 4 5 6 7
	16. DEALING WITH THE PUBLIC	1 2 3 4 5 6 7
	17. OBSERVANCE OF RULES, REGULATIONS, AND PROCEDURES	1 2 3 4 5 6 7
	18. OFFICER SAFETY	1 2 3 4 5 6 7
ADAPTABILITY		
	19. PERFORMANCE IN NEW SITUATIONS/ACCEPTANCE TO CHANGE	1 2 3 4 5 6 7
	20. PERFORMANCE UNDER PRESSURE	1 2 3 4 5 6 7
	21. PERFORMANCE WITH MINIMUM INSTRUCTION	1 2 3 4 5 6 7
PERSONAL TRAITS		
	22. APPEARANCE	1 2 3 4 5 6 7
	23. ATTITUDE TOWARD POLICE WORK	1 2 3 4 5 6 7

Continued

Figure 16.2
Redondo Beach Sworn Personnel Evaluation Form

supervisor-employee relationship or a periodic source of irritation, depending on the way it is used. Periodic performance evaluation and counseling is the very best method available in improving relationships with employees and helping them to fulfill their needs for satisfactory recognition and growth.

Information for Evaluations

Law enforcement managers responsible for evaluation must record all information as soon as possible after an incident is observed. A form for each officer the manager rates should be maintained. It is impossible to remember such information over long periods. A simple form and notation are all that is required, as Figure 16.4 illustrates.

When it is time to complete the formal evaluation form, all the information will be available. This lessens the tendency for information gathered closer to the time of the formal evaluation to overshadow information gathered months before.

SPECIFIC JOB CLASSIFICATION FACTORS

POLICE OFFICER/AGENT

24. DRIVING SKILL 1 2 3 4 5 6 7
25. FIREARMS 1 2 3 4 5 6 7
26. INTERVIEW TECHNIQUES 1 2 3 4 5 6 7
27. INVESTIGATIVE SKILL 1 2 3 4 5 6 7
28. RADIO PROCEDURES 1 2 3 4 5 6 7

SUPERVISION/MANAGEMENT (SUPERVISORY & MANAGEMENT PERSONNEL ONLY)

29. APPROACHABILITY 1 2 3 4 5 6 7
30. BUDGETARY MANAGEMENT 1 2 3 4 5 6 7
31. DELEGATION 1 2 3 4 5 6 7
32. DISCIPLINARY CONTROL 1 2 3 4 5 6 7
33. EVALUATING EMPLOYEES' PERFORMANCE 1 2 3 4 5 6 7
34. FAIRNESS AND IMPARTIALITY 1 2 3 4 5 6 7
35. TRAINING AND INSTRUCTION 1 2 3 4 5 6 7
36. SUPPORTIVE OF POLICY AND PROCEDURE 1 2 3 4 5 6 7

TOTAL NUMERIC RATING ______________

NUMERIC AVERAGE ______________ (TO SECOND DECIMAL PLACE)

*PROMOTABILITY/ASSIGNMENT FACTOR (NUMERIC AVERAGE x 3.58)

*PROMOTABILITY FACTOR TO BE APPLIED AS 25% OF FINAL SELECTION PROCESS SCORE FOR PROMOTION AND 50% OF THE OVERALL SCORE FOR ASSIGNMENT SELECTION.

RBPD Form 345 11/87

Figure 16.2
(Continued)

Reprinted by permission.

REDONDO BEACH POLICE DEPARTMENT
PERFORMANCE PRE-EVALUATION FORM

Name ______________________________

Date ______________________________

You are encouraged to complete this form to provide a more meaningful exchange of information during the performance evaluation.

If you wish, you may provide a completed copy to your supervisor prior to being evaluated on your performance.

1. Describe individual accomplishments, noteworthy achievements and/or projects that you feel should be considered. Also, discuss those situations you feel required special consideration or which involved extenuating circumstances.

2. What personal/professional growth has there been during this time period?
   (a) For yourself?

   (b) For your staff? (Supervisors/Managers ONLY)

3. What additional experiences or training would you like to obtain to enhance your professional development and job proficiency?

4. Do you have any ideas or suggestions that would enable you to function more efficiently/effectively?

RBPD Form 344 5/86

Figure 16.3
Redondo Beach Pre-Evaluation Form

Reprinted by permission.

Information for Performance Evaluation

City of: ______________________

Employee evaluated: ______________________

Date: ______________________

Description of information: ______________________

____

____

____

____

____

____

____

Figure 16.4
Information for Evaluation

The information may be about specific incidents such as a high-speed chase, a shooting by an officer or a public-relations-type incident. Enter such information immediately after the occurrence while facts are remembered.

Dees (2001, p.15) suggests that computers can be used to monitor areas such as officers' records of assignments, both in geographical area and job function, personnel complaints, commendation notices, disciplinary records, training completed, use of sick and vacation time and shifts worked. He recommends that officers' performances be compared against those of their peers who work under similar conditions.

Common Types of Performance Evaluations

Numerous types of performance evaluations are available to managers.

Among the performance evaluations are the following:

- Ratings by individual traits or behaviorally anchored rating scales (BARS)
- Group or composite ratings
- Critical incident ratings
- Narrative, essay or description
- Overall comparison ratings
- Self-evaluation

Opinions vary on the value of each type of evaluation.

Evaluation of Subordinates by Managers, Supervisors and Others

Any of the preceding common types of performance evaluations can be used to evaluate subordinates.

Ratings by Individual Traits

Behaviorally anchored rating scales (BARS) are individual trait ratings usually done by the manager immediately above the employee in rank. Various factors concerning individual employees and the job are rated on a scale of 1 to 5 or 1 to

10. For example, a factor such as dependability would be rated from 1 to 10, with 1 being poorest and 10 being outstanding or excellent. It is fairly easy to perform this type of rating. The Redondo Beach Evaluation Form in Figure 16.2 is an example of this type of evaluation.

Differences arise over how to do individual trait rating. Some think managers should rate the first item for all employees before proceeding to the second item. Others think all factors for one employee should be rated at once before going to the next employee rating.

Unless department policy dictates otherwise, raters should try both ways to decide which works better. The total score is the composite rating. Some think that poor and excellent ratings should be justified by performance evidence. Trait categories fall into those related to *performance* measured by quantity and quality, accuracy, efficiency and amount of supervision required; *personal qualities,* such as personality, attitude, character, loyalty and creativeness; and *ability,* which involves knowledge of job, mental and emotional stability, initiative and judgment. The traits must be job related.

Group or Composite Ratings

Many departments are changing from individual to group ratings, where traits are rated by a group instead of one manager. For example, rather than having a sergeant rate the patrol officers, a group of three or four people of different ranks in the department might evaluate the patrol officers. This might include one officer from the same level as the person rated, overcoming single-rater bias. Varied percentage weights may be applied to different raters according to rank. Or employees could be rated by all members in the organization of the same rank or a section of first-line supervisor, a higher manager, their peers or other group members. Some departments use a member of the personnel department to interview those associated with the employee, and this interviewer makes the rating for the personnel file. This method involves more time.

Critical Incident Ratings

Most managers keep *critical incident logs* that record all good and bad performances of employees (see Figure 16.5).

Keeping such logs is time consuming, but the information is of great value when it is time for the formal performance appraisal. If an officer did an excellent investigation or made an excellent arrest, this would be recorded. If the officer made a bad arrest or a poor investigation, this would also be recorded. All incidents would be discussed with the employee.

Narrative, Essay or Description

In this method, raters use a written description of what they observed rather than a rating scale. It is also possible to combine numerical and narrative in the same form, with words replacing numbers.

Overall Comparison Ratings

Managers review all their subordinates and then rate which one is top and which bottom. They then arrange the others on a comparative scale.

CRITICAL INCIDENT REPORT

EMPLOYEE: ______________________________

SUBJECT: ______________________________

COMMENTS: ______________________________

____

____

____

____

____

____

SUPERVISOR SIGNATURE	DATE
*EMPLOYEE SIGNATURE	DATE

*Employee's signature does not necessarily indicate agreement with this report. This form may be used for the purpose of preparing performance evaluations.

WHITE-FILE YELLOW-EMPLOYEE PINK-SUPERVISOR

Figure 16.5
Sample Critical Incident Report

Self-Evaluation

Self-evaluation is becoming more popular. Self-evaluation forms allow subordinates to rate themselves. There is value in people comparing how they perceive themselves with how others perceive them. Self-evaluation assists in getting employees to accept other types of evaluations. In some instances, individuals are more self-critical than external raters, simply because they know things about themselves others do not. These ratings have substantial value if no other evaluation exists.

Evaluation of Managers and Supervisors by Subordinates

One form of performance evaluation allows subordinates to evaluate their supervisory and administrative personnel. This gives command personnel a new source of information and a reasonably accurate assessment of subordinates' perceptions. A form such as that shown in Figure 16.6 can be used to evaluate first-line supervisory personnel and others who directly supervise field personnel.

Higher level managers and the chief or sheriff might also be evaluated by their subordinates using an instrument that includes management and leadership skills. Although subordinates evaluating managers is not common, it has value. Rating managers could help both managers and the organization, and the same rating method would be used for managers and subordinates. Subordinates should have as much right to rate their managers as managers have to rate their subordinates.

Performance Evaluation of Supervisory Personnel by Subordinates

This evaluation should be completed by the employee and submitted to the designated proctor for processing. Deviation from this procedure may invalidate this evaluation.

Rated Supervisor: ______________________________

Evaluating Employee: ______________________________

Proctor: ______________________________

Using the graphic scales, rate the performance against the criteria listed. A 10 indicates total agreement or outstanding performance; a 1 indicates total disagreement or unsatisfactory performance. Place a check in the "Not Observed" (N.O.) column if you have not observed performance in that area or if you feel you are not qualified to rate in that area.

Leadership Skills		N.O.
1. Subordinates are encouraged to excel through the positive, professional attitude and action of this supervisor.	1 2 3 4 5 6 7 8 9 10	____
2. Innovative ideas are encouraged from subordinates for improving the effectiveness of the unit.	1 2 3 4 5 6 7 8 9 10	____
3. Departmental needs, plans, information and goals are communicated to subordinates.	1 2 3 4 5 6 7 8 9 10	____
4. Plans, projects and objectives are consistent with departmental needs, goals and resources.	1 2 3 4 5 6 7 8 9 10	____
5. *Composite leadership rating:*	1 2 3 4 5 6 7 8 9 10	____
Judgment and Decision Making		
1. Makes decisions in a timely manner.	1 2 3 4 5 6 7 8 9 10	____
2. Demonstrates decisiveness when faced with options.	1 2 3 4 5 6 7 8 9 10	____
3. Decisions rendered conform with departmental rules and regulations, policy and procedure, and all applicable laws.	1 2 3 4 5 6 7 8 9 10	____
4. Personnel assignments reflect proper use of manpower resources.	1 2 3 4 5 6 7 8 9 10	____
5. *Composite judgment and decision-making rating:*	1 2 3 4 5 6 7 8 9 10	____
Direction of Personnel While under Emergency, Unusual or Stressful Conditions		
1. Supervisor is present as appropriate.	1 2 3 4 5 6 7 8 9 10	____
2. Situation is correctly analyzed, and appropriate actions are taken to control situation.	1 2 3 4 5 6 7 8 9 10	____
3. Available resources are properly deployed.	1 2 3 4 5 6 7 8 9 10	____
4. *Composite stress performance rating:*	1 2 3 4 5 6 7 8 9 10	____
Application of Departmental Rules, Regulations, Policy and Procedure		
1. Sets a good example by adhering to established policy and regulations.	1 2 3 4 5 6 7 8 9 10	____
2. Policy and directives are explained when necessary.	1 2 3 4 5 6 7 8 9 10	____
3. Violations are identified, and timely corrective action is taken.	1 2 3 4 5 6 7 8 9 10	____
4. Rules are applied fairly and impartially to all subordinates.	1 2 3 4 5 6 7 8 9 10	____
5. Subordinates receive evaluation and counseling in an objective manner and in line with established procedure with constructive suggestions as to how performance can be improved.	1 2 3 4 5 6 7 8 9 10	____
6. *Composite application of rules rating:*	1 2 3 4 5 6 7 8 9 10	____

Figure 16.6
Subordinate Evaluation of Supervisors

Continued

Training Ability and Communication Skills

1. In-service training needs are identified, and efforts are made to provide proper training. 1 2 3 4 5 6 7 8 9 10 ____
2. Information given is relevant and timely. 1 2 3 4 5 6 7 8 9 10 ____
3. Ideas are presented in a clear, concise and understandable manner. 1 2 3 4 5 6 7 8 9 10 ____
4. Presentations are logical, organized and in compliance with current policy and standards. 1 2 3 4 5 6 7 8 9 10 ____
5. *Composite training and communications rating:* 1 2 3 4 5 6 7 8 9 10 ____

Composite Supervisory Rating

Consider the above criteria and those areas not specifically addressed by this evaluation. Rate the supervisor on overall capability to perform effectively as a supervisor.

Comments

Please use this section to explain any answers and/or address other points not covered that you feel are significant. Attach extra sheets if more room is needed. Your interest and cooperation are appreciated.

Figure 16.6
continued

Source: Thomas S. Whetstone. "Subordinates Evaluate Supervisory and Administrative Performance." *The Police Chief,* June 1994, p.62 Reprinted from *The Police Chief,* Vol. LXIII No. 6, June 1994, p.62. Copyright held by the International Association of Chiefs of Police, Inc., 515 N. Washington St., Alexandria, VA 22314, USA. Further reproduction without express written permission from IACP is strictly prohibited.

Performance Interviews

Performance interviews are private, one-on-one discussions of the performance appraisal by manager and subordinate. The performance interview should be based on comprehensive, accurate records and should focus on employee performance and growth. The appraisal form is the basis for the performance interview. Although rating forms and managers vary, it usually takes two to three hours of preparation time for each person rated. Many managers mark the evaluation forms lightly in pencil in case the interview brings facts to light that change the rating.

Managers should allow 45 minutes to an hour for each performance interview. They should prepare in advance so as not to omit important items. Planning includes the time and place, preventing interruptions and topics to be discussed. A starting point is to review the evaluation form.

Performance interviews open with a statement of purpose and should seek to make the employee feel at ease. Personalize the interview so it does not appear "canned." After rapport has been established, the employee's accomplishments are usually discussed. The appraisal form can serve as the foundation for the discussion. Compare it with the last appraisal. The tone throughout the interview should be positive. Ask employees to indicate what they see as their strengths and weaknesses. Ask what you, as manager, can do to help improve the weaknesses. Encourage participation.

The performance appraisal interview should help employees do their jobs better and therefore improve individual performance and productivity.

All employee performance interviews should be private. Employees are normally apprehensive about evaluation. They are concerned about the manager's perceptions and how these compare with their own. An interview is a chance for managers and employees to establish rapport. If the interview is conducted properly—inviting input from employees—it will decrease controversy. Emphasize strengths rather than weaknesses.

Interviews of this type may identify conditions, distractions, lack of resources, training or equipment to do the tasks required or other obstacles, none of which may have been known to the manager before the interview.

A positive approach is likely to produce positive responses. A negative approach normally generates defensiveness and lack of cooperation. This does not mean everything needs to be "hearts and roses." Criticism is necessary for development, but it should be constructive.

Law enforcement managers are employee problem solvers. During performance appraisal interviews, employees will be concerned about any low ratings and individual problems. They should be encouraged to mention perceived problems. Explain precisely what makes performance unsatisfactory, and do not apologize for discussing the matter. As a supervisor or manager, correcting your subordinates is your responsibility. Ask whether the employee understands the problem and has any ideas on how to approach it. Offer help in resolving the problem. If the problem is resolved at the first meeting, follow up by further monitoring. Congratulate the employee if the problem is corrected.

If the employee's position is one you cannot immediately discuss further or resolve, tell the employee of your next step. Set a time and place to continue the discussion. Explain that in light of what you have been told, you will investigate further and will reach a decision as soon as possible. Follow through within a day or two.

In some extreme cases of intentional misbehavior, for instance an officer who abuses alcohol or drugs, it may be necessary to suggest termination if immediate remedies are not available.

Agree on important issues discussed, set future expectations, discuss training opportunities available for personal improvement and summarize the entire meeting with a positive ending. If you agree to do certain things, follow through.

The Redondo Beach Evaluation Manual (pp.14–15) contains the following suggestions, based on experience and research:

- Plan the appraisal interview in advance. Define your objectives and outline the key points you want to cover.
- Plan and schedule the interview for a time and place that will give you and the employee privacy and allow your undivided attention to be devoted to the subject.
- Get right into the appraisal at the outset, but encourage the employee to speak his/her mind about any portion of the appraisal the employee thinks is incorrect or unfair.
- Listen to the employee during the interview—especially immediately after negative feedback has been given.

SUPERVISOR SIGNATURE DATE

EMPLOYEE SIGNATURE* DATE

*Employee's signature does not necessarily indicate agreement with this report. This form may be used for the purpose of preparing performance evaluations.

WHITE-FILE YELLOW-EMPLOYEE PINK-SUPERVISOR

Figure 16.7
Supervisor and Employee Signature Lines and Statement

Your attitude and interest regarding the employee are more important than any counseling technique you might use. If employees see that your prime objective is to help them do a better job, the appraisal is on its way to a successful result. If you put yourself in the role of a judge and the employee is the defendant, the appraisal will in all likelihood be a waste of time.

The appraisal interview should not be the only time you talk with employees about performance. Appraisal, to be effective, must be continuous.

Most employee rating forms require signatures of the rater and the person rated as evidence the employee has seen the evaluation, not necessarily that he or she agrees with the results, as illustrated in Figure 16.7.

Before concluding the performance interview, many managers give the employee an opportunity to discuss their performance as a supervisor. This is done after the formal performance evaluation to increase the likelihood that the person being evaluated will be at ease and discuss more frankly. At the end of the interview, allow for a summary and future action statement. Set objectives for future performance, and also set a date for the next appraisal meeting (opinions vary on how frequently such meetings should occur).

The most common recommendation for frequency of performance appraisals is twice a year and more frequently for employees who perform below expectations.

When the interview is completed, managers should make appropriate meeting notes immediately. These should be part of the permanent personnel file. Another file should contain any agreements reached that must be performed before the next appraisal, along with the date of the next appraisal.

Generally, appeals regarding ratings can be made to the next higher manager and on up to the head of the department. There may even be provision for an appeals board. The decision of the appeals board is usually final. Appeals should be required within a specified time and hearings held as quickly as possible.

Guidelines for Evaluating

The following guidelines are summarized from the Redondo Beach Police Department Evaluation Manual:

- Communicate your expectations in advance.
- Appraise performance for the entire period. Critical incident reports can highlight performance over the entire rating period.

- Keep the appraisal job-related. Don't let your attitude toward individuals or their personal attitudes bias your evaluations.
- Employees should participate. During the appraisal interview, the supervisor may choose to alter his/her appraisal after the subordinate provides additional information and insights regarding performance.
- Avoid the halo effect.
- Use descriptive statements to support your evaluations. Describe the performance on which you base your evaluations.

Problems of Performance Evaluations

Every employee evaluation system has shortcomings.

Some problems of performance appraisals are the following:

- Lack of faith in any appraisal system
- "Late-inning" results count most
- The halo or horn effect
- Inaccurate numerical or forced-choice methods
- Unfair percentage ratings
- Rating personality rather than performance
- Rater bias
- Rating at the extremes

Lack of Faith in Appraisal Systems

Some managers have a defeatist attitude about performance rating. "It won't work." "Employees should not be compared with one another." "It all depends on the rater." "Managers are not trained to be evaluators." "Employees don't like it." "The seniority system is good enough for me."

A defeatist attitude can arise from excessively high expectations about performance evaluations. Perfection is not the goal; growth and development are. Sometimes choosing the best method is a problem. Any formal performance appraisal is better than no appraisal if it is **valid,** meaning it is well grounded, sound, the factors rated are job related and the raters are trained.

Late-Inning Results Count Most

When ratings are performed annually, the actions and performance in the final months of the rating period are often better remembered and given more weight. This works both ways. Employees may have a good first nine months and a bad last three months or vice versa.

The Halo and Horn Effects

The **halo effect** is the tendency to allow an employee's performance in one area to unduly influence the ratings in other areas. Some evaluation experts use a narrower meaning of the halo effect, reserving that term for allowing highly positive attributes in one area to carry over into rating all characteristics positively. When the opposite happens and a highly negative attribute causes other attributes to be rated low, this is called the **horn effect.**

Inaccurate Numerical or Forced-Choice Methods

Numerical ratings do not provide the information needed for improving employee performance because they do not indicate specifics about individuals. Managers who do the ratings are not put to the test of really knowing their employees.

Unfair Percentage Ratings

When raters must place a percentage of employees in the upper, middle and lower third of ratings scales, they tend to be unfair. The same unfairness exists when raters place all employees at or near the average or middle of the scale. Employees should be rated on the basis of their actual performance, regardless of how many are upper, middle or lower. Some managers do not have the courage or training to do such ratings. In other instances, managers have a problem of being either high, low or middle raters.

Rating Personality Rather Than Performance

Some raters tend to use their personal prejudices to rate employees. Instead of looking at each task or criterion and considering it individually, raters use a personal opinion of the individual based on a single experience. They may also rate on prejudice based on education, race or other factors.

Rater Bias

Closely related to rating personality is allowing one's personal biases to interfere with the evaluation, for example, preferring men over women or nonminorities over minorities.

Rating at the Extremes

Some evaluators rate in extremes of too lenient or too strict. This is especially true with marginal employees. Rather than terminate an employee who is liked, managers give a higher rating than the employee deserves. The opposite is true if the rating supports termination because the employee is not a "yes" person but performs other tasks well.

Other rating problems arise when managers rate employees in higher-level positions higher than those in lower-level positions, especially when raters have no training in rating or when raters do not care about the process. Other problems arise when the instructions are unclear or the terms and standards are not clearly defined.

Automated Performance Evaluations

The Cheney Police Department has developed an **automated performance evaluation,** a system to evaluate officers' "production" using a computerized point system. This system assigns points to all possible activities and allows officers to develop their minimum baseline production points any way they wish. Minimum point requirements are set in areas such as parking citations—for example, three points for each traffic citation written. Responding to any type of call is worth one point. Officers are tracked by computer from the time they come to work until they go home. Supervisors can award bonus points for whatever they are focusing on during any given period. Point values can be raised or lowered by the administration as its priorities shift.

Legal Requirements in Performance Evaluation

Performance evaluation rating forms have changed over the past 20 years to meet legal criteria and to make them more directly related to improvement of employees.

To meet legal requirements, performance appraisal criteria must be *job related.*

In times past, fired employees and their families were the only ones to suffer financially, but now it is quite different. Fired employees are suing to get their jobs back—and often winning not only their jobs but also back pay and even damages for emotional injury.

To avoid such lawsuits, any system of performance rating must be based on rating items specific to the tasks performed on the job. For example, law enforcement civilian employees do not use firearms; therefore, the form used for sworn officers is not directly related to civilian employees even though they both work for the same agency.

Fitness-for-Duty Evaluations

As Kenny (2000, p.58) points out: "Police work requires great endurance, strength and agility—attributes that can mean the difference between life and death." Schultz and Acevedo (2000, p.34) note: "Individual officer fitness cannot be overstressed as it can have a tremendous impact on how well a department functions. Studies have consistently demonstrated that healthy and fit officers improve work productivity, lower absenteeism rates and reduce health risks." Griggs and McCorquodale (2001, p.58) add: "Police professionals respect the skill and wisdom mature officers bring to the profession and recognize that improved health maintenance and medical care can mitigate some of the effects of aging and prolong law enforcement careers."

In addition to physical fitness standards, most states have statutes that define psychological suitability for peace officers. To determine whether officers meet this standard, a fitness-for-duty evaluation (FFDE) may be appropriate. Rostow and Davis (2002, p.58) explain: "The purpose of an FFDE is to notify the police executive and department of information that touches upon behavioral, mental illness or personality issues that may diminish an officer's performance of his or her official role." The issue of mental stability comes under the purview of the Americans with Disabilities Act (ADA), whose primary benchmark is whether or not an individual's condition prevents him from performing "essential job functions."

Benefits of Evaluation

Performance evaluations benefit all levels of a police department. First, they benefit the *organization as a whole* by accurately assessing its human resources so informed decisions can be made about assignments. They provide a permanent written record of the strengths and weaknesses of the department, which can help determine salary changes, promotions, demotions, transfers, court evidence and so on.

Second, they benefit the departments' *supervisors* by giving them a clear picture of their subordinates' abilities and allowing them input into officer development. Areas in which training is needed become more obvious.

Third, they benefit the department's *officers* by letting each know exactly what is expected and identifying areas needing improvement. Once employees come to recognize personal weaknesses, they should be stimulated to set goals for self-improvement. Perhaps most important is that they document officers' good work.

Martin and Matthews (2000, pp.191–192) suggest five reasons to measure an agency's performance: "First, measurement should provide a foundation for improving agency performance. . . . Second, measurement should increase agency accountability to policy-makers and the public to use all resources effectively and efficiently. . . . Third, measurement should promote integrity and ethical behavior. . . . Fourth, measurement should help determine agency progress in following an articulated strategic direction. . . . Fifth, measurement should promote leadership development within departments."

The Evaluation Cycle

Evaluation, like training, should be continuous, and each evaluation should identify areas for improvement. The evaluation cycle is diagrammed in Figure 16.8. Continual feedback, both positive and negative, on each employee's performance is provided throughout the year, giving employees a chance to constantly improve.

Evaluating the Team

Although it might be tempting to think that adding up all the individual performance ratings would be sufficient to evaluate the team as a whole, this is not the case. Periodically, managers and supervisors should formally assess the effectiveness of their teams. A form such as that in Figure 16.9 might be used.

Abilities to evaluate include how the group works together; effective use of individual skills; competence in addressing community issues; ability to engage the citizenry, other city departments and community groups in addressing local problems; adaptability to change; ability to function as part of the organization; ability to problem solve and reach a consensus on methods to define solutions; and the quality of solutions produced.

Evaluating Training

Perhaps the most obvious evaluation occurs during the FTO program and the probationary period. According to Kaminsky (2001, p.32): "The concept of 'probation' has been with us for some long time. The avowed purpose of the proba-

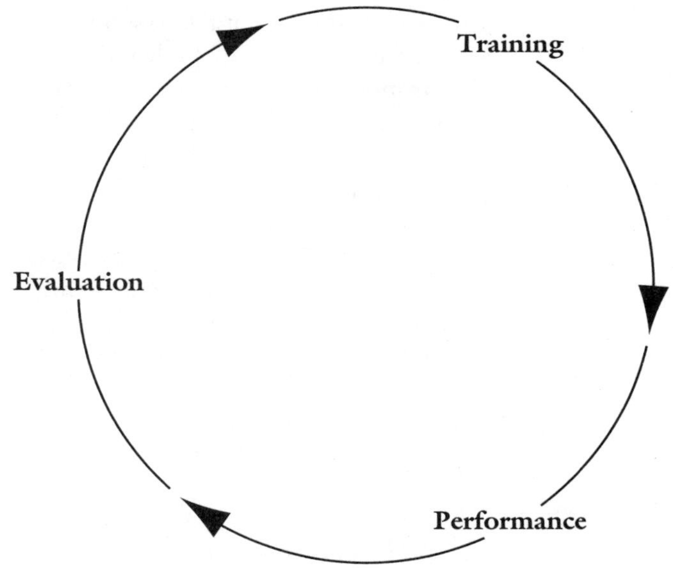

Figure 16.8
The Evaluation Cycle

TEAMWORK ASSESSMENT

Listed below are characteristics of effective, productive work teams. This assessment seeks feedback about (1) how important you feel each characteristic is and (2) how well you feel your team exhibits the characteristic. Please use a rating scale of 1 to 10, with 1 indicating lowest rating and 10 highest rating.

Characteristic	*Importance*	*Performance Rating*
Officers work toward common goals, known and understood, that serve both individual officers and the agency.	____	____
Officers know their individual responsibilities as well as those of their team.	____	____
Officers have the skills and knowledge to accomplish the job.	____	____
Team morale is high. Officers are enthusiastic and upbeat.	____	____
Productivity is high. Officers work hard and perform to the best of their ability.	____	____
Officers have confidence and trust in their team members.	____	____
Officers cooperate rather than compete with one another.	____	____
Officers can disagree without being disagreeable.	____	____
Communication lines are open. Officers can openly discuss their ideas and feelings, and they also listen to their team members.	____	____
Officers are not threatened by change. They are eager to try new approaches to routine tasks.	____	____
Officers take pride in their team and its accomplishments.	____	____
The team frequently evaluates how well it is doing.	____	____

Figure 16.9
Team Evaluation

tionary period is to provide some protection to an organization while it determines whether or not the new employee is all that the organization hoped they would be when hired." Evaluation is continuous during this period. The performance of the FTOs should also be evaluated. As Meehan (2001, p.30) stresses: "The purpose of the evaluation should be to ensure program and departmental accountability, identify problems and remedial strategies and recognize conscientious, hard-working FTOs."

The importance of ongoing training was a focus in Chapter 8. It is important that training efforts also be evaluated. Bumgarner (2001, p.34) suggests: "In doing full-fledged training evaluations, favorable evaluation results can be used to demonstrate the usefulness of training and the appropriateness of expending training dollars." He describes the Kirkpatrick Model's four levels of evaluation.

The Kirkpatrick Model of training evaluation has four levels: reaction, learning, behavior and results.

The *reaction* level focuses on the participants' perceptions of the training. This is the most common type of evaluation. The *learning* level focuses on the knowledge or skill acquired, ideally through a pre-post test. The *behavior* level looks at whether the knowledge or skill is actually applied on the job by observing the participants using what was learned. The *results* level focuses on the department's return on investment, for example, cost savings, increases in work output or quality. Bumgarner (p.36) recommends: "For criminal justice managers to know that the organization has truly benefited through the training of its employees, all four levels should be examined."

Evaluating the Entire Department

Evaluation must also consider the entire agency and how well it is accomplishing its mission. Again, this cannot be done simply by looking at the performance of individual officers or even of the teams making up the organization.

As managers evaluate the department as a whole, they should remember that people tend to use crime rates, number of arrests and case clearance rates to measure how the police are doing. Such measures have several problems:

- Low crime rates do not necessarily mean a police agency is efficient and effective.
- A high arrest rate does not necessarily show that the police are doing a good job.
- A high ratio of police officers to citizens does not necessarily mean high-quality police services.
- Responding quickly to calls for services does not necessarily indicate that a police agency is efficient.

Kramer and Fiedler (2002, p.164) summarize the problem well: "Traditional measurements, such as the Uniform Crime Reports, the NIBRS report, arrests and tickets tabulate only events. They do not measure whether the activities were

© Jim Shaffer

Positive officer-citizen interaction is extremely important because when an officer interacts with a citizen both may be informally evaluating each other.

completed efficiently and effectively, and they don't describe what impact the activities had on the community." Rather than looking at crime rates, number of arrests and response time, evaluation should assess whether the agency is effective in fulfilling its responsibilities to the community and might focus on three areas: organizational, technical and personnel.

When evaluating the effectiveness, efficiency and productivity of the entire department, managers must focus on their mission statement. They must also consider what citizens want and expect from their protectors. Most citizens want to live in safe, orderly neighborhoods. Recall from the discussion of productivity in Chapter 15 that police are considered effective when they produce the perception that crime is under control. Reduction of fear is a very important measure. A fear and disorder index allows police to measure citizens' concerns and also sends a message to citizens that the department is addressing their fear of crime and neighborhood disorder.

Citizen approval or disapproval is generally reflected in letters of criticism or commendation, support for proposed police programs, cooperation with incidents being investigated, letters to the editor, public reaction to a single police-citizen incident or responses to police-initiated surveys.

Citizen Surveys

One way to assess citizen approval or disapproval is through citizen surveys, which can measure trends and provide positive and negative feedback on the public's impression of law enforcement.

Community surveys are often a win-win situation—citizens are better served and officers receive positive feedback. Community surveys can also be key in establishing communication.

One citizen survey developed by the Plainsboro Township (New Jersey) Police Department uses a closed-end form (answer yes or no) asking very specific questions to assess the performance of individual officers (see Figure 16.10).

Surveys can be conducted by mail or by phone. Mailed surveys are less expensive and reduce the biasing errors in phoned surveys caused by how the person doing the phoning comes across to the respondent. However, they require that the person receiving the survey be able to read, which might not happen. The major problem with mailed surveys is their low response rate. However,

Call-for-Service Contact

We have started a Citizen Response Survey as part of our continuing effort to provide professional and efficient police service to the residents of Plainsboro Township and other individuals with whom our police officers come in contact. Your name has been selected at random from among those who have had recent contact with one of our officers.

Your response will be used internally to help us recognize potential deficiencies, acknowledge officers who continually perform in the manner expected and evaluate our procedures and methods. The feedback you provide will facilitate the improvement of future relations between the police and the public, aid in the evaluation of individual officers and provide an important means of acquiring additional citizen input into how we serve the community.

Please return the questionnaire in the enclosed envelope. It is the policy of this department to follow up unfavorable comments. However, if you do not wish to be contacted, please indicate in the space provided. Thank you.

Sincerely,

Clifford J. Mauler
Chief of Police

Citizen Response Questionnaire

1. Did the officer respond quickly to your call for service? Approximately how long did it take for the officer to respond after being called? ____________	Y____	N____
2. Was the officer courteous?	Y____	N____
3. Was the officer neatly attired?	Y____	N____
4. Did the officer identify himself by name?	Y____	N____
If not, do you think he should have?	Y____	N____
5. Did the officer speak clearly? Were you able to understand him?	Y____	N____
6. Were you satisfied with the service provided by the officer?	Y____	N____
7. Did the officer appear knowledgeable?	Y____	N____
8. Did he obtain all information that would seem pertinent under the circumstances of this contact?	Y____	N____
9. If applicable, did you feel satisfied with the supplemental investigation conducted by the officer?	Y____	N____
10. Upon completion of this police contact, did you feel satisfied with the general quality of the service rendered?	Y____	N____

11. Additional comments:

____

____

____

Signature ____________________ Date ____________

Figure 16.10
Cover Letter and Citizen Response Questionnaire

Source: Elizabeth Bondurant. "Citizen Response Questionnaire: A Valuable Evaluation Tool." *The Police Chief,* November 1991, p.75. Reprinted from *The Police Chief,* Vol. LVIII, No. 11. November 1991. p.75.

King (2001, p.253) found that postcard surveys have yielded response rates between 77 and 100 percent with only one or two waves of mailing.

Phone surveys have a much higher response rate but are also much more expensive unless volunteers can be enlisted to make the calls. In addition, individuals who do not have a phone cannot be included.

No matter which form of survey is used, the expense is small relative to the continued positive police-community relations. Citizen surveys might also help set organizational goals and priorities, identify department strengths and weaknesses, identify areas of improvement and needed training and motivate employees.

In addition to citizen ratings, the department should also conduct a self-assessment, perhaps through a committee established for this purpose.

As with individual performance evaluation, the department evaluation should be a continuous cycle of evaluating performance, identifying areas to improve, making adjustments and evaluating the results.

Partnerships

Another way to obtain community input is through focus groups, forums or roundtable discussions, which usually take about three hours and have three phases. First, citizens talk and management listens. Second, together they brainstorm ways to work together, using a 10/10 target, that is, coming up with 10 creative ideas in 10 minutes. They then evaluate the ideas and select those with merit. Third, they focus on implementation, setting up teams or task forces to implement and track the ideas. Groups should be kept small—eight to twelve participants—and should exclude competitors and have a trained facilitator.

A more formal approach to evaluating the entire department is through accreditation.

Accreditation

Accreditation is a process by which an institution or agency demonstrates that it meets set standards. Schools, colleges and hospitals frequently seek accreditation as recognition of their high quality. Institutions that lack accreditation are often considered inferior.

In 1979, four law enforcement agencies—the International Association of Chiefs of Police, the Police Executive Research Forum, the National Organization of Black Law Enforcement Executives and the National Sheriff's Association—established the Commission on Accreditation for Law Enforcement Agencies (CALEA). The purpose of CALEA was to set national standards against which agencies could evaluate themselves. The program is voluntary but involves a great amount of time and expense. Costs can range from $5,500 for small agencies to $22,000 for larger agencies. Currently CALEA has more than 500 agency members. Some states have also established standards and a process of accreditation, including California, Colorado, Idaho, Kentucky, New Hampshire, New York and Washington.

Accreditation consists of meeting a set of standards established by professionals in the field authorized to do so. Currently, accreditation may be granted by the Commission on the Accreditation of Law Enforcement Agencies (CALEA) or by some state agencies.

Accreditation provides a number of tangible benefits, including controlled liability insurance costs, fewer lawsuits and citizen complaints, stricter accountability within the agency and recognition of a department's ability to meet established standards. Intangible benefits include pride, recognition of excellence and peer approval. Everyone involved in the process gains a broader perspective of the agency, which ultimately leads to improved management.

Accreditation is not without its critics, however. In addition to the expense, some think that local and regional differences in agencies make a national set of standards unrealistic. Many agencies think the number of standards is simply overwhelming. Smaller agencies must usually meet 500 to 700 standards; larger agencies must usually meet more than 700 standards. Other critics contend that accreditation is like having a "big brother" overseeing their activities. Further, most of the standards deal with departmental administration rather than with its mission.

Sharp (2000, p.92) reports: "A recent poll of randomly selected law enforcement agencies indicated five major arguments against accreditation: too expensive, too time-consuming, dubious benefits, hard to justify to community government and department administration does not believe in accreditation." In this same poll, 54 percent responded that accreditation has an appreciable impact on how well an agency performs. Sixty percent said accreditation establishes accountability within the office. Sharp (p.95) also reports on a study conducted by the Intergovernmental Risk Management Agency which found that the number and severity of claims against departments dropped considerably in a comparison of CALEA and non-CALEA agencies: "The number of claims per 100 officers is reduced by 17 percent in frequency and 35 percent in severity when agencies are accredited by CALEA."

Accreditation and Community Policing

Controversy exists regarding the compatibility of accreditation standards and efforts to implement community policing. According to Cordner and Williams (1999, p.372): "Community policing and law enforcement agency accreditation are two of the most significant police reform initiatives of the late 20th century. Whether these two major developments, one primarily operational and the other mainly administrative, are compatible or in conflict emerged as a serious issue in the late 1980s and early 1990s."

After analyzing a variety of data, Cordner and Williams (p.377) conclude accreditation and community policing are compatible; accreditation does supports community policing to a limited extent; and the two reform strategies do not conflict directly, but there are some indirect tensions and strains in that COP and CALEA compete for resources and attention. Table 16.2 summarizes the degree of support found for various hypotheses regarding the relationship between community policing and accreditation.

Table 16.2
Summary of Support for 14 Hypotheses about the Relationship between Community Policing and Accreditation

Hypotheses	Support
The Anti-COP Hypothesis: accreditation directly conflicts with COP	Little or nor support
The Anti-POP Hypothesis: accreditation directly conflicts with POP	Little or no support
The Rigid Bureaucracy Hypothesis: accreditation creates formality which interferes with COP	Some support—mixed opinion
The Efficiency Hypothesis: accreditation's internal focus deflects attention from substantive problems in the community	Some support—mixed opinion
The Thin Blue Line Hypothesis: accreditation emphasizes accountability within the organization to the detriment of accountability to the community	Little support
The Style Over Substance Hypothesis: accreditation focuses attention on process rather than outcomes	Some support—mixed opinion
The Incident-Driven Hypothesis: accreditation takes an incident-oriented view to the detriment of the problem-oriented approach	Some support—mixed opinion
The Professional Model Hypothesis: accreditation implicitly favors the professional model over COP	Some support—mixed opinion
The Scarce Resources Hypotheses: accreditation and COP compete for resources and attention	General support
The Police Politics Hypothesis: supporters of COP and accreditation compete for status and influence	Little support
The Support Hypothesis: accreditation directly supports COP/POP	Some support—mixed opinion
The Neutrality Hypothesis: accreditation is neutral toward COP/POP	Some support—mixed opinion
The Flexibility Hypothesis: accreditation does not interfere with COP/POP because of the flexibility of the standards	General support
The Null Hypothesis: no conflict because supporting one or the other (or both accreditation and COP) has no real impact	Some support—but not from chiefs or experts

Source: Gary W. Cordner and Gerald L. Williams. "Community Policing and Police Agency Accreditation." In *Policing Perspectives: An Anthology*, edited by Larry K. Gaines and Gary W. Cordner. Los Angeles: Roxbury Publishing Company, 1999, p.377.

Evaluation and Research

This chapter has focused on evaluating individuals, teams and entire departments. Sometimes, however, administration wants to evaluate specific problems. In such cases, research is needed. One approach is using the SARA problem solving approach introduced in Chapter 4, identifying problems, analyzing current responses and available resources, exploring alternatives and assessing the results of implementing alternatives. Swope (2000, p.28) notes: "Program evaluation can provide departments with measures of success and show which plans, tactics and initiatives should be abandoned. Resources can be more efficiently and effectively directed as a result of program evaluation."

Two kinds of statistics are generally helpful in such research: descriptive statistics and inferential statistics. **Descriptive statistics** focus on simplifying, appraising, and summarizing data. **Inferential statistics** focus on making statistically educated guesses from a sample of data.

At other times administration wants to determine how well a specific program is working. In such instances administrators might want to familiarize themselves with the National Institute of Justice's "Research Partnerships in

Policing." The NIJ partnership program in policing complements the basic premise of community policing: working as partners achieves more than working alone. Such research partnerships typically consist of a local police department or other law enforcement agency and a local university and make extensive and effective use of graduate students. A valuable resource for departments wanting to undertake research is the Justice Research and Statistics Association (JRSA) whose Web site is www.jrsa.org. As Cordray (2000, p.401) cautions: "Randomized field experiments can provide trustworthy evidence about the effects of interventions. But, investigators have limited control over important features of the field experiment (e.g., program implementation, receipt of intended and unintended services, retention of participants in the study). Unchecked, these factors can limit the technical adequacy and utility of the study."

Challenging the Status Quo

Research can help evaluate traditional practices that may no longer be productive. Consider the story of the four monkeys and the cold shower:

> In a conditioning experiment, four monkeys were placed in a room. A tall pole stood in the center of the room, and a bunch of bananas hung suspended at the top of the pole. Upon noticing the fruit, one monkey quickly climbed up the pole and reached to grab the meal, at which time he was hit with a torrent of cold water from an overhead shower. The monkey quickly abandoned his quest and hurried down the pole. After the first monkey's failed attempt, the other three monkeys each climbed the pole in an effort to retrieve the bananas, and each received a cold shower before completing the mission. After repeated drenchings, the four monkeys gave up on the bananas.
>
> Next, one of the four original monkeys was replaced with a new monkey. When the new arrival discovered the bananas suspended overhead and tried to climb the pole, the three other monkeys quickly reached up and pulled the surprised monkey back down. After being prevented from climbing the pole several times but without ever having received the cold shower, the new monkey gave up trying to reach the bananas. One by one, each of the original monkeys was replaced, and each new monkey was taught the same lesson—don't climb the pole.
>
> None of the new monkeys ever made it to the top of the pole; none even got close enough to receive the cold shower awaiting them at the top. Not one monkey understood why pole climbing was prohibited, but they all respected the well-established precedent. Even when the shower was removed, no monkey tried to climb the pole. No one challenged the status quo.

What implications do this story and its lesson hold for managers? The realization that precedents, enacted into policy manuals, and training programs can far outlive the situational context that created them. Simply telling officers, "That's the way it's always been done," can do a great disservice to the organization as a whole. When officers don't know *what* they don't know and, worse yet, aren't even aware *that* they don't know, they are kept from empowerment, and problem-solving efforts are seriously compromised.

Encouraging officers to think creatively, tackle public safety issues through innovative problem solving and question the status quo if necessary are basic challenges facing law enforcement managers and certainly affect the future success of their agencies. This is the focus of the next chapter.

Summary

Evaluation can be informal or formal. Groups, organizations and individuals can all be evaluated.

Law enforcement managers' attitudes toward evaluation and their ability to evaluate are critical factors in whether an evaluation system works successfully. Managers who provide the most immediate direction of subordinates should do the evaluation. Purposes of evaluation include promoting common understanding of individual performance levels, needs, work objectives and standards; providing feedback and suggesting specific courses of action to take to improve, including training needs; and setting objectives for future performance. Evaluation may also help identify department-wide training needs and make decisions about promotions, reassignments, disciplinary actions and terminations. Basically, the purpose of performance evaluation is to improve employee performance.

Job standards make it easier for employees to meet requirements and managers to determine whether they have been met. Standards may include areas such as physical energy to perform and emotional stability while performing law enforcement tasks; individual judgment, reliability, loyalty and ability to get along with the public, fellow employees and managers; creativity and innovation; attitude; knowledge of tasks; competence; and amount of management required. By-the-numbers evaluation makes evaluation more objective by using a numerical scale for each dimension.

Evaluation should have consequences. Those who rate in the acceptable range might be considered for promotions, special assignments or pay raises. Those who rate below the acceptable range might be given counseling, training, a demotion, salary reduction, probation or, in extreme cases, termination.

Among the types of performance evaluation available to managers are ratings by individual traits or behaviorally anchored rating scales (BARS); group or composite ratings; critical incident ratings; narrative, essay or description; overall comparison ratings; composite ratings; and self-evaluation.

Performance interviews are private, one-on-one discussions of the performance appraisal by manager and subordinate. The performance appraisal interview should help employees do their jobs better and therefore improve individual performance and productivity. The most common recommendation for frequency of performance appraisals is twice a year and more frequently for employees performing below expectations.

Some problems of performance appraisals are lack of faith in appraisal systems, late-inning results count most, inaccurate numerical or forced-choice methods, unfair percentage ratings, rating personality rather than performance and rating at the extremes. To meet legal requirements, performance appraisal criteria must be job related.

In addition to citizen ratings, the department should conduct a self-assessment, perhaps through a committee established for this purpose. It might also consider seeking accreditation, which consists of meeting a set of standards established by professionals in the field authorized to do so. Currently, accreditation may be granted by the Commission on Accreditation of Law Enforcement Agencies (CALEA) or by some state agencies.

Discussion Questions

1. What are the advantages and disadvantages of informal evaluation? Formal evaluation?
2. What can law enforcement managers do to prepare for employee evaluation interviews?
3. What main change would you recommend for future performance evaluations?
4. Should performance evaluations be used for promotions? Transfers? New assignments? Pay increases?
5. Who should rate subordinates? One person or several?
6. What type rating do you like best?
7. What are some uses of performance evaluation?
8. Have you been formally evaluated? What was your opinion of the evaluation? Should such appraisals be retained?
9. What are the advantages and disadvantages of having subordinates evaluate their managers?
10. Do you favor or oppose national accreditation? State accreditation? Why?

InfoTrac College Edition Assignment

Use InfoTrac College Edition to answer the Discussion Questions as appropriate.

Find an article on *evaluation in law enforcement.* You might find it under different names, for example, *performance appraisals* or *assessment.* Summarize the article and include the full reference citation. Be prepared to share your summary with the class.

References

Bumgarner, Jeff. "Evaluating Law Enforcement Training." *The Police Chief,* November 2001, pp.32–36.

Cordner, Gary W. and Williams, Gerald L. "Community Policing and Police Agency Accreditation." In *Policing Perspectives: An Anthology,* edited by Larry K. Gaines and Gary W. Cordner. Los Angeles: Roxbury Publishing Company, 1999, pp.372–379.

Cordray, David S. "Enhancing the Scope of Experimental Inquiry in Intervention Studies." *Crime & Delinquency,* July 2000, pp.401–424.

Dees, Tim. "Performance Assessment and Review System." *Law and Order,* February 2001, pp.15–16.

Griggs, Thomas and McCorquodale, Staphanie. "Effective Medical Screening Can Safeguard an Aging Law Enforcement Workforce." *The Police Chief,* January 2001, pp.58–62.

Kaminsky, Glenn F. "First the Academy, then the FTO Program and Next . . .? Effective Utilization of the Probationary Period." *The Law Enforcement Trainer,* March/April 2001, pp.32–33.

Kenny, Sean. " 'S.W.A.T.' for Survival." *Police,* April 2000, pp.58–59.

King, William R. "Mailed Postcards as a High-Response-Rate-Data-Collection Instrument." *Police Quarterly,* June 2001, pp.253–258.

Kramer, Lorne C. and Fiedler, Mora L. "Beyond the Numbers: How Law Enforcement Agencies Can Create Learning Environments and Measurement Systems." *The Police Chief,* April 2002, pp.164–173.

Martin, Jeffery. "Making Appraisal Writing Easy." *The Police Chief,* May 2002, pp.49–53.

Martin, John A. and Matthews, Kurt. "Measuring an Agency's Performance." *Law and Order,* October 2000, pp.191–194.

Meehan, Mike. "Performance Evaluations of Field Training Officers." *The Police Chief,* November 2001, pp.25–30.

Moore, Mark; Thacher, David; Dodge, Andrea; and Moore, Tobias. *Recognizing Value in Policing: The Challenge of Measuring Police Performance.* Washington, DC: Police Executive Research Forum, 2002.

Rostow, Cary D. and Davis, Robert D. "Psychological Fitness-for-Duty Evaluations in Law Enforcement." *The Police Chief,* September 2002, pp.58–66.

Schultz, Ray and Acevedo, Art. "Ensuring the Physical Success of the Department." *Law and Order,* December 2000, pp.34–37.

Seiler, Roger. "Performance Appraisal System Gets High Marks." *Law Enforcement Technology,* May 2000, pp.107–108.

Sharp, Arthur G. "Accreditation: Fad or Fixture?" *Law and Order,* March 2000, pp.92–98.

Swope, Ross E. "Measuring Success." *The Police Chief,* March 2000, pp.28–37.

Book-Specific Web Site

Go to the *Management and Supervision in Law Enforcement* Web site at http://info.wadsworth.com/0534616054 for student and instructor resources, including Internet Assignments and Case Studies.

CHAPTER 17

Challenges in Managing for the Future

The best way to predict the future is to create it.
—Peter Drucker

Do You Know?

- What currently is most important in management skills?
- How the public will change in the future?
- What role technology will play in law enforcement work?
- What the major challenges facing law enforcement are?
- What four broad obstacles face local and state law enforcement in fighting terrorism?
- What the three basic principles of futuristics are?
- What the fundamental premises of futuristics are?
- What the three primary goals of futuristics are?
- What the boiled frog phenomenon is?
- How change should be viewed?

Can You Define?

bifurcated society	environmental scanning	privatization
boiled frog phenomenon	futuristics	

INTRODUCTION

Several changes in the law enforcement organization have already been discussed. Among the most important changes likely to affect management in the future are the following:

- Participative management, the manager as a leader
- Flattening of the organizational hierarchy
- The necessity to provide more services with fewer resources
- Better-educated law enforcement officers who are less willing to accept orders unquestioningly
- A shift in incentives, with intrinsic rather than extrinsic rewards becoming more motivational
- Implementing community policing and problem-oriented policing, including being proactive rather than reactive
- Developing partnerships with other agencies as well as with the public
- An increasingly diverse public to be served
- Privatization of services

This chapter examines global trends and the ways in which they will affect law enforcement, including what the future will demand of the law enforcement manager and the skills a manager will need to meet future challenges. Then, the changing U.S. population and advances in technology are examined. Next is a look at law enforcement's challenges in fighting drugs, violence and terrorism. This is followed by a discussion of privatization as well as futuristics, its potential for managers and how creativity and innovation are needed for managing law enforcement agencies of the future. The chapter concludes with a revisiting of change and the various ways it might be viewed by progressive managers to positively shape the future of law enforcement.

Megatrends—Looking to the Future

Naisbitt and Aburdene's *Megatrends 2000* (1990) noted the following worldwide trends:

> We are moving from an industrial society to an information society. Children are learning computer skills in school; adults will need special training to catch up to them.
>
> We are moving from forced technology to high tech/high touch. Although technology is stressed, it will not replace the need for human interaction.
>
> We are moving from a national economy to a world economy. To be successful is to be trilingual, that is, fluent in English, Spanish and computer-ese.
>
> We are moving from a short-term orientation to a long-term orientation. We need to pay attention to future trends and engage in long-range planning.
>
> We are moving from centralization to decentralization. More decisions, including major life decisions, are being made at the local level.
>
> We are moving from institutional help to self-help.
>
> We are moving from representative democracy to participatory democracy. Today's leaders need to be facilitators rather than order givers.
>
> We are moving from hierarchies to networks. The old power structure is disappearing, being replaced with teamwork, quality circles and participative decision making.

We are moving (physically) from the north to the south. Spanish is becoming more necessary.

We are moving from an either/or orientation to one of multiple options.

These global trends continue into the twenty-first century and have implications for our country, its citizens and those whose job it is to protect and police them.

Law Enforcement for the Future

Significant trends and challenges can be seen within law enforcement, most of which have been alluded to throughout this book. Having a clear mission is imperative for all law enforcement agencies. The mission statement of the Delray Beach (Florida) Police Department is exemplary (Dale, 2000, p.117): "We will be an organization that is fully trained and culturally acclimated to a partnership approach with the rest of the community to resolve problems, not only crime problems, but also problems involving social disorder and quality of life issues." To this statement the challenge of homeland security might be a fitting addition.

Dale surveyed 100 officers to identify the most pressing concerns for the future. Six major concerns were identified:

1. Employment—Hiring and retaining professional, ethical, educated, culturally diverse personnel
2. Budget—Competitive salary, unions, grants, taxes
3. Technology—Internal/external communication, training, managing technology
4. Crime—Juvenile, elderly, white-collar, computer, drugs
5. Growth—Population, diversity, geographic, build-out
6. Quality of life issues—Effective community policing, strategic management planning

A Basic Change in Needed Management Skills

One reason changes have been so overwhelming in past decades and will continue to be in the decades ahead is that the required management skills have changed.

Technical competence used to be most important. Now and in the years ahead, "people skills" are most important.

Woodward and Buchholz (1987, pp.13–14) explain it this way:

> One way to visualize this tactical, people-oriented approach is with a bicycle. The two wheels of a bicycle have different purposes. The back wheel powers the bike; the front wheel steers it. Extending this analogy to an organization, "back-wheel" skills are the technical and organizational skills needed for the organization to function. "Front-wheel" skills are the interpersonal "people management" skills. Corporations tend to rely on their back-wheel, that is, their technical skills.
>
> Typically, however, when change comes, the response of organizations is primarily back-wheel response—do what we know best. But the real need is for front-wheel skills, that is, helping people understand and adapt to the changing environment.

Winning coaches know that games are not won or lost in the fourth quarter or the ninth inning. The outcome of any game is determined by the amount of preparation. Law enforcement managers must possess a combination of technical skills and people skills to successfully guide their departments through the new millennium.

A Changing Public to Be Served

One of the most significant changes for modern law enforcement is the increasing diversity of the U.S. population. Numerous social changes have affected law enforcement and will continue to affect it in the future.

The public to be served will include more two-income families, more single-parent families, more senior citizens and more minorities. The educational and economic gap will increase, with those at the bottom becoming more disadvantaged and dissatisfied.

The necessity for two-income families has increased the need for daycare centers, some without security-checked personnel. This has produced problems of child and sexual abuse, which have gained national attention. On the other hand, development of work-at-home programs has helped those who want added income but also want to remain at home to care for their children. Preset performance standards make this possible without regard for when or where the work is actually performed.

The high rate of divorce has changed family relationships. R. Morton Darrow, speaking at the National Press Club, stated: "With growing divorce and remarriage, the United States is moving from a nation in which parents had many children to one where children have many parents. This results in different needs and pressures in the family."

In addition, our population is aging. The baby boomers have turned 50, and by 2010 one-fourth of all Americans will be at least 55 years old. More efforts will need to be spent on crime prevention and on support programs for older adults. Minorities will also increase, requiring law enforcement officers to be able to deal with many divergent social and ethnic groups.

Another change is that the educational gap is increasing, with those at the bottom becoming even more disadvantaged. As the gap widens, economic opportunities dwindle and frustrations increase. The gap between the haves and the have-nots is widening significantly, with the likely result being social unrest. The United States is becoming a **bifurcated society,** with more wealth, more poverty and a shrinking middle class.

The smokestack America of the early 1900s has been battered by the most accelerated technological revolution in history. Computers, satellites, space travel, fiber optics, fax machines, robots, bar coding, electronic data interchange and expert systems are only the most obvious manifestations. All this has been combined with globalization of the economy, rising competition and many social and cultural changes as well.

Advances in Technology

Brown (2001, pp.1, 20) notes: "Law enforcement, like every other profession in America, has been hard-pressed to keep up with the lightning speed of technological change. Every task required by law enforcement work has been transformed by more sophisticated computer software programs, thermal imaging cameras, DNA testing, face scanning technology, voice recognition software . . . the list is endless."

Scoville (2001, p.27) contends: "In the field, we've become walking, talking circuitry [officers], with cameras on our dashboards and lapels. We carry microcassette recorders in our pockets and run subjects on our MDTs. We're decked out in improved ballistic vests, using safer traffic radar and getting quicker access to pertinent information. Throughout, we're only a click of a portable away from backup." He (pp.28–29) believes that the top five innovations for officers on the line have been ballistic vests, the portable video camera, the automated wants and warrants system, portable radios and laptops.

Technology will continue to enhance law enforcement in communications, records, evaluation and investigation. Rapid availability and dissemination of restricted and confidential information assists investigators and results in increased apprehensions of criminals. At the same time, technology reduces the need for traditional reports and record keeping. Officers spend less time completing official reports and have more time for field activities.

Technology will expand in all phases of law enforcement and will greatly enhance efficiency. It will be increasingly imperative for most law enforcement personnel to be computer literate.

AP Photo/Pittsburgh Tribune–Review, Warren L. Leader

Advances in technology will continue to enhance law enforcement in communications, records, evaluation and investigation. A technician at Eltech Security Systems in Allison Park, Pennsylvania, demonstrates a remote wireless camera.

Technology allows administration to know better how time is actually being spent and how it should be spent. Tracking officer activities can be more immediate, but it should not be done to the point where officers lose their sense of reasonable freedom and control over decisions.

Keeping abreast of innovations in technology can be a major challenge, especially for smaller departments. According to the IACP (Deck et al., 2001, p.43): "The acquisition and use of technology has redefined policing in America, and law enforcement technology use promises to grow. The IACP views this explosion of technology and the uses as predominantly positive." The IACP offers several resources and initiatives to help agencies select and use emerging technologies. Their publication *A Best Practices Guide: Acquisition of New Technology* includes an acquisition plan, acquisition and delivery, and implementation and training recommendations. The guide is available on the Internet at decke@theiacp.org.

Major Challenges in the Twenty-First Century

In addition to the challenges of drugs and violence, law enforcement is heavily focused on homeland security.

The Drug Problem

The national and international drug problem has placed law enforcement officers on the front line, not only in enforcing drug laws but also in establishing drug undercover operations and participative community programs. The drug problem is of such magnitude that no single individual, segment of society or government can resolve the problem, which means that no segment can move ahead alone. An attack on one segment of society must be accepted as an attack on all.

In 1989 the drug problem was the largest single issue and concern in the nation. The public still expects law enforcement organizations to deal with this problem. Many federal resources will have to be devoted to it, and law enforcement entities must develop new approaches to meet the local challenge. Resolving the problem may involve reducing individual civil liberties in the interest of overall social well being.

In February 2002, President Bush set a goal of cutting drug abuse by 25 percent in five years through greater efforts toward prevention, treatment of addicts and improved law enforcement ("Bush Goal. . .," 2002, p.A7). Suggested approaches to address the drug problem include crime control, punishment, rehabilitation, prevention and legalization, as summarized in Figure 17.1.

These approaches should support the five goals of the *National Drug Control Strategy* (2000, p.1): (1) to educate and enable America's youths to reject illegal drugs as well as alcohol and tobacco, (2) to increase the safety of America's citizens by substantially reducing drug-related crime and violence, (3) to reduce health and social costs to the public of illegal drug use, (4) to shield America's air, land and sea frontiers from the drug threat and (5) to break foreign and domestic drug sources of supply.

Military measures may have to be instituted to support law enforcement's efforts to control the militant and terrorist tactics of drug lords to protect their

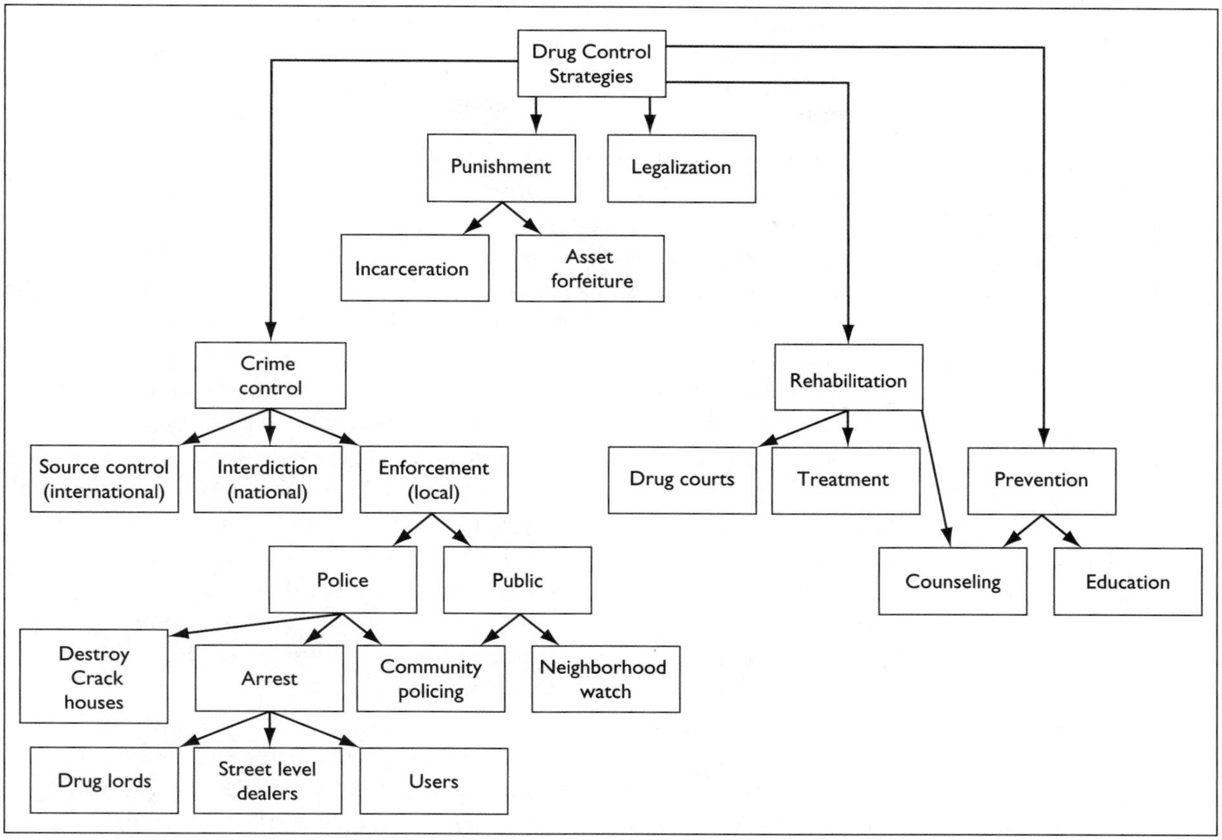

Figure 17.1
Overview of Drug-Control Strategies

Source: Henry M. Wrobleski and Kären M. Hess. *Introduction to Law Enforcement and Criminal Justice*, 7th ed. Belmont, CA: Thomson/Wadsworth Publishing Company, 2003, p.304.

huge monetary rewards. This is a war in which all willing and unwilling participants have been losers, either financially or in terms of human distress and suffering. Drastic measures will be necessary to bring about a resolution.

A closely related problem, often linked with drug dealing and gangs, is violence.

Violence

One of the greatest challenges facing law enforcement is increasing violence. The Los Angeles riots following the Rodney King verdict caught the nation's attention. But this was not an isolated event. In Chicago in 1992, for example, after the Bulls won their second NBA title, violence erupted. Two police officers were shot, and more than 90 others suffered injuries.

Domestic and family violence is increasingly drawing the attention of law enforcement, including not only spousal abuse, but also child abuse and elder abuse. The Internet has complicated this challenge, with adults stalking other adults and children online. In addition, violence has taken its toll in our schools across the country with mass shootings. According to Small and Tetrick (2001, p.3): "Crime and violence in schools are matters of significant public concern, particularly after the spate of tragic school shootings in recent years." Workplace violence has also captured national headlines. According to a survey of Fortune 1000 companies, workplace violence was found to be the leading concern of security managers at America's largest corporations for the third straight year ("Violence in the Workplace . . .," 2001, p.42).

Yet another challenge is urban terrorism, which was vividly illustrated in the sniper-shooting spree in the fall of 2002 with 13 people shot, 10 of them fatally, over a three-week period on the nation's east coast. The country was transfixed, and yet, Wexler (2002, p.11) questions why the American public does not show the same "angst over other homicides." He notes: "During the same time, the Washington region experienced 18 'routine' homicides related to gangs, drugs, domestic violence and other common causes. There were also numerous automobile fatalities and accidents. Why have we not shown the same fear, anxiety and demand for action each month when such violence occurs in our cities?" He concludes: "And while we would like to think this is the end of such senseless violence here at home, there is a sense that the other shoe will someday drop. Many fear it is not the end, as various forms of terrorist threats loom." Indeed, preparing for and appropriately responding to terrorist attacks has become a top priority at all levels of law enforcement.

Homeland Security

Olin (2002, p.27) observes: "September 11 marked a profound and fundamental change in the terrorist conflict. The United States was attacked with resulting mass casualties, destruction of property valued at more than a hundred billion dollars, an economic crisis, and deployment of troops in a war to disrupt future terrorism against our country." He notes: "How tens of thousands of law enforcement officers and thousands of law enforcement agencies evolve in handling the future threats against our country will, in large part, determine how modern civilization fares against a determined foe." According to Olin: "Every law enforcement officer needs basic information on the terrorists' motivation, tactics and threats." In addition, he (p.28) stresses: "Every law enforcement agency in the United States should continue with its community policing emphasis to strengthen the connections between citizens and government."

Samuels (2002, p.6) contends: "The seeds of despair sown by the events of September 11 can yield gardens of hope. . . . The roles we perform and the responsibilities we bear are evolving as a result of a shared and willful commitment to combat terrorism." Hoover (2002, p.1), likewise, notes: "State and local police agencies are facing a significant challenge in the wake of September 11. The federal government is asking for their substantive involvement in the homeland security effort." He outlines four broad categories of obstacles facing state and local law enforcement agencies in the terrorism intelligence effort.

Four broad categories of obstacles facing state and local law enforcement agencies in the terrorism intelligence effort are technological, logistical, political and ethical.

The need for homeland security was brought to the forefront by the events of September 11, 2001. A rescue helicopter surveys damages to the Pentagon Building as fire fighters battle flames after terrorists crashed an airliner into the U.S. Millitary Headquarters, outside Washington, DC.

According to Hoover (p.1): "The *technological* issue that most challenges state and local participation in any national anti-terrorism intelligence effort can be summarized by one word—interoperability. The inability to exchange information on a regional and statewide level is overwhelmingly the primary issue." He suggests: "Some existing programs designed for drug trafficking information sharing might be able to serve concurrently as a homeland security database, hastening the implementation process." According to Hoover (p.4): "Data entry is the most problematic of the *logistical* issues. It is observed that if intelligence officers spend all day entering data, they are not doing very much intelligence analysis."

Of the four obstacles, Hoover contends: "By far the most serious impediments to establishing a national interconnected antiterrorism database are *political.* There are several levels of political issues. . . . First and foremost among these is the issue of 'who pays for this.' " Other political issues include linkages to the Immigration and Naturalization Service (INS), relationship with the FBI and with state police, the need for confidentiality (viewed as secrecy by many local agencies) and the role of intelligence.

The final obstacle is *ethical,* including the possibility of racial profiling, the problem of open records legislation and new concerns about infringing on individuals' privacy and civil rights through new wiretapping laws.

In July 2002, the first *National Strategy for Homeland Security* was released, providing direction for steps that can be taken by local and state law enforcement agencies, private companies and organizations and individual Americans

("National Strategy for Homeland Security Released," 2002, p.7). The *Strategy* lists the strategic objectives of homeland security in order of priority as:

- Prevent terrorist attacks within the United States.
- Reduce America's vulnerability to terrorism.
- Minimize the damage and recover from attacks that do occur.

The new Department of Homeland Security (DHS) brings together 22 entities with critical homeland security missions, providing a single federal department whose primary mission is to protect our nation against terrorist threats.

Doubtless, community policing efforts can and must play a large role in homeland security, with citizens serving as eyes and ears for local law enforcement. In addition, privatization will become increasingly important.

Privatization

One significant trend in law enforcement even before September 11th was **privatization,** that is, either contracting out or working collaboratively with private security agencies, other governmental agencies and individuals or organizations that can help a police department fulfill its mission. Private laboratories may be used to test seized evidence, and private companies may screen applicants or do civilian fingerprinting. Private security officers may be stationed in courthouses, government buildings and airports.

The gap between private sector industry and public law enforcement is narrowing. One good indication of this is the formation of the IACP's Private Sector Liaison Committee (PSLC). The PSLC was founded in 1986 to develop and implement cooperative strategies for the enhancement of public law enforcement and private sector relationships in the interest of the public good. Among the areas the committee is addressing are drugs in the workplace, combating workplace drug crimes, false alarm perspectives, combating workplace violence and most importantly after September 11th, working together for homeland security. As Samuels (pp.6–7) stresses: "Private-sector security represents a vast and vital resource, and we must strengthen our existing partnership with this profession. The events of September 11, the frequency and impact of public protests resulting in civil disobedience or criminal violations, and the fiscal and psychological consequences of Internet-related crimes demonstrate a need for greater communication and cooperation."

According to Dominguez (2001, p.134): "By partnering with local residents, associations and police, companies can help create programs that benefit the whole community." Paynter (2000, p.6), likewise, suggests:

> Privatization of policing services appears to answer some of policing's present woes. By partnering with private organizations, law enforcement may be able to address the public's calls for increased policing services and better focus on its primary function, which is to combat crime.
>
> The public employs police officers to maintain order, enforce the laws, patrol the streets and keep the roadways safe. But other policing functions, such as general assistance, administrative support services and other tasks, might be offloaded to the private sector.
>
> A private firm could provide services such as funeral escorts, directing traffic around an accident, citing parking violations, responding to burglary alarms

(95–99 percent of which are generally false), etc. These services do not require police training, but can occupy up to 80 percent of an officer's time and waste an agency's limited resources.

How much privatization will occur, in addition to how effectively law enforcement will meet the special challenges ahead of it, are addressed by futuristics.

Futuristics

As a profession, law enforcement has relied too heavily on experience and not enough on innovation. Futuristics is a new tool for criminal justice executives. People who study the future use **environmental scanning,** that is they identify factors likely to "drive" the environment. Three categories of change likely to affect the future criminal justice system they study are:

1. Social and economic conditions (size and age of the population, immigration patterns and nature of employment and lifestyle characteristics)
2. Shifts in the number and types of crimes and disorder challenges
3. Developments in the criminal justice system itself, including community involvement in all aspects of the system

Futuristics is the science of using data from the past to forecast alternatives for the future and to then select the most desirable.

Forecasting, a form of futuristics, is similar to the headlights on a car being driven in a snowstorm. The lights provide enough illumination to continue but not enough so the driver can proceed without caution. What lies ahead is still unknown. Futuristics is not something mystical or prophetic. It combines historical facts, scientific principles and departmental values with vision to imagine what could happen in the future. The Society of Police Futurists International was founded in 1991 by Dr. William Tafoya. PFI is dedicated to futures research in policing, and to stimulating new ideas on a variety of policing theories and practices. Futuristics rests on three basic principles or assumptions about the nature of the universe and our role in it (Tafoya, 1983, p.13).

The three basic principles of futuristics are as follows:
- The unity or interconnectedness of reality
- The significance of ideas
- The crucial importance of time

The *unity* or *interconnectedness of reality* suggests that we operate in a "holistic universe, a huge mega-system, the activities of whose systems, subsystems and components interface and interact in synergistic fashion."

The *significance of ideas,* the second basic principle of futuristics, emphasizes the quest for new and better ways of doing things—exploring divergent new ways to deal with old problems and imagining new ways to anticipate potential problems.

The third basic principle, the *importance of time,* suggests a future focus. Rather than being absorbed with today's problems and holding on to traditions, futurists think five years ahead and beyond. Futuristics often uses the following time frames (p.15):

Immediate future	Present to 2 years
Short-range future	2 to 5 years
Mid-range future	5 to 10 years
Long-range future	10 to 20 years
Extended-range future	20 to 50 years
Distant future	50 years and beyond

Law enforcement managers tend to focus on the immediate future, dealing with problems that need resolution, trying to stay "on top of things" and "putting out fires." No wonder they do not notice a mere 2 to 4-percent annual increase in the crime rate. The crisis faced today is probably a minor one that was ignored yesterday. Time is significant. Do not let it be said of the future that it is "that time when you'll wish you'd done what you aren't doing now." According to Richards (2000, p.8): "Planning stands not as an attempt to predict the future but as the best chance for survival in a world that is constantly changing." He (p.10) stresses: "Administrators should not allow time constraints imposed by outside influences to short-circuit the planning process."

Futurists also operate under three fundamental premises (p.15):

Fundamental premises of futurists are the following:

- The future is not predictable.
- The future is not predetermined.
- Future outcomes can be influenced by individual choice.

The third premise is critical to managers because the choices that are made today *will* affect law enforcement in the future. As has been said, "The future is coming. Only you can decide where it's going." How can futuristics be used in law enforcement management? Tafoya suggests three primary priorities or goals (p.17):

Goals of futuristics:

- Form perceptions of the future (the possible).
- Study likely alternatives (the probable).
- Make choices to bring about particular events (the preferable).

> If people are to influence future outcomes, perceptions of the future must be formed. . . . Be alert to risks as well as opportunities. What is possible is what "could be;" this key role is characterized as *image-driven.* . . . What is required

> is breaking the fetters of one's imagination. It is the vital, *creative goal* of futuristics.
>
> Once new images have been generated, likely alternatives must be studied. The probable path to the future must be analyzed; quantitatively as well as qualitatively. . . . What is probable is what "may be;" this aim is characterized as *analytically driven.* It is the detached, systematic and *scientific goal* of futuristics.
>
> Having imagined the possible and analyzed the probable, it is necessary to make choices among alternatives. . . . What is preferred is what "should be;" this intent is characterized as *value-driven.* It is the *managerial, decision-making goal* of futuristics.

Remember: The future never comes. It is like tomorrow. We can only function in today—but what we do today will influence all the todays to come. Managers must be forward looking and willing to accept changes as well as opportunities.

The Need for Creativity and Innovation

Creativity and innovation in law enforcement must continue in the decades ahead. Considerable impetus for innovative projects was provided through past Law Enforcement Assistance Administration (LEAA)-funded programs. Much of this impetus has been retained mentally but slowed by decreased funding. Many improvements in law enforcement can be continued or developed within existing budgets and with existing personnel. These programs involve improvements in everyday activities.

One responsibility of managers is to examine and be creative about each task to be performed. Determine how each task can be done better and involve the task-doer in the process. Give subordinates input and control over what they do to increase a sense of contribution and well being on the job and to reduce stress. Many law enforcement tasks generate a high degree of stress. Stress experts state that lack of control on the job is an additional stress producer. Getting the job done better and reducing stress at the same time is one key to future healthy officers.

Management should encourage creativity even at the cost of failures. Experimentation failures must be accepted as part of the process of growth and development. Edison did not fail 25,000 times to make a storage battery. He knew 25,000 ways NOT to make one.

Officers who know that punishment will follow failure will not take the risks necessary for individual and departmental growth. Therefore, managers should encourage reasonable risk taking. They might encourage subordinates to think creatively and take risks by posting slogans such as the following in prominent places:

- Don't be afraid to go out on a limb. That's where the fruit is.
- Don't be afraid to take a big step if one is indicated. You can't cross a chasm in two small jumps.
- If you're made of the right material, a hard fall will result in a high bounce.

Those involved in research understand that failures are the stepping-stones to success. "Nothing ventured, nothing gained" remains true for the future and applies to law enforcement managers at all levels and to their subordinates.

Creativity and innovation do not automatically involve large amounts of money. Often they require only the present level of personnel and equipment but used more efficiently. The future of law enforcement depends on federal financial and research assistance, supported by state and local willingness to support creativity and freedom on the job.

Creativity results from extending, searching into the unknown and trying the untried. It is risky. It may fail. In law enforcement, creativity means viewing a police problem in a new way, having a new idea.

Everyone can create, but few do. Studies indicate no relationship between high I.Q. and creativity. What is unique about creative people is that they keep trying. In the process they make mistakes but accept them and move on to the next idea. Creative people take time to dream.

Everyone reading this book can be creative. Have you ever said to yourself, "Why didn't I think of that before?" Creativity is nonconformity, not in the destructive sense of being difficult to get along with but in the useful, positive sense.

In police work, every task can be accomplished better. We need police who use their minds to create these better ways. Creativity means thinking of a better technique for handling domestics and, when successfully applied, thinking of an even better way. To give creativity a chance to work, try some of the following options:

- Take time out to research a specific subject.
- Delay a decision until you have time to think about it and perhaps sleep on it.
- When you feel mentally blocked, take a walk down the hall or outside the building.
- Expand your mental capabilities by going beyond what is known.
- Concentrate on a small part of the problem and deal with that.
- Consider different options and alternatives.
- Instead of everyone sitting down at a meeting, stand up.

Thinking traps and mental locks described in Chapter 4 are relevant as a department strives for innovation. Other obstacles may exist in the form of politics, restrictions mandated by union contracts, local ordinances, special interest groups and so on.

Change Revisited

Sewell (2002, p.14) notes: "According to some futurists, changes in a society occur in several major areas, directly affecting law enforcement." These include changes in the society itself, in technology, in the economy and in the environment, as well as political changes. McLagan (2002, p.26) points out: "Change is an increasingly important focus of attention in today's organizations. Globalization, advances in information and workplace technology, and increasing sophistication of the social sciences are some of the reasons for the big interest." As noted by Sewell (p.14): "The needs of communities and constituencies, rapid technological growth and enhancements, and the changing capabilities and structures of law enforcement demand that agencies regularly examine and improve their ways of operation."

Change can occur in one of two ways—changing individuals or changing the organizational structure. The changing process itself involves three phases:

1. Unfreezing of an old pattern or relationship
2. Changing to a new behavior pattern
3. Freezing the new pattern

It often takes a catastrophe such as the attacks on America on September 11, 2001, to bring about change. Without such an impetus, initiating change may be difficult. Sparrow (1988, p.1) makes a classic analogy, comparing changes in policing to driving a 50-ton semi:

> The professional truck driver . . . avoids braking sharply. He treats corners with far greater respect. And he generally does not expect the same instant response from the trailer, with its load, that he enjoys in his car. The driver's failure to understand the implications and responsibilities of driving such a massive vehicle inevitably produces tragedy: if the driver tries to turn too sharply, the cab loses traction as the trailer's momentum overturns or jackknifes the vehicle.

Police organizations also have considerable momentum. Having a strong personal commitment to the values with which they have "grown up," police officers may find hints of proposed change in the police culture extremely threatening.

Buggé (2001, p.40) explains that change is a process: "Like any process, it goes through stages. Your job will be to properly manage or coordinate those stages." The first stage is planning. During the planning stage, it is important to create a concept officers can rally behind. The second stage is implementation. Buggé (p.42) suggests that at this stage you call the change an experiment, which some call the Delta Technique. He notes that people fear change but they seldom fear experiments. The third stage is assimilation: "Full assimilation eventually will follow if the change process is managed correctly" (p.44).

Often what is needed is change in the very culture of an agency. Fullan (2002, p.19) contends: "Transforming culture—changing what people in the organization value and how they work together to accomplish it—leads to deep, lasting change."

Sparrow (p.2) notes: "A huge ship can . . . be turned by a small rudder. It just takes time." The amount of time needed will vary from agency to agency, but managers should avoid becoming victims of the boiled frog phenomenon.

The Boiled Frog Phenomenon

The **boiled frog phenomenon** suggests that managers must pay attention to change in their environment and adapt—or perish.

The boiled frog phenomenon rests on a classic experiment. A frog is dropped into a pan of boiling water and immediately jumps out, saving its life. Next, a frog is placed into a pan of room-temperature water that is gradually heated to the boiling point. Because the temperature rise is so gradual, the frog does not notice it and sits contentedly in the bottom of the pan. The gradually rising temperature initially makes the frog comfortable but eventually saps its energy. As the water becomes too hot, the frog has no strength to jump out. It boils to death.

Planning for the Future

Richards (2000) suggests that: "Administrators should anticipate potential contingencies, continuously prepare for them and regularly review any existing plans." Richards (p.12) concludes:

> Law enforcement administrators can free themselves from their long-held belief that planning for the future stands as a tedious and formidable task by following some basic procedures. These include developing the plan through defining the problem, gathering relevant facts, developing alternative approaches and evaluating the effects. Once they have completed these planning phases, administrators can decide on their course of action, develop a written plan and then test it for potential problems. . . .
>
> Administrators also should encourage and challenge their subordinates to plan for the future. All law enforcement professionals should remember that those who fail to plan, fail to achieve.

Acceptance of Change

Change is inevitable. No person or organization can stop it. Managers must accept that the only constant is change. Whether change is positive or negative is characterized by Enright (1984) this way:

> A branch floats peacefully down a river whose waters are high with the spring run-off. Although the branch is floating rapidly and occasionally bumps gently into a rock, it is almost effortlessly motionless in relation to the water it floats in.
>
> A similar branch has become wedged between some rocks and is thus resisting the swift flow of water around it. This branch is buffeted, whipped and battered by the water and debris floating past it, and will soon be broken by the pressures against it (unless it dislodges and "goes with the flow"). If branches could experience, the one wedged into the rocks would be experiencing change with intense pain and distress; the floating one would experience ease and, paradoxically, comfortable stability even in the midst of rapid motion.

Change is inevitable. View it as opportunity.

The future is not a result of choices among alternative paths offered by the present but a place that is created—created first in mind and will, created next in activity. Ten two-letter words sum it up: *If it is to be, it is up to me.*

> We have trained [people] to think of the future as a promised land which favored heroes attain—not as something which everyone reaches at the same rate of 60 minutes an hour, whatever he does, whoever he is.
>
> —C. S. Lewis

> The future is not some place we are going to, but one we are creating. The paths are not to be found, but made, and the activity of making them changes both the maker and the destination.
>
> —John Schaar

Summary

The law enforcement career will be a continuous process of everyday learning at a rapid pace. Technical competence used to be most important. Now and in the years ahead, people skills are most important.

The public to be served will include more two-income families, more single-parent families, more senior citizens and more minorities. The educational and economic gaps will increase, with those at the bottom becoming more disadvantaged and dissatisfied. Technology will be used in all phases of law enforcement and will greatly enhance efficiency. It will be imperative for most law enforcement personnel to be computer literate. In addition to the challenges of drugs and violence, law enforcement is facing the challenge of homeland security. Four broad categories of obstacles facing state and local law enforcement agencies in the terrorism intelligence effort are technological, logistical, political and ethical. In planning to meet the challenges facing law enforcement, managers can benefit from futuristics.

Futuristics is the science of using data from the past to forecast alternatives for the future and to then select the most desirable. The three basic principles of futuristics are (1) the unity or interconnectedness of reality, (2) the significance of ideas and (3) the crucial importance of time. Fundamental premises of futurists are that the future is not predictable, the future is not predetermined and future outcomes can be influenced by individual choice. Goals of futuristics include:

- Form perceptions of the future (the possible).
- Study likely alternatives (the probable).
- Make choices to bring about particular events (the preferable).

The boiled frog phenomenon suggests that managers must pay attention to change in their environment and adapt—or perish. Change is inevitable. View it as opportunity.

Discussion Questions

1. What should be law enforcement's role in the drug problem? In the violence problem? The challenge of homeland security?
2. Do you think creativity can be learned? Why or why not?
3. What would be the advantages of "flattening" the hierarchy? Disadvantages?
4. What trends do you foresee in the future of policing?
5. What is the importance of innovation and creativity in a law enforcement organization?
6. What do you see for the future development of your law enforcement agency?
7. How would you meet the decline of law enforcement resources?
8. What changes do you think are needed in the selection of future officers?

9. What major changes have you experienced in the past year? The past five years? How well did you handle them?

10. How can you best prepare for the inevitability of change in your life and your career?

InfoTrac College Edition Assignment

Use InfoTrac College Edition Edition to answer the Discussion Questions as appropriate.

Find one journal article on *the future* in general. Find another article on *the future of law enforcement or criminal justice.* Summarize each article, including the full reference citation. Be prepared to share your summaries with the class.

OR

Read and outline one of the following articles:

- "Planning for the Future" by Robert B. Richards
- "Managing the Stress of Organizational Change" by James D. Sewell

References

Brown, Cynthia. "Struggling to Keep Pace." *American Police Beat,* April 2001, pp.1, 20–23.

Buggé, Brian. "The Art of Managing Change." *Security Technology and Design,* December 2001, pp.40–44.

"Bush Goal: Cut Drug Abuse 25% in Five Years." Associated Press, as reported in the (Minneapolis/St.Paul) *Star Tribune,* February 13, 2002, p.A7.

Dale, Nancy. "Survival Strategies for the Next Decade." *Law and Order,* October 2000, pp.117–122.

Deck, Elaine; Hicks, Jennifer; and Nichols, Laura J. "Law Enforcement in the 21st Century: IACP Technology Initiatives." *The Police Chief,* September 2001, pp.43–48.

Dominguez, Louis G. "How Can Security Help the Community?" *Security Management,* October 2001, p.134.

Enright, John. "Change and Resilience." *The Leader Manager.* Eden Prairie, MN: Wilson Learning Corporation, 1984.

Fullan, Michael. "The Change Leader." *Educational Leadership,* May 2002, pp.16–20.

Hoover, Larry T. "The Challenges to Local Police Participation in the Homeland Security Effort." *Subject to Debate,* October 2002, pp.1–10.

McLagan, Patricia A. "Change Leadership Today." *TD,* November 2002, pp.26–31.

Naisbitt, John and Aburdene, Patricia. *Megatrends 2000: Ten New Directions for the 1990s.* New York: William Morrow & Co., 1990.

National Drug Control Strategy, 2000 Annual Report. Washington, DC: Office of National Drug Control Policy, 2000. (NCJ 180085)

"National Strategy for Homeland Security Released." *NCJA Justice Bulletin,* July 2002, pp.7–10.

Olin, W. Ronald. "Why Traditional Law Enforcement Methods Cannot Win the War on Terrorism." *The Police Chief,* November 2002, pp.27–31.

Paynter, Ronnie. "Privatization: Something to Think About?" *Law Enforcement Technology,* September 2000, p.6.

Richards, Robert B. "Planning for the Future." *FBI Law Enforcement Bulletin,* January 2000, pp.8–12.

Samuels, Joseph, Jr. "The Challenge Before Us." *The Police Chief,* November 2002, pp.6–9.

Scoville, Dern. "Ch-Ch-Ch-Ch-Changes." *Police,* July 2001, pp.26–29.

Sewell, James D. "Managing the Stress of Organizational Change." *FBI Law Enforcement Bulletin,* March 2002, pp.14–20.

Small, Margaret and Tetrick, Kellie Dressler. "School Violence: An Overview." *Juvenile Justice,* June 2001, pp.3–12.

Sparrow, Malcolm K. "Implementing Community Policing." *Perspectives on Policing,* November 1988, pp.20–49.

Tafoya, William L. "Futuristics: New Tools for Criminal Justice Executives: Part I." Presentation at the 1983 annual meeting of the Academy of Criminal Justice Sciences, March 22–26, 1983, San Antonio, Texas.

"Violence in the Workplace: Still Number One Security Threat for Fortune 1000 Corporate Security Managers." *Security Products,* July 2001, p.42.

Wexler, Chuck. "A Form of Terror." *Subject to Debate,* October 2002, pp.2, 11.

Woodward, Harry and Buchholz, Steve. *Aftershock: Helping People through Corporate Change.* New York: John Wiley and Sons, 1987.

Book-Specific Web Site

Go to the *Management and Supervision in Law Enforcement* Web site at http://info.wadsworth.com/0534616054 for student and instructor resources, including Internet Assignments and Case Studies.

APPENDIX A

Sample Application Form

DEPARTMENT OF ADMINISTRATION
4801 West 50th Street • Edina, Minnesota 55424-1394
(612) 927-8861 TDD(612) 927-5461

DATE RECEIVED

OFFICE USE ONLY

Employment Application

THE CITY OF EDINA WELCOMES YOU as an applicant for employment. Your application will be considered with others in competition for the position in which you are interested. It is our policy to provide equal employment opportunities to all. Individuals are evaluated and selected solely on the basis of their qualifications.

Please furnish complete and accurate information so that the City of Edina can properly evaluate your application.

Be warned that the use of false or misleading information or the omission of important facts may be grounds for immediate dismissal. Also note that information you provide herein may be subject to later verification and/or testing.

You may attach to this application any additional information that helps explain your qualifications.

Please print clearly or type.

Personal Information				
Name	Last	First	Middle	Previous
Present Address	Street	City	State	Zip Code
Permanent Address	Street	City	State	Zip Code
Telephone	Residence	Business	May we call you at work? ☐ Yes	☐ No
Are you between the ages of 16 and 70?		☐ Yes	☐ No	If "No", state date of birth:
Do you have a Social Security Number?		☐ Yes	☐ No	

Work Preferences	
Position for which you are applying (or type of work in which you are interested):	*Are you interested in . . .* ☐ Full-Time ☐ Part-Time ☐ Seasonal ☐ Paid on call ☐ Volunteer ■ Date available for work: ____________________

General Information

Have you previously been employed by the City of Edina? ☐ Yes ☐ No — If "Yes," Dates ______ Position ______

Do you have relatives or in-laws working for the City of Edina? ☐ Yes ☐ No — If "Yes," who:

How did you hear about a job at the City of Edina?

☐ Came in on my own ______	☐ Other (Specify) ______
☐ City employee ______	☐ Newspaper (Specify) ______
☐ School (Specify) ______ (Counselor) ______	☐ Employment Agency ______ (Specify) ______

Have you ever been convicted of a crime for which a jail sentence of more than 90 days could have been imposed? ☐ Yes ☐ No

Have you ever been convicted of a felony? ☐ Yes ☐ No

You may answer "No" to these questions if the conviction or criminal records thereof have been annulled, expunged, sealed, set aside or purged, or if you have been pardoned pursuant to law. Before any applicant is rejected on the basis of a criminal conviction, he or she will be notified in writing and will be given any rights to processing of complaints or grievances afforded by Minnesota Statute Chapter 364. If the answer to this question is "Yes," please attach a separate sheet of paper giving full particulars.

If you are not a citizen of the United States, do you have a valid work permit? ☐ Yes ☐ No Number______

Do you have a valid Drivers License? ☐ Yes ☐ No State:______ Class:______

Are you subject to a child support or spousal maintenance order? ☐ Yes ☐ No

If "Yes," are you subject to withholding for child support or spousal maintenance? ☐ Yes ☐ No

Education

School Name and Location	Attendance Dates From (mo/yr)	To (mo/yr)	Graduate	Type	Degree, Diploma or Certificate and Major/Minor	Academic Standing Grade Average, eg, (3.2/4.0)
High School last attended			☐ Yes ☐ No			
Vocational, technical school			☐ Yes ☐ No			
College or university			☐ Yes ☐ No			
College or university			☐ Yes ☐ No			
Other (skilled trade training, etc.)			☐ Yes ☐ No			

Please list academic honors, scholarships, fellowships, memberships in professional and honorary societies, and any other extracurricular activities:

Special Skills/Training/Licenses

Clerical Skills	What is your present speed per minute?	Typewriter	Shorthand	Speedwriting	Can you operate	Dictating equipment ☐ Yes ☐ No	Computer/terminal ☐ Yes ☐ No
	Other office equipment you can operate (including word processing, database management, spreadsheet and other software): Do you have experience in a skilled trade? If so, please describe the extent/nature of experience.						
Skilled Trade Skills, Licenses, Certifi-cations	Have you completed an apprenticeship in a skilled craft? ☐ Yes ☐ No	If yes,	What craft?	Where did you complete it?			
	List all machines and equipment you have operated:						
	List all current licenses and/or certifications together with an identification of the granting authority:						
	Do you have Advanced First Aid, EMS First Responder, Crash Injury Management (CIM) or EMT certification? ☐ Yes ☐ No						

Employment History

Please give accurate, complete and part-time employment record. *Start with present or most recent employer.*

Company Name	Telephone ( )
Address	Employed (State month and year) From To
Name of Supervisor	Salary ☐ Hourly ☐ Monthly ☐ Yearly $
State job title and list your duties/responsibilities beginning with the duty that consumed the greatest proportion of your time:	Reason for leaving

Company Name	Telephone ( )
Address	Employed (State month and year) From To
Name of Supervisor	Salary ☐ Hourly ☐ Monthly ☐ Yearly $
State job title and list your duties/responsibilities beginning with the duty that consumed the greatest proportion of your time:	Reason for leaving

Company Name	Telephone ( )
Address	Employed (State month and year) From To
Name of Supervisor	Salary ☐ Hourly ☐ Monthly ☐ Yearly $
State job title and list your duties/responsibilities beginning with the duty that consumed the greatest proportion of your time:	Reason for leaving

Company Name	Telephone ( )
Address	Employed (State month and year) From To
Name of Supervisor	Salary ☐ Hourly ☐ Monthly ☐ Yearly $
State job title and list your duties/responsibilities beginning with the duty that consumed the greatest proportion of your time:	Reason for leaving

If you need additional space, please continue on a separate sheet of paper. Be certain to complete both sides of this application.

Public Safety Applicants (Please Respond)

Date and location of POST licensing exam Date:

Skills course attended

Date of graduation from skills course

Are you currently licensed? ☐ Yes ☐ No If so, License Number

If you are currently licensed, status of license? ☐ Active ☐ Inactive ☐ Part-time ☐ Other__________

Additional Experience and/or Training

Describe any additional experience or training that qualifies you for this job.

Important facts concerning information on your application

MINNESOTA LAW AFFECTS YOU AS AN APPLICANT with the City of Edina. The following data is public information and is accessible to anyone: veteran's status, relevant test scores, rank on eligibility list, job history, education and training, and work availability. All other personally identifiable information is considered private, including, but not limited to, your name, home address and phone number.

If you are selected as a finalist for a position, your name will become public information. You become a finalist if you are selected to be interviewed by the City of Edina.

The information requested on the application is necessary, either to identify you or to assist in determining your suitability for the position for which you are applying. You may legally refuse, but refusal to supply the requested information will mean that your application for employment may not be considered.

If you are selected for employment with the City of Edina, the following additional information about you will be public: your name; actual gross salary and salary range; actual gross pension; the value and nature of your fringe benefits; the basis for and the amount of any added remuneration, such as expenses or mileage reimbursement, in addition to your salary; your job title; job description; training background; previous work experience; the dates of your first and last employment with the City of Edina; the status of any complaints or charges against you while at work; the final outcome of any disciplinary action taken against you, and all supporting documentation about your case; your badge number, if any; your city and county of residence; your work location and work telephone number; honors and awards; payroll timesheets and comparable data.

Anything not listed above which is placed in your application folder or your personnel file (such as medical information, letters of recommendation, resumes, etc.) is made private information by law. For further information, refer to Minnesota Statute, Chapter 13.

I understand that any false information on or omission of information from this application (including additional information required for Public Safety Applicants, if applicable), or failure to present the required proof, will be cause for rejection or dismissal if employed.

Public Safety Applicants Only: In consideration of being permitted to apply for the position herein, I voluntarily assume all risks in connection with my participating in any tests the City of Edina deems necessary to determine my fitness and eligibility, and I release and forever discharge the City of Edina, its officers and employees from any and all claims for any damage or injury that I might sustain.

Tennessen Warning. The purpose and intended use of the information requested on the application is to assist in determining your eligibility and suitability for the position for which you are applying. You may legally refuse to give the information. If you give the information, that information, or further investigation based on it, could cause your application to be denied. If you refuse to give the information, your application for employment may not be considered. Other persons or entities authorized to receive the information you supply are: Staff of Edina Police Department, Bureau of Criminal Apprehension, Hennepin County Warrant Office, Ramsey County Warrant Office, State of Minnesota, Drivers License Section, Hennepin County Auditor, and other governmental agencies necessary to process your application.

Applicant's Signature

Date

The City of Edina's policy and intent is to provide equality of opportunity in employment to all persons. This policy prohibits discrimination because of race, color, religion, national origin, political affiliation, disability, marital status, sex or age (except when sex or age is a bona fide occupational qualification).

The City of Edina is an equal opportunity/affirmative employer.

APPENDIX B

Sample Interview Rating Sheet

CITY OF ANYWHERE, U.S.A.
Oral Interview Board
Police Officer

Candidate's Name: ______________________________

Total Score: ______________________________

A. Interview Questions

Instructions: Do not permit candidates to give a "yes" or "no" answer to the following questions. Ask for justification or explanation of candidates' positions.

1. You and your partner have just stopped a driver for speeding. You observe the driver hand your partner some money and drive off. When your partner returns to your police vehicle, he offers you part of the money. What action would you take?

   6 7 8 9 10 _____

2. Give three good reasons why you have become a candidate for the position of police officer.

   6 7 8 9 10 _____

3. Do you think you could use deadly force, if necessary, to make an arrest? Justify your position.

   6 7 8 9 10 _____

4. What changes do you foresee having to make in your lifestyle to become a police officer?

   6 7 8 9 10 _____

5. What is the role of the police in crime prevention?

   6 7 8 9 10 _____

6. When did you decide to become a police officer? What preparations have you made toward that goal?

   6 7 8 9 10 _____

7. Is there anything else you would like to say about yourself with regard to this position?

NOTATIONS (FOR QUESTION 7 ONLY): ______________________________

____

____

TOTAL SECTION "A":_______

B. Personal Characteristics

1. Appearance: Consider the candidate's personal appearance, bearing in mind the requirements of the position. Does the candidate give a satisfactory appearance as a representative of the local government?
   (Observe: dress, neatness, posture, sitting position, facial expressions, mannerisms)
   6 7 8 9 10 _____

2. Voice and ability to use the English language: Consider the quality of the candidate's voice in relation to the subject position. Does the candidate speak clearly and distinctly? Is his/her voice pleasant or harsh? Consider the candidate's choice of words, sentences, phrases, use of slang or needless technical jargon.
   (Observe: use of simple and correct English, logical presentation, coherence of thought)
   6 7 8 9 10 _____

3. Self-Confidence: Consider self-control. Is the candidate nervous or ill at ease? Is he/she poised and relaxed? Does he/she appear to be uncertain or hesitant about his/her ideas?
   (Observe: embarrassment, stammering, tension, poise, hesitation, confidence, timidness, over confidence)
   6 7 8 9 10 _____

4. Ability to get along with people: Consider the candidate's attitude toward the examiners. Does he/she seem over-sensitive? Is there antagonism, indifference, a cooperative attitude?
   6 7 8 9 10 _____

5. Suitability for this position: Consider whether the candidate will work out on the job. Does he/she reply readily to questions asked? Are his/her ideas original? Are statements convincing and appropriate? Is there evidence of leadership? Does he/she speak out voluntarily at proper times? Does he/she have a definite interest in this work?
   (Observe: alertness, responsiveness, tact, cooperation, enthusiasm)
   6 7 8 9 10 _____

TOTAL SECTION "B": _______

GRAND TOTAL: ___________

REMARKS: ____

____

____

____

____

____

SIGNATURE OF RATER _________________

APPENDIX C

Accessibility Checklist for Complying with the ADA Regulations*

Parking Lots

- ☐ Designated parking spaces should be located near the building, and they should not be occupied by maintenance trucks, employee cars or the cars of able-bodied guests.
- ☐ If parking spaces are not close to the building, valet service should be available at curbside.
- ☐ Verify that access from the parking lot to the building is free and clear. (No gravel or loose impediments.)
- ☐ The approach should be flat and smooth.
- ☐ If the weather is bad, is access to the building covered?
- ☐ Are curbs adjacent to designated parking spaces?
- ☐ Are the angles on the curbs sharp?
- ☐ Watch out for open stairs. Are handrails present?

The Building

- ☐ The approach to the entrance should be a hard surface at least five feet wide.
- ☐ There should be space for a wheelchair lift to be lowered flat to the ground (not on curb).
- ☐ Is the doorsill raised?
- ☐ How heavy is the door?
- ☐ If there are revolving doors, are the side doors unlocked and easy to open?
- ☐ A single-door entrance to the building must be at least 32 inches wide (a standard wheelchair is exactly 32 inches wide). The ideal width for a single-door entrance is 36 inches.
- ☐ A double-door entrance must be at least 48 inches wide.
- ☐ Once inside, is there signage? What is the height? Is it easily visible from a wheelchair?

The Front Desk

- ☐ Most front desks are uncomfortably high. If inaccessible for wheelchair users, can registration be moved to the concierge table, or to another table to the side of the front desk, or can the guest use a clipboard to complete registration forms?

The Elevator

- ☐ Are the control panels low enough to be accessible by wheelchair users?
- ☐ Are the floor numbers in Braille for the sight-impaired?
- ☐ Elevators must be a minimum of 48 inches deep and 22 feet square to permit the wheelchair user to turn around and face the door.
- ☐ The door must be at least 32 inches wide.

The Guest Room

- ☐ Door handles on the outside door and all inside doors should be levers.
- ☐ Once inside the room, all doors and hallways must be a minimum of 32 inches wide.

---

*By January 1993, any major construction required for public accommodations must comply with ADA standards. Both tenants and owners of facilities are responsible for insuring that areas of public accommodation and where public services are offered are accessible. This is a comprehensive checklist for use in site inspections to make sure your site meets ADA standards.

*Note: Although developed for meeting sites, this checklist can be used for any public facility, including police departments.

Source: Cindy Alwood. "Checklist: Does Your Meeting Site Obey the ADA?" *Successful Meetings,* December 1992, pp. 131–132.

Reprinted with permission from the MPI Education Research Foundation Research Center's "Americans with Disabilities Act & Meeting Planning" research subject package.

- ☐ Mirrors in a guest room should be not higher than 40 inches from the floor.
- ☐ In rooms with two beds, there should be a space between the beds or along the outside.
- ☐ Phones, remote controls and light switches should be located next to the accessible side of the bed.
- ☐ Maneuverability is important in a guest room, so check for poorly placed furniture.
- ☐ If the room has a thermostat, it should be no more than 40 inches from the floor.
- ☐ If the temperature controls are on the heating/cooling unit itself, make sure furniture does not block the unit.
- ☐ The closet bar should be 40 inches from the floor.
- ☐ The peephole in the outside door and all locks should be low enough for a person in a wheelchair.

The Bathroom

- ☐ There should be a cutaway under the sink to allow wheelchair users to roll up to the sink.
- ☐ There should be space to maneuver along the bathtub.
- ☐ The bathtub should be equipped with grip bars, ideally with both vertical and horizontal bars low to the tub.
- ☐ Check for stability of grip bars. Poorly mounted grip bars might not withstand a strong pull.
- ☐ Towels should be within reach of someone in a seated position.
- ☐ Toilets should not be higher than 29 inches off the floor, urinals not higher than 17 inches.

Lounge

- ☐ Is access to the restaurant/lounge a flat surface?
- ☐ Are there stairs or a ramp?
- ☐ Is there adequate space between tables for a wheelchair?
- ☐ Check out table heights.
- ☐ Is there access to the dance floor?
- ☐ Are the restrooms accessible by wheelchair?
- ☐ The upper edge of the drinking fountain should be no higher than 36 inches from the floor.
- ☐ Phones should feature coin slots that are no more than 54 inches off the ground.
- ☐ At least one phone should have hearing amplification in the handset.
- ☐ A phone equipped with TDD (telecommunications device for the deaf) should be available.

Meeting Rooms

- ☐ Aisles should be a minimum of 32 inches wide.
- ☐ If you are using a riser, consider its accessibility: Risers require ramps with a slope of no more than one inch vertical to every 12 inches horizontal.
- ☐ Noisy heating/cooling systems in older facilities can make hearing difficult.
- ☐ Chandelier and fluorescent lighting are hard on the eyes.
- ☐ If your meeting has recreation time built into it, recreation facilities—the pool, locker rooms, sundeck—should be accessible.

Staff

- ☐ Staff should be sensitive to greeting and working with persons with disabilities.

In the event of emergencies:

- ☐ Is there a sprinkler system?
- ☐ Are fire alarms 40 inches from the floor?
- ☐ Are there flashing lights to alert deaf or hearing-impaired guests?
- ☐ Is there a voice alarm for guests who are blind or sight-impaired?
- ☐ The door to the bathroom should open out. If the door does open out, make sure it does not block access to the outside door.

APPENDIX D

Sample Affirmative Action Questionnaire

The following information is necessary for the city of Anywhere to evaluate its recruiting and hiring practices and to prepare reports required by law for the state and federal governments. We ask your help in filling in the blanks that apply to you. The Civil Rights Act, Title VII, makes it unlawful to discriminate in employment on the basis of race, color, religion, sex or national origin. Federal and state laws prohibit discrimination in employment on the basis of disability or age. This form will be detached from your application and the information will not be used to make any employment decisions that affect you.

_______ American Indian or Alaskan Native (All persons having origins in any of the original peoples of North America.)

_______ Black (Not of Hispanic origin): All persons having origins in any of the Black racial groups.

_______ Asian/Pacific Islander (All persons having origins in any of the original peoples of the Far East, Southeast Asia, or the Pacific Islands. This area includes, for example, China, Japan, Korea, the Phillipine and Hawaiian Islands and Samoa.)

_______ Hispanic (All persons of Mexican, Puerto Rican, Cuban, Central or South American, or other Spanish culture or origin, regardless of race.)

_______ White (Not of Hispanic origin): All persons having origins in any of the original peoples of Europe, North Africa, the Middle East, or the Indian Subcontinent.

Birthdate: ___________ Age_______ yrs. Sex: Male _____________ Female _____________

Do you have a physical, mental or addictive handicapping condition which substantially limits a major life activity?

Yes ________ No ________ If yes, explain: ____

Exact Title of Position for Which You Are Applying: ______________________________________

DATE: _______________ NAME: ____

APPENDIX E

Offenses and Their Penalties—Progressive Discipline

		Penalties*		
Offense	**Explanation**	**1st Offense**	**2nd Offense**	**3rd Offense**
1. Failure to carry out assignment/insubordination a. Minor	Deliberate delay or failure to carry out assigned work or instructions in a reasonable period of time.	R	R to 5 days S	R to D
b. Major	Refusal to obey legitimate orders, disrespect, insolence and like behavior.	R to D	R to D	D
2. Absence without leave a. Minor	Unauthorized absence of 10 hours or less, repeated tardiness, leaving the job without permission.	R	R to 5 days S	R to D
b. Major	Unauthorized absence of more than 10 hours (If misrepresentation is involved, see #8).	R to D	R to D	D
3. Neglect of duty a. Minor	Unauthorized participation in activities during duty hours which are outside of regularly assigned duties. The offense is usually considered minor when danger to safety of persons or property is not acute or injury or loss is not involved.	R	R to 5 days S	R to D
b. Major	The offense is usually considered major when danger to safety of persons or property is acute or injury or loss is involved.	R to D	D	
4. Careless workmanship or negligence a. Minor	When spoilage or waste of materials or delay in production is not of significant value.	R	R to 5 days S	R to D
b. Major	When spoilage or waste of materials or delay in production is extensive and costly; covering up or attempting to conceal defective work.	R to D	D	
5. Violation of safety practices and regulations a. Minor	Failure to observe safety practices and regulations and danger to safety of persons or property is not acute.	R	R to 5 days S	R to D
b. Major	Failure to observe safety practices and regulations and danger to safety of persons or property is acute.	R to D	D	
6. Loss of, damage to, unauthorized use or willful destruction of city property, records or information a. Minor	When loss or damage is of small value and such loss or damage is not knowingly perpetrated.	R	R to 5 days S	R to D
b. Major	When loss or damage is knowingly perpetrated.	R to D	D	
7. Theft, actual or attempted, in taking and carrying away city property or property of others	Penalty will be determined in part by value of property.	R to D	D	
8. False statements or misrepresentation a. Minor	When falsification, concealment or misrepresentation has occurred, but has not necessarily been done deliberately.	R to 10 days S	D	
b. Major	Deliberate misrepresentation, falsification, exaggeration or concealment of a material fact, especially in connection with matters under official investigation.	R to D	D	

Continued

*Note: R in table means reprimand. The abbreviation S means suspension. The abbreviation D means dismissal.

Offense	Explanation	Penalties 1st Offense	2nd Offense	3rd Offense
9. Disorderly conduct a. Minor	Rude, boisterous play which adversely affects production, discipline or morale; use of disrespectful, abusive or offensive language; quarreling or inciting to quarrel.	R to 5 days S	R to D	D
b. Major	Fighting, threatening or inflicting bodily harm to another; physical resistance to competent authority; any violent act or language which adversely affects morale, production or maintenance of discipline; indecent or immoral conduct.	R to D	D	
10. Gambling a. Minor	Participation in gambling during working hours.	R	R to 5 days S	D
b. Major	Promotion of, or assisting in, operation of organized gambling.	R to D	R to D	D
11. Use of intoxicants a. Minor	Drinking or selling intoxicants or controlled substances on duty or on city premises.	R to D	D	
b. Major	Reporting for duty drunk, under the influence of controlled substances or intoxicated and unable to properly perform assigned duties or to be a hazard to self or others.	5 days S to D	D	
12. Misconduct off duty	Misconduct which adversely affects the reputation of the employee or reflects unfavorably on the city.	R to D	R to D	D
13. Failure to honor valid debts	Garnishment of an employee's wages by an appropriate court order.	R (the first offense requires more than one garnishment before applicable)	R	R to D
14. Discrimination a. Minor	Any action or failure to take action based on age, sex, race, color, religion or national origin of an employee, former employee or applicant which affects their rights, privileges, benefits, dignity and equality of economic opportunity.	R	R to 5 days S	R to D
b. Major	If the discriminatory practice was deliberate.	R to 20 days S	20 days S to D	D
15. Fiscal irregularity	Misappropriation of city funds which came into the employee's possession by reason of their official position; falsification of payroll records for personal gain.	D		
16. Political activity	Engaging in types of political activity prohibited by these personnel policies.	R to D	R to D	R to D
17. Violation of code of ethics	Acceptance of gifts or favors influencing discharge of duties; use of position to secure special privileges or exemptions; disclosure of information adversely affecting the affairs of the city; transaction of city business where personal financial interest is involved; deliberately thwarting execution of a city ordinance, rule or official program.	R to D	D	
18. Violation of the city charter or personnel or departmental personnel policies not already covered above. a. Minor	Violation of a policy which has little adverse affect on production, employee morale, maintenance of discipline and/or the reputation of the city.	R	R to 20 days S	R to D
b. Major	Violation of a policy which adversely affects production, employee morale, maintenance of discipline and/or the reputation of the city in a direct way.	R to D	D	

Source: City of Boulder City, Nevada, Police Department. Reprinted with permission.

APPENDIX F

Sample Community Policing Implementation Profile

Complete the profile questionnaire to analyze the degree that different community policing activities are integrated into your police agency and community. For each activity listed, circle a number between 1 ("not implemented") and 5 ("fully implemented") to indicate the degree that you feel the activity is currently implemented.

Build Partnerships with the Community	Not Implemented			Fully Implemented
1. Police communicate the community policing philosophy through news media, community newsletter or citizen meetings.	1	2	3	4	5
2. Police discuss with citizens what community policing can do and cannot do.	1	2	3	4	5
3. Police at all organizational levels participate in two-way communication with citizens and community leaders.	1	2	3	4	5
4. Police use each neighborhood's own public safety priorities to guide department activity in that neighborhood.	1	2	3	4	5
5. A partnership form documents joint department and citizen group responsibilities concerning specific problem-solving activities.	1	2	3	4	5
6. Police include elected officials in the community policing planning process.	1	2	3	4	5
7. Police involve relevant community agencies in the community policing planning process.	1	2	3	4	5
8. Police coordinate problem-solving activities with appropriate social service agencies.	1	2	3	4	5
9. Police and community agencies track police social service referrals.	1	2	3	4	5
10. Police distribute an information package that gives a realistic picture of community policing.	1	2	3	4	5
11. Top police managers conduct press briefings to explain community policing.	1	2	3	4	5
12. All police personnel are authorized to speak directly to the media about their work.	1	2	3	4	5
13. Police personnel have organized an internal speakers bureau to promote community policing.	1	2	3	4	5
14. Police sponsor public seminars on community policing.	1	2	3	4	5
15. Individual employees participate in civic groups trying to solve crime problems.	1	2	3	4	5

Build Partnerships within the Police Department	Not Implemented			Fully Implemented
16. Frequent personal communication from top management disseminates community policing philosophy to all personnel, sworn and nonsworn.	1	2	3	4	5
17. All personnel participate in community policing planning processes that affect their own work.	1	2	3	4	5
18. Management recruits people who respect community policing values.	1	2	3	4	5
19. Management seriously considers the merits of all internal suggestions for improvement.	1	2	3	4	5
20. Employees are rewarded for doing community policing activities.	1	2	3	4	5
21. Employees help design their own performance evaluation criteria.	1	2	3	4	5

Decentralize Police Decision-Making	Not Implemented				Fully Implemented
22. Management practices emphasize broad-based participation in policy formation.	1	2	3	4	5
23. Problem-solving groups are composed of many different ranks.	1	2	3	4	5
24. Problem-solving groups have the authority to implement their decisions.	1	2	3	4	5
25. The general rules and regulations have been streamlined to emphasize broader guidelines to appropriate action.	1	2	3	4	5
26. Management practices are consistent with the large amount of individual discretion that patrol officers exercise.	1	2	3	4	5
27. Patrol officers accept having increased accountability along with increased decision-making authority.	1	2	3	4	5
28. Management has reduced the rank level of approval required for many decisions.	1	2	3	4	5
29. Management authorizes officers to commit police resources when working with citizen groups to solve problems.	1	2	3	4	5
30. Patrol areas conform to natural community boundaries.	1	2	3	4	5
31. Officers who work in the same neighborhood areas attend frequent meetings with each other to plan their problem-solving activities.	1	2	3	4	5

Restructure Police Training and Education	Not Implemented				Fully Implemented
32. Management works to change state police academy curriculum to teach more community policing skills.	1	2	3	4	5
33. Department training emphasizes community policing skills.	1	2	3	4	5
34. Management rewards patrol officers who take outside courses that help them to do community policing.	1	2	3	4	5
35. Department policies encourage managers to take outside courses in participatory management skills.	1	2	3	4	5
36. Management uses citizen complaints about police conduct to identify training deficiencies.	1	2	3	4	5
37. Management uses patrol officers who are successful in community policing to help train other officers.	1	2	3	4	5

Go Beyond 911	Not Implemented				Fully Implemented
38. The department emphasizes using an alternative phone number to 911 for non-emergency police contact.	1	2	3	4	5
39. Citizens are provided a method to directly contact their neighborhood patrol officers.	1	2	3	4	5
40. Police employees have accurate information for correctly referring citizens to other agencies for problem-solving assistance.	1	2	3	4	5
41. The department uses alternatives to automobile patrols.	1	2	3	4	5
42. The method for evaluating the performance of police officers includes monitoring officers' progress on self-generated problem-solving plans.	1	2	3	4	5

Source: Reprinted by permission from *The Police Chief,* Vol. LXIII, No. 10, October 1994, p. 118. Copyright held by The International Association of Chiefs of Police, Inc., 515 N. Washington St., Alexandria, Virginia 22314, U.S.A. Further reproduction without express written permission from IACP is strictly prohibited.

APPENDIX G Sample Goals, Daily Routine, Methods, Responsibilities and Duties of a Community Policing Officer

The following are examples of goals, daily routine, methods, responsibilities and duties of a community policing officer:

Goals

The following are goals of the Neighborhood Foot Patrol:

1. To decrease the amount of actual or perceived criminal activity.
2. To increase the citizen's perception of personal safety.
3. To deliver to Flint residents a type of law enforcement service consistent with the community needs and the ideals of modern police practices.
4. To create a community awareness of crime problems and methods of increasing law enforcement's ability to deal with actual or potential criminal activity swiftly and effectively.
5. To develop citizen volunteer action in support of, and under the direction of, the police department, aimed at various target crimes.
6. To eliminate citizen apathy about crime reporting to police.
7. To increase protection for women, the aged and children.

Daily Routine

The following is an example of a Neighborhood Foot Patrol officer's *typical* day:

1. Report to roll call.
2. Report to base station.
3. Office call-in time, check notes and messages.
4. Establish priority list for complaints received.
5. Make decision as to which complaints would be better handled by another department. For example, garbage complaints would be referred to the Sanitation Department.
6. Start walking beat.
7. Go door to door, make security inspections of home, take complaints of neighborhood problems and concerns.
8. Follow up on written recorded complaints and refer to the proper agency those that cannot be handled.

9. Make person to person contact with residents, including distribution of a personal "letter of introduction" to each home and business.
10. Make contact with families of any juvenile who appears on the juvenile sheet and lives in beat area.

Methods

The Neighborhood Officer

The neighborhood officers themselves are the most important factor in achieving the goals of this program.

The officers who have been selected under this program are operating under a full-service role model, as opposed to the basically narrow, vocational one based primarily on law enforcement alone. A full-service model contains these goals: professionalism, human relations, community relations and law enforcement. The goals are defined as follows:

PROFESSIONALISM: Characterized by independence in decision making which is guided by a code of ethics and the systematic application of a body of knowledge; actions are geared to the needs of the client rather than self-interest; self-monitoring and ultimate accountability to one's own peers.

HUMAN RELATIONS: An awareness of interpersonal dynamics expressed by the utilization of alternatives to physical force; primary focus is on verbal and social interaction skills; a problem-solving orientation in which the police officer becomes a source of support, strength, and authority.

COMMUNITY RELATIONS: A collaborative approach to law enforcement in which liaison with the service community is maximized; cooperation and information flow are enhanced through various attempts to reduce social distance; coordination efforts with community members and resources.

LAW ENFORCEMENT: Characterized by a recognition that the power and authority vested in the police officer is a responsibility to be exercised in consideration of the needs of the individual citizen (victim and criminal alike) and the best interest of society. Law enforcement in the context of "law and order" is feasible only as a *joint effort* of the *police and the citizens of the community.*

The Neighborhood Foot Patrol officer's job is to encourage Flint citizens to work with the Flint Police Department to reduce crime and to develop a community crime prevention network.

The following is a summary of the neighborhood officer's responsibilities and duties:

1. Increase citizen awareness of the problem of crime by analyzing the neighborhood crime patterns and reporting the actual crime problems confronting individuals who live in the target area.
2. Conduct public education programs on crime prevention geared specifically to the various groups in the neighborhoods.
3. Confer with residents and businesses regarding problems relative to the police department, city government and other criminal justice and governmental agencies.
4. Gather and contribute helpful information to the Flint Police Department concerning social problems involving individuals, families and/or neighborhoods.
5. Maintain a high degree of contact with the existing citizen action groups operating within the neighborhoods and involve them in planning, designing and evaluating neighborhood crime prevention programs.
6. Patrol streets to strengthen lines of communication with citizens and prevent crime and delinquency.

7. Attend neighborhood block clubs and services as a resource person relative to crime prevention and police problems, activities and procedures.
8. Attend School Advisory Councils in area assigned.
9. Inspect residential and business premises and make recommendations to improve physical security.
10. Investigate selected crimes against the person or individual and support community education programs to prevent reoccurence.
11. Prepare written crime prevention material for community newsletter.
12. Create an environment of safety for the elderly by encouraging self crime prevention techniques such as direct deposits for income; the use of checks and credit cards instead of cash to decrease chances of monetary loss; and transporting the elderly to banks and shops to further reduce chances of attack by criminals.
13. Maintain an ongoing juvenile delinquency prevention program for our youth through the medium of the Police Athletic League (PAL). This activity will incorporate the traditional sports games that youth enjoy, as well as field trips to museums, art fairs and the theater to culturally enrich those among us who are deprived of such outlets.
14. Inspect the total turf of the beat for any violation of city codes or ordinances. Contingent to the basic concept of the Foot Patrol, the officer has a close personal relationship with all sectors of the populace, both private and commercial. With this in mind, enforcement may be procured on a voluntary basis rather than punitive, thereby not only enhancing the image of the officer, but abating the problem at hand. Areas where the officer may realize this concept in daily activities fall under a myriad of duties.

    The aesthetic beauty of the community is enhanced with the officer's enforcement of abandoned vehicle violations, trash and garbage complaints, and the noncompliance with the sundry animal ordinances.

    In effect, the foot patrol officer becomes a code enforcement officer, and the close rapport established with the public within the beat configuration enables compliance with, and abatement of, ordinances and violations observed through this personal relationship.

    The officer will actively seek out any grievances that the citizenry may have, and seek to alleviate them. Street lights that are inoperative, trees that need to be trimmed, all have an impact on the citizen's view of the environment. The act of actively seeking out complaints such as these and procuring abatement of the problem at hand will improve not only the image of the officer to constituents, but the aesthetic beauty and safety of the assigned area.
15. Work with the elderly to develop programs and activities to help ensure safety and comfort in their living and social environment.
16. Work with youth to develop activities to decrease their opportunities to become involved in delinquent behavior.
17. Routinely review community resources to ascertain what's needed to improve the quality of life in the area.
18. Perform other duties required of a Flint Police Officer.

Source: Flint, Michigan, Police Department, "Neighborhood Police Foot Patrol Instruction Manual." Reprinted by permission.

APPENDIX H

List of Abbreviations and Acronyms

AAP	Affirmative Action Program
ABC	Activity-Based Costing
ABM	Activity-Based Management
ADA	Americans with Disabilities Act
ADEA	Age of Discrimination in Employment Act
ADR	Alternative Dispute Resolution (Program)
AED	Automated External Defibrillator
AHA	American Heart Association
AIDS	Acquired Immune Deficiency Syndrome
AIM	American Indian Movement
AMP	Assessing and Managing Performance
ASLET	American Society of Law Enforcement Trainers
ATCB	Architectural Transportation Compliance Board
ATF	Alcohol, Tobacco and Firearms (Bureau of)
ATV	All-Terrain Vehicle
BARS	Behaviorally Anchored Rating Scale
BFOQ	Bona fide occupational qualification
BJA	Bureau of Justice Assistance
BJS	Bureau of Justice Statistics
BVP	Bulletproof Vest Partnership
CAD	Computer-Aided Dispatch
CAD	Computer-Assisted Dispatch
CALEA	Commission on Accreditation of Law Enforcement Agencies
CAPE	Computer-Assisted Police Evaluation
CBO	Community-Based Organization
CBT	Computer-Based Training
CEO	Chief Executive Officer
CFS	Calls for Service
CISD	Critical incident stress debriefing
CLS	Court Liaison Sergeant
COP	Community-Oriented Policing
COP	Citizens Observer Patrol
COPPS	Community Oriented Policing and Problem Solving
COPS	Community Oriented Policing Service
COPS	Concerns of Police Survivors

CPA	Certified Public Accountant
CPA	Citizen Police Academy
DHS	Department of Homeland Security
DLT	Distance Learning and Training
DOJ	Department of Justice
EAP	Employee Assistance Program
EBB	Electronic Bulletin Board
EEO	Equal Employment Opportunity
EEOA	Equal Employment Opportunity Act
EEOC	Equal Employment Opportunity Commission
EMS	Emergency Medical Service
EPA	The Equal Pay Act of 1963
EPA	Environmental Protection Agency
ERP	Enterprise Resource Planning
EW	Early Warning
EWS	Early Warning System
FCC	Federal Communications Commission
FEMA	Federal Emergency Management Agency
FFA	Force-Field Analysis
FFDE	Fitness-for-Duty Evaluation
FLETC	Federal Law Enforcement Training Center
FLSA	Fair Labor Standards Act
FTO	Field Training Officer
GAAP	Generally accepted accounting principles
GIGO	Garbage In/Garbage Out
GIS	Geographic Information System
HIV	Human Immunodeficiency Virus
HUD	Housing and Urban Development
IA	Internal Affairs
IACP	International Association of Chiefs of Police
IAD	Internal Affairs Division
ICS	Incident Command Systems
INS	Immigration and Naturalization Service
JDL	Jewish Defense League
JRSA	Justice Research and Statistics Association
KISS	Keep It Short and Simple
LEAA	Law Enforcement Assistance Administration
LEOBR	Law Enforcement Officers' Bill of Rights
LESTN	Law Enforcement Satellite Training Network
LETN	Law Enforcement Television Network
LLEBG	Local Law Enforcement Block Grants
MBO	Management by Objective
MBTI	Myers-Briggs Type Indicator
MBWA	Management by Walking Around
MIS	Management Information System
MMPI	Minnesota Multiphasic Personality Inventory
MORE	Making Officer Redeployment Effective

MPO	Master Patrol Officer
NAFTO	National Association of Field Training Officers
NAPO	National Association of Police Organizations
NASA	National Aeronautics and Space Administration
NCJOSI	National Criminal Justice Officer Selection Inventory
NCJRS	National Criminal Justice Reference Service
NIJ	National Institute of Justice
NLRB	National Labor Relations Board
OC	Oleoresin Capsicum (pepper spray)
OCFAF	Open Case Fired Ammunition Files
OJJDP	Office of Juvenile Justice and Delinquency Prevention
OJP	Office of Justice Programs
OJT	On-the-Job Training
OVC	Office for Victims of Crime
PC	Personal Computer
PDA	Personal Digital Assistant
PDM	Participatory Decision Making
PERF	Police Executive Research Forum (Foundation)
PIN	Pager Information Network
PIO	Public Information Officer
PMO	Police Motorcycle Officer
PMP	Patrol Management Program
PODSCORB	Planning, Organizing, Directing, Staffing, Coordinating, Reporting and Budgeting
POP	Problem-Oriented Policing
POST	Peace Officer Standards and Training
PSLC	Private Sector Liaison Committee (of the IACP)
PSOB	Public Safety Officer's Benefits (Program)
PSOEA	Public Safety Officer's Educational Assistance (Program)
PTSD	Post-Traumatic Stress Disorder
PWC	Personal Watercraft
Q & A	Question and Answer
QID	Qualified individual with a disability
QPP	Quality Performance Plan
QWL	Quality of Work Life
R&R	Rest and Relaxation
RFP	Request for Proposal
RISS	Regional Intelligence Sharing System
RMS	Records Management System
SBC	Suicide by Cop
SCA	Sudden Cardiac Arrest
SDP	Supervisor Development Program
SMART	Specific, measurable, attainable, relevant, trackable
SMILE	Stress Management in Law Enforcement
STAR	Small Town and Rural (Training Program)
TEAM	Traffic Enforcement and Management System
TQM	Total Quality Management

UCR	Uniform Crime Reports
VIPS	Volunteers in Police Service
VIPS	Volunteers in Public Service
ZBB	Zero-Based Budgeting

Glossary

Number in parentheses is the chapter(s) in which the term is discussed.

ABILENE PARADOX—begins innocently, with everyone in a group agreeing that a particular problem exists. Later, when it comes time to discuss solutions, no one expresses a viewpoint that differs from what appears to be the group's consensus, even though many secretly disagree with it. Finally, after the solution has been implemented, group members complain privately about the plan and look for someone to blame for its development. (4)

ABSTRACT WORDS—theoretical, not concrete, for example, *tall* rather than *6′10″*. (3)

ACCOUNTABILITY—makes people responsible for tasks assigned to them. (1)

ACCOUNTING—the process by which financial information about an agency is recorded, classified, summarized and interpreted and then communicated to managers and other interested parties. (6)

ACCOUNTING PERIOD—the time covered by the income statement and other financial statements that report operating results. (6)

ACCREDITATION—the process by which an institution or agency proves that it meets certain standards. (16)

ACTIVE LISTENING—includes concentration, full attention and thought. (3)

ACTIVITY-BASED COSTING (ABC)—a modern version of the program budgeting system, except that rather than breaking costs down by program, the approach breaks down costs by activity. (6)

ACUTE STRESS—severe, intense distress that lasts a limited time and then the person returns to normal. (14)

ADMINISTRATIVE DECISION—middle-management level decision. (4)

ADMINISTRATIVE SERVICES—supports those performing field services. Includes recruitment and training, records and communication, planning and research and technical services. (1)

ADMINISTRATIVE SKILLS—include organizing, delegating and directing the work of others; writing proposals, devising work plans and developing budgets. (2)

ADMINISTRATOR—plans, analyzes, organizes. (9)

AFFIRMATIVE ACTION PROGRAM (AAP)—a written plan to ensure fair recruitment, hiring and promotion practices. (7)

AFTERBURN—a stressful incident that greatly affects an officer's family and leaves damaging emotional scars. (14)

AGENDA—a plan, usually referring to a meeting outline or program; a list of things to be accomplished. (3)

AGGRESSIVE PATROL—proactive patrol, focuses on preventing and detecting crime by investigating suspicious activity. Also called *proactive* patrol. (15)

ALIGNED ON PURPOSE—having a sense of common purpose about why a team exists and the function it serves. (2)

ALL-LEVELS BUDGETING—everyone affected by the budget helps prepare it. (6)

ANDRAGOGY—the art and science of helping adults learn. (8)

APPEAL—request for a decision to be reviewed by someone higher in the command structure. (11)

APPROACH-APPROACH CONFLICT—selecting between two positive alternatives. (13)

APPROACH-AVOIDANCE CONFLICT—selecting one positive alternative that will also produce a negative consequence. (13)

ARBITRATION—turning a decision over to an individual or panel to make the final recommendation. (7, 12)

ASSESSMENT CENTER—places participants in the position of actually performing tasks related to the anticipated position. Incorporates situational techniques in a simulated environment under standardized conditions. (10)

ASSETS—items of value owned by an agency. (6)

ASYNCHRONOUS LEARNING—learning in which interaction between teachers and students occurs intermittently with a time delay. Opposite of synchronous learning. (8)

AUDIT TRAIL—the chain of references that makes it possible to trace information about transactions through an accounting system. (6)

AUTHORITY—the power to command, enforce laws, exact obedience, determine or judge. The ability to get things done through others by influencing behavior. (2)

AUTHORITY/COMPLIANCE MANAGEMENT—emphasis is on achieving production goals by planning, directing and controlling all work, with good relationships viewed as incidental. It is inner-directed and suppresses conflict through authority. (2)

AUTOCRATIC LEADERSHIP—managers make decisions without participant input. Completely authoritative, showing little or no concern for subordinates. (2)

AUTOMATED PERFORMANCE EVALUATION—officers are continuously evaluated and awarded points, which are kept track of by computer. Supervisors can award bonus points. (16)

AVOIDANCE-AVOIDANCE CONFLICT—selecting between two negative alternatives, commonly referred to as "the lesser of two evils." (13)

AVOIDERS—people who put things off, procrastinate or physically absent themselves to keep from getting involved. (13)

BACKGROUND CHECK—investigating references listed on an application as well as credit, driving record, criminal conviction, academic background and any professional license required. (7)

BALANCE OF CONSEQUENCES ANALYSIS—a grid used to analyze problem behavior and the consequences that follow the behavior in an attempt to understand how the consequences might be to altered to change the problem behavior. (11)

BALANCE SHEET—the financial statement that shows the financial position of an agency at a specific date by summarizing the agency's assets and liabilities. (6)

BALANCED PERFORMER MANAGERS—develop subordinates' and an organization's capabilities. (9)

BALANCING—unfairly stopping unoffending motorists to protect officers from the "statistical microscope" individually or collectively. (9)

BEHAVIORALLY ANCHORED RATING SCALES (BARS)—specific characteristics for a position are determined. Employees are then rated against these characteristics by on-the-job behaviors in each area. (16)

BIFURCATED SOCIETY—a society in which the gap between the "haves" and the "have nots" is wide, that is, there are many poor people, many wealthy people and a shrinking middle class. (1, 17)

BLIND SELF—that part which others can see but you do not know about yourself. (9)

BLOCK GRANT—grant awarded to states or localities based on population and crime rate. Also called a *formula grant.* (6)

BLUE FLAME—the symbol of a law enforcement officer who wants to make a difference in the world. (14)

BODY LANGUAGE—messages conveyed by gestures, facial expressions, stance and physical appearance. (3)

BOILED FROG PHENOMENON—based on a classic experiment, suggests that managers must pay attention to change in their environment and adapt—or perish. (17)

BONA FIDE OCCUPATIONAL QUALIFICATION (BFOQ)—a requirement that is reasonably necessary to perform the job. It may on the surface appear to be discrimination. (7)

BOTTOM-LINE PHILOSOPHY—allows shifting funds from one expense category to another as long as expenses do not exceed the total amount budgeted. (6)

BRAINSTORMING—a method of shared problem solving in which members of a group spontaneously contribute ideas, no matter how wild, without any criticism or critique. (4)

BUDGET—a list of probable expenses and income during a given period, most often one year. (6)

BUDGET REDUCTION—see *cutback budgeting.* (6)

BULLIES—people who attack verbally or physically, using threats and demands to get their way. (13)

BURNOUT—occurs when someone is exhausted or made listless through overwork. It results from long-term, unmediated stress. Symptoms include lack of enthusiasm and interest, a drop in job performance, temper flare-ups, a loss of will, motivation or commitment. (14)

BURST STRESS—to go from complete calm to high activity and pressure in one "burst." (14)

BY-THE-NUMBERS EVALUATION—makes evaluation more objective by using a numerical scale for each characteristic or dimension rated. (16)

CAPITAL BUDGET—deals with "big ticket" items such as major equipment purchases and vehicles. (6)

CASE STUDY—a detailed analysis of a specific incident used to instruct. (8)

CERTIFIED PUBLIC ACCOUNTANT (CPA)—an accountant licensed by a state to do public accounting work. (6)

CHAIN OF COMMAND—the order of authority; begins at the top of the pyramid and flows down to the base. (1)

CHANNELS OF COMMUNICATION—how messages are conveyed; usually follows the chain of command. (1, 3)

CHIEF EXECUTIVE OFFICER (CEO)—manager at the top of the hierarchy, usually the chief or sheriff. (2)

CHRONIC STRESS—is less severe than acute stress, but is continuous. (14)

CIRCADIAN SYSTEM—the body's complex biological timekeeping system. (14)

CIVIL RIGHTS ACT OF 1964—prohibits discrimination based on race, color, religion, sex or national origin by private employers with 15 or more employees, governments, unions and employment agencies. (7)

CIVILIAN REVIEW BOARD—a group of citizens designated to investigate and dispose of complaints against the police. (12)

CIVILIANIZATION—refers to hiring citizens to perform certain tasks for law enforcement agencies. (15)

CLOSED SHOP—prohibits management from hiring nonunion workers. (7)

COACHING—one-on-one field training. (8)

CODE OF SILENCE—encourages people not to speak up when they see another officer doing something wrong. (9)

COLLECTIVE BARGAINING—the process whereby representatives of employees meet with representatives of management to establish a written contract setting forth working conditions for a specific time, usually one to three years. (7)

COMMAND DECISION—a decision managers make on their own with little or no input from others. (4)

COMMON COSTS—costs not directly traceable to a segment of an agency such as a department or division. They might include a municipality's insurance costs. (6)

COMMUNICATION—the complex process through which information is transferred from one person to another through common symbols. (3)

COMMUNICATION BARRIERS—obstacles to clear, effective communication, including time, volume of information, tendency to say what we think others want to hear, failure to select the best word, prejudices and strained relationships, judging, superiority, certainty, controlling, manipulation and indifference. (3)

COMMUNICATION ENHANCERS—techniques for reducing or eliminating barriers to communication, including properly encoding messages, selecting the best channel, describing, equality, openness, problem orientation, positive intent and empathy. (3)

COMMUNICATION PROCESS—involves a message, a sender, a channel and a receiver; it may also include feedback. (3)

COMMUNITY EMPOWERMENT POLICING (CEP)—advances community policing to a new level focusing on building crime-free neighborhoods. (17)

COMMUNITY ERA—characterized by police authority coming from community support, law and professionalism; provision of a broad range of services, including crime control; decentralized organization with greater authority given to patrol officers; an intimate relationship with the community; and the use of foot patrol and a problem-solving approach. (1)

COMMUNITY POLICING—decentralized model of policing in which individual officers exercise their own initiatives and citizens become actively involved in making their neighborhoods safer. This proactive approach usually includes increased emphasis on foot patrol. (1)

COMPLAINANT—a person or group filing a complaint. (12)

COMPLAINERS—people who find fault with everything and everyone. (13)

COMPLAINT—a statement of a problem. (12)

COMPREHENSIVE DISCIPLINE—uses both positive and negative discipline to achieve individual and organizational goals. (11)

COMPUTER-ASSISTED POLICE EVALUATION (CAPE)—using computerized rating forms that provide printouts to be used by law enforcement managers and subordinates. (16)

CONCEPTUAL SKILLS—problem-solving ability, planning ability and the ability to see the big picture and how all the pieces within it fit. (2)

CONE OF RESOLUTION—narrowing in on the geographic locations of crime. (15)

CONFLICT—a mental or physical fight. (13)

CONFRONTATION TECHNIQUE—insisting that two disputing people or groups meet face-to-face to resolve their differences. (13)

CONSENSUS DECISION—a decision made democratically by a group; a joint decision often made by members of a committee. (4)

CONSIDERATION STRUCTURE—looks at establishing the relationship between the group and the leader. (2)

CONSULTATIVE DECISION—a decision that uses input and opinions from others, with the final decision still made by the manager in charge. (4)

CONSULTATIVE LEADERSHIP—employees' ideas and input are welcomed, but the manager makes the final decision. (2)

CONTENT VALIDITY—the direct relationship between tasks performed on the job, the curriculum or training and the test. (8)

CONTINGENCY FUNDS—money allocated for unforeseen emergencies. (6)

CONTINGENCY THEORY—Morse and Lorsch's motivational theory that suggests fitting tasks, officers and agency goals so that officers can feel competent. (10)

CONVERGENT THINKING—focused, evaluative thinking. Includes decision making, choosing, testing, judging and rating. Opposite of divergent thinking. (4)

COORDINATION—ensuring that all members of the department perform their assigned tasks and that, together, the department's mission is accomplished. (1)

COST ANALYSIS—examining how resources are spent for specific services and specific results. (6)

COUNSELING—one-on-one field training. (8)

COUNTRY CLUB MANAGEMENT—win friends and influence people; sees production as incidental to good relations; supervisors establish a pleasant work atmosphere and harmonious relations between people; very "other" directed; avoids conflict by conforming to the thinking of the boss or peers. (2)

CREATIVE PROCRASTINATION—delaying decisions, allowing time for minor difficulties to work themselves out. (4, 5)

CREATIVE TALENTS—applying individual talents and creativity. (2)

CREATIVITY—the process of breaking old connections and making new connections; being innovative; originality. (4)

CRIME TRIANGLE—a model illustrating how all three elements—motivated suspect, suitable victim and adequate location—are required for crime to occur. (15)

CRITICAL INCIDENT—an extremely traumatic event such as a mass disaster or a brutally murdered child. (14)

CRITICAL INCIDENT STRESS DEBRIEFING (CISD)—officers who experience a critical incident such as a mass disaster or crash with multiple deaths are brought together as a group for a psychological debriefing soon after the event. (14)

CROSS FLOW & CROSS TELL—one department alerts other departments about a mistake revealed during inspection. (5)

CRUNCH—a major problem. (12)

CULTURAL AWARENESS—understanding the diversity of the United States, the dynamics of minority–majority relationships, the dynamics of sexism and racism and the issues of nationalism and separatism. (9)

CUMULATIVE STRESS—less severe but continues and eventually becomes debilitating. Sometimes called *chronic stress.* (14)

CUTBACK BUDGETING—providing the same or more services with less funding. Also called *budget reduction* or *reduced expenditure spending.* (6)

CYBERTRIBE—a group of bright people all sharing the same enthusiasm for their organization's goal, but bringing a wide range of complimentary skills to bear on the effort. (2)

DAILY VALUES—how people actually spend their time and energy. (9)

DATA—facts and figures. (4)

DECENTRALIZATION—encourages flattening of the organization and places decision-making authority and autonomy at the level where information is plentiful; in police organizations, this is usually at the level of the patrol officer. (1)

DECISION—a judgment or conclusion, making up one's mind or settling a dispute. (4)

DECISION-MAKING PROCESS—a systematic approach to solving a problem for example, QUID/QUOD, force-field analysis, nominal group technique or the Delphi Method. (4)

DECODE—decipher a message. (3)

DELAYING TACTICS—stalling during negotiations. (7)

DELEGATION—assigning tasks to others. (1)

DELPHI TECHNIQUE—a way to have individual input; uses open-ended questionnaires completed by individuals. Answers are shared and the questionnaires are again completed until consensus is achieved. (4)

DEMOCRATIC LEADERSHIP—does not mean every decision is made by a vote, but rather that decisions are made only after discussion and input of employees. (3)

DEMONSTRATION—modeling or showing how to do a task, for example, how to administer CPR. (8)

DEMOTION—places an employee in a position of lower responsibility and pay. Often a part of progressive discipline. (11)

DEPENDENT (STAGE OF GROWTH)—when someone is just learning the job and is very dependent on others—rookie stage. (9)

DEPRECIATION—the process of allocating the cost of a long-term asset to operations during its expected useful life. For example, squad cars will depreciate as they are used. (6)

DESCRIPTIVE STATISTICS—focus on simplifying, appraising and summarizing data. (16)

DESYNCHRONIZATION—the body's circadian rhythm is negatively affected by a deviation from the night-sleep, day-wake pattern. (14)

DEVELOPMENTAL CELLS—a small unit within an agency where a change is first implemented. From within this unit leaders are selected to implement change within other units. (17)

DIRECT EXPENSES—operating expenses that can be identified specifically with individual departments. This would include such things as salaries and benefits. (6)

DISCIPLINARY ACTIONS—steps taken, verbally or in writing, to reprimand undesired behavior. Should be done in private. (11)

DISCIPLINE—training expected to produce a desired behavior—controlled behavior or administering punishment. Also a state of affairs or how employees act, in contrast to morale, which is how employees feel. (11)

DISCRETIONARY BUDGET—funds available to be used as the need arises. (6)

DISCRETIONARY GRANT—awarded based on the judgment of the awarding state or federal agency. (6)

DISCUSSION—interchange of ideas. (8)

DISEQUILIBRIUM—being out of physiological balance. (14)

DISMISSAL—termination of employment. Usually the final step in progressive discipline. (11)

DISTRESS—negative stress. (14)

DIURNAL—day-oriented. Humans are by nature diurnal in their activities. (14)

DIVERGENT THINKING—free, uninhibited thinking. Includes imagining, fantasizing, free associating and combining and juxtaposing dissimilar elements. Opposite of convergent thinking. (4)

DOG SHIFT/WATCH—late night, early morning shift, typically from midnight to 0800 hours. (15)

DOWNWARD COMMUNICATION—messages from managers and supervisors to subordinates. (3)

DRIVING FORCES—forces that foster goal achievement. (4)

EDUCATING—generally refers to academic instruction that takes place in a college, university or seminar-type setting and deals with knowledge and mental skills. (8)

EMPLOYEE ASSISTANCE PROGRAM (EAP)—may be internally staffed or use outside referrals to offer help with stress, marital or chemical-dependency problems. (14)

EMPOWERED—given legal authority to act on their own discretion. (1)

ENCODE—place a message into a form to be transmitted. (3)

ENTREPRENEUR—uses vision and creativity to address problems. (9)

ENVIRONMENTAL SCANNING—identifying the factors that are likely to "drive" the environment, influencing the future. Includes social and economic conditions. (17)

ENVIRONMENTAL/INSTRUCTIONAL VARIABLES—refers to the *context* in which learning or training takes place, including physical setting, amount of practice, knowledge of results and incentives. (8)

EQUAL EMPLOYMENT OPPORTUNITY COMMISSION (EEOC)—enforces laws prohibiting job discrimination based on race, color, religion, sex, national origin, handicapping condition or age between 40 and 70. (7)

EQUAL IN CRIME POTENTIAL—means that, based on history of requests for law enforcement services and updating factors, the probability of a patrol car being needed in any of the patrol areas at any given time is the same. (15)

EQUILIBRIUM—the problem in force-field analysis—the equilibrium is not where you want it to be. (4)

ETHICAL BEHAVIOR—that which is "moral" and "right." (9)

ETHICS—standards of fair and honest conduct. (9)

EUSTRESS—helpful stress, stress necessary to function and accomplish goals. (14)

EVALUATE—to determine the worth of, to find the amount or value of or to appraise. (16)

EVALUATION—determining the worth of, finding the amount or value of, appraising. May be formal or informal. (16)

EXECUTIVE MANAGER—top management, usually the chief or sheriff. (2)

EXONERATED—a complaint or grievance in which the investigation determines that the matter did occur, but was proper and legal. (12)

EXPECTANCY THEORY—Vroom's motivational theory that employees will choose the level of effort that matches the performance opportunity for reward. (10)

EXPENSES—the cost of providing services. (6)

EXPLODERS—people who yell and scream. (13)

EXTERNAL COMMUNICATION—messages sent from within the agency to citizens or other organizations or vice versa. (3)

EXTERNAL COMPLAINTS—statements of a problem made by a person or group outside the law enforcement organization. (12)

EXTERNAL MOTIVATORS—see *tangible rewards.* (10)

EXTERNAL STRESS—tension produced by real threats and dangers, for example, being shot at. (14)

FACE TIME—time spent in the agency or department long after a shift ends and on weekends when not on duty to make sure you are seen putting in extra time by those with the power to promote you. (5)

FACILITATORS—assist others in performing their duties to meet mutual goals and objectives. (2)

FACTUAL QUESTIONS—test students' grasp of the concepts presented, for example, "What are the elements of second-degree murder?" (8)

FAIR LABOR STANDARDS ACT OF 1938—established the 40-hour week as the basis of compensation and set a minimum wage. (7)

FEEDBACK—the process by which the sender knows the receiver has understood the message. (3)

FIELD SERVICES—directly help accomplish the goals of the department using line personnel. Main division is uniformed patrol. Also includes investigations, narcotics, vice, juvenile and the like. (1)

FIELD TRAINING—learning that occurs on the job, usually under the direction of a field training officer (FTO). (8)

FIELD TRAINING OFFICER (FTO)—an experienced officer who serves as a mentor for a rookie, providing on-the-job training. (8)

FINANCIAL BUDGET—see *budget.* (6)

FINANCIAL STATEMENTS—periodic reports that summarize the financial affairs of an agency. (6)

FIRST-LINE MANAGERS—those who supervise the officers actually doing the work—the line staff. Usually called supervisors; usually are sergeants. (2)

FISCAL YEAR—the 12-month accounting period used by an agency. A calendar year runs from January 1 through December 31. This may or may not be the same as an agency's fiscal year. (6)

5P PRINCIPLE—proper planning prevents poor performance. (5)

FIXED COSTS—expenses that do not vary in total during a period even though the amount of service provided may be more or less than anticipated, for example, rent and insurance. Also called *overhead.* (6)

FLAT ORGANIZATION—one with fewer lieutenants and captains, fewer staff departments, fewer staff assistants, more sergeants and more patrol officers. (1)

FLEXIBLE BUDGET—a projection that contains budgeted amounts at various levels of service. (6)

FOCUS GROUPS—usually consist of people from the educational community, the religious community, Neighborhood Watch groups and the like. (4)

FOCUSED ON TASK—keeping meetings or other activities focused on results. (2)

FORCE-FIELD ANALYSIS (FFA)—identifies forces that impede and enhance goal attainment. A problem exists when the equilibrium is such that more forces are impeding goal attainment than enhancing it. (4)

FORMAL EVALUATION—efficiency ratings, employee appraisals, service ratings, progress reports, performance appraisal, employee performance review, merit ratings or appraisal interview. (16)

FORMAL ORGANIZATION—how a group of people is structured on paper, often in the form of an organizational chart. (1)

FORMULA GRANT—awarded to states or localities based on population and crime rates. Also called a *block grant.* (6)

FOUR-SYSTEM APPROACH—Likert's management system that divides managerial approaches into four different systems going from System 1, a traditional, authoritarian style, to System 4, a participative management style. (2)

FREE-REIN LEADERSHIP—leaderless, laissez-faire management. (2)

FUTURE FOCUSED—seeing change as an opportunity for growth. (2)

FUTURISTICS—the science of using data from the past to forecast alternatives for the future and to then select those most desirable. (17)

GAME THEORY—a strategy, a mathematical plan so complete it cannot be upset by criminal action or an act of nature. (15)

GARRITY PROTECTION—a written notification that an officer is making his or her statement or report in an internal affairs investigation involuntarily. (12)

GENDER BARRIER—differences between men and women that can result in miscommunication. (3)

GENERALISTS—officers who perform most functions, including patrol, investigation, juvenile and vice. (1)

GENERALLY ACCEPTED ACCOUNTING PRINCIPLES (GAAPs)—the rules of accounting used by agencies in reporting their financial activities. (6)

GENERATION XERS—those born during the years 1961 to 1981. (7)

GHOSTING—falsifying patrol logs to make the numbers come out right. (9)

GIGO—computer acronym for "garbage in, garbage out." (4)

GOALS—broad, general, desired outcomes; visionary, projected achievements. What business calls *key result areas.* (1)

GRAPEVINE—informal channel of communication within the agency or department. Also called the *rumor mill.* (3)

GRATUITY—a favor or gift, usually in the form of money, given in return for service, for example a tip given to a waiter in a restaurant. (9)

GRIEVANCE—a formally registered complaint. A claim by an employee that a rule or policy has been misapplied or misinterpreted to the employee's detriment. (12)

GRIEVANT—the person or group filing a grievance. (12)

GROUP DECISION-MAKING PROCESS—any one of several techniques used to achieve consensus among group members as to how to solve a particular problem. (4)

GROUPTHINK—the negative tendency for members of a group to submit to peer pressure and endorse the majority opinion even if it individually is unacceptable. (4)

GUIDING PHILOSOPHY—the organization's mission statement *and* the basic values to be honored by the organization. (1)

GUNNY SACK APPROACH—occurs when managers or supervisors accumulate negative behaviors of a subordinate and then dump them all on the employee at the same time rather than correcting them as they occurred. (11)

HALO EFFECT—tendency to rate one who performs above average in one area above average in all areas or vice versa. (7, 16)

HANDS-ON LEARNING—learning by doing. (8)

HAWTHORN EFFECT—workers are positively affected by receiving attention. This affects research efforts. (1)

HEALTHY CONFLICT—challenges the status quo and offers constructive alternatives. (13)

HIDDEN SELF—that which is secret and which you do not share with others. (9)

HIERARCHY—a group of people organized or classified by rank and authority. In law enforcement, typically pyramid shaped with a single "authority" at the top expanding down and out through the ranks to the broad base of "workers." (1)

HIERARCHY OF NEEDS—Maslow's motivational theory that people have certain needs that must be met in a specific order going from basic physiological needs to safety and security, social, esteem and self-actualization needs. (10)

HIGH COMMUNICATION—creating a climate of trust and open, honest communication. (2)

HIGHLIGHTING—using a special pen to graphically mark important written information. Should be done *after* the initial reading of the information. (5)

HOLISTIC MANAGEMENT—views personnel as total individuals who make up their team. (2)

HOLISTIC PERSONAL GOALS—includes all aspects of a person's life: career/job, financial, personal, family/relationships, spiritual/service. (9)

HOMEOSTASIS—the process that keeps all the bodily functions in physiological balance. (14)

HORIZONTAL (LATERAL) COMMUNICATION—messages sent between managers or supervisors on the same level of the hierarchy and between subordinates on the same level. (3)

HORN EFFECT—allowing one negative trait to influence the rater negatively on other traits as well. (16)

HOT SPOTS—specific locations with high crime rates. (15)

HYGIENE FACTORS—tangible rewards that can cause dissatisfaction if lacking. (10)

IMPOVERISHED MANAGEMENT—don't rock the boat; avoids problems or defers them to others; does not get involved in conflict. (2)

INCENTIVE PROGRAMS—programs designed to motivate. (10)

INCIVILITIES—signs of disorder. (15)

INDEPENDENT (STAGE OF GROWTH)—can perform job on their own. (9)

INDIRECT EXPENSES—costs that cannot be easily assigned to a particular department when transactions occur and are recorded. Some indirect expenses, such as depreciation, have a meaningful relationship to individual departments and can be allocated based on this relationship. Other indirect expenses must be allocated on the most logical basis possible. (6)

INDIVIDUAL VARIABLES—learner characteristics such as age, sex, maturation, readiness, innate ability, level of motivation, personality and personal objectives. (8)

INFERENTIAL STATISTICS—focus on making statistically educated guesses from a sample of data. (16)

INFORMAL EVALUATION—making judgments whenever necessary, often very casually. (16)

INFORMAL ORGANIZATION—groups that operate without official sanction but influence department performance. (1)

INFORMATION—analysis of facts and figures. (4)

INFORMATION TECHNOLOGY (IT)—using computers to process information, as well as such devices as fax machines to transmit it. (18)

INFORMATION VARIABLES—relates to *what* is to be learned: knowledge, skills or attitudes. Also called *task variables.* (8)

INITIATING STRUCTURE—looks at how leaders assign tasks. (2)

INNOVATION—a new idea or way of doing things. (4)

IN-SERVICE TRAINING—in-house training. (8)

INSUBORDINATION—failure to obey a lawful and direct order from a supervisor. (11)

INTANGIBLE REWARDS—internal motivators such as goals, achievement, recognition, self-respect, opportunity for advancement or to make a contribution, belief in individual and department goals. (10)

INTEGRATOR—like a negotiator, takes individual goals and transforms them into group goals. (9)

INTEGRITY—steadfast adherence to an ethical code. (9)

INTELLIGENCE—ability. (4) See also *multiple intelligences.*

INTERACTORS—communicate with other groups and agencies: the press, other local government departments, the business community, schools and numerous community committees and organizations. (2)

INTERDEPENDENT (STAGE OF GROWTH)—cooperate, care for, assist and support the team effort. (9)

INTERFACERS—coordinate law enforcement agency's goals with those of other agencies within the jurisdiction. (2)

INTERNAL COMMUNICATION—messages within the agency or department, whether downward, upward or lateral. (3)

INTERNAL COMPLAINTS—statements of a problem made by an individual or group within the law enforcement agency. (12)

INTERNAL MOTIVATORS—see *intangible rewards.* (10)

INTERSUBJECTIVITY—people's mutual understanding of and respect for each other's viewpoints, a kind of reciprocal empathy. (13)

INTERSUBJECTIVITY APPROACH—uses 3-by-5-inch cards as a means to get people in conflict to share their most important ideas about a problem and to come to a mutual understanding of and respect for each other's viewpoints. (13)

INTERVAL REINFORCEMENT—presenting information several times, with breaks between the repetition. (8)

INTUITION—insight; knowing without using any rational thought process. (4)

JARGON—nonsense or meaningless language, often called *legalese,* for example, party of the first part, hereafter referred to as . . . . Also, specialized language of a field, for example, *perpetrator.* (3)

JOB DESCRIPTION—detailed, formally stated summaries of duties and responsibilities for a position. (9)

JOB ENLARGEMENT—assigning additional responsibilities to an existing job. (10)

JOB ENRICHMENT—similar to job enlargement except that in job enrichment the focus is on the quality of the new jobs assigned rather than on the quantity. Emphasizes adding variety, deeper personal interest and involvement, increased responsibility and greater autonomy. Appropriate for any highly routine job. (10)

JOB ROTATION—changing the job assignment or shift. (10)

JOHARI WINDOW—a model to illustrate how people can learn more about others and themselves. (9)

JUST CAUSE—a reasonable, fair, honest reason. (11)

KEY RESULT AREAS—the goals of an organization. (1, 9)

KILLER PHRASES—judgmental, critical statements that serve as put-downs and stifle others' creativity. (4)

KISS PRINCIPLE—axiom in communication: "Keep It Short and Simple." (3)

KNOW-IT-ALLS—people who are highly opinionated, speak with great authority, have all the right answers (or think they do) and are impatient with others. (13)

LAG TIME—time elapsed between the occurrence of an incident and it being reported to the police. Often more important than response time. (15)

LAISSEZ-FAIRE LEADERSHIP—involves nonintervention; let everything run itself without direction from the leader; there is little or no control. (2)

LANDRUM-GRIFFIN ACT OF 1959—required regularly scheduled elections of union officers by secret ballot and regulated the handling of union funds. (7)

LATERAL (HORIZONTAL) COMMUNICATION—messages sent between managers or supervisors on the same level of the hierarchy and between subordinates on the same level. (3)

LEADER—influences others by example, guides people, motivates, instills courage and the like. (2)

LEADERSHIP—influencing, working with and through individuals and groups to accomplish a common goal. (2)

LEARNING CURVE PRINCIPLE—if you do a group of similar tasks together, you can reduce the amount of time it takes, sometimes by as much as 80 percent. (5)

LECTURE—instructor presents information orally to a group of learners. (8)

LEFT-BRAIN THINKING—primarily using language and logic. (4)

LINE PERSONNEL—those who actually perform most of the tasks outlined in the work plan. (1)

LINE-ITEM BUDGETING—identifies specific categories (line items) and dollars allocated for each. Line-item budgets are usually based on the preceding year's budget and anticipated changes in the upcoming year. (6)

LINE-ITEMS—specific expense categories, for example, personnel, maintenance, training. (6)

LINES OF COMMUNICATION—similar to channels of communication. May be downward, upward (vertical) or lateral (horizontal); internal or external. (3)

MAJORITY WORLD VIEW—beliefs held by those in the majority. (9)

MANAGE—to control and direct, to administer, to take charge of. (2)

MANAGEMENT—the process of combining resources to accomplish organizational goals. (2)

MANAGEMENT BY OBJECTIVES (MBO)—involves managers and subordinates setting goals and objectives together and then tracking performance to ensure that the objectives are met. Term first used by Peter Drucker. (2)

MANAGEMENT INFORMATION SYSTEMS (MIS)—software programs that organize data to assist in decision making. (4, 15)

MANAGERIAL ACCOUNTING—an internal reporting system that gives management financial information for use in decision making and long-range planning. (6)

MANAGERIAL/LEADERSHIP GRID—Blake-Mouton's management theory describing five styles: task management, country-club management, impoverished management, middle-of-the-road management and team management. The "ideal" management style is an integration of high concern for both people and production, resulting in an energetic team approach. (2)

MANAGERS—those who control and direct, administer, take charge of. Those who accomplish things through others, blending resources—human, material and financial—to accomplish organizational goals. (2)

MARGINAL PERFORMER—employee who has demonstrated ability to perform but who does just enough to get by. (13)

MASTER BUDGET—a projection that includes a detailed operating and financial budget. (6)

MATURE EMPLOYEE THEORY—Argyris' management theory that views employees and their organization as interdependent. (2)

MECHANISTIC MODEL—divides tasks into highly specialized jobs where job holders become experts in their fields, demonstrating the "one best way" to perform their cog in the wheel (Taylorism). The opposite of the organic model. (2).

MEDIATION—bringing in a neutral third party to assist in negotiations. (7, 12)

MENTAL LOCKS—thinking patterns that prevent innovative thinking. Also called *thinking traps.* (4)

MENTOR—a wise, trusted teacher or counselor. (9)

MIDDLE MANAGEMENT—the middle of the hierarchy, usually lieutenants and captains. (2)

MIDDLE-OF-THE-ROAD MANAGEMENT—firm but fair; seeks a balance between high production and sound relations in conflict; supervisors stay neutral and carry out established procedures; samples opinions, manipulates participation, compromises and then sells final solution; deals with surface tensions and symptoms only. (2)

MINORITY WORLD VIEW—beliefs held by those in the minority. (9)

MISSION—the reason an organization exists. (1)

MISSION STATEMENT—a written explanation of why an organization exists. (1)

MODIFIED DELPHI TECHNIQUE—uses objective rather than open-ended questions. (4)

MORALE—a person or group's state of mind, level of enthusiasm and involvement with work and with life. How employees feel; in contrast to discipline, how employees act. (10, 13)

MOTIVATION—an inner or outer drive or impetus to do something or to act in a specified manner. An inner or outer drive to meet a need or goal. (10)

MOTIVATOR FACTORS—intangible rewards that can cause satisfaction. (10)

MULTIPLE INTELLIGENCES—theory of Gardner that people have six intelligences: linguistic, musical, logical-mathematical, spatial, bodily-kinesthetic and personal. (4)

NARROW EYE SPAN—occurs when a reader focuses on one word at a time rather than taking in groups of words or phrases in one look. (5)

NATIONAL LABOR RELATIONS ACT OF 1935 (WAGNER ACT)—legalized collective bargaining and required employers to bargain with the elected representatives of their employees. (7)

NATIONAL LABOR RELATIONS BOARD (NLRB)—the principal enforcement agency for laws regulating relations between management and unions. (7)

NEGATIVE CONFLICT—disagreements that are destructive. (13)

NEGATIVE DISCIPLINE—punishment or reprimand in an effort to compel expected behavior. (11)

NEGATIVE REINFORCEMENT—punishment following an undesired behavior that tends to decrease the behavior. (10)

NEGLIGENT HIRING—failure to use an adequate selection process resulting in hiring personnel unqualified or unsuited for law enforcement work. Often includes failure to check for prior offenses of misconduct. (7)

NEGLIGENT RETENTION—failing to terminate an employee when justified. (11)

NEWS MEDIA ECHO EFFECT—occurs when a highly publicized criminal case results in a shift in processing for similarly charged but nonpublicized cases. (3)

NOMINAL GROUP TECHNIQUE—an objective way to achieve consensus on the most effective alternatives by using an objective ranking of alternatives. (4)

NONACTOR LIABILITY—any officer present at a scene where use of force is in question and is obviously excessive and the nonactor officer did nothing to prevent it; that officer is also held liable by the courts. (13)

NONVERBAL COMMUNICATION—messages conveyed by body language as well as tone of voice. (3)

NORMS—the attitudes and beliefs held by a group of individuals. (9)

NORRIS-LAGUARDIA ACT OF 1932—regulated court injunctions against unions and made yellow-dog contracts illegal. (7)

NOT SUSTAINED—a complaint or grievance in which the investigative facts are insufficient, that is, the evidence does not support the accusations. (12)

OBJECTIVES—specific, measurable ways to accomplish goals. They are more specific than goals and usually have a timeline. (1)

OMBUD—designated neutral or impartial dispute resolution practitioner whose major function is to provide confidential and informal assistance to managers and employees. (13)

OMBUDSMAN—a liaison between police and residents. (12)

ONE MINUTE MANAGING—Blanchard's approach to giving one minute praises and reprimands. (11)

ON-THE-JOB TRAINING (OJT)—occurs during field training, in-house training sessions and roll call. (8)

OPEN DISCUSSION—issues are debated and resolved in a win-win situation. (7)

OPEN SELF—what you know about yourself and what you show to others. (9)

OPERATING BUDGET—a budget that contains projections for income statement items as well as expenses. (6)

OPERATING EXPENSES—costs that arise from the normal activities of the agency. (6)

OPERATIONAL DECISION—first-line supervisor level decision. (4)

OPERATIONAL ISSUE—involves a more limited scope of less than one year, usually involves day-to-day activities. (4)

OPERATIONAL STRESS—the total effect of the need to confront daily the tragedies of urban life; the need to deal with thieves, derelicts and the mentally deranged; being lied to and so on. (14)

OPINION-BASED QUESTION—questions asked to get students to share their personal feelings about topics presented. There are no right or wrong answers, for example, "What type of weapon would you prefer to carry?" (8)

ORGANIC MODEL—a flexible, participatory, science-based structure that will accommodate change. Designed for effectiveness in serving the needs of citizens rather than the autocratic rationality of operation. The opposite of the mechanistic model. (2)

ORGANIZATION—an artificial structure created to coordinate people or groups and resources to achieve a mission or goal. (1)

ORGANIZATIONAL CHART—visually depicts how personnel are organized within the department. Might also depict how the department fits into the community's political structure. (1)

ORGANIZATIONAL STRESS—tension produced by elements inherent in the paramilitary character of law enforcement agencies, constant adjustment to changing schedules, working at odd hours, requirements that detailed rules and procedures be complied with. (14)

OTHER EXPENSES—costs not directly connected with providing services. (6)

OVERHEAD—see *fixed costs.* (6)

PARADIGM—a model, theory or frame of reference. (1)

PARADIGM SHIFT—a dramatic change in how some basic structure is viewed. (1)

PARETO PRINCIPLE—20 percent of what a person does accounts for 80 percent of the results. (5)

PARKINSON'S LAW—the principle that work expands to fill the time available for its completion. (5)

PARTICIPATIVE LEADERSHIP—managers build a team and view themselves as a part of this team. (2)

PARTICIPATORY DECISION MAKING (PDM)—employees have a say in the decision-making process. (4)

PASSIVES—silent, unresponsive people who seldom offer their own ideas or opinions. (13)

PATROL MANAGEMENT PROGRAM (PMP)—reorganizes the patrol division into teams and platoons to increase continuity and to clarify lines of authority. (15)

PEDAGOGY—the science of helping children learn. (8)

PEOPLE SKILLS—being able to communicate clearly, to motivate, to discipline appropriately and to inspire those within the organization for whom they are directly responsible. (2)

PERCEPTION—how one views or interprets things. (10)

PERFORMANCE APPRAISAL—formal evaluation of on-the-job functioning; usually conducted annually. (16)

PERFORMANCE APPRAISAL ATARI—a phenomenon in which those being rated anticipate the specific criteria on which they are rated and meet those criteria to the letter, without any regard for the spirit of the criteria. (16)

PERFORMANCE BUDGETING—allocates dollars based on productivity. Budget defines the agency's objectives for the year, the specific activities or programs needed to achieve those objectives and the cost. Also called *planning-programming-budgeting system* or *PPBS.* (6)

PERFORMANCE INTERVIEWS—private, one-on-one discussions of the performance appraisal by manager and subordinate. (16)

PERKS—tangible rewards. (10)

PERP WALK—where suspects are paraded before the news media. (3)

PERSONAL STRESS—tension generated by an officer's racial or gender status among peers. (14)

PESSIMISTS—people who always say "no" and see "gloom and doom" in every situation. (13)

PETER PRINCIPLE—people rise to their level of incompetence. (8)

PETTY CASH FUND—a cash fund of a limited amount used to make small expenditures for which it is not practical to write checks. (6)

PINCH—a minor problem. (12)

PINCH MODEL—illustrates the importance of communication in dealing with complaints and the consequences of not communicating effectively. A *pinch,* a minor problem, can turn into a *crunch,* a major problem. (12)

POLICE CULTURE—sum of the beliefs and values shared by those within the organization, serving to formally and informally communicate its expectations; may include the code of silence, a sense of solidarity and a them vs. us mentality. (9)

POLICE LOGS—record of requests for services, time, nature of the request and time the incident was completed. (15)

POLITICAL ERA—characterized by police authority coming from politicians and the law, a broad social service function, decentralized organization, an intimate relationship with the community and extensive use of foot patrol. (1)

POSITIVE CONFLICT—see *healthy conflict.* (13)

POSITIVE DISCIPLINE—uses training to foster compliance with rules and regulations and performance at peak efficiency. (11)

POSITIVE REINFORCEMENT—rewards following a desired behavior that tend to increase that behavior. (10)

POSTERIORITIES—tasks that do *not* have to be done, have a minimal payoff and have very limited negative consequences. (5)

POST-TRAUMATIC STRESS DISORDER (PTSD)—a psychological ailment following a major catastrophe such as a shooting or dealing with victims of a natural disaster. Symptoms include diminished responsiveness to the environment, disinterest, pessimism and sleep disturbances, including recurrent nightmares. (14)

POWER—the ability to get things done with or without legal right. Uses persuasion. (2)

POWER GAP—occurs when supervisors feel powerless to successfully claim acceptable work from their subordinates. (18)

PRE-EVALUATION—a procedure to allow those being evaluated to have input by completing a form outlining their accomplishments. (16)

PREREQUISITES—necessary background needed to master a given skill. (8)

PRICE METHOD—Blanchard's five-step approach to employee performance problems: Pinpoint, Record, Involve, Coach, Evaluate. (11)

PRINCIPLED NEGOTIATION—pays attention to basic interests and mutually satisfying options. Avoids positional bargaining that tends to produce rushed agreements that can lead to damaged relationships. (13)

PRIORITIES—tasks that must be done, have a big payoff and avoid negative consequences. (5)

PRIVATIZATION—is either contracting out or working collaboratively with private security agencies, other governmental agencies and any other individuals or organizations that can help a police department fulfill its mission. (17)

PROACTIVE—involves recognizing problems and seeking the underlying cause(s) of the problems. (1)

PROBLEM—a deviation from what is desired, a difficulty. (4)

PROBLEM EMPLOYEE—exhibits abnormal behavior to the extent that the behavior is detrimental to organizational needs and goals as well as the needs and goals of other law enforcement agency personnel. (13)

PROBLEM-ORIENTED POLICING—management ascertains what problems exist and tries to solve them, redefining the role of law enforcement from incident-driven and reactive to problem-oriented and proactive. (4)

PROBLEM-SOLVING POLICING—in contrast to the traditional reactive approach of simply responding to calls for service. (1)

PROCRASTINATION—putting things off. (5)

PRODUCTIVITY—converting resources to results in the most efficient and effective way possible. In law enforcement, productivity is achieved through people. Measured by what types of services are provided and how well. (15)

PROFESSIONAL MODEL—crime control as the primary function, a centralized and efficient organization, a professional remoteness from the community and an emphasis on preventive motorized patrol and rapid response to crime. (1)

PROGRAM BUDGETING—see *performance budgeting.* (6)

PROGRESSIVE DISCIPLINE—uses disciplinary steps based on the severity of the offense and how often it is repeated. Steps usually are oral reprimand, written reprimand, suspension/demotion, dismissal. (11)

PROMOTABILITY/ASSIGNMENT FACTORS—an attempt to make evaluation "count for something." (16)

PROPORTIONATE ASSIGNMENT—area assignments are determined by requests for services, based on available data. (15)

PSYCHOLOGICAL HARDINESS—the ability to successfully cope with stress. (14)

PYRAMID OF AUTHORITY—the shape of the typical law enforcement hierarchy, with the chief at the peak and having full authority down through managers (captains and lieutenants) and supervisors (sergeants) to those who accomplish most of the tasks (officers). (1)

Q & A—question and answer method of teaching. (8)

QUALITY CIRCLE—a group of five to ten employees who volunteer to meet to solve problems in their workplace. (15)

QUALITY OF WORK LIFE (QWL)—a general name given to a variety of programs and projects used in business to help employees meet their needs. Might include rewards, job design, employee influence, interpersonal relations, the physical environment and job facilitation. (10)

QUID/QUOD DECISION-MAKING PROCESS—a quantified interpersonal decision-making process for deciding between two alternatives individually (QUID) or as a group (QUOD). (4)

QUOTA—a specific number or proportional share that each officer is expected to contribute or receive. (15)

RACIAL PROFILING—any police-initiated action that relies on the race, ethnicity or national origin rather than the behavior of an individual or information that leads the police to a particular individual who has been identified as being or having been engaged in criminal activity. (9)

RANDOM PATROL—officers on patrol are unsystematically (randomly) assigned areas to cover. (15)

RAPID RESPONSE—identifying and acting on opportunities. (2)

RAPPORT—a comfortable relationship, a feeling of mutual understanding and trust. (7)

REACTIVE—simply responding to calls for service. (1)

REDUCED EXPENDITURE SPENDING—see *cutback budgeting.* (6)

REFORM ERA—characterized by police authority coming from the law and professionalism, crime control as the primary function, a centralized and efficient organization, a professional remoteness from the community and an emphasis on preventive motorized patrol and rapid response to crime. (1)

REGRESSION—tendency to look back over previously read material. (5)

REINFORCEMENT THEORY—B. F. Skinner's motivational theory that behavior can be modified by using positive and negative reinforcement. (10)

REPRIMAND—formal criticism of behavior. May be oral or written. (11)

RESPONSIBILITY—answerable, liable, accountable for. (1)

RESTRAINING FORCES—forces that impede goal achievement. (4)

REVERSE DISCRIMINATION—giving preferential treatment to women and minorities, to the detriment of white males in hiring and promoting. (7)

RHETORICAL QUESTION—question to which an answer is not expected. The purpose is to get the listener thinking about a topic. (8)

RIGHT-BRAIN THINKING—primarily using images and emotions. (4)

RIGHT-TO-WORK LAWS—make it illegal to require employees to join a union. Established by the Taft-Hartley Act of 1938. (7)

ROLE PLAYING—a learning method that casts individuals into specific parts to be acted out. (8)

ROLL CALL—brief period before each shift when officers check in and receive their briefing prior to going on duty. (2, 8)

ROTE LEARNING—memorization, not necessarily with understanding. (8)

RUMOR MILL—informal channels of communication within a department or agency. Also called the *grapevine.* (3)

SCANNING—reading material rapidly for specific information. (5)

SCUTTLEBUTT—one employee complaining to another, uninvolved employee who cannot remedy the situation about an adverse action taken by upper management. (1)

SEAGULL MANAGEMENT—manager hears something's wrong, so flies in, makes a lot of noise, craps on everybody and flies away. (2)

SELF-ACTUALIZATION—refers to achievement, to meeting individual goals and fulfilling one's potential. It is fostered by the chance to be creative and innovative and by being given the opportunity to maximize skills and knowledge. (10)

SELF-DISCIPLINE—self-imposed rules for self-control. (11)

SELF-FULFILLING PROPHECY—the theory that people live up to expectations. If people believe they can do a job, they usually can. If people believe they cannot do a job, they usually cannot. (10)

SELF-MOTIVATION—acting in an expected way from personal choice. (10)

SEMI-VARIABLE COSTS—expenses that have characteristics of both fixed costs and variable costs. For example, utility expenses. (6)

SHARED RESPONSIBILITY—a work culture where all team members feel as responsible as the manager for accomplishing the team's goals and objectives. (2)

SHIFT—time span to which personnel are assigned. Most agencies have three eight-hour shifts. Some agencies call this time span a *watch.* (15)

SIMULATION—imitation of a process. (8)

SINGLE HANDLING—not picking up a piece of paper until you are ready to do something with it. Applies particularly to the daily stack of mail. (5)

SITUATIONAL LEADERSHIP—leadership viewed as an interplay between the amount of direction (task behavior) a leader gives, combined with the amount of relationship behavior a leader provides *and* the maturity level that followers exhibit on a specific task the leader is attempting to accomplish through the individual or group (Hersey and Blanchard). (2)

SKIMMING—reading information rapidly for the main ideas, usually the first and last paragraph, the first sentence of all other paragraphs and the captions of any charts or figures. (5)

SMART GOALS AND OBJECTIVES—objectives that are **s**pecific, **m**easurable, **a**ttainable, **r**elevant and **t**rackable. (2)

SNAP DECISIONS—deciding rapidly, making decisions on the spot. (4)

SNIPERS—people who do not attack openly but engage in subtle digs, cheap shots and innuendos. (13)

SPAN OF CONTROL—how many people one individual manages or supervises. (1)

SPECIAL EMPLOYMENT GROUPS—groups included in affirmative action programs such as African Americans, Asians, Eskimos, Hispanics, homosexuals, immigrants, individuals with AIDS, individuals with disabilities, Middle Easterners, Native Americans, religious group members, substance abusers, Vietnam veterans, whites (reverse discrimination), women, young and aging individuals. (7)

SPECIALISTS—those who work in a specific area; investigators, juvenile officers, SWAT officers and the like. (1)

SPOILS SYSTEM—motto, "To the victor go the spoils," resulted in political interference with policing. (1)

STAFF PERSONNEL—those who support line personnel. (1)

STAKEHOLDERS—those affected by an organization and those in a position to affect it. (1)

STANDARD ENGLISH—language that follows the grammatical rules of American English. (3)

STANDARDS—targets to be met, including level of performance. (16)

STRATEGIC DECISION—executive-level decision involving long-range plans. (4)

STRATEGIC ISSUE—one directly related to the department mission and requiring a comprehensive response. (4)

STRATEGIC PLANNING—long-term planning. (2)

STRESS—tension, anxiety or worry. Can be positive, *eustress,* or negative, *distress.* (14)

STROKE APPROACH—using positive strokes rather than negative, crooked or plastic strokes. (11)

SUBCONSCIOUS SELF—that part of you neither you nor others have yet discovered. Also called *undiscovered self.* (9)

SUBVOCALIZATION—the contraction of the tongue and other speech-related organs made during learning to pronounce each letter of the alphabet. Becomes ingrained and can slow down adult readers. (5)

SUMMARY DISCIPLINE—discretionary authority used when a supervisor feels an officer is not fit for duty or for any reason the supervisor feels a need for *immediate* action. Also called *summary punishment.* (11)

SUMMARY PUNISHMENT—see *summary discipline.* (11)

SUNK COST—a historical cost that has already been incurred and is thus irrelevant for decision-making purposes. For example, the purchase of a K-9. Other costs associated with the dog, however, will continue. (6)

SUPERNORMS—overriding expectations of a given work group, for example, do not volunteer or do not criticize. (9)

SUPERVISION—overseeing the actual work being done. (2)

SUPERVISORS—first-line managers; usually sergeants. (2)

SUSPENSION—being barred from a position for a period of time. May be with or without pay. Often part of progressive discipline. (11)

SUSTAINED—complaint or grievance in which the investigative facts support the charge. (12)

SYNCHRONOUS LEARNING—real-time, instructor-led online learning in which all participants are logged on at the same time and communicate directly with each other. Opposite of asynchronous learning. (8)

SYNERGISM—occurs when the whole is greater than the sum of its parts; the team achieves more than each could accomplish as individuals. (2)

SYNERGY—where the whole is greater than the sum of its parts. (9)

TACTICAL PLANNING—short-term planning. (2)

TAFT-HARTLEY ACT OF 1947—balanced the power of unions and management by prohibiting several unfair labor practices, including closed shops, which prohibited management from hiring nonunion workers. (7)

TANGIBLE REWARDS—external motivators such as salary, bonuses, insurance, retirement plans, favorable working conditions, paid vacation and holidays, titles and adequacy of equipment. (10)

TASK MANAGEMENT—produce or perish; sees good relationships as incidental to high production; supervisors achieve production goals by planning, directing and controlling all work; inner directed, depending on own skills, knowledge, attitudes and beliefs; takes a win-lose approach to conflict, seeking to win its own points. (2)

TASK VARIABLES—relates to *what* is to be learned: knowledge, skills or attitudes. Also called *information variables.* (8)

TAYLORISM—time and motion studies pioneered by Winslow Taylor (1856–1915). (5)

TEAM—consists of two or more people who must coordinate their activities regularly to accomplish a common task; builds on the concept of synergism. (2)

TEAM MANAGEMENT—people support what they create; such a team sees production resulting from integrating task and human requirements; good relationships and high production are both attainable; supervisors attain effective production through participation and involvement of people and their ideas; seeks emergent solutions as the result of debate, deliberation and experimentation; confronts conflict directly, communicating feelings and facts as a basis to work through conflict. (2)

TECHNICAL SKILLS—all the procedures needed to be a good law enforcement officer, including interviewing and interrogating, searching, arresting, gathering evidence and the like. (2)

TECHNOPHOBIA—the fear of using technology because of unfamiliarity or uncertainty as to how it works. (15)

TERMINATION—being fired from employment. Usually the final step in progressive discipline. (11)

THEORY X—McGregor's management theory that assumes workers are dull and lazy and need control by coercion, threats and punishment. They want secure jobs above all else. (2)

THEORY Y—McGregor's management theory that assumes workers are willing workers who can be trusted to do a good job and should share in decision making. (2)

THINKING TRAPS—habits people fall into without recognizing what they are doing, including either/or thinking, deciding too quickly, deciding based on personality rather than facts, being a victim of personal habits and prejudices and being unimaginative. Also called *mental locks.* (4)

TICKLER FILE SYSTEM—a set of file folders, organized by year, month and day, into which lists of tasks to be accomplished are placed. (5)

TIME ABUSERS—activities or tasks that waste time, for example, socializing, drop-in visitors, telephone tag. (5)

TIME LOG—a detailed list of how time is spent each day, usually broken into 10- to 15-minute segments. (5)

TIME MANAGEMENT—dividing and organizing time to accomplish the most tasks in the most efficient way. (5)

TONE—emotional effect of language, for example, an angry tone of voice. (3)

TOTAL QUALITY MANAGEMENT (TQM)—Deming's theory that managers should create constancy of purpose for improvement of product and service, adopt the new philosophy, improve constantly, institute modern methods of training on the job, institute modern methods of supervision, drive fear from the workplace, break down barriers between staff areas and eliminate numerical goals for the work force, remove barriers that rob people of pride of workmanship and institute a vigorous program of education and training. (2)

TOUCHSTONE VALUES—what people say is important to them. (9)

TRAFFIC ENFORCEMENT AND MANAGEMENT SYSTEM (TEAMS)—uses participatory management and measures productivity by the degree to which management's traffic goals are accomplished. (18)

TRAINING—generally refers to vocational instruction that takes place on the job and deals with physical skills. (8)

TRAIT THEORISTS—those who research special characteristics that leaders possess. (2)

TRAITS—personal characteristics. (2)

TRANSFORMATIONAL LEADERSHIP—treats employees as the organization's most valuable assets. Is employee-centered and focuses on empowerment. (2)

TRAUMATIC STRESS—is severe, extremely intense distress that lasts a limited time and then the person returns to normal. Sometimes called *acute stress.* (14)

TWO-FACTOR THEORY—Herzberg's motivational theory that employees' needs can be classified as hygiene factors and motivator factors. Hygiene factors are tangible rewards that cause dissatisfaction if lacking; motivator factors are intangible rewards that can cause satisfaction. (10)

TWO-WAY COMMUNICATION—information is freely exchanged, with feedback occurring during the process. (3)

TYPE A PERSONALITY—describes people who are aggressive, hyperactive, drivers who tend to be workaholics. (14)

TYPE B PERSONALITY—describes people who are more laid back, relaxed and passive. (14)

UNDISCOVERED SELF—that part of you neither you nor others have yet discovered. Also called *subconscious self.* (9)

UNFOUNDED—complaint or grievance in which the act did not occur or the complaint/grievance was false. (12)

UNION—any group authorized to represent the members of an agency in negotiating such matters as wages, fringe benefits and other conditions of employment. (7)

UNION SHOP—must belong to or join the union to be hired. (7)

UNITY OF COMMAND—means that every individual in the organization has only one immediate superior or supervisor. (1)

UPWARD (VERTICAL) COMMUNICATION—messages conveyed from subordinates to supervisors and managers or from supervisors to managers. (3)

VALID—well grounded, sound, the factors rated are job related and the raters are trained. (16)

VALUES—the beliefs, principles or standards considered worthwhile or desirable. (1)

VARIABLE COSTS—expenses that vary in total directly with the amount of service provided. For example, personnel costs including overtime. (6)

VARIANCE ANALYSIS—comparing actual costs against what was budgeted and examining the differences. (6)

VERBAL CHANNELS OF COMMUNICATION—one-on-one conversations, phone conversations, radio dispatch, interviews, meetings, news conferences and speeches. (3)

VERTICAL (UPWARD) COMMUNICATION—messages conveyed from subordinates to supervisors and managers or from supervisors to managers. (3)

VICARIOUS LIABILITY—the legal responsibility one person has for the acts of another. Managers, the entire agency and even the jurisdiction served may be legally responsible for the actions of a single officer. (7)

VIDEOCONFERENCING—simultaneous, interactive audio and video communication. (8)

WAGNER ACT—see *National Labor Relations Act of 1935.* (7)

WALLENDA EFFECT—the negative consequences of fear of failure. (2)

WATCH—see *shift.* (15)

WHOLE-BRAIN THINKING—using both the logical left side and the emotional right side of the brain together for best results. (4)

WOLF PACK SYNDROME—a vestige of primitive male hunting groups within which no weaknesses were tolerated. Any deficiencies were attacked by other members of the group. (1)

WORK PLANS—the precise activities that contribute to accomplishing objectives. Detailed steps or tasks to be accomplished. (1)

WORKPLACE CULTURE—the sum of the beliefs and values held in common by those within the organization which formally and informally communicate what is expected. (9)

WRITTEN COMMUNICATION—notes, memos, letters, reports, manuals, bulletins, policies, etc. (3)

YELLOW-DOG CONTRACT—makes union membership illegal under the penalty of discharge. (7)

YES PEOPLE—super-agreeable people who are vocally supportive in your presence but rarely follow through. (13)

ZERO-BASED BUDGETING (ZBB)—begins with a clean slate, justifying each expenditure anew. All budget lines begin at zero base and are funded according to merit rather than the preceding year's funding level. (6)

Author Index

Subject Index

U

Credits

This page constitutes an extension of the copyright page. We have made every effort to trace the ownership of all copyrighted material and to secure permission from copyright holders. In the event of any question arising as to the use of any material, we will be pleased to make the necessary corrections in future printings. Thanks are due to the following authors, publishers, and agents for permission to use the material indicated.

Chapter 1. 24: Tony Freeman/Photo Edit

Chapter 2. 51: © Jim Shaffer

Chapter 3. 94: REUTERS/Brian Snyder/© Reuters NewMedia Inc./CORBIS; **97:** ©David Young-Wolff/PhotoEdit-All rights reserved.

Chapter 4. 111: © Spencer Grant/PHOTOEDIT

Chapter 5. 153: © Shepherd Sherbell/CORBIS SABA

Chapter 6. 165: ©Spencer Grant/PhotoEdit

Chapter 7. 212: © Jim Shaffer

Chapter 8. 240: © Spencer Grant/PhotoEdit; **245:** © Mikael Karlsson/Arresting Images

Chapter 9. 273: © Jim Shaffer; **277:** © Michael Newman/PhotoEdit

Chapter 10. 298: ©Spencer Grant/PhotoEdit

Chapter 11. 334: AP Photo/Angela Rowlings

Chapter 12. 364: © Tom Carter/Photo Edit; **369:** © Jim Shaffer

Chapter 13. 393: AP Photo/Diane Bondareff

Chapter 14. 407: AP Photo/Danny Johnston; **425:** © Michael Newman/PhotoEdit

Chapter 15. 448: ©Jeff Greenberg/PhotoEdit-All rights reserved; **457:** Gail Burton/APWide World

Chapter 16. 495: © Jim Shaffer

Chapter 17. 507: AP Photo/Pittsburgh Tribune-Review, Warren L. Leeder; **511:** © Reuters NewMedia Inc./CORBIS;